THE WOMEN

The Women

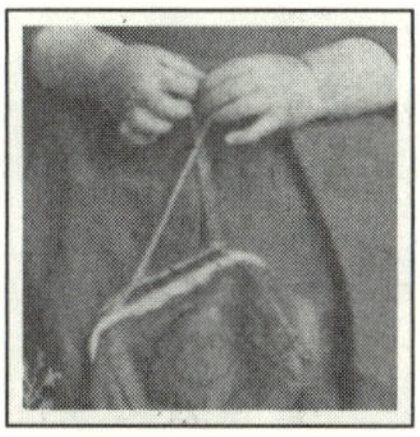

KERRY WILLIAM BATE

The University of Utah Press | Salt Lake City

The Defiance House Man colophon is a registered trademark of the University of Utah Press. It is based on a four-foot-tall Ancient Puebloan pictograph (late PIII) near Glen Canyon, Utah.

20 19 18 17 16 1 2 3 4 5

Library of Congress Cataloging-in-Publication Data

Names: Bate, Kerry William, author.
Title: The women/Kerry William Bate.
Description: Salt Lake City : The University of Utah Press, [2016] | Includes bibliographical references and index.
Identifiers: LCCN 2016019374| ISBN 9781607815167 (cloth : alkaline paper) | ISBN 9781607815174 (ebook)
Subjects: LCSH: Steele, Catherine Campbell, 1816–1891—Family. | Utah—Biography. | Women—Utah—Biography. | Mormon pioneers—Utah—Biography. | Mormon women—Utah—Biography. | Mormon families—Utah—Biography. | Mormons—Utah—Biography. | Mormon women—Utah—Social conditions. | Women—Utah—Social conditions. | Utah—Social conditions. | BISAC: SOCIAL SCIENCE/ Women's Studies.
Classification: LCC F826.S74 B38 2016 | DDC 305.409792—dc23
LC record available at https://lccn.loc.gov/2016019374

Printed and bound by Edwards Brothers Malloy, Inc., Ann Arbor, Michigan.

This book is dedicated to my great-aunt

REBA ROUNDY LEFEVRE

without whose cheerful cooperation it couldn't have been written.

CONTENTS

PREFACE AND ACKNOWLEDGMENTS

I am indebted to numerous individuals for their assistance in bringing this volume to fruition. I acknowledge and thank my wife Marilyn and children, the late David Bate as well as Doris, Marilee, Jennifer, Becca, Gwendolyn, and Joseph, for the price they have paid for this project. My sister Tonia Ann Bate did important interviews for me; generously gave me two books that had belonged to our great-great-grandmother, Young Elizabeth Steele Stapley; and gave this manuscript a thorough reading. My late mother, JoAnn Sylvester Bate, consented—sometimes reluctantly—to be repeatedly interviewed, and also recorded an important interview with her aunt Reba Roundy LeFevre. Despite tiring of being recorded, she was excited about this book and I especially owe her a debt of gratitude for her wise advice about these women: "They were, (Mama [Sarah Roundy Sylvester] and all) struggling human beings, so no use throwing a silk mist over their lives." [1]

The late J. Clive Davis, who had enough foresight to write some personal histories and record an important oral history interview with his aunt Leola Amelia Stapley Anderson. Clive's late widow, Mae Jensen Davis, kindly shared these records with me. Gary Hall Callister was especially obliging and his collection of John Steele papers cast much light on Catherine Campbell Steele and more on John himself. Hilga Frier, who served as an officer in the Steele Family Association, searched her voluminous files and was generous in sharing them with me. Ileen Judd Johnson, Hilga's sister, traveled to Australia and recovered copies of some of John Steele's correspondence with his Australian relatives and kindly shared those letters.

Genevieve Sooy Jensen and Jennifer Jensen Stephens sent me important information, including transcripts made by Iona Jeanne Poling of a portion of the Steele papers that were in the possession of the Jensen family. Wanda Steele Cox was also generous in giving me copies of the letters John Steele received from his Australian sister, Elizabeth Steele Connelly. Australian cousins—Janet O'Hara Ellis, Edith Meredith, and Jean Aileen McMurtrie Curry—provided letters John Steele sent his Australian niece, Letisha Connelly Todd and shared other information.

The late Dr. Wesley P. Larsen, once owner of the John Steele home in Toquerville, was generous in every way possible. Dr. Larsen took me on a personal tour of part of the Escalante trail and reintroduced me to the flora and fauna of southern Utah. He shared many leads with me and gave me several useful books about southern Utah, including some of his own about Toquerville, which are rich compilations drawing on a wide variety of sources.

It was Dr. Larsen who told me that an oral historian, Fielding Hyrum Harris, had been through Iron and Washington counties in the years 1968–1970, and tapes of those interviews were on file in the Special Collections Library at Southern Utah University in Cedar City. They have provided some pivotal insights and I wish to acknowledged Harris's foresight and express my thanks. This book would not have been possible without Dr. Larsen's continual encouragement, support, and interest.

He also introduced me to Blanche Clegg, the patient and courteous Southern Utah University Special Collections librarian, whose assistance went far beyond her responsibilities and included finding ways to entertain my very tired twelve-year-old daughter when I had run out of ideas about how to keep her busy. Blanche was followed by Janet Burton Seegmiller, and then Paula Mitchell, both of whom were helpful to me in my research. The records in their collections, especially the William R. Palmer papers, are priceless for the historian of southwestern Utah. Sheila Johnson of Southern Utah University provided me a transcript of my grandmother Sarah Elizabeth Roundy Sylvester's grades. Mamie Talbot opened the Daughters of the Utah Pioneers Museum in Panguitch and allowed me to photograph an anonymous history of Mahonri Moriancumer Steele Sr.

Lorana Fish Mineer generously gave me her impressions of Strabane, Tyrone, Ireland. Velma Stapley Ryder wrote her recollections of Young Elizabeth Steele Stapley and those memories have proven very helpful. Shanna Lea Sanford read an earlier draft of the manuscript and made important suggestions that helped me clarify for myself a woman's opportunities and limitations in pioneer Utah. Bob Bauer and Brad Lee Wolverton made copies of old photographs for me. Brad, a close friend of well over forty years and a professional artist, drew maps to illustrate the Roundy and Stapley Kanarraville homesteads.

Josephine Kay Garfield invited me into her home, showed me Catherine Campbell Steele's clothing kept in the "brown box" in her attic, and shared many photographs, some old letters, and her mother's brief but buoyant diary.

I have benefitted from five more recent readers: my sisters Tonia Ann Bate, Shannon Ritchie, and Sara Jo Merrill, my cousin Maureen Smith Bryson, and my niece Harvest Merrill.

William W. Slaughter of the Church History Library, Church of Jesus Christ of Latter-day Saints, along with his genealogist wife, Shari, are friends of many decades; Bill has been an inspiration to me and helped locate photos and documents. Linda Haslam was a great help as well. Lavina Fielding Anderson reviewed several of my writings in the 1980s and 1990s, and encouraged the writing of this book. Her suggestions and corrections were incredibly effective teaching tools; she has also been an informed guide to the strange world of publishing. Thank you, I admire your mind and your integrity. I have drawn inspiration from the fun and fearless historian Will Bagley; benefitted from guidance on a tricky point from Floyd O'Neil; and also appreciated Floyd's talented wife and my longtime friend, Shauna O'Neil, for her interest in my work. Ardis Parshall and I exchanged information and resolved the problem of a misdated letter; I appreciate her thoughtfulness in responding to me.

John R. Alley of the University of Utah Press has a knack for telling complicated truths in such a simple way I would find myself puzzled until I had a day to think over his suggestions, and then the wisdom would be so apparent I would wonder why I hadn't thought of it myself.

The readers of my manuscript, Todd Compton and Colleen Whitley, were cogent, generous and thorough in their reviews. I can't begin to express how much I appreciate their thoughtfulness and encouragement and the resulting book is much improved thanks to them. A third (anonymous) reader offered a bracing and enlightening response.

Elizabeth Oberdick Anderson, my copyeditor, has saved me from many mishaps and improved the clarity and professionalism of the resulting book and rescued me from innumerable blunders and run-on sentences. The remaining mistakes are my own.

I have been gifted with encouraging and supportive cousins. Javotte Pickering made copies of her mother Ruth Sylvester Pickering's photos available to family members and some of them enrich this book; Cynthia Sylvester Schlant shared another important photograph. A more distant cousin—the late Jesse Lenard Warner, an accomplished genealogist—provided me critical information on the Roundys. The late William Marden Stapley shared photographs and provided me a copy of his father William Tarbet Stapley's autobiography. That autobiography gives the only known account of the details surrounding Sarah Elizabeth Roundy (Sylvester)'s birth.

Brent Pace Prince transcribed and posted online the Kanarra and Harmony Stock Company Minute Book, 1874–1898; this helped me with some important details. Lyman de Platt published a thorough history of the Platt family that was helpful to me and also generously sent me an electronic update.

My distant Kanarraville cousin, Ron Williams and his wife Joan, were very kind to me. Joan provided me copies of photos from her extensive collection and shared town lore. Charles "Chas" Peterson would be surprised to find his name here but he sent Wes Larsen an excerpt from the Carlos Badger papers that led me to that man's diaries and illuminated several interesting points.

One of my late friends, Morris Shirts, was also an inspiration and provided information. My late cousin Sylvester Arthur Gregerson allowed me to photocopy his mother Maud Sylvester Gregerson's manuscripts, some incomplete but helpful for the Sylvester and Hanks families.

Teresa Truman Orton, my fifth grade classmate, gave permission to reproduce two excellent photographs of John Steele and Catherine Campbell Steele owned by the Daughters of the Utah Pioneers McQuarrie Museum in St. George. Thank you.

I have particularly benefitted from the L. Tom Perry Special Collections at Brigham Young University; the Special Collections at Southern Utah University (Cedar City) and Dixie University (St. George); the records at the Church History Library, Church of Jesus Christ of Latter-day Saints; the Family History Library, Salt Lake City; the Utah State Historical Society and Archives; the Washington County Library; online Utah newspapers provided at digitalnewspapers.org by the University of Utah; and online newspapers at chroniclingamerica.loc.gov and newspaperarchives.com. I have also read microfilmed copies of newspapers at the Utah State Historical Society and the University of Utah Marriott Library.

And finally there are those persons mentioned in the text and sources who consented to be interviewed by me or by others. The contemporary records are the scaffolding upon which I have built this book; the oral history interviews have served as my bricks and masonry to fill it out and make it presentable to the world. Without all of these persons, this could not have been completed: Dr. George Russell Aiken, Leola Amelia Stapley Anderson, Fredrick Wilford Balser, JoAnn Sylvester Bate, Hazel Eagar Bringhurst, Norma Bringhurst Empey, Ruthell Roundy Bryant, Bessie Elizabeth Davies, David Elmer Davies, Arvil Hanks Davis, Leonard Davis, Verna Platt Davis, Homer Y. Englestead, Albert Emil Fitzpatrick, Martha Rosalia Landon Fitzpatrick, Josephine Kay Garfield, Emil James "E. J." Graff, Leila Platt Heap, Sylvia Batty Hunt, Gwen Sylvester Hunter, Zona Russell Jensen, Florence Beatty Leavitt, Carl LeFevre, Reba Roundy LeFevre, Thelma Berry Lovell, Everett Blair Maxfield, Arthur

Olds, Charles Andrew Olds, Franklin Kent Olds, Lottie Dodge Olds, Ruth Sylvester Pickering, Rulon Berry Platt, Lela Berry Pollock, Lynn Reeves, Ella Batty Reeves, Jesse Kay Roundy, Karl G Roundy, Nancy Lillian Eagar Roundy, Varsel Clair Roundy, Ellis Alonzo Russell, Estella Roundy Russell, Edwin Kenneth Slack, Elsie Kay Smith, Elton Williams Stapley, Lena Stevens Sylvester, Leon R Sylvester, Rex J Sylvester, SueZanna Wittwer Sylvester, Jesse Peyton Warner, Plorn J. Williams, Rebecca Alenna Stapley Williams, Sylva May Davies Williams, Nell Sylvester Wilson, Harriet Arvilla Ford Woodbury and Ferl Leona Davis Zohner.

The challenge of turning verbal reminiscences into text is surprisingly difficult. Does one include "crutch" words like "ah," "see," "and that"? While for the most part I transcribed my interviews quite literally including all the hems and haws, I have used traditional journalistic practice in this book—that is, eliminating "crutch" words and using standard spelling regardless of pronunciation.

I thank *Dialogue: A Journal of Mormon Thought* and the *Utah Historical Quarterly* for allowing me to use portions of the following articles originally published in their magazines:

Kerry William Bate, "Promise to Grandma," *Dialogue: A Journal of Mormon Thought* 19, no. 4 (Winter 1986): 123–36.

Kerry William Bate, "Diary of Mary Elizabeth (May) Stapley, a Schoolteacher in Virgin, Utah," *Utah Historical Quarterly* 60, no. 2 (Spring 1992): 158–67.

Kerry William Bate, "John Steele: Medicine Man, Magician, Mormon Patriarch," *Utah Historical Quarterly* 62, no. 1 (Winter 1994): 71–90.

Kerry William Bate, "Kanarraville Fights World War I," *Utah Historical Quarterly* 63, no. 1 (Winter 1995): 24–49.

I apologize to those I've forgotten to name: a project that takes thirty years to complete includes some memory casualties along the way. And I conclude by exonerating those named in my acknowledgments from responsibility for my conclusions, but without them there would be no story to tell.

INTRODUCTION

This is the story of four women spanning the years 1816–1949, mothers and daughters who faced all that men, environment, and God could throw at them. It's the story of fights, cooperation, failings, and triumph in a world that valued women cheaply, granted nothing cheerily, and dismissed them easily. Though their stories are framed by Utah and Mormonism, their lives represent the experiences of many women of their era.

Sources for the marginalized, including minorities and women, necessarily vary considerably from those who ruled. "It was formerly the most invariable practice of great houses in Venice to form a cabinet of manuscripts as an adjunct to the library," wrote the early nineteenth-century German historian Leopold von Ranke. "It was in the nature of things that these would relate principally to the affairs of the republic. They represent the part taken by the respective families in public affairs and were preserved as records and memorials of the house for the instruction of its younger members."[2]

Three of the women in this volume left among them only five discoverable letters, three written by amanuenses; the fourth and last woman apparently did not leave any correspondence.

Catherine Campbell Steele's husband, John, knew his life was important and he saved family letters and papers in an old honey-colored trunk that four times followed him across the Atlantic Ocean. In the summer of 1986, I was lucky enough to meet Toquerville's hospitable and witty historian Dr. Wesley P. Larsen, who introduced me to Gary Hall Callister, a distant cousin and conscientious guardian of the Steele trunk. Gary allowed me to make an inventory of the trunk, take pictures, and photocopy the documents.

Gary told me that over the years the trunk had been partly depleted, sometimes through gifts of documents to others and sometimes perhaps in less generous ways. I learned the truth of this when I found out that a cousin-in-law in Henderson, Nevada, Genevieve "Gen" Sooy Jensen, had additional documents from the trunk. The Jensen documents had been very accurately transcribed by Jeanne Iona Jensen Poling and mimeographed; Gen shared copies of these with me. Later, when I learned that Gary Callister made Brigham Young University (BYU) the depositary of his John Steele collection, Genevieve Jensen asked me if she should do the same. I thought recombining these documents was important and supported her decision to do so.[3]

A study of these reunited documents show that the collection is still incomplete, as, for instance, the series of letters from Mahonri Moriancumer Steele Sr. and Joseph Fish to John Steele. This was confirmed when letters from the Steele trunk began appearing on eBay.

On February 25, 1980, thirty-seven-year-old Janet O'Hara Ellis of Lithgow, New South Wales, Australia, posted a letter to me explaining she had been given my contact information by the Church of Jesus Christ of Latter-day Saints. She proved to be a distant cousin, a descendant of John Steele's sister Elizabeth Steele Connelly. This led to information exchanges and friendships with additional cousins Edith Meredith and Jean Aileen McMurtrie Curry in Australia, while our Utah network expanded to include Wanda Steele Cox, Hilga Judd Frier, and Ileen's sister, Ileen Judd Johnson.

Ileen visited the Australian cousins while Aileen and her husband John William Curry visited Utah cousins. This also led to exchanges of family records, including the Utah branch providing Australian kin copies of letters sent to John Steele by his Australian relatives and the Australians providing copies—and in three instances, the originals—of some of John Steele's letters to his niece Letisha Connelly Todd of Essington, New South Wales. I have since donated to BYU my Steele memorabilia, including these Steele-Todd letters and the only letter I've seen written by Catherine Campbell Steele.

The greatest lacuna in the Steele papers are letters from John Steele's wife Catherine Campbell Steele. If some had been present and others missing I would suspect they weren't especially valued by John—though letters from his daughters survive. My guess is that Catherine's were removed and may yet surface, allowing for a more sophisticated appraisal of this somewhat elusive woman.

This book is also illuminated by the collections of the Church History Library, Church of Jesus Christ of Latter-day Saints. Housed there, for instance, is a letter from John Steele to George A. Smith announcing the marriage of his daughter Young Elizabeth Steele (Stapley). The records of the Toquerville and Kanarraville wards were especially important to me. (I actually first went to the Church History Library in 1967 or 1968 and was easily batted away by the fierce Will Lund; later historians have been much more accommodating with an historical collection that can only be described by a researcher as luscious.)

By the time we get to the latter half of the life of Catherine's daughter Young Elizabeth Steele Stapley—around 1903—a lot of useful information also becomes available from weekly county newspapers. These represent secular community diaries as many little towns had a (usually anonymous) correspondent who reported to the county at large. In Kanarraville, at least part of the time, that correspondent was Young Elizabeth Stapley's son William T.

My next major source for this study—the one Theodore Rosengarten used with such effect for his stunningly powerful *All God's Danger: The Life of Nate Shaw* (1974)—was oral history. The memories of living persons serve as the Venetian library cabinet of working class people, with the disadvantage that it can't reach back hundreds of years and the happy prospect that it can be cross-examined. The right person can speak knowledgeably about events a hundred years ago. My great-aunt Reba Roundy LeFevre could talk with some accuracy about her ancestors' days in Nauvoo, though her people were exiled from that community in 1846. When I asked her what family members weren't Mormon, she explained John Roundy wasn't—and he was born in 1726! Of course there's a lot of difference between witnessing something and repeating stories about it, but the historian always has to test and evaluate sources anyway. "A history in which every particular incident may be true may on the whole be false," wrote Thomas Babington Macaulay.[4] And I may conversely say that sometimes in oral history the story used to describe a character may not be strictly accurate but the characterization itself exact.

Though I didn't begin to conceive of this book until January 25, 1985, and I didn't write the first sentence until February 12, 1986, I actually did my first recorded interview with my great uncle, Eugene Perry, on January 29, 1972, as a history assignment at Weber State College. I did a few more, then went for six or seven years without doing any, but in the meantime I continued collecting family history. When I got a job in downtown Salt Lake, I found myself so close to the Church History Library I was occasionally able to spend my lunch hour there researching. In addition, I often traveled statewide and began taking along a tape recorder to gather information.

Oral history, like any other subjective source, including diaries and after-the-fact memoirs, has shortcomings. We live our lives sequentially but we relive them episodically. Like all sources, reminiscences—oral or written—must be tested against other evidence. In a paper pointed out to me by Colleen Whitley, Laurel Thatcher Ulrich skillfully demonstrated how to do this in her Leonard J. Arrington Mormon History Lecture Series, *Rachel's Death: How Memory Challenges History* (2004). Ulrich expanded on family records and traditions by squaring them with contemporary accounts, the two sources enriching each other.

Because so much of this book is based on sources not always available to the general public—private family histories, diaries, letters, and especially oral histories—I have deposited copies of some of these sources at the Utah State Historical Society.

My great-aunt Reba Roundy LeFevre (1904–2001) is central to this story: three generations earlier than her is Catherine Campbell Steele, the first American emigrant; three down is my own generation. Reba stayed close to home. Her grandmother lived with Reba and Reba's parents until Reba was thirty-four; both parents were living when she left home at the age of forty-two to marry G. I. Carl LeFevre in a match arranged by the relieved mothers of the bride and groom. No one knew more of the facts, legends, and tribulations of these women. She also had family documents that were invaluable to me, including the only Catherine Campbell Steele letter I've found. Reba knew that despite the official family hagiographies, these women worked cunningly and endlessly to subvert God's curse on Eve: "I will greatly multiply thy sorrow and thy conception. In sorrow thou shalt bring forth children; and thy desire shall be to thy husband; and he shall rule over thee" (Genesis 3:15).

Because of her willingness and patience in "telling all," I dedicate this study to her.

FAMILY PEDIGREE

- Arthur Knox
b. ca. 1750
of Strabane, Ireland
= Margaret Graham
b. ca. 1752
  - Arthur Knox Jr.
(1774–1829)
= Mary J. Inch
(ca. 1792–ca.1879)
    - Dr. John Knox
(1817–1889)
= Lucy C. Macon
grandniece of
Pres. James Madison
  - Mary Knox
(1783–1854)
= Michael Campbell
(1781–1852)
    - Catherine Campbell
(1816–1891)
= John Steele
(1821–1903)
      - Mary Campbell Steele
(1840–1874)
= Thomas LeFevre
(1838–1913)
= Joseph Fish
(1840–1926)
      - Young Elizabeth Steele
(1847–1938)
        - *next page*
      - Mahonri Moriancumer Steele
(1849–1923)
= Emily Bunker
(1849–1921)
= Mary Ellen Jepson
(1851–1887)
      - Susan Adams Steele
(1851–1927)
= William A. Bringhurst
(1839–1912)
      - *next page*
  - John Knox
= Rebecca Keith
    - William Knox
(1830–1904)
= Rachel Hamilton Elliott
(1839–1909)
      - William Elliott Knox
(1862–1927)
banker
      - Margaret Knox
(1866–1934)
educator
      - Arthur Knox
(1874–post-1938)
Columbia Law School
      - *others*
  - *others*

Family Pedigree

- Catherine Campbell (1816–1891) = John Steele (1821–1903) = Mary Jane Ould (1851–1910) = Tamar Elizabeth Booth (1867–1914)
  - John (1840–1845)
  - Margaret Campbell (1844–1845)
  - Young Elizabeth Steele (1847–1938) = James Stapley (1838–1920)
    - James Steele Stapley (1864–1926) = Harriet Louisa Berry (1867–1948)
    - Sarah Catherine Stapley (1866–1949) = Joel Jesse Roundy (1864–1949)
      - *next page*
    - William Tarbet Stapley (1869–1954) = Lucy Emmeline Allred (1880–1964)
    - John Alma Stapley (1872–1950) = Lucretia Jane Higgins (1881–1938)
    - Mahonri Moriancumer Stapley (1875–1954) = Rebecca Almeda Williams (1877–1961)
    - Mary Elizabeth "May" Stapley (1878–1955) = John S. Kay (1873–1929)
    - Joseph Henry Stapley (1884–1886) Rebecca Stapley (1886–1886)
  - John Alma Steele (1853–1931)
  - Jane Catherine (1855–1903) = John Peter Jensen (1851–1932)
  - Robert Henry (1857–1858)

Family Pedigree

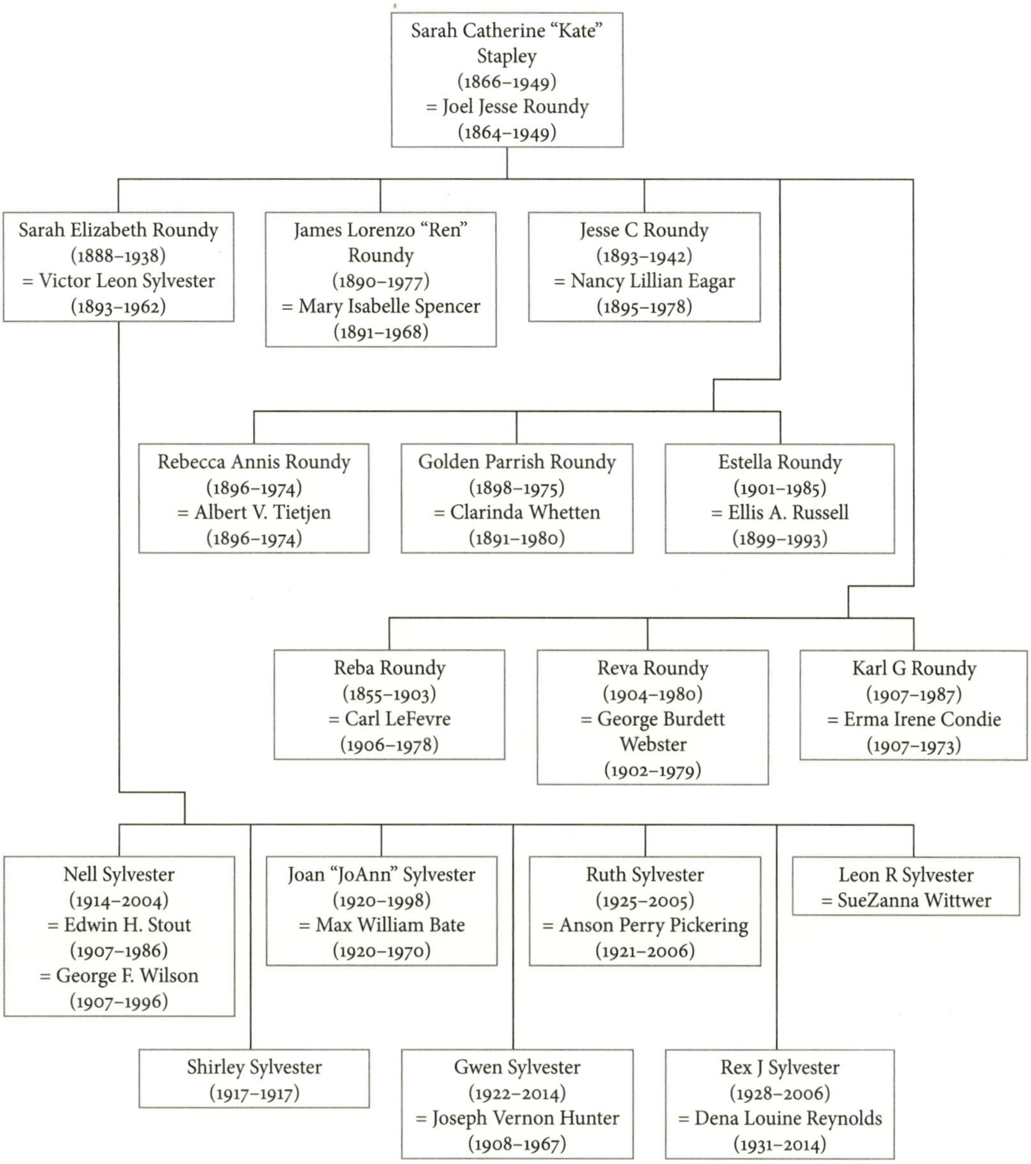

1

"Husband What Is Thy Will?"

Catherine Campbell Steele

"Where the summer sun spends the winter!" lied the St. George Chamber of Commerce in billboards showing a glorious orange sun. It was a late Friday night in January 1985, and the sky was actually dark with brooding, wet clouds. Still, my great-aunt Reba Roundy LeFevre was happy to see me when I stopped by. She generously fixed the kind of semivegetarian dinner we both liked—beans, onions, boiled eggs, and buttermilk.

While we ate we visited. I loved listening to her—the bumpy, gritty cadences of a voice echoing the language and idioms of rural nineteenth-century Utah. Southern Utah was what the historian Juanita Brooks called "The Ragged Edge," tough, frontier pioneering that was slower to change and adapt to modernism than northern Utah.[1] Aunt Reba reflected that Rip Van Winkle stoppage of time, while her unquestioning religious certainties were as fascinating and integral a part of her as her crinkled skin.

We ended up talking about Reba's sister, my individualistic, talented, assertive grandmother, Sarah Elizabeth Roundy Sylvester. For the first time in seventy-one years Reba explained my grandmother's speedy and passionate courtship and failed marriage.[2] It was a startling conversation, and I suddenly realized the importance of the story of the women in our family.

Reba's great-grandmother, Catherine Campbell Steele, lived in the Mormon haven of Nauvoo, Illinois, before trekking across the Great Plains with the Mormon Battalion. When she gave birth in the Great Salt Lake Valley to Young Elizabeth Steele on August 9, 1847, the baby was the first Mormon born in the new Zion. Elizabeth, as she was called, lived to be over ninety, her life symbolizing the Mormons' successful conquest of their Great Basin home. A strong-minded and accomplished if nearly illiterate midwife, Elizabeth was celebrated as "The First White Child Born in Utah," riding in parades, adorning floats, and in one noticeable instance sharing a platform with a president of the

United States. She had such a strong sense of adventure and love of fast travel that when she took her first airplane ride in her late seventies she declared that, finally, the speed was "just right!"[3]

Elizabeth's daughter Catherine—named for her mother and known as Kate—was Reba's mother and an accomplished community leader in her own right. She organized her town's considerable supportive efforts for World War I, even though townspeople were less than enthused about that adventure. Kate's daughter Sarah was a gifted seamstress who could make a dress after looking at a picture in a magazine. Her great practical skills and her role in a cooperative family matriarchy allowed her to successfully navigate the Great Depression, notwithstanding the unreliable support of the husband she warred with most of her married life and whom she repudiated on her deathbed.

Despite, or because of these and other talented women, men are often conflicted about the mystic powers of the opposite sex and blame them for dissension and iniquity, whether it's Pandora letting loose vice and disease or Eve enticing Adam with an apple. Capable women are a threat.

"God made the earth, then He rested. Then He made man and rested, then He made woman, and since that time neither God, man or the devil have ever rested," said Kanarra's George Berry in his 1906 Fourth of July toast,[4] a sentiment echoed by Sarah's cousin-in-law, ninety-year-old Jesse Payton Warner, who explained, "But, boy, how true it is! The Devil's going to work through the women. You never saw a woman smoking on a billboard before that [1904]. But since then, you've seen women drinking, taking dope, things like that."[5]

It was Mr. Warner who supplied me with the title of this study of the failures, achievements, and complexities of four generations of gifted individuals: *The Women.*

"My dear Wife," Mormon missionary John Steele wrote from 124 New Castle Street off Stratford Street, Hulme, Manchester, England, to his wife Catherine in Toquerville, Utah Territory, USA, on May 26, 1878. "As Everybody in this world has to have their ups and downs I Sopose you think yours are the worst that Ever was but nevertheless if I Could only have a little peace from home affairs I think I Could manage all the other little Itams, if not to Suit other people, So that I Could Manage to get along and about all I ask my family to do is for them to do as I want them, and I will Manage all the rest, Oh gentle dames it gars [?] me Greef to think how many Counsils Sweet, and so forth, if you have any more Such please dig a large whole in the Sand in the Creek ^for them^[6] and perhaps when one of thos[e] floods Come down they may Go on down to the Gulf of California, and Should I Call around that way I will make Some inquiry."[7]

This contrasted with John's pleas for letters and his claim that "I am glad to hear from You of home affairs," or "Catherine your letter of Sept 14 is just Come to hand this Morning, and I am very Sorry to hear that you are in Such trouble you are Sore perplexed and I have felt it very much and have prayed for you and my Friends, and my Enomays as well and you may rest assured the Lord will remember both" or "as for you working so hard take it Easy there is more days than one take Care of the things and do the best you Can."[8]

John himself was memorable, his grandson Mahonri Moriancumer Steele Jr. describing John as "a man of many accomplishments which helped might[i]ly in building up a new country. He was a sailor, a soldier, mason, shoemaker, surveyor, and had a good clerical education for a man of his time; delved in astronomy and withal took the place of physician and surgeon . . . He had a firey temper, and keen sense of right and wrong, and the man never lived that he feared. All in all he was one of the most remarkable men I ever knew, and I fondly cherish his memory." Mahonri Jr. found his grandmother Catherine "in many ways as remarkable a woman as Grandfather Steele was a man."[9]

Despite John's sometime sympathy and Catherine's talents, she had plenty of problems. She was sixty-one, ailing, had fallen and badly hurt her finger.[10] She was living in Toquerville in southern Utah Territory, a settlement so isolated that one woman, Sarah Bryant Stapley, complained "neither God nor the Devil will ever find us here."[11]

Catherine's small three-room house—unbaked adobe brick on a limestone foundation, walls ten inches thick with a four-inch thick plank floor—was hardly spacious or comfortable,[12] so haphazardly plastered inside with mud that Hazel Eagar Bringhurst, a later occupant, said "somebody must have done that when they was drunk!"[13] The leaking roof threatened to melt the red dirt walls and by late May it was getting hot. The house faced the eastern Black Hill, an abrupt rise of Navajo sandstone and limestone covered by volcanic rock interspersed with sentinels of purple-fruited prickly pear and the white trumpets of poisonous loco weed, occasionally dampened on the southern end by a feeble spring. This spring was supposed to supply water power for John Nebeker's cotton mill but its efforts were half-hearted and it gave up early every summer, leaving the mill paralyzed.

The locust trees growing on the main street (now rather grandly known as Toquerville Boulevard) joined with the hill to shade Catherine's home until ten o'clock in the morning, by which time the house began to heat up despite that cooling adobe.

Catherine's garden was watered by an irrigation ditch served by Ash Creek—the stream that John was suggesting she bury her troubles in so they'd flow to California. Her only cash crop was wine but a drought the preceding summer stunted the grapes. Still, the vines needed their annual trimming. There was no hope from last year's new orchard—the fence had fallen down and hungry cows and calves had eaten up all the young trees.[14]

Catherine was also trying to tend to John's business affairs. She couldn't get anyone to buy his tank of quicksilver and no one wanted his mine. John had been dismissed from his postmastership after fifteen years but Catherine was still being hounded by the government about a missing package. And John's assurances from overseas that the dissatisfied Edwin Lamb, Steele's partner in a mill and arrastra (a poor man's version of a mining stamp mill), had no legal right to take their home didn't stop bushy-headed Lamb from making threats.[15]

John repeatedly reminded Catherine that he'd signed a power of attorney to Martin Slack, by most accounts a capable community leader and certainly a friend of Steele's, though a newspaper who sponsored a failed rival candidate for the legislature unfairly characterized Slack as "a hide-bound, semi-animated mummy."[16] Slack was apparently unable to help.

When John took the census in 1880, he described their twenty-five-year-old strapping and handsome six-foot son John Alma (Almy) as a "wood man & miner."[17] But at the time of John's mission, Almy was hurt from his wagon capsizing and dumping a load of wood on him—John suspected carelessness[18]—and even in good health he was too often incapacitated by Toquerville wine—Valley Tan.

"I am sorry Alma has such poor health," Catherine's son Mahonri Moriancumer—quite sensibly called M. M.—wrote his mother. "Nothing will cure him but a good big Chunk of vally tan I am certain he cant stand it much longer, if he dont [get any]." But wine was a major cash crop for his parents and Catherine herself enjoyed a glass. M. M. also wrote Catherine, "I don't want any wine but I'd just like to chat with you long enough for you to sup a glass of Dixies best I would tell you lots of things about England Ireland and America but I[']ll save it till I come home."[19]

John, knowing seamstress Catherine's love of fabrics and fine clothing, wrote in March 1878, "I Should like about \$100^{00} and M M needs \$100^{00} to help him home, there are many things here I would like to take home with me if I had the money for Instance there are good Wool Shall's for 21 shillings or 4 dollars that would Cost 20 $ there and Cutlary Very Cheap dress patrens of 16 yds of Marino for 8 Shillings the best Broad Cloth at 13 Shillings pr yd or 3 dollars double width, so that if I had some money when I got ready to Come I Could bring some things home with me, and the way for you to do if you Can Get hold of Some Money is to go to Rob Lund and deposit $100[oo] with him he will Charge you about $1,50 and he will Send a draft to me on the London bank and I can draw it here. You need not talk it very loud away from home as there is no necessity for any body knowing it but my self and no one knowing it there but yourself, I do not want it known at this Leverpool office if I Can help it."[20]

He also held out the allure of "Gloves ribbons and Cashmere dress,"[21] but Catherine couldn't or wouldn't rise to the bait: on September 12, 1878, he borrowed "Fifteen pounds 18/2 sterling" from his church to return home, a debt later "Cancelled by order of Pres John Taylor."[22]

John might get her a cashmere dress. John might get himself another wife. He wrote frankly to Catherine about sexual matters. "There are Some as handsom Men and woman here as you would like to look at and others that you would think ware begoton in a wind storm and Set up against a Crooked Fence to dry and they Got badly warped while Soft," he observed. "There is no difficulty about Geting a wife here as there are more woman than there are men for them, and the Law is rather Monogamic, in its Nature, but polygamic in its practice So that there are but few woman who live to the age of 80 years, but what Know that it takes a man and a woman to make a man."[23] His search for women included inviting Catherine's niece Maryanne Campbell to immigrate to Utah. But Maryanne didn't want to go, and anyway she was confined in the Belfast Insane Asylum for religious mania.[24]

Catherine had to take his courtship insinuations seriously. It had been less than ten years since, at age forty-eight, he'd taken an eighteen-year-old South African, Mary Jane Ould, as a second wife. However, in fifteen months the marriage disintegrated and he thriftily kept the divorce decree for notepaper, recording on the back the "Diference in Time between London England and Toquerville Utah 7" hours 34' minutes 5"."[25]

When Catherine commented unhappily about John's proposed womanizing, he snapped back: "As for the Beauties you spoke of, I should think you would thank them for taking Care of your better half just a little, and Make them welcom[e] when they bring him home all right and Sound, and for taking Care of him While traveling through this lower world."[26]

John asked Catherine to congratulate their daughter Susan on once again making them grandparents, then referred allegorically to Catherine being beyond the age of childbearing: "All I am Sory for is that my loom was out of order or I might have had a web in of my own, there are Plenty of Looms idle here and they go begging for Some one ^to^ fill them with warp and they will waft them & weave them themselves and not Charge a Cent."[27]

John sent Catherine endless lists: Almy should fix the roof, haul rock for a fence, fetch fifteen loads of wood and a load of flour, "Keep from Wine and Carousing with drunkards and bad Company," and get married. Catherine should call James Lewis's bonds if he continued to be troublesome; make David Williams pay for his lumber; plant a garden; sell the quicksilver to merchant and church leader Joseph F. Birch; ignore Lamb's threats; organize a neighborhood "bee" and fix up the place. John could tell by the tone of Catherine's cool responses that "When I Come home I am redused to the bed rock once again."[28]

And John had other complaints. He read a letter Catherine had written her poor and widowed Belfast sister, Margaret Campbell Johnston. John thought Margaret had been an ideal candidate for conversion, but Catherine's letter hadn't helped. "If [I] had thought you would have wrote Whining I would not have Sent you her address," John objected. "I had made a good impression upon her and her daughters and Gave her money and Could have done Something for her But that letter of yours nocked it all in the head."[29]

Catherine passively ignored John and instead wrote M. M., who passed on the news to John, which brought another angry blast. "I am glad you find time to write to Somebody if you have not time to write to me . . . I sopose I need not feel atall disapointed if I do not get a letter once a month, if that is all you can offer me, I sopose I must be Content with Small favors and large ones in proportion, <u>when</u> <u>they</u> <u>come</u>," and he castigated her for not acknowledging receipt of a photograph he'd sent—"But I sopose it Makes no Matter its only <u>Me</u>."[30]

John's history was so important to him that he saved dozens of letters and kept detailed journals but like most nineteenth-century men he wrote little about his wife. Since Catherine's correspondence hasn't been found we're mostly forced to see her through the scraps of paper her husband kept and his letters to her; the reader must understand we've concentrated on the tensions in their relationship in order to better understand her.

Still, we know that Catherine was patient and philosophical. As a descendant of Presbyterian Covenanters who fled from Scotland to Ireland because of religious persecution, she was familiar with her Bible and knew of God's terrible misogynist curse: "I will greatly multiply thy sorrow and thy conception.

In sorrow thou shalt bring forth children; and thy desire shall be to thy husband; and he shall rule over thee" (Genesis 3:15).

There must have been times when Catherine asked herself how she came to be ruled by a short, stubborn, willful Scotch-Irishman who'd dragged her halfway around the world to build a religious utopia—the Mormon "Kingdom of God."

Life's journey began for her as Catherine Campbell, daughter of Mary Knox and Michael Campbell, on November 16, 1816, in Strabane (pronounced Strabon), County Tyrone, Ireland. "A populous Market town on the banks of the Mourne," Strabane was well known for its provision trade[31] and, as Catherine's descendant Lorana Fish Mineer described it, "a beautiful hamlet down in the valley nestled by rolling hills" with "little thatched roofed cottages."[32] John also remembered it as a "Beautiful Town,"[33] but in Catherine's youth the Campbells moved to fast-industrializing Belfast in the center of Ulster.

"In the long winter evenings when she [Young Elizabeth Steele Stapley] stood at the spinning wheel her mother [Catherine Campbell Steele] told the children gathered about her of the days in Belfast, Ireland[,] and of the story in her family that the Campbells had descended from royalty."[34]

The Campbells, like the Knoxes, were tradesmen: Michael Campbell and his brothers Robert and Ephraim were tobacconists, suggesting it was a family trade learned from their father Henry. Robert married Matilda Arbuckle, niece of Joseph Arbuckle, a prominent Belfast merchant. The trades of the Campbells and Arbuckles and their spouses included a printer, merchant, schoolmaster, bootmaker and leathercutter, publican, plumber and coppersmith, farmer, baker, and carpenter.[35] Mary and Michael Campbell's children married, respectively, a shoemaker, blacksmith (he was called a machinist in his later years), iron moulder, and whitesmith (tinsmith). The couple's son Robert was a carpenter who became an architect and estate manager for Hugh Annesley, Earl Annesley of Castlewellan, Viscount Glerawly and Baron Annesley of Castlewellan. Robert married the daughter of a shopkeeper.[36] (When John Steele wrote of Margaret Kirkwood—a cousin of the wife of his brother-in-law Robert Campbell—that she "has property on her account" he was linking her with the minor gentry.)

These occupations are far removed from royalty and nobility, but some children of royalty descended to nobility, some of those descended to gentry, and some gentry to merchants; as a result, there was fluidity between social classes, with some rising and some falling.[37]

The Campbells and Knoxes likely had kin of higher as well as lower rank (contemporary Campbells and Knoxes are County Tyrone and County Down gentry), and once Catherine's Knox cousins were liberated from Old World constrictions with their immigration to New York, they rose quickly and in some cases became members of the highest social classes. Catherine's cousin Arthur Knox—her grandfather's namesake—was president of his Columbia Law School class.[38] Cousin William Elliott Knox became president of the Bowery Savings Bank, second largest savings bank in America, and served a term as president of the American Bankers Association; he owned a home in New Rochelle and another on Park Avenue before succumbing to depression and taking his own life in 1927, two years before suicide became a career exit for bankers.[39] Cousin Dr. John Knox graduated from the University of Virginia and married twice into the Virginia bluebloods—his first wife, Lucy Conwayella Macon, a grandniece of President James Madison.[40] Catherine's cousin, Hunter College graduate and author Margaret Knox, became such a noted educator that her death earned a ten-paragraph story in the *New York Times*.[41]

We know very little about Catherine's mother, Mary Knox, except she was a daughter of Arthur and Margaret (Graham) Knox. A "Mrs. Campbell" is in *Matier's Belfast Directory 1835–1836* at "7 King st., dressmaker,"[42] apparently before Catherine's family moved there, but may have been a relative as Catherine was a "trained tailor," her sister Mary Ann a "Dress Maker," sister Rebecca a "seamstress," and younger sister Eliza a "Drefsmaker."[43] (John Steele is shown in 1840 as a shoemaker at "18 King-street" so could have met her through the otherwise unidentified "Mrs. Campbell" who had a shop nearby.)[44]

Michael and Mary were at "7 Hope's court," Belfast, in 1843 but by 1847 had moved to "26, Bank lane," where they remained until 1852, when their place was taken by William Butler, "bootcloser."[45]

Michael Campbell's grandchildren proudly cited Campbell family traits. Campbells are youthful and long-lived: "I have seen father climb up a ladder to the top of a 6 storey building and go over scaffolds when he was about 80 years of age," recalled Catherine's nephew William, writing to an elderly first cousin he believed had inherited the family spryness. "He was very youthful even at a very old age," William's sister Maryanne added. And the Campbells were musical—cousins boasted of their public performances and claimed that humor and drollery were special family inheritances.[46]

Family members also said Catherine's son Mahonri bore a striking resemblance to her father, which suggests Michael Campbell was prematurely bald, exaggerating his rounded cranium, and big-eared with slightly hollow cheeks.

His deep-set, dark eyes were from his father John; a picture of Catherine's brother Robert Campbell displays the same features.

Catherine's photograph shows us a woman with a thin mouth, firm nose, serious eyes, and one eyebrow raised skeptically. She was delicate and loved fine clothing. Family legend says she was taller than John and had sandy-red hair. The light eyebrows in her photographs suggest a fair complexion. Catherine was also a well-educated woman for her time and wrote in a clear and uncrowded hand—spelling better than John, who was himself educated above the average for his time.

John was born in Holywood, County Down, famous for its Maypole, said to be the oldest in Ireland and dating from 1700.[47] He was a person whose outsized ego contrasted with an undersized frame. What kind of a man could we expect him to claim as a founder of the Steele clan? Naturally, *The Ancestor* should have brothers who peopled the world by migrating to Scotland and America to found foreign branches of this illustrious house; he should outlast six fruitful wives; father eighteen or twenty children; boast sons all six feet tall; and live for a hundred and ten years.[48]

John assures us such a one was Arthur Steele of Glenavy, County Antrim, a Scotchman who married an Irish wife named Mary Shannon, who was required to bear him the requisite seven sons—"and some daughters," John added, perhaps apologetically.

After that, the family seems positively feeble. Arthur's son, also named Arthur, fathered only fifteen children by two successive wives, Elizabeth Greenfield and Jenny Higgins (but had enough vinegar to abandon the second), and with the special longevity standard established by his father, died in his prime at eighty-eight. Arthur was followed by John, an Irish sergeant who first married Susan Williams, a niece of the colonel of his regiment, and second, Nancy Kennedy of the respectable Holywood Kennedys. This John was dismissed from the Duke of Kent's First Regiment of Foot after twenty-one years for "Being woarn out."[49] By Nancy Kennedy, John had two daughters, Elizabeth (born 1818) and Jane (born 1819), and John Jr.—our John—born March 21, 1821, when the old Peninsular War soldier was forty-seven years old.[50]

John Jr.—whom we'll call John—was a short man with deep, inquiring eyes and vigorous health who wrote a cramped, hasty hand. He crammed each page with more information than it could hold, then ran sentences up around the borders—sometimes found that inadequate and added afterthoughts to the top of the first page. Catherine, if we can judge from a single letter, wrote in a leisurely hand and was untroubled by empty white space.

John's temper mirrored his letters, spitting like overheated oatmeal and burning wherever it landed. Frank Beckwith,[51] probably relying on John's papers—which he studied and partially published—and on descriptions by Catherine's granddaughter and namesake Catherine (later she used "Cathren") "Cassie" Steele Riding, described John as "this irascible old pepperbox[,] this Irish midge no bigger than a pint o' soap after a hard day's wash[,] took no sass from anybody big or little, just itched for a fight and when he saw a scrap begged for permission to get into it. Was a good judge of whiskey and a tease to the women—what an ancestor!" Beckwith added later that Steele was "a fighter who cared not for size or brawn . . . who walloped his school master and then walloped the bully who hit the master."[52]

"All the Steeles had been military men," explained Reba Roundy LeFevre, John's great-granddaughter. Because John's father had been a soldier, John was "brought up as a military man. You was strict with what you done. You done exactly what they said. And that's what he came up with, he said, well, he's a military man, why then everything had to be right on the dot." Reba summed up this authoritarian philosophy as, "You do as they say! That's what he told all his kids: 'You do what they say.'"[53] And that's what he told Catherine: "All I ask my family to do is for them to do as I want them."[54]

In an unfortunately too succinct paragraph, John summarized his young manhood, courtship, and early married life. "I went to Belfast and commenced business for myself and kept a boot and shoe shop in my 18th year, and in my 19th year I got acquainted with Miss Catherine Campbell, daughter of Michael and Mary Campbell. And on the 1st day of January 1840 at 10 o'clock in the morning, I married her."[55] The marriage was probably performed by the Rev. James Morgan, DD, graduate of Glasgow University and minister of Fisherwick Place Church in Belfast, "a voluminous writer" and one whom John thought enough of to have posthumously made a Mormon,[56] through a special religious ritual of baptizing for the dead.

"Things did not prosper with me at this time," John wrote. "Many trials were we caused to pass through, which caused us to think the world was an enemy to its own."[57] The nature of these trials probably was not only poverty, but John's personality—"flighty,"[58] Reba said, picking the perfect adjective.

In January 1841, a few weeks after his father died, John left Belfast for Glasgow in Scotland, found work, and sent for Catherine and their infant daughter, Mary Campbell Steele. Years later Catherine's brother Robert recalled their life in Glasgow, writing in admiration for the progress they'd made "since you left Great Doo Hill in overcrowded Glasgow with all its pinching poverty and misery."[59] John III was born June 2, 1842, in Glasgow, and Margaret on June 17, 1844. Catherine seems to have philosophically accepted the world while John funneled his resentments into all the radical utopian causes to change it: a strike agitator in labor-torn Glasgow; leader in a workman's insurance organization called the Raccabite Club; subscribing to the principles of the Chartists, endorsing socialism and later claiming a great role in strikes and promoting workers' rights—though he is not mentioned in either *The Chartist Circular* (1839–1842), published in Glasgow, nor in *The English Chartist Circular* (1841–1844). He was also too radical for the Covenanter Presbyterians and became obsessed with religion and searched for the one true church.[60]

His story of conversion to Mormonism was typical of many others: he heard of the religion founded by the self-proclaimed American prophet Joseph Smith, read Apostle Parley P. Pratt's *Voice of Warning*,[61] also read power loom tender Graham Douglass's copy of the revelation called the Book of Mormon, "believed what it contained, and in the evening of the 10th of April I was baptised, 1843." Catherine was not so enthused: "My wife did not believe until I preached the Gospel to her, and in a few weeks she was baptized also, May 3, 1843."[62]

John's conversion meant Catherine was on her own while he went off preaching. When he decided, thanks to a legacy from his half-brother William, to migrate to the United States in 1845 to help build the Kingdom of God, Catherine was also dragged along—though he told the story so succinctly he forgot to mention he had anyone with him: "Soon shipped on board the ship *Palmyra* for New Orleans, a distance of 5000 miles, and set sell from the Marsy Rise [in Liverpool] on the 21st of January. Had 9 days storm and after a pleasant voyage of six weeks and three days arrived at New Orleans on 7th of March, 1845. And on the 11th of March, left the ship for the steam boat and proceeded up the river" to St. Louis, Missouri.[63]

Here in St. Louis John carefully inventoried all their worldly goods including Catherine's personal trunk full of her valued Irish linens. He appraised everything they owned at thirty dollars and then cheerfully gave three dollars to Erastus Snow as tithing. They worked for a Mr. Bates on 3rd Street at boot making.[64] Catherine, a skilled seamstress,[65] did the fine stitching and John sided and bottomed them up. After three months they went on to Nauvoo, Illinois, the Mormon gathering place.

Joseph Smith and his brother Hyrum had been murdered in June, 1844. When Catherine arrived in Nauvoo in July 1845, she spent her first night in the "Mansion House," the hotel God ordered built for Joseph Smith and now run by his widow Emma. Despite the impressive newly built city and nearly completed temple, the Mormons were facing expulsion. Still, the young family soon had a home, with Catherine settled into homemaking and probably seamstress work while John made shoes for the Nauvoo Tanners and Shoemaking Association.[66]

The lower part of Nauvoo is a low, broad green field that juts out to the Mississippi River. A few restored buildings dot the marshy field but the present town sprawls across a hill northeast of the foundation of the temple. In Mormon prophet Joseph Smith's day, he lived on and owned much of the low field and marketed that land to his followers. Rival land speculators on the hill were so angry by his neglect of their interests that some were accused of complicity in his murder. Unfortunately this low land was swampy and malarial and Catherine, like many others, found her family sick with "fever and ague and soon with fatigue."[67] Only four-year-old Mary was well enough to wait on them. John III, aged three, died on December 10, 1845, followed by eighteen-month-old Margaret eight days later.[68] Catherine knew firsthand what God meant when he promised to multiply her sorrow.

"Mother" Bullock, probably church clerk Thomas Bullock's wife Henrietta, visited the sick family and said she might as well take Mary as everyone else was going to die. That's probably just what feisty John needed—anger enough to keep him alive. He rose up and informed Bullock, "I would not die, nor my wife should not die, and I would not give her Mary."[69] They recovered and he went to work as a carpenter on the Nauvoo Temple until their leaders agreed the Mormons would leave the city.

On May 4, 1846, they abandoned Nauvoo and like many others couldn't take all their personal property. John insisted Catherine's precious cedar chest be left behind. According to a family story it was filled with "good linen and lace and everything that was made in Ireland," including "a beautiful looking glass and all her fineries." It was so full that Catherine had to sit on it so John could fasten the lid. "Now Sister Steele, don't never look back!" the people warned Catherine. "Don't be like Lot's wife, don't never look back." "But she couldn't take it," her great-granddaughter Reba Roundy LeFevre explained. "When she got so far out she looked back and she saw a big old ax come right down on the top of all her good linen and everything else . . . She never got over it."[70]

The refugees migrated to Mt. Pisgah, Iowa, where U.S. Colonel James Allen found them and, authorized by President Polk, raised a battalion for the United States' war with Mexico.[71] John enlisted as a soldier on July 18, 1846, and his later recollection, perhaps with hyperbole as it was in the form of a eulogy, was that when they got "the call from our nations Chief [to] fight the Battle of our Countary and to Compell a foreign foe to Give up part of her vast domain even 350 leagues long upon the Shores of the Great Paciffic Sea She [Catherine] Sh[irked?] not but Said wee'l go."[72]

Catherine was one of twenty women who signed up as a laundress, with five-year-old Mary one of the few children to join the march. John and Catherine celebrated that night with music and dancing and next day were each issued a blanket, tin cup, knife, fork, and spoon.

"Provisions were scarce," explained an early Steele family history, "but the soldiers shared with the child, rather than leave her behind." When Catherine was sick, which was most of the time—she became pregnant during the latter part of the trek—she rode in the wagon. Colonel Allen, John tells us, was especially solicitous of Catherine's health. She cooked with buffalo chips for their mess—including irascible Levi Savage, shoemaker Ezra Fatoute, and Hayward Thomas. She slept on the ground in a tent and waited patiently while the Brethren admired Indian ruins which they identified as ancient Book of Mormon "Nephite works."[73]

When the Americans approached San Miguel they saw Spanish women sitting on top of a one story, flat-roofed adobe home eyeing Catherine and little Mary. Soon an aged man, who proved to be the father of these women, invited them in. "Then when my women got out of the wagon," John wrote, "there was such a hugging as I had never seen before, as that is their manner of saluting." John, spying a crucifix in the home, made the sign of the cross and this so won over the Mexicans that Catherine and the whole family were treated like lost kin. But John worried about his team, insisted his family move on, and justified it later by arguing the Mexicans had plans to "steal my little girl."[74]

At Santa Fe the new commander, tall and lean Philip St. George Cooke, announced the women, children, and sick would be sent to Bent's Fort and the married men would travel on alone. John tried to organize a protest over the separation but he could only get John Hess to support him, and Hess had to be fortified with whisky; Steele claimed it fell upon him to argue with Colonel Cooke. When Steele was so angry he felt like he "could have thrashed the ground with him," Hess said the Colonel pointed out that he too left his wife behind and Hess replied, "Colonel, I suppose you left your wife with her friends, while we are required to leave ours in an enemy's country in care of a lot of sick, demoralized men." Hess thought that "seemed to touch a sympathetic cord."[75]

Cooke relented and eighty-seven men and twenty women and at least one child, John and Catherine's Mary, were detached for Pueblo, Colorado, with Catherine's husband driving a wagon full of women. Their supplies were limited: when they got to Bent's Fort they were down to four ounces of food a day. At Bent's they replenished their stores and when they arrived in Pueblo on November 18, 1846, they were feeling better until they spent the winter under the command of Captain James Brown.

Catherine was no doubt unhappy listening to the men quarreling over Brown's alleged dishonesty, profanity, and authoritarianism, and noticed that they resented the other officers as well. Once John had her try to give a message to Benjamin Roberts, who had been tied to an anvil as punishment. Because the rules forbade any conversation with the malefactor she wasn't successful. "We all feel the hands of tyrants," wrote John in his journal. John said Brown's "common word is 'God Dam their soul! to hell', 'But I will have their God-damned throats cut,' just as if we were as many niggers in the south."

When Captain Nelson Higgins asked the one hundred and thirty men to pray for the leaders, only six or eight grudgingly admitted they would. Higgins was once especially abusive to the women, probably including Catherine since John angrily wrote about it in his journal. Higgins had gotten into a public fracas with some men and then turned on the curious female spectators, shouting that "they were like an old goose that had wore all the froth out of their tail and did not know their arce from a hole in the ground."

Catherine must have welcomed May 25, 1847, when they picked up camp from Pueblo for the Mormon trail to take them to the Salt Lake Valley. The trip was mostly uneventful, but Reba Roundy LeFevre recalls family folklore not corroborated by Steele's irregularly kept journal, but perhaps a distorted version of the story of their arrival in San Miguel. "On the way back, why, Grandma got tired 'cause she was with child. She got tired and Grandpa said, 'why, there's a house right over there. Let's go over and see if we can spend the night there.'" They went over and the woman at the house said they could stay until her husband got there. "But when Grandpa got back out to the wagon" Catherine said, "we're not staying here!"

"We're not?"

"No," Catherine announced with rare assertiveness, "get in the wagon, we're leaving."

They went on, camped elsewhere, and next morning the others caught up with them and told them of the danger they'd been in from anti-Mormons. "That place where you were going to stay, they were going to kill all of you. Going to kill every one of you," John and Catherine were informed. "So Grandpa said, 'my wife was a little wiser than I was that time,'" Reba chuckled, adding that this was the first of the two times Catherine defied John.[76]

On August 1, 1847, they arrived in the Salt Lake Valley, just a week after the first Mormon pioneer band led by Brigham Young. They left Mt. Pisgah looking fresh and light-skinned but now they were as sunburned and weather-beaten as the mountain men. They were dressed in moccasins, beads, and buckskin with fringes and porcupine quill decorations—as fancy as so many Native Americans, and showing Hispanic-Mexican influence by riding on Spanish saddles and using Spanish bridles with "jinglers." In this finery they made camp, went next day to the hot springs and bathed and—refreshed—began planting buckwheat and turnips.[77]

Even before they arrived, Young had laid out their future in a July 28 sermon for all of the "Camp of Israel." He pointed out that the valley had enough water for a city of a hundred thousand. The Camp unanimously voted to settle the Great Salt Lake area. Brigham Young—whose millennial utopianism was, except in economics, usually balanced by hardheaded practicality—outlined exactly what his plans were. According to pioneer diarist Norton Jacob, there were to be forty acre blocks, streets eighty-eight feet wide, sidewalks twenty feet, each lot to contain one and one-quarter acres, eight lots in a block, houses set in the center of the lot, twenty feet back from the street. "A man may live here with us & worship what God he pleases or none at all, but he must not blaspheme the God of Israel nor dam old Joe Smith or his religion, for we will Salt him down in the lake!"

Young also called for a Mormon autarky, a self-contained economy because "The Kingdom of God cannot rise independant of the gentile nations until we produce, Manufacture, & make every article of use, convenience, or neces[s]ity among our own People." His plan was that they eventually "need no commerc[e] with the nations" because this would be the place, independent, self-sustaining and holy, where Christ would find his Kingdom when he soon returned to earth.[78]

"Well," Young continued, "I have a Sermon to Preach to the Sisters concerning <u>their</u> duty, and I believe I will give some of it to you now."

"Let us have it, says Several voices."

Young did.

"I will begin by saying there's not a woman in this Church that Knows her duty. My Wife probably Knows as much as any woman in the Church, & she does not Know her duty!!" Just as Brigham's duty was to inquire of God, "Lord what is thy will?" wives should inquire, "Husband what is thy will?" His will,

Young declared, was "that you take care of my clothes & keep them & your house clean," take care of the children, instruct and teach them, and don't let them run about the streets and associate with bad companions. He concluded that if a woman "will continual[l]y resist all temptation she will be blessed herself, & the body of her child will be larger, more strong & robust, the Spirit mild & tractable, & [in] this way our race will become improved, until the age of Man shall be as the age of a Tree."[79]

These sentiments of command and control fit John's temperament quite nicely; making clothes, cleaning house, righteous living, and mothering were things Catherine apparently did willingly and patiently.[80]

Catherine had ten days or so to contemplate the millennial plans for the valley before she went into labor on a buffalo robe with a government-issued Mormon Battalion tent over her where the east wall of the Salt Lake Temple now stands.[81]

"Monday 9 August 1847," wrote Camp historian Thomas Bullock in his journal, "—About one hour before day break [3:40 a.m.] Catherine Steele Wife of John Steele was safely delivered of a daughter named Young Elizabeth by Ruth Abbott."[82] Ruth Markham Abbott, wife of Mormon Battalion soldier Joshua Chandler Abbott, was a fellow battalion laundress and undoubtedly a friend of Catherine's.[83]

Cries from a new baby were probably welcome because the company was made up almost entirely of adults, as Bullock had noted two months before: "Sunday 6 June 1847. Fast Day—a cloudy morning. Heard a young child cry [from a nearby "Gentile" camp], which is quite a novelty to us, in the Pioneer Camp of Israel."[84]

John recorded the historic birth in his journal: "This morning before break of day my wife was delivered safely and speedily of a fine daughter, being the <u>first</u> <u>birth</u> in this great city, named Young Elizabeth."

And John composed a verse to celebrate:

It was on the ninth of August
Before the sun was up
There was a little stranger
Came to my board to sup
With flaxen ringlets
And cheeks of rosy hue
My pretty little young one
This morn, how do you do?[85]

Though Young Elizabeth (named for Brigham Young and John's sister Elizabeth)[86] was Catherine's fourth-born child, two had been buried in Nauvoo and the huge, nearly empty Great Salt Lake Valley must have seemed a forbidding place to bring forth another. The Mountain Man Jim Bridger had supposedly assured John that he would give them a thousand dollars for the first ear of corn raised in this valley because, Bridger claimed, "it froze every month in the year."[87]

Three days after Elizabeth's birth (no one called her "Young") she was blessed by Heber C. Kimball and John got to work making her a pair of shoes. Years later it was reported that "old grandfather Steele is said to have said this in a Pioneer celebration on the Twenty-fourth of July: 'I made the first last in Utah; I made the first shoe that was made on the last; I made the first foot that went into the shoe.'"[88]

Apostle Charles C. Rich's wife Sarah De Armon Pea Rich remembered that fall of 1847. "One of the families of the Mormon Battalion let us have two small rooms to live in until we could get a room built. This was a great accommodation to us," she wrote.[89] That family may have been the Steeles, for Sarah was fond enough of Catherine to send her news ten years later, and John wrote in his diary on April 16, 1848, "Several of our neighbors would come and get butter and milk" from a cow the Steeles bought for ten dollars on the Platte River, "and swap us measure for measure and our butter brought us meat or flour, especially from Gen. [Charles C.] Rich and family. He always stood by us in our trials and was kind under every circumstance."[90]

Despite hunger, John solaced himself with the honor paid him because the 29th Quorum of Seventies met at his home, Catherine preparing for the priesthood brethren and cleaning up afterward.

Catherine and John joined the Scottish dances as William Park played the fiddle to dance to old Scottish ditties like the Laird O'Cockpen who wooed Jean Lee, "A penniless lass wi' a lang pedigree."[91] Spring of 1849 they moved onto their city lot on the northwest corner of Seventh East and Fifth South where they ploughed and planted.[92] On May first at 9:45 a.m., assisted by Elizabeth Edwards and a Mrs. Hamilton, Catherine bore a son in the cellar. They named him Mahonri Moriancumer, his peculiar name said to have been that of the brother of Jared, a Book of Mormon character.[93]

2

"Convicts to Bondsman's Lands"

Catherine and Elizabeth Steele

In the fall of 1850, Catherine and John were called to go under command of the rotund Mormon Apostle George A. Smith to found a settlement more than two hundred miles south of Salt Lake.[1] Their mission was to exploit rich coal and iron resources in what became Iron County, with the home manufactured iron contributing to building the Kingdom.[2]

Catherine, by now an experienced frontierswoman, drove a large yoke of oxen pulling a wagon loaded with cooking tools and a stove.[3] They stopped in a big, open valley on January 13, 1851, and John, Tarleton Lewis, and two or three others found enough timber in the mountains to encourage a settlement. They laid out the city of Parowan ("mean" or "evil" water in Paiute[4]) at the base of a canyon that knifed through the red hills. The pioneers got a city charter, elected a mayor, chose John as marshal, and built a log meetinghouse.

John's sketchy journal barely mentions Catherine. He was building God's Kingdom, occupying every week with prayer meetings, exploring, serving as a major in the Iron Battalion, and participating in Indian expeditions (John played a typical and shameful role in Native American displacement). In 1853 he was city mayor—at the same time serving as Iron County judge and recorder, besides being counselor for a time to tall, thin schoolteacher and Stake President John Calvin Lazelle Smith.[5] He had many talents and wasn't afraid of leadership. Sometimes that leadership meant social opportunities for Catherine as she occasionally accompanied John on visits to other settlements, as shown in Henry Lunt's journal on June 18, 1853: "About 11 A.M. J[ohn] C. L. Smith[,] John Steele and Ladies, and some 8 more brethren and their Ladies drove up to my House in 2 carriages and 4 Horses each and 1 carriage and 2 [horses]." The group drove on to Harmony with Lunt where John D. Lee "slaughtered a sheep—the brethren made us very welcome and in the evening we enjoyed ourselves in the dance, in a large room of bro Lee's."[6]

And there were more Steele children, though John's journal entries forgot Catherine: "I had a daughter born to me on the 28th day of April at 22 minutes to 8 p.m. in the year 1851, on Monday, named Susan [Adams] Steele." And later: "On the 6th of April [1853] . . . my son John Alma was born at 9 o'clock a.m. on Wednesday." He took time out to organize and direct a town drama club, and then Catherine's fecundity proved itself again: "Jane Catherine Steele, born Thursday, April 26, A.D., 1855, about 9."

John was released as stake counselor in 1855 to help found Las Vegas, Nevada. James H. Martineau wrote Apostle Smith about the Pentecostal-like send-off Parowan gave their two Las Vegas missionaries: "We gave a party to John Steele and W. C. Mitchell Jr. which was powerfully influenced by the Holy Spirit and your wife Zilpha spoke most powerfully in tongues to the missionaries and the sisters, prophesying many things, which Br. [John] Calvin [Lazelle Smith] interpreted and others also. She prophesied many things, both to the missionaries and of the church."[7]

Catherine supervised things at home and John returned a few times, but spent most of the next two years in Las Vegas making adobe brick, exploring, baptizing Indians, furtively searching for silver and openly prospecting for lead, sometimes quarreling with mission leadership—except when he was in charge—and doing his own domestic work. "I still get along first rate and wash make & mend like some old woman," John assured Catherine on October 13, 1855.[8]

Zilpha probably didn't prophecy that the wheat John planted before he left on his mission would be destroyed by grasshoppers before fall harvest. "When I hear that there is mo [no] meal in they barrel & they Bishop has now and no money to Buy any with in the Treasury It Makes me feel as if: my little Babeys are hungary," John wrote to George A. Smith on October 1.[9]

Catherine, hardened with experience, was equal to the challenge. She sold her cow, "old, poor, and blind of one eye" for fifteen bushels of wheat to James Henry Martineau.[10]

Catherine had other problems not of her making. On July 13, 1856, Jedediah M. Grant, a raw-boned, youthful Mormon apostle whom John considered a special friend, called upon the sinful residents of Provo to reform. "The Church needs trimming up, and if you will search, you will find in your wards certain branches which had better be cut off."[11] This began a chapter in Mormon history known as the "Reformation." In some settlements a few took literally doctrines like "blood atonement," where one should kill the guilty and let their blood run to atone for their sins.

Brigham Young had a penchant for vengeful language, as the sermon he gave four days after arriving in the valley showed when he talked about the fate of a hypothetical opponent: "Salt him down in the lake."[12] And Young had advice for pesky federal officials who were starting to show up: "He hoped to live to lead forth the armies of Israel to execute the judgements & justice on the persecuting Gentiles & that no officer of the United States should ever dictate to him in this valley, or he would hang them on a gibbet as a warning to others."[13]

Parowan, far from being exempt, was on the hardscrabble southern Utah frontier. Apostle George A. Smith—cousin to the murdered prophet Joseph Smith and Parowan founder—hated federal intrusion and federal judges and preached on December 26, 1853, "All the business I want to come before the Court in Iron Co next summer, is for all to become democrats who are mind to. Do not carry news to [federal] Judges. Let the Bishop or teachers kick any man's ass and land him in G. S. Lake & pickel him in saleratus of salt who shall carry news to the judge."[14]

"You know my feelings with regard to Californ[i]ans," wrote Apostle Smith's cousin and Parowan resident Jesse Nathaniel Smith. "Salt em at once rather than have them eat up the Saints but if you do, Salt em down so that their—may not rattle bells to the no Small annoyance of Settlers."[15]

A by-product of the Reformation was the promotion of early marriages, considered a fornication preventive and sure to increase the number of saints in Zion. A new Parowan stake president, excitable but timid William H. Dame, took special delight trying to promote matches amongst the teenagers,[16] perhaps to subconsciously compensate for his own sterility and the consequent inability of any of his three wives to present the world with new Dames.

John Steele wrote a poem about sex entitled "Forbidden Fruit" and explained that in his ideal world marriages would be consummated early:

> I'd have the young united Stand
> From fourteen years and up
> To eighteen years of measured time
> Before they'd taste the Cup.[17]

John and Catherine's sixteen-year-old daughter Mary was vulnerable. A lively girl who was described by her second husband with the adjectives sociable, quick-witted, high-minded, ambitious, and hardworking, Mary was interested in dark-haired, scholarly fifteen-year-old Joseph Fish. John would have nothing to do with the match because of the age of the proposed groom. Mary must marry eighteen-year-old Thomas LeFevre, a member of Steele's militia.[18]

"He was a poor worthless fellow," Fish wrote of LeFevre in an early draft of his memoirs, but later softened it slightly to read, "He was rather a trifling person and belonged to that worthless class of young men who were neither very good or very bad."[19] LeFevre's uncle wrote a brief memoir and spoke respectfully of Tom, though it must be admitted that by 1875 LeFevre was described by the anti-Mormon *Salt Lake Tribune* as a man who "once belonged to the [LDS] church, but has been a free man for a number of years."[20] Mary objected that she loved Fish and not LeFevre, but John only had to recall efforts to set new community standards, like Isaac Haight preached a year later: "The Gentile custom of Sparkification was done away so that the passions may not be aroused and undue advantage taken of the chastity of the Daughters of Zion by these pernicious habits &c.," and "Marry first and spark after."[21]

When Mary asked for more time, John knew Brigham counseled men to "Get good young Women when you Get them that can be controld."[22] And given the nature of Steele's own personality—Fish described him as "one of those stern characters who compelled their children to obey them in all things"[23]—he insisted she get married, he insisted she get married now, and he insisted she get married to Thomas LeFevre.

This was done in February 1856, and when John learned of the young couple's subsequent marital problems he wrote Catherine on April 23, "tell Mary to do the best she Can and talk good all the time tell Thomas he must be a good boy and I shal bless him," and then, perhaps remembering the schoolgirl that Mary still was, he lectured, "I want Mary to continue to write as it will improve her hand tell her to take more pains and put all the Letters into the words."[24] This loveless match, doomed to failure, was a dramatic demonstration of John's attitudes toward women and courtship. "She went over and married him," her grandniece Reba Roundy LeFevre said, "and she lived there—I don't know, a month or—two or three weeks, and she said, 'I don't want him! I don't want him at all. I wanted Joe Fish,'"[25] and they were soon divorced.

Mary's romance with Joseph Fish may have started at an outing to Panguitch Lake, for her brother M. M. later joked of "a certain 'fish' which his sister caught swimming in the lake many years ago, 'who' was six feet 'long'; his other name was Joseph. Otherwise the fine mountain trout which abounds in the lake seldom exceeds one and a half pounds in weight."[26] After the divorce, Mary married Fish—her first choice—a talented, self-educated diarist, historian, and community leader.

A possible consequence of the Reformation included the attempted murder of John Tobin, son-in-law to Catherine's friend Sarah D. Rich. Brigham Young sent letters warning local Mormon leaders about two ex-convicts headed south, Thomas Betts and John G. Ambrose, writing William H. Dame, Parowan stake president, to "Be on the lookout now, & have a few trusty men ready in case of need to pursue, retake & punish. We do not suppose there would be any prosecutions for false imprisonments, or tale bearers for witnesses . . . Make no noise of this matter, & keep this letter safe. We write for your eye alone, & to men that can be trusted."[27]

Betts and Ambrose joined others to make up a party of eleven or twelve but they split south of Parowan with John C. Peltro, John Tobin, John Williams, and perhaps a Mr. Smith going on. Peltro's group got to Santa Clara Creek February 17, where it was so cold they kept their fire burning all night. At four a.m. they were attacked by small arms fire and when Tobin rose up in bed he was shot under his right eye and through his cheekbone. John Williams lost two fingers and a bullet grazed one of the other men in the back of the neck while Peltro returned fire. No one died but the suspicion was that a group sent by Dame had attacked the wrong party, thinking they were Betts and Ambrose.

Catherine wrote a now missing letter to Sarah D. Rich reporting the attack and what she said can be inferred from Rich's response. "Dear sister," Rich replied, "I Suppose your have heard by this Time Some of my troubles concerning Mr. Tobin . . . there was reports out that he was killed and your letter is The firsd we had heard cerTain aboud his gitting away." Rich concluded,

> Sister Steel if I could see you I could talk a whole week about what has transpired since you was hear We now have The besd meetings I was ever at The refermation has done a work long to be remembered in this city as well as in other places I hope you have good times out thare now . . . Plese to write every chance give my love to Brother Steel and Mary and all the family Sarah Jane sends her best regards to you and Brother Steel and Mary Tell Brother Steel that he never saw the like of the marrying among the old men that there is this winter even old Ellick has taken 2 young girls lately and hundreds of others.

She signed off, "good Knight Sarah D. Rich."[28]

Catherine saw how much further fanaticism could go later in 1857. Ongoing problems between the Mormon theocracy and the federal government culminated when President James Buchanan ordered troops to Utah to replace Brigham Young as governor and quell a supposed rebellion. The Mormon reaction was hysteria and fear of more mobbing and was not tempered by the red-hot responses from Brigham Young, George A. Smith, and other angry leaders. Smith went on a preaching tour to Parowan to rouse the settlers and was so busy with his fiery oratory that John Steele acted as amanuensis for a letter to Smith's London-based missionary brother John L.

We know John L.'s response: "br Geo when I think about Unkle Sam's raising his puny arm against the Saints of the most high, & Sending 2500 (as we are Informed) Soldiers to revolutionized Utah & hang up The leaders it makes my (shall I Say Smith Blood, or Mormon Blood) boil to think I am not there to take part in the strug[g]le if strug[g]le there be," and adding "on my return I Intend bringing a pair of 'Colts' which I already have & an Enfield Rifle or a Mine' [Minié ball] if I can obtain one."[29]

Catherine was in Parowan due to deliver a baby when the "Gentile" Fancher party tried to make its way from Arkansas to California through the excited settlements. The Fancher group reached Cedar City on September 4 and after friction with the settlers, camped west of town. They couldn't have been in a more dangerous community, for in 1853 most of Cedar's independent-minded families left Utah after mutinying against the heavy-handed way their cattle had been taken during the Walker Indian War. Their disgruntlement led to numerous court-martials for most of the dissidents and those who didn't abandon Cedar City were the most obedient to authority.[30]

The party headed west toward Mountain Meadows while Cedar City's Isaac C. Haight—a onetime Nauvoo policeman and member of the posse that destroyed the *Nauvoo Expositor*—was now mayor, legislator, and militia leader. Haight sent young John Chatterley to Parowan with a note apparently requesting permission from William H. Dame and the high council to murder the emigrants through the use of Indian allies. Years later Chatterley identified John Steele as one of the council members who debated Haight's message.[31]

According to historians Ronald W. Walker, Richard E. Turley Jr., and Glen M. Leonard, "The council decided that 'all possible means should be used to keep the peace until the emigrants should leave and proceed upon their journey.'" They say, "Dame sent a letter in answer counseling peace, and for them not to regard their [the emigrants] threats, as, according to Parowan leader James H. Martineau, 'words are but wind.'"

Massacre participant and onetime Cedar City bishop Philip Klingensmith testified later that "Haight went to Parowan to get instructions and then he received orders from Col. Dame to decoy the emigrants out and spare nothing but the small children who could not tell tales," countermanding the order for peace, if such an order was given. This fits Dame, who was a weak-willed man according to Steele's son-in-law Joseph Fish—"a man that wished to push off all the responsible things that were not agreeable for him to shoulder on to those of others."[32]

Haight proceeded to organize an Indian attack on the Fanchers. After John died, his son M. M. told Carl Ashby Badger that John "always insisted that Dame at Beaver [Parowan, not Beaver], was the guiltiest party. It was said that Dame moulded the bullets that were used at the massacre."[33] Steele and Dame didn't always get along, Steele once saying "he thought Br. Dame wished to crowd him down, and referred to some past circumstances as proof."[34] John would have reasonably blamed Dame for responsibility if the irresolute man had reversed the council's decision to let the travelers go in peace.

When the Fancher party put up a heavy and successful resistance the Cedar City militia was sent to Mountain Meadows. Mormon Indian agent John D. Lee enticed the emigrants out of their redoubt under a white flag and promise of safety, but once the prisoners were defenseless a signal was given and the Mormons and their Indian allies murdered all but seventeen children. As many as 120 met their deaths on September 11, 1857, in the bloodied meadows.[35]

John Steele's papers record another event ten days earlier: "Robert Henry Steele, born September 1, 1857," showing Catherine gave birth to another son.[36]

"Have you any Roberts in your family, or Henrys? Your [Campbell] uncles names were these,"[37] wrote Maryanne Campbell Wilson to her cousin Mahonri fifty years later. Alas, they had not. Steele's replacement in the stake presidency, James Henry Martineau, got a letter from his wife Susan in Parowan initially dated May 30, 1858, reporting, "we have just heard of the death of sister Steeles baby [Robert Henry Steele] you remember it had a breaking out on its head and face and they gave it some Calomel which made the disease strike in and killed it."[38] John Steele's journal reports that the baby "died June 1, 1858, aged 9 months; buried at Parowan" and a paper in his old trunk gave what was probably meant for a tombstone inscription for his young son:[39]

> Sacred to the memory of Robert Steele
> Who departed this life
> June . . . 1858 Born Sept 1
> Aged 9 months

But did John associate this boy, born so near the day of the mass killings, with that event? He wrote some very odd notes on the other side of this paper (I have completed the scriptural references in square brackets):

> REVEL 14 AND 13
>
> Blessed are the Dead Which Die in . . . [the Lord from henceforth: Yea, saith the Spirit, that they may rest from their labours; and their works do follow them]
>
> REV 16 AND 6
>
> For they have Shed the Blood of Saints [and prophets, and thou hast given them blood to drink; for they are unworthy] Come out of her my people [that ye be not partakers of her sins, and that ye receive not of her plagues] &c Rev 18 & 4
>
> REV 18 AND 24
>
> And in her was found the Blood of prophets, [and of saints, and of all that were slain upon the earth.]
>
> REV 18 AND 20
>
> Rejoice over her ye heavens ye Holy apostles [more correctly: Rejoice over her, thou heaven, and ye holy apostle and prophets; for God hath avenged you on her.] &c
>
> REVELATIONS 17 AND 4 TO 6TH
>
> And I saw the woman drunken with the B[lood] of the Saints and the Blood of the martyres [of Jesus: and when I saw her, I wondered with great admiration] &c—the plagues Revelations 15 erd [*sic*] to . . .

Catherine never resigned herself to the loss of this son with the Campbell family names and thirty years after leaving Parowan, when she knew she was going to die, she demanded her body be taken back and placed next to Robert Henry's. John was not one to mourn: "Dont worrey about those who are Dead," he counseled his niece Letisha Todd: "They are far better off than those who are alive."[40]

Years later, when Dame was brought before Judge McKean at the third district court in Beaver for his murky role in the massacre, he was viewed with anything but friendliness by the judge. John's reaction was decidedly interesting, too, for shortly afterward Joseph Fish wrote Catherine, "Dear Mother Steele I have neglected to answer yours for I expected Bro Steele along every day Bro. Durham saw him at Springville he said that he was going around by Gunneson but it is time that he was here. I do not know that there is any danger of his being indicted I have not heard anything of it but I have not been to Beaver for some time. I should have been over there this term of Court but Mary is so sick . . . I have thought that Bro Steele was gone so long that perhaps he had gone around by Pangwitch for the purpose of avoiding Beaver but I do not apprehend any trouble from that direction at present."[41]

Catherine obviously felt John was at risk of indictment while Judge McKean was investigating the Mountain Meadows Massacre and other crimes, and John was subpoenaed as a witness in the summer of 1875 when Dame and John D. Lee were coming up for trial.[42]

John later wrote defensively to Catherine, "As for Bro O M[43] I have had my hands full of Such men and like the Refirmation I have got through with it and I do not think of Going back over the past for improvement there has been many things of the past that has been forsed upon me by the Circumstances of the Case, But on my own account I have very few things on my own account to Blame Myself with . . ."[44] Whether his conscience bothered him for Reformation activities, Mountain Meadows, or something else is unknown to us, but Catherine knew. John himself was so fearsome that as late as 1887, Dr. Singleton Husted, a Gentile graduate from the College of Physicians and Surgeons in New York City and married to a Mormon, examined him for a Battalion pension and then wrote fearfully to Hon. John C. Black, Commissioner of Pensions, "He is a Mormon and in this part of the Country my wellfare and life would scarcely be safe should he know of the nature of the report."[45]

When Lee was executed for his role in Mountain Meadows, Steele's neighbor and onetime Mormon Battalion messmate, Levi Savage, wrote coolly in his journal, "My birth day[.] John D. Lee having been condem[n]ed to be executed for a horable massacree he was concerned [in] 18 years ago he was shot on the notable ground of the Masacree. about 11 O'Clock today."[46] Steele's son M. M. provided a burial place for John D. Lee in Steele's own Panguitch family plot—the grave described in 1905 as graced by a "half-rotted board at the head" with "J. D. Lee" cut "in rude letters" and nearby an old tin can that once held flowers.[47] Allowing the burial was a generous gesture given how Lee had become a pariah even to Mormons. (After visiting Catherine's Knox relatives in New York, John had written, "as they all believe what we teach only

Jo Smith and poligama We get along very well about Lee that is not as bad as Poligama."[48])

Catherine's children were growing up in these pioneering times. Her daughter Elizabeth, a healthy young girl with brown eyes and curly auburn hair,[49] told of the time they had Chief Walker over for dinner, "and how orderly her parents told her and her brother and sisters they must be while he was there."[50] Steele himself hadn't always been so "orderly" around the Indian chief—Richard A. Benson later related the time Steele challenged Walker to a fistfight.[51] That meal must surely have been tense even for a woman with Catherine's serenity.

Elizabeth watched the Native Americans carefully and years later explained they "had considerable trouble there [in Parowan] with Indians," whose land the white settlers squatted on. The men, which she or her interviewer called bucks, were "dressed in woven wool blankets with buckskin string around the waist." The women "were dressed in capes made of rabbit skins, cut in long strips and sewed together. Capes came below their knees. Some wore moccasins of buskskins [*sic*], others were barefoot. Some of the bucks wore buckskin leggings." They "lived in wickiups made of willows. When they moved they burned the wickiups. They were about seven feet high with the willows coming to a point; large enough to lie down in and cook in them." While John compiled a "Utah Indian Language This 4th day of December 1851" and learned to talk Paiute, Elizabeth didn't know their language.[52]

Elizabeth had her own adventures; one time she went to the creek for water and the bridge she was standing on collapsed. She was carried downstream before a neighbor boy saw her and gave the alarm, resulting in a rescue.[53]

Elizabeth's education was so limited, that her granddaughter Reba explained, she "never learned how to do anything, only just how to read . . . she never learned how to write, and she never learned how to do a lot of things like that, arithmetic and things like that she never learned. She could count your money out and all that stuff, but when it come to doing this and that, until her last daughter was born and went out as a school teacher, Grandma never learned how to do anything, only just how to read." Reba stated, "What education she got she learned by tongue. By listening to people talk and people telling their stories and things like that."[54] Elizabeth signed her name with a mark, and letters from her were written by someone else. "She had to take the hard blunt of the world," Reba concluded.[55]

"If I'd a went to school like my sister Susan," Elizabeth lamented, "I would a learned to read [better] and I would a learned to write." Elizabeth told Reba that M. M. was also favored because John did things with him and took him places while she stayed home and worked.[56] But Elizabeth blamed Susie and M. M. more than their imperious father. "Don't you talk against my father!" she told Reba. "Don't you talk against my mother either."

And getting Catherine and John's children an education in Parowan was challenging. "Tell the Children to Learn all the[y] can at School," John wrote Catherine on April 23, 1856.[57] But schooling was irregular and community support unreliable. Elizabeth's first teacher was John Calvin Lazelle Smith,[58] a young Yankee schoolmaster, something of a twin to Sleepy Hollow's Ichabod Crane. Washington Irving's description of the latter conveys some sense of the former: "He was tall, but exceedingly lank, with narrow shoulders, long arms and legs, hands that dangled a mile out of his sleeves, feet that might have served for shovels, and his whole frame most loosely hung together. His head was small, and flat at top, with huge ears."[59]

Schoolteacher Smith was as superstitious as Crane, but unlike Crane he was good-natured and beloved, unlikely to whip a thick-headed child and diligent in his work (in a letter to E. W. Thompson on June 22, 1855, he ordered several things including "a Spelling Book").[60] He was also an admirer of Elizabeth's father John, his counselor in the stake presidency. (Smith chose John to accompany him when he led the first Mormon explorers into what is now Zion National Park, as well as the site of what became Panguitch, Utah.)[61] Smith, who died young, was followed by Margaret "Peggy" Jane Meeks, daughter of Elizabeth's father's friend and Parowan's Thomsonian herbal doctor Priddy Meeks and "an ardent Latter-day Saint."[62] She was succeeded by a cheerful and good-natured young townswoman named Susan West, destined soon to become a plural wife of Apostle George A. Smith.[63]

Elizabeth's last teacher, Isaiah Moses Coombs, may not have looked like Ichabod Crane but he had much of Crane's spirit. He found Parowan's schoolhouse was as poorly built as the one in Sleepy Hollow, noting, "Such a thing as a school house can not be found in all Parowan," and complained, "I have been teaching ever since I have been here in what they call the 'Council House,' an old dilapidated log building which was used in ancient times as a block house, so open that two large fires are not sufficient to warm it and [so] destitute of glass that the children have to study by fire light."[64] The school benches were made of split logs trimmed flat on one side, with round sticks plumped into auger holes serving as legs. They had no backs so "lolling" was impossible, and students' laps served as desks. During times of Indian troubles, guns were stacked in the corner of the room.

Coombs had arrived in Parowan in the fall of 1858 and was soon dividing his attention between lusting after his wife's thirteen-year-old sister[65] and interpreting every Parowan slight to education as a personal insult. When Coombs tried to stir up interest in building a new schoolhouse he found that "a very evil spirit prevails, a spirit that will lead this people to destruction unless it is put down."[66] Not particularly appreciating his unflattering descriptions of their spiritual state, town members chose to ignore him. Only six people showed up at his meeting to promote a new schoolhouse and no business was transacted.

At this point a surprising diplomat appeared. "Br Jno. Steele having heard that I was on the point of removing from the place paid me a visit this evening for the purpose of dissuading me from such a step," Coombs confided to his journal. "I think that the president [William H. Dame] sent him. He says that the people will repair the old house so that it will do for a school this winter."[67] Coombs ignored the gesture and began closing out his affairs. Bishop William Stockbridge Warren had fallen into disrepute for, among other things, trading with Gentiles and keeping company with rowdies and cattle rustlers and Brigham Young specifically named Warren among those "who are a stink in my norstrails."[68] But whatever moral authority the bishop had left he used to preach to the members in Parowan about education and the teacher found seventy scholars for the 1860–1861 term.

If Parowan's hospitality was mixed, Catherine herself was always a capable hostess. John had numerous interactions with Brigham Young and other Mormon general authorities and Mormon apostle and later Church President Wilford Woodruff took John exploring with him and apparently spent the night at Catherine and John's home.[69]

John C. L. Smith's wife Sarah was awakened one night in February 1854 by cries of distress; she woke her husband, who got Jesse N. Smith, John Steele, and Edward Dalton and they discovered explorer John C. Fremont's stranded and starving expedition and put them up. John never forgot Fremont making off with his maps; but Catherine was probably left with pleasanter memories as hostess.[70] Coombs also enjoyed Catherine's hospitality for he stayed on and when he organized a school exhibition he held at least one rehearsal at Catherine's home, though the agenda doesn't list any of her children as participants. But there wasn't the kind of support in Parowan that Coombs was looking for, his affair with his wife's sister ended in a brawl with his mother-in-law, and in the spring of 1862 he moved to Payson.[71]

"There has been no school here since you left," Isaiah's brother Hyrum reported from Parowan in 1863, "with the exception of one taught by a certain

Mr. [Martin] Slack, and he being Slack by name, and Slack by nature, and not appreciating the great privilege of teaching the Parowan youth, and receiving for pay bread and borrowed buttermilk, speedily removed to Cedar." (Hyrum's sister Mary added a postscript to this letter saying that John Steele "must have been drunk" when he reported to Isaiah that she could not travel.)[72]

"They liked Parowan and all but their father wanted to remain but of course they did as their father directed,"[73] explained a family history Elizabeth dictated. According to John's autobiography he left Parowan in 1861 because an epidemic of grasshoppers caused a scarcity of wheat. He went to Salt Lake to get Brigham Young's permission to move and when that was given, went to Toquerville.[74]

John doesn't mention another reason. Historian David Bigler wrote that "from 1847 to 1874, not one candidate chosen in advance by Mormon leaders failed to win election."[75] Bigler missed two. In early 1861 John Steele and Nelson Hollinshead were nominated by "the Priesthood" to be Parowan city aldermen.[76] A priesthood nomination was tantamount to election because religious etiquette meant no other nominations were supposed to be made, but the candidates were so unpopular—and religious authority so frayed after Mountain Meadows—that Richard Benson and a Mormon named William Laney[77] (the latter brain damaged by being brutally beaten because he gave needed supplies to members of the Fancher company shortly before they were murdered) got up an opposing ticket. They were James McGuffie and a Mr. Gregory, the former a crude but courageous trader who owned a small store and found fault with the controversial Stake President William H. Dame, and had apostatized from the Mormon Church. In 1877 John wrote his wife, "while I see James McGuffie has deigned to mention my name in Connection with pres Young and others, the Devil will get all his own by & by."[78] Possibly Mr. Gregory was the John Gregory who was court-martialed in Cedar City in 1853 with a group of other dissidents.[79] The unorthodox candidates won the election.[80]

The public repudiation of having been beaten by the anti-Mormon ticket in a day when votes were public was likely the most significant cause of John's abrupt move—only weeks before he had been begging Coombs not to leave town.

The failed election was in February 1861. On June 5, Parowan's blacksmith Calvin Pendleton wrote William Dame, then on a British mission, "Judge [James] Lewis, John Steele, E. Newman, H. M. Alexander and others, are talking of making a home on the Rio Virgin above Grafton or Tinneys settlement. They have the Prests [Brigham Young's] sanction I believe."[81]

Eleven days later John bought a place in Toquerville from his friend John D. Lee and then sold his Cedar City lots to his militia colleague and lifelong friend, the volatile George Wood.[82] He was so anxious to leave Parowan that he moved to Kanarraville, settled only that spring, and stayed a short time before moving further south.[83]

"The cause of the settlement [of Toquerville] was," Steele wrote later, "there was a large spring of good water and a creek called Ash Creek from the great quantity of ash timber growing here." He admitted that "The appearance of the country to the first settlers was very forbidding."[84]

This little town about forty miles south of Parowan was even more on the edge of the Mormon frontier, circled on the north and west by Ash Creek, on the east by the Black Hill, and on the south by uncultivable hogbacks and ravines. It was inhabited by several of the Mountain Meadows Massacre participants and may have been founded because it was so remote that they would have safety there. Toquerville was described in 1862 as "a pleasant little village of one street, lined on either side with a fine growth of cottonwood shade trees." While the soil was only of "medium" quality the mild climate meant grapes could go through the winter "without freezing." A three-year-old fruit tree had a bushel of produce; alfalfa yields were as high as sixty tons per acre with five and even six cuttings a year. Toquer and other communities in Washington County were destined to be the wine and fruit sources of the state[85] while Seth Johnson reported from Toquerville that "the principle game we have is the <u>Lizzard</u> the <u>Horned</u> <u>toad</u> the <u>chipmunk</u> the <u>mountain</u> <u>rat</u> & the <u>grasshopper</u>."[86]

Catherine, John, and all of the children except Mary, who was married, moved from Kanarraville to Toquerville "in January during a long rain storm," Elizabeth's history explains.[87] The winter of 1861–62 was so wet and windy that it caused the collapse of houses in New Harmony, killing John D. Lee's children George A. and Margaret Ann. "The creeks were flooded," continued Elizabeth's history.

> The roads were rocky and conditions were very unpleasant. Ash Creek was so full of mud and water it was thought unsafe to cross, so they swam the cattle across first. They went over safely so the wagons followed. They arrived at their new home, rather down-hearted and added to their troubles their adobe house was flooded with mud and water. They cleaned it up and made the best of it but seemed to wish they were back in Parawon.[88]

Catherine was joined by her children in resentment at John for making them move because far southwestern Utah was unwelcoming and not just to Catherine and her children. "At one time England sent her convicts to

Bondsman's Land; Russia sends hers to Siberia, but Utah—or the church at that time—sent hers to the cotton farms of southern Utah,"[89] wrote another southern Utah settler, George A. Hicks. (Pioneering here was so hard it had the most unstable population of all Mormon settlements.[90])

Catherine and John's homestead in Toquerville was made up of several acres of land, a farm, and an unstuccoed adobe one story, double parlor, vernacular house in a desert climate blessed with such warm weather that years later John bragged to his Australian niece Letisha Todd that in February "our treese are now Showing Signs of putting forth their blossoms, Apricots, & peech," and he commented on the "beautifull Climate here in these vallies where I live."[91] By late March he said "I am now putting in my garden, potatoes, & peas," and added that "I have just got my peaches, apricots, and apples trim[m]ed and will commense on the grapes now."[92] In August he reported, "I have perhaps 500 bushels of fruit lying upon the ground uncared for, apples, peaches, apricots, and currans dried upon the bushes for want of help to take care of them."[93] By September it was worry over "the hurry of Fruit drying and taking care of my Stock, Cutting and Securing hay for the Winter."[94]

John, who was quite literate by frontier standards, was a talented leader and always had plenty of jobs: short, local preaching missions; Justice of the Peace; Kane County Surveyor; Kane County Assessor and Collector; silver prospector; 1880 census enumerator and self-trained doctor.[95] In the late 1860s he was asked to move to the "Muddy," a hopeless, malarial-cursed colony on the lower Virgin River. "I've moved as far as I'm going too," Reba reported her great-grandmother Catherine told John. "I'm not moving another step." And she reinforced the point. "You can go where you want to, but I am not going any farther."[96] Reba says that was the second—and last time—she defied John. They stayed in Toquerville.

Catherine continued to be a gracious hostess. John D. Lee visited John and Catherine in Toquerville on June 12, 1866, and recorded that "by pressing invitation we spent the Night with Maj. John Steele & Lady. Kind Reception. Spent the eving Cheerfully & agreeably."[97] When James Henry Martineau went through Toquerville and lunched with the Steeles he described them as "old Parowan friends."[98] That meant something because the generally good-natured Martineau moved away so angry he confided his resentment in his journal: "Left Parowan with my family, happy to leave behind us a set of hypocritical leeches and scandal mongers."[99]

Meanwhile the family letters show Catherine maintained her friendships with other women. One of these, as mentioned, was Sarah D. Rich, who wrote,

"I went to The Store This afternoon and god [got] what you directed I hope you will be suited The calico is The besd I could find and Such as I should fancy for myself, so I Think you will like The same Times are verry hard wiTh us This winter money and every thing else is out of our reach at The present, every thing but bread," and, "Sister Steel if I could see you I could talk a whole week about what has transpired since you was hear."[100]

A letter from Catherine's friend going back to Mormon Battalion days, Isabella Wilkin, made up in enthusiasm for gaps in spelling when she reminisced of the days when "we felt eaqual to the Battle of life under such fe[e]ling & influence aure friendships was formed, ther[e]fore we must always regard each other with a Sickred [sacred] & tender feeling & rejely [?] and triels through which we pass togeather Sarve to bind aur hearts togeather in the hard times Sister Steele & me learned to get along with a very little, do you ever think of those times."[101]

Another peek at Catherine involves millinery. Catherine was "a lady tailor" and she had a favored dainty purple and white hat—a modest, fairly close-fitting production that included a black lace top with a shell-like string holding it together. This hat, which she was wearing when she had her picture taken with John in 1873, has come down to posterity; along with a favored dress of dark blue velvet, boasting a lace collar with scalloped beadwork on the sleeves and a round black decorative button between each scallop. That it was well worn is shown because the garment has been rent on the right side and repairs appear to have been darned in.

It also tells us she had a twenty-seven-inch waist. The flounce is seven inches and straight, not pleated. Below the flounce is a one-inch-high row of box pleats and the flounce has the same brown-gray lining as the blouse. Though the garment is handsewn, the beadwork appears to have been mass-produced and then attached.[102]

This dress and hat can tell us a story—a subtle one, but plausible. Catherine likely stood something under five feet, six inches and was a slender, high-waisted woman. She loved lace, as the story of her losing her Irish laces and linens also attests, and she found beads attractive. She probably had few other fine clothes and valued these enough to keep them through her life. The women who followed her recognized the importance of the clothes to Catherine for they saved and passed them on. The elegance of the hat, combined with its simplicity, also suggests that she favored tastefulness over flamboyance. (Her sister Mary Ann favored a dark, heavily pleated material with big triple ruffles in the skirt in her formal portrait.[103])

At an LDS Conference in St. George on April 7, 1877, John Steele and his twenty-eight-year-old son Mahonri M. heard their names read by Mormon Apostle George Q. Cannon as being called on missions "To Europe."[104] After the mission, he returned home to Toquerville on October 20, 1878, with five cents in his pocket. "I was gladly welcomed home" he admitted to his journal, and then added a curious clarifying comment in a later postscript. I "was welcomed by all my friends," implying that maybe the whole reception wasn't so warm. But perhaps Catherine relished his return so he could manage his own business affairs. He looked over the homestead and then complained bitterly to his journal—and probably even more harshly to her—that "everything that I had left when I went away [had] gone to wreck and ruin. Fences all down, stock very badly scattered and all my former prospects gone to ruin."[105]

Catherine, who dealt with him passive-aggressively, likely responded with outward equanimity. A newspaper reporter interviewed Catherine's daughter Elizabeth at some length in 1937, and described Catherine's personality as "serene."[106] Catherine also consoled herself with a conviction that the family had seen better days. Reba LeFevre attributed her great-grandmother's passivity to "royal blood." Reba explained, "Well according to the way that this here royal people are raised, they're raised that they're calm. They don't never get excited. They don't get angry. They're raised to be just peaceable clear through . . . You just take it as it comes and let it go as it goes."[107]

What Reba is referring to aren't entirely imaginary traits associated with "royal blood" but the gentlemanly—and gentlewomanly—conduct expected of upper class, well-bred British aristocrats of her time.

Catherine, her grandson Mahonri M. Steele Jr. explained, was much calmer than John. She was "in many ways as remarkable a woman as Grandfather Steele was a man. She belonged to the Scotch Campbell family and was very proud, refined and well educated." Then he clarifies Catherine's role in the marriage: "She always seemed to be a balance wheel to the exuberant spirit of her husband." Mahonri Jr. also writes a sentence that seems puzzling. Catherine "carried herself like a queen and seemed more or less out of place in the hardships of pioneer life."[108] Puzzling because family folklore and tradition insists she was an excellent housekeeper, good cook, accomplished seamstress, and proficient at the domestic arts. As her grandson James S. Stapley recalled, Grandma "was a verry faithful and energetic woman, always ready and on hand to assist in every thing she was able to do."[109] Pretensions to ancestral splendor are fairly common. In what way would she be out of place?

Likely Catherine was a conventional, believing church member, but there's a possibility that she wasn't and we have a clue if we go back to John Steele's account of Catherine's conversion to Mormonism: "My wife did not believe until I preached the Gospel to her."[110]

Another hint is from Catherine's granddaughter Emily, who recalled in 1933 that her grandmother "was engaged to a Kings guard[sman] before meeting Grandfather who was a fancy shoemaker and said she couldn't see how she ever married Grandfather but guessed she was to be tried thru all the trials she had to encounter."[111]

In a letter from John to Catherine dated October 13, 1855, he announced that he worried constantly about her spiritual state. "I never go to sleep but what the welfare of you & thy children are last on my mind and I pray Continuely to the Lord for you & them that he will watch over you and keep you from going astray."[112] And maybe it was her indifference to Mormon proselytizing that led her to write a frank letter about Utah and the Mormons to her sister, Margaret Johnston, where she said things that didn't confirm the picture John had drawn of the New Zion.[113]

As in most contemporary western societies, men were in charge in Mormon country. Brigham Young advised his priesthood brethren that women's "council & wisdom (although there are many good women) don't weigh as much with me as the weight of a Fly Tird. Excuse me for my vulgarity. It is not common for me to use such Language, but I know of no Language to mean to suit the case before us,"[114] the "case" being a trial where a woman allegedly defrauded John D. Lee. John Steele's letters seem to echo the sentiment but less crudely.

On the other hand, Mormon women had always been able to vote in church meetings and they were among the first in the United States to vote in political elections, gaining that right in 1870. A "gentile" traveler, Leonard Swett, passing through Beaver in 1879 wrote his mother that "Out here the women vote, and I saw whole families come to the polls together. One woman was so enthusiastic that she brought her wagon three times full of women."[115]

They could bless people,[116] heal by laying on of hands, in certain sacred rituals could be ordained "Queens" and "priestesses," and the 1842 organization of the Female Relief Society created one of the first (and longest lived) women's organizations in the United States. In some ways polygamy itself was liberating for it allowed individual wives to pursue careers and share household burdens in ways that matched the talents of each—though not all of them enjoyed the success of polygamist wife Martha Hughes Cannon who was the first woman state senator in the United States, beating her husband, Angus M. Cannon, who had five other wives to console him.

The women of Toquerville had their own social organization: the Toquerville Relief Society was organized June 11, 1868, with Catherine as a charter member and treasurer. She also served twenty years as appraiser,[117] an important position when almost everything was done by barter and item values needed to be individually established.

As the name implies, one of the Society's primary responsibilities was to relieve the needs of the poor. Joshua Boyer, who was John and Catherine's farm hand when the 1880 census was taken, was one of the perennial charity cases. Catherine was given credits in the Relief Society accounts for providing meals to Boyer, the ladies made him "A Summer hat & A pair of over alls" because "he needed them sadly," provided him bedding, and Catherine also washed his clothes. (When the community had to defend itself from a charge in the *Salt Lake Tribune* that it squandered money from a charity dance, the reply included that beneficiary "J. Bowyer" got five dollars.)[118]

How tactfully this was done or how humiliating Brother Boyer found it is open to question since Martha Jackson reported once that he "syd he did not want the sister[s] to visit him eney more."[119]

They visited more welcoming families to see to their needs or, as the Society's secretary put it, went "teachering."[120] The women collected carpet rags, day books, gloves, towels, wine, and yarn, and even sold Catherine a linsey-woolsey quilt. She was a leader in trying to establish the silk industry, was appointed to a committee to arrange a program for an annual ball, gave the benediction, donated cash for a "sis[ters] Convention," made quilt blocks, donated flour, wine, and calico, carpet rags and cash, tea and sugar, dried apples and spices, and knitted socks, all to be given to the poor. The women established a "Ladies Store," collected money and grain, and put Catherine on a committee that organized a dance where they were entertained with German songs and a horn pipe. She must have especially enjoyed quilting. When the sisters picnicked, they quilted and sashed quilts, favoring those with a Magnolia design.[121]

She didn't get angry and boycott meetings like her good friend, the onetime first counselor in the presidency, Fanny Spilsbury,[122] but either through ill health or a loss of interest Catherine asked on April 6, 1870, to be dropped from her leadership position.[123]

Soon she attended only about half the time.[124] Did she find no independence in a women's organization that was dominated by men? It was true that the women invented a new office for young ladies: "Deaconess."[125] This seems to have been a female variant of the Mormon priesthood office of deacon, and likely meant the young women were responsible for getting firewood and keeping the Relief Society building clean and warm. Catherine's daughter, Jane, was one of Toquerville's deaconesses. But the office of deaconess disappeared quietly from the records.

Grain collection was a project perhaps organized by the men, and it fell to Charles Stapley Jr. to exhort the sisters to redouble their efforts. Judging from John's missionary letters to Catherine, she wasn't in much sympathy with the sisters who used the meetings to lament the threat of their husbands going to prison for polygamy, and lectures against "Backbiting and talking about our neighbors" were probably more usefully directed toward John than her.[126]

She had no political independence, though women in Utah Territory had been given the franchise. She must use her vote to uphold the male priesthood and plural marriage. Sister Kleinman reminded the Relief Society sisters of this when she addressed them "in a spirited manner" and "urged us to be united as one[,] spoke of the necesity of voteing and doing all we could to hinder the enemy from taking away our rights and freedom . . ." The rights and freedom that were threatened were the rights and freedom of John to find "Beauties" in England. A United States congress, frustrated that Mormon women didn't use their franchise to rebel against polygamy, eventually took their vote away.

By 1883 the Relief Society had saved a hundred dollars. Catherine's son-in-law Bishop William A. Bringhurst borrowed it on "intress" for an organ for the church hall. But instead of getting the money back, the women were "encouraged" to donate seventy-five dollars of the debt to the ward and give the remainder to the church's emigration fund.[127]

Though the women were organized, it was for the aspirations of a male-dominated theocracy. Ladies had to be content with parties and socials honoring each other's birthdays. Catherine was told to pursue the plans of others and the strategies to accomplish them were dictated by men. Lack of choice could have made her seem skeptical, aloof, and out of place to the more conforming. John made it quite plain: "All I ask my family to do is for them to do as I want them, and I will Manage all the rest."[128]

He only asked for the rights guaranteed to him by the God of the Old Testament and advocated by Brigham Young. Despite her seeming obedience, Catherine firmly, yet passively, made her own way.

3

"Letting Posterity Come In"

Elizabeth Steele Stapley

"The community all feels like Brothers & Sisters," John wrote from Toquerville to his Australian niece Letisha Todd.[1] He was designated justice of the peace as early as October 16, 1869.[2] He tried to convince himself that he was the patriarch in his house and no one was in a better position to consider the parallels between town and family life.

But underneath a general sprinkling of Christian platitudes, conflict ran deep in Toquerville: a drunken Horace Slack—"he was a fighting little devil," remembered his nephew Edwin K. Slack[3]—calling stockbreeder Hamilton Wallace a "goddamned son-of-a-bitch!"; Willie Savage beating up this same Slack with brass knuckles; Yorkshire-born constable John Batty arrested for assaulting Lyman W. Dodge; Dodge in court for fighting with watermaster George Batty; Tom Crowt prosecuted for setting up a wheel of fortune; Thomas Reed guilty of carrying on a lottery with a "Jewelry Spinner"; Horace Slack's more docile brother Vernon Slack joining Horton Haight in a pleasant drunk and then robbing George Spilsbury's store;[4] and colorful Zettie Stapley accused in sacrament meeting of "keeping a disorderly house"[5] (the church records don't explain what was meant by the term).

John and Catherine's son M. M. definitively dismissed two townsmen: "So far as [William Brown] Hill & [Levi] Savage are concerned I want nothing to do with them. Both drunkards And Savage was never Known to live in peace in any community & for cuch [such] society I need not go out side of Pangwitch."[6]

Toquerville earned such a bad reputation that Mormons from Arizona were advised to bypass it "on account of apostates."[7] "[T]here has been a good deal of the Spirrit of Evil Contained in that little Town for many years," John confided to his daughter Susan, the bishop's wife, "and So far as I am Concerned I Could feel just as well if I should make An entire new Start."[8]

John often repeated this threat to Catherine, and on August 12, 1883, M. M. wrote from Panguitch that "I will look around, & see what I can do for you in the shape of land, House & lot Etc. and let you know," but that it would be best to "find out what you can get for your place & what Kind of pay & then you will know how to deal in the purchase of a place out here."[9] But Catherine's refusal to move was not negotiable and John always retreated.

The family, like the town, suffered from conflicts and rivalries. "You and I are rebelleous and bad," Jane wrote sadly to her carousing brother Almy on January 1, 1883,[10] when she was ignored by the more successful and pious M. M., who was even then busily earning a column and a half in the *LDS Biographical Encyclopedia*.[11] Almy's grandniece, Reba Roundy LeFevre, traced her uncle's rebellion to John's imperiousness. "Well his dad was trying to boss him too much," she explained. "That's why kids don't get along with their dad, isn't it? They try to force them to do this and force them to do that, and John always said, 'Now you do this and you do that'—the rest of them would do it, but he wouldn't."[12]

"Tokerville is a wine Destrict," wrote a grateful John D. Lee.[13] The summer afternoons in this desert community were ushered in by heat so relentless that the air became thick as gelatin and smelled powerfully of the unpleasant aroma of steeping Mormon tea, broiled by the sun from a plant the Paiutes called Tuttumpin, while the very dust was baked a reddish-brown. Dogs took to the shade, children disappeared over the Ash Creek banks and into the cover of purple tamarack plumes, men and women sat on the wide porches spitting, dozing, or praying vainly for the attentions of the stingy god of breezes, and Almy fled with like-minded souls to the shade of the arbors of the vine and tippled "Valley Tan." "Uncle Alma . . . always took my part when things went wrong," remembered his niece, Della Fish Smith. "He was naturally a very refined and gentelmanly man, large and strong but unfortunately became addicted to the use of Dixie wine and thus ruined his usefulness for himself and his ability to render happiness to others."[14] Della said that this wine "was like taking a dose of castor oil." A gentile observer, Don Maguire, claimed it "was villainous stuff, containing about as much of the juice of the yellowjacket and wasp as it does of the grape," and "So rascally is the nature of this drink that people of Arizona and Nevada claim that a man who drinks a quart of it will get up in the night and steal his own clothes."[15]

John took Almy's addiction personally. Almy's brawls and scrapes included getting part of his ear bit off one raucous night,[16] which so enraged his impatient parent that eventually John denied fathering him: "As for John Alma he is a stucco or made of mud, there is no Steele in his composition if his mothers husband had been like him he would have been Fatherless."[17] That also failing, John attacked his wife: "Why don't you put him in his place?" Catherine refused: "You're the one that does that!"[18]

At other times John tactlessly tried to use sex to make Almy more docile, writing from England promising him "a Splendid Girl" he'd recently converted if Almy would "Keep from Wine and Carousing with drunkards and bad Company."[19] Almy died at seventy-seven, still a bachelor.

M. M., confident in his obedience—his temper maybe softened by his mother's genes—had wit but could be as censorious as his father. He described his brother at twenty-four as "the boy" and suggested to Catherine that Almy "is becoming fit for nothing—like the Salt of the earth but to be cast out & trodden under foot—I feel like he was not filling up the measure of his creation."[20] Still, M. M. was sympathetic to his mother, as shown by a letter to her dated February 20, 1878, after John's blast at Catherine for telling her sister about Utah: "So far as I am individually concerned, I build no air castles for any one in this land, for I expect they will be sadly disappointed when they get home to Zion."[21]

Catherine's daughters saw their brothers as a contrast in self-righteous obedience and tortured rebellion, but their own psychology wasn't so symmetrically tidy. Mary, the eldest, seems most like Catherine—extremely hard working, quick witted, possessing a genial disposition to make friends, and outwardly obedient.

Though her husband Joseph Fish wrote of Mary fondly in his autobiography, the marriage wasn't untroubled. This sociable woman loved to go dancing while her scholarly husband preferred staying home and working out math problems. When he finally did socialize it was to court Eliza Jane Lewis, a talented cook and capable nurse.[22] "He come and said he wanted a consent to marry this other woman," Reba reported, "and she said, 'I will not consent to it.' And he said, 'I want you to consent that I can marry this other woman.' And she said, 'No! I can never do it; I will never do it.' She said, 'You can go marry if you want to but you're not coming back here.'"[23]

Yet somehow he reconciled her and on July 17, 1869, Joseph and Elizabeth went to Salt Lake City to be married, Mary unhappily tagging along to give her grudging permission. She was "quite blue," Fish remembered, and he explained that she "did not like the move very much. It was hard for her to get over it, but this is natural and could hardly be otherwise."[24] Thereafter Mary seemed to retreat into childrearing and genuinely bad health.[25]

Mary's children often stayed with their grandmother Catherine, including her namesake Delphina "Della" Catherine Fish. Della remembered "Grandma was a very Cultured and dignified woman and tried hard to make me walk the straight and narrow path even if she did not always succeed. Her dresses had to be faultless, her house keeping makes me wonder why I cannot make a better job of it and she was always a good Mormon."[26]

John and Catherine's daughters Mary, Susan, and Elizabeth were each married at sixteen but Jane, the oval-faced, dark haired, self-described rebel was not married until she was twenty. Jane had a flirty romance with Nathaniel Goodman, an English-born carpenter who worked for her brother-in-law, Joseph Fish, and who helped plant Mary Steele Fish's garden in 1874. Mary liked "Nate" and wrote Jane:

> do you feel bad about the affair with you and nate I hope that you do not, for the more a boddy sees of him the better they like him but don't let one word that I say weigh in the balance he is here now in the morning Joseph and him starts for the canion in the morning when he was here before he was as blue as indigo because he could not hear from you but as soon as he came back again and the very minute that I laid eyes on him I new that he had herd from you he said that one letter was wourth a thousand dollars to him I dont think that any man thought more of any woman than he does of you they will be in the canion all the rest of the winter.[27]

That long winter apparently proved too much for the romance—by spring Jane married another. Nate later married Ada Emeline Weeden in Minersville, perhaps to Jane's benefit for Goodman was remembered in his family's history as a man with "a very lovable disposition, but it was marred by a violent temper" and his marriage ended in divorce.[28]

When an adobe maker named Alexander Watson was called to settle Toquerville he took along twelve-year-old John Peter Jensen, a Danish-born apprentice. By age fourteen, Peter, as he was known, set out on his own, living a rough life lumbering and freighting until he returned to Toquer where he lived with the Spilsbury family and, staked on his savings, went to school where he claimed "he learned more in that six months than his grand children do now in six years." Jensen, lanky and jug-eared, married Jane in early 1874. He described her as "Miss Catherine Jane Steele," and "the baby daughter of John and Catherine Steele"[29] but told us little else about her.

Mary Steele Fish's daughter Della loved her Aunt Jane Steele Jensen, who "lived in Grandpa's old house after she was married, it was near the new one, and sometimes when Uncle Peter was away she would ask me to sleep with her. She took great pains to tell me the right kind of stories, especially did she try to inspire me . . . to live a pure life. Her teachings have never [been] erased . . . I still thank her for the good lessons she gave me."[30] The Jensens lived a few years in Toquerville, were called to join "the Hole in the Rock" expedition to San Juan County, and finally ended up in Taylor, Arizona, near Jane's brother-in-law and community leader—Arizona state legislator, Joseph Fish.

Peter read and approved if not dictated a history of himself that reported "he had horses when he arrived [in Taylor] and gave one of them for the [W. C. Baldwin] place. The next year his other two horses died just about the same time and left him just a little filly. This was the straw that broke the camel's back and his wife had to give up to tears. She was the baby of the family and had been raised to know no want." Indeed, Jensen recalled, "In all their experiences and hardships of their travels she had been able to stand the trials without a murmur"[31] up to that point.

If Peter was inadvertently minimizing Jane's role, their son Raymond Mahonri offers additional information: "Mother was a good cook and it seemed she always found something for us to eat. She was a good entertainer. She was a good singer and a good manager, and did all of Daddy's writing for him. Daddy said that he only went to school three [six] months, but he could read the newspapers and could always tell me whether I was right or wrong with my arithmetic."[32]

"I heard that you were all mad at us and I thought you would not care to hear from us that is the reason I have not written before," Jane wrote her mother defensively from Arizona, "but if I have done any thing to hurt your feelings I am sorry for it and I ask your forgiveness." Catherine wasn't angry. A postscript from Jane thanked her for a parcel just received.[33]

Susan "Susie" Adams Steele, later Bringhurst, was neither rebellious nor obedient. She had a square face, flattened nose, and with her hair brushed fiercely back she looked wise and humorless as an owl. "Aunt Susie was a tall, handsome woman" remembered her niece, Della Fish Smith. "She occasionally chideg [chided] me for uncouth actions which I doubtless deserved."[34] Toquerville resident Edwin K. Slack confirmed she was tall: "She's a very stout, large, she's close to six feet, very beautiful woman. Yep."[35] Della went on to write, "All my mother's relatives were very anxious for me to 'walk the straight and narrow path,'" that sentence inspired by a reference to Susie.

Susie was generous in her donations to the Toquerville Relief Society, the record for 1870–71 explaining: "Susann Bringhurst calico .20, 1 woollen block & 2 calico blocks for quilts Jan 7th 1 days sewing 1 linsey block, July 30 1 block, April 28th 1 lb of carpet rags, 1870 June 9th 1 calico block, Nov 3rd 1 lb of carpet rags .30, Feb 11th 1871 1 calico quilt block Novr[?] 13th 1 linsey block."[36]

Susie was also a leader, chosen for a committee overseeing boys hauling fence posts to the Relief Society lot, an appraiser with her mother Catherine, assigned to "take charge of the quilting," serving more than once on the committee putting together the Annual Ball, and was asked to get "Sister Mary An[n] Stapeley" for a surprise party when Mrs. Stapley was moving to Arizona. But Susie was also formidable, something of her father's favorite, and the second of three wives to Toquerville's bishop, William A. Bringhurst. Bringhurst was so intimidating that his third wife, Mary, referred to him as "Brother Bringhurst," and "cranky" and "grouchy" were two adjectives Toquerville old-timers used to describe him. "Hell," said ninety-two-year-old Edwin K. Slack, "if you had three wives it'd make anybody irritable anyhow!"[37]

Susie worked hard in the Relief Society and relied more on God for moral support than on Bringhurst; perhaps even more on her Mormon sisters. She was a strong preacher of unity: "She talked to us and urged us to be united as a bunch of sisters gave us good advice which if carried out will benefit us all" and "said she wanted to be one with the rest. The Lord said unless ye are one ye are not mine. Then let us be one we have a good band of sisters in Toquerville. The opportunity is always before us to do good" and confessing "I can say i feel my weekness in standing before you but with out the Lord we are nothing."[38]

The spelling was that of a Society sister without Susie's education. John made sure she was well trained and a surviving letter from her to her brother M. M. working out the intricacies of an insurance policy is intimidating with its brisk, cold efficiency, though she preferred periods over commas. "Your welcome letter recd. and contents noted," she wrote. "In regard to the policy. You will note on that envelope that I sent you that it was to be an anual payment, and at that rate it would be due on a certain date and that date was not due for three days after his death. but what ever papers of importance there was. I sent them to Will." Susie instructed her brother to "take good care of that envelope, for if this firm refuse me anything I will try another." She thought "all this fuss about paying it is just to kill time. and get out of paying it." Her concluding line was formidable: "Now dear brother do the best you can for me. and we will talk about pay afterward."[39]

"Why dont you say something about Susan," Mary once questioned Jane, "you never mention her name."[40] Jane may have been resentful toward Susie. Elizabeth certainly was. "Aunt Susan come over—they used to come over to Hurricane to conference all the time," explained Reba, "and they'd come over and stay with mother and eat dinner and go back. Aunt Susan thought she was so nice and handsome looking—beautiful, I'll say, not handsome. Men are handsome. She was beautiful and she always colored her hair so it don't go gray. And she got too much color in it one time, came over, and her hair was green!"[41]

Reba went on, "They teased her about, 'Well Susan, you got green hair today!' 'Oh I have not!' she said. 'Oh you sure have.' So she must not have had a glass to look in the back. But the next time she come over the dye was out. It wasn't green anyway. And her daughter, thought she'd color her hair, and she colored her hair and got it purple."[42]

This report suggests that Susie's kin thought she was a little vain and they enjoyed telling a story that showed her up. Elizabeth described Susie as "the favorite" and Reba quoted John as saying to his daughters, "'Now Susan, you do this, Susan you go here, Susan you go there; now, Elizabeth, you stay here and do the work.'" Elizabeth's testimony was, "I always had to stay home and let her do it" because "My Dad told me I was the one that had to do all of this and all of that, and Susan . . . got all the education, and she got all of the going out into the public and everything."[43]

John and Catherine's Utah-born daughter Elizabeth was nearly fourteen years old when she moved to Toquerville, at which time her schooling ended. John worked her hard and there was plenty for her to do. "When a girl I spent whole days gleaning heads of grain from the fields after harvest," the *Deseret News* reported her as saying. "I picked cotton, plowed and helped make molasses."[44] "She learned to work and did large washings when she was only 12 years old," added a family history written at her direction. "She could also bake and cook over the fireplace with much skill . . . She knew what hardships were and had danced barefooted many times in the boweries."[45]

The *Washington County News* of December 16, 1937, said that in Parowan "Elizabeth learned from her mother the art of carding and spinning wool."[46] Catherine, who carded enough cotton at one time to make thirty-five yards of cloth, taught Elizabeth how to spin it and a family history reported that Elizabeth "kept her spinning wheel all her life and spun much yarn for her own children." She also took wool to the cotton factory in Washington to be spun and an almost golf-ball sized bundle of black yarn that belonged to Elizabeth has been handed down in the family. "When Grandma died it was left there," Reba remembered. "Mother had it. And when mother died, it was still there. Nobody would take it, so they left it to me, so I took it."[47]

Reba explained that her grandmother "went out and helped milk, she helped do the chores, she helped do the garden, she helped do the hard work all the time."[48]

Elizabeth was, according to her own account, "one of the young people of Toquerville [who] became the life of the town," and years later enjoyed telling the story of the time the young folks had a narrow escape from tragedy. They fitted up a new wagon with bows, cover, and spring seats and set out for Pocketville (Virgin). One of the girls, in an attempt to drive up the "twist" to Northup, managed to overturn the wagon. "Uncle" Thomas Stapley rescued the excursionists, but the boys wouldn't go back to town until it was dark "because they were ashamed of the dilapidated appearance they made."[49]

By the age of fifteen Elizabeth was thinking of marriage. The Toquerville Stapleys were a family of some importance, despite the doubtful morals of the later Zettie Stapley of "disorderly house" fame. "Uncle Thomas's" respectable brother Jim Stapley courted Elizabeth. If the Steeles claimed descent from a mystic race of long-lived giants and the Campbells assured themselves that they had once nested in the Scottish highlands and been addressed as lairds, the Stapleys then or later pronounced themselves kin to the English Stapleys of Framfield, landed gentry in county Sussex. This gave them the opportunity to borrow a Stapley coat of arms, with (in the quaint language of heraldry) "two dragons' heads erased, or"—which meant the dragons weren't erased at all but decapitated and painted gold or yellow.[50]

The Stapleys who sported dragons on their shields produced the only members of the family to earn a place in Great Britain's *Dictionary of National Biography*, thanks to another decapitation. Anthony, claimed by the Toquerville Stapleys as a distant kinsman, is introduced as a "regicide" and was one of Charles I's judges. When Cromwell's New Model Army deemed it necessary to remove that king's head from his shoulders in order to impress upon His Highness the importance of keeping one's word, Anthony Stapley was one of those who signed the death warrant. Anthony's son John somehow endeared himself to the future Charles II and despite parental sins was knighted and baroneted.

But alas for the pious patrons of genealogical dot-to-dot. Laborious research takes the Toquerville Stapley pedigree back to William Stapley of Battle, born about 1662. The Framfield Stapleys reach down, but the gap is too wide to bridge and there is no evidence outside name and place of any relationship. Twenty years after the death of the knighted Sir John, George, the son of William of Battle, marries and parish registers announce his occupation as "labourer." Only a pauper had lower social standing.

While the landed Stapleys tumbled into an effete extinction, the laboring Stapleys of Battle spread across the land, into Udimore, then Seddlescombe, and across the Kentish border into Rolvenden. In 1836 Charles Stapley and his wife Sarah Bryant sailed from England on the *Westminster* to Australia where their son James was born in New South Wales two years later. Mormon missionaries scoured them out and cleansed them by baptism in February 1853. One year later they sailed to California, lived with fellow Mormons in San Bernardino, and joined the 1858 evacuation to Utah.[51]

"Charles Stapley Sr. was a very quiet man," the Stapley family history tells us. "He minded his own business, and wound the clock every Sunday morning."[52] The implication that the Stapleys all stuck to regimen with imbecilic regularity is slightly softened with the knowledge that Charles's son—Charles Jr.—was a good singer and danced barefoot to his brother Tom's fiddling,[53] and the other brother, James, challenged John D. Lee to a horserace down Toquerville's dusty red boulevard.[54]

The courtship between sixteen-year-old Elizabeth and twenty-six-year-old James probably took place at community dances in Toquerville, though she may have married him simply because her father ordered her to. She was about five foot tall, had auburn hair and her father's deep blue eyes with a firm, serious mouth. Despite her lack of education she had a quick, inquisitive mind, was hardworking, fun loving, and dominating. With a very strong belief in her own dignity she insisted on being called Elizabeth and resented James's nieces and nephews addressing her as "Libbie,"[55] though they ignored her objections.

James was handsome, five foot four inches, had brown hair with blue eyes and a high forehead. He was an excellent farmer but if he was related to the Stapley regicide, the genes of rebellion were recessive and James was completely practical and depressingly orthodox.

The Kanarra blacksmith Joseph Henry Pollock related the story of the time he and James were called out with the "Minute Men" to pursue marauding Navajo Indians who had stolen most of the town's horses. The Minute Men found dead and mutilated horses all along the route until finally late at night they came to the Indian camp. As they were wearily preparing to attack, a dog that had been following them began barking wildly. The alerted Indians got away in a fusillade of bullets, but the white men did recapture all of their own horses except for Johnny Hamilton's, killed in the firing. The men camped near a beautiful lake—called Duck Lake but eventually changed to the more tourist-friendly Navajo Lake in honor of this expedition—and began fixing dinner at one o'clock in the morning. While they were eating, one of the horses ran away and James Stapley promptly mounted up to give chase. But the same dog that had so helpfully warned the Indians now began barking and chasing the runaway horse. "Mr. Stapley pulled his six-shooter out and shot the dog," Pollock recalled succinctly, confirming James wasn't sentimental.[56]

James and Elizabeth were married in Toquerville on Sunday, February 21, 1864,[57] by Bishop Joshua Thomas Willis, known as Thomas and described as "a native of Kentucky [he was born in Illinois of southern origins], but was an old Mormon" and "a man without education."[58] Later, Elizabeth talked about her wedding with Katharine Miles Larson of the *Washington County News*, who reported that Elizabeth "worked for weeks to earn her wedding dress, which was made of muslin with tiny red rose buds in a sprig design upon it." The shoes she wore to her wedding dance had been half-soled by her prospective bridegroom and wedding refreshments were molasses cake and rice pudding sweetened with molasses. The young couple was so poor that Elizabeth's trousseau consisted of a regular sheet and a linsey sheet, a pair of pillowcases, and a quilt. James added all of his own possessions to that—a set of knives and forks.[59]

A week after the marriage, John wrote his old friend and mentor Apostle George A. Smith to announce "there are always some changes going on in this wour[l]d" and explained, "I Write to inform you that the Baby born on the Temple Block sixteen years ago last ninth day of August at four Oclock A m on Monday 1847 has on last Sunday Been married by Bishop Joshue T Wellis to Brother James Stapley of this town." John complained that another claimed "the Honor of Being the first white Child Born in the Valleys of the Mountains" and "when the Deser[e]t News gets in run[n]ing order again as to have it Published <u>I will pay all Expenses</u> by refer[r]ing to the record Made by Brothe[r Thomas] Bullock you will Se[e] that her name is Young Elisabeth Steele Born Temple Block Gr S Lake City Monday 9th August at 4 Am 1847 Blefsed by Broth[e]r Heber C. Kimball on the third day after her birth."[60]

A note at the top of the letter, "1.00" was apparently the cost for publishing the following notice in the *Deseret News* on March 30, 1864:

MARRIED: . . .

At Toquerville, Washington co., by Bishop Joshua T. Willis, on Sunday, Feb. 21, 1864, Mr. James Stapley and Miss Young Elizabeth Steel[e]. The

> bride has the honor of being the first white child born in the Territory of Utah. She was born in the camp of the Pioneers, Now the Temple Block Salt Lake City, August 9, 1847 at 4 a.m.[61]

And a separate article in the same newspaper reported:

> The First Born—Among the notices of "keeping the commandment" in today's paper we observe the claim for one of the fair ones that she was the "first born" of Israel in the mountains. Over a year ago, there was a similar claim made in good faith; but we think the records award the honor to the present claimant, born August 9th 1847. How time flies! Israel has reason to be grateful.

A few years later Catherine got a letter from Isabella Wilkin, her Scottish friend whose husband David was born in Catherine's native county of Tyrone. "Your children whom you name in your letter I can not remember only Mary & Elisabeth I think it was Elisabeth but I can not remember" Isabella wrote, "but it was the Baby which was born in the old Fort the furst gril [girl] in Salt Lake—when hir Mother come to See me & of corse brought hir beening [bringing] the baby I had to put my watter bucket out of the way and dish rag too or She mad[e] a fine business for me, well, well—She is married Oh! how time passes on."[62]

Elizabeth and James's first son, James Steele Stapley, was born November 15, 1864,[63] and five months later they moved north to the much colder town of Kanarra (it took the name Kanarraville when it was incorporated after World War I), a small place between Parowan and Toquerville. The trip was arduous as thirteen of the twenty-four miles between Toquerville and Kanarra are over the Black Ridge. Traveler John V. Long wrote that it was "literally covered with a loose kind of volcanic rock which must, at some remote period, have been belched forth by some now extinct volcanoes into this narrow valley and the adjacent mountain gorges."[64]

"The first town of Kanarra was among sand banks," Elizabeth's history explains. "When the wind blew the sand piled up and covered fences and made it very disagreeable for the citizens, so the town was moved to its present location," about one mile southwest.[65] In 1872 Elizabeth Wood Kane wrote that "the wind had driven the settlers [from the first Kanarra]. Absolutely nothing, not even a potato, they told us, could be grown there . . . one day the settlers were threatened with being buried alive, and the next, perhaps, a still stronger wind would sweep away sand, fences, roofs, and walls, and leave the plain smooth and naked as a sea-beach."[66]

Elizabeth, still on the forefront of pioneering, gave birth on October 28, 1866, to Sarah Catherine, who "has the distinction of being the first white child born in the new town."[67] In "new" Kanarra James built a one-room log cabin and then added a lean-to; Elizabeth lit the rooms with mutton-tallow candles. "I was as happy as I could be in our two-room log cabin," the *Deseret News* reported Elizabeth as saying. "Many of the amusements of the young people were in our home as they all seemed to enjoy meeting at our home."[68]

Elizabeth was happy in her choice of work as well, and we'll move ahead of our story to summarize. Though she possessed the sewing skills of her mother, Elizabeth chose to follow the interests of her father. John took immense pride in his skills as a self-proclaimed doctor, describing himself in the 1880 census as "Dr. & surveyor." His herbal remedies included generous doses of opium for cholera and colic, and maybe he was able to keep some of the women in his life docile by prescribing marijuana for "Nervous Debillity in Females," as well as for amenorrhea, or absence of menstruation.[69] Toquerville's aged residents were once accident-prone youths, and more than one remembered "Old Doc Steele" setting broken bones. "They said he was a perfect bonesetter," Reba explained.[70] John also took an early interest in female physiology, as shown by his purchase of Thomas Andrew's *A Cyclopedia of Domestic Medicine and Surgery. . . . Diseases of Women and Children*, inscribed "John Steele's Book | Glasgow Scotland | 1841."[71]

Midwifery was almost the only calling outside that of wife and mother where women were highly valued, as is shown by one of Elizabeth's books.[72] "That females can make competent *Accoucheurs,*" wrote Frederick Hollick in *The Matron's Manual of Midwifery*, "is proved by numerous well known instances." Whether men ought to act in that capacity was open to debate. Hollick argued that females "would be the *best* assistants, to say nothing of their being the most *proper*. There are many things experienced by females in such situations, which can never be understood by a man at all, though they are readily appreciated by one of their own sex, particularly if she has been a mother herself. With each other also there would be less disposition and less occasion for reserve in delicate communications, and less repugnance to necessary examination or manipulation, which could therefore be more efficiently practised." But Hollick believed claims that male midwifery led to "wide spread Profligacy and Adultery" were exaggerated.[73]

Midwives held the high moral ground; they had tremendous community standing (their dedication "was the kind of thing that made the midwives of the time worshipped," recalled eighty-nine-year-old Rulon Berry Platt),[74] and midwifery boldly challenged God's threat, "In sorrow thou shalt bring forth children."

Modern doctors weren't always impressed with the village midwives and nurses. Dr. George W. Middleton was born at Hamilton's Fort, near Kanarra, the same year as Elizabeth's daughter Sarah Catherine. He graduated from the University of Utah and became a fine medical doctor and an expert surgeon, but in his memoirs he wrote of "the old ladies of the village" who nursed one of his friends to death, relying on herbs and stale air. "That same summer, in the same town," wrote Middleton, "there were not less than six or seven young women who died in childbirth, of puerperal fever. The same old lady would swab out the throat of a child suffering from virulent tonsillitis, or apply fomentations to a person suffering with erysipelas, and without even washing her hands would go to the lying-in room to disseminate a fatal infection."[75]

If Middleton would have shuddered at Elizabeth, he would wretch at her father's methods. "I take great delight in Doctering up our sick and wounded and don't charge one cent for it," John Steele wrote Letisha Todd on December 24, 1897, explaining "my Daughters are good nurses & midwives and we have plenty to do." Perhaps it was more than coincidence that every one of John's daughters chose medicine as a calling. Wasn't it a perfect way to announce their value as women and refuse to accept a passive role? Jane was a nurse and Susie a midwife. ("Well, to me she was an angel from on high. Aunt Susan was everything to me cause she brought me into the world," Edwin K. Slack said. Then he added, "[I] don't know whether she got a nickel for bringing me or not; if she did, why, my folks lost money on it.")[76] The most talented family midwife was Elizabeth, whose skills became part of southern Utah legend. "She was a marvel!" remembered Rulon Berry Platt.[77] "Everybody just thought the world of her!" recalled Lynn Reeves.[78] "An awful good woman," added Sylva Davies Williams.[79]

"Her Dad was a quite a doctor," Reba explained. "She learned doctoring under her father . . . He set bones and things like that. But he didn't medicate like she did. But he set bones and he told her this and that." Her disposition was something like her father's, too, and she made her patients obey her. Elizabeth was "strict on this," said Reba. "She's got that strict deal" because "she wanted to run the whole roost . . . She was like Grandpa Steele. She asked you to do anything she wanted you to right now. Didn't want you to wait around. 'You do it right now!'" And James was "very pliable to what she done," even though midwifing rarely paid. "She done it as a free will . . . She said she never even kept track of as many babies as she brought into this world." Her only insecurity was in later years when she feared the dark and always took a black mongrel dog named Rover along with her lantern and valise on night deliveries. And, she maintained, deliveries "always happened in the middle of the night."[80]

John used magic, mysticism, and herbs for cures. He got his patients' birthdates and birth times so that he could draw their horoscopes and find out what the problem was with their "Solar Biology."[81] Elizabeth's methods were less eclectic. She is said to have trained under an otherwise unidentified Dr. Christopherson. She had two medical books, Hollick's, already mentioned, and Horton Howard's *An Improved System of Botanic Medicine. Founded upon Correct Physiological Principles; Together with an Illustration of the New Theory of Medicine to Which is Added, a Treatise on Female Complaints, Midwifery, and the Disease of Children in Three Volumes.*[82] (Elizabeth apparently only had one volume.) This was her standby and had originally belonged to her Toquerville and Kanarra neighbor (and Mountain Meadows Massacre participant) Samuel Pollock (signed "Samual Pollocks Doctors Book | Samuel Pollock ss"). Both of her medical books had pictures of female anatomy and childbirth, and the Hollick book boasted color plates.[83]

Elizabeth walked the streets of Kanarra and rode to nearby ranches and towns with Rover, practicing the same role as her century earlier predecessor, Martha Ballard, "simultaneously a midwife, nurse, physician, mortician, pharmacist, and attentive wife."[84] One can add to that herbalist, therapist, housekeeper, and spiritual healer. She found "cures" among plants and flowers of the area: multi-joint Brigham tea (also called ephedra: it "cleared your system"), hairy-looking bluebells, red bells, fat-chinned lady's slipper, wolf flowers or Indian paintbrush (used as a condiment by some Native Americans), edible sego lily, and wild sage ("clear your blood"), pine gum, turpentine, flaxseed, sheep dip, and even cow manure made into poultices to draw out infection. Tansy was avoided by pregnant women as causing abortions. Green tea was a cure-all for stomach ache, headache, and when "you didn't know what was wrong with you." Raw potatoes killed worms, balsam eased coughs, a Denver mud plaster and daily beefsteak combatted pneumonia, catnip calmed nerves and fought scarlet fever, castor oil with iodine and cheese weed made a tea that cleaned kidneys, licorice relieved coughs and colds, horehound prevented hoarseness, garlic helped the liver, elm bark cured gallstones, black tea prevented morning sickness, coffee was a "physic," golden seal healed cankers, spearmint dissolved gas, whiskey combatted ulcers, and Dixie wine killed everything left over.[85]

Traditional Mormon faith healing was done by men whose priesthood guaranteed them special consideration from God. But blessing and anointing often included administering to the afflicted parts and therefore it was questionable for men to anoint pregnant women. Elizabeth gave expectant mothers blessings to assist them in labor, as Reba remembered. "[You] pray over them. You just have a group of Relief Society people come in and they all circle around the bed and they gave a prayer and then if some of the others wanted to join in and continue praying around, they did that." There was a long-lived Mormon tradition that women could heal with faith, prayer, and anointing, a practice not formally abolished until July 29, 1946.[86]

Elizabeth Stapley not only anointed pregnant and ill women, she blessed babies as well. "They anointed them for health," explained Reba. "But they did not anoint them with the priesthood. That is, they did not use the priesthood in this service." Reba explained that the women in the Relief Society would make a prayer circle around the bed of the afflicted, put their arms on each other's shoulders, and pray and ask for a blessing. "I have seen them do that when I was a kid," Reba explained, "and they got better."[87]

Midwives didn't just deliver babies. "Everybody knew them as house doctors," explained salty old Rulon Platt incorrectly. "That was their name in those days. It wasn't midwives. They didn't know anything about this damn mid-stuff!"[88] The diseases Elizabeth was called upon to fight were varied, the remedies often ineffective, but her dedication unquestioned. John Johnson Davies, an early Kanarra diarist, mentions townsfolk dying in childbirth, from "quick consumption" (tuberculosis and pneumonia were usually described as consumption), cramps and vomiting, accidents, "brits decase [Bright's disease]," blood poisoning, dropsy, and rattlesnake bite.[89] Church minutes record epidemics of scarlet fever, measles, and influenza. There was no end to the afflictions turned over to Elizabeth.

And even in her tiny community she had medical colleagues. Elizabeth didn't always appreciate that her neighbor Priscilla Parrish Roundy—who ran a store and used a magic charm to cure toothaches—inherited the skill of midwifery from her Irish mother, and quite humanely believed that medical practitioners should give patients what they craved. Reba said of Priscilla, her paternal grandmother, "If they asked for a sour pickle, she give it to them." Elizabeth complained, "I don't like what she does because she gives them this and that, if they want it. She gives it to them even if it kills them."[90] As JoAnn Sylvester Bate, Elizabeth and Priscilla's great-granddaughter said, "Grandma Stapley knew what was best for the patient, and Grandma Roundy felt that the patient knew what was best for the patient."[91]

Elias H. Blackburn, a "faith doctor," gave out Mormon patriarchal blessings and used simple conviction to cure goiters and cancer.[92] George Wood, a close friend of John Steele's, set broken bones so expertly that Dr. Middleton wrote admiringly of his skill.[93] Dr. John Huston Brown found a mixture of powerful opiates effective in relieving pain.[94] Irona Hanks Davis, Amelia Flowers, and James's sister Sarah Stapley Reeves all did some nursing and midwifing in Kanarra. "I guess everybody down there that had guts enough was doing babies!" laughed Elizabeth's granddaughter, Leola Stapley Anderson.[95]

The midwives often worked cordially together. Both of Lazell Stapley's midwife grandmothers, Elizabeth Stapley and Amelia Flowers, were at his birth and when the delivery got tough they called in Becky Berry.

But there was also competition among the women. Elizabeth midwifed the birth of Zina Parker Pollock's first five children, but when Zina was pregnant for the sixth time she was angry at Elizabeth. She had someone else help, probably Hannah Williams, at the birth of her twins, Echo and Esther. "Grandma Stapley never forgave Zina for that," noted a Parker family historian.[96]

Elizabeth loved midwifery. "She was 'letting people in,'" Reba explained. "She said, 'I'm letting posterity come in.'" In a typical pregnancy the expectant mothers

> went through their housework and things like that and then when the sign come that they was going to be delivered, why then they had her come. Some took longer time than others to born their babies but she was there at the same time. And she just worked according to the way that the people worked. She got her hot water and her antiseptics [sometimes carbolic acid] ready and then just the process of it being born. Maybe sometimes she helped them in some ways and some ways maybe she didn't. Maybe they just born them naturally . . . [After the birth she] just come in and took care of her in the morning. I mean, come back at night and see if everything was okay, but she made two trips a day . . . [She would wash the mothers and have] them lay in a certain way in bed so the uterus would go back into its position.[97]

She also took care of the new baby.

> She would wash it and see how it was breathing and how its heart was beating and see what she could do for it to help the baby along better. Some babies are strong and healthy and some are weak. A Ford woman

> had a baby, weighed two pounds. And now, I don't know whether Grandma took care of this baby [at her place] or whether they took care of it in its own home. But they put the oven door down and made a fire and kept the fire so that this heat would come out on the oven door. And they raised the baby. They saved it. They didn't have no inkoo-bators for them then but then she kept it on this oven door. And mother said it only weighed two pounds, and they said, "Oh, that'll be a puny little kid," but when it was grown it was over six foot.[98]

Midwives not only helped at the birth but often did the housework for the mother for several weeks afterward. When Henry Pollock's son Joey was born at Dry Creek, Elizabeth went down and served the family until finally, in boredom, she called her son John A. on the telephone and said, "Come and get me! I'm tired of waiting on these people."[99]

Elizabeth was always interested in the children she delivered. Fredrick Wilford Balser, born on March 30, 1900, called Elizabeth his "godmother" because that was the designation given when "instead of having a doctor you have a lady deliver you. She always more or less called me her boy," Balser remembered proudly. "She was a wonderful woman; she was a most gracious person. I used to always go and visit her, 'cause there was a closeness there. Pancho Villa, the Mexican outlaw? It was night when I went up there, [and] I used to forget what time it was and she'd say, 'Now you'd better hurry up and go home because Pancho Villa is'"—and here Balser broke into gay laughter, concluding rather abruptly—"He was clear down in Mexico, and this was in Kanarra! Oh dear!"[100]

The weapons Elizabeth had in her war against God's curse of childbirth and disease were faith, herbs, common sense, and the gradual recognition that germs played a vital role in illness.

Naturally the use of faith was important in health care. Non-Mormon historian J. Cecil Alter pointed out that the practice resulted in "undoubted success . . . and there are scores of unquestioned cases of miraculous healing through faith and prayer in the records of the early Mormons."[101] This was a belief shared by Mormons then and now, high and low. In fact, when Apostle (later President) Heber J. Grant spoke in Kanarra in 1916, he "Bore his testimony and told how he had been heald when the doctors said he must die," and then sang a song in his monotone voice, which had unfortunately not been cured.[102] Very conservative and orthodox Mormons had their faith shaken to learn that high church officials visited trained doctors.

The women of the Mormon Relief Society played an important role in improving rural life. They gleaned wheat, raised silkworms, and collected donations for the poor. But their most outstanding contribution was made early in the twentieth century, when they began educating the public about the causes and cures of disease, especially diseases killing their children. The Kanarra Relief Society sponsored a series of lectures that explained the role of germs in spreading epidemics. These women found they could conquer diphtheria and typhoid through better sanitation. They encouraged the men to pipe in clean water so they would no longer have to drink out of the ditches.[103] They also battled the curse of disease by eagerly patronizing the modern Cedar City doctors, Ernest Flint Green (who was accused of purposely spreading disease to increase his patronage), George W. Middleton, Menzies Macfarlane, and young Jacob Bergstrom who would deliver Elizabeth's great-granddaughter JoAnn Sylvester; all of these doctors were educated at eastern universities, and did all they could to subvert God's curse.

And there was the aid of common sense. Even the water taps were frozen in Kanarra in January 1917. John William Platt was in Parowan on jury duty (among the cases was "Wm. D. Leigh vs. George Wood. Motion for new trial denied")[104] but Dr. Macfarlane was luckily on hand when Platt's good-natured, big-hearted wife Mina ("My-nie") began her labor six weeks early, with Mina's sister Hannah Berry Williams assisting. Mina was in excruciating agony with an ulcerated tooth and a difficult delivery in the northwest bedroom of her red brick house, a big fireplace burning cedar or pine. Finally a little four-pound girl arrived (Verna), followed fifteen minutes later by a slightly larger boy (Vernon). He was so weak and frail that Macfarlane said he didn't think Vernon's survival possible and sent for Mina's husband. Mina would need a lot of help recuperating from the delivery. Dr. Macfarlane went to William C. Reeves's house because he had a telephone and called Parowan to get word to Mina's husband, John. Then he sent for Elizabeth.

Elizabeth sized up the situation, quickly took charge, and then clung to her duty with the kind of Mormon tenaciousness that made the desert valleys blossom. "She sit by the open fire place," Verna reported, in a wooden chair cushioned by a quilt and pillows, "and just held him—Vernon . . . [on a pillow] on her lap for three weeks. Never left him, day or night, only she'd give him to my aunt while she went and had a 'spit bath' she called it, or to the outhouse. Never left him off her lap, other than that." At night she used a chamber pot, which her brother Rulon had to empty. She fed the twins lime water with medicine droppers and when Vernon began to turn blue she said shrilly, "He's getting hidebound! He's hidebound!" and "she'd just rub him and rub him tell he'd look pink."[105]

"Why don't you lay down with Mina and rest?" Mina's husband John asked thoughtfully.

"No." She didn't trust John to watch Vernon.

Mina had no milk but Hannah Reeves Davis had just had a baby girl named Elda and, according to Mina's older son Rulon, Hannah "was a great milk producer"—and Platt held his cupped hands out in front of him to indicate an amply bosomed woman. "She used to milk her nipple and then they'd put that milk in the boy's mouth with a medicine dropper," Platt explained.[106] Verna, too, was fed with a dropper. "Rulon'd come over to my place and get my mother on a horse" remembered Hannah's son Leonard Davis. "Snow about that deep [motioning two feet] and bring her over here and she'd nurse these twins."[107]

The tactic worked: less than two weeks after their birth, the *Iron County Record* noted, "The twins of Mr. and Mrs. John W. Platt, which were born January 26, and for a time were very delicate, are thriving nicely now."[108] Elizabeth stayed for three or four weeks to make sure they were doing well. Years later Elda Davis, who turned out to be smaller than the Platt twins, joked that they'd gotten the better of her dinner. But Elizabeth was given credit for saving the two babies. "The doctor later said that only the constant vigil and fire in an open fireplace kept us alive," wrote Verna.[109]

Elizabeth "kept in touch with them," Reba reported, and she also kept a picture of the Platt twins. "I think she kept track of all she had," Reba explained. "We said, 'how many children did you have in?' She said, 'oh, about five hundred; I won't say for sure.' And we said, 'Well, you must have been—kept track of a whole lot of them and she said, 'Well, I did.' . . . She could tell you where a lot of them went and lived."[110] Verna remembered that her own mother kept track: "Whenever Grandma Stapley come to town my mother had to clean us up and send us up to see Grandma Stapley." The resentment "wasn't we didn't like her" but it was "making us go see an old lady that we didn't want to go see!" laughed Verna. Elizabeth had "a lot of whiskers coming out of her chin," which puzzled Verna, and "she was white as snow"—her hair, her skin. And then "they kept her so clean and pretty. She always had a nice dress and a white apron on it."[111]

"Here comes my twins! Here comes my twins!" Elizabeth would shout with pleasure when she saw them and then "she'd have to pick us up, one on each side of her, and hold us and kiss us and tell us how little we were, an she didn't think we'd live; we weren't worth having! And all this stuff. . . We'd have to tell her what we'd been doing" and "what grade we were in and who our teacher was . . . We were taught to love her and appreciate her and believe me, now we do."[112]

Besides treating the townspeople in Kanarra, New Harmony, and outlying villages, Elizabeth was friends with and proud to help the nomadic Paiute Indians. She told Katharine Miles Larson, correspondent to the *Washington County News*, "Never once was I frightened or refused to accompany the Indians to their wickiups." She told a *Deseret News* reporter that "One day an Indian came and told me his squaw was 'heap sick.' I went alone with him to his wickiup and nursed her. Later he called at my home and said: 'You good woman; you made my squaw better.'"[113]

Sadly, she was not always successful. Poincum, a friendly Paiute, flat nosed and dark skinned, had ridden with the white men against the Navajos in the raids of 1869. Thereafter he came through Kanarra every fall with his wife U-wink-ipe, known to the whites as Blind Mary, selling pinenuts and buckskins, and U-wink-ipe was sometimes hired to do laundry. Jim Davies, who could speak their language, always bought hides for his cobbler work and gave U-wink-ipe a free biscuit to put in the flour bag she carried. She called Jim "Wino," which he thought was the Indian word for "good" but might have reflected the taste for liquor some of the Davises/Davieses had. "They came all dressed up and painted, with their long, black, shining braids and beaded bands around their heads" on the Fourth of July, remembered Esther Parker Robb. Bishop Lorenzo Roundy always welcomed them and later his son Joel had an apple tree reserved for Poincum.[114]

Poincum and U-wink-ipe were such regulars that when a town youth wanted to call a playmate an Indian he would shout out derisively, "Oh, you poincum!" U-wink-ipe had had tough pregnancies and came to Elizabeth and said, "I want you to bring my children here."

"You want me to take care of you?" Elizabeth questioned.

"Yes."

So when the time came Elizabeth took U-wink-ipe into her house, put her in bed, and nursed her. When the first baby was born Elizabeth set it aside, realizing there would be a second.

"I don't know what's wrong with me," U-wink-ipe said, "I feel funny."

"Well, you have twins," Elizabeth explained.

"I have twins?"

"Yes, you have twins."

But despite Elizabeth, one twin died. The Indians took it to a low hill at the foot of the Kanarra Mountain on the east side of town and cleared off a place, laid the body down, and then built a rock cairn over it. A few days later the second one died, and townspeople asked U-wink-ipe if they could bury both of them in the Kanarra cemetery. When she agreed, the deaf carpenter John Smith made a casket while Elizabeth took her white petticoat with wide eyelet embroidery—"All her clothes were just snow white," remembered her niece Sylva Davies Williams[115]—and made burial clothes. The twins were interred in a grave in the southeast corner of the cemetery. When Poincum and U-wink-ipe's sons Wiley and Russ were later buried in Grafton, blankets and guns were interred with them to help in the afterlife; perhaps some treasures were added to the graves of these twins.

Thereafter on every Decoration Day, Elizabeth, then her children, and eventually her grandchildren and great-grandchildren, laid flowers on the unmarked grave.[116]

Despite failures, midwifing was not only enjoyable, it thwarted God's curse on Eve. But Elizabeth didn't see herself as a rebel against God. She accepted unquestioningly the faith she was born into, though she was disinterested in theological details and didn't talk about religion unless others brought it up. Her belief was shown in her church participation, where her statements were always orthodox, and by the steel engraving she put over her mantel of the Mormon prophet Joseph Smith in his general's uniform astride his favorite horse Duncan; a picture of her mother, Catherine, also was in pride of place.[117]

When the Mormon practice of forbidding hot drinks began to be more rigorously enforced, someone heckled her over her love of green tea. "I didn't think you was that good of a Mormon and [would still] drink tea!"

"Get out of here!" she said. "Get out of here!"

She tried once to give it up, got sick, decided it was medicinal, and promptly announced, "Give me my green tea back," and cajoled, "I'll settle with the Lord for that, now you give it to me!"[118] Elizabeth was confident of her power to negotiate with God over some of His foolish rules.

4

"Nicest Great Grand Baby You Have Got"

Catherine Steele

Three miles south of Kanarra is the northwest tip of Zion National Park where the geology speaks of a race of prehistoric giants: the Great White Throne, Checkerboard Mountain, Towers of the Virgin, the Three Patriarchs and the Court of the Patriarchs, Weeping Rock, Temple of Sinawava, Angels' Landing, and Kolob (Mormons define Kolob as the planet or star nearest the throne of God). Like most of southern Utah, Zion is a geologic collage of deep narrow canyons, sheer rock walls, hanging gardens, streams, and waterfalls, all as rich with color as a heap of crayons melted by a winking preschool deity and presented to the traveler as magnificent and powerful and naked as Christ in Michelangelo's *Pieta*. "Color Country," brags the Utah Travel Council, but the vivid reality enfeebles the cliché.

Kanarra, intimidated by splendor that took a thousand million years to create, sits meekly at the foot of the magnificent Kanarra Mountains, the village a forgettable collection of unimpressive houses—except for the two-story home of Charles Parker, and he was the town misanthrope.[1] Other Mormon pioneers built memorable churches, tabernacles, temples, and mansions. But the only sign of manmade aspiration in this dusty place, besides the handsome Cobble Crest Dance Hall,[2] is a brass "Founders Plaque" in the town square next to a 1950s church. The plaque is securely fastened to a large boulder, as though recognizing that only geology comes close to being eternal as it announces the names of the men who first called Kanarra home.

"I think James S[tapley] lacks a little energy to get out of Kanarrah where he can get land & something for his boys to do," M. M. wrote his father August 12, 1883.[3] Can we call James and Elizabeth's stubborn fidelity to this little town a deficiency of ambition or imagination? Maybe they stayed because James was gradually accumulating much of the farmland south of town. Of fourteen Kanarra farmers listed in the *R. L. Polk & Company's Utah State Gazetteer,*

1903–04, James Stapley ranked number four in terms of acreage owned—252 acres—and number six in the dollar value against his name ($675). His son-in-law Joel J. Roundy, by contrast, ranked eleventh (160 acres) and eighth ($200).[4]

Stapley's business interests and potato peddling took him on many trips (his brother-in-law, M. M. Steele, wrote on June 17, 1888, "James Stapley stayed with us last night & left for East Fork for wool, & sheep business")[5] and he became a prosperous farmer, stockman—he was a charter member of the Kanarra and Harmony Stock Raising Company[6]—sheepman, and beekeeper.

These temporal goods could have held him to Kanarra, but maybe it was more than that; maybe it was the grandeur of the country itself. Situated on Kanarra Mountain was James and Elizabeth's 120-acre ranch where she, like many Iron County people, spent the hottest months of the summer. The view was unexcelled. Directly to the west was the blue Pine Valley Mountain, to the south she could see the Cedar Valley tottering, then collapsing into the ravine-ridden beauty of the Virgin River Basin, with Zion National Park to the southeast. The valley stretched to the north as bumpy as the curious heads that patronized nineteenth-century phrenologists. "The fresh mountain air, the cool spring water, beautiful scenery and fat cattle all went to make her life [at the ranch] happy," wrote her son Will.[7]

The Stapleys, like others, generally went up in June or July, the *Iron County Record* reporting July 24, 1903, under a Kanarra byline that "Mr. James Stapley and family moved today to their ranch on the mountain and will spend a couple of months there making butter and cheese," a job under Elizabeth's direction.[8] "A lot of people here had cattle," explained Lynn Reeves of Kanarra. "But they had no place to run them." So in the summertime they'd take them to the mountain and "all those old-timers would make butter and cheese and then they'd bring it down and sell it."[9]

"I don't think the boys did much up there," recalled Elizabeth's grandson Elton Stapley. "That is, they were big enough to work on the farm, why, they stayed down and did farm work in the summer while the women folks did the dairying on the mountain."[10]

"They milked the cows, then they set it on the stove and warmed it to a certain temperature [84–86°] and put some rennet in it," said Reba, describing how the women made cheese.[11]

> Now the rennet curdles it. And they worked it till they got the whey out of it. Now the whey is the juice that comes out with the rennet. They

> took the rennet out, took the juice out, and then they fed it to the pigs and the cows and calves and they used to keep a pitcher full and drink it theirselves. And the curd. The curd, they mix it up until it curds, and then they'd put out a pan here of curd to eat through the day and then they put this cheese in a press and then they'd press it down and they wanted a bit of cheese like this, about like this [motioning in a circle], they had the press for that one thing you put it in, you press it down, till you get it where you want.[12]

It took from six weeks to two months to cure. They made five or six wheels of cheese annually and each one was six or eight inches high. Wax was too precious to waste on cheese. "They always rubbed it with butter," Reba recalled. "After they get it through, they always rubbed it with butter, and then set it on the shelf to cure, they called it. And this butter would get hard. Just as hard as hard. And it kept the juice in the cheese. And that's the way they fixed it."[13]

"I've eaten Grandma Stapley's cheese they'd make on the mountain, and they'd make there at home," recalled Rulon Platt with enthusiasm. "Marvelous! Marvel." Asked if the Stapleys sold cheese he answered, "Oh man, yes! I should say so."[14] Elizabeth's granddaughter Leola Stapley Anderson agreed. "She run a dairy up there, and she'd pack butter in crocks and then in the fall of the year Grandpa would get what harvest stuff he had and take that and he'd come in to Salt Lake and bring that in and trade it for commodities that they needed down there. And it'd take him about six weeks to make the trip."[15]

Elizabeth's children and eventually grandchildren loved staying in the Stapley house at the mountain ranch where the nearby Ponto Springs Ranch boasted "Ponto Rock" sitting over Ponto Spring. Despite being no bigger than an overstuffed chair, the rock seemed huge to children.[16] The ranch was also a place to joke and tease. Blair Maxfield reported that one night his mother Lella, Elizabeth's granddaughter, heard "two range bulls bellering as they come down this fence [at the ranch], one on each side. They got to the opening in the fence and one bull pushed his head in and bellered, and mother shouted, 'Come in, Aunt Lynn!'" referring to Rebecca Williams Stapley's sister Lynn, whose boisterousness was apparently well known after spending a year living with her sister and M. M. Stapley.[17]

The families on the mountains usually moved back to town in September, where Elizabeth used a lot of the cheese herself because, as her Bible illustrates, her family was growing:[18]

Family Record
Births.
James Stapley Nov. 4, 1838
Elizabeth Stapley August 9, 1847
James S. Stapley Nov. 15, 1864
Sarah C. Stapley Oct. 28, 1866
William T. Stapley June 3, 1869
John A. Stapley July 21st, 1872
Mahonri M. Stapley June 7, 1875
Mary E. Stapley March 14, 1878
Joseph H. Stapley April 6, 1884
Rebecca Stapley Oct. 2nd, 1886

Marriages.
James Stapley Feb. 21st, 1864 to Elizabeth Steele.
James Steele Stapley Feb. 23rd, 1887 to Harriet L. Berry.
Sarah Catherine Stapley March 11, 1887 to Joel J. Roundy
John Alma Stapley June 9, 1899 to Lucretia Jane Higgins.
Mahonri M. Stapley May 12, 1898 to Rebecca Almeda Williams.

Deaths.
Joseph H. Stapley Oct. 29th, 1886
Rebecca Stapley Oct. 2nd, 1886

We have a glimpse of baby Rebecca's brief life and Elizabeth's longing for her mother Catherine in times of hardship in a short letter James wrote John and Catherine just after Rebecca's death: "I take this opertunity to let you know how we are and of our misfortion Ǝlisebeth gave birth to A little girl about two oclock this Morning it Shoed Sines of life for about 15 or 20 minutes and pas[s]ed A way Elisebeth is Smart and wants her mother to come I will send Willie With the team he Will be there this eve Ready to Start in the morning pleas[e] get ridy Yours James Stapley."[19]

Elizabeth's interest in parenting was expressed in the Relief Society minutes where her favorite topic was child-rearing. "Sister Stapley . . . felt like doing all she could in training her children in the write way" said one entry, and in another she argued parents should "set a good example for our children,"[20] and "spoke of the many little duties which we should perform to encourage the young."[21] (Husband James sounds a little dull with his predictable complaint that children have "more privilidges now than he had in his days.")[22] Elizabeth's idea of good parenting meant lots of hard work and stern direction.

Of Elizabeth's eight children, six lived to maturity. James Steele "Jimmy" (1864) was the first-born child, given his father's first name and his mother's maiden name. He was followed less than two years later by Sarah Catherine (1866), named after her grandmothers Sarah Bryant Stapley and Catherine Campbell Steele, and called Kate. Jimmy and Kate had a special camaraderie, shown by a tintype taken of them about 1868 when Jimmy was four and Kate was two. We see a little boy with playful eyes and blushing cheeks, his just-wet hair leaping up on his broad forehead. He is wearing double-hooked suspenders thrown over a white shirt and buttoned into dark baggy pants, one hand at his side and the other tentatively circling his sister. Kate's hair is slicked down, a dark ribbon coming out from behind her ears to the top of her head and fastened in a flat bow, her chin obediently held high and her eyes cast correspondingly down, wearing a high-waisted, ankle-length striped dress.

Kate, at about ten or eleven, got her own little chair with a rawhide bottom; her mother guarded it so zealously that Kate reported later, "My mother would never let me have it. She always kept it."[23] Maybe that's why it lasted Kate's whole life and was a treasured heirloom when she died.

Jimmy and Kate were followed in 1869 by William Tarbet Stapley, his middle name a throwback to an ancient Stapley grandmother. Will's earliest recollection was of "being rocked in the green colored, two handled cradle by mother while she sang me to sleep." He himself was a singer and a performer, practicing recitation on the range.[24]

John Alma (1872) and Mahonri Moriancumer (1875) had names that neatly honored respectively Elizabeth's reprobate and respectable brothers, both of these sons lively and intelligent.

These additions to the growing family were exciting but in 1874 a heartbreaking event struck. Mary Campbell Steele Fish, the daughter of John and Catherine Campbell Steele (who had been with them on their Mormon Battalion trek) suffered from poor health for some years after her marriage. In October 1874, her husband Joseph Fish, who was working in Beaver, received a telegram that Mary's chronic condition was much worse and their baby was sick, too. About the same time, Brigham Young, suffering from rheumatism and unable to attend meetings, went to Parowan with his nephew, Dr. Seymour B. Young, and Joseph had the latter examine Mary. Dr. Young announced she had heart disease, made a prescription and charged ten dollars, but it didn't help.

While the Mormon community was aflutter with the capture of John D. Lee,[25] Mary's condition got so bad that Joseph wrote Catherine, "Mary is so sick. She is very bad and has been for a week but I think that She is a little better this morning. She is considerable the Same as she was when Jesse was born. She has considerable difficulty in breathing and her heart seems badly affected. We take the best care of her that is possible I have been at home Six weeks and expect to remain here and not go back to Beaver." He added that he was expecting John to arrive from the north, which happened two days later.[26]

John was appalled at what he found and wrote about it four years later when he saw how ill his sister Jane Steele McClelland was, telling Catherine of his sister Jane,

> Sometimes when I look at her I can see Mary in her as plain as can bee—and She is Suffering Just as Mary suffer[e]d She is Swelled up like a barrel and has to Sit up in a Chair Just like Mary and the prospect is that I may See the last of her on this Earth before I leave She is fast Sinking and no one knows the day when She may drop of[f] the feet & legs are badly Swollen the face is thin & oh So much lik[e] Mary I am Glad I am here to sooth her a little I try to Joke but lik[e] Mary <u>Oh Father don't Joke any more as I Cannot laugh it hurts me So, it is Just the Same with Jane She cant Laugh it hurts her so.</u>[27]

Mary died the day after her father arrived, December 12, 1874, not quite thirty-four years old, and Catherine was immediately sent for. Her husband Joseph described Mary as "5 ft. 2 inches in height, weighed about 120 pounds, being rather heavy set. She had very light brown hair, dark eyes and a very white transparent skin. She was of a very sociable disposition, was very good company, being rather quick-witted."[28]

While we don't know directly Catherine's reaction to Mary's death, she was probably as pained as John, who—reminiscing three years later on those who had passed on—mentioned "not forgeting our on little Mary, among the rest, who upon Mention of her name I Can Scarcely hold my feelings leval."[29] The hiatus in John Steele's papers from the end of December 1874 to May 1875 may partly reflect a deep depression from Mary's death.

Elizabeth named her next child after her sister and herself, Mary Elizabeth ("May," 1878), who turned out to have the same genial disposition as her aunt and namesake. Elizabeth's youngest surviving child May was scholarly and received a good education.

Elizabeth's sons Jimmy, John, Will, and Mahonri Stapley all took a turn at sheepherding, as their father was a stockholder and director of the Kanarra Co-op Sheep Company and responsible for butchering and selling the company's mutton. Will started herding with his father at Dry Creek when he was about ten. The outfit consisted of a covered wagon box, a frying pan, a Dutch skillet, a coffee pot, and a kettle for cooking beans, rice, and potatoes. It was Mahonri who at the age of four or five summed up the boys' attitudes toward the animals: "Whew!" he announced grandly. "Some folks says sheep stinks like hell."[30]

Twelve years older than May, Elizabeth's Kate did much of the housework. "She learned the trials and hardships of pioneer life very young," wrote Kate's daughter Estella Roundy Russell. "She learned to scrub the family wash when she was so small she had to stand on a box to reach the tub . . . She learned to card wool, spin yarn, knit her own stockings, do the household tasks, and care for the children. She was real handy at making dresses, shirts, and pants, even men's suits. Her grandmother Steele was a trained tailor in the old country."[31]

"She had to take care of the house while Grandma went out nursing," Reba explained of Elizabeth's expectations of Kate. "And she had to do the cooking and all of the things because she was the oldest girl. She was the second child but she was the oldest girl and she had right from the beginning do the housework and everything when Grandma wasn't there. And they went to the dances and they had parties and sewing bees. She went to Relief Society and was put in secretary of the Relief Society when she was fifteen."[32]

Kate and Jimmy, as Elizabeth's oldest, were especially close and their cousin, motherless Della Fish, remembered stopping at Kanarra as a child on a trip to Toquerville to see Grandpa and Grandma Steele, riding in a lumber wagon with affable Uncle Almy. We "remained overnight at Kanarra with my aunt Elizabeth Steele Stapely," Della recalled. "Her husband, Uncle Jim, cared for us very gallantly. The children seemed delighted to see us. The oldest boy Jimmy a little older than myself and Kate a little younger showed us fine cows they owned but the best thing was the large clean cellar and splendid buttermilk."[33]

Della went on to Toquerville, which she found "a pleasant surprise. Nestling down there like a lovely little blossom just dropped down" among the black volcanic rocks. "It did not take Grandma [Catherine Campbell Steele] long to introduce me into my room nor did it require much time to carry in my suitcase." Della, whose middle name was Catherine after her grandmother, was soon put to work picking, cutting, and drying peaches until the job "be[c]ame very irksome . . . I did not regret saying goodbye to the big patches of peaches I had helped to pick, cut, and spread."[34]

Stopping in Kanarra on her way back from drying peaches, Della remembered that Uncle James and Aunt Elizabeth's "flock of happy children greeted us. They were Latter-day Saints [in] very deed and proud of the fact. They had a robust family of boys and girls." Cousins Jimmy and Kate "showed me around in great style. Aunt Elizabeth asked me to remain with them for a while and it did not take long to get me in the notion. Be sure the treatment was first class."[35]

Other relatives dropped by, including Elizabeth's nephew Joseph Campbell Fish when he brought his fiancée Katie Reidhead to Utah to be married. "On the way to Parowan and again on the return trip they stayed overnight in Kanarraville at the home of Joseph's Aunt, Young Elizabeth Steele Stapley," reports Fish's biography. "As they returned through Kanarraville [from a wedding dance in Parowan], Aunt Elizabeth and family had a warm welcome ready and had prepared a delicious meal in their honor."[36] They stopped, too, with John and Catherine in Toquerville.

Elizabeth didn't find the small town confining. "They all just seemed to be one big family," Reba said, "and they had sewing bees and rag carpet deals and everything else. They'd make rag carpets in church. They'd have one day they were sewing carpet rags . . . Every afternoon if they had anything to do why someone would bring out their quilt blocks or they would bring their rags and that and have a sewing bee or quilt blocking bee."[37] The town also had some friction but less than Toquerville.

Everyone in the family worked hard and James and Elizabeth put up travelers at their home, especially church officials. "The church leaders come to their place," Reba explained. "The church leaders come to Grandma's as they went from St. George, back and forth. They took them in as travelers. They stayed there one night, including Brigham Young." Years later Elizabeth remembered, "At one time when there was a deep snow between Kanarra and Bellevue [now Pintura] a posse of boys were sent to break a path so Brigham Young could come from Bellevue. My husband was among the group. I have kept a piece of the tape I made for Brigham's boots, so he could pull them up as he waded through the deep snow."[38]

Besides being a hostess, Elizabeth was a good cook. "I don't think there was anybody that could make bread like Aunt Libbie," recalled Sylva Davies Williams. Elizabeth made the bread in black roasters that held four to eight loaves, cooked in her black iron Majestic stove purchased in Cedar City from Leigh Furniture and Carpet Company.[39] "She was a breadmaker," explained Sylva. "And I was really flattered because I was just a young girl, and she was ill one day and she wanted me to mix bread for her, and I said, 'that's the greatest compliment I ever had!'" Williams explained the circumstances: "I was just a kid because I remember one night, they were having a hayrack ride. Well I was too little to go on the hayrack ride and I thought, 'gee I wish I was old enough that I could go.' So while they were on their hayrack ride I went and mixed Aunt Libbie's bread for her. She used to mix at night and it set overnight, you know. Lot of them used to do that."[40] (Elizabeth had a fondness for Sylva, saving a Valentine's card that said "So Lonesome without you," signed in a child's hand "From Sylvia," before Sylva shortened her name.[41])

"She loved respect," explained Kanarra's Rulon Platt, whose grandmother Becky Berry was a sister midwife. "She was entitled to it. She was a marvelous woman. Good cook! Oh man!" he said enthusiastically. She cooked "anything you want. Pies, cakes, it didn't make any difference."[42]

James worked as hard outside of the house as Elizabeth did inside. "As far as I got it in my head," remembered Elizabeth's granddaughter Reba, "he run the outside and she run the inside. She'd come out and say, 'Why don't you do this or that?' and he said, 'Why don't you go back in the house!' So she'd turn around and go back in the house."[43] Besides hosting peddlers and drummers, James made extra money keeping bees.[44] He also had dairy cows in town when they weren't at the ranch. "Marvelous corrals, clean! Mighty well swept!" explained Platt. The barns had hay in the lofts and sported shingled roofs. James's "stockpens were well cared for. Clean! Good gosh! You could sit down on the cow pen in the barn and eat your bread and butter and never wonder—it was that clean."[45]

The family garden was about thirty by fifty feet, weed free, and the rich red soil was fertilized with manure from their cows and horses. ("The fertilizer they had was good cow shit and cheap shit!" chortled Platt.[46]) James raised rhubarb, beans, squash, corn, onions, and lots of potatoes. "The rows was as straight as you could make them," explained Reba. "Never had a weed in it, and never had one row crooked. They was all straight."[47] The tasty melons James grew in his garden were proverbial. "Hellfire, I can see his melon patch now!" exclaimed Platt. "Take this damn kid down there and let him steal melons from old Brother Stapley!" Elizabeth preserved the vegetables by drying them and the fruit was dried or put up in five-gallon cans and covered with molasses. They frugally saved corncobs to fire the smoke house where they cured ham and bacon.

The hard work paid off and by 1884 Elizabeth and James built a new home, the red bricks baked at the Jim Davis brickyard. Davis was a hard drinking, loud-singing Welshman whose philosophy was, "Why be poor when two bits of wine will make you rich?"[48] (Davis's wife, Polly, was famed for her colorful profanity.[49]) Jimmy and John A. Stapley hauled lumber for the house, barn, and fences from a mill near Bryce Canyon. The new Stapley home dwarfed the old, with its two stories boasting two rooms upstairs, and a downstairs with front room, bedrooms and kitchen.

Elizabeth worked her children hard and demanded the respect ordered by God in the Fifth Commandment: "Honour thy father and thy Mother: that thy days may be long upon the land which the Lord thy God giveth thee" (Exodus 20:12). She was scrupulously obedient to this charge as well, making periodic visits to Catherine to help her mother garden, boil grease into soap, and dry the Toquerville fruit.

"I am pretty tired," an amanuensis, probably one of her sons, wrote for Elizabeth to Catherine in late March 1883, after returning home from one trip.

> I found the children all right and doing well. Sarah Reeves [James's sister] has got a little girl [Amanda Ellen] it was born monday morning it weighed 11 1/2 pounds both are doing well, please tell Grandpah [Charles Stapley Sr.]. The brown beens are called case knife beens. When they come up put a stick long side of them to hold them off from the ground. I send you a bucket of lard, and a pocket, and the note to send for your name. Kind love to all and except a good share your self. I forgot your soap grease, if you will send it up the first chance I will make it up. E. Stapley.[50]

On May 8, 1888, she sent another missive to her parents thanking them for a letter, notifying them that some goods they sent her weren't received, and explained that "Jim and John Started to Corncrick this morning with a flock of Sheep he thinks he will be gone about three weeks. Sister Spillsberry called a little while in the evening but was so independent she camped in her wagon. Mother if you are able to come up I will send one of the Boys for you. I think an out will do you good. Will Corn do for your chickens. as we have no wheat." George Wood had been trying to collect a debt Kanarra's one-time schoolteacher Eugene Schoppman owed Catherine. "Jim thinks if you will write to Bro: Schoppman you can get your money Bro Wood says he is tired of asking him for it." Wood's wife Janey was probably dying, Elizabeth had a bad cold and cough, and "Kate and children join in kind love to you all not forgetting yourselves. Write soon from your loving Daughter Elizabeth."[51]

Catherine's only known surviving letter is to Elizabeth:

May 11th/84
My Dear Daughhter [*sic*] Elizabeth

I received your very welcome letter Sometime ago was glad to hear that you and baby [Joseph H. Stapley] were getting along So well I hope you are Still continue[ing] in well doing we are haveing very high water in the creek it is almost impossible to cross they people have to Swim their cows across yesterday billy Forsyth tried [to] cross and came very near getting Drownd and so did Henry Kliman and David Spillsbury they were helping him the Waggon upset he lost all his bedding and everything else that he had in it every body was trying to help him it was a great excitement the Boys were all under water horses and all Bill Jackson he tried to cross the Vergin he had a hard time to Save himself and his Boy he lost his bedding and his Waggon came apart I heard he had found it again

Well I don't know when I will have a chance to get to See you there aint much travel through town on account of the high water it is washing their farms away, up the river at Kanab it has washed a gulch 50 feet deep I presume high water is universal you will Soon be able to . . . get around again I had a letter from [granddaughter] Josie [Fish Barraclough] She Said her baby [John Lindsay Barraclough] was Sick felt a little better when She wrote had a letter and a present of a nice tidy from [granddaughter] Della [Fish] they were all well my health is some better than it was Father is gone to Washington to preach in company with Brother Spillsbury [as a home missionary] he went yesterday Susie as usual dont feel very well please to write Soon accept my Kind [regards] to your family God Bless you and yours is the prayer of your ever loving Mother C Steele[52]

Catherine enjoyed being grandma and the grandchildren enjoyed her, as her grandson M. M. Jr., explained: "She always made us children, when we went to visit her, feel at home."[53] Della wasn't the only one to visit in the fall and help harvest and dry the fruit (it was only after Catherine's death that John speaks of fruit rotting on the ground for want of care).

One gets a sense of the respect her children held for her because each of those who became parents named a child after her: daughter Mary Campbell Steele Fish had Delphina Catherine Fish;[54] daughter Young Elizabeth Steele Stapley had Sarah Catherine Stapley; son Mahonri Moriancumer Steele had Catherine Steele; daughter Susan Adams Steele Bringhurst had Eleanor

Campbell Bringhurst; and her youngest daughter June Catherine Steele Jensen had Mabel Catherine Jensen. Each of them named a son John, too.

Family members loved writing to Catherine. "I do not know how to thank you enough for the stockings for baby," granddaughter Josie Fish Barraclough wrote from Beaver on May 20, 1888, "they are so nice and pretty, and they Just fit her, you must have tiard your self out knitting them."[55] Della Fish (later Smith) wrote a pleasant, unaffected letter from Snowflake, Arizona, on June 10, 1884: "Am glad you were pleased with the tidy I sent, it is not so nice as I would like to have sent but it is my own work, and I knew you would like it for that." Answering Catherine's inquiry whether Della planned to get married in Utah, Della explained that "I, like yourself, have heard so but there is no more truth in that report than in the one that I had joined the Methodist church. It may be that I will some time but am not contemplating such a thing at present."[56]

"Dear Grandma," wrote Frances Fish Carson from Parowan on April 29, 1882, "you aught to see your only great Grandchild [Joseph Clair Carson] he is as fat as he can be I wish you could come up here and stay a while this summer I think an out would do you good and you could have a good time with all your old friends they often ask me how you are gitting along."[57] And on July 8, 1882, gushed about the baby, "I know you would think he was the nicest Great Grand baby you have got."[58] Josie challenged Frances when she wrote her grandmother on December 9, 1883, from Salt Lake City about great-grandchild John Lindsay Barraclough: "I think any one would do fine if they had as grand a baby as I have got, I do not think that you will ever have a great grand baby to begin to compare with him." And Josie thanked John for working out the boy's horoscope: "he will make a sensation if he turns out as Grandpa says he may do, that is to be a preacher or yet a stage actor. I am glad that Grandpa drew a figure for him as I like to know what planets he was born under."[59] Sadly for John's predictions, little John Lindsay Barraclough died before he was three years old.

"You are generally so punctual in writing," explained Josie on April 18, 1884. "I would like to be there to do some thing for you if I could help you any way, but I am sattisfied if you would come up here that it would do you good and make you feel better."[60]

Catherine sent fruit to M. M.'s wife Emily in 1877, with the expectation Emily would market it. Because Emily was expecting, her mother Emily Abbott Bunker wrote back that "Emily has a fine Son [Arthur Steele] born July the 16 ha[l]f past 4.am. Emily is doing as well as could be expected we recieved the fruit all right. many thanks for it. Emily Says She can not do anything with the apricots untill She gets well and then She will do the best She can with them She will Send you 6 of butter & Alma's pants pattern." And toward the end added, "She has let a pound & a half of apricots go for a pound of butter if you want any more for them Send word. She got the fruit you Sent by Miles Sevy & haveing her some preserves made this afternoon."[61] M. M. also regularly sent sugar and brine-pickled fish to Kanarra, which Elizabeth forwarded to their parents.

Emily knew of Catherine's love for fine things and commented in a letter from Panguitch, "Samuel Crosby left here for home a few days ago I sent by him 12 yds delane [delaine, a woolen cloth] & 2 yds toweling to be left at Kannarrah for you; I hope you will get them all right; & the delane will suit you."[62] Catherine's daughter Jane Jensen also wrote from Taylor, "Well Mother I send you some lace for your Pillow Slips I hope you will get it all right," and she asked do you "still have your white Flannel under Skirt if so how menny widths is there in it be shure and tell me and I will Knit some Lace for it well I will quit for this time hopeing to hear from you soon with Kind love to you all. Peat and the Children Join in love to all. I remain your loveing Daughter."[63]

Many of the grandchildren visited and some, like the Fishes, had extended stays. Elizabeth's children Kate and Jimmy visited their grandmother Catherine in the fall of 1877 while John was on his British mission. They both wrote to their grandfather of the event—he enjoyed several letters he got from them on his mission and mentioned them in his journal—and each received a kind reply. "I am glad you & Jamie went down to Toquerville and helped Grand Ma last peech cutting time," John wrote Kate, "there is no peech cuting here [in Lancashire] nor apples either the trees are little pretty scrubby things of 50 or 100 years old and are not as large as my apple Treese at home and their apples are not the Size of Mine." John didn't write to Jimmy, a future justice of the peace, about apples: "the law Shal Go forth from Zion and the Boys Such as you will be the Very Men by & by when you are well learned to administer the Law and Justice as a servant of God."[64]

Kate visited a number of times and was impressed with Catherine. "She says she was a good cook, she kept her house clean, she done everything just perfect," Reba remembered. And Kate carefully watched her grandmother's interactions with her touchy grandfather.[65]

Today the south side of Catherine's house is a lush green carpet of purple-eyed myrtle.[66] At one time John had his shop here, an adobe building that may have been the house his daughter Jane lived in when she first got married. It held a shoe last and awl that John used to make his own shoes (otherwise he had given up shoemaking as "a lost business and Even if well followed, it don't pay"[67]). This is also where he kept his anvil, and the shop smelled of pungent drying herbs. (*Phallus vulgaris* still grows wild on the lot.)

Here the little man with a whitening mane of hair circling his fierce eyes and powerful mouth would mix his potions and putter and hammer. Disorderly and cluttered, John still knew where everything in the shop belonged. One day Catherine, in a burst of enthusiasm, tidied it all up for him. When he found out he came into the house screaming.

"Just leave my shop alone!" he ordered, "I don't want you in there!"[68] He claimed he couldn't find anything and Kate noticed Catherine never cleaned it again.

There were two other incidents that caught Kate's attention. Catherine made John a shirt but the sleeves were too long. He contemptuously cut off a cuff and handed it to his wife. "Now put that on right!"

"Oh well, that's just a man for you," Catherine confided to Kate. "It won't do any good to say anything so I'll just take a little piece of cloth and fix it." Another time, at noon, Catherine was slow with lunch ("dinner" she called it) because she'd been interrupted by company. John marched in with military precision at exactly twelve o'clock, looked around and announced "No food on the table," then stomped back out to his shop.[69]

Catherine, seemingly oblivious to the slight, sat down with Kate and they ate their meal, the grandmother carefully putting the leftovers away. "He'll come in when he's hungry," she said.

"She was well patient," Kate said of her grandmother. "She'd have to be to live with him. She was well patient, nothing interfered with her."[70] "I never did see her get upset."[71]

Kate's younger sister May had the same impression of her grandmother that Kate did. "She was a quiet little woman," May recalled of Catherine: "You used to listen to Grandpa Steele talk, why you'd think he had the kids and did everything; Grandma didn't do anything!"[72] Years later May named her first daughter Kathryn and carefully preserved her grandmother's elegant—but worn—velvet dress, and purple and lace hat, already referred to. These were stored in a little brown trunk John built May, and ironically the only memento of his in the trunk is his old black leather wallet and perhaps a green tobacco tin.

But Elizabeth's daughters didn't have too much time in their childhood to visit relatives. Besides housework, there was schoolwork. James Stapley, poorly educated himself, was a firm believer in education and as Sunday School Superintendent he reminded the young that they should "read good books and be delegent in School for they would see the time when they would be glad they had done so and would never regret it." Later he said that "we should improve our minds. Said we should learn to read and understand what we read," and he exhorted Kanarra youngsters "to be a little better and a little smarter than the people of the world [non-Mormons]."[73]

We wonder how much the Stapleys believed study applied to women. Kate's brother John kept minutes for the Kanarra YMMIA during the early 1890s, and he wrote a beautiful hand. Will was ward clerk prior to 1912, and—like John and Mahonri Stapley—had impressive handwriting. Kate wrote a legible hand but without the ornate flourishes of her brothers, and she also lacked their grammatical and spelling skills.

"As for school," wrote Kate's daughter Reba, "My mother said they went about 4 month[s] a year, at first no books, no pencils, they used slaights of rock to write on. I[t] wyapt off eas[i]ly. they study spelling as well as reading and mathematics. A good fo[u]ndation. They would see who could stay up the longest." The teachers were boarded with local families, and Reba said that the school "had spelling bees and they had times tables and then they took turns reading. And she only went three or four months a year."[74]

An early teacher was Rufus Albern Allen,[75] a long-faced, bewhiskered man who looked like a rabbi. He was injured in a farm accident, attended the University of Deseret and then became a teacher, collector, and assessor for Piute County, bishop, and finally a representative at the Utah State Constitutional Convention. He was followed by old George Sprague. Sprague used to take a pencil and twist it into the hair of unruly students, leading them in a trot around the room. Sunday School Superintendent John W. Brown was followed by the most colorful teacher in southern Utah history, Eugene Schoppmann. Schoppmann was a Munchausen-like boaster, though an inspiration to many of his pupils, including Dr. George W. Middleton who remembered him with great affection "as unique [a] character as Falstaff."[76]

Will Stapley dismissed Schoppmann rather tersely as one that "many people thought was a splendid teacher" who insisted on good penmanship and taught geography.[77] Either because, or in spite of Schoppmann, Will also developed an excellent hand but his sister Kate remembered Schoppmann as the man with a German accent who called her Cat-Rine (she vowed she'd never name a child Catherine because they'd call her "Cat"). She hated Schoppmann for this perceived slight and as a practical joke she and some friends starched his shirts and pajamas as stiff as the school's brass bell.[78] Kate's childhood friend and future sister-in-law, Hattie Berry Stapley, described him as a "drifter, German by birth" who "before many months of school" had "drifted out as he had drifted in" and after he left "parents aided their children in their education."[79] Kate's education was limited to the Fifth Grade Wilson reader.

Kate's brothers—Catherine's grandchildren—were also growing up. Jimmy and Will were singers, gave recitations, participated in "Dialogues" (joint readings), lectured and played the piano and mandolin.[80] John was a great practical joker ("He was all for the fun he could get out of it" Reba said), and along with their brother Mahonri sang and played the guitar.

"Well, I'll tell you," recalled Reba. "You get them three brothers together and they could sing any Irish song you ever heard of. They were all good singers. The girls couldn't sing. But the boys was real good singers. They could sing and laugh and carry on—oh, they'd just be—just a lot of fun."[81] Kate thought "the boys was all [the] musicians in the family and the girls didn't have any." Music and singing were Campbell family traits.

May was eleven years Kate's junior and Kate lamented that "I didn't know what it was like to have a sister,"[82] and like her mother before her she did much of the household work. When her little brother Joseph was born in 1884, seventeen-year-old Kate took such tender care of him she felt like she was his mother. She said his death in 1886 "was like my son dying."[83]

Kate grew up in a Mormon society at war with the larger American culture. The war wasn't about patriarchy—most everyone accepted that—it was mostly over polygamy, but also about the Mormon theocracy. Mormon doctrine said a man couldn't reach his full glory in heaven unless he had more than one wife.[84] But during the 1870s and 1880s the United States Congress passed increasingly severe laws against multiple marriages. Kate's relatives began feeling the pressure and some had second thoughts. The Toquerville Relief Society minutes record that community's insecurities. "Sis[ter] Bringhurst spoke of the Bishop hearing that some of the Sisters had spoken against Plural Marige she hoped we would not talk against it for it was a true principle."[85]

M. M. Steele, Kate's uncle, had successfully courted Emily Bunker, one of the beautiful daughters of Bishop Edward Bunker celebrated in Dixie folksong:

> Bishop Bunker's daughters were proper sort of girls.
> Bishop Bunker's daughters were as pretty as pearls.
> If I was a Mormon, a monkey or an Earl,
> By Jingo, I'd marry Bishop Bunker's other girl.[86]

Five years after his first marriage, M. M. was comfortable enough to take a second wife, Mary Ellen Jepson of Virgin. But by the late 1880s, M. M. was threatened with prison and he complained at a Pioneer Day celebration that "the present administration [is] legislating and enacting special laws against the people called 'Mormons,' compelling them to renounce and totally deny their religion, to do this or be forever deprived of their franchise."[87] The next year he wrote his father that "the hoops are being driven tighter," and "our enemies are increasing their endeavours to entrap our feet and the power of oppression is being made manifest to a greater degree, and those of our people who will not go to the pen must go into exile for a time." He reported that "I expect by the end of this year to be on wheels for Mexico. I am shaping every string to that end at present."[88]

At first his good-natured, fun-loving, mother-dependent wife Ellen made light of the threat of prosecution, even composing a carefree song about the deputies and the "raids," but eventually the pressure proved too much for her.[89]

When she was captured by the marshals in the last stages of pregnancy she couldn't be taken to Beaver for trial; they took her eleven-year-old daughter Nellie instead. The family came back from court just in time to see Ellen give birth and die. Joseph Fish blamed the federal marshals. "How is M. M's case going to terminate thought that perhaps they would dismiss it they ought after murd[er]ing his wife you might call it murder for I suppose the fright was the cause of her death."[90] In fact Ellen's timely death did free M. M. from further worries and Emily, faced with raising the children of the other wife, fell into a long-term invalidism after a year. Nevertheless, she took care of them with good cheer (she was remembered as one who "managed her home and family from her bed" and protected the children from their father's stern discipline[91]) and was cured about the time the last child left home; the family credited Cedar City's Dr. George Middleton for her improved health.

Kate's uncle and Toquerville's Bishop, William Augustus Bringhurst, also went into hiding. The deputies came so close to catching him once that he had to run off half-naked through his field. Bringhurst's bravado made him quite a hero to some, but M. M. disapproved. "I heard of W. A. B. taking through the lot in an undress uniform. Well he had better go slow, for they have his case in B[eaver]. & five years is not so funny."[92] A Toquerville neighbor turned in Bringhurst for the $2.50 reward, he was captured February 14, 1888, paid a twenty-five dollar fine and spent six months—not five years—in the state penitentiary.[93]

Other angry letters came to John Steele, the old Toquerville patriarch. Joseph Fish, once husband to Steele's daughter Mary and since married several times over, wrote December 31, 1886, of the killing of Parowan polygamist

E. M. Dalton by Deputy Marshall Thompson, "I see that the war still goes on in Utah and in a shameless manner. the killing of E. M. Dalton was a cold blooded murder."[94]

"I see that the people in Dixie are being looked after quite close by Uncle Sam," Fish wrote May 15, 1888.

> It looks is [as] if, they would get all the polygamists unless they leave the Territory, it is indeed a close sive and many will drift off with the chaff. One of our old Iron County Pioneers is living in one of my houses expect to locate there and make him a place it looks hard to see old men who have spent the best years of their lives become exiled because they do not turn their wives and children out of doors and disown them.[95]

Elizabeth's husband James needed an additional wife for he was becoming increasingly important in the Kanarra church organization and though the office of bishop seemed hereditary in the extended Roundy and Berry families, he eventually held every other calling of importance. "I can remember my Grandmother telling me that Grandfather was close to 50 when he stopped the use of tobacco," remembered Elizabeth's granddaughter Lella Stapley Maxfield, "because he was called to be 2nd Counselor to [Roundy brother-in-law] Bishop William Patterson Willis."[96] Chewing tobacco—"a piece of the horse's butt" according to Rulon Platt[97]—was probably why James retained a nervous habit of chewing the rest of his life. Arvilla Ford Woodbury said he "had that jaw just a going all the time."[98] A second wife would assure James's place in heaven and show his commitment to Mormon orthodoxy. The Stapleys seem to have been unenthused with polygamy—neither James father nor his brothers took additional wives—and Elizabeth couldn't have been very happy about the idea either.

At one point James was looking for a mail order bride from his father-in-law, for John Steele wrote Catherine from England, "I am very Much pleased to hear from James & Elisabeth Jamey and Kate God Bless them tell James I will think about that other woman if he would Send a Box with a Lock & Key And 75$ I might get her Safe across, he must remember this is England I am in, and things here does not wear pad locks, or if they do as they are very seldom used, But there is noble Exceptions to all General Rules."[99]

Whether he didn't have a box with lock and key, seventy-five dollars—or all of the above—we don't know, but we do know no English bride graced his Kanarra home. Instead, practical minded, he and Elizabeth found another solution since only illusions separated the living and the dead. After Joseph Smith's death many women had been "sealed" as wives to the uncomplaining prophet. Elizabeth's dressmaking Aunt Mary Ann Campbell immigrated to Philadelphia and died there in early 1885 at the age of 74. Unmarried, unless a husband was found for her posthumously, she would be a servant in the eternity.

She had hardly been receptive to Mormonism. John wrote Catherine, "how did Aunt Mary Ann write you I have no hopes that any one of your family (unless Eliza) will Come into the Kingdom of God on the earth perhaps the [celestial] prison house may do Something for them, as for them there is no faith."[100]

Why not seal Mary Ann Campbell to James and give him his quota of wives for full celestial glory? Mary Ann, in that Mormon post-life "spirit prison" for non-Mormons, would have plenty of time to accept the divine truth. And meanwhile Elizabeth would have thirty or forty more years to shape her husband into the kind of man she wanted before she'd have to share him. This was done, so they found an answer that avoided threats of the penitentiary.[101]

By 1887 Catherine's granddaughter and namesake, Kate Stapley, was twenty-one years old—an old maid by her grandfather Steele's standards. A photograph taken of her about this time shows a pretty young woman with large, deep eyes and a wave of hair on her forehead. She was dressed in an attractive dark gown with lace over the shoulders, and in the most approved Victorian fashion she was buttoned up from her neck to her toes with only her hands exposed, one finger sporting a ring. (This was a favored dress: years later, when it was beginning to look a little faded, she is still wearing it in a photograph with her husband and four children.)

Kate, recipient of a "Reward of Merit" for her Sunday School work, was ambitious, pretty, and had a wide range of beaux—young and old, single, widowed, and married.[102] None of them were dead, though twenty-seven-year-old Andrew Huston Perkins sometimes seemed close to it. He was a member of Kanarra's Mutual Improvement Association (MIA), a youth group that provided social activities for both men and women. "Perkins tried to step [court] her," explained Reba, "and he would go to sleep. He had this disease that when he come in and sat down, he would go to sleep, no matter who he was with or where he was . . . She said she wasn't going to marry a sleeping guy." He eventually married Almaretta Spencer.[103]

Then there was a thirty-seven-year-old Englishman and snare drum player in the Kanarra martial band, John Charles Roe.[104] Roe had fathered three children, had two living, and had recently lost his wife in childbirth. This beau had a penchant for droll stories, such as one he told about faith in the Mutual Improvement Association. The discussion "put him in mind of an old lady that he had heard of about having the faith of a grane of mustard seed could move a mountain! She thought she had faith anuff to moove a little hill that was in front of her chicken coup so she went to Bed with good faith and thought that the hill would Be mooved away in the Morning so she gets up in the morning and goes out and lo and Behold the hill was thare yet. 'thare that's just as i expected it would be,' the woman announced triumphantly."[105]

Roe's own faith—in prospecting—took him over the mountain to Panguitch. He asked his good friend Joel Jesse "Dode" Roundy to keep an eye on Kate while he was away. "Gladly," Joel said.[106] Roundy was a handsome twenty-three-year-old man with a carefully waxed handlebar mustache, stood five feet eleven inches, and weighed 150 pounds. His good nature was proverbial and proven by a phrenologist who assured him that his head had a "bump of compassion" and therefore he was gifted with "a kind and tender heart."[107]

The Roundys were a loyal and credulous family who were good friends to the Spafford, New York, Pulsiphers. According to Spafford folklore, "Swamp Angel" Pulsipher and his gullible relatives waited up one night for the resurrection of a dead child. Impatient with God's dilatoriness, "Swamp Angel" dressed himself in white robes and tinkling bells and tried to assist in the ascension, only to be captured by skeptical unbelievers who had been watching.[108]

Spafford people assured themselves it was only logical that the Pulsiphers be the first to join the Mormon faith, with its tales of a golden bible and heavenly visitations, and Zerah Pulsipher's friend Shadrach Roundy was also one of the earliest converts. Shadrach and his son Lorenzo dedicated their lives to the new church, serving with such unquestioning obedience that a non-Mormon observer, Elizabeth Wood Kane, wrote "father and son had adhered to the faith with the tenacity of mastiffs."[109] This loyalty cost the younger Roundy his life when, in 1876, Brigham Young ordered Lorenzo to lead a Mormon expedition to Arizona and Roundy was drowned crossing the Colorado River.[110]

He was survived by his second and third wives, Susannah Wallace and Priscilla Parrish, the latter a frugal half-Yankee, half-Irish businesswoman who brought up her brood in the most orthodox Mormon fashion; son Joel was the most faithful of her children. Priscilla had a strong impact on Joel. "They raised their grain and they frailed [flailed] it," her granddaughter Reba reported, "and grandma and her children used to go out in their aprons and pick the heads of wheat so they could have enough wheat to eat."[111] Like Joel, she was poorly educated, devoutly religious, and mightily superstitious.

Joel was good friends with Jimmy Stapley partially because he was attracted to Jimmy's sister Kate. "They run together, and what one done, the other thought that was just perfect," explained Reba of Joel and Jimmy.[112]

They all grew up in Kanarra and Joel, Jimmy, and Kate attended the Kanarra Sunday School where Jimmy was secretary, old James Stapley was Superintendent, and Joel sometimes took minutes for Jimmy. With his assignment from Roe to "keep an eye on Kate," his friendship with Jimmy, and common interests in church, Joel was set for a successful courtship.

Some of their wooing must have taken place in the Sunday School where Jimmy's minutes record that they listened to Assistant Superintendent Brown lecture on "Parents teaching their children to prey [pray]," heard James Stapley explain that "we have a great many trials and dificulties to contend with," and probably nodded off while Bishop William Patterson Willis lectured "the young men to leave of[f] drinking liquor and useing tobacco, spoke of governing our tongue[s] and to be careful what we say, also to shun the company of the evil doer."[113]

Kate was a Sunday School teacher and she "give some very good instruction to the pupils in keeping the Sabbath day holy," according to Jimmy, after which their father "spoke, said it was a duty devolving upon him to talk to the pupils once in a while, spoke of punctuality and of improving our time."[114]

They were part of a special Sunday School program in April 1886, where Kate gave a dialogue, Joel a speech on "Trust in god and do the right," and Joel's mother gave a recitation.[115] In October 1886, Joel's elder brother Sam gave a parting sermon before leaving on his mission, urging the young "not [to] get drunk," and to "do that which is right," after which Kate's grandfather John Steele "said that being raised in the church we should remember that we have a work to do," and urged even more missionary efforts.[116]

The young couple set their marriage for March 9, 1887, in the St. George Temple with a double ceremony including Jimmy and his fiancé, the studious schoolteacher Hattie Berry. Kate, like her mother and grandmother, was an accomplished seamstress. "Grandma told me about the beautiful wedding dress she made and the many hours she spent embroidering and sewing in lace and tucks and such," recalled Kate's granddaughter JoAnn Sylvester Bate.

> She also showed me the petticoat she was married in which was about 5 yards around and had I think 3 series of tucks with 5 or 7 in each series around the whole thing and fancy cut work and satin stitch embroidery between the series of tucks. When she went to hurry into her clothes to

> get married, she only got her petticoat. They wouldn't let her wear her wedding dress as it was too fancy for the Temple. She was always hurt about that because she felt that no matter what she made it was far short of being worthy to go to the Temple. She put so much into making the dress to go before the Lord.[117]

Jimmy and Hattie couldn't wait for the double marriage ceremony and got married February 23, so Joel and Kate went to St. George without them. No marrying took place on March ninth so they waited until the tenth. Still they weren't marrying anyone. They were told on the eleventh that "we're not going to marry you today, either." If they weren't married before the twelfth, they would have to buy a license. Kate was disappointed when she went back to where she was staying "to get her clothes changed and she was just half undressed when someone came down and said, 'Come on! Come on! Come on! They're going to marry. You better get up here.'"

"I slammed my clothes on!" Kate recalled later, meaning the clothes she was allowed to wear, not the ones she wanted to wear, and they were promptly married, March 11, 1887.[118]

When they got back to Kanarra, Kate's entry in the Sunday School class roster was changed from "S. C. Stapley" to "S. C. Roundy,"[119] and they moved in with Joel's midwife-mother, Priscilla Parrish Roundy. "I received a letter from M. M. a short time since he said that quite a number of the young folks were marr[y]ing off two of, Elizabeth's children among them hope they will all do well," Joseph Fish wrote to John in Toquerville April 27, 1887.[120] Soon Joel went to work out of town and Kate went home to stay with her mother until he came back. After that "they found a shack of their own and stayed together," said Reba.

When Roe "come back he said, 'Did you take good care of my wife?' 'You bet I did!'" Joel replied, "'She's the Missus now!'"[121]

Soon Joel was busy with another courtship. His father, Lorenzo Wesley Roundy, had been a polygamist and his uncle Jared Roundy was a polygamist husband to Nellie White, one of Mormonism's especially courageous women. Questioned closely by a federal attorney about the secret temple rituals, Nellie refused to answer; her obstinacy won her a cell in the state penitentiary and wide applause from her coreligionists.[122] It was natural that Joel be committed to the principle that had brought him into the world, but Kate wasn't enthused about polygamy. "If that was the law and the way that it should go," Reba said, "well, she would do it. But if that wasn't the law she didn't want to do it."[123]

Polygamy was against the law of the United States, but not against the "higher law" of the church.

Margaret Ahlene "Maggie" Davies was the twenty-year-old daughter of Kanarra's Welsh town diarist and musician, John Johnson Davies; her mother died three hours after giving birth to her. Maggie's brother Henry "Hennie" was married to Joel's sister Annis. Maggie "was crazy about dad," recalled Reba. Kate also liked Maggie, confiding to Reba that "we could of got along all right."[124]

Like her father and many of Kanarra's other Welsh people, Maggie was a singer, entertaining the MIA in duets and quartettes. Once after Maggie sang, Joel proposed a toast and then his brother Wallace Roundy warbled "The Old Man's Drunk Again," suggesting the exuberant good time everyone enjoyed.[125]

As Maggie and Joel were ready to set the date there were hints the Mormon Church might abandon polygamy. "We'd better see how this is going to turn out first," Joel advised.[126] Three months later Wilford Woodruff, the aging prophet, issued a press release called "The Manifesto," which prohibited further plural marriages. The wedding was called off. Not only was Woodruff's statement the beginning of the end of church-sanctioned plural marriage, it also signaled giving up on the theocracy that was to build the Kingdom of God in Utah; eventually the Kingdom was redefined to be the whole earth and "gathering" to Utah was discontinued.

Maggie married Robert Madison Mulliner, but her marriage was a failure and she died less than five years later of Bright's disease in Cedar City, leaving a small daughter, Effie. The funeral was postponed while the family hunted down her absent husband. Afterward he disappeared again, not to be seen in Kanarra for another twenty years when, again wifeless, he showed up at his daughter Effie's with four more motherless children.[127]

Maggie had more trials to pass through after she died. Since Mulliner was unlikely to take her into the Mormon Celestial Kingdom her family felt she should be sealed to a worthier man. Her brother-in-law Reese J. Williams raised Effie, and consequently Maggie was sealed to him on June 1, 1915. But Williams, a four-term Iron County commissioner, was discredited when his son took a legacy left to the Kanarra Ward by a wine loving Swiss-American peddler and trader, John Kunzler (known to everybody as Johnny Kinsley), and used it to buy his father's farm for the church. There were accusations this was self-interested and shady. The sealing was cancelled soon after Williams's death in the 1930s and Maggie was posthumously united to the suitor of her youth, Joel Roundy.[128]

Kate wasn't entirely happy with the resolution to this problem because when Joel talked to Effie about being sealed to Maggie, Effie said "I'm perfectly satisfied the way it is." Joel complained about this to Kate.

"Well, maybe she don't want you," Kate commented tartly.

"Well, she don't understand," Joel replied.[129]

But perhaps she did.

5

"She Wanted Her Own Rights"

Sarah E. Roundy

John Houston Brown is the only doctor buried in the Kanarra cemetery, his black marble monument terse (the inscription reads: BROWN Dr. J. H. 1852–1895), dignified, and out of place among the verbose inscriptions on the sprawling gray memorials erected for his contemporaries.[1] This is a monument to a man and to a mystery. How and why did Dr. Brown die so young?

"People say he was a suicide," Joan Norman Williams explained. "I went down there once to find out. Suicides are buried facing away from the sun when they rise on the morning of the first resurrection. Otherwise they're buried facing toward the sun. Well, I went down there. But I couldn't tell which way he was buried."[2]

Lynn Reeves, whose father bought Brown's carpenter tools from his widow Margaret, gave a different version. "He took an overdose of laudanum for something, whatever was wrong with him, and it killed him."[3]

The latter story, not necessarily contradicting the first, is circumstantially supported by Dr. George W. Middleton who wrote of early southern Utah doctors: "At a later date a southerner called Doctor Brown, drifted into the area. He used to mix cocaine with ditch water in any uncertain, unmeasured quan[t]ity and inject it into the gums before pulling the teeth. The wonder is that people did not die of cocaine poisoning, but so far as I recalled he had no fatalities."[4]

Brown was born in Henderson County, Kentucky, and married in Illinois to Margaret Josephine Wilson, first cousin of Joel Roundy's brother-in-law, Kanarra bishop William Patterson Willis. "Pat" Willis baptized the couple while on an 1880s Illinois mission and they followed him back to Kanarra where Brown built one of the finest residences in town, a six-room brick house with a closed porch and separate entrance to the cellar.

The summer of 1888 Brown was minding sheep at Shiver Creek on the Kanarra Mountain. Kate was home with her first labor. A terrible storm blackened the evening sky with only an occasional flash of lightning providing any visibility. Elizabeth was midwifing her first grandbaby into the world, but when the labor became complicated and the situation dangerous, she fitted up her younger son Will on "Old Button" to go up the steep mountain road for Doc Brown. Will was afraid and lonely in the black night. "When I arrived at the top where timber of various kinds was plentiful, and where a trail crossed my way, the old horse turned on to that trail and took me perhaps a quarter of a mile when I discovered I was going in the wrong direction, and in trying to turn and get my bearings I became tangled in the thick timber," he wrote.[5]

Will stopped, lost and frightened. Finally he got down from the saddle and stood by Old Button in fervent prayer, asking God to "open the way that I might be successful in my undertaking." The clouds parted in the south, providing enough moonlight so that he found his way to the main road. The grateful boy took time to thank the Lord for divine assistance and then headed into Brown's camp. The Doc was astonished to see him but saddled up and followed Will down the intimidating trail in the middle of the night. By the time they got to Kanarra it was early morning on July eleventh. Kate was feeling better, and she soon gave birth to Sarah Elizabeth Roundy, named after her mother Kate (Sarah Catherine) and her grandmother Elizabeth. This troubled beginning foreshadowed Sarah's difficult life.

"I was married the eleventh of March and on the eleventh of July I had a baby," Joel said.

"Why, Dad," said a surprised son-in-law, "I didn't think you were that kind of man!"

"Well, I didn't say what year. Eighty-eight," Joel laughed, the closest he ever came to a risqué joke.[6]

The earliest photograph of Sarah shows a very sad two-year-old abstractedly clutching a chain-handled purse decorated with a large flower. A stylish woman her whole life, even here she is sporting finery: a dark dress with a flower and stem sewed over each sleeve and knee, her neck circled by a lace collar and her feet encased in high button-up boots.

Though Kate's first pregnancy had been hard, with one exception she enjoyed good health. The exception was an affliction she shared with others in southern Utah, a poisoned goiter.[7] This malady was so common in the days before iodized salt that in my own youth in the 1950s and 1960s some old women still had goiters. In earlier times John Steele had a special remedy for it: two teaspoons each of salt, borax, and alum dissolved in two spoonfuls of water and applied three times a day—whether internally or externally his prescription doesn't make clear.[8]

The condition didn't win any sympathy from younger people, as Arvilla Ford Woodbury makes plain. Between the Ford and Platt home were

> these big currant bushes, wild currants. Well, they was my brother and me and my sister that Momma sent up to pick these wild currants to bottle. And I don't know why, we was just little kids, but this old lady, Verna [Platt Davis]'s mother [Mina Berry Platt] had a great big neck [because of a goiter]. And I don't know why we got talking about her, but we just got talking about her, three of us, little bits of kids, and come to find out she was on the other side picking currants. So she yelped at us, and gosh we took our little buckets of currants and if we didn't go down to Momma's on the run! She knew darn well we'd done something, so we finally told her what we'd done. And oh she was mad. She said, "you get right up there and ask her forgiveness for what you done!" So we walked up there. We ended up there on the other side of the fence, and she was still picking currants. And we says—here the elderly Mrs. Woodbury stood up, dramatically bowed very low and with her hands held high in supplication—and said, "Forgive us, old Big Neck!"[9]

Mina Platt's mother, Becky Berry allegedly died on the operating table getting a goiter removed (her death certificate says the cause of death was "canser of throat"[10]) and though Mina eventually had hers taken out, her sister-in-law, Susannah Elizabeth Williams Berry, was never operated on. Mina's brother, Bishop John William Berry, "just felt like he'd lost his mother, he didn't want to lose his wife too, so he'd never consent to it," remembered his daughter Thelma Berry Lovell.[11]

In the late nineteenth century, Elias H. Blackburn, who had less training than John Steele, promoted himself as a healer and was licensed by the Utah Board of Medical Examiners as a doctor. "Oh, he kind of wanted to be a medicine man like an Indian," Rulon Platt recalled, and said Blackburn "was kind of a neighborhood–country doctor" around the Loa, Wayne County, area.[12] Joel's brother Myron S. Roundy, a couple of years before his early death from pneumonia, touted him in the Kanarra church because people had "received immediate aid thru the administration of the Faith Doctor, Bro. Blackburn."[13] Maybe John Steele's remedy failed, as Kate went to Loa to get treated by Blackburn.

"Mother had a goiter, she went to Loa for that," Reba remembered. "She went over and stayed with him [Blackburn], and by having faith and doing what he told her to, and rubbing it with olive oil, it killed it. Killed the goiter, and she didn't have to have it operated on."[14] So closely interwoven were medicine and religion that while Kate was in Loa she had Blackburn give her a Mormon "patriarchal blessing" too, and he promised she would be healed.[15]

It was good that Kate was healthy because Elizabeth expected Kate to put more energy into being a daughter than a mother. Elizabeth "was a perfectionist," recalled her granddaughter Lenna Stapley Williams. "Nobody but Kate could do it good enough."[16] Lenna's cousin Josephine Kay Garfield laughingly agreed that Kate "did everything that Grandma wanted her to, even at the expense of her kids and everybody!"[17] Every day Kate went to her mother's and did the housework and took care of her mother's younger children, while Joel accepted this arrangement uncomplainingly and assumed much of the responsibility in his own household.

At the same time, Elizabeth had her own mother to worry about for Catherine's health had worsened. Repeated energetic requests that Catherine "come visit" were made by many of her children and grandchildren. As, for instance, from son M. M., who tactfully suggested he would welcome both his parents, but really seemed to be addressing his plea to Catherine: "I wish you would bring Mother out. If you can not bring her and you both can not leave at once, if you will send word when she can leave I will send the carriage for her. I want her to come out & spend a short time rusticating."[18] But as her health worsened she seems to have stopped traveling.

"My wife is very low and has been bedfast for nearly four months but my Children and grand Children take care of her & the prospects are that she may yet live a long time," John wrote Letisha Todd on November 16, 1890. Then he added almost tenderly, "This day is her Birth day 75 years ago She first Saw the light of day in that Beautifull Town Called Straban[e] in the County Tyrone Ireland nine miles from the City of Londonderry. We are making a Birthday for her when her Children, and Grand, and Great Grand Children Several of whom will be present, but it would take a larger house than I have at present to hold them all as there is about 80 of them all told," and then he went off into a diatribe about Genesis, and the sun and moon, and breasts and womb, Deuteronomy, Abraham, Isaac, and Jacob.[19] When he finally came up for air he managed to say he had "one picture" of Catherine, and "she looke right Smart looking and to think she is the Mother of 5 living Children and 4 dead, as it Seems but yestarday" since they were married.[20] (Little Sarah Elizabeth Roundy, Elizabeth's first granddaughter and namesake, was almost certainly taken down to her great-grandmother Catherine's party and we can easily imagine the elderly woman coaxing a smile from her serious little descendant.)

In March 1891, six or eight weeks after the Kanarra meeting house burned down,[21] John reported to Letisha that his posterity numbered "about a hundred in all," defended polygamy to his unsympathetic correspondent ("So how Many Eves did god make & put With Adam?" Letisha had curtly questioned[22]) and announced, "Your Aunt is much on the improve and I think She will ralley once more."[23]

As early as May 1887, Sister Rosalia Naegle reported to the Relief Society ladies that "all felt well but sister Steel and she was quite sick." By December Catherine was well enough to attend Relief Society meeting, motivated by the death of her dear Salt Lake friend, Eliza R. Snow, "one of the most celebrated Mormon women of the nineteenth century. A renowned poet, she chronicled history, celebrated nature and relationships, and expounded scripture and doctrine,"[24] and was widow of both Joseph Smith and Brigham Young. The minutes give a paraphrase of Catherine's remarks: "siste[r] Cathrin Steele spok[e] of her early a^c^quaintants with sis Eliza and how she has labor[e]d in the C[h]urch but she could not tolk for her hart was to[o] full."[25]

A few years later Catherine's health again became a source of concern to the women. Ann Savage "asked the Lord to bless . . . Sister Steele and comfort her while she lived," the minutes reported on October 2, 1890; and in December, "Sister Sarah Stapeley and Regular Naegle gave a good report of the 1 dis[trict] found all well but Sister Steel she was very sick was pleas[ed] to see . . . the teachers."[26]

Catherine's neighbor Levi Savage wrote on January 11, 1891, "I made Sister Ste[e]l a short visit. She seems to be improveing a very little, but her age is against her."[27] There was a rally, for M. M. wrote his parents on February 12, 1891, "I am pleased to learn that you are all on the improve."[28] "[A]ll well an doing well but sister Cathrine Steel and she was get[t]ing better," the Relief Society sisters heard in April.[29]

Despite M. M.'s hopes and John's prediction that Catherine would get better, she died on June 15, 1891. Levi Savage, coming into town after listening to B. H. Roberts's St. George conference address, made a note in his diary: "I rode for home w[h]en I arrived a little after 12 noon. As soon as I was off my horse, I was tolde that Sister Steel died yesturday about 4 P. M. The funeral services was postponed this morning or forenoon, and had started the friends with the body to the Parowan Burying ground for Burriel, the news of her death was telligraffed to Bishop Bringherst yesterday at 4 P.M. but we heard nothing of it until we got home."[30]

Her Relief Society friends mourned. Sister Eliza A. Slack said, "In speaking of Sister Steele['s] death . . . the scriptures say blessed are they that die in the Lord for they shall have eternal life."[31] The 1891 financial accounts that closed Catherine's Relief Society career reported, "Dide Toquervill[e] June 15 1891 She left a Husband and 9 Children 4 dead 5 living (Absent but not Forgoten[])]."[32]

Saddened and depressed, John sat down on the day of Catherine's death to pencil a tribute on the handiest piece of paper he could find—the back of an 1889 form letter to agents of *The Contributor* magazine: "In watching by the Beadside of Some Dear . . . [paper torn] A Wife, a mother, Sister Dear, fast drawing near her end of this frail life, with Cares and woes and and sorrows great, and with the weight of three score years and fifteen upon her head," he began with tender lack of coherence.

> Who's shadows are past and gone, and children many, yea and grand children not a few, waiting around the bed to see the last frail spark of mortal life depart it's clay, and to return to immortality from whence it came. To give an account of the many acts of good or evil through which it has passed while tabernacled here in this frail mortality, having traveled many weary thousand miles from that far land that gave her birth, to gather with the saints of God and help with her small mite, to rear a kingdom where the will of God might here on earth be done as it is in heaven . . ."

He then fell completely into his old pattern and went on and on, called down the wrath of God on the persecutors of the Latter-day Saints, mourned their exile to Utah, cursed Missouri and Illinois "whose soil has drunk the blood of God's best men," and finally concluded Catherine "was one of those noble souls who bravely took up her cross to follow Christ and gain that crown of glory and eternal life, whose brightness shines more brilliant than the noon day sun."[33]

So before her body was buried the process of posthumous sanctification began, reinforced since by descendants who made a typescript of John's comments on Catherine's death and bravely titled it "Reflections" (maybe hoping no one would notice that the lengthy document tells us little about Catherine but, as with all John's records, a lot about him). Her deification continued with enthused family historians drawing upon her life's resume, the process reaching its apogee in a history that united them in death as they'd never agreed in life: "They were both deeply religious. They had a firm conviction that Joseph Smith was a prophet of the living God . . . They were firm believers in the hereafter . . . They believed that man's existence here on earth is one phase or schooling . . . They believed that their mission here on earth was to spread the truth . . . No sacrifice was too great."[34]

But perhaps one sacrifice was too great—being buried in Toquerville.[35] John took Catherine's body almost fifty-six miles over some of the roughest roads in Utah—including the notorious Black Ridge[36]—to Parowan for interment. There Bishop Charles Adams conducted services on June 17. "Remarks, kind and complimentary to the deceased, and consoling to the husband and children, who were present, were made by a number of speakers," explained Joseph Fish's fearless, prosperous, and half-blind brother-in-law William Campbell McGregor in an obituary of this Campbell clanswoman. "It was Sister Steele's desire that after her death her body should be laid in the Parowan cemetery, by the side of a married daughter [Mary] and yoong [*sic*] son [Robert Henry], who died here some years ago. All who had the pleasure of an acquaintance with Sister Steele speak of her as a kind, self-possessed, brave and noble woman. The blessings promised in the Gospel will be her eternal reward."[37]

The most convincing tribute to Catherine came from Joseph Fish, a man with four mothers-in-law. Fish wrote about visiting Catherine after a long absence:

> "I went over to Parowan where I found my mother-in-law Mrs. Steele. I had not seen her for two years, and I was pleased to meet her for she was not like most relatives of this class [mother-in-law]. She was one of my very best friends and we were always on the very best terms with each other."[38]

Her tombstone inscription was long and wordy:

Catherine Campbell
Wife of John Steele
Born Nov. 16th 1816
in Strabane
Tyrone co. Ireland
came to Utah
July 29th 1847
Moved to Parowan
in 1851
Died June 15th 1891
in Toquerville
Washington Co.[39]

Catherine was a passive resister in God's war against women. John did his best to "rule over" her and she gave every outward indication of acquiescence. But she only heard what she chose to hear. When John's letters became too abusive she refused to write back; when his advice was unwelcome she paid it no heed; when his tantrums seemed unbearable she announced philosophically that he'd have to get over them. His severity toward her suggests the depth of his resentment for her unwillingness to really surrender. It was left to the women who followed her to battle patriarchy more directly. And in the way of the Mormon people—like other pioneers, she has never been forgotten—her story and her skills, especially with the needle, passed down from one generation to the next.

On June 21, 1891, Levi Savage again confided in his diary: "I called on Bro. John Steel, he has lately returned from Parowan, where he attended to the buriel of his late departed wife, he seems lonely."[40] A letter John wrote M. M. showed the old man was still grieving in mid-July; M. M.'s response was,

> I certainly sympathize with you in your lonely condition O! how lonely it must be. The bud certainly has a bitter taste, the flower we trust may be sweet. I can realize now that a home will be with-out a mother. She will rest in peace till the resur[r]ection. While we will continue to labor untill our labors are finished, then and not till then, will we be able to fully see the justice of Our Father separating us in this life. We will have our heart strings streached all they Can bear before we can reap the blessings.[41]

Kate carefully saved a tiny piece of russet-colored paisley cloth with vertical black lines, enclosing blue and red designs, as a memorial to her namesake. Years later she pinned a note to it: "this is a piece of Grandma Steele's dress, at least 50 years ago," and on the back, "This is 1933."[42] Kate's brother Jimmy, on a mission in Belfast, wrote to console his grandfather. "I was not surprised to hear, but was glad to hear that she passed away so easy. Poor soul she had to suffer so much I know that death was a relief to her. She has born her trials verry patiently, and in company with you she has passed through a great many hard scenes, and trials." He added that "time and space will not permit me to explain my feelings with regard to her, but suffice it to say if we can all live so as to be able to meet her after leaving this probation it will be well with us."[43]

"Well Grandpa," Jimmy wrote in September. "You no doubt feel lonely, now that your loving companion is gone, but when a man can look back upon his past life and can say that he and his companion lived togather in peace and love all their days he has nothing to regret." Perhaps thinking about Catherine's silent suffering, he added, "We seldom realize the benefit of a good thing until we have lost the use of it, that is, to the extent we should."[44]

As John Steele's life was reduced to unwanted solitude, his daughter Elizabeth found her own family growing up and marrying. Elizabeth's son Mahonri Moriancumer Stapley, a handsome young man with dark eyebrows, full mustache, and short brown hair, married Rebecca Almeda Williams in 1898—she a practical joker, more than a head shorter than him. "He went with her seven years before he married her," Reba chuckled. "He was going like Jacob, he was going to get seven years in."[45] Mahonri spent part of this time earning a wedding stake and he took his fiancée to Salt Lake City where they were married in the temple, after which they spent nearly all their twenty-dollar gold pieces, partly through putting on a great wedding dance. By the time their honeymoon was over, they had one gold piece left and were forced to move in with Elizabeth.[46]

"Mother spent the first nine months of her married life living in Grandma's home," said Rebecca's oldest son Elton. The experience with her dominating mother-in-law embittered Rebecca so much that she asserted, "I wouldn't have a daughter-in-law of mine come into my home [to live] if she had to live in a tent."[47]

They moved to Loa in Wayne County, seemingly a safe distance away. But when Mahonri got deathly ill in May or June 1905, Rebecca's mother and both Mahonri's parents, James and Elizabeth, went to Loa to nurse him. The paper reported: "Mahonri Stapley, who has been very sick with typhoid pneumonia, but is much better now, being able to sit up a little."[48] (Tradition says Mahonri's temperature got up to 107 before it could be brought under control.)

Besides her brother John Alma Steele, Elizabeth worried about her son John Alma Stapley.[49] The latter "got in with a bunch of boys in his age and they just went through the town a terrorizing people," said Reba. The Groves children were special targets of cruelty by John and his friends.[50] (Four of the eight Groves children were sent to the State Mental Hospital in 1919, but were refused admittance because they were improperly diagnosed as "insane" when they were, the hospital said, "feeble-minded." Still, eventually five of them ended up at that institution.[51])

"They used to just tease the life out of" the Groves children, Reba said. "They'd make noises, they'd make this, they'd make that. If they was going out and taking their cows up to Spring Creek to feed they'd follow and split the cows up and they'd go all in every direction." John's adventurousness was eventually subdued by a mission call, marriage to Lucretia "Louie" Higgins, and then lifelong snickering by his family because he and Louie were married in June and their son Alonzo Lazell was born in September. A photograph of John and Lucretia taken early in their marriage shows a thin, handsome man with a light colored mustache, holding chubby baby Lazell while Lucretia stands nervously behind John, her dark hair in ringlets and wearing an elaborate, lacy dress. To the end, John A. Stapley shared his uncle and namesake's love of music, a good time, and a little wine.

A few weeks after recovering from illness in early 1903, John and Louie went with his parents to St. George to do temple work. Later he moved with his brother James "Jimmy" Steele Stapley to Loa. Jimmy became a politician—Republican candidate for county clerk and recorder in 1908[52]—while John and Louie farmed before moving back to Kanarra. On May 31, 1912, the *Iron County Record* reported, "John Stapley has rented the [Kanarra] home of Mrs. John Reeves and is now living there."[53]

In the fall of 1900, Elizabeth's daughter May left home to teach school in Virgin, Utah. She was a vivacious, spontaneous woman, confiding in her journal during her first year in the class room that "school teaching is hard on the nerves I feel as tired as if I had been washing when I get home." She noted disapprovingly, "There are some very notty little fellows there and it puts me at my wits end to know what to do with them."[54]

May flirted, and particularly liked Joel Roundy's rather unromantic nephew and cousin Othello "Thell" Roundy. She received a postcard, probably from Thell, dated Alton, April 24, 1909, which showed a young lad surrounded by tubs of wash and captioned, "Young Lady wanted to keep house for Single Young Man (State salary required)." A handwritten inscription added, "If you will except this, please notify all the Bachelors. Alton, Utah."

After she left Virgin, May attended the Branch Normal School in Cedar City, graduating on May 29, 1902, and continued her teaching career. She took her father to the National Education Association Conference in Los Angeles in the summer of 1907, and they looked up his California sister, Charlotte Stapley Hawker. Aunt Charlotte's colorful husband, Thomas Hawker, had careened through life as a shoemaker, highway robber, was transported to Australia in lieu of a death sentence, there became an escapee, thief, and bush ranger—all of which prepared him for life as a prosperous California rancher and real estate investor.[55] James also visited his sister Hannah Maria Stapley Rawling, said to have been married three times and, the family picture suggests, hardened into the grimness of a steel ax by life's ordeals.[56]

May was given a "Grammar grade life diploma" by the State Board of Education in April 1909, and that summer the local paper reported, "May Stapley is attending the summer school at Salt Lake City," along with her Mona friend, Eliza Williams.[57]

She went to Eliza's hometown to spend a weekend and was introduced to a thirty-six-year-old bachelor named Jack Kay. Jack, according to his daughter Josephine, "was a hard person to get acquainted with. People didn't really take to him at first, but if they got to know him they liked him better."[58]

May and Jack shared a love of music and she got to know and like him better. They were married December 15, 1910, in the St. George Temple with her mother Elizabeth, father James, and brother Will present.[59] Afterward they settled in Mona in northern Juab County, where Jack ran a farm and raised grain, horses, and milk cows while May concentrated on bringing up her family, including daughter Kathryn she'd named for her grandmother Catherine Campbell Steele. She sometimes taught school in Mona or Nephi, besides making her husband his favorite delicacy, dandelion wine.

Will T. Stapley, lean, clean-shaven, and jug-eared with light-colored bushy eyebrows and ferret-like eyes, stayed on in Kanarra, a bachelor and ward clerk. Reba remembered him as

> a very pious man. He didn't like to have anything stirred up. If he had this here all done and somebody come moved a book he didn't like it. This is what I knew when I was a kid. He was to home; the rest of them was all married. He was to home, and him and Grandpa farmed and us—Grandma would say, "go out and gather the eggs," because he wouldn't climb around in the hay, and Grandpa didn't want to. She said, "Now you kids go out and gather the eggs." So one time we were gathering the eggs and Leola and Arvil [Stapley] and Harold come down and so we was out getting them. "You kids get right down out of there!" he said. "Get out of this corral! Get right out of this corral! You don't know but what a cow or a bull will chase you. Get out of this corral," he says. "Now get right out of here!"[60]

While Elizabeth's other children were courting and marrying, her daughter Kate's family grew and she soon had enough athletic boys to make up a big share of the town's Westside baseball team. Ren, Jesse, and Golden served as shortstop, catcher, and pitcher and could beat all comers. "They said the Roundy boys never lost," laughed Reba. Her twin, Reva, like Jesse, was a renowned runner: "Reva could beat anybody, in short distance."[61]

"James Lorenzo [Ren] Roundy was a happy Christmas Present for his parents on Christmas Day 1890," wrote Reba.[62] He was very bashful but reliable and hardworking. When he was just a young boy Joel took him to the Co-op

Ranch on the East Fork to care for the cattle for the summer, and in 1904, when he was only fourteen, he went with his uncles John and Mahonri Stapley to move their cattle to Loa, riding back alone.

Kate and Joel's son Ren was followed by Jesse C, born in 1893. "My grandmother [Elizabeth] put the 'C' in because her mother was a Campbell," Reba remembered. "She put the 'C' in, it doesn't stand for anything, only 'C.'"[63] When Jesse was a baby, Joel and George Berry were "called" to spend twenty weeks at BYU. George was outgoing; Joel was bashful so he always told his friend, "Now, George, you ask them." The two of them discovered bananas in Provo and Joel was pushed almost to his limit when he had to sit at "a big long table" and "they always put him down by a girl. Oh, he hated that." When he took bananas back to Kanarra, his father-in-law, James Stapley, delighted, said, "Mmm! Mmm! Bananas! Bananas! Give me a banana Dode!"—Joel's nickname—"Give me a banana," and he peeled one, which was the first time Joel knew the proper way to open it. James explained that on ship from Australia the Captain said, "If anybody will go up and get that stem of bananas," hanging from the rigging, "they can have it." So James went up and, he said, "I haven't had one of them since I left Australia."[64]

Jesse was good-natured—a great, but tender tease—and like his brothers, powerfully built. He was "a good athlete and he was a good LDS," recalled Lynn Reeves, whose father Will C. Reeves employed young Jesse at Reeves's Kanarra Mountain coal mine.[65] (Reba remembered Will Reeves, a cousin, as "a nice fellow. He was a good-hearted man and he had to work, and he supported his family fairly well,"[66] so Jesse probably enjoyed working for him.) Ren and Jesse liked practical jokes and once played a prank on the town grocer, Riley G. Williams. Williams stood about five foot five and, like his mother, walked in an oddly shuffling, hunched over way. He was generous in giving candy to Reba and Reva, and since he couldn't tell them apart, one girl could go back for more, pretending to be the other.

Jesse, Ren, and their crowd of boys took Riley's buggy apart and placed it over the steps of the chapel, about twenty-five or thirty steps up from the ground, put it back together, and braced it so it wouldn't fall. Not surprisingly, Reba reported, "He didn't like that one bit!"[67]

Rebecca Annis came to Kate and Joel in 1896 and, when older, proved herself a capable seamstress, like so many women in her family. She made many of the rugs in town on her mother's loom. "She was a nice looking girl," recalled Hazel Eagar Bringhurst, who used to have her sewing done by Annis.[68]

Next was Golden Parrish (1898), like his brothers another great athlete. "I was herding sheep one spring," Lynn Reeves explained about Golden, and

> They was sporting up here on the corner of the [town] square. He came up and he had an old four buckled overshoe on one foot, and a cowboy boot on the other. And oh, kind of a slicker on, you know, it was kind of—and that. And somebody said, "can you get up to that mark?" in a hop-hop-jump. If you've ever heard that. They'd take two hops and then they'd jump. And he said, "Oh, I think so." They said, "Well, there's the mark and nobody else can get up to it." And they used what they called car links. That's the links between railroad cars if you've ever seen one of them. And they used them for weight, to help them push, you see, to jump farther. And he took that, and swung a couple of times, and hopped out there, and he went over it about three feet. And nobody could get anywhere around it. They tried to get him to put on a pair of [matched] shoes to see how far he could go, but he wouldn't do it.[69]

Estella ("Stella") was born in 1901, when Joel was building a new brick house, so the birth took place next door at Zephyr Kelsey Nixon's. Zephyr, a friendly woman with a spotted dog named "Sport" had three consecutive husbands and was suspected—without any evidence—of poisoning one or two of them.[70] But that was probably because her nephew Frank P. Kelsey was tried and acquitted for poisoning his wife. And charges against him for the attempted poisoning of his mother and grandparents were dismissed—but suspicions were never lifted.[71]

Zephyr had an extra bedroom and Kate stayed there for two weeks recuperating from Stella's birth. "They had them stay in bed about fourteen days," Reba explained. "And then if they felt better, if they felt good in fourteen days they got up but if they didn't they stayed longer."[72]

Uncle Will Stapley—Kate's brother—had broken his leg. It healed badly and he had it broken and reset by Dr. George W. Middleton because, the *Salt Lake Tribune* joked, "it was not straight enough to suit Mr. Stapley's ideas of physical beauty and convenience."[73] Will's brother M. M. came down to help James with the farm and Elizabeth went with Will to Cedar City for the January 20, 1904, operation. "The patient is getting along nicely, so the doctor says," was the subsequent newspaper report, and later, "After having served six weeks in bed Wm. T. Stapley will try wooden legs." Will recalled, "I'm sure [Dr. Middleton] did a perfect job, but owing to my riding in a saddle too soon after stock it became bent and has given me more or less pain ever since."[74]

What Elizabeth missed while she was in Cedar with Will was two births announced in the February 27, 1904, *Iron County Record*: "Mrs. James Stapley came home from Cedar Sunday night in a hurry and was happily surprised to find a pair of twin girls at the home of her daughter, Mrs. J. Roundy." These vivacious and pretty identical twins came in a blizzard and were named Reba and Reva, Kate's only children assisted into the world by Elizabeth's midwife rival, Priscilla Parrish Roundy. Their oldest sister Sarah made a layette for them.[75] Curiously, Kate credited the family sewing skills to Joel's mother, not her own grandmother: "Sarah is a lot like Grandma Roundy, so mother said," Reba reported. "Grandma Roundy could look at anything in church and go home and make it. Knitting, crochet or dresses she'd look at them and she could go home and make them. She wouldn't wait a week or two to make them, either, she made them right when she got home."[76]

Reba also reported that her father "always told me afterwards that he took care of me and my mother took care of Reva. And I guess he said he pulled me through on catnip tea because in them days they didn't have what they have now for babies," and her "mother didn't have enough milk for both of us." That, she thought, made a lifelong difference: "I'm better off than she is. I'm a lot healthier all my life than she's been, and I do a lot more things than she's done."[77] (Kanarra twins who followed them were their cousins Echo and Esther Pollock in 1916, and Verna and Vernon Platt in 1917.)

And last of all the Roundy children was Karl G (1907). Karl described himself as "the black sheep of the family" who "raised more hell,"[78] but others remembered him as a handsome, tow-headed boy who was a little spoiled. A picture of him at three shows a cute little boy with a very wicked grin.

Kate was quick-witted, courageous, and strong, as Fred Balser explains. Corral gates at the turn of the century were built by craftsmen. A good one had heavy, two-inch by eight- or ten-inch planks with heavy iron hinges. A pine pole six feet longer than the width of the gate was balanced over the top of a heavy cedar gate post and pinned with a steel pin running through the pole and into the top of the gate post. At the end of the six foot pole, farmers built a frame and placed rocks or scrap iron to act as a balance to make the gate operate smoothly. A well-functioning gate could weigh two or three hundred pounds.

When it was working properly it was a pleasure to watch the heavy equipment move so lightly on its hinges and a simple matter to swing it back and forth. But with so much weight it could be deadly. "The most vivid thing I can remember is when my mother broke her leg," Fred Balser reminisced. "I was about three years old," the accident happening on October 20, 1903. His tiny, dark-haired mother Hattie Balser was going into the corral intending to milk the cows.

> In opening the gate it come off its hinges, knocked her down and broke her leg [in the thigh]. And of course all the animals moving around was starting to move, walk over this gate, get out or get in, one or the other . . . I remember her laying there on the ground with this gate on top of her and all the animals looking at her, you know, didn't know whether to attempt it or not . . . She kept trying to tell me to go and get somebody. Well, I'd start out and I'd get just so far and then I wouldn't want to leave her, so I'd go back. So she'd send me again to go get somebody.

Hattie didn't have the strength to lift the gate and crawl out, and in a matter of moments she might be stampeded by the nervous stock.

While Hattie was trying to convince Fred to find help, Kate—at five foot two, the same height as Hattie but more powerfully built—"came to the door and she seen what was happening, so she threw away whatever she was doing and come a running and lifted the gate up and I don't know how she ever done it. But she lifted the gate up and I guess mother crawled out, you know, the best she could and so got free from the gate."[79] Kate's later comment was "I went to see if I could help her; I never dreamed that I could help her but the Lord helped me move the gate off from her . . . and it didn't take me one little bit," and then "[I] got her out of the way of these running cattle."[80] Fred credited Kate with saving his mother's life, and though the broken bone was set by the town carpenter, John Smith, and though the newspaper claimed that "at date of our information [Mrs. Balser] was doing as well as could be expected under the circumstances," the leg never healed properly and afterward she had a noticeable limp.[81]

Kate was practical as well. "Mom, if I don't give them some raisins they're going to beat me up and kill me!" Karl told her when he was threatened by a group of aggressive cousins. "You're not giving them any raisins," she said resolutely, and after Ren cracked the culprits' heads together, "they was a little bit more careful how they attackeded him," Reba recalled.[82]

Joel's nasty-tempered and mentally ill niece-in-law Rachel Griffin Roundy lived in Joel's old house. She enticed Golden's lambs to her place and tied them up with carpet rags. Kate advised the anxious teenager to "just wait 'til they get hungry, then go out and call them. They'll come." Sure enough, an hour after feeding time, Golden called "Lammie, Lammie, Lammie!" and, said Reba, "they went just like that, right through the hole in the fence and broke the carpet rag strings. Then that made her angry, because she was going to make him pay for the damage they'd done."[83]

Kate wasn't willing to see her children bullied but she hated fights. Reba explained that on holidays like the Fourth of July, there used to be

> horse races and buggy races and they had all kinds of foot races and everything and they went and got in the buggy to go to one of these and Mother was a little bit too slow. Dad didn't like it. "Hurry up we got to get there and see it! We got to get there! You're losing out! Come on!" So they got in the buggy and when they was having it, somebody was having a fight. Two people got angry at each other and so they was having this fight. And he says, "Here hold the reins of the horses!" She says, "Take care of them yourself!" And so he didn't get to see the fight. And the sheriff come along and he said "Dode [Joel's Kanarra nickname], did you see that fight?" And he says, "No, I didn't see it." "Why didn't you see it?" He says, "My wife wouldn't let me!"

"And so they had a court over it," Reba said. "And one man who bragged 'Oh yes, I saw it all,'" was called up to testify. Joel told Kate, "'I'm glad you wouldn't hold the horse's reins.' And she says, 'Why?' and he says, 'Because, I'd have been in court.' He says, 'I didn't see any of it. That taught me a lesson. Just don't get into things like that.'"[84]

Kate, who had worked for fifty cents a day in her youth, spent her married life working for her mother Elizabeth for nothing. "She had to work too much" to enjoy town activities, Reba remembered.

> She always done her work and then went up to Grandma's and never got home until ten or eleven o'clock. So I don't think she went out much . . . Grandma said she was a midwife, and she was away and from home all the time. And she went there and helped cook and do the washing and clean the house . . . She was up there most of the time. And you had to scrub on the board, you didn't have electric lights, you didn't have anything to wash your clothes with . . . You put them on the board. You put your water and then you scrubbed them on the board and then you

> put them in the kettle and let them steam and get hot and then you took them out and cooled them off a little bit and scrubbed them a little more and then rinsed them and hung them out.[85]

Kate spent so much time at her mother's her children didn't see much of her. "Oh, my mother, far as I can remember, she'd come home—she was home at night, in my early life," Reba remembered.

> She was home quite a little bit, but it seemed like every day she had to go up to her mother's, up to Grandma's. It seems like most mothers turn to their daughters . . . [Grandma Stapley] said we had a large family of girls; we didn't need that many. So they could take care of the place and she could have mother . . . Because of that, we always went with our dad. I didn't pay much attention to my mother. We was always with our dad, anything that we wanted we went to our dad for 'cause he was home and we was trained to go with him. And he said that, he'd always took care of us, and this one time they went up north to take my grandmother, or, take her up to her daughter's, and that was at Mona, Utah, and they stayed there a day or two . . . When they come back my mother said, "Did you miss us?" and I says, "Well, I didn't miss you but I missed my father!" [Reba laughed, but added] That cut her. I was too young and ignorant to even think about what I was saying, but anyhow it give her something to think about. She's thanked me a lot since then to do that, 'cause she didn't know she neglected us that much. She knew we were all right as long as we was with our father. So she told our grandmother that she was going to start staying home more. And that's when I really started to get acquainted with my mother.[86]

Kate was busy with other things, too. James Stapley kept bees and gave a half-dozen or more hives to Kate and Joel, and when he decided to end his bee work the Roundys ended up with twelve or fifteen stands.

"Women ought to be better bee-keepers than men," opined Julia Allyn in the *Ladies Home Journal* in 1891, "for they have, usually, a finer, gentler touch than men,"[87] but Joel joined Kate in the apiary, putting their hives between the red Astrakhan apples and the garden. That made treating oneself to these delicious June apples risky and Reba confirmed, "We got stung, too," but added, they put soda or black mud on it and laughed, "we got paid for our thieving, we called it!"[88]

Kate wasn't the only one who kept bees. In 1910 there were 707 hives in the county and 21 in Kanarra, enough that the county hired a bee inspector who required owners of hives diseased with things like foul brood to destroy them. "She had to put her veil on, and go right out there and stay right with him [Joel]," Reba remembered.

> They had a big vat and you whirled it around this way, you put your honeycomb rack . . . [in, and] you stand them in down like this, and then you turn this around like this way, and that flips the honey out . . . And she was there to catch the honey. Dad would turn it, and she was there to catch the honey and put it in to the different containers that was around there. Keep them clean, keep the porcupines from coming in. They liked honey. We had a heck of a time keeping them out. Skunks like honey, too.

Reba said that the bees "sure stung you. Dad didn't seem to get stung too much. He said he was too sour, they didn't like him!" The honey was extracted three times a summer and stored in five gallon cans for home use, to sell and trade. "We always had honey candy," Reba also remembered. "We'd have candy bees."[89]

Joel's saintly, even temper assured that the household was generally peaceful, even when Kate was gone to her mother's. "Once in a while, her and Dad had a round," Reba said, and then "they spoke sharply to each other, but as a general rule, they didn't speak sharply." Kate wasn't passive like her grandmother Catherine, but not demanding like her mother. "If she got really excited or got het [heated] up" then she'd speak her mind "but that was only once in a great while."[90]

She would have occasion to speak her mind.

"Our dad was sickly," but Kate was busy. Joel's poor health was a constant worry because he had a "sore stomach." "'Now you go down and stay with your dad,'" she advised the twins when he went out to work on the farm. "So we'd go down and we'd stay with him," Reba remembered. "He'd plow two or three rows around with the horse, then he'd stretch out on the ground and rest awhile. Then he'd plow some more around. That's the way he farmed . . . One day we were down there, helping him clear the grass, or the brush up on the land, and he said—he'd just bought us new coats. And we said, 'We'll hang them right here on this post and then we'll burn this brush.' Well, when we got ready to come home we didn't have any coats" because they got burned up.

For as long as Reba could remember, "about twenty years, I can remember [him] being sick. He was thrown off from a horse and it hurt his stomach some way. Fell on his stomach or something but anyhow his stomach was sick. He'd just get sick and then he couldn't do anything. He didn't want to stay in bed; he knew he had to work so he just stood up and worked anyway."[91]

Being a twin presented more special opportunities than just spending time with Joel. "We never had a school teacher that could tell us apart," Reba said.

> We went to school one day and Val Hafen was our favorite teacher, and he said, "Now, if you'll stay just like you are today"—we had a skirt and blouse on and we had different blouses—"if you'll stay just like you are today, I can tell you [apart] all day long." And so when we went out at recess, we changed blouses, when we come at noon, we changed blouses, went back out at recess, we changed blouses. And he said, "I'll give up."[92]

The children were soon growing and Kate's oldest, Sarah, was an especially clever, stubborn, and independent girl. "Mother said she [Sarah] didn't like to wash dishes and she'd go slip up in the tree and take a book and set there and read all day, rather than come in and wash the dishes," Reba remembered. Kate was tolerant: "At least she wasn't under my feet."[93] Sarah was soon sewing her own clothes, and later she and Annis took a millinery course. Her mother Kate was quoted as saying of Sarah, "[I] never could make a dress that suited her. She was ten years old and wanted this new dress and I couldn't do it to suit her, and I just said, 'do it yourself.' So she did! And she did a good job of it. And then she started making her own clothes and she started making clothes for all the girls."[94]

Kate, dominated by her mother to the point of almost being henpecked, refused to rule her own children that way. "Mother was raised up, you do what the other person says. And when it come to her [Sarah], why, she wanted her own rights, so [when she got] so old she give it to her. She also give it to the rest of us."[95] This was more freedom than Catherine Campbell Steele had ever had. But maybe Kate's refusal to raise her daughters the way she had been raised by Elizabeth was the same kind of passive resistance Catherine had shown John when she wouldn't battle with him—but also refused to accommodate all of his wishes.

6

"Do Their Own Doing"

Sarah E. Roundy

"There has been great discrimination among a certain class of Doctors, who profess to monopolise the healing art," John Steele wrote his state legislator, James Duffin, on January 31, 1897. He continued in his humorously caustic manner:

> and who have amalgamated themselves together as a Board Excluding Every other Person who have not been, or, are not able to answer certain questions of Greek and Latin, in medical practice, from practicing the healing art, although they may have Served the Public for Twenty, or Forty years, doing much good . . . and heretofore the History of medicine Legislation, and its Enforcements in this state, whereby a Ring of Professionals, have held Controle, Shutting out from practice all who could not understand Alpha, Beta, Gamma, Delta, Epsilon, Zetta, of Greek Or the Latin, ah, bay.
>
> Having Spent a Couple of years in some institution of learning . . . [and] come out a full fledged Doctor with a Diploma as long as your arm, with the Privilige of charging a fee as long as your leg . . . The medical Law now in Utah is a Tyranical monopoly Ring . . . Set the people free . . . [and questioned] If you were to Examine the Medical Examining board you would find ninety Percent are young men lately from College What can they know about Disesaes of Woman, and Children?[1]

This was a perfect Thomsonian response to university-educated doctors restricting the practices of the untrained. It had carried much greater weight in the 1830s than in the 1890s when medicine made such great strides and germs were discovered to be the cause of many afflictions.[2]

Despite his periodic threats to leave Toquerville, the old man stayed. The *Deseret Weekly News* described him on November 23, 1894, as "the late John

Steele" though he was very much alive.[3] He complained to his congressman Frank J. Cannon that he needed a bigger pension for back and kidney injuries, and described himself—somewhat pitifully—as "now so Cripp[l]ed up that I am entirely unable to work and have forwarded Docters Certifficates about Eight times all to no purpose I am now 76 years old."[4] About the same time he bragged to his Australian niece Letisha Todd that "My Health is very good for a man of my years," and that he could "Climb a tree faster than any of the Boys & Ride a Horse over the plains at top Speed when I am hunting Cattle."[5] He was seemingly gifted with eternal life despite his hostility to the new medicine, proud that despite his years he was vigorous and strong, though he sometimes suffered from rheumatism and other ailments.[6] But, as he wrote after Catherine's death, "I was lonely,"[7] so lonely that Panguitch's thoughtful Joseph L. Heywood wrote with a suggestion: "After my last conversation with you upon the subject of matrimony a personage was presented to my mind & that the widow of the late Wandall Mace of Kanab Kane Co. a most estimable lady & true Latter Day Saint. Sister Mace may be something over Fifty years of age, has never had any children, I have had some Corispondence with her of late as she has been making up her husbands History."[8]

Wandle Mace's autobiography became an important part of early Mormon history but his attentive wife, Rebecca Elizabeth Howell Mace, did not become the third Mrs. John Steele. Evidently John was considering someone though, as his St. George friend David Milne concluded a letter to him in September with, "Well may God bless you and yours and your intended."[9]

At seventy-two he went to the Salt Lake Temple dedication in early April 1893, ran into a young woman—twenty-five-year-old Tamar Elizabeth "Lizzie" Booth Cheatham Renick—whom he'd confirmed after her baptism when she was a child in England. He married her after a two-day courtship and took her back to Toquerville, unaware she'd not been divorced from either of her two previous husbands.[10]

The marriage startled Toquervillites, especially when his fellow townsman and age-mate Augustus E. Dodge married a young widow, as reported by the *Deseret News*: "Probate Judge [Seth M.] Blair has married two couples from Toquerville within a week. In both cases the bridegroom had reached the ripe age of seventy. In the one instance the bride [Lizzie] had seen twenty-five summers, while over the fair head of the other [Martha Jane Calvert Dockstader] twice that number had passed."[11]

John's ecstasy with his young bride was short-lived—"I soon found my new made wife was a regular termagant and scold."[12] Repeated travel from

Toquerville to Salt Lake over the course of the next several years, and distressed and angry letters to and from her mother complicated any hope of matrimonial bliss. John's Boston astrologer Oliver Ames Goold wrote, warning him he should never have married ("Had I been advising you early in life I should have counselled you to have not married any woman in the world"[13]). And, to add to the fray, there was plenty of neighborhood gossip ("Brother Steel and his wife quarreling was mentioned. Some proposed to arrest them for disturbing the peace, others thought a better way could be adopted. The matter rested here," journalized his neighbor Levi Savage[14]). John exchanged letters with the LDS Church hierarchy,[15] with the result the marriage eventually sputtered out—not without drama—for in one rage Lizzie beat him, broke his dishes, smashed his windows and doors, and threatened to kill him.[16]

The year 1897 was the fiftieth anniversary of the arrival of the pioneer band into the Salt Lake valley. A large celebration was planned in Salt Lake City and free railroad passes were given to the surviving members of the 1847 group, including Elizabeth and her father John.

John, with a *Pierce's Memorandum Account Book* in hand, wrote a Salt Lake shopping list ("Two wagon tyre 15 F 3 inches," "4 lengths Stove piping," "1 Tea Kittle," and so on) and, curiously, listed two addresses for "Mrs. Elizabeth Booth," which can only be his recently divorced wife: "9th South 7th East Stevens Row in the Arear [*sic*] of Lake Street" and "65 Grape St." and used the remainder of the *Account Book* as a diary of this trip.[17]

Elizabeth, her husband James Stapley, and their neighbors, Reese Jones Williams and his wife Martha, as well as a Williams son—perhaps Reese James Williams[18]—outfitted a good team and wagon. They were joined by John and his daughter Susie during a rainstorm on July 14. After a day refitting, they left for Salt Lake on July 16—with it still raining—and had dinner with Enoch Jones in Cedar City and camped out on their way to the train.

Next morning, after "Breakfast by a Sage brush fire," they made their way to Minersville where they left their team, then on to Milford to board a train so packed, "there ware Scarcely Standing room for the Crowd on Board." They arrived in Salt Lake on Sunday, July 18, at 5:10 a.m., and stayed at the home of his granddaughter Mary Elizabeth Bringhurst Duffin, at 273 West First North.

Elizabeth was joined by her daughter May and by son Jimmy's oldest boy, future Carbon County commissioner William B. Stapley. M. M. Steele Sr. also joined the group.

John rode the train to Lagoon in Farmington "with all manner of amusements and a Collection of South Sea Island[e]rs performing in native Costume and Dance," and the next day he took in "Salt Ayer" at the Great Salt Lake. On July 23, John, Elizabeth, and other family members toured the three-year-old sprawling Richardsonian Gothic Salt Lake City and County Building.

They climbed "clear to the top where the Masinery of Clock works are and had a good view of city and Surrounding Countery." Surprisingly, John's pocket diary doesn't mention what he must have seen, but perhaps wasn't aware of—Catherine's head carved in stone at the east entrance of the building to commemorate her as one of the twenty women who marched with the Mormon Battalion and mother of the first Mormon child born in the valley. She stares down from an angelic perch with large almond-shaped eyes, her mouth pulled into a perpetually triumphant smile, maybe thinking of John down there peering up.

At Savage's Gallery the tired travelers had a four generation photograph taken. John sits on a wooden chair with his grim face in a frown and looks more old than fiery. His pioneer badge and gold medal glitter on his chest while his pocket watch chain tries to sneak out of the bottom of his jacket. The only elegance is a beautiful and delicately carved cane in his left hand. Standing next to him is solemn eight-year-old William Berry Stapley, his left hand nervously playing with the fingers of his right. Behind John is Elizabeth's daughter May, a woman with a broad forehead, her hair ruffled around her sad-looking face. Deep-eyed Elizabeth, in the first photograph we have of her, stands behind William wearing a black dress with a black lace collar and puffed sleeves, hair held tightly against her head. (James also had his picture taken alone and with Elizabeth at this time. He has intelligent, playful eyes and his neat beard seems to hide a smile.)

Elizabeth and John were honored on July 24—fifty years to the day after Brigham Young first rode into the valley—and each was given a memento for the occasion. "I Sat on the Stand when our Beloved presidant Wilford Woodruff was crowned with lorrals by his great grand Daughter," John wrote to Letisha Todd on August 2, 1897. He described the scene as grand. "I did not See any person the worse for drink I did not See any person look Cross or Speak Cross."[19] They marched in the pioneer parade and John was surprised to see his estranged wife Lizzie, the "termagant and scold," and he wrote in his retrospective rather than contemporary journal, "While the [parade] procession was forming, my wife Lizzie came and put her hand into mine and she walked all the way with me during the procession." (The relationship did finally peter out; Lizzie died in the state insane asylum aged forty-five, her death certificate reporting the cause as "Apoplexy," with "Manic Depressive Psychoses" as a contributing factor.[20])

John and Elizabeth also went to the Parowan Pioneer Day Celebration on January 13, 1902, and the *Deseret Evening News* reported that "Father John Steele of Toquerville, 82 years of age, was among the most agile and active."[21]

He didn't see much of his daughter Jane but they kept in touch, John writing his Australian niece Letisha Todd about his family and explaining in 1901, "Then Comes Jane C Steele, She is married and has a large family & lives in the State of arizona about 1000 miles South of me Born ^ April 26 1845 [1855]^ . I Just got a letter from her when I got yours this morning."[22]

Jane didn't inherit her father's vigorous health, suffered from heart trouble like her sister Mary, and became very ill in December 1902. When John was ordained a Mormon "patriarch" on March 13, 1903[23] (a church office allowing him to give blessings that provide individual guidance and direction for the faithful), Jane was dying. The *Holbrook Argus [Arizona]* reported,

> Died, March 21st [1903], Mrs. Jane C. Jensen, wife of J. P. Jensen. She leaves a husband and nine children to mourn her untimely loss. Two daughters are married and seven are still at home. The funeral services were held at the hall at 10 o'clock Monday morning and the remains were buried in the cemetery here. Much sympathy is expressed for the bereaved ones. Mr. Jensen and children have moved back to the ranch.[24]

The reporter for Shumway also reported that "nearly everybody from this place attended the funeral of Mrs. J. P. Jensen at Taylor Monday."[25]

This was hard for her husband, Pete. Brother-in-law Joseph Fish, married so many years before to Jane's amiable sister Mary, wrote, "I have seen Pete twice since Jane died he seems quite lonesome as he naturally would."[26] And John's granddaughter Josephine "Josie" Fish Barraclough reported similar sentiments from Jane's bereaved children: "Had a letter from Fannie [Fish Carson] a short time ago she had got home safe and sound from her trip to Arizona. said that she had such a nice time with them all but it was so short she was only there two weeks, she went up to see Aunt Janes children, she says that she feels so sorry for them."[27]

"I promised Mama I would keep the children together and do the best I could with them," recalled her husband Pete. "He always speaks in the most tender terms of his wife," recorded his dictated history. "He spent some long lonely years since then," never remarrying, he said, to keep his promise of doing "the best I could" with the children.[28]

But John's vigor seemed unabated. On Elizabeth's fifty-seventh birthday, August 9, 1903, John was in good spirits as he and Susie joined other family members at the Stapley ranch on the Kanarra Mountain for Elizabeth's party.[29] It seemed nothing could wear him down.

But then, "he stepped on a nail and they didn't do it right," explained Reba, "and it turned to gangrene."[30] One of his many remedies said that "Cantharis, Spanish Fly good in burning, itching of Skin rawness, Soreness of the whole body inflam[m]ation, gangrene of the parts Convulsions of limbs,"[31] was a cure but in the end self-medication with the old-fashioned remedies wasn't good enough. Elizabeth went to Toquerville to take care of him.

> He had to take so many drops of medicine. I don't know what kind of medicine it was. But, now you—they didn't have a medicine dropper. "Now you count them drops and you make just exactly what they are, no bigger, nor no littler." The drops has got to be the same size. Then he would take his medicine. If he didn't, he wouldn't take it. And he's very strict. You done this. You done that. I think that's where Grandma got her strictness from.[32]

"I heard he got gangrene," remembered his great-granddaughter, Elsie Kay Smith. "And I thought that my mother [John's granddaughter May Stapley Kay] told me that—and his foot and leg, it just kind of went—you know how it would go up your leg and first it would be a fiery red and then it would turn black. And she said to her grandfather, 'Oh, doesn't that hurt?' And he said, 'Oh, my dear, if you only knew!'"[33]

In the last few weeks of his life, John gave Elizabeth a blessing that confirmed her success in escaping Catherine's servitude. "Thou art a chosen vessel of the Lord to come forth in this day & generation and be numbered among the 144,000 redeemers in Israel to redeem the people of the house of the Lord therefore thou art Called to do a great and a mighty work in these last days, and were called to come forth in a very prominent time," and "The Lord will give unto thee in his own due time the Holy priesthood in fullness."

He concluded with recognition of her midwifing and nursing abilities. "Thy hand shall ever be opened to assist the afflicted and thy house continually be a house of prayer in behalf of those who are distressed. Now my dear daughter thou art true & faithful in keeping the commandments of the Lord and not one word of this blessing shall fall to the ground without its fulfillment."[34]

He gave this blessing in Toquerville on December 6, 1903, probably just before Elizabeth took him to Kanarra where she could care for him in her home. A year before he had been preaching "general principles" of the gospel in church, but now the old fire-eater was having the fight of his life. "We are pleased to recall the statement in last week's issue concerning Gran[d]father Steele, and say: He is surprisingly smart at the age of 82 and were it not for his foot he could no nout [doubt] as he says, walk a mile in ten minutes. He is now at the residence of Jas Stapley of this place," commented the *Iron County Record,* December 26, 1903.[35]

Under a December 17, 1903, Kanarra byline, the *Iron County Record* reported, "Father and son George Wood, were down to see their old friend, Jno. Steel and try to console him if possible." In the same issue there was another report from Kanarra, this one with a December 24 byline—"Grandfather Steele is gradually climbing the ladder to the other side. His sons and daughter have been telegraphed for."[36] He clung on until nearly the New Year, dying on the last day of December. Two days later he was buried in Parowan next to Catherine, as he had requested.[37] The issue of the *Record* reporting his burial is missing, but the story was picked up by the *Salt Lake Telegram* and the *Salt Lake Tribune,* adding their own gloss:

> A pioneer well known in Salt Lake recently died at Kanarra. The Cedar City [*Iron County*] Record says of him: "Father John Steele, who was buried in the Parowan cemetery last Saturday, had the distinction of being one of the Mormon battalion, a pioneer into the Salt Lake valley, a pioneer into Parowan Valley, and the father of the first girl baby born in Salt Lake, and he had reached the good old age of 83 years."[38]

John's death was a blow to Elizabeth, and she immediately went into formal mourning while at the same time assuming the prerogatives of clan matriarch to replace the loss of the family patriarch. But the rule-defying demands of a younger generation of women were hammering at her door and times had changed since the old pioneer was in his prime. As Alice Louise Reynolds wrote in the LDS Church-sponsored *Young Woman's Journal* in 1899, "The woman of today very soon realizes that the demands made upon her Puritan and Pioneer grandmother, are no longer made upon her. The spinning-wheel which was as conspicuous in the early home, as is the cook-stove of today, is now no longer seen; and the long hours spent in stitching with the little steel needle are, through the sewing-machine, now spent in other ways."[39] Elizabeth still had her old spinning wheel, but granddaughter Sarah had new ideas.

"When he died," explained Reba of the death of John Steele, "that was during the holiday time, see, right after Christmas, and they always go to each holiday [dancing] and Sarah wanted to go to the dance and Grandma said you can't go. And Mother said she couldn't see any reason why she couldn't go. Grandpa'd been laid away for a week. She didn't know why she couldn't go. And so she let her go and Grandma got after her, got after my mother for letting her go."

"She shouldn't be going to the dance yet!"

"What you got to do?" Kate said. "He's gone, you can't just sit here and worry."

"You had no right doing that," Elizabeth expostulated.

"I did have a right to let her go," Kate countered. "She's my daughter, and if I want to let her go, I'll let her go!"[40]

Elizabeth lost the round, and after that there was often a wary distance between her and her independent-minded granddaughter. Sarah was too much like Elizabeth to take orders. "I have a mind of my own!" she announced to her mother. "Let me use it."[41]

"Before that," Reba explained, "you always told the kids what to do and they done it. And this time of the year, everybody was wanting to do their own doing. That was the change of the turn of the century. So Sarah says to my mother, 'Now you let me do it my way, and I'll do it. But I'm not going to do it this way.' And mother said okay. So Grandma said, 'Now you do it this way,' and she says, 'I'll talk to my mother.'"[42]

James and Elizabeth were traditional, though they weren't exactly Norman Rockwell grandparents. "My mother and my grandmother used to send me up there to get a start of yeast to make bread, you know," remembered James and Elizabeth's grandnephew Leonard Davis. "They'd always send me up to Aunt Libbie's to get a start of yeast. She'd always have to give you a piece of bread and butter or cookie or something . . . She's just a nice old lady. I thought the world of her because she'd always give you a piece of bread and butter, things like that."[43] Elizabeth's granddaughter Leola Stapley Anderson also remembered that Grandma would "always have something for you when you'd go, you know, cookies or just warm bread and butter or something."[44]

"I liked to follow Grandpa around while he did chores," said Lella Stapley Maxfield, who spent the winter of 1910–1911 with the Stapleys. He "was always busy." She remembered him once "sitting on the front step eating apples that he picked from his trees. He scraped his with his pocket knife as he had no teeth. His teeth were kept in the cupboard in a cup. I asked Grandmother about that once when I was washing the cupboard out, as her teeth were in the cupboard also. She said they didn't fit so they didn't wear them. I had an idea they were mail order teeth."[45] (Good dental care was problematic: a roving dentist named Dr. Elijah Smith pulled and replaced a lot of teeth in Iron County,[46] possibly including James and Elizabeth's.) "She's just a gummer," Reba said of her grandmother, whose teeth had been pulled before Reba's 1904 birth.[47]

Grandchildren like Leola who came to the Stapleys to borrow for their parents had to identify those parents. "Well, who's your father?"[48] James would ask before lending the shovel, ax, or other tool.

"Grandpa Stapley was a quiet man," Reba remembered. "I never did—only time I ever seen him angry was when Uncle John's kids come down and when they come down they always wanted to tear everything up and do everything—tip it upside down and everything. He called them 'Hell' and 'Damn.' 'Ah, here comes Hell and Damn,' he says. They'd climb the trees, they'd do this, they'd do that. Anything that'd disturb him."[49]

> Now when we went to Grandma's, we always went out and played on the lawn. We didn't go in the garden. We didn't go out in the fruit . . . unless they wanted us to do it. If they wanted us to go out and pick currants, we went and picked currants. If he wanted to pick cherries, we picked cherries. And they had a place out in the garden where you could climb up on a raft [fruit rack] somewhere and spread out fruit to dry. That's the only time we ever went out in the garden. Unless we went out to tell Grandpa dinner was ready.[50]

But everyone, including Reba and Reva, raided his sour cherries.

> We was just on top of the fence, reaching out, off from the fence, you know, and getting them. He come up and he says, "I told you kids, now get out of that cherry tree." And they said, "We're not stealing them." And he said, "I told you to get out." And they said, "We're not stealing them." And he said, "Now get out!" And Reva and I got out. When he said, "Get out," we got out. We went to the house. And then he said, "I never have anything them kids don't come down here and try to get rid of it." If you'd just ask him for it, he would give it to you. But he didn't want them coming down helping theirselves.[51]

Anyway, Reba reasoned, they weren't stolen if they were picked off from that part of the tree that hung over the walk and road. People "didn't steal them—they were on the public . . . They took them off from his tree, but it was not stealing, because it was on the public. But he didn't like it that way. He said, 'If they'd come ask me, I would let them come and get some cherries.' But, you know, kids's got to steal some anyway. They taste better!"[52]

James and Elizabeth had few public disagreements. She paid lip service to the patriarchy. "She always talked the man was the head of the house," Reba recalled.

> She would leave him and go to her midwife work. And sometimes he thought she was just gone too much. But I don't think that one bossed the othern any more than the othern bossed the othern. 'Cause when it come election time, Grandma turned out to be a Republican and Grandpa turned out to be a Democrat. And the only time they had any trouble, mother said, is when election come. They wouldn't speak to each other for two or three months.[53]

James took especial pride in his beautiful yard and big weed-free garden as well as his healthy red currants and fruit trees heavy-laden with plums, apples, and cherries. He gave away rhubarb by the armful. Sometimes Elizabeth would interfere with his outside work, as grandchildren Leola Stapley Anderson and her cousin Dee Stapley found when they were quietly playing in a hedge of irises. Behind the house was a hard path, made by throwing dish water out the back door, and at Elizabeth's direction James was sweeping it. "Now James, you sweep here and there!" she ordered. "Jimmie you sweep here and there!" This kept up for some time, with James getting more and more irritated.

Finally he threw down the broom in frustration and hissed, "Take your damn broom and do it yourself!"

"We both just really died laughing to ever hear Grandpa swear," chuckled Leola.[54]

But there was much they worked on together, especially in matters of religion. James often addressed the "sisters" at Elizabeth's Relief Society meetings and when Elizabeth was in charge of grain collecting for the organization she stored it at their home. As a counselor in the bishopric, he regularly presided over Sunday services, and Elizabeth helped him with those responsibilities. "[Grandpa] used to have a little brass bucket," remembered Leola, "about a quart, maybe, or more. And Grandma always just had that shined to the fare-thee-well. And a nice linen napkin that went over the top of it. Every Sunday Grandpa carried that down from their place down to the church, 'cause you didn't have running water everywhere, an he'd carry that down for the sacrament."[55]

Reba's older cousin Elton, another Stapley grandchild, didn't see the marriage as a relationship between equals. Elizabeth "liked a lot of attention and demanded a lot of attention, to my estimation," he chuckled. He thought "she would of made a good queen because she liked to dictate."[56] ("Dad used to call her the queen bee," laughed Elton's cousin Leola Anderson.[57]) Elton said "she saw that Grandpa had plenty to do to keep him busy. If he wasn't, why, she'd find something for him to do . . . She kept him hoeing the weeds and sweeping the yard and carrying the water."[58]

Lenna Stapley Williams, daughter of Jimmy Stapley and Elton's cousin, agreed with Elton. "She was a perfectionist. She made everybody handy around and do it for her though. I never did see her do much work." Lenna added, "Aunt Kate and Stella, one of Aunt Kate's daughters, did all of her work, all of her laundry, all of her scrubbing. I never did see my grandmother turn a hand." James "had a lot of patience with Grandma . . . He'd come in from doing chores and put his feet on the heater. She'd say, 'Get your feet!—Jim! Get your feet off that heater!'" Laughing, Lenna concluded, "I can remember her just shouting that, 'Jim! Get your feet off there!'"[59]

Grandma was formidable. "She'd try to boss you around," Reba recalled.[60] Many of Elizabeth's grandchildren wouldn't go to her house because of her domination. "Boy, she could work them!" remembered Elton.[61] She resented any sign of independence. Once she put herself in charge of combing the twins' hair, coming down every day to do so. "She always got Reva because Reva cried," Reba said. "I think she done it just to make her cry." Elizabeth would take the hair and "skin it back up, even pulled her skin up." So the twins decided to hide by some wild rosebushes and outwait their grandmother. "We was down there about four hours. We figured Grandma had gone home and went up and there she set."

"Where you been?" Kate asked anxiously.

"I don't want to tell you," Reba said.

"Where've you been?" she demanded again.

"Now listen, Mother. I'll tell you but you got to do one thing. We went down and played in the rosebushes so Grandma wouldn't comb Reva's hair. You comb Reva's hair now. If you don't, we're going right back down there in the rosebushes. Now you make sure from now on you comb Reva's hair."

"Okay," she said.

Inside the house Elizabeth was grimly waiting with a hairbrush. "It's about time you was getting here to get your hair combed," she announced. Reba walked over and sat down, offering her head to be combed.

"I'm not combing your hair!"

"You're combing my hair but you're not going to comb anybody else's."

"I'm combing Reva's hair this morning," Kate explained.

Elizabeth grudgingly pulled Reba's hair up tight but wasn't able to make her yell. "Oh well, you won't cry," Reba remembered her saying.

"Nope. If you pulled it out I wouldn't even cry."[62]

That brought an end to this particular contest of wills.

Reba was as blunt and frank as Elizabeth. "Aunt Reba is the one that could straighten Grandma Stapley out," explained Reba's perceptive niece Gwen Sylvester Hunter, one of Elizabeth's many great-grandchildren. "She'd just tell her straight out, 'Now Grandma, you've got to let people do what they want to do, and as long as they're not hurting you, you just forget about it.'"[63]

Surprisingly, this didn't create resentment. Elizabeth once told Kate that this granddaughter was the only one that never talked back to her.

"You little hussy!" Reva objected to Reba. "You're always telling her off!"

"But I have the right way of doing it," Reba explained. "I was always telling her back—only I done it in a different way . . . I just used my psychology a little bit better . . . I learned a long time ago that you have to use your psychology like you do with kids."[64]

James Stapley's brother Charles had an adopted stepson, John Edward Stapley (nee Rodwell), who was known as "Deef John," because when he was ten years old he "had an accident . . . and a wheel ran over his head and it made him deaf," recalled Edwin Kenneth Slack.[65] He was described by a newspaper reporter in 1896 as "a sort of an imbecile" who "could not tell ten cents from a dollar and could not count twenty."[66]

Despite that, Mormon missionaries arranged for him to marry a Swiss convert named Elizabeth Zetta Hubschmid, or Zettie.[67] She had an inheritance that enabled her to buy cattle and she knitted and watched her investment dwindle to nothing. But she was as controversial as her husband and was so famous for cursing that Slack said, "We used to mimic her—'You dirty, lurdy, low-down dirty son-of-a-bitch!' She could call you off! . . . She was lamented," he summed up, and blamed it on her husband. "I think I'd a went crazy too if I'd a have to live with [him]."[68] Besides that, she became such a drain on the charity of the Toquerville ward they finally just wrote "Zettie" in their account book and didn't bother with a last name.[69] She was also accused by some townspeople of allowing young boys to gamble and "keeping a disorderly house."[70] (Whether this literally meant a bordello is unknown; Slack thought not.)

Somehow the two of them had six children, but by 1896 the marriage was blowing apart. When John Edward Stapley's brother signed an affidavit that Zettie was insane the case was heard before Judge E. V. Higgins in St. George on May 5, 1896. She effectively defended herself, showing "about as much intelligence as the other witnesses." And, after hearing testimony from doctors Fredric Clift and Agnes Thompson and other evidence, the *Tribune* reporter was convinced that Stapley "has abused the poor woman till she has almost become distracted, and at times uses a great deal of profanity. It is suggested by some that the proper remedy would be to give the woman a divorce and send the husband to the asylum." Zettie was "adjudged . . . not insane and she was discharged."[71]

She seemed to take the hint that ending the marriage might be a good idea because that fall she was back in court for a divorce. She was successful again, Judge Higgins ruling, "Divorce granted and plaintiff has exclusive custody of eldest son and two youngest children and half of the common property, and defendant has the other three children and pay plaintiff allimony and costs of suit."[72]

But a third court appearance on September 7, 1899, didn't go so well and four days later she was sent to the State Insane Asylum in Provo.[73] (The tactful Parkinson family historians described Zettie as leaving "Toquerville in a state of mental exhaustion."[74]) Zettie was given custody of the two youngest, Selinda (called Salindia in the 1900 census[75] and known all her life as Linda) and George. While she was in Provo they were living with Toquerville's kindly midwife, Regula Benz Naegle,[76] and described by the census taker as "orphans" despite both of their parents being alive.

Eight-year-old Linda apparently wanted to get out of Toquerville. Reba says that she "got on Grandma and Grandpa's mind and nerves so much that they said come up and live with us."[77] A few months after the census was taken, Elizabeth's daughter Aunt May went to Virgin to teach school. After the Christmas holidays James took May through the rain back to the town of Virgin and on his way home stopped in Toquerville. "He took little Linda Stapley back [to Kanarra] to live with us," May noted in her diary. "If all is well I will have a little sister when I go home."[78]

Linda stayed on for several years with her great-uncle and great-aunt, the *Iron County Record* reporting April 23, 1904, "James Stapley and his sister Sarah

Reeves left here this morning for Toquer to attend the funeral services of their eldest brother Chas. who passed peacefully away yesterday about 4 p.m. They were accompanied by his (Charles') granddaughter Linda Stapley, who is making her home at the residence of James Stapley."[79] Her uncle and aunt, Charles and Jane Stapley, moved to Beaver in late November 1904, and she may well have gone with them; her foster sister, Elizabeth's daughter May Stapley, was teaching in Beaver by late 1906. In any case, Linda was there by 1910, boarding with widow Elizabeth Limb while doing domestic work.[80]

The relationship between Linda and her great-aunt Elizabeth must have been good because in 1912 Linda sent Elizabeth a Christmas postcard with a note, "Dear Aunt How are you? I am well and hope you are the same. Tell every body hello for me, wish you all a marry xmas and a happy new year, Love to all Linda."[81]

After Linda left, Elizabeth became convinced that one of her granddaughters should stay with her to do the housework. John's daughter Vilda said she wasn't available. Lella, Mahonri's oldest, spent one winter there and refused to stay again, announcing she "wouldn't be her slave!"[82] "Aunt Hattie would never let her kids go over to Grandma's very much," Reba said, explaining that Lenna Stapley Williams's mother only had one daughter who survived and "was afraid . . . she would have to leave her over there."[83]

Overall, Elizabeth's health had been remarkably good, though on December 30, 1883, Wilford Woodruff recorded in his journal a visit to Kanarra but then crossed it out, "We administered to Young Chizabell Shapley [*sic*]."[84] (She was not among those he "set apart" as a midwife unless, as this entry suggests, he was confused.)

But Elizabeth became more insistent for help after December 15, 1911, when she was stricken at 4:30 a.m. with what the family and the newspapers called lockjaw.[85] She was rushed to Cedar City's new doctor and city health officer, Alonzo N. Leonard (he'd only come to town the previous June), who treated her with hot bandages, which suggests she had some kind of inflammation or dislocation. "They made quite a fuss about it when they took her to Cedar," remembered Reba. "They didn't have a doctor that could put her jaw back the way it's supposed to so it stayed."[86] This brief disability had more long-range consequences.

After the attack Elizabeth slept with pillows "placed on top of each other," wrote her granddaughter, Velma Stapley Rymer. They "propped Grandma up so she slept in a sitting position instead of being down. She didn't always fully close her eyes when she slept and we giggled & laughed to think she could sleep with her eyes open."[87] "I've seen Aunt Kate fix her pillow," granddaughter Lenna Stapley Williams explained. "Didn't work. Nope, that didn't fit. Aunt Kate would pound it and pat it and shake it and put it back. Nope. No. That didn't fit. Half a dozen times. She should have thrown the pillow at her!"[88]

The "lockjaw" also made her "scared of the dark," Reba said. "She must of had it in the dark. And she was scared of the dark and she always left the [coal oil] lamp burning all night. If anybody called her anything, day or night, she was to go, she went . . . As long as she could see that light when she woke up, she was okay. But if she didn't she smothered. She fought for breath. Until she died. She always had that light until she died." Reba explained it as "her hypertension just goes up to a smother."[89]

"I don't know whether Grandpa wouldn't get up and do what she wanted him to or not," Reba remembered, but thereafter he slept upstairs on a bedroll. Reba asked her mother why James and Elizabeth didn't sleep together after all the years they'd been married. "Well, I guess she'd had enough husband!" Kate laughed.[90]

That may have been literally the fact—in 1918 Elizabeth had an operation for "female trouble."[91] That generally meant one of two things: a hysterectomy or a uterine suspension. Elizabeth's quick recovery suggests that she had the latter, required for uterine retroversion, or a tilted uterus, causing painful intercourse,[92] so maybe she literally had "enough husband" and that's why she preferred to sleep alone.

Soon after her surgery Elizabeth joined her two sons James S. and John A. to visit Will and M. M. in Millard County and only hurried back because "James Stapley returned from the conference at Parowan sick and has been in bed ever since. His wife and two sons who were in Millard County were wired for and made haste to reach his bedside. He is in his 80th year, but is some better at this writing."[93] By summer both James and Elizabeth were well enough to make another visit to the Delta country and probably went on to Mona to see their daughter May as well. Their son John A. stayed on trying and failing to sell his four room house and 160-acre dry farm, hoping to move to Idaho.[94]

Once she returned from traveling, Elizabeth redoubled her efforts to get one of Kate's children. "You got too many girls," she said. "Now you let me have one of them." "When my mother's kids went to stay with her, she wanted them to do what she wanted them to do, not what they wanted to do," Reba reported. Reba's sister Sarah stayed for a while "and she says, 'I'm not going [to] stay to Grandma's no longer!' and she went home." Sister Annis had the same experience and was soon back.[95]

Elizabeth's brother Almy was in Toquerville, a sometime undertaker, the popular bass drum player in the town band, and such an enthusiastic caller at dances that town leader Rhea Higbee Wakeling said after hearing him "one couldn't help but dance." But Edwin Slack recalled "the night he [Alma] broke his hip" in the fall of 1909: "We had a little play—we had to entertain ourselves in them days, so we had lots of plays, and in their enthusiasm some of them sat up on the—instead of setting on the bench you set up on the back of the bench, and he was setting back there with a bunch of kids, and I guess that something happened that some of them got off and it tipped over; it broke his hip there."[96]

Elizabeth took him into her home to nurse him back to health. "He reports himself as feeling better from his crippled condition," the county newspaper announced on December 10, 1909, and the day before Christmas explained that "J. A. Steele, who has been for the last two months hobbling around on crutches, is about to throw them away, as he is learning to walk without them."[97]

Alma went back to Toquerville where he was such a fixture that Edwin Slack remembered "Almy" playing the snare drums and walking beside "Rone" Spilsbury in parades, Edwin following "behind them on the Fourth of July at four o'clock in the morning throwing out half a stick a dynamite ever once in a while to blow up the town!"[98]

Almy struggled along in Toquerville, but finally the *Washington County News* reported that "J. Alma Steele left yesterday [10 February 1914] to live at Kanarra with his sister, Mrs. Elizabeth Stapley. Al has been quite an invalid since sustaining a very painful injury to his hip a few years ago. He is a member of the Indian War veteran company of this place."[99]

With Elizabeth having a sometimes ailing husband, and a partly crippled brother—not to mention her own need for attention—she insisted again that someone come to help her out. Stella was the only one willing to go and "went to live with them," Reba said. Stella complained that "Grandpa had to go upstairs to sleep, and I had to sleep with Grandma."[100]

Stella liked her grandfather. "He was a good old guy," she said, "and I liked him so much and he was always so good to us."[101] But at ten years of age, she soon resented Elizabeth. "She got tired of it," remembered Stella's friend Arvilla Ford Woodbury. "She used to do everything for her. Her dishes, clean house, cook, and lot of times she'd want to be off playing and she had to go to Grandma's first and see about Grandma." Woodbury said, "I used to feel sorry and I'd go up on Sundays and help her do her dishes and things so we could go out to play for a little while . . . You know, she was up there really more than she was home. But we always got together, we was real pals."[102]

Elizabeth struck Stella's friend as "kind of a cranky little old lady. I liked her but she just wanted Stella on the job all the time." Stella was "good natured, she was a good little gal, and she was willing, you know, to do things for her, but she just had too much for her to do . . . I think she figured that was her job and she had to take whatever the old lady told her to do." Stella "really had a kind of a bad life when she was young. And I don't think she ever had a fellow even, or a date around here until they moved to Hurricane."[103]

There was no pay for this job. "She just went free will," worked hard, and everything "Grandma wanted done she had to do it," Reba said.[104] This included attending to the fifty-gallon water barrel. In 1909 the town had voted to install a new $5,000 water system, piped three-quarters of a mile from the Kanarra Creek's "cement reservoir." Plumber H. E. Peterson made so much money putting in new water systems he was able to buy a car and invest in the county newspaper. But Peterson was accidentally shot in the face by an overenthusiastic colleague on a town rabbit slaughter, blinded in one eye, and moved to Springfield, Missouri, before Kanarra folk learned the system wasn't built for the long haul. On January 26, 1917, the Kanarra correspondent reported that "Nearly all the water taps in town are frozen up, necessitating the carrying of most of the drinking water for the families."[105]

Therefore, Stella had to care for the water barrel. "This barrel was filled each morning whether anything else got done or not," remembered Lella Stapley Maxfield. It nestled in the shade of four giant lilacs and was filled early before the stock muddied the ditch.[106] After the dirt and the "wigglers" settled to the bottom the brave could use the long handled dipper and flirt with typhoid.

Preparing Elizabeth's clothing was a big job too. Her skirts and petticoats were "starched until they was stiff. You could just stand them up and they wouldn't shrink down," Reba remembered. Stella "ironed one and it wasn't—she didn't get it starched good enough. And it slumped down."

"Now," Elizabeth said, "you put that back on there and iron it over again."

"Won't do any good to iron it over again, it'll slop down again," Stella explained, and so she dipped it into the starch and let it dry and was finally successful.[107]

"It wasn't good enough if they didn't stand by itself," Reba said.

> And you had to look so no wrinkles was in it. If you had a wrinkle in it you had to wet it and iron it out so that it'd be gone. She had a flannel petticoat, and then she had this white petticoat which was starched. The other one wasn't, but this white one was starched. Sometimes she

> wore a red flannel petticoat and sometimes she wore a white one. But she always had about two or three petticoats on . . . [And she also] used to wear a shimmy. A shimmy would come to her knees, then these petticoats on top of it.
>
> [The shimmy was] like a dress. But it didn't have the long sleeves in it. It just had short sleeves here and it just went straight. It didn't have any waist to it or anything. It just went down straight. That's what they had to keep them warm in cold weather.

The many clothes were used because "it was warming" and "the starch in the petticoat kept the air out. So she kept warm."[108]

All this work made Stella resentful. "I couldn't hardly think that my Dad would let me go there and do that," she complained.[109]

"I don't think it was all my Dad," Reba remarked. "I think it was quite a bit my mother [and Stella] was the only one that would consent to go. Reva and I was too young and the others was too old and they wouldn't go 'cause they didn't like Grandma. They didn't like her bossing them around, telling them what to do."[110] Stella's cousin Lenna Stapley Williams said Stella "was very good natured about it," and added with a chuckle, "better than I would have been!"[111] Reba remembered that Elizabeth "had the teachers of the school come and stay with her because Stella done the work, done the ironing and everything."[112]

But even Stella's patience wasn't endless. "Stella got so—the last year she was there, she was getting quite rebellious because she couldn't go out and play with the girls," Reba remembered. "I've been there long enough," she told her father, "now I think it's somebody else's turn."[113] Joel agreed she could come home.

Before she left, Uncle Will insisted that Elizabeth should give Stella a cow as appreciation for all she'd done. "He says, 'She's been here and helped you all this many years, you ought to give her a cow. You got a whole lot of them out there. Now you ought to give her a cow!'"

"All right. Which one should I give her?"

Will pointed out the cow. When Stella got ready to go home Will reminded her, "Take your cow with you."

"Do you think Grandma will let me?"

"Well, I'll see that she does."

So Stella took the cow home.

"And then when Grandma seen that the cow was going, why that felt like they was taking part of her away, so she said, 'Bring the cow back.' Now she'd had it down, I guess maybe two or three days, so she told Stella, 'Bring the cow back.'"

"It's my cow," Stella said. "I'm not bringing it back."

"Bring the cow back!"

So Stella told her father.

"Well, there's two ways of looking at that, now," he said. "Let's look at it different ways. If you've had the cow, and you had a calf, and you wanted some money, you wanted to sell the calf to get some money to do this or that, why she'd want part of your money. If you sold the cow, she'd want part of your money. Now, let's look at it the other way. If you turn the cow back to her, she's got to feed her. You don't have to feed her. You've got to feed her. You don't get anything from her, but you don't have to give her anything, either."

And he consoled her. "If you want a cow, I'll give you a cow."

"Yeah, but I didn't work for that," Stella said.

"Oh yes you have. You've lived in my family a long while, and I'm going to give you a cow."[114] And in fact he gave each of his daughters a cow as a wedding present.

Stella never forgave her grandmother. "She never paid any more attention 'til she got older," Reba said. "And when she got older she just set around and thought. 'This and that. If I'd a done this or that in my life it would of been different. Or if I'd a done this or that over here it'd a been different.'" And a major unresolved problem in Stella's long life was that early betrayal when Elizabeth took back the cow.

When Stella quit, "Reva and I had to take turns sleeping with her at nights," Reba remembered. Grandpa James Stapley slept upstairs with a bedroll in the summer and downstairs in the winter. "After we slept with her two years, Aunt May come down and stayed with her a little while."[115]

Elizabeth was never aware of how deeply offended Stella was—and had she been, she'd likely have done nothing different. She was more used to healing troubled bodies than troubled minds. "Mrs. Elizabeth Stapley was called on short notice to Harmony to assist in taking care of the sick," reported the *Iron County Record*, December 8, 1905. "She has not yet returned. The patient is improving."[116]

Almy's hobbling, the town's scarlet fever, and general sickness couldn't prevent a lively party on the Stapleys' fiftieth wedding anniversary in 1914. "Will Stapley went to Lund today to meet his brother Mahonri and wife, his sister and possibly his own wife, who are expected home to participate in the celebration of the golden wedding of Mr. and Mrs. James Stapley," reported the *Iron County Record*. "An elaborate dinner party will be given for the occasion on Feb. 21."[117]

James retired from farming, dividing his farmland equally among his daughters and sons, and asked John A. to come down from Corinne in northern Utah and farm the Stapley acres. "Well, Dad thought they would give him a place to build him a house on or something," remembered John's daughter Leola. "But they said no, that all that [town] property was Uncle Will's. So he didn't get a lot there, he had to go up in the other end of the town where it was just rock and like that, so he just had to start from scratch up there."[118]

As James aged, climbing the stairs to sleep in the upstairs room became more difficult. "They had very steep stairs," Lenna Stapley Williams remembered. "He was getting a little out of balance as he got older and it was hard for him to climb the stairs and a little dangerous. And my grandmother had the bedroom downstairs all to herself." Frustrated at Elizabeth, Jimmy went over to confront his mother and, as Lenna said, "he told her off."

"I'm bringing my dad's bed downstairs," Jimmy announced. "I'm putting it in the living room and you can like it or you can lump it. I'm moving him. He's not climbing those stairs anymore!"

Elizabeth's reaction was predictable. "Oh, she was upset!" remembered Lenna with satisfaction. "She said, 'I have never been talked to by one of my children before like that!' She was really upset. [But] he moved the bed. Granddad came downstairs."[119]

Perhaps Elizabeth wasn't as sympathetic as she might have been because she was still so active herself. Sometimes she'd have John drive her into Cedar City in James's white-topped buggy. "Nobody in town had one quite like Grandpa," remembered Leola. Elizabeth would say to her son, "Whip them up John! Whip them up!" because "the faster you'd go, the better she liked it."[120]

And she "always had a quilt on," Leola remembered. "Seemed to me like she had these big old hooks up in the top of her kitchen, and you'd put the quilt down here on ropes, and everybody would get around and quilt and then when it would come time for dinner, why up would go the quilt and it'd get out of sight."[121]

Her career as midwife was still as busy as it had ever been, the *Iron County Record* announcing on May 1, 1914, in the Kanarra column: "Born, last Sunday [April 26], a son [Delile] to Mr. and Mrs. Albert Davis. Mother and child doing fine with Sister Stapley in attendance."[122]

Elizabeth was still vigorous, joining her brother M. M. Steele at Parowan's homecoming where they ate Dixie fruit, visited with friends, and enjoyed a concert. "Old men clasped each other in their arms, and old women shed tears of joy at beholding friends of long ago," reported the *Parowan Times*.[123] It would also have been an opportunity to pay respects at the grave of their parents. Both were growing older, M. M. a brother she could be proud of—he had built himself such a beautiful two-story home it became an historic landmark in Panguitch, known as "The House of Nine Gables." Like his father and several of Elizabeth's sons, he was called on frequently for his clerical abilities—ward and stake clerk, historian, tithing clerk, clerk of Garfield County, Panguitch Stake presidency, school trustee, and superintendent of schools.[124] He was such a significant—if occasionally controversial—player in Republican politics[125] that he received an appointment from Governor William Spry to a coveted position on the State Land Board.[126] His talented daughter Catherine was candidate for Garfield County recorder at age 21. M. M.'s equally gifted—and politically connected—son, M. M. Jr., received a federal post office agent appointment, became a senate candidate, and a significant Republican "insider."[127] The local newspaper reporting Parowan's homecoming reminded its readers that M. M. Steele Sr., was "A YOUNG PIONEER. An interesting feature of the public auction is the fact that M. M. Steel[e], who had immediate charge for the [land] board, is one of the youngest pioneers of Parowan. He went to that place in his mother's arms in January, 1851, when he was only 18 months old."[128]

Elizabeth remained as tough and as formidable as she'd ever been. John Steele might have died, but his replacement as family leader shared many of his characteristics, and demanded every emblem of respect that Steele had expected.

FIGURE 1 (above left). Catherine Campbell Steele. Courtesy of the McQuarrie Memorial Museum, St. George, Utah.

FIGURE 2 (left). John and Catherine Campbell Steele. Written on the back: "Toquerville Kane Co. Utah Territory, North America April 4th 1873."

FIGURE 3. Robert Campbell, an architect, holds a rendering of a building. On the back: "Taken on the 25th/8/1885. Uncle Robert Campbell, Grandma Steeles Brother." And "Hutchinson photographer and portrait Painter Londonderry."

FIGURE 4. Mary Ann Campbell, Philadelphia seamstress, Catherine's sister, and posthumous wife of James Stapley.

FIGURE 5. John Steele. Courtesy of the McQuarrie Memorial Museum, St. George, Utah

FIGURE 6. Mary Campbell Steele Fish.

FIGURE 7. John Alma Steele on white horse. Written on the back: "1. James S. Stapley 2. John Alma Steele 3. Arch Kleinman are Rone."

FIGURE 8. Left to right: Mahonri M. Steele, Young Elizabeth Steele Stapley, Susan Adams Steele Bringhurst, and John Steele in 1897.

FIGURE 9. Susan Adams Steele Bringhurst.

FIGURE 10. Catherine Campbell Steele carved in stone on east side of the Salt Lake City and County Building.

FIGURE 11. Catherine Campbell Steele hat, worn by her great-granddaughter, Josephine Kay Garfield. Courtesy of Josephine Kay Garfield.

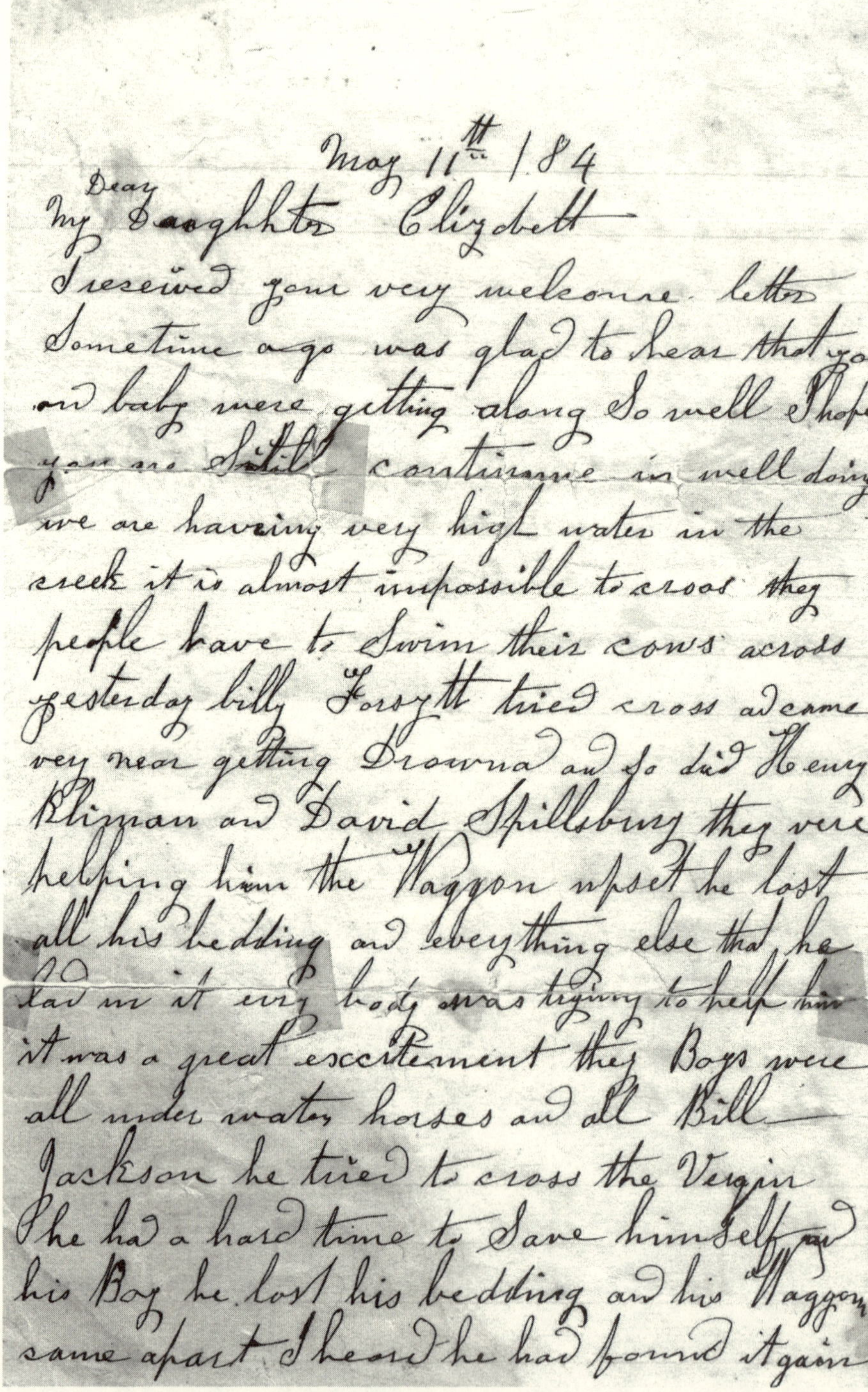
May 11th 184
My Dear Daughhter Elizbeth
I received your very welcome letter
Sometime ago was glad to hear that you
and baby were getting along So well I hope
you are Still continue in well doing
we are having very high water in the
creek it is almost impossible to cross they
people have to Swim their cows across
yesterday billy Forsyth tried cross and came
very near getting Drowned and so did Henry
Kliman and David Spillsbury they were
helping him the Waggon upset he lost
all his bedding and everything else that he
had in it every body was trying to help him
it was a great excitement they Boys were
all under water horses and all Bill
Jackson he tried to cross the Vergin
she had a hard time to Save himself and
his Boy he lost his bedding and his Waggon
came apart I heard he had found it again

FIGURE 12. Catherine Campbell Steele letter to daughter Elizabeth, page 1.

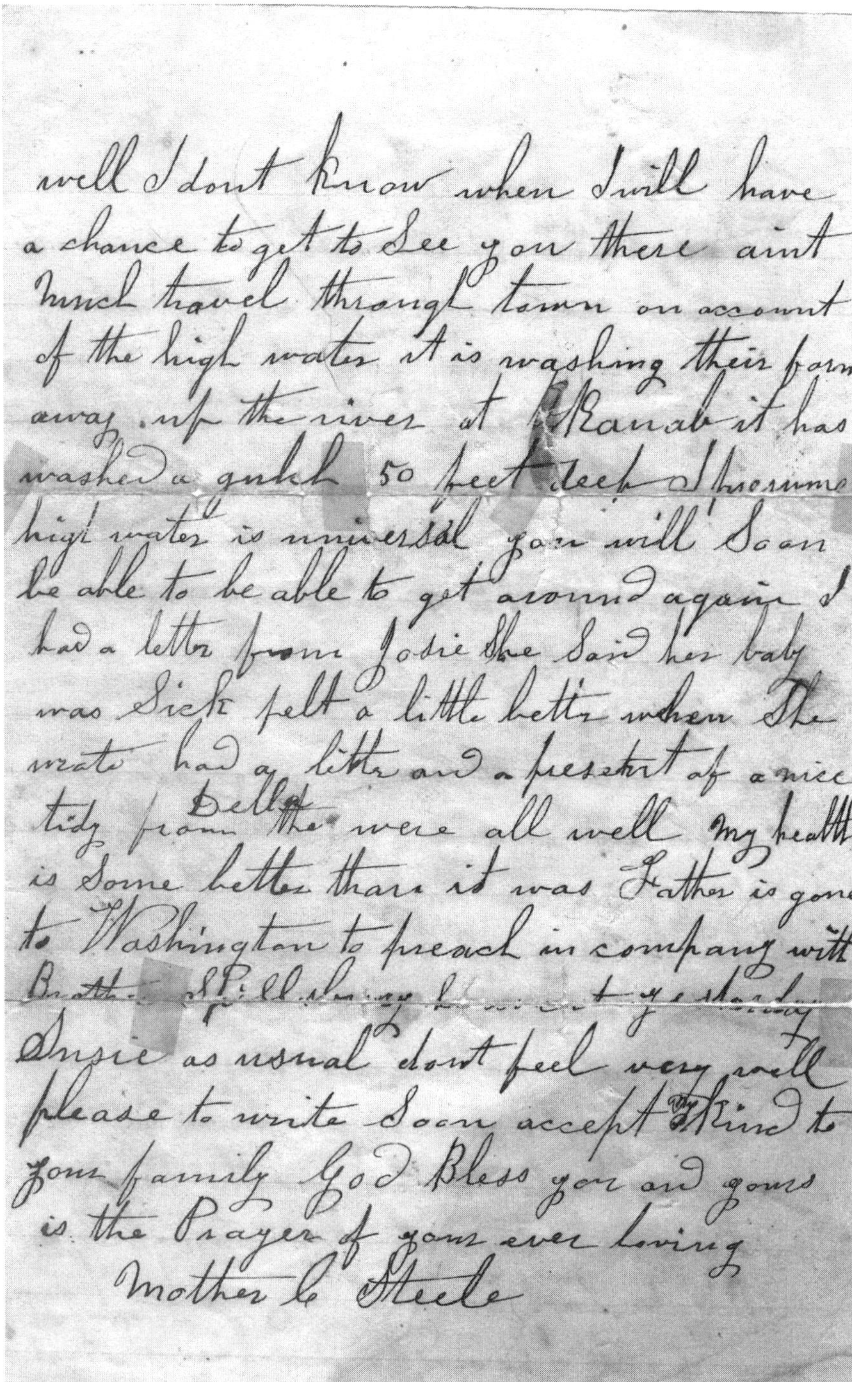

well I dont know when I will have
a chance to get to See you there aint
much travel through town on account
of the high water it is washing their farms
away up the river at Kanab it has
washed a gulch 50 feet deep I presume
high water is universal you will Soon
be able to be able to get around again I
had a letter from Jodie She Said her baby
was Sick felt a little better when She
wrote had a letter and a present of a nice
tidy from Bella the were all well my health
is Some better than it was Father is gone
to Washington to preach in company with
Brother Spillsbury went yesterday
Susie as usual dont feel very well
please to write Soon accept my kind to
your family God Bless you and yours
is the Prayer of your ever loving
Mother C Steele

FIGURE 13. Catherine Campbell Steele letter to daughter Elizabeth, page 2.

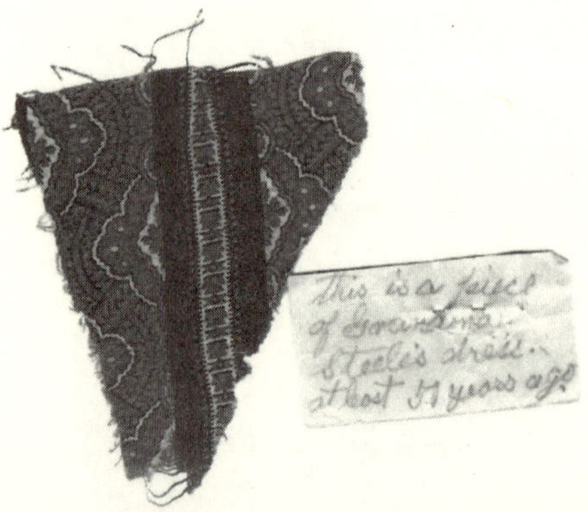

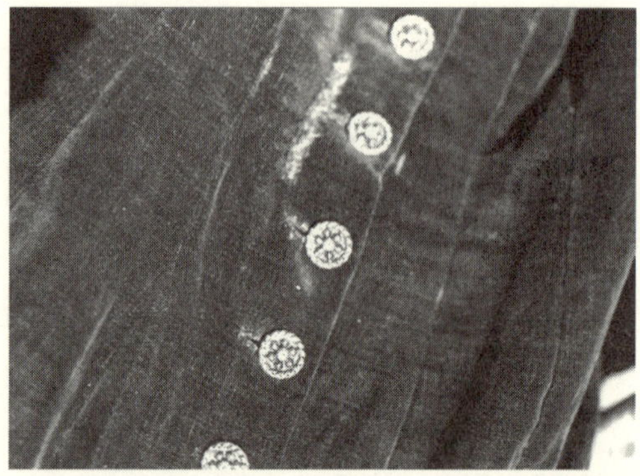

FIGURE 14. Paisley material that belonged to Catherine Campbell Steele, with a note by Sarah Catherine "Kate" Roundy: "This is a piece of Grandma Steele's dress at least 50 years ago." The other side of the note indicates it was written in 1933.

FIGURE 15. Catherine Campbell Steele dress detail. Courtesy of Josephine Kay Garfield.

FIGURE 16. James Stapley and Young Elizabeth Steele Stapley, 1897.

FIGURE 17. James and Elizabeth Stapley home, Kanarraville, Utah.

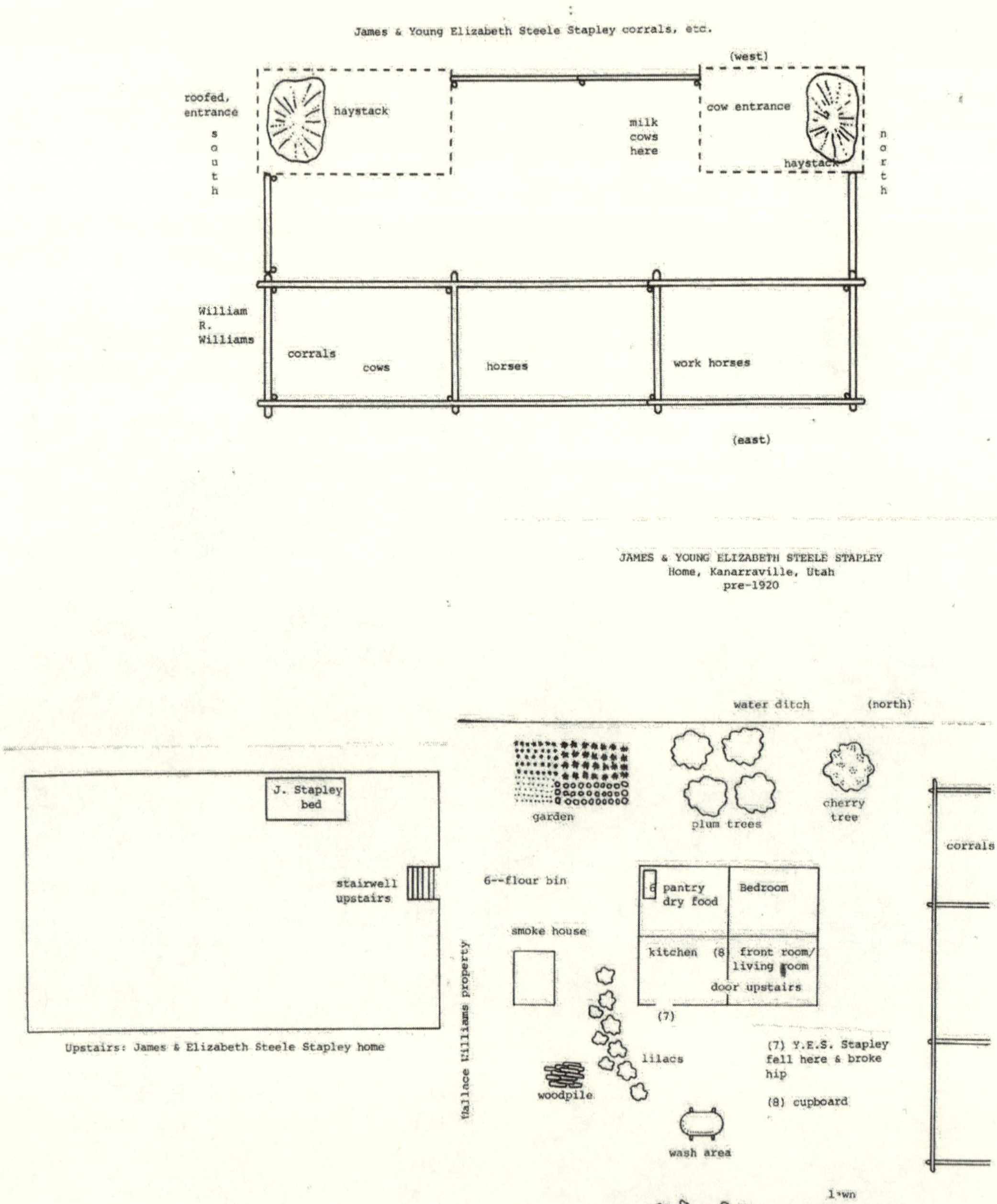

FIGURE 18. James and Young Elizabeth Steele Stapley homestead in Kanarraville. Illustration courtesy of Brad Lee Wolverton.

FIGURE 19. The Platt twins, Verna and Vernon; picture owned by Young Elizabeth Steele Stapley.

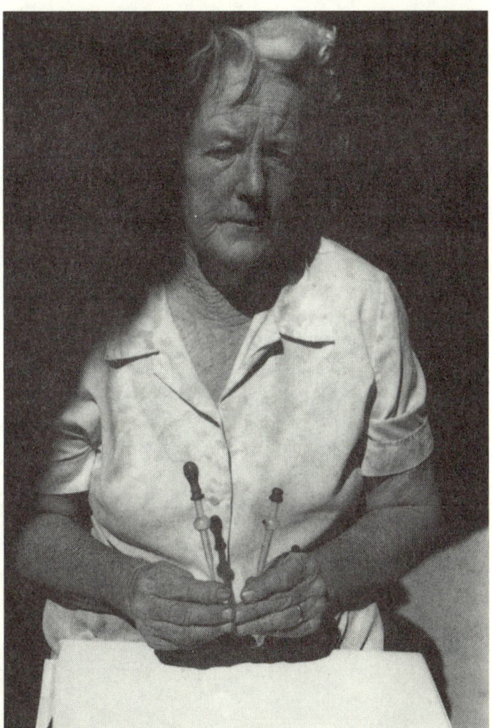

FIGURE 20. Verna Platt Davis holding the eye droppers she and her twin brother Vernon were fed with by Young Elizabeth Steele Stapley at their birth. Picture taken October 4, 1990.

FIGURE 21. Mary "May" Elizabeth Stapley (Kay). On the back: "May To. Y. E. S."

FIGURE 22. Young Elizabeth Steele Stapley wearing Pioneer medallion at neck.

FIGURE 23. James Stapley.

FIGURE 24. Paiute-made basket (partially burned from a subsequent house fire) holding one of Young Elizabeth Steele Stapley's medical books, which is open to a color print of a uterus; cards with birds addressed, respectively, to James Stapley and Elizabeth Stapley; and card with eggs to the Stapleys. In front of the basket is a larger ball of Elizabeth's yarn, dark blue, from the Washington Cotton factory and a smaller ball of black yarn; also, a second open medical book belonging to Elizabeth Stapley.

FIGURE 25 (left). Postcard (1917), left to right: Sarah Catherine Stapley Roundy, Nell Sylvester with doll, Sarah Elizabeth Roundy Sylvester, and Young Elizabeth Steele Stapley. On the back, in Sarah Catherine's hand: "Dear Son Lorenzo from Mother."

FIGURE 26 (above). Young Elizabeth Steele Stapley on left, President Warren G. Harding, and his wife, Florence Harding, Toquerville, June 27, 1923.

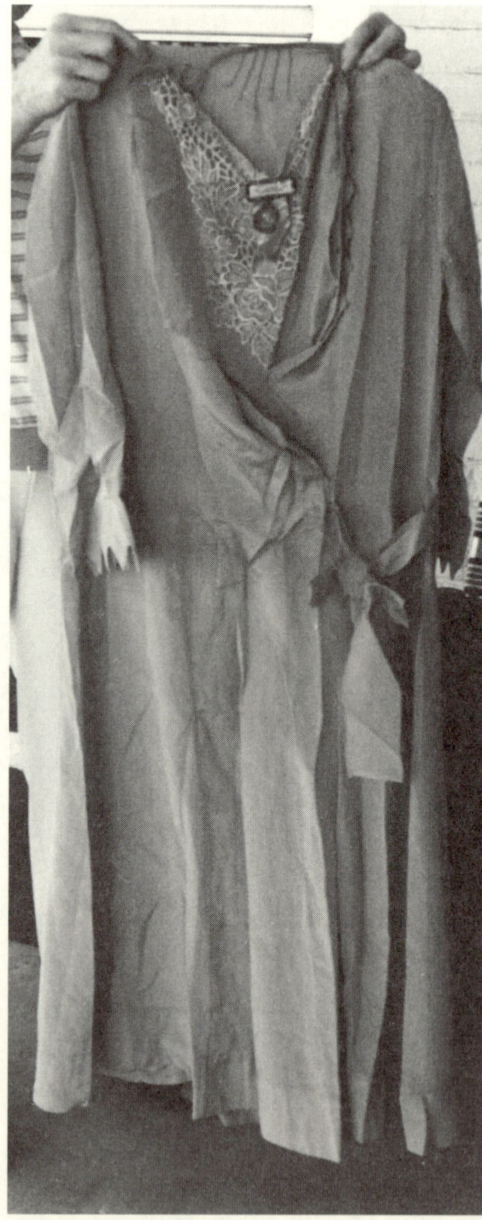

FIGURE 27. Elizabeth Stapley's photo of the Arizona Wranglers. Written on the front, "Best Regards from The Arizona Wranglers and 'The Sheriff.' Radio K.N.X." Identified on the back as: "Sleepy Cal Short, Slicker Laverne Castello, Hungry Joe Ivans, Dynamite Len Dossey, Nubbins J. E. Patterson, Irontail Chas Hunter, Sherriff Loyal Underwood."

FIGURE 28. A dress made by Annis Roundy Tietjen for her grandmother Elizabeth Steele Stapley, who wore it at the 1931 Pioneer Day parade (note the medallion and badge). Courtesy of Josephine Kay Garfield.

7

"She Can Do It"

Sarah E. Roundy

Capable women are a threat. Certainly Kate's daughter Sarah displayed a level of confidence that was disconcerting. "Sarah was limited," said Rulon Berry Platt. "Balance! Mental balance!" She "never treated everybody on the same level." Wasn't she intelligent? She was "Very smart. Very smart." The problem was "she just kind of built up a little bit of a cat stare . . . and she let it get the best of her!"[1]

In a word, uppity.

"No one was quite as good as the Berrys," Reba answered, referring to Platt's mother's family. Lynn Reeves elaborated. Rulon's maternal grandfather, William S. Berry, "was killed [on a mission] back in Tennessee and they thought they was just a little bit better. They said that their salvation was secure because their father was killed."[2]

"Oh well," responded Platt dismissively, "that's—that's peoples' opinions. Let them have it. That's a good deal. That's all right. Let them think it. I don't give a damn." But even Platt had to concede that his father's biggest disappointment "was having to cope with the in-laws."[3]

Sarah had an unassailable answer for the Berrys. Her grandfather Lorenzo Wesley Roundy was drowned while crossing the Colorado on a Mormon expedition. When she got "riled up" about the bragging Berrys she said, "Well my grandfather is [a martyr], too. He gave his life to go on a mission."

"Before she said that why it was always the Berrys this and the Berrys that and the Berrys something else," Reba remembered. "That's all you heard. And she said, 'why don't you talk about the Roundys?' Well, that put a block in the wheel. They shut up. And people in town said, 'Well, I'm sure glad, Sarah, you talked. 'Cause,' they says, 'we heard something besides the Berrys.'"[4]

Platt, son of Kanarra's schoolmaster, admitted Sarah was intelligent, and those who knew her agreed. The town offered the equivalent of an eighth grade education in the basement of the log church until it burned down.[5] Then for several years classes were held in private homes like that of storekeeper George A. Williams or the Welsh choirmaster John Johnson Davies; and once a class spilled over into "Aunt" Viny Berry's spare room. When the basement of the new church was finished, school was held there.

Joel was a school trustee who oversaw the construction of a new school, during which he won reelection on a write-in vote, much to the irritation of his neighbor Riley G. Williams—a candidate whose name was on the ballot. But generating interest in the school was challenging, as shown when the annual report and salary plan for trustees was presented for a vote at a 1904 town meeting. "There were only two voters present," reported the *Iron County Record*, "one representing the poorer class and the other the more wealthy position. One was liberal minded and advocated giving $75; the other more conservative and thinking that $60 was sufficient. The latter won by one vote and the last named amount was fixed as the compensation."[6]

Platt was Sarah's teacher. "I don't know who the rest of them was, but John was the last of them," Reba remembered, and

> he come up to Dad, when she was in eighth grade, he come to Dad and said, "Sarah's capable of graduating, she's got the knowledge and everything, but she's just lazy and won't do it! She won't even take the exam." He said, "It's up to you if she gets graduated." So, it went on for a day or two, and they was setting there one day, and he says, "Well I understand that you're not going to graduate." "Who said I wasn't going to graduate?" "Well," he says, "it's rumored around that you're not going to graduate. You won't take the exam, and you won't do nothing." "Who said that?" He said, "Well, I don't know, just noised around," and she went over and told John Platt she wanted that exam, and she passed it like that [and Reba snapped her fingers].[7]

"Most of the children went to the 8th grade," explained Marvin J. Christensen in recounting his mother Rosella Pollock Christensen's memoirs of Kanarra's school, and "that was the end of their education." But "if you had enough money to go to Cedar and stay you could attend high school."[8] Sarah, having passed the minimum age of fifteen, enrolled as a first-year student at the Southern Branch of the State Normal School at Cedar City, Utah, second semester in early 1906. The school had only been open for eight years, boasted two large new buildings, and held daily chapel. There was no tuition, and board and room was $2.50 to $3.50 a week. Because there were several other students from Kanarra—some of them Sarah's cousins (Esther Parker, who was graduating in spring; Charles Parker, May Smith), as well as Andy and William Berry, Victor Ford, and J. E. Ingram—Sarah likely boarded with friends. Sarah went two semesters, taking first-year courses in algebra, arithmetic, drawing, English, music, and U.S. history and civics, as well as what her school transcript calls "Phy.," which could be Physiography, Physiology, or Physical Education. Despite the school being the equivalent of a high school, a graduate could get a teaching certificate[9] like her aunt May Stapley Kay—though May went on to take classes at the University of Utah and made teaching a career.

The school gave numerical instead of alphabetical grades. Sarah's lowest score was 60 in algebra, followed by 70 in English and 75 in "Phy." She got 85 in U.S. history and civics, 87 in music and also in reading, with 88 in drawing. Her semester average was 78.86, but it's hard to translate that into a letter grade since we don't know the range; if we applied 78.86 to the current Wesleyan GPA this would equal a C+.[10]

Sarah's first teaching job was likely in church where she was set apart as a Primary teacher on March 4, 1906. This class focused on small children and she took her work seriously. When there was a Primary convention in Cedar City the following June, she and several other townswomen attended. She was apparently effective juggling Primary and the Young Ladies Mutual Improvement Association (YLMIA), for in March 1907, she gave a story for the latter, and on November 20, 1907, she was sustained again as an aide in Primary—but also an aide in the YLMIA. A year later she became Literary Class leader in the latter; she was always available in the YLMIA to sing or give recitations. Yet she continued her Primary work, and when it was reorganized in April 1912, she was chosen as counselor to "Sister Johanna Ford" and she promptly attended another Primary convention.[11]

After Branch Normal School (BNS) Sarah "went out to Alamo [Nevada], [to] teach school, that one year," Reba said, "and they called her Beth out there. And she come back and she still wanted them to call her Beth, and they said, 'No, you're Sarah, we're not going to call you Beth.'" She was five foot nine and she put on too much weight. "While she was out there she got up to 200 pounds. When she come back home she said, 'I'm too heavy,' so she put it down to 168."[12]

She was in Kanarra the winter of 1909–1910 when the Kanarra schooteachers were a husband-wife team, William O. and Hettie Sullivan Bentley, and they boarded with Vinnie Sylvester Berry.

Hettie had a beautiful voice and was a popular soloist and had taught in Kanarra the previous year while her husband was at the BNS in Cedar City, but her second year at Kanarra with her husband as principal didn't go well for her.

In early December 1909, the county newspaper reported Hettie "accidentally fell and fractured her ankle last week, [and] is obliged to rest up for a little while. Miss Sarah Roundy is taking her place in the school room." Her recovery was slow; by the second week in January the paper said, "The advanced grades of the school are now in session but it is doubtful if Mrs. Bentley is yet able to attend to her division." Then Hettie was diagnosed with Bright's disease in May and had a relapse in June. Sarah finished out Hettie's teaching term.[13]

Sarah was "rather temperamental," Rulon B. Platt said, "She didn't get along. Now let me say she could have been a marvelous school teacher . . . but with [her] temperament she couldn't handle it . . . She just [had] a, sulky sad disposition. And when you get that way, no child [is] going to listen to you."[14] Reba preferred to call her "plain spoken" and noted that she had many friends.[15]

Sarah's brother Ren graduated from the eighth grade in May 1909, at the age of nineteen and enrolled that fall in the Normal School in Cedar.[16] But he and Kanarra's John Layron Williams had to quit temporarily in early 1910, "having begun to get the swell head [mumps]."[17] On Sunday, August 14, 1910, Professor J. E. Hickman, principal of the Beaver Branch of Brigham Young University in Beaver, commonly called Murdock Academy, by "driving at breakneck speed from Hurricane" was able to talk in Kanarra's church and urge the people to support education. "His object was to get before the people the necessity of proper school training while in their youth," and Murdock had a lot to offer. Courses included high school studies, iron work, domestic science, domestic art, and agriculture—besides special courses in elocution, bookkeeping, and stenography. Despite impressing Harvard geologist James Walter Goldthwait as one "who thinks he knows it all, which is far from true when it comes to geology,"[18] Hickman's remarks were so well received that "after the meeting it was agreed by the body of priesthood remaining to at once sign a joint note for the amount due the Murdock Academy as assigned to this Ward some time ago and send the money immediately."[19] After all, "the school stands for thrift, character, and scholarly attainment."[20]

Sarah and Ren registered at Murdock on September 19, 1910, and roomed together. Ren studied carpentry and "ironwork" (blacksmithing) and also had classes in theology, English, zoology, ancient history, and physiology.

The term began registration day at the old military fort turned high school in a community described by an anonymous young woman visitor in spring 1910 as "the prettiest little inland town I have visited . . . The tall poplars of the long established Beaver homes gave us the breezes through their pretty green leaves, the lilacs gave us of their perfume," and she mentioned "the beautiful situation of Murdock Academy."

Sarah had relatives in town, including Linda Stapley and Charles A. Stapley—as she had kin in many towns in southern Utah—and the student body president was John H. Batty, member of a prominent Toquerville family and one of the five-member Murdock orchestra.

The school had a very strong track team—Alma Richards, destined to be the first Utahn to win an Olympic gold medal, was a member the previous semester[21]—and the enthusiasm of church members and other boosters, including students, funded a building expansion while Sarah was there. The *Murdock Lever*, the school newspaper, was in its second year and a newly acquired grand piano adorned the Assembly Hall.

Sarah took a course in woodworking (cost: two dollars in 1905) and learned carpentry (grades: an A and a B); ever after she was an expert at home repair, fixing sagging doors, and building boxes. The school was a big booster of vocational training. She also took domestic art (received two As), and drew "a perfe[c]t head and put all the veins in it," Reba wrote.[22]

She had a 3.9 grade point average: As in theology and Physiology, a B and an A in English, as well as the grades listed in the preceding paragraph. She rounded out her activities by joining the choir. (Ren's grades were good—he had a 3.0.)

A picture of Sarah and Ren at Murdock shows her fashionably dressed in an attractive white blouse sporting a large spray of lilacs and Ren in suit and tie with his hair carefully parted down the middle, also with lilacs.

Joel brought up fruit and, as Rulon Berry Platt recalled, "anybody else they'd have that would be coming in that direction, the people in the community would usually send a box of something, a box of fruit or a sack of potatoes or something."[23]

The school had interesting lecturers, from Rev. Elmer Goshen to LDS Church leader Levi Edgar Young, and the town itself had more Gentiles—and Jews—than any other place Sarah lived. On April 28, 1911, the students were "up on the side of the mountain this morning giving the big M its usual spring cleaning," the paper reported (despite landscape artist Lewis A. Ramsey objecting to defacing nature by painting giant school letters[24]).

Final exams were held in early May, with first-year student commencement exercises at 8 p.m. on May 25 and 2 p.m. on May 26, a week after "one of the heaviest winds ever known" swept over the valley. Sarah could have gone back to teaching but didn't.

By summer 1912 Sarah was working for her uncle—her grandmother Elizabeth's son John A. Stapley—doing housework and tending children. "I remember, she was so darn ornery!" laughed John's daughter Leola Stapley Anderson.[25] She didn't forget Murdock and when the Branch Normal School in Cedar City sent teams to outlying rural areas to "talk up" their school, Sarah volunteered to speak for Murdock. She joined John Reeves and her grandfather or uncle—the record says only "James Stapley"—to go to a freshly sprinkled and cooled down New Harmony on August 27, 1911. "Miss Sarah Roundy from Kanarra was here today in the interest of the Murdock Academy. She put up a good talk in behalf of the school," reported the New Harmony correspondent to the *Washington County News*.[26] She also did some midwifing, helping her friend and cousin-in-law Hettie Davis Pollock during Hettie's first delivery. "Lay across me here," Sarah said and then, Reba explained, Hettie "laid across her chest and she said, 'Now do this and do that,' and finally they got the baby," who was Roma, born November 26, 1912.[27]

Sarah joined her father in spring 1913 to visit his sisters in Venice, Utah, and then worked for Lula Jane Mathis in New Harmony, whose husband Albert—a wealthy sheep man—was a first cousin to "Zettie" Stapley.[28] But what Sarah really was interested in was the town's stimulating cultural and church life.

The musical tradition for Kanarra went back to 1866 when John Johnson Davies organized the first choir. By the 1890s the town had vigorous martial, harmonica, and school bands. Favorite songs included "I'll Bear It Like a Man," "Homeless and Alone Tonight," "Home Sweet Home," "When the Swallows Homeward Fly," "My Old Cabin Home," "Little Brown Jug," "Dat Baby of Mine," and colorful Jim Davies insisted that at his funeral they sing, "A Hot Time in the Old Town Tonight."[29] (The tune for "Hot Time" was also the air to Sarah's BNS class's "Hallowe'en Song": "All the spirits demoniacal/The enemies of right,/ Will try to scare the '05 Class/And fill our hearts with fright."[30])

Though Joel loved music, Rulon Platt said, "I don't know of one of his children that had a damned bit of music in them." Actually, most of them were in the town band and Sarah had a good voice and sang her first duet in church at the age of eleven with her cousin and friend, Hulda Pollock ("one of her main friends," Reba remembered).[31] Sarah "could sing beautifully," recalled Sarah's own daughter JoAnn years later. "She said she couldn't but she could. She had a beautiful singing voice, like a contralto rather than like a regular alto or soprano."[32] Sarah was a member of the church choir in Kanarra as early as 1905.[33]

The town's famous dance tradition was as old as its musical one, though more controversial.[34] The Mormon apostle, Hyrum M. Smith, grandnephew of the first Mormon prophet, visited Kanarra in 1902 and commented "how, when he was here before, the meeting house was dirty and filthy but what a difference now. He thanked the Lord that his and Apostle [Abraham O.] Woodruff's words had been appreciated. He wished to impress upon the people the necessity of fencing the public square. He was very much in favor of good Dramatic Associations and down on dancing."[35] A dozen years later the *Iron County Record* reported that Apostle Hyrum Smith's brother, Apostle Joseph Fielding Smith Jr., told Parowan Stake Conference attendees that "he does not believe in public dances, people should be there because they're invited, no man should go without a partner."[36]

Like most unworkable religious strictures, the townspeople yearned to comply and yet ignored the Smiths' rulings. They danced "quadrilles, hop-scotch [Schottisches], and the highland fling, Virginia reels . . . They waltzed then too . . . [and] turkey trots," Reba remembered.[37] "Basket Dances" were also popular, where the women made a lunch basket and the men drew to see who got what basket with what girl. Bessie Davies remembered the time her brother Elmer won Sarah, who was eight years his senior.[38] Sarah "liked to dance" and Reba said "she was always to the dance."[39]

So was everyone else. "Families would take their children and all and they'd make beds on their benches and they'd put their kids to bed and they'd all dance 'til the wee hours of the morning and then pick up the kids and go home," remembered Sarah's cousin, Leola Stapley Anderson.[40]

Nothing could stop their dancing. "It rained so hard that they couldn't hardly dance so they just pulled off their shoes and danced in their stockings and their bare feet," Lynn Reeves said, and his wife Ella stated matter-of-factly that Kanarra "was noted for their dancing, and that's all there is to it!"[41]

Arvilla Ford Woodbury said, "I remember when I used to get up early in the morning when I'd be so sleepy I could hardly stand. But I knew that my dad and mother wouldn't let me go out to the next dance if I didn't get up. We had work to do. Dishes and housework, and we all knew that if we didn't get up and get that work done, that next night we wouldn't get to go to the dances." She said that "On New Year's Eve we'd dance all night long!" and that "we just danced our heads off." During holidays they danced every night for a week, always regretting when the orchestra played the "Home Waltz," signaling the last dance.[42]

They also danced to raise money for the school band, for missionary work, or for repairs on the church. Despite Apostle Smith's censoriousness, everyone was invited to the public dances—people came from as far away as Toquerville and Hurricane—and Dixie wine was as popular an accompaniment as Sam L. Pollock's lively fiddle.[43] Asked why Kanarra dances were so well attended, Ella Batty Reeves laughed and said, "We don't have as many cops here as they have in other towns!"[44]

Sarah, like her great-grandfather John Steele, loved dramatics. Kanarra's drama club—approved by Apostle Hyrum Smith—was first organized in December 1898 by her uncle Will Stapley and teacher John W. Platt, and reorganized periodically thereafter. A story in the *Iron County Record,* refers facetiously to the "Kanarra Opera House" and explains the goals of the club of which Sarah's father Joel was vice president:

> Kanarra Dramatic and traveling troupe has again been reorganized. Within an hour after its resurrection parts were assigned for "The Old Wayside Inn," and it is expected that they will play first at the Kanarra Opera House three nights in succession, after which they will make a tour of southern Utah. The officers are R. G. Williams president, J[oel]. Roundy, vice-president, aids, Jos. S. Williams, Ethel Williams, and Amanda Reeves.[45]

Joel was in many plays, Reba recalled. "He always took the Dutchman's part, always talked backwards, and that's where I learned to talk backwards. We were always with dad, wherever dad went, we went . . ." An example Reba gave of talking backward was to say, "The cow set on the stool," or "The stool set on the cow," but however much that handicapped her when she started talking that way, she thought this was also the beginning of Joel's remarkable story-telling ability.[46]

And Joel wasn't the only one in the family who could act. His sons Ren and Jesse were good and so was Annis as well as Sarah, who was "a good player," Reba recalled. "She could learn her scripts good, Sarah could," she "was smart, and she could remember and she never had to study very much, it always come easy for her . . . She didn't maybe take the leading part, but she was in them."[47] Platt averred she took "little girl parts, young lady parts" as well as "the grandmas and the mothers" and "the part of a nice maiden or the aunt," and he said she was "very good. She learned that in her dramatics up at Murdock Academy in Beaver."[48]

Sarah's real service to the ward came in 1912. "She was the town clerk or something there [in Kanarra]," recalled Lela Berry Pollock. "No, not the town clerk; that would be a man. She was something to do with the clerking part there when I was a kid but I don't remember what it was."[49]

Pollock was elderly, trying to reconcile current realities with her memories of early twentieth-century Mormonism. In fact, Sarah did hold a "man's job" in her community, a job held only by men before and after her. She was Kanarra ward clerk from 1912 to 1914, succeeding her pinch faced, but capable and pious uncle, Will Stapley.

Will had seemed certain for eternal bachelorhood and looking after his father's farming and ranching interests but change came abruptly. "Our little town was unusually excited recently, by the news of a bachelor, who has lived without his full amount of ribs for 42 years," the *Iron County Record* wrote. "At last he (Will Stapley) was struck by a piercing arrow of Cupid, and left for Hinckley to secure a valentine in the shape of Miss Emmeline Allred, the missing rib. They were married last week in the Salt Lake Temple. It seems he is ashamed to return, judging from his secret departure, and will locate at Hinckley for the pre[sent]."[50]

Apparently no one could do a better job replacing him as ward clerk than his niece. And it was appropriate that Sarah be selected as ward clerk in 1912. She had proven her worth in Primary and Mutual assignments, she was twenty-four, and it was the Progressive Era. Despite tiny Kanarra's isolation, it was much infected with new ideas. Progress was in the air. The U.S. Congress was passing laws regulating trusts and monopolies; the Utah State Legislature was restricting child labor, establishing minimum wages, mandating prison reform; and the towns of Utah were making all kinds of civic improvements.[51]

Cedar City twice elected socialist mayors (one, Daniel T. Leigh, on the Republican ticket), and Kanarra Ward members heard lectures from their bishop to "improve"—and they did. They built the new, not very effective water system and installed telephones. The town also bought a new piano for community dances, farmers looked at new farming techniques like dry farming, and townspeople pointed out shocking paragraphs in their county newspaper—such as a police-provoked "Wobblie" riot in Salt Lake City where six men were shot,[52] and an exciting tale of women in Portland being arrested for wearing "x-ray dresses."[53]

The Roundys were up-to-date, too. Joel Roundy thought candles were too dangerous because of the potential of fire and he and Kate were among the first in Kanarra to install gas lighting. The light was in the ceiling but they also got a gas-powered iron for ironing clothes. Annis did the ironing and Jesse took care of the gas light until they got electricity two years later.[54] In 1903 there were hints of telephones coming into Iron County and on February 13, 1904, the *Iron County Record* published a rumor that a phone might be going into the

Williams Hotel in Kanarra. Bishop Berry, who was considered well off, had a phone by June 1904, and in 1905 the Kanarra correspondent to the newspaper could phone in the town's report.[55]

Rees Williams, Uncle John Stapley, and Sam Pollock eventually took over Kanarra's Farm and News [Telephone] Company, which had competition ("The Iron County Telephone Co. and the Farm and News Co. here are having quite a bit of annoyance due to too close connection of the lines, which we have not been able to locate yet," reported the newspaper).[56] By July 1908 Frank Anderson of Anderson's Junction was a lineman for Bell Telephone from St. George to Kanarra.[57]

Kate and Joel got a telephone in 1910. "Everybody had one," Reba remembered, "and all you had to do was ring one ring and you could talk to a dozen people at the same time. Us kids used to go play, and then we'd say, 'We'll run home and call you, and see which one gets home first.' . . . then they got so that everybody—every time the phone rang, everybody would lift the receiver and listen to what was going on and everybody's business."[58]

In short, in the years around 1912 when Sarah was chosen as ward clerk she was a member of a respectable family in a dynamic, forward-looking community. Still, it was unusual to move a woman into a man's job, which is what happened when Sarah was called to be ward clerk on April 14.[59] Bishop John William Berry "figured she was worthy of the calling or he wouldn't of called her," said his daughter, Thelma Berry Lovell.[60]

"They couldn't get a man to take it," Reba recalled, so they selected Sarah because "she's smart and she can do it." Sarah thought it over, consulted her father—who was in the bishopric—and with his encouragement said, "Well, if you think I should, I should," and accepted. Her fellow townspeople were at least grateful—"they was glad she got it because they wouldn't have to do it," Reba said. As ward clerk she kept minutes, vital statistics, and financial records. She efficiently set to work, sketching in the minutes as well as she could during the two-month hiatus.[61]

On the same day she was sustained as second counselor in the Young Ladies' Mutual Improvement Association, a group which organized many town social events. She served as ward clerk until the end of January 1914, and took her clerking seriously. She was conscientious, recording minutes fully and consistently during her tenure in office, something not all ward clerks did. Once she wrote, "No minutes kept Sept. 8, 1912. Ward Clerk at Mutual Convention." She used adjectives to help better describe the nature of talks and church activities: a returned missionary gave a "beautiful account" of his mission, the bishop gave "excellent warning," Sister Ethel Ashdown delivered "an instructive talk," and her father preached an "interesting and consoling" funeral sermon.[62]

Her spelling was not always orthodox—we find "Parawon" for "Parowan," "Seccion" for "Session," "Convercttion" for "conversation" and a phonetic "posponed" for "postponed." The trials of polygamy were already receding so far that its spelling proved a trial ("pylogamy"—but her grandfather John Steele had trouble with that word, too, once writing "polygamee"[63]), and genealogical work was of so little interest that it comes out "genology." Randolph Andrus, a state champion orator and Kanarra school principal and teacher, who was so beloved for raising money for the school band that the town presented him with an expensive chair, is given a mystery name choice in her minutes, among them "Randolph," "Andolph," or "Audolph."[64]

The congregation of approximately one hundred was treated to a few frank details of the personal lives of their neighbors, and Sarah did not flinch from recording them. "Charles Parker Sen. expressed his desires to fulfill his marriage vows to his wife," John Platt (for good reason, as will appear), reminded ward members of the "sin of scandal," and one father publicly confessed that his daughter had fornicated "with her husband" before marriage. The congregation, after the bishop gave "excellent warning to the young people," extended "a unanimous vote of forgiveness."[65]

As ward clerk Sarah attended the only "Bishops Trial" held during her tenure. Asked who the gossips were in town, Reba answered very succinctly: "Everybody!"[66] One of them, however, took tale telling too far. On October 13, 1912, Sarah's former teacher John W. Platt charged Sarah's paternal cousin by marriage—Rachel Griffin Roundy—with promoting the story that, nearly twenty-five years before, Platt had an affair with his own sister-in-law, Hattie Berry Stapley. Hattie, the proudest and grandest of the proud and grand Berry clan, was married to Sarah's uncle Jimmy Stapley. Rachel alleged the affair took place while Jimmy was on his Irish mission and resulted in a pregnancy and miscarriage.[67]

Rachel pleaded not guilty and "asked for other witnesses, some of her friends, not enemies," and finally fell back on her husband, Byron Alma "Toot" Roundy, who asked for "coencided evidence."[68]

Rachel was controversial. She'd been active in the Young Ladies and Young Men's Mutual Improvement Associations, giving readings and recitations[69] and she married Joel's hotheaded nephew "Toot" and moved into Joel's old house. Reba remembered Rachel as one who would "cook the dinner all ready—and a good looking dinner, too, Dad said—and just as soon as she saw him [Toot] come up, she'd take and dump it all out on the porch step." "'Well, you're not here,' she says, 'and you can't have it.' So she'd dump it all on the step. I don't know. She was weird." [70]

Elizabeth told the story of the time she went to deliver one of Rachel's babies, and Toot brought over some flour and sugar. "She took it out and put it under the tap and let it wash away!" Elizabeth exclaimed, summarizing Rachel as "the meanest woman I ever seen." Rachel was so ill-tempered and unbalanced that Reba concluded, "We'd call her handicapped now, but we called her crazy."[71]

According to Reba, Rachel made it her special mission to see if she could get a reaction from Joel Roundy.

> She moved to the next house over from my dad, and every so often she'd come to the fence—she'd never come in, she'd come to the fence—and she'd yell, "Mr. Roundy! Mr. Roundy! Come out here!" And so he'd walk out into the middle of the lot and she'd call him every name she could think of. Every hard name she could think of—never a kind one. And she'd talk until she'd give out. And he'd just stand there, never say one word. And then she'd go and not come back. And then she'd take—we found out afterward—she stayed there about three or four years—and we found out just before she left, she told some of the neighbors she come down here to make my dad angry, and she never succeeded.[72]

Platt's son Rulon was no more charitable toward Rachel than Reba was, charging over seventy years later that she was "a bullshitter" and "prevaricator" who would "hatch up a story and tell it" because "she was just an off breed" that "fell off the log and got bumped."[73]

The affidavits Sarah copied into the ward records show that Rachel had made the charges and she didn't give any evidence at the trial. The case was postponed, but eventually Platt prevailed and on December 29, more than two months after first hearing the accusations, the bishop—Hattie's brother—announced the outcome from the pulpit ("There was no truth in the charge") and urged communal unity.[74]

Like many of the girls in Kanarra, the now twenty-five-year-old Sarah found her first beaux among the young men of nearby New Harmony. Her named is linked to sheep herder Orson Hammond's in at least friendship, a Davies in some possible romance, but a New Harmony goat herder of Swiss parentage, Andy Schmutz—"very fine looking" and "very religious," according to Rulon Platt[75]—was said to be her most serious suitor. She was blue-eyed, dark-haired, about five feet nine, weighed 168 pounds, and was blind in the right eye because of a childhood accident. "I don't know if it was cutting wood or what, but something flipped and split the pupil right there in two. She had a little streak right through the pupil, and a little black pupil . . . And I used to say, 'Sarah's blind in one eye and [brother-in-law] Burdette's blind in the other,'" Reba remembered.[76]

Sarah was always dressed in the latest fashions, clothes made by her own expert hands, though the unsympathetic Platt said she "didn't have a very good presentation. Wasn't good looking, a little bit awkward, slight. Didn't have this millionaire"—and he paused dramatically, then added—"sex appeal."[77]

Her personality could be off-putting, too. Reba described Sarah as "plain-spoken like Grandma. Mother said she was more like Grandma Roundy than any child she had. Grandma Roundy could go to a meeting and look at a collar or a dress or anything, and go right home and make it. Didn't have to have no measurements or anything, go right home and make it. And Sarah could do the same thing." Grandma Priscilla Roundy was headstrong, determined, and more intimidating than intimidated. Furthermore "Grandma Roundy was—according to Aunt Jane—was a big-framed woman. And Aunt Jane says, 'She takes after her mother. I take after my father; he's more refined,'" and Reba laughed.[78]

Despite giving up half braids for dark long hair—which she stylishly curled for special occasions with a curling iron—and wearing fashionable clothes, Rulon noted that Sarah was "not too goodly, rather large, rather composed," and he gave what was probably the official town position on her: "She was getting up in years."[79]

8

"Nothing Too Refined"

Victor L. Sylvester

New Harmony wasn't the only town with a potential suitor for Sarah E. Roundy. Bellevue was described in 1869 by Joel H. Johnson as "located 8 miles north of Toquerville and 13 miles South of Kanarrah." He explained, "We have a town laid off here but only six families at this time," and though he expected "many more soon," the town never grew much despite his opinion that it was one of the "best places in the territory." "I have only been here a little over 1 year Shall have from fifty to one hundred bushels of peaches besides pears apples plumbs Apricots cherries Currents goosburies strawburies Grapes &c all of which kinds of fruit flourishes here the best of any place I ever saw."[1]

The tiny town couldn't grow as Johnson anticipated because it was pinched in by mountains and hills, with little room for expansion and young folks had to leave for opportunities. While some expected Sarah to marry New Harmony's Andrew Schmutz, a twenty-year-old man from Bellevue came to town to work as a sheepherder for his cousins Jim and Andy Berry. Victor Leon ("Lee-own" in the local pronunciation) Sylvester had a heritage of culture and curses. The Sylvesters were musicians and poets, loving nothing better than aping Tennyson with their verse, and applying middle-class English landscaping to their homestead, boasting lush flowers, vigorous gooseberries, and a very fine organ.[2] His great-great-uncle Charles Sylvester was a British engineer who corresponded with the Wedgwoods, wrote revolutionary poetry (published anonymously to avoid prosecution) and articles for the *Encyclopedia Britannica,* was a scandalous atheist, helped usher in the railroad, and had his bust molded by Francis Chantry.[3]

Victor's mother, Jane Hanks Sylvester, was a great-granddaughter of James Bean, who suffered from Brigham Young's malediction along with David Miller, when Young wailed that "they shall be cursed and you will see it!"[4] Years later Young thundered against the capitalist class in Parowan and cursed

Jane's father, Ebenezer Hanks.[5] (Victor was born in Hanksville, named after this grandfather, a high desert area so isolated and dry that it was later chosen by NASA for robotic testing to simulate Mars.[6])

Vic's father, Joe, was a sometime cowboy and stage coach operator and driver,[7] while Jane was a gentle, well-bred woman. "Our boy is so big and fat that I can't hardly carry him around," Vic's mother wrote of him in 1898,[8] when he was five years old, but she died when he was eleven.[9] Jane's mother, Sarah Jane Casper Hanks Burnell, was formidable and still angry at her own father, William Wallace Casper, for beating her with a whip when she was fifteen to force her to marry Ebenezer Hanks, a man thirty years her senior.[10] Sarah Jane lived into Vic's adulthood but wasn't taken with grandchildren so he didn't get motherly nurturing there. However his father furnished him with a stepmother, the *Iron County Record* reporting, "A marriage license was issued December 14th to Mr. Joseph Sylvester of Bellevue and Mrs. Emily Stewart of Washington. They were married [in St. George] by President Edward H. Snow the same day."[11] Joe was tipsy when he stood up for the wedding vows but he got through it.[12]

Vic's stepmother, who was actually named Emeline, was the postmistress of the town of Washington at the time of the marriage, a kindly woman with some important connections including her brother Judge John Foy Chidester—long since having lived down allegations of firing a neighbor's haystack when a boy.[13]

Vic also inherited some stepbrothers and sisters and became pals and business partners with one of them, Wallace Stewart. Subsequently his father and stepmother had two children, giving him a half-sister Jane, and half-brother LaVell, both of whom were very fond of him.

Vic had his own anger and bitterness; he was described by a nephew not given to profanity as "the orneriest bastard that ever lived,"[14] and Vic's younger sister Gladys said he was "a mean brat" who "teased me constantly and I hated him when I was a kid."[15]

"I knew him when I was a lad," recalled ninety-two-year-old Edwin K. Slack. "He used to beat the hell out of me every once in a while. We both lived at Bellevue. We rented a home there and that would be about when I was just eight or ten years old. He was older than me but we played together and he was quite a bit older, so naturally he beat the devil out of me when he wanted to. But anyhow, we did grow up together."

"I wouldn't say he was quarrelsome," Slack explained, "but nobody stepped on his toes without getting smashed a couple of times."[16]

"He was kind of rough," Lottie Dodge Olds agreed. "He just grew up on a farm. They were nothing too refined."[17] Lottie's eighty-nine-year-old husband

Arthur remembered that when kids were crouched over the ditch in the morning to get a drink Vic would "come along and just take like that"—shoving his open hand roughly forward—"and push a kid's head right down in the water. He thought that was quite a joke. He'd do that pert near every morning."[18]

Arthur's older brother Andrew Olds, Vic's schoolmate and future brother-in-law, said Vic "was smart. But he just couldn't get along with the teacher. He wanted to be teacher and pupil too, you know . . . The teacher would tell him to do this, do that. No: he wouldn't do that. He does as he damned pleased . . . Old Vic was quite smart in one way or another. And he didn't want to learn. He didn't want anybody to tell him anything." Andrew's most vivid recollection of Vic in grade school was when the teacher—Kate's step-cousin George R. Bringhurst—would stand that young man in a corner, both hands uplifted, one holding a dictionary and the other a geography book, punishment for bad behavior.[19]

He had good qualities, credited by Slack with generously donating fifty dollars toward a Toquerville town project, being "honest to a fault,"[20] and was described by an admiring Platt as "a natural-born, self-made comedian. You could laugh at anything that crazy guy would say."[21] Vic loved a good fight, liked a little wine, and hated a bully. "He was rougher than Halifax," Slack asserted.[22] Andrew Olds agreed: "Oh, he was a rough, tough little bugger."[23]

Vic's father Joe had inherited the moribund family acres in Bellevue (now known as Pintura). His only cash crop was wine made out of sweet, black California grapes.

One observer explained that "Kanarraville is a strange little settlement. It always has a cold wind blowing down upon it. The very inhabitants seem to share in its bleakness, and the reputation of the town for drunkenness seems to suggest that the people indulge in spirits as a means of keeping warm."[24]

This gave Joe a good market for his wine: he "used to trade lots of it in Kanarra," recalled his son-in-law Andrew Olds. "He'd get a load of coal, and he'd get some, little hay, you know. And whatever them Kanarra fellers had, he'd get, but he didn't get too much money from them. Younger fellers would buy the wine but the older ones would trade with him." Olds chortled that so many Kanarra people patronized the Dixie winemakers that church authorities "had a hell of a time getting bishops out there!"[25]

Joe not only made wine, he religiously drank his tithe of it, his occasional bouts with drunkenness a trial to his successive wives, Jane and Emeline, as well as his children.

Vic was bright—his sister Maud wrote later that "his teacher at school said they never had seen a child with such a memory as Victor had"[26]—but he wasn't interested in education. Still, his father and stepmother enrolled him, his sister Gladys, and stepsister Mary in school in the town of Washington in the fall of 1910.[27] But he had no more luck in graduating than his mine-promoting Uncle Andrew Gregerson did in his failed attempt that fall to beat the Democrats and get himself elected Washington county commissioner.[28]

Maud remembered that "Mother's great worry befor[e] she died, was about eleven-year-old Victor. She knew the family would pay a lot of attention to eight-year-old Gladys. She knew that Victor would take a lot of love and patience."[29] He quit school before finishing the eighth grade and later referred to college as a "paid vacation." He worked at cow punching with his father and stepbrother Wallace Stewart, then bought an elegant cowboy hat that he proudly wore on the dusty red streets of Toquerville.[30] "The loftier the hat was, why—it was just right," remembered Andrew Olds.[31]

After a few years of working with cows, Vic and Wallace leased Joe's Bellevue land, hopeful that new agricultural methods would wring a living from the dying acres. "The old man rented the farm to Vic and Wallace," Andrew Olds remembered,

> and I knew it at that time, and they went out and pruned the grapevines and plowed it up a little and plowed up some of that old alfalfa that they had. Been in there twenty or thirty years, you know, it was spoilt. They plowed up some of those plants some more. That's what the parting started with. The old man got mad and he beat the hell out of old Vic and Wallace and told them to get the hell out of there. And they hitchhiked up to Kanarra, and never come back home after that.[32]

Vic went to Salt Lake to visit his university-educated older brother Frank, who wrote a postcard to their sister—"Vinnie" or "Dick"—on August 25, 1911: "Went to Saltair yesterday and had a swim. Victor seems to enjoy himself."[33] Maud reported that Frank also "made a trip home after graduating from the University [of Utah]. He talked to Victor about going in to school and thought he had made all the arrangements with the teachers at the B.N.S. [in Cedar City] but then [cousin] Jim Berry talked him out of it. I asked Frank why he thought Victor didn't go on, and he says Victor hadn't mothers influence."[34]

Instead, in late 1912 Vic and Wallace went to work for Vic's cousin Jim Berry on the Berry ranch two and a half miles north of Kanarra, now known as Suicide Ranch; so named because "some feller kicked his bucket over there—purposely," recalled Andrew Olds.[35] Vic did cow punching and sheepherding. Rulon Platt, a "shirt-tail cousin," since both were related to the Berrys, herded sheep with Vic. Platt greatly admired the older man, and remembered eating "many a plate of fried onions and potatoes in the camp with him. Many of them," describing Vic as "a very good hard working person in his field. Now, he wouldn't go out and pitch hay. He hated it. But he was a marvelous man with livestock. Good worker."[36]

This prickly, handsome, wiry-haired young cowboy, five years Sarah's junior, courted her at the dances. "He'd always come in and he'd take her to the dance and there was no ice cream parlors or anything like that in those days" recalled Platt. "A lot of times they'd have a bean bust after a dance, or go out and have cookies and coffee. Oh, they always generally had some kind of a little social after a dance. Vic was always mixed up in that kind of a thing, he liked it. Vic liked friends, but he was not a woman hunter, woman chaser."[37]

It must have soon been obvious to everyone that Vic liked to drink a little wine—"He'd have a drink or two, and then he was really a high stepper," his daughter Gwen recalled later.[38] The wine relaxed him enough to dance or sing, but unlike his father he wasn't an alcoholic. Vic and Sarah "just got started going together and she didn't have boyfriends and she was just a kind of a loner and he was just one of those kind of guys that was just a loner,"[39] was Platt's understanding of the courtship.

Sarah was an inordinately independent minded woman—her own mother had seen to that. And it seemed everyone was getting married in 1913, including her fun-loving and sheepherding cousin Joe Ingram to Kanarra's Naomi Wood. Stockman Reese J. Williams's daughter Julia married the Cedar City athlete Percy Wilkinson, who was Kanarra's onetime schoolteacher and earned fame as the carpenter who—upon the completion of the Cedar City Rock Church—stood on his head on the steeple. Kanarra schoolteacher Arthur Fife, famed for his band (which included Sarah's brothers Ren Roundy on the bass horn, Jesse Roundy on the slide trombone, Golden with the trumpet, and sister Annis on the clarinet) married Sarah's cousin Florence Williams. Andrew Olds' brother Will from Bellevue married Sarah's happy-go-lucky cousin Lizzie Williams. Noel Williams married Sarah's sweet-tempered cousin Lena Parker, and Branch Normal students Riley B. Williams and Irva Dalley married.[40]

"An epidemic has struck Kanarra which has taken away quite a number of the young people, and a few more have a very high fever," quipped the Kanarra correspondent to the *Iron County Record* on August 15, 1913, "but the best part of the malady is that it is not a quarantine type, so the health officer has nothing to say. It has been diognosed [*sic*] and pronounced Matrimonial Fever, as there has been seven weddings since April 1st, with three more in the near future."[41]

Apostle Joseph F. Smith Jr. explained at the Parowan Stake Conference in March 1915 why not only marriage, but marriage in LDS temples with proper rituals, was eternally important.

> Said that he was informed that in this stake the marriages performed outside of the temple outnumbered those solemnized within the temple, which he said showed a lack of faith on the part of the people. The speaker quoted from the Doctrine and Covenants to prove that men and women thus married would not be reunited in the world to come, and that they would be merely ministering angels, without exaltation, to those who complied with this ordinance while on earth.[42]

There was hope with a civil marriage that it could later be confirmed in a temple, but unmarried women couldn't be "exalted." Sarah's grandmother Priscilla Parrish Roundy said that God's curse on unmarried women was that they "would be servants hear after."[43] Reba said that a spinster could go to the highest Mormon heaven: "She goes into the Celestial Kingdom, but she just is an angel." Everyone else could become a wife, a mother, and a goddess. Temple rituals of being "sealed" to men are necessary, and it's there a woman gets a new name. "If you don't have this new name when you get to the judgment seat, why, he'll ask you what your name is, and if you tell him Kerry Bate—'I don't know you.' But if you have your name in the Lamb's Book of Life—that's what the Lamb's Book of Life is, your temple recommend, then he will say, 'come in.'"[44]

Lottie Olds thought Sarah was the aggressor in this relationship because she followed Vic to the sheep herd and down to Bellevue.[45] "Sarah couldn't find a boyfriend," Platt asserted. "And she wanted to be married so badly . . . But I do know this! She wanted to be married! Now I remember that. Stella did. And boys didn't take to them. Why? The boys around town was all drinking, and that didn't go in the family. Got it? That's where the break came from." Asked why the family tolerated Vic's drinking, Platt replied, "She was old enough to think for herself. She said, 'I'm going to have a man!'"[46]

But Reba had different memories, recalling Sarah was pursued by Victor. "Vic was always talking about the birds and the bees, the birds and the bees, doing what the birds and the bees done."[47]

Vic, whose arm had been set in 1900 by John Steele,[48] didn't like Sarah's grandmother Elizabeth, whom he called "Old Lady Stapley," and according to Platt he would "torment her" by pricking Elizabeth's legs and teasing her. "She about laid on him with an ax!" Platt laughed.[49] If he teased Elizabeth, he was more respectful toward Kate and Joel. Still, they discouraged Sarah from marrying him. Kate was particularly upset about Vic's lack of religious commitment. Platt said Vic never talked about church "but he was a scriptorian. Don't you ever think he didn't know the Bible or the Book of Mormon. He spent his days reading and herding sheep. He knew it! He could quote it to you!"[50] Platt added that "A lot of sheepherders read trash. Things that never do them a damn bit of good. But Vic, I'll tell you this, Vic knew the Czarism. The Czars of Russia? He read about those cusses, he could tell you all about those things. I borrowed books from Vic that he'd read about the czars. He was intellectual."[51] (On the other hand Andrew Olds averred Vic just read "old wild west books," and attributed Vic's skepticism to the fact he "kind of liked to doubt a fellow, you know, and then have the other fellow prove it if he could."[52])

The family was tongue-tied about sex despite Elizabeth's father John Steele being an earthy man who could be quite direct in writing Catherine from England, "There are but few ^woman^ who live to the age of 80 years, but what Know that it takes a man and a woman to make a man."[53] He had even run across homosexuality in New York City, noting indignantly in his journal on June 7, 1877, "While I was passing along the bottom end of Broadway today a slim, gaunt young man came and whispered in my ear, 'Do you want a man?' I made no answer but thought of Sodom."[54]

As a midwife, Elizabeth was particularly informed on sexual matters, and one of her medical books had engravings—some in color, explaining the birthing process itself—but she was far from willing for her children to be educated about such matters and watched over their reading materials. "She was fussy about what her kids had to read and one thing an another," chuckled her grandson Elton Stapley. Just before Elton's father, Mahonri Moriancumer, was getting married in 1898, someone gave him a copy of Sylvanus Stall's, *What a Young Man Ought to Know*. That it was written by a minister and "Dedicated to The Young Men who should be Pure and Strong" didn't matter to Elizabeth. "Grandma got ahold of it and locked it down the bottom of her trunk!" laughed Elton.[55] (When it was proposed to teach "sex hygiene" in the schools in 1914, national educators were appalled,[56] but by 1920 lectures on the topic could be publicly given.[57])

It is no surprise, then, that Elizabeth's daughter Kate didn't explain sexuality or menstruation to her daughters. "I don't think anybody knew anything about it, only just got married, and you learned as it comed along," Reba explained.

> If you'd ask them a question or two, they say go ask your Dad and if you asked your Dad, go ask your Mother. And we knew we'd never get an answer. We got most of our answers listening to people talk, kids talk out in the town . . . When we were a, um, what was it thirteen, I guess, we was about twelve or thirteen, we went for a horseback ride and Reva started to menstruate first, and when she got off from the horse she saw all the [blood] on her pants and so she went out in a ditch and washed it off. And when Mother saw what she was doing, why then she told us. But they give us books to read on it. They didn't talk very much about it, but they give you books.[58]

The *Young Woman's Journal* did talk about menstruation, and LDS "Sister Hannah Sorensen" published a book, *What Women Should Know,* that apparently covered that and other sensitive subjects.[59]

"I think it was too much secret, secret. They didn't talk about anything," and, Reba concluded, "if anybody got in trouble in sex, you never heard anything about it. It was hush, hush."[60]

On Tuesday, September 26, 1913, the church Mutual Improvement Associations gave a farewell party to honor two departing missionaries. One was Sarah's cousin, William Berry Stapley, who as a young boy went to Salt Lake City with his grandmother Elizabeth Stapley and great-grandfather John Steele. He had since grown up, a handsome, square-jawed man, and worked for the Consolidated Wagon and Machine Company in Salt Lake until he returned to Kanarra in early 1913. He was now headed to the Southern States Mission where his grandfather William S. Berry had been murdered August 10, 1884.[61] The other missionary was John Henry Williams, a blue-eyed sheep herder of medium height who was headed to the Eastern States. The farewell culminated in a shared cash gift of the money raised, including a donation of twenty-four dollars from the Young Ladies, besides the bundle shower the women gave the night before when "each received twelve pairs of colored socks and a handkerchief from those in attendance."[62]

It was probably that night Vic and Sarah quietly left Joel and Kate at the dance. They went through the block from the church to Sarah's house and, instead of turning on the gas lights or coaxing up a fire, Vic urged Sarah to show her love for him and promised that in return he would investigate the Mormon faith. That odd combination worked. They crawled under the homemade patchwork quilts in her parents' bed by the window facing the schoolhouse and made love. Reba and Reva, in their shoulder to ankle nightgowns, were supposedly sleeping in the same bedroom and it was very dark, but "we just heard the bedsprings squeaking, that's how we knew something was going on." Vic suddenly heard the twins whispering—they were trying to figure out what was causing the noise—and realized they were awake. "Shh!" he said. Then he and Sarah lay there quietly until the girls did fall asleep.[63]

The consequences were quick. Sarah soon suspected she was pregnant. A proud woman, she could hardly relish following her Kanarra neighbor Ratie Balser Wood's example by sending her father to Sunday Services to beg the gossipy town's forgiveness.

There had been other humiliating town sex scandals. One of Sarah's relatives was on a mission for three months serving God and the church when he got a letter demanding he come home because a girl in town was pregnant and identified him as the father. He wrote back and said he "had no business with her at all."[64] The church authorities wrote again and demanded he come home. He went back to Kanarra and the social pressure was so intense that he married the girl, and—so an unconfirmed report says—she later confessed to him that her stepfather had sired the child.

Furthermore, unmarried intercourse—fornication—was unlawful and prosecuted. In 1920 Velma Stapley, a grandniece of James Stapley, had an illegitimate son, Richard Weldon Stapley, by a blue-eyed farm hand named Heber C. Kimball Jenson—grandson of John Steele's friend George Wood.[65] Within a year, Vic's cousin Viola Davis had an illegitimate daughter that she said was fathered by Sarah's cousin William Basil Williams, nicknamed "Dill." (Viola made up a marriage to a "Mr. Brown" and her daughter was known in the family as "Lorna Brown.")

Williams and Jenson each pled guilty to fornication. They could have been jailed for up to six months and fined up to a hundred dollars. Judge D. H. Morris—described as "short, florid, self-confident and even bombastic, at times"[66]—was disgusted that the county jail had "been condemned by the health officers as unsanitary." (C. F. Emery, the state Board of Health Inspector, bluntly warned four years earlier that it smacked "of the Siberian dungeons of years ago" and said it was so bad it should be sealed "so that no one can get into it."[67]) Judge Morris couldn't imprison them so he fined each of them a hundred dollars and "expressed regret that a heavier penalty could not be imposed." He commented that "recently a young man had been convicted of stealing one sheep and under the law the court was compelled to sentence him to the State prison for a period of not less than one nor more than ten years;

and it looked like more value was placed upon one sheep than the virtue of a young girl."[68]

Without a marriage, Victor could look at jail—if it was sanitary enough. And besides the public humiliation, Sarah had the dead weight of her sainted ancestors. None of them was ever known to have committed such indiscretions and few to have even acknowledged human sexuality; John Steele's earthly sensuality was the exception. Overwhelmed with fear, she wrote a very emotional letter to Vic that was paraphrased by someone who read it as, "Now I've proved my love for you, you prove your love for me and keep your promise."[69]

Vic asked Joel for Sarah's hand, and then with Joel's permission, the young couple hurried on the bumpy road to Parowan to be married so quickly on October 28, 1913, that Sarah borrowed a wedding dress from Vic's sister Maud.[70] They were married by merchant and prematurely balding but mustached Mormon Stake President L. N. Marsden, a familiar figure in Kanarra. Annis Roundy and Sarah's Murdock Academy fellow choir member—Marsden's pretty daughter Florence M. Joseph—were witnesses. (Perhaps they were served Mrs. Joseph's award-winning "Matrimonial Cake," a recipe she picked up in Canada and that was later published in the *Salt Lake Tribune*.)[71]

Everybody liked a wedding. "Hell, they'd coax you to get married so you'd give them a dance!" recalled Andrew Olds.[72] The *Iron County Record* noted that "Mr. and Mrs. Victor Sylvester gave the public a wedding dance last Monday night."[73] Further details were provided by Olds who said the dance "was the main thing," and blue-eyed Dan Barney of New Harmony, married himself the year before, played the fiddle—"he was a fiddling son-of-a-gun!"—with occasional intermissions when Barney would be escorted to the back door, given a drink of wine to refresh him, and then the fun would commence again.[74]

The Mutual Improvement Association minutes for November 9, 1913, show that the young people heard a "story by Mrs. Victor Sylvestor [*sic*]. Recitation by Rulon Platt," and a week later "the lesson was treated by Bp. J. W. Berry, Victor Sylvester & Otto Reeves." That is the complete extent of the written record of Vic's attempt to "get religion."[75]

Gossipy townspeople thought the marriage was a little too rushed and could hardly have approved of their church clerk marrying a man they called "Swearing Vic" because of his bad language.[76] "I know the town was all up in airs about her getting married," Reba said.[77] On January 26, two months after the marriage, pregnant Sarah wrote her last minutes as ward clerk. "They was all up in the air, and when Nell was born they was all up in the air again," Reba commented. She explained the change in ward clerks as being unrelated to suspicions about Sarah's morality. "Soon as they said they got a man to put in it she just handed it over to them and said that's okay."[78] However, the man who succeeded her, R. J. Williams Jr., seems to have always been in town and at least theoretically available for some time.

There was no public confession, and Sarah's name drops completely and permanently out of the sacrament meeting minutes.

On June 28, 1914, during light rainy weather, Elizabeth ushered into the world her first great-granddaughter, Nell Sylvester, followed by Sarah's slow recovery from this pregnancy. She developed milkleg and was kept in bed for two months and dosed alternately with castor oil and coffee. But Sarah and Vic loved their new baby. "Every morning Dad had to take me out to the gate and back after I was born," Nell said. "He must have wanted a boy when I was born because he called me Tommy all of my life . . . Dad used to sing to me by the hour . . . He could sing any kind of song under the sun."[79]

Sarah was busy with the baby, dressing her in long clothes, using flannel and old blankets for diapers, feeding her with a cup and spoon and weaning her after a couple of years. She could also note she and Vic had a lot of commonalities: both loved to read, were good singers, and avid dancers. In addition, they were talented, he at drawing horses, braiding, and finger weaving; she in sewing, crocheting, needlework, and handicrafts. His family was probably more enthusiastic about this marriage than hers for he was following the advice his Aunt Almira "Midey" Hanks McDougall gave his Aunt Irona "Rony" Hanks Davis when Vic's cousin Wallace Davis married Sarah's cousin Vilda Stapley: "Tell walace I wish him and wife all the prosperity and hapiness in the world I honor his jugment in a wife I dont go much on these buterflyes Powder and paint."[80]

Sarah's daughter Nell was cute, fiery, and bossy—traits amply attested to by her pre-school pictures that show a well-dressed, pretty blonde girl with an erect posture, feet firmly apart, her pageboy haircut topped by a large white ribbon, and a look of smug certainty on her face. "Sara and Victor are doun for a visit," wrote Vic's sister Gladys in 1916. "Little Nell has groun lots and is awfully sweet."[81]

But not everyone remembered her as sweet. "She'd come in to your house and tell you what to do," Sarah's cousin Leola Stapley Anderson remembered. "She was a character when she was little." James Stapley's fine garden was carefully fenced in and "When you go in there, you must ask Grandpa," Leola explained.

> Never go into that garden without asking Grandpa. You went round to the back gate and he'd let you in, and he'd lock the gate when you'd come

> out. And he had cherries and things, and we'd go in and get some and eat them, and he had rhubarb all along the top of the garden. You could always get a big armful of rhubarb. Well, she came over there one day and she didn't stop to go through the gate, she went right through the fence, she pushed the wire down and went right through there. Grandpa he just went over and cut him a little willow and boy, he just tingled her right out of there!

Here Leola laughed, and then in a high-pitched tone of mock disgust mimicked her grandfather, "That child! That child!"[82]

Nell couldn't even win over her Uncle John Stapley's dog Gyp. "We had a dog that hated her. They lived just above us. Every time she'd come that way why, that dog would . . . just nail her. But . . . come to find out, she was throwing rocks at it every time she'd come to our place."[83]

Nell spoke warmly of her early childhood. "I was the only kid and the only grandchild for six years," she laughed. "Now you wonder why I'm spoilt!"[84] It seemed everyone in town was a relative and Nell's mother's cousin Joseph Stapley and her father's cousin Hillman Davis were playmates just Nell's age. Her grandfather Stapley's house seemed huge, the transoms over the windows magnificent, and the carved lintels unforgettable.

After the marriage, Joel and Kate gave Sarah and Vic a granary across a lane to the west of their home to live in and gave them some farmland. On March 20, 1915, Vic also filed a homestead entry for land southwest of Kanarra[85]—a great place to get cedar fence posts[86]—but some were skeptical of Vic as an agriculturalist. "Now Vic never was a farmer," Platt explained. "You give him a shovel and he'd probably cut you in two with it, he just wouldn't have anything to do with it. And he was not good with an axe. That kind of labor didn't interest Vic."[87]

Within two years of Nell's birth Sarah turned her energies elsewhere: she helped organize the Kanarra Poultry Club, probably in spring 1916. The women of Kanarra made money selling eggs; efficient egg and meat production were not casual interests but the serious dollars-and-cents activities of practical businesswomen.

Sarah was chosen president, and many of the other ladies in the town joined the club, including Sarah's mother Kate, grandmother Elizabeth, Aunt Louie Stapley, and cousins—clarinet-playing Jennie Reeves and crocheting Sadie Williams.[88] Sarah Isabelle Hales Davis was one of the more colorful members, a woman whom Lynn Reeves explained was memorable because "she always took a red bandanna handkerchief [to public dinners]. And when this party or dinner was over, she'd take some sandwiches and cakes and stuff and put it in that," claiming she was just "taking it home for George!" Then her three children, too young to be invited, would "see her coming, why they'd run down so they could get some."[89] Midwife Hannah Berry Williams was also a member, a woman who "said what she thought. It didn't make no difference who it hurt," remembered Lynn Reeves. When Martha Peterson was moving, Hannah went down, looked over Martha's house, and then announced, "You stay in one place 'til you get it so filthy you have to move to another place!"[90]

Attendance sometimes exceeded thirty, 10 percent of Kanarra's entire population, and more than the Mormon Relief Society could get out for its weekly assemblies.

Sarah's favorite chickens were Rhode Island Reds, a handsome rust-brown and heavy layer, and Barred Plymouth Rocks, a cold-hardy, gray and white bird; she thought these two types a good compromise between heavy layers and fast meat growers and could order laying eggs from the latter for ten dollars per hundred.[91] She was interested in incubators and encouraged their use, though the *Iron County Record* reported April 2, 1915, that her coal-oil incubator caught fire and burned up nine dozen eggs, a "substantial granary," two work horse collars, one pair of lines, breeching for a set of harness, and a pair of nosebags.[92] Still, that didn't discourage her; the club was organized several years later.

The club also subscribed to *Everybody's Poultry Magazine*, which had all the latest information about poultry, featured advertisements and articles about every kind of chicken from Anconas to Wyandottes, as well as stories about ducks, guinea pigs, rabbits, pigeons, pheasants, turkeys and the paraphernalia associated with these types of animals. It also threw in little stories and homilies ("Jim—'My wife's been nursing a grouch for a week.' Joe—'So you've been sick, have you?'").[93]

In 1917 proud club members were photographed displaying a white hen, the March issue of the magazine, and their numerous children. They also invited speakers to their meetings, like Branch Academy College animal husbandry professor David Sharp of Cedar City, who lectured about modern poultry methods.[94]

In addition, the club met social needs so well that Leola Stapley Anderson didn't realize they had a serious side. "I don't think it was anything to do with poultry," she said. "They just made quilts and they done—more like a women's club. They just called it the Poultry Club, I don't know why."[95]

"Well, they was all in it together," remembered Reba. "They all tried everything. They was going to see which one could be the best . . . [at] raising chickens!" And they'd "get together and have a good time, that's what they said. Said, 'Well, if we don't do any other thing but just set here and talk we'll learn a little bit about chickens,' said 'we can just sit here and talk an get acquainted with each other.'"[96]

The socializing fit in well with Sarah's personality. Her daughter JoAnn later recalled her as loquacious: "She'd talk-talk-talking and she'd talk-talk after they got through talking, and she'd decide to go home, and they'd walk all the way out to the gate, and sometimes half the way home, and then she'd walk back with the lady or something—we'd always say she got hung up by the tongue."[97]

The club sponsored banquets, a character dance, and enjoyed vocal and instrumental music. At one dinner the paper reported that "the meeting was well attended and at the close of the lecture, an appetizing lunch was served, the charge being twice the amount represented by the size of the shoes they [the guests] wore." The *Iron County Record* reports this 1916 outing as well:

> Last week Thursday the Poultry Club took a hike onto the mountain, stopping at the Will C. Reeves ranch, where they had dinner. Those participating in the hike were, Mrs. Sarah Sylvester, president of the club; Mesdames Jesse Williams and Charles Parker Jr., Mr. and Mrs. John Stapley, Mrs. Hannah Williams, Miss Jennie Reeves, Mrs. W. C. Reeves. The mountain road being washed out, the party went on horseback. After dinner they all went over to the LaVerkin. Some returned home the same day and some not until the next day. The young people both male and female intend going to the mountain again Saturday and stay over Sunday.[98]

Leola remembered this as the time the grownups "went horseback up from the mountain and my mother, that's the only time I ever saw her in a pair of pants! She put on Dad's bib overalls."[99] The last mention we have of the Poultry Club was a report that "Dr. Merrill and Mr. Sanborne were here yesterday [March 27, 1918] lecturing to the members of the Poultry Club and other persons on various conservation topics at 2 o'clock."[100] Sarah's activities with the Poultry Club continued until her second pregnancy was well advanced, her husband was threatened with the draft, and the townsfolk turned their attention to events in Europe.

9

"Mother of the Ward"

Sarah Catherine Stapley Roundy

In March 1917 Joseph T. Wilkinson—teacher, lawyer, bibliophile, and former Cedar City mayor—was honored at the home of his eldest daughter, Elizabeth McConnell, for reaching his seventieth birthday. Eleven of his thirteen children were present including Kanarra's slender, twenty-seven-year-old red-headed school principal and teacher, Stephen R. Wilkinson.[1]

Kate's daughter Stella remembered the younger Wilkinson as a staunch Democrat and a dynamic history teacher who would read history "until it got so fascinating that we kept hollering at him all the time to read and he'd read to us and sometimes he'd get to the end of the chapter [and we'd say], 'Oh, let's just read a little bit more, just another chapter.'"[2] He was also a big believer in exercise and even took a group of students to Hurricane to put on a gymnastics demonstration.[3]

But Wilkinson didn't teach long in any one place (Modena, 1914; Cedar City, 1915–1916; Kanarra, 1916–1917), despite publishing treatises on education,[4] and he could be hot-tempered. Once he came into the classroom and saw a verse on the blackboard: "Stephen R. Wilkinson all freckled and frail, | Took his honeymoon trip on a Toquerville Rail," and resented this slur against his pretty Toquerville wife, Veda Bringhurst Wilkinson, a cousin to Kate Roundy. It was written by Elden Reeves, short stop in the town's west-side baseball team, but the teacher blamed Fred Balser. "He was red-headed and freckled," said Balser ruefully, "but he wasn't frail." Once or twice parents threatened to "go down and take care of Stephen R." because they didn't like his methods of discipline, but Balser's father wasn't one of them.[5] Neither was Stella's.

Wilkinson unexpectedly raised the unforgiving ire of his cousin-in-law Kate Roundy. He had the disconcerting habit of leaving his classes to direct themselves, as, for instance, in mid-November 1916 when a Cedar City column in the *Parowan Times* reported he "spent the latter part of last week here visiting relatives."[6] The same thing happened when he went to Cedar to attend his father's birthday celebration and lingered too long. The students stayed in class like he told them but the next day Wilkinson wasn't there again. "Well, this is the first time we ever did anything mean," Stella remembered, "but we all went home and got our lunch and went for a walk—the whole school." Wilkinson, ostensibly in Cedar to observe the school there, telephoned the Kanarra School and asked either Rhoda Bryant or Eula Barton to look in on his students. The teacher informed Wilkinson that "you're just too late. They've all been home and got their lunch and gone for a walk and they're out of town, just out of town." Wilkinson was upset and angry.

"He come back home. He got home before noon," Stella remembered. By then some of the students had gone back to school. "Shoot, why we going back to school?" Stella asked the rest. "There's no school up there. We're all down here anyhow." "Down here" was just a half mile from the Roundy Camp Creek farm, and Stella, who was tender footed, waited to catch a wagon ride home with her brothers.

Next morning Stephen R. ordered Stella to stay after as punishment for not coming back to school. When Kate heard that she was furious. "Mother, she don't get on her ear very often, but she did that time," Stella recalled. Then Wilkinson kept Stella after school a second day. The morning of the third day Kate marched across the street to the school and tore into Wilkinson in front of the students. "You wasn't there! You don't know how many hundred times you left that school house with those kids alone and let them teach their own classes!"

Wilkinson argued that most of the students came back.

"Yes, but how many times didn't you come back!"

Wilkinson still didn't back down. When Kate told Joel about it, he was critical. "You mean you went in there and give him a going over right before the whole school? You could have waited until you had him alone. You hadn't ought to embarrassed him that way."

"Well, I was so mad I didn't care whether I embarrassed him or not," Kate said.

Wilkinson kept the girls after school once more and this time Kate talked to the county school trustee, James W. Williams, a prosperous onetime Republican candidate for county commissioner.[7] The next morning Wilkinson was reading to his class. "Everything was just as quiet as a mouse," Stella said. "All you could hear was him reading." Suddenly there was a sharp rap, and before Wilkinson could open the door Williams came in. Red with embarrassment,

Wilkinson abruptly turned pale when Williams suggested the class be dismissed for recess. "It isn't quite time," the teacher countered cautiously.

"Let them go!"

The children were dismissed, Williams and the teacher had a long private talk, and Stella was never kept after school again.[8]

At the end of that school year Stella remembered how Wilkinson summed up his Kanarra teaching career in the Mormon Fast Sunday sacrament meeting. "I had the best kids of any kids I've ever taught," he was remembered to have said. "Those kids stayed there, they didn't tear around, they didn't rant around, they gave the classes like they was assigned to, they was the best kids I've ever seen."

"There was one woman—they've talked about me all over town. And I've been ridiculed, and talked about, and cussed and everything you can think about. There's only one woman in this town that had the courage to come tell me what she thought about me to my face," and that was Kate Roundy.[9]

Though family and friends from Kanarra remembered Kate as a homebody who "wasn't out in the public"[10] because, as she confessed at a Relief Society meeting, she "felt well in coming to meeting [but] said it was a great task for her two rise to speak to the sisters."[11] She was a determined woman and eventually held the most prestigious position a woman could hold in town. Her grandmother Catherine's mixed participation in the Relief Society was compensated by her mother, Elizabeth, who supervised grain collection, held meetings at her home, and donated to various Society projects to help the poor. (Their help wasn't always welcome. Elizabeth Davies Parker threatened her daughters that if they didn't get the dishes done, she would "call in the Relief Society ladies" to make their dresses, a chilling threat that prompted the girls' immediate attention and obedience.[12])

Reba explained why Kate was given this much responsibility at such a young age. "She told me she went to the Relief Society and when she was fifteen they put her in secretary 'cause there wasn't very many people there then and so everybody had to do their due."[13] That was probably only a slight exaggeration: in a Relief Society meeting on February 3, 1900, "Sister Sarah Roundy bore her testimony and felt like pressing forward. She had been a member of the Relief Society since she was 16. And felt well when she attended the meetings."[14]

Young girls carried chips from home to start a fire in the meeting house. The earliest minutes were lost in one of Kanarra's two church fires, but Kate is named in the earliest surviving Relief Society records. She made a cash donation of twenty cents in February, apparently in 1890, when she "said she hasent been to meeting for some time but she felt like comeing to meeting," and next month she donated half a bushel of wheat.[15] (Her mother-in-law, Priscilla Roundy, kept the minutes, apparently in pencil and they're unpaginated and hard to read). Considering the statistical report for July 31, 1890, shows that there were nine meetings held with an average attendance of fifteen and they had ninety-four cents in cash and $1.82 in property, Kate's donations weren't insignificant. She read from the "history of Heber C. Kimbel" and served as secretary several times,[16] as did other members of her family including her sister-in-law, Hattie Stapley.[17]

This was a family affair: in March 1892 her father "said he felt his weakness in addressing the sisters though felt willing gave some very encouraging remarks spoke upon Home duties and the duties of husbands to their women and asked God to bless us," and there were "remarks by counselor Elizabeth Stapley which was very interesting."[18] The meetings were sometimes held at her mother's house and occasionally at Kate's, and both of them continued to make contributions of cash, goods, and their time.[19] They frequently spoke. In January 1894, "Counselor Stapley then arose and spoke . . . Related some of Apostle [Heber J.] Grant's remarks while at conference said he was satisfied that the gospel was true. Spoke of the many little duties which we should perform to encourage the young also spoke of the benefit of the Primary. Prayed to God to bless us that we might magnify our callings." Kate's father, James Stapley, gave the closing prayer.[20]

A typical entry from the minutes reads:

> Sister Elizabeth Stapley said she felt like being one with the rest of the sisters. Said that she knew that this was the true Gospel and was willing to do her part. Sister S[ophia Roundy] Parker spoke and gave some very good advise and was willing to do all the good she could and spoke of being healed by the laying on of hands twice and had seen a good many healed by administration . . . Sister Kate Roundy said she was satisfied with the society and hopeded we would have a good time togather.[21]

The donations they made helped the poor, so collecting wheat was important. In addition, they also donated cheese, butter, quilt blocks, merchandise, sewed carpet rags, contributed cash, fixed meals for the bereaved, did housekeeping for the disabled, babysat, baked, bottled, and donated a nickel each per month. Despite shyness, Kate occasionally spoke: "Sister Sarah Roundy felt like bearing her testimony to the sisters. For when she bore her testimony it strengthened her. She had her prayers answered and felt like it was her duty to come to meeting and ask the Lord to bless us at all times."[22]

Being a young mother and attentive daughter hindered her participation, as she mentioned in 1905 when she reported to the sisters "she had so many responsibility at home she could not come to meetings as she would like to but had not forgotten her duties in the work of the Lord."[23] The society seemed to struggle, even though as Kate's children got older she had more time to contribute. A typical minutes noted that from August 1906 to February 1907 no meetings were held, "first two months owing to neglect on the part of the Presidency. Next three months the weather not being fit to get out to hold meeting."[24]

Finally in November 1911, church leaders completely reorganized the Society by putting in mostly younger officers. Kate was selected as president and when called upon to speak, "Said She felt weak in trying to fill her position She was called to."[25] Undoubtedly she was strengthened by the capable women who were assigned to be her coworkers. Frances Rebecca Pollock Williams was Joel's niece and Kate's first counselor, a tall, stately woman described by Thelma Berry Lovell as "very energetic" and "a pusher." Williams was not only a Relief Society officer; she ran the post office, supervised the telephone switchboard, and revived the town drama club. When her position was announced she said she "felt weak in being called" because she "was the youngest member of the association," but she went to work.[26]

Kate chose as her second counselor the bishop's wife, Susannah "Susie" Elizabeth Williams Berry; she was also Joel's niece, and one of the kindest and most thoughtful women in town. "She had black eyes," Reba remembered. "Real black eyes." When Kanarra's Myrtle Spendlove Davis was divorced she commented that Susie Berry was one of only two townspeople who would never talk about her—an especially useful trait in a bishop's wife. (The other discreet townsperson was Charlie Parker Jr., whose wife Emiah had been subject to gossip.) Besides her discretion Susie was famed for her cream pies, Washington cakes, huge loaves of delicious bread, and her generous contributions to town projects. When she was called as second counselor to Kate she spoke in an upbeat manner about the new job.[27]

Kate's secretary, Betsy Parker Smith—another Roundy cousin—had an excellent voice and used to team up with John Alma Stapley to sing, "For the Mormons Shall Be Happy" at Fourth and Twenty-Fourth of July celebrations. She was described by Lynn Reeves as "quite a public-spirited woman." "She was a person that would tell you what she thought right now," remembered Reba. "If you come in and she said something a lot of times, 'I'll tell you what I think. You don't need to get upset over it,' she says. 'I just got to tell you what I think and then you can take it for what it is.'"[28]

At first even this reorganization seemed halfhearted: Kate, Frances, Susie, and Betsy were not formally set apart for their new positions until March 1912 when Kate, encouraged by twelve attendees, said that "she was pleased to see so many out."[29] The Relief Society had to do all its own fundraising, so Kate worked with the sisters to make and sell quilts. In the fall, on wood haulers day, "they'd go out and haul wood then the women would fix a big dinner and then they'd have a dance at night to celebrate," Thelma Berry Lovell recalled. They also had "pie dances," where the women made pies and the men bid for them, the winner spending the evening with the woman whose pie he won. "Aunt Kate Roundy, she had a loom and she did most of the rugs for the town with that loom," Lovell explained, a job shared with the Relief Society sisters and made part of their fundraising.[30] Under Kate's lead more regular meetings were held, the women raised cash and collected grain, and by the end of 1912 they could report $4.20 in cash of total assets of $46.91, besides two hundred bushels of wheat. They had twenty-four members, held seventeen meetings during the year with an average attendance of nine, and recruited three new members.[31]

When Kate had first attended Relief Society the older women reminisced about Nauvoo and pioneer Utah. Under her stewardship they increased their teaching efforts by visiting women's homes, studied current events and disease prevention, and completed their own Relief Society Hall on the town square across the street from the Roundy home. The building, a half-basement structure locked with a huge bar over the front door, was solid and serviceable,[32] but hardly an architectural attraction: when townsfolk got too rowdy with Dixie wine on the Twenty-Fourth of July the Relief Society Hall doubled as the jail.[33]

A major reason for a new water system for the town was to protect people from typhoid. But in the summer of 1912, the James L. and Irona "Rony" Hanks Davis family stayed at their Dry Creek farm where the water was impure and both Vic Sylvester's Aunt Rony Davis and cousin Viola caught the disease. Rony's new baby, Arvil Hanks Davis, was only seven months old so Kate, as Reba said, "didn't want the baby to die, so she said she would take it and keep it, until everything was okay."[34]

Dr. C. M. Clark, the family physician who charged fifty cents a mile to visit Kanarra (discounted 20 percent if paid in cash the same day), said "he anticipate[d] no difficulty in controlling the disease."[35] Mary Jane Stout, who with other Mormons fled Mexico because of turmoil in that country's revolution,[36] stopped in Kanarra on her circuitous way to Rockville and "her services were obtained [to nurse the Davises] until Miss Minnie [Vinnie] Sylvester can come from Salt Lake. Miss Sylvester is expected in about a week."[37] Dr. Clark was back in Kanarra on September 1, when he lectured in church "on the dangers of flies and the necessity for doing everything possible to exterminate them," and the newspaper reported "The typhoid patients are progressing nicely."[38] Vinnie, Vic's literary sister and Aunt Rony's niece, had received her nursing degree in Salt Lake City on May 19, 1910,[39] and was apparently on the job by mid-September, when Stout returned to Rockville.

But before baby Arvil could be returned home, his sixteen-year-old brother Lemonde caught the disease, which developed into peritonitis. He died on Monday, September 30, and was buried the same day. "Monte was a bright youth and will be sadly missed by the community," lamented the newspaper, and explained, "His mother and sister are just recovering from the same disease and were unable to attend the funeral. We all deeply sympathize with them in their sad misfortune."[40] The Davises were left to carry on as best they could, poor and facing a delinquent property tax bill of $82.83 that winter.[41] For the rest of her life Aunt Rony saved a birthday card to Lemonde from Sarah Jane Casper Hanks Burnell, the grandmother Lemonde shared with Vic Sylvester.

The day before Lemonde's death, Joel's eighty-three-year-old Aunt Sophia Roundy Parker was buried, a woman who "was personally acquainted with the Prophet Joseph Smith of whom she has often spoken; has heard him speak to the people many times and witnessed the persecution of the Mormons in Nauvoo, being in her fifteenth year when the Prophet and his brother Hyrum were murdered."[42] With both young and old dying, Reba reported that the Davises "fumigated the house and everything, and then they took Arvil back to its mother." He had been with Kate and her family for over two months.[43]

Kate probably helped prepare Joel's Aunt Sophia and Lemonde for burial because that was another job of the Relief Society. Speaking of the bodies, Reba reported,

> They didn't keep them. They put ice on them. Cold, wet—cold rags, cold wet cloth, that's the only thing they had to keep the bodies from deteriorating. No one to take or anything them days. I don't think they ever got real stiff. They got limber . . . They didn't keep them for three or four days like they do now . . . If they could keep them a day and a

> night, or two days and a night, something like that. Or two days and a night, they did it.[44]

Susie Berry's most important Relief Society job was to help dress the dead. "It was always her job to make the shoes because she was so particular," explained her daughter Thelma Lovell. "She would do such a pretty job that no one else would try to compete with her and they'd just give her that job."[45] Because bodies had to be buried so quickly she sometimes had to work all night. The women, especially Kate's daughter Sarah, also "sat up" with the dead as a sign of respect. "She stayed a lot of times with them [when they were dying] because she told me that's where she learned the death rattles," Reba reported of Sarah.[46]

Still, Relief Society attendance generally didn't exceed a dozen (the Poultry Club could draw nearly three times that) and Ella Perkins Reeves reported other problems when she "said that some visiting had been done but the weather had been so bad that the teachers didn't get through but hoped they could do more this month." The minutes conclude, "The rest of the time was spent in sewing rags."[47] But in 1917 the Society played a dramatic role in the international crisis.

The war in Europe had been in the news since 1914. "Ireland is not so badly off as England or Scotland," wrote Elizabeth's cousin Maryanne Campbell Wilson from Dublin on January 3, 1915, to M. M. Steele. "She has peace as far as the war is concerned, save for the men she has sent to the front . . . So that this dreadful war might be brought to an end. Yes there has been talk about peace, but I am afraid it will not come yet." Maryanne added that "People are afraid to cross the ocean. Now so many ships have been sunk by the cruel Germans, who seem to have no pity for women or children."[48]

Democrat Woodrow Wilson campaigned in 1916 that he'd kept the United States out of war, which was so appealing that Kanarra's Phebe Reeves Davies, a lifelong Republican and Kate's cousin, voted for him and subjected herself to neighborly ribbing.[49] Blatant anti-Semitism asserted itself in the 1916 campaign in Utah because Simon Bamberger, the Democratic candidate for governor, was Jewish. The *Iron County Record* gave a page each to the Republican and Democratic women in the election of 1916. Cedar City's tireless and tiny-minded librarian, Emily Crane Watson—sometime Republican candidate for county office—oversaw the "Poetical Department" for her party.[50] It was rife with personalities and "Hebrew" stereotypes, including providing the public with an anti-Semitic song, "Jew-tah, We Love Thee."[51]

Anti-Semitism has never been a winner in Utah and Watson's strategy failed: the headline in the next number of the *Record* reported,

> Sweeping Democratic Victory
> Election Proves a Very One-Sided One in County, State and Nation
> Every Nominee on County Ticket Wins[52]

and left it to a Kanarra wag—perhaps grateful to Bamberger for campaigning in the little town two years earlier[53]—to get in the last word. Writing anonymously and tongue-in-cheek to Dr. A. N. Leonard, Republican precinct chairman, the correspondent opined: "There must be a great 'meny' more women and men 'to' that are not intelligent, by the way the election has 'went.'"

"Hurrah for Jew-tah."

The Republican-leaning editor enthusiastically headlined the piece: "We Share This Opinion."[54]

Even before Wilson's second inaugural, the public realized American involvement in the war was almost inevitable because of Wilson's response to Germany sinking neutral ships and the U.S. tilt toward the Allies. Calling it an "irony of fate" after the recent election, the *Record* editorialized February 9, 1917, that war would "be somewhat of a disappointment to those fond but hysterical wives and mothers who cast their votes for Wilson for the sole reason that he had 'kept us out of war.'"[55]

By April war was declared and Phebe Davies was so incensed that despite living to be 102 she never voted for a Democrat again.[56]

Proclamations from the Governor of Utah and the president of the Utah Agricultural College called upon the people to organize and cooperate in increasing productivity for the war. Locally, school superintendent L. John Nuttall lectured to "a good sized audience" in Kanarra "on the subject of war and the need of more and better cultivation of our farms."[57]

Even during the enthusiastic early days of the war a note of caution was sounded by the Kanarra correspondent to the *Iron County Record*. "Registration Day June 5th seems to worry some of the young men," commented the reporter. "Also some of the women don't feel any too well about it. They feel that if the men could do their scrapping on our own land it wouldn't be so bad."[58]

But Kanarra people turned registration into a patriotic celebration and registered thirty-two young men, including Elizabeth's grandsons William B. Stapley, Leland Campbell Stapley (who inherited Elizabeth's red hair[59]), Jesse Roundy, and grandson-in-law Victor L. Sylvester. (Ren Roundy was on a southern states mission.)[60] Nine Kanarraites subscribed eight hundred dollars to the first Liberty Loan, but missing were any members of Elizabeth, Kate, or Sarah's families,[61] and townspeople had such a low-key celebration on the Fourth of July that some felt like the holiday had never really been acknowledged.[62]

When the first conscription list of 202 was drawn for the county's quota of 48 men, Jesse came up at 72, Leland 110, Vic 177. Those numbers weren't comforting. "Owing to the fact that so many of the men examined last week were found deficient, and to the further fact that a heavy percentage filed affidavits of exemption, it was found necessary to call for some 62 additional men to take the examination," the *Record* reported on August 17. Jesse and Leland were examined in the first group and both "found physically fit and did not claim exemption."[63]

The second examination reaffirmed Victor Sylvester as one able to serve, the newspaper headline reading, "Men Who Will Fight Our Battles."[64] Sarah couldn't have looked forward to this, though she later playfully had her picture taken in Jesse's army uniform. By mid-July she was seven months pregnant. Because she'd had two miscarriages since Nell's birth she was cautious and worried. On July 22 she went into premature labor and, with her grandmother Elizabeth assisting, was delivered at three a.m. of a little girl she named Shirley. The baby lived only ten minutes—Reba said the baby was two months premature.[65]

"Mother come up and said that Sarah had a baby," Reba recalled.

> Reva and I took down to the house to see it. And we had a [sewing] machine that had a cover just over the head of the machine. And they had her stretched on this cover. And we dashed down in there, I seen her on this cover and I picked her up and sat down. Mother got down there, I was rocking her. Grandma says, "You can't do that!" I says, "Why can't I?" I says, "It's a baby isn't it?" She says, "Yeah, but you can't do that!" I said, "Why not?" She said, "'Cause it's dead." But I went on rocking it anyway. I rocked it for about five minutes. I said, "It won't hurt it any more, five minutes, than it's already done." So when I got up to put it back, Reva took it, and she set down in the chair and rocked it, and then we put it back on the top of the machine.
>
> . . . She was a perfect baby, all but her head. And when her head come down this way like this, she had this skin out here like this that wasn't developed over her head . . . It just hadn't matured out enough [and wasn't] quite filled out.[66]

No physician was in attendance, and the death certificate was filled out by Kate's cousin William C. Reeves who listed cause of death as "unknown," and the informant as Victor Sylvester.

"If I'm going to lose them all, why, I guess I'll die in the end," was Sarah's sad comment.[67]

Victor wasn't with the first group of four draftees who left Kanarra on September 19:[68] fun-loving Jesse Roundy, good-natured sheep herder Wells Williams, Sarah's go-getting cousin George E. Roundy, and another cousin, mischievous Leland Stapley ("I'm going to grease your head and swallow you whole!" Leland used to growl menacingly at his little cousin, Leola Stapley Anderson[69]). When draftees were organized by classes, Victor Sylvester's name was among those least likely to be drafted.

Elizabeth's returned missionary grandson William B. Stapley (son of "Uncle Jimmy") followed his brother Leland into the service, reporting to the local board on June 14. "That upset my dad, my mother," recalled William's sister, Lenna Stapley Williams. "It was hard to get communication at that time, World War I. Telephone, newspaper. We didn't have TVs or radio then. I know it was a big worry."[70] William B. used his first army paycheck to buy Joel's cousin, the elegant young Sophia Parker, an engagement ring.[71]

William was followed two weeks later by Vic's cousin Wendell "Wennie" Davis, the snare drum player in the martial band, who until then had been herding sheep in Panguitch.[72] By July parents got word that Leland Stapley and Wells Williams (despite brown-haired, blue-eyed Williams's claim to have chronic appendicitis and a broken foot[73]) were to be sent overseas. In late August more Kanarra boys were called up: fiery Will Roundy's irritable son Marion, and a dour young German-born farmer, Gustave Henry Pingel.

Twenty-nine more Kanarra men were registered in fall 1918, including Kate's son Golden and her nephew Lazell Stapley.[74]

Iron County deaths were not long in following these drafts. Henry M. Jones of Enoch, whose appeal for continued exemption from the draft was denied,[75] and Elmer Jesperson of Cedar City were the first reported fatalities. (Ironically, half of Cedar City's eventual war fatalities died from influenza.) Vic Sylvester's brown-eyed step-brother Wallace Stewart[76] was among the first registered in Washington County and he drew draft number fifty-nine. Before being drafted, however, Wallace enlisted in the Marines, along with Toquerville's Maurice Peterson Naegle and blue-eyed Moroni Kleinman.[77] The town had a party for them on July 28, 1917, and next day they left for Salt Lake City. Kleinman, who had been herding sheep on Kolob for Will Adams, was so enthused he had tried three times to join before being accepted, and in an excited letter to his mother about his trip from California to Virginia he marveled: "I never had any idea there were so many Negroes in the world as I saw in Louisiana; it seemed like they were all colors."[78]

Kleinman's fate was reported under the headline, "First Dixie Boy to Lose Life on Battlefield." He was wounded June 23 at Chateau Thierry and died June 25; the American Legion Post in Toquerville was named for him.[79]

In August 1918, the Sylvesters got word that Wallace had also been killed. It wasn't until late October that his sister Evelyn received a letter and found "he is well and still fighting the Hun." Stewart was gassed, commissioned as a lieutenant, and came back in excellent health. All the members of his unit were awarded the *Fourragére* for being mentioned in dispatches.[80]

Leland Stapley, the 91st Division bugler who just missed being killed when three soldier companions went down around him, gave the *Record* a description of his overseas duty. Stapley enjoyed the French wine, resented not being able to smoke after dark, and said, "It is impossible to describe the noise made by the cannon. Hundreds of them firing at the same time with huge shells bursting all around. The lights of Broadway are mere glimmers when compared with the lights of battle," and he concluded that "one's nerves sure go to pieces in time under shell fire." Tripping over skulls, avoiding shrapnel, and trying to dodge gas was frightening and unforgettable.[81] After the war ended Leland was reticent to discuss his experiences.

The drafts and consequent placement of Kanarra's young men on the frontlines had a dramatic effect on war bond sales. Joel Roundy and James Stapley each subscribed a hundred dollars to the Second Liberty Loan. On the Third Liberty drive Joel pledged another hundred dollars and the United States government received fifty dollar pledges each from James Stapley, and his sons John Alma and Jimmy, and Jimmy's son William B. Stapley.[82] Jimmy's daughter Lenna remembered that "they were patriotic, I've never seen more patriotic people than they were then. We bought war bonds, even the school went out, I can remember I was only a fifth grader or something, we went out and gleaned beans, sold them, and bought a war bond."[83]

The last U.S. "crusade" that had such a dramatic impact on townsfolk had been the abolition of polygamy. Unlike the resistance generated by the "raids" of the 1880s and 1890s, the drafts and loan drives of the war years had the support of the Mormon Church. Church leaders preached from the Kanarra pulpit the importance of buying war bonds. Joel was an optimist, and explained in church that "he looked for good to come out of the war."[84] His soldier-nephew

William B. Stapley later argued that "he believed the gospel had been spread more by soldier boys than by Elders in the same length of time."[85] It was more comforting to think of soldiers like Kate and Joel's son Jesse serving a mission the same as his brother Ren than it was to imagine him killing people.

As president of the Relief Society, Kate played an important role in the town's war effort. Unfortunately, the minutes of the organization from 1915–1920 either were not kept or are missing so we're forced to rely on other church records, newspaper accounts, and oral histories to discover what that role was. The Rocky Mountain Division of the Red Cross organized chapters throughout the state and asked members to canvass for contributions door to door. The Mormon Relief Societies in Utah accepted most of the responsibility for this work.

Kate was in charge of the Kanarra efforts and the *Iron County Record* reported the busy scenes in local Relief Society halls:

> White-haired grandmothers, whose fingers have not forgotten their skill, are using all their spare moments to knit warm socks and sweaters for the soldier boys; busy mothers are leaving their home duties undone to go to work rooms and sew on hospital supplies; school girls are turning out surprising quantities of Red Cross garments; even the tiny tots are begging to be allowed to clip rags or make wash cloths, or do something to help win the war.[86]

"Our front room was twenty by eighteen," Reba explained, spacious enough to set up two quilts with eight women at each one. "They'd get around the quilt—Grandma says, 'Now come on you girls, now, thread the needles.' So we went around and threaded the needles and when it come time we clipped the clips. Well we didn't sit around doing nothing."[87]

The Red Cross needed crutch pads, wash cloths, ambulance pillows, comfort pillows, pillow cases, socks, sweaters, pajamas, bed shirts, bandages, napkins, tray clothes, ice bags, and hot water bottle covers.[88] Kate's Relief Society sisters did "all of that," Reba remembered. "They knit their sweaters and they knit their socks and they done all this other stuff," spurred on because so many of them had relatives in military training camps.[89] "My mother used to make a lot of that stuff," Lynn Reeves recalled. "I can remember her making those knitted sweaters, you know, sleeveless sweaters . . . and she was a good seamstress . . . All the women in town here just buckled right in and really done whatever they could to help."[90] Lenna Stapley Williams agreed: "I got so I could even knit," she laughed, "but I can't now."[91]

Sometimes they worked in the Relief Society Hall, though it was used as an elementary school during the week. Asked what they did in the hall, Reba explained, "They have lessons, they have quilts put on, they're like in the World War why there was knitting, and they was knitting socks, they was knitting sweaters, they was making anything they could wear." Heated with a potbellied stove burning coal from Will Reeves's mine, the warm hall was as comfortable as Kate's home for working and talking.[92]

March 1918 stands as a month of special accomplishment. At the first of the month Kanarra women contributed ten pajama suits and were at work on socks, napkins, and handkerchiefs. By the middle of the month they had completed ten napkins, thirty-two ice bags, twenty-eight tray cloths, eleven pairs of bed socks, nine handkerchiefs and twelve wash cloths. At the same time they staged a fundraising melodrama—"In Dixie"—to a packed house, planned another play, and at the end of the month they had contributed an additional ten suits of pajamas, four sweaters, and many more socks. They were even instructed to contribute to the war effort by saving candy and gum wrappings made of tin foil and worth sixty cents a pound.[93]

When it was time to select people to serve on the official Red Cross fund-raising committee, men were listed instead of women like the shy Kate,[94] but it was the women who did most of the work. "The Red Cross made another call on us for funds," the Kanarra correspondent reported in the *Iron County Record,* June 7, 1918. "The ladies from the Relief Society who are Red Cross members, took up the canvass, carrying Kanarra 'over the top.'" And then in the querulous tone this correspondent adopted during the war, continued: "We feel that we are called on pretty heavy to keep up the war activities. With only a population of 300 we have 11 men in service now and more expecting to go this month."[95]

The old-time Relief Society practice of gleaning wheat and collecting eggs continued under Kate's leadership, but now the wheat was sent overseas and the eggs were sold for materials for the soldiers and civilians in Europe. "They had to knit sweaters, they had to knit socks," explained Reba. "And she went around, and they all got together and done that, and she still had to take care of the sick. And Reva and I used to—she'd make us go with her. If she went to visit the sick, we had to go too. And so we went with her too. And take care of the dead, and anything else that had to be done. She was the mother of the ward. She had to see that everything come her way."[96]

Kate Roundy presented at a special sacrament meeting March 17, 1918, commemorating the founding of the Relief Society but focusing on war work.

"Sister Sarah C. Roundy gave a report of the Relief work and conservation," the minutes reported, and the rest of the time was devoted to discussing victory gardens and the virtues of Red Cross founder Clara Barton.[97]

To President Wilson's discredit he denounced Senate war critics who briefly delayed the declaration of war as a "little group of willful men." They were threatened and taunted while the Second Amendment's guarantee of free speech was essentially suspended and those who differed were persecuted, prosecuted, and jailed.[98] War paranoia was encouraged at the highest levels and the town of Beaver was gripped with suspicion aimed at a blue-eyed, blond, Dutch-born, Spanish-American War veteran (12th Regiment, New York Volunteers), Fredrick Bernhardt Carl Eilersficken. Eilersficken had practiced in California as a doctor, "osteopath and clairvoyant healer," as well as hypnotist—who promised "Your Rheumatism Neuralgia, Paralysis, Cancer, Tumor, Kidney Trouble, Constipation, etc., can be cured." He then trained as a chiropractor at the Palmer School of Chiropractic in Davenport, Iowa. With a German name and Dutch accent he was suspected of espionage, forcing his American-born, Daughters of the American Revolution-enrolled wife May to offer a twenty-five dollar reward for anyone calling him a spy.[99]

It may have been his notoriety that drew Sarah's attention as she brooded over not having more surviving children after Nell; she had had two miscarriages and then a premature birth. "You can have seven miscarriages," explained Reba, drawing on folk wisdom, but "on the seventh it kills you." Perhaps Sarah saw a notice in the newspaper in June 1918 that "F. B. C. Eilersficken, a chiropractor from California, has located in Parowan and is attracting quite a little attention there." She got the idea that he could cure her miscarriage problems, so she said to her father, "Let's get in the car and go up and see him!"

"What do we want to go up there and see him for? We've got doctors here."

"Let's go up and see him. He's different."

"Well, if you think that's what we ought to do, that's what we ought to do!"

So they drove to Parowan where Eilersficken put her face down on a table and "went down her spine and he said, 'your spine is like this, you've got four joints out right here, and come back. That's why you can't have any more babies. And that—those four spines keeps you from having a baby.'" He allegedly put the bones back in place and then he turned to Joel, who had had continuous stomach problems for years. "He said his stomach bone was out," Reba reported. "He rode a horse a long time ago, and he got threw off it, and it knocked his stomach bone out and he was never able to put it back in, and that was what made his stomach sore."

He didn't do Joel any good but according to Reba, when Sarah "got these four bones put in right there, she didn't have any more miscarriages."[100]

When the war abruptly ended, Kanarra townsfolk were disillusioned and suspicious that the whole thing had been a great job for British imperialism. But—after waiting out a terrible flu epidemic—the survivors celebrated the return of the "soldier boys" with dances and parties and listened avidly to their war stories.[101] "Elder William B. Stapley took up a portion of the time telling about life in the camp where he trained," reported the Kanarra Ward minutes January 26, 1919. "Said the discipline was very strict but was allright when he got used to it. Said he enjoyed most of the time."[102] But privately he told family members that his fellow soldiers were just "a waiting for the sergeant to get up front and get on the battle line so they could all shoot at him."[103]

Jesse ended up in a logging camp in the state of Washington. "Elder Jesse C. Roundy told about some of his experiences in the lumber camp," the church minutes explain, also on January 26. "Said it was a pretty rough life but not so bad as it might have been. Said he was not sorry of the time he had been in the training camp."[104] (Vic's stepbrother Wallace Stewart and Maurice P. Naegle were the last of Toquerville's "soldier boys" to return, the newspaper reporting their arrival on September 4, 1919. Naegle was presented the Distinguished Service Cross by General Pershing and also won the Navy Cross and Silver Star Citation.)

Reba explained that Kate and Joel believed that World War I "was something that shouldn't be done. And they didn't think our folks should have been over that. But they would have kept on warring until maybe we'd of been worse than ever, so we just went over and ended it right there . . . they were horrified to think that France and England and all of them would send over here for soldiers to come over there and fight [for] them." Elizabeth had definite opinions as well. "She thought it was just put on. Thought they was no use of having that war," Reba said. "Lot of people in Kanarra said it wasn't called for. Just somebody wanted to gain and they just stuck the war on." And Sarah agreed with her grandmother, saying "it was uncalled for."[105]

Even church officials had trouble deciding what it all meant. Brother William H. Lyman spoke in the Kanarra Ward on May 18, 1919, "of the effect of the War and the speculation as to what is going to take place now the war is over. Said he wondered what would happen if Germany refused to sign the peace terms," and then in typical Mormon fashion compared it to something that seemed more real and close to home: the "first great conflict took place in heaven, and the war here is satan and his hosts trying to destroy the souls of men."[106]

Elizabeth and James did their part in the war effort—Elizabeth's granddaughter Leola Stapley Anderson speculated that the older woman "was probably telling them how to do it!"[107] And, despite advancing age, Elizabeth was active until April 1919, when—just two months after Kate had recovered from a serious bout of pneumonia[108]—Elizabeth caught her foot in the carpet while throwing a wash basin of water out the back door. She fell, cracking her hip, and was rushed to Dr. Macfarlane's ultramodern and comfortable hospital in Cedar City (once Uriah T. Jones's ten thousand dollar "mansion house"). She stayed there for about a month under the not very successful care of Macfarlane's nonchalant partner, Dr. Jacob Bergstrom. Reba said the doctors put a cast on the leg, which became so swollen that seventy-one-year-old Elizabeth was given morphine to keep her calm until she died. "We'll take her home then," Kate said hotly, arguing that Elizabeth "can die to our place as easy as she can die here." The doctor took the cast off to let the blood circulate and sent her home.[109]

Sarah asked Eilersficken to look at her grandmother. He made a trip to Kanarra—the town was his last known Utah address in May 1919—and he felt Elizabeth's spine. "Well, there's not much I can do about that" he said, "but I can do something with this leg right here." He told her family to "take her out in the sun and put her leg on the table . . . and strip everything off from her and get some of these here burdock leaves, big burdock leaves . . . and let them stay there . . . that'll draw the poison out." When they did that the water ran out for three weeks until the swelling went down and her leg improved, but she never again walked without crutches or a chair, and gave up her midwifing career. (Her son John A. cut her crutches off periodically because she was getting smaller as she aged. He finally gave it up when they were sawed off clear up to the crotch.)[110]

This even incomplete recovery surprised the doctors, as the newspaper explained on May 2, 1919. "Sister Stapley has returned home from Cedar where she has been in the hospital since early last month. The cause of her confinement being a fractured hip. She is doing very well, but her advanced age making it more difficult, she has the honor of being the first white child born in Utah."[111] Because of their age and additional infirmities, Elizabeth and James no longer went to church. "I never did see Grandma go to church. I never did see Grandpa go to church," explained Reba, and once again Reba and Reva stayed at night with Grandma because of the broken hip.[112]

Elizabeth struggled with hip pain all summer and in early September she went to her old hometown of Toquerville. "Mrs. James Stapley of Kanarra is here receiving treatment for a badly injured leg, and is taking advantage of the beneficial use of the Zion canyon sanitarian [*sic*]," reported the *Washington County News*. The "Zion canyon sanitarian" meant soaking in the La Verkin hot sulfur springs to ease the aches.[113]

Elizabeth's condition reinforced her demands that her granddaughters serve her and Stella Roundy and Vilda Stapley took turns staying at the home. This responsibility wasn't any easier. When Vilda brought the thirsty Elizabeth water in a quart bottle, the latter felt she was being degraded. "I won't drink out of that!" she announced. "Well," said the normally good-tempered Vilda, "I guess you'll go thirsty then."[114]

Nationwide flu epidemics killed tens of thousands just as the war ended, and people were quarantined repeatedly. In addition, there was cynicism and bitterness in response to the Treaty of Versailles. The sacrifices to "make the world safe for democracy" seemed a mockery as the world became safer for British imperialism, and a national mood of restlessness swept the country.

Townsfolk remodeled or built new homes, finished plastering the new school building, boasted that at last they had a junior high, and Otto Reeves, Ren Roundy, and Grant Platt returned from their southern states missions at the same time as the last of the soldiers.[115] All of this called for dances and parties, but that didn't satisfy the urge to move on.

"John Stapley is in Idaho looking up prospects for the purchasing of a home," the Kanarra correspondent to the *Iron County Record* reported June 13, 1919, of one of Elizabeth's sons. "If he finds one that is satisfactory he will sell out here."[116] Kate's sons Ren and Golden and their cousin William B. Stapley got summer jobs at the Joseph Fife sawmill on the mountain. In 1920 Sam Bateman made plans to move to Elsinore. Elizabeth's grandson Leland Stapley moved to St. George; another grandson, Parley Stapley, was living in Salt Lake City but soon moved to the coal mining town of Helper, in Carbon County.[117]

Reba successfully warded off the flu—which killed Bishop Berry—by eating "onions every night for supper."[118] The flu epidemic was mixed with an agricultural depression while prices were rising. "With grain out of sight, loose alfalfa hay at thirty dollars per ton and other commodities in like proportion," the last really good farming year in Kanarra had been 1913, excepting the 1917 potato harvest.[119] Coal was up fifty cents a ton.[120] Jobs were scarce, and that winter William B. Stapley was the first of many Kanarra men to leave town for the Castle Gate coal mine in Carbon County, Utah.[121] "It had been real dry," remembered Rulon Platt, "and there just wasn't anything there. They went to

Las Vegas. They were just starving to death for something to do, something to live on; it [Kanarra] just disintegrated at that time."[122]

On November 28, 1919, the newspaper carried a surprising story by Kanarra's irrepressible W. G. Platt. "Mr. Joel J. Roundy has sold his home and farming land in the Kanarra field to W. W. Roundy. Joel has bought Joseph Haslam's home in Hurricane. This change will necessitate a new superintendent for our Sunday School, which position Elder Roundy has held for 20 or more years. Also, the Relief Society will be left without a president, which position has been held by Mrs. Roundy. Kanarra's loss will be Hurricane's gain." Platt repeated this sentiment the next week: "We regret to lose Mr. Roundy for he has long been an ardent worker in the ward. He has been Sunday School superintendent for a great many years and also served a faithful term in the ward Bishopric. We can assure the citizens of Hurricane that they have a worthy man in their midst for ecclesiastical as well as temporal work."[123]

Late December was unusually warm; the snow melted and tricked buds into coming out. The town organized races and ball games and "a most touching farewell program was rendered Joel J. Roundy and family Tuesday afternoon," reported Platt. The event was held at the church with the following agenda:

> Singing, by congregation.
> Prayer, James W. Williams.
> Reading, Winnie Williams.
> Address, Wm. B. Stapley.
> Song, Lorenzo and Sadie Williams.
> Talk of appreciation, Riley G. Williams.
> Address of Thanks for Relief Society, Zina Pollock.
> Presentation of Present, James W. Williams.
> Talk, Joel J. Roundy.
> Violin Solo with Piano Accompaniment, Melbourne Williams and Arvilla Ford.
> Games and refreshments.
> A dance with the music furnished by the town orchestra was enjoyed at night.
> We regret greatly to lose this family; Brother Roundy from the Sunday School and Sister Roundy as president of the Relief Society. But we heartily wish them Godspeed and welcome more of their type to our midst. Mr. Roundy's health is the cause of the move . . . I wish you all a happy, prosperous New Year.—Wm. Grant Platt.[124]

Why Hurricane? The weather was radically warmer and the Roundys and Stapleys had been familiar with it since its founding; the nearby town of Toquerville was pioneered by Elizabeth's family. Distances were great in southern Utah but the area was lightly populated. A St. George journalist wrote of "Kanarra, so close to us that it almost seems as if we know everybody there," adding, "and most of the people of that place are well known here."[125] That was true, for as Reba remembered, "The people from Hurricane used to come up peddling [Dixie fruit], they'd stay at our place overnight. And then go peddling their things around and stay that night and then come on home next day. Mann Stanworth, Henry and Joe Gubler, the Hardys, Savages come up there quite a bit from Leeds, and most anybody that peddled." Emmanuel (Mann) Stanworth, was a special friend of Joel's. "He come peddling up [to Kanarra]. He bought pelts and things and he come peddling around and he talked him into coming down to Hurricane 'cause his health was bad, so dad decided to come."[126]

Joel, fifty-five years of age, gave a number of reasons publicly and privately for leaving the town he had lived in since 1868. The newspaper said "Mr. Roundy's health is the cause of the move." But he had other concerns, including his increasingly demanding mother-in-law. "Somebody told me he moved to Hurricane to get away from her," Reba remembered, and added, "I think there was a little bit of truth in it. And I also think that we were too related in Kanarra, and he was afraid we'd marry cousins . . . So he said he'd move out and get new blood in the line."[127] If health, in-laws, and cousin marriages were the reasons he left, he was partially successful. His health improved, his daughters and sons married outside their extended families, but his mother-in-law was destined to spend many more years with him. Some of Kate and Joel's children—Golden, Ren, Sarah, and Jesse—stayed behind, Golden to finish his agricultural studies at the B.A.C. in Cedar City. He and Ren also partnered to run the family farm.[128]

10

"Let's Go Over and See President Harding"

Joel J. Roundy

John Steele and James Jepson organized the Hurricane Canal Company, which—after eleven years of toil and incredible hardship—laced seven and a half miles of canal along sheer cliffs, through nine tunnels, over rock fills, and along trestles to the Hurricane Bench. The first irrigation water arrived seven months after Steele's death. Within a few years Hurricane, the newest and most prosperous town in Washington County, boasted four saloons and two houses of "ill fame." In addition to a nearby temporary oil boom, the warm "Dixie" climate was an attraction.[1] Kanarra, on the other hand, "was the coldest place in the country" because of the terrible winter winds, Kate's daughter Stella recalled.[2]

When Kate began preparations to move south Elizabeth decided to go. With Elizabeth's father's role in the town's founding and its closeness to Toquerville she must have felt a bit like she was returning home. And given her age, crippled condition, and James's poor health, Elizabeth looked at Hurricane as a pleasant place to spend the winter away from Kanarra's icy blasts; besides, she could always soak in the nearby La Verkin hot springs if her bones began to ache. "She wasn't going to be alone up there," Reba recalled. "Uncle Jimmy's wife wouldn't go over and do anything for her, and she wouldn't let Uncle John's . . . Uncle Almy couldn't do anything 'cause he's laid up too. And Mother'd always had to go up there every day to her place, and I don't think she was going to get away from her like that! No sir."[3] James was unenthused and refused to go, staying instead with son Jimmy.

The family moved to La Verkin in the Buick that Joel bought in 1918 from J. A. Kopp of Cedar City.[4] "I think they took all the furniture and everything in the wagon and brought it down, but we come down in a car,"[5] Reba remembered. Henry W. Gubler, a prosperous farmer, Dixie peddler, sometime county commissioner, and old family friend, "was the one we used to trade with, grapes and molasses and fruit and melons and everything else, we used to trade with him," remembered Reba. The Gublers spent the winter of 1919–1920 in St. George so their children could attend school and the Roundys rented their home until May 1920, when stockman Joe Haslam would be out of the newly purchased Roundy home in Hurricane. Gubler's LaVerkin house "was on the main street," Reba continued. "It was about—what? two or three blocks from the church house. Big brick house" with one story and a basement.[6]

Though Golden stayed in Kanarra, the La Verkin town correspondent for the *Washington County News* reported January 15, 1920, "Mr. and Mrs. Golden [Joel] Roundy and family of Hurricane have come here to spend the winter."[7]

The 1920 census taker found a population in La Verkin of 173. The town was nestled on the north side of the Virgin River between Toquerville to the north and Hurricane to the southwest. The bridge to Hurricane was unsafe, but additional work had been done at the sulfur hot springs sanitarium since Elizabeth's visit in the fall of 1919 and La Verkin was busy building a cement culvert between Toquerville and Hurricane.[8]

In late January T. H. Pratt and his son arrived in LaVerkin from the town of Hinckley. Pratt had come to bathe in the local hot springs, but his son developed symptoms of flu or influenza. Hurricane had already been effectively closed because of the flu quarantine, "all meetings being forbidden and school work being suspended until further developments," thanks to Sam Wright also developing flu symptoms. Influenza soon devastated nearly all of southern Utah and was so bad in Cedar City that the district school was converted into an emergency hospital. There were nearly forty cases in nearby little New Harmony. H. S. Prisbrey of the town of Washington, had his three flu-stricken boys sleeping outside in a tent. He went out one night to check on them and, in lighting a match, he accidentally set the tent aflame. Luckily, the boys were unharmed. By February, Dixie Normal College's robust president, Erastus S. Romney, "a big, strong man full of life and vigor," was dead from the contagion.[9]

Vic's grandmother Sarah Jane Casper Hanks Burnell left Hanksville—named for her first husband, Ebenezer Hanks—in fall 1919. Irritable and crippled from seven years of rheumatism, she intended to spend her remaining years with her daughter Irona "Rony" Davis in Kanarra. "For the last two months [she] was almost helpless," reported the *Iron County Record*. In her weakened condition she was in no position to battle the flu and died on February 19, 1920, about the same time as another elderly Kanarra matriarch, Orilla Williams.[10]

Besides flu, the Roundys' New Year was welcomed in by unusually wet and, for Dixie country, cold weather. In two days there was over one inch of rain and an inch and a half of snow. In February the storms were so severe the mail was delayed and "freighting altogether out of the question," reported the *Washington County News*. February brought more rain—over two and a half inches—and was warmer, enough so that almond and apricot trees began blooming. "The weather is unusually cold and backward, but visitors tell us Dixie is a paradise compared to other places in the north, and say they are glad to get here and enjoy the warm sunshine," the *News* reported in April. The Roundys, new to Dixie, saw this first winter and spring as very mild.[11]

Whooping cough developed at Uncle Jimmy Stapley's in Kanarra in late February, perhaps brought in by his son Parley and family, who visited from Helper, and eventually passed on to their LaVerkin kin. Reba recalled:

> While we was in LaVerkin we got the whooping cough . . . Grandma would never let us have the whooping cough. Anybody that come in town had the whooping cough, they could not come to my mother's place. Nobody that was sick could come in that house. So we didn't get the whooping cough. And then we went down to LaVerkin, I didn't know anybody had the whooping cough around there. I'd never heard of it before. Well, all at once I started to whoop. And Grandma says, "You've got the whooping cough!" And I said, "Is that what's wrong with me?" And she says, "Yes, you have the whooping cough." Reva got it. We just about lost her. She was sick. She couldn't keep anything down. She just whooped, whooped 'til you'd think she was going to die. We had her administered [by Mormon elders] two or three times. She couldn't take olive oil, it made her sick. And I'd drink olive oil. And I wasn't half as bad as she was.
>
> . . . And I give it to Grandma. And she was seventy-five. She had kept us away from the whooping cough until she was seventy-five but she got it—we moved to Hurricane and she still had to go over there but it wasn't so severe as Reva's was and finally she got over it.[12]

The La Verkin correspondent reported to the *News* on April 15, "Mrs. Roundy and family who have been spending the winter here have moved to their new home at Hurricane." The Hurricane Ward records show that on April 11, 1920, Joel "bore his testimony to the truthfulness of the gospel. If we live the gospel as we should we will be better men and women. He related incidents that showed the results of earnest prayer. He expressed himself as being glad to become a member of this ward." Kate was placed on the Relief Society rolls and bore her testimony on June 1, but only attended seven times during the remainder of the year; she spent much of 1920 back in Kanarra.[13]

Hurricane was now purer than River City because the brothels were long gone and D. P. Cheney's pool hall had just been run out of town.[14] The moralists had a new target when the president of the General Board of the Young Ladies Mutual Improvement Association, snub-nosed Martha H. Tingey, approvingly quoted a friend that "ragtime dancing is to dancing what profanity is to English."[15] (Tingey, who had turned sixty-two three days before this pronouncement was perhaps not the best-placed person to represent "Young Ladies" in the era of "Flappers"; besides, as she spoke, jazz was already replacing ragtime.)

James initially stayed in Kanarra where he was well known and had an Indian war pension to supplement a life of living frugally,[16] but Elizabeth wasn't separated from him for very long because he was soon convinced, rather unwillingly, to move to Hurricane. "Are you going to take me over there to die?" he inquired querulously and asserted, "I would like to have peace for ten years."[17] But in Kanarra the flu was also intense, with 196 of the town's approximately 300 residents sick in early 1920,[18] so there was no safety at home either.

James's health problems had increased over the years. In March 1915 his hand was so badly infected he had John Alma take him to the Cedar City doctor for treatment. A more serious incident occurred in May 1917, when James got so sick at conference in Parowan that, anticipating his death, family members telegraphed for Elizabeth, who was visiting Mahonri and Will in Delta. But James recovered and in the summer of 1918 visited those sons and then went to see daughter May in Mona.

He was suffering from "men's trouble," Reba explained. "Postrate gland. They didn't know what to do with it then. That was way back in the twenties and nobody knew—doctors didn't know what to do with it then but now they can take care of it." When James began to get sick he was given the northeast bedroom of the Hurricane brick bungalow and Elizabeth slept alone on the porch. They had so little furniture that the room was almost bare except for James's dresser and bed.[19]

They'd only been in Hurricane a few weeks when James became mortally ill. The Roundys telegraphed for James's children. Reba remembered:

> All the family was there, circled around his bed. But that's the only people I ever seen that had the whole family around when they died . . .

> He was in the bed . . . and the people was all around here, and we was in there about an hour before he died. He'd breath, and then he'd kind of hesitate a little bit, and then he'd go, "ah-ah-ah-ah-huhhh!" Well, he done that about four or five times, and I says—very insistently—"Can't somebody do something for him?" and they says, "Shhh! he's dying!" And about three times he done that, and he didn't breathe anymore . . .
>
> Grandpa set on the foot of the bed after he died . . . That night I had to sleep in that bed. I don't know why. They always told about setting up with the sick, the dogs howling, the cats meowing. They really did it that night! . . . The dogs did howl and the cats did meow. . . . He sat on the foot of the bed and sang to me every night. Yes, it spooked me . . . Scared me half to death! Mother and us kids slept on the front room floor. And we had some beds down into the basement. The menfolks slept down there. But I said, "It's queer. Everything that has to be done, I have to do it."

Elizabeth and Reba were both still sick with whooping cough and Reba's great-grandfather, John Steele, prescribed "Cuprum, Copper good in Convulsions, Cholera, Hooping Cough Diarrhea Epiliptic," but Reba credited her cure to Aunt Mina Hinton's cocklebur tea. She and her sister Annis missed the funeral to take care of the sick. ("Aunt Mina" was later one of the few neighbors to the Roundys on the west side of Hurricane. "Everybody loved her," recalled Reba.)[20]

The death certificate said James died of "Old Age (no Physician in attendance)" and listed the informant as "Hiram" Roundy of Hurricane.[21]

There was no obituary in the *Iron County Record* but the *Washington County News*, burying the story under the headline "Hurricane for Roads and Reclamation," reported on May 27, 1920, "Brother James Stapley of Kanarra, died at the age of 83, at the home of his daughter, Mrs. Joel Roundy of Hurricane. The deceased was taken to Kanarra for burial."[22]

Leola Stapley Anderson remembered her grandfather's funeral. "It was in May, it was hot weather, they didn't have undertakers to embalm you in those days. And they had lilacs and lilies and it was all over that lawn of theirs, and at night they took him out and put him on the lawn. I don't know why they kept him so long. All the children were there. But they had to have a certain day to bury him, I guess." A hundred people were present, with John M. Sorenson presiding. James's old friend Riley Williams gave the prayer and also spoke, suggesting "Bro. Stapley's work as a L. D. S." was "well worth patterning after." Following a song, "O Grave Where Is Thy Victory," "Brother John D. Williams spoke praisingly of Brother Stapley. Told of some of the offices which brother Stapl[e]y had held with honor, from the time he was superintendent of the Kanarra Ward Sunday School, thru the bishoprick unto the present."

There were a lot of speakers—Leola remembered "that funeral lasted from in the morning some time, 'til—it was dark before the men got back from covering him up. Those funerals were so long. Every old man in Cedar, it seemed like, talked at that funeral." John D. Williams was followed by "Brother Henry Leigh of Cedar City [who] spoke of the honesty and integrity of brother Stapley as an early settler from a foreign land, having come from Australia." And wealthy Uriah T. Jones of Cedar City, a significant founder of what is now Southern Utah University, said he "thot it to be consoling to the mourners to know that they had the sympathy of the people as is manifest by the well filled house." Stake President Lunt also had some comments, "spoke of the Restoration of the Gospel thru the Prophet Joseph Smith. Brother Sorenson spoke a few moments. Said he hoped it could be said of himself as it had been of Brother Stapley."[23]

It was no wonder the funeral was lengthy.

During the services Hattie Berry Stapley "could hear someone singing," Lenna Stapley Williams explained. "And she said it was just a soft, jest a kind of a hum, you know, and she thought it was my dad because that was the way he did things, humming. And she asked him after the funeral why he was humming during the funeral. And he said, 'I didn't. That wasn't me you heard.'" Hattie concluded she had heard a spiritual manifestation meaning James "must be happy in his death" and it was "the right thing that had happened to him. He was happy to go."[24] Though this was another sign of God's interest in the family, there was little family effort at formal sanctification of James Stapley—no posthumous memoirs, reminiscences, or life sketches except a charming little text about James and his wife Elizabeth years later by granddaughter Lella Stapley Maxfield. In his death as in his life, James's individuality was overpowered by his authoritative wife.

Reba viewed James's death philosophically. "Grandpa told Dad he would like to have peace for ten years, just before he died. 'I would like to have peace for ten years. I would like to have peace ten years, before anything happens.'" She theorized the following years when James was separated from Elizabeth by his death were those peaceful years he had been looking for. "Now, Grandpa had a wife over there," Reba explained. "Not very many people knew that. But Grandma's mother had a sister [Mary Ann Campbell] that didn't get married. Whether she died before they sealed her to Grandpa or not, I don't know, but over here in the temple she has been sealed to James Stapley. So he was living with her, over there, eighteen years" without interference from Elizabeth.[25]

Uncle Jimmy filed a $3,000 bond and was appointed administrator of his father's estate and, working with attorneys Shay and Lunt, probated the property before the end of the year.[26]

Soon after, Joel shaved off his mustache.

> He always had a big mustache, big one, out here, and he'd go like this. He'd put rosin on it and put it for his handlebars. And he decided—we'd only been there about maybe a month or two—and he went down to the barber shop and had it shaved off. And he came home and knocked on the door and he says, "I was wondering if I could rent a room tonight." And our mother said, "Why I don't suppose you can. We've got a big family, and we don't have room for strangers." And he went on a kidding around a bit, and finally grinned, and she says, "Oh darn you!" He got a big kick out of that. He never did let it grow on again.[27]

Elizabeth decided to go back to Kanarra. "She was always talking about going back to Kanarra, back to her home, that was it, she was going back to her home. So dad said, 'Okay, we'll take you back home.' She had a brother up there [Almy], she said, 'We'll take care of ourselves.' So he [Joel] said, 'All right. I'll take you back home.' So he took her back home."[28] Almy slept on a cot in the kitchen and Elizabeth resumed her place in the master bedroom. But the old bachelor still limped from his accident a decade earlier, was nearly as crippled as Elizabeth, and despite a small Indian war pension—thanks to the work of his grand-nephew William B. Stapley—the arrangement to share the work of running a house wasn't very successful.[29]

"Why don't you come up and stay with me?" Sarah asked Reva, and so Reva agreed to spend the summer in Kanarra, helping her oldest sister Sarah, who was pregnant again. "Grandma wanted her to go down and stay with her, too," Reba explained. "But she says, 'Well I'm staying with Sarah,' she says, 'She's going to have a baby and I can't leave her.'" Elizabeth was angry. "Well, we can't get along down here, Almy and I can't live alone down here, either. Nobody comes in and helps us." Elizabeth tried to talk Stella into going back, but Stella refused; that missing cow still hurt. Reba said if the family went to take care of Elizabeth in Kanarra, "We'd a had to kept going that way. We wouldn't do it. Or else mother would have to come up and do it." But eventually Kate stayed with Elizabeth "because nobody else would take care of her."

Kate "might of stayed there for that summer, but Dad wouldn't let her stay any longer," Reba chuckled.

> He moved down there to [Hurricane to] get away from her [Elizabeth], but she still followed. She said she couldn't live anywhere's else because nobody had the priesthood like my Dad. "I don't feel good where they are," she says, "They don't have the priesthood." Now she had two sons and a son-in-law. The son-in-law [Jack Kay] made whiskey. But then when she went to her sons' place, their wives wasn't receptive to her, so she didn't feel good there, so she said she wasn't going to stay, there was no priesthood. She didn't feel the priesthood there like she did home.[30]

Kate's daughter Sarah enjoyed the society of lifelong friends in Kanarra but she missed her family and enjoyed them visiting as she turned her creative talents more and more to crocheting, cutwork, tailoring, and handicrafts. "I do remember how Sarah would spend most of her time crocheting," Arvilla Ford Woodbury recalled. "She could make beautiful things, and I think that was mainly her life, just to crochet you know, and she'd crochet a lot when she ought to be up doing her housework."[31]

This sentiment was repeated and amplified by Sarah's much younger cousin Leola Stapley Anderson. In response to the question, What was Sarah like?, Leola answered with one word: "Lazy!" Then she explained that "As I remember she used to live in a house just above our folks and Vic would go out and work and you'd go up there and she'd be just in a pile of yarn and stuff. She knit, she crocheted a lot and like that. She'd never do anything around in the house. She'd just go off and leave it," Leola laughed, "or go off down to her mother's and someplace and like that. But she never really seemed ambitious to me, about doing anything."

Anderson qualified this comment with, "I don't think that her health was too good," and admitted Sarah "did beautiful work. She did beautiful work but she was"—and here she stopped to chuckle again—"Dad [John A. Stapley] always said, 'Sarah's just lazy.' He'd go up there and he always seen that she had wood cut, and stuff, so she'd have a fire. My dad would never want anybody to be cold." Leola concluded that Sarah "wasn't ambitious about housework."[32] Sarah's cousin Elsie Kay Smith agreed, remembering Sarah:

> loved to read, and she loved—she was so clever, she could draw, artist, she could paint, she could sew. All that sort of thing. Really gifted, but

> somebody told the story, and I don't know—I don't think they made it up, but they said that they went to her house. Maybe you heard it, but anyway, she had some shelves there with some fruit on it, and I—she was sewing. She just couldn't be bothered with this stuff. And one of the bottles of fruit had spoiled and it kind of hissed, you know and she said, "Oh, damn you, spit! I'll throw you out tomorrow!"

Elsie broke into laughter and added, "I just loved that, I thought that was so funny!" Elsie laughed again, and asked about housework she laughed and said, "Who wants to bother with that?"[33]

But Sarah was immensely practical, as Elsie also recalled, describing a visit to her Aunt Kate Roundy's.

> I kind of had to, seemed like, cross the bridge over a ditch that went there, and I barely got to the gate and these hornets came after me! Oh! They scared me to death and I, I thought there must have been a hundred. When you're a child, you know, things are exaggerated, maybe there were ten, I don't know. But I was jumping up and down, just screaming. And course Sarah came running out, every—the kids all came, they thought somebody had killed me, and these things were crawling up me like this, and they stung me, but Sarah grabbed me and she got mud and daubed on me and, but I'll never forget that. I'm scared to death of a bee to this day![34]

Sarah expected a full-term delivery, which she credited to Dr. Eilersficken's ministrations. The result was advertised in the *Iron County Record* on October 29th: "The stork visited the home of Mr. and Mrs. Victor Sylvester October 16 [at 5:10 p.m.], leaving them a fine baby girl. All concerned doing nicely." This baby, whom they named Joan and pronounced "JoAnn" (which spelling she later adopted), was my mother. Undoubtedly those at the birth were not only the baby's grandmother Kate, but her great-grandmother, Elizabeth, while newlywed Dr. J. W. Bergstrom also assisted and signed the birth certificate.[35]

Nearly a month after Sarah's baby had arrived, Elizabeth packed up her "bed and a chifforobe for her dresses, her clothes, a wardrobe, that was there," explained Reba. "She called it a chifforobe. Ah, maybe a washstand, or something like that,"[36] and the *Washington County News* for November 18, 1920, reported the sequel under a Hurricane byline: "Mrs. Kate Roundy has returned from Kanarra where she has been spending the summer; her mother 'Grandma' Stapley came with her."[37]

Eventually Kate, Elizabeth, and Elizabeth's daughter May agreed that Elizabeth would spend the summers with May in Mona, where it was cooler, and the winters with Kate in Hurricane, where it was warmer. Sometimes she also stayed with her sons Mahonri or Will in Delta or John or her brother Almy in Kanarra.

Meanwhile the power struggle was still on between Elizabeth and her twin granddaughters.

> We had a room here, and we had a clock right here, and Grandma would get on this side so she could see the clock. She had good eyes. She could see the clock, and when we went to school, if we didn't get home at a certain time, why, we got told off. She didn't tell us off. She told mother off. And we had a cantata going along the end of the school and we had to go practice at night.
>
> "Now you get home!" she said, "You get home!" And we said to mother, "We can't come home 'til they get through practicing—it was about nine or ten o'clock. "You get home!" So, they went to bed. Mother said, "I'm tired and give out. You got to go to bed," so mother put her to bed and she watched this clock and when we come in—we come in about ten-thirty, maybe eleven. We turned the kitchen light on, and got us a drink and the clock struck one—I think it was eleven—the clock struck one. And I said, "Let's have some fun." Reva says, "Okay. What you going to do?" And I said, "I'm going to put some cotton under the striker. She can't hear it." So she said, "Okay, let's do it." So I put some cotton under it. She saw me open the door to the clock. She saw me do something. It just struck one. Well, it struck one again. And we stayed there. We fooled around there until twelve o'clock, and it just struck one then. Then it struck one at twelve-thirty, and then one at one-thirty. She told mother, "Them kids done something to that clock! It just struck one all night!"[38]

On May 5, 1921, the *Washington County News* announced that Reba and Reva were graduates of Hurricane School,[39] and soon there was another crisis between Elizabeth and her granddaughters. The older woman's everyday dress of whites, blues and grays, plaids, and checked ginghams covered an enormous array of undergarments, including a heavy red flannel petticoat, a white petticoat, and a regular petticoat as well as a shimmy. Starching and ironing them was a fulltime job, as Stella had learned.

Summers in Washington County could be unbearably hot. Urie Macfarlane, a stout man missing his left thumb and "Government weatherman" in St. George recorded that between June 23 and June 30, 1926, the lowest temperature was 78 degrees and in the heat of the day it averaged 107.25. July and August were worse; when John L. Heywood's house burned in Veyo the family saved their bedsteads and bedding because they had been moved outside where it was cooler.[40]

"It was real hot," explained Reba.

> Run at about a hundred and ten in Hurricane in the summer time. It was just too hot. And out to our place we just had the thin walls, and it was hot in the house, too. Mother went off one day and we was taking care of her, Reva and me decided we was going to take one of them petticoats off from her. She said, "Well, I have to have them both on!" We said, "No you don't have to have them both on, because it's too hot. Now you just let us take one of them off and let's prove it to you." Well, it took her awhile to get her to let us do it, but she finally consented to let us take her petticoat off. And we said, "Now, you sit in the chair." She had a rocking chair of her own. "You sit in your chair now and see if it isn't more comfortable." She sit in the chair, and she hated to admit it, but she said, "It is more comfortable." So she told mother when she come back, "I won't put the other one back on."
>
> Now, she used to wear a shimmy. A shimmy would come to her knees, then these petticoats on top of it . . . She figured she still had to have that . . . We got this shimmy of from her . . . She said, "Them darn kids, they don't give you any peace 'til you do want they want you too!" But anyhow we took the shimmy of from her.

But that wasn't the end of Reba and Reva's efforts to convince Elizabeth to wear cooler clothes.

> When it got hotter we took the petticoat off from her just left the one thin—what you might call the bleached petticoat [and] the one that was starched stiff. She said that was cooler, too. Well, we didn't like to iron them petticoats, Reva and I, because we didn't like them. Stella always ironed her petticoats, always ironed her clothes. We didn't iron her clothes, so one day we said, "We're not going to iron the petticoat. We're not going to starch it that stiff." Mother says, "I don't know how

you're going to get around it." And we said we could work it. So when it come time to get dressed the next morning, why we said, "We're bringing your clothes in so you can dress, and going to change them and put some clean clothes on." She said, "What about the petticoat?" We said, "We lost it. We don't know where we put it." "Well, don't give me that." "We did. We lost it. We don't know where we put it." We took and hid it. She called Mother in and she said, "I want my other petticoat." And Mother looked around and she said, "I can't find it!" She looked here and looked there and looked everywhere in the drawers and cupboards and everything else and she said, "I can't find it. What did you kids do to it?" We said, "We lost it."

So, we got this petticoat in. It was slimsy [unstarched]. "I can't wear that kind of a thing." And we said, "Yes you can. You're not going outdoors. We haven't got cold weather down here so you'll have to wear this." So Mother says, "How you going to get that on her?" We said, "We'll get it on her." So we just put it over her head and put it down. She was about a yard around the waist. And we made it so that we measured her waist and measured—put the slip in the petticoat and then buttoned it. And we made the opening so it would go down over her head. We knew that would be okay. We put it on her and fastened it up. "I'll freeze to death! I'll freeze to death!" And Reva said, "Well, let's try it and see." "Okay." So she let us put it on, put her dress on, and she had to have an apron on top of that.

Sarah put the lace on Elizabeth's aprons because she was such a fine seamstress.

And the apron went clear to the floor, from the waist to the floor. And about that wide, a yard wide, or a yard and a half, and you always had to have them cross stitches on the bottom of them. So we put her slimsy petticoat on, and we put her dress on, and we put this apron on . . .

And we put it on her, and she sit for a while, then she said, "You know, that does feel more comfortable." And Mother said, "Do you think you can last it through the day?" "I'm going to try it!" she said. So she put it through the day, and as she went on she said, "Don't believe I'll wear my petticoat again. Let them stay lost," she said.[41]

Sometimes Elizabeth would get irritated at Reba:

> We come in, Reva and I, with our friends. There's a fireplace in this corner. We just come in and walked through, we didn't say hello to Grandma or anything, just walked through. Soon as we got out of sight, "Kate! Get in here!" she says. "Them kids was very insulting. They never even introduced me to their friends or said hello to me or anything else." So mother said, "You come back here and beg your Grandma's pardon." Well, we'd go in there and said we're sorry for this or that, and I said, "Well, we didn't know you wanted to meet our friends or anything like that." So I says, "Here they are. Right here. Just meet our friends."[42]

Kate found the "Dixie" weather "was cold in the wintertime," Reba explained. A year after moving to Hurricane the town "was visited with a destructive wind Saturday night," reported the county newspaper. "The barn of Wm. Sullivan was blown down, several trees were blown over and some windows and doors blown in; much of the remaining fruit was destroyed."[43] Toquerville lost half its fruit and several barns. Maybe it was this storm Reba reported on when she said, "We was setting out on the south side of the house one day, and a windstorm come up—we always wondered why they called it 'Hurricane'—down there it's 'Harricane.' We always wondered why it's called—and down there we had a five gallon can there, half full of dirt. That wind picked up that five gallon can and brought it way down here. Mother said, 'That's why they call it Hurricane.'"[44]

A personal hurricane was about to hit the Roundys. Melbourne DeMill, the original builder of their home, had served a two-year mission to the eastern states, was a home missionary in Washington County, and after his move to Monroe became a bishop and a member of the stake high council. DeMill's business interests were wide—he and his brother-in-law Charles B. Petty moved the old DeMill store in Rockville to Hurricane in 1909, spotting the town's potential long before others. DeMill bought beehives in April 1913, purchased land in Hurricane, and became a director of two different banks. He was willing to invest his money in worthy projects, like the ten dollars he donated to the St. George Academy, and pledges to the World War I Liberty loan drives. In 1918 the county newspaper reported, "There are four new dwelling houses in the course of construction . . . Melbourne Demill is having a small bungalow constructed on his lot and it adds much to the looks of that corner of town." That referred to the Roundy home. DeMill was, among other things, a real estate speculator and even after leaving the county Charles Petty looked after DeMill's interests.[45]

When the Roundys bought Melbourne DeMill's house from Joe Haslam, the latter used the money to buy Hyrum Corry's Cedar City place, "which consists of three city lots, a brick house and a large barn."[46] Corry was heading to the Delta country where Elizabeth's sons M. M. and William T. Stapley were farming, and where Corry hoped to get enough acreage to put his sons into the farming business. What Haslam didn't do is pay off his mortgage to DeMill and after three years DeMill was ready to collect. The newspaper reported on April 26, 1923, that "Melbourne DeMill and wife of Monroe are here looking after property and visiting relatives."[47] The property he was looking after was the Roundy house with the secret—and long-delinquent—mortgage. Charles B. Petty "was watching us ever[y] minute to make sure that DeMill got it back," Reba recalled. "He had sold several places there in Hurricane and people didn't come through with the money and then he'd repossess them." Joel had no way to pay for the house a second time. "We had to give it up," Reba said. "If we'd fought the case maybe we could of saved it but Dad thought everybody's as honest as he was so he just let it go."[48]

Haslam, unabashed, continued his annual livestock buying trips to Hurricane and other towns until, with seventeen-year-old Cyril Wittwer at the wheel, his truck—overloaded with cattle and hogs—hit a bad curve on the way to the Las Vegas market and Haslam was thrown out and the truck and its cargo rolled over and killed him. Besides the stockman's death, "three steers were killed in the crash, and three others together with six pigs were so badly injured that they had to be slaughtered." And, in the way these things work, Haslam's daughter Percia later married Joel's grandnephew Lloyd Wallace Roundy, son of "Toot" and the unbalanced Rachel Griffin Roundy.[49]

The Roundys rented a room for four months in Jode Heaton's house—a onetime Alton farmer who became a Hurricane sheep man. He knew Joel's Roundy kin Napoleon and Lauren Roundy, but the Roundys left Heatons abruptly. "We was all outside," Reba recalled, always referring to herself in the plural in order to include her twin, Reva:

> and I think we was going to change our dress and go somewhere to—I don't know whether it was to Mutual or to some entertainment of some kind and Dad said, "Go up and get your dress changed so we can go," so we went up and—we knew they was mice there, because we heard them running around. So we went up to take our dresses off and she picked her dress up to put it on—it was hanging over the bannister. And she said, "Come quick Reba! Come quick!" And I said, "Why?"

> And she said, "Grab it right there! Grab it!" So I put my hands on it. It was a mouse. So she finally—we got it turned around and that time they heard us yelling so they come to see what was the matter, and told them we had a mouse. They said, "How do you know it's a mouse?" I said, "I know it's a mouse." And so they put their hand over mine an squoze it so we could, ah, dumb it a little bit—numb it—so it couldn't move and so I opened my hand and there was a mouse. And so Dad said, "well, it's about time we were moving then," so we went up and got this other place.[50]

"Hurricane Making Substantial Growth," headlined the *Washington County News* in 1924. The story related that despite drought and late frosts, "Hurricane continues to show growth and development." The school was literally bursting with 340 students and from poor construction (the heavily patched roof eventually splayed out the walls and threatened to collapse the building); it was overseen by eleven teachers and town business was booming. The "new business block" included the Petty Mercantile Co. store, C. B. Petty and Stanley Bradshaw's Hurricane Garage Company, the Hurricane Café and Bakery, Hurricane State Bank, and the Worthen Meat Market. In addition, "many new residences have been built."[51]

One of those residences was not of a type to get front page coverage in the local newspaper. It was Joel and Kate's next home. Late in 1923 Joel traded two horses to Morris Hinton, his new neighbor, for two lots and scavenged a corrugated lean-to and hauled it to the lot to make a three sided, dirt floor, partly roofed building. "The open side was on the east side," Reba remembered. "We had a door in the north and a door in the south. And then we put a partition in it to make two rooms." It was made of rough boards with

> cracks about an eighth of an inch, and it was breezy and it was in the winter time. So we decided the only way we could ever break the wind from it was to get a lot of newspapers and make some paste and paste them on there and let them dry and the more paper we could put on it, the warmer it got. So we got about eight papers on it, on the inside . . . When we got tired and wanted to do anything, we'd go around the walls and read [she chuckled].[52]

The corrugated tin roof panels were about one tin short of covering the house and when the first rain and snow came on December 29, 1923: "Next morning when we woke up, Annis and Reva and I was in one bed and when we woke up we had snow on us. So Dad said, 'Well, that won't do,' so he worked around with it until he got another tin and put on there."[53]

At first Elizabeth's bed in the Roundy house was in the kitchen with Reva and Reba, but later she had her own room. Still later, "We decided to have a commode put in the room where Grandma was . . . so we wouldn't have to go outdoors so far. So we was digging around outside, and he [Dad] made a hole in the ground, and dug in a bit more, and went down to the ground. The dirt kept going down, down, and down." In most places in Hurricane bedrock was so close to the surface that it was impossible to dig a basement. "And he said, 'Well, why don't we just put it right there and use that as a cesspool?' So we did. So she didn't have to go outdoors so much then."[54]

Settled in at last, Kate finally took Joel to Cedar City to see about his stomach problems. "We are glad to learn that Uncle Joel J. Roundy who was operated on at the county hospital, was not afflicted with ulcers of the stomach as was feared," the *Iron County Record* reported early in 1924. "His trouble was caused by a diseased appendix, which was removed. He is reported as getting along nicely."[55] Reba said Joel's appendix "was just like—steel. Throwed them on the floor . . . His appendix was hard," she amplified, "and they said as the food left the stomach and hit the appendix it threw it back into the stomach and that made the stomach sore, because it didn't digest. Or digested too fast." Dr. Menzies MacFarlane said, "That's what's been giving you the trouble," and added, "You won't be bothered with that anymore."[56]

But that didn't stop the pain and his cousin Minerva "Nerve" Williams told him that Hurricane's Dr. Russell Aiken said he had cancer. Joel was concerned enough he prayed in the chaparral at his own little sacred grove on a hill northwest of his home where he went to meditate, reminiscent of the grove of the founding prophet of his faith, Joseph Smith. He secreted himself in the thickets of the shrubs and challenged God: "Lord, I've found out what's wrong with me. Now, with your help and the medicine, if I'll do what's asked me in the church I expect you to cure me." And, Reba said, "From that day on, everything they asked him to do, he never turned it down. He had as high as twelve, thirteen jobs in the church and he never turned any of them down no matter how sick he'd be in bed. They asked him to come and do something he'd get right up and do it. And he cured the cancer by faith."[57]

But he didn't rely just on faith: he confronted Aiken about not telling him about the cancer. Aiken is reported to have said, "I was afraid you wouldn't do anything, most people are scared when they got cancer." "Well I'm not," Joel responded, and asked for a diet. Aiken told him to just drink milk, but Joel's daughter Sarah, who had studied nutrition, told him, "You can't live on milk up to the farm," and they both went back to the doctor, who told him to also eat cornflakes.[58]

Reva got him to add chicken soup to his diet and when he recovered he visited Dr. Aiken, who had moved to Kanab. "You don't have any cancer," Aiken allegedly told him. "You never have had any cancer." On his ninety-fourth birthday I visited Dr. Aiken, who remembered Joel Roundy. "The family tells the story that he had a stomach cancer that you diagnosed and that he lived on milk and cornflakes for a year and a half and that cured it," I said.

"Oh you bet! You bet. Wonderful!" was the enigmatic response.

"Do you remember anything about that?"

"No," Dr. Aiken laughed. "I don't remember that part."[59]

For the Roundys, Hurricane poverty meant hard but often interesting and enjoyable work. Joel, who loved experimental gardening, planted a garden with black currents, grapevines, Himalaya berries, and vegetables, and built a chicken coop. "The Lord will bless them that's poor," Joel asserted. "He'll bless me. If I don't make too much here I'll get it there." Reba remembered that:

> We didn't have much money so we had to herd our cows. So Dad would get out in the morning and take them out around through the ditch banks and along the fields and along the country there and feed his cows. We could sell milk so we sold enough milk to keep us eating—and when he got back then I took the turn of going around. And we were out there—we done that quite a little bit—went to work for somebody and got some wood and we had a wood stove, worked and got some wood. We planted trees and we planted Himalaya bushes. We put the corral there and then finally he got enough money and built his own barn . . .
>
> So I stayed there and helped. I raised the garden and milked the cows.

In the summer Joel worked on the Kanarra farm with sons Ren and Jesse and helped with ditch work to keep the family water rights. In the winter Joel lived and worked at the Hurricane homestead.[60]

"But we worked there and went into the stores and run a little bill and then paid off part at a time. [Emanuel] Stanworth helped him out several ways. Some of the others helped him and we got along all right. Then he worked in, for the church," Reba recalled.[61]

Joel attributed his problems to evil forces.

> The devil was always after my Dad and if he got a chance to sell a cow or a yearling, why if he didn't sell it right then, the next day it would be dead. He had six or eight, I don't know which, yearlings that were just ready, top price, and ready to sell but somebody come and offered to buy them and he thought they ought to be just a little bit more. Ren and Jesse was in Beaver going to school [the winter of 1912–1913], and so he turned them down, and [said] "Let's wait 'til tomorrow," and next morning, why, they was all dead. If he had a chance to sell a horse—we raised horses—not as a living, we just had horses, and if the mares had colts, why—one day he come up, we had one, that Mann [Stanworth] come down and wanted it and he said, "Take it." He said, "It'll be dead in the morning if you don't take it." That's what he told him. And he said the devil was always after him, and he was after him all the time. And he never was once what you call plentiful of money. He kept enough to feed his family and that, but never had any spare.[62]

Someone else was having problems in the spring of 1923. In late May, Joel learned that President Warren G. Harding was making a western tour—"the Voyage of Understanding"—and was going to dedicate the new branch of the Union Pacific Railroad in Cedar and go through Toquerville on his way to visit Zion National Park. The "Voyage" itself would end in Alaska, where the president hoped to settle territorial and administrative conflicts. Harding had specific reasons for leaving Washington: his crony Jess Smith had recently committed suicide, the scandals of the administration were beginning to surface, and the president wanted to focus attention on his accomplishments and whip up enthusiasm for the World Court.[63] In addition, Harding's unlikely pal Utah Senator Reed Smoot showed the president and his wife pictures of southern Utah and got them excited to visit.[64]

"Come on, Grandma," Joel told Elizabeth on the day the president was to arrive, "let's go over and see President Harding."[65] Both were Republicans—Joel had been a member of the committee on credentials of the Iron County Republican party in 1906 and chosen to attend the state convention.[66] Neither needed convincing that this was one of the country's finest leaders and both appreciated the fact that Harding was the first President of the United States to visit southern Utah. County Commission Chair, Henry T. Atkin, was so excited he declared the day a "County Holiday" so people could see their president, and a good omen was a refreshing and welcome rain—the first in three months—when the news was announced.[67]

"A Great Day for Utah's Dixie," blared the *Washington County News*, announcing "Wednesday, June 27, 1923, will go down in the history of Washington county as a red-letter day for on this day the beloved president of this great republic visited them, spoke to them, and shook hands with them, making them feel that he was one of them and one with them in all true and lofty ambitions for our great country."[68]

Under the shady old locust trees on the east side of Toquerville's main street and just north of the old church house, town members built an elegant platform carpeted and draped with red, white, and blue, covered with flags, and perfumed by vases full of fresh flowers. On a tall poplar near the platform was St. George's large national flag, and everywhere flags, bunting, and patriotic displays reminded townsfolk of the event. Even the ropes reserving part of the roadway for the president were entwined with "national bunting." A large white banner stretching across the street announced, "Welcome to Washington County, Utah's Dixie."[69]

The American Legion Moroni Kleinman Post 103 was out in full uniform, with Post Commander Edwin K. Slack serving as marshal, overseeing the medal-sporting "boys" who were assigned to maintain order in an obedient crowd that needed no officers.[70] Maurice Naegle, with his impressive medals, stood out.[71] Inquisitive Leland Bringhurst, treasurer of Post 103,[72] and Harry Slack—crippled by tuberculosis of the hips and injured by A. C. Peterson in a reckless car accident[73]—took Harding's Secret Service men to George Judd's bootleg outlet in LaVerkin. And, remembered Edwin K. Slack, got "them drunker than a Lord and when they come back they was wearing the badges and things of these guards,"[74] which may have been why two policemen and Governor Mabey's chauffeur were misplaced on the trip.[75] Or, as the tactful *Salt Lake Tribune* put it, "The journey was broken by restful stops for refreshments."[76] (Judd was arrested before year's end and fined one hundred dollars for illegal possession of liquor.[77])

"As the presidential party topped the hill approaching Toquerville," wrote Nell Murbarger, "the old town bell began pealing vigorously and was kept ringing until the nation's chief executive was seated."[78]

Elizabeth was invited to join other dignitaries on the stand with the president. "On the rear of the platform on which the president was to speak, were situated pioneers, early settlers and two elderly ladies of the first handcart company to cross the plains, Mrs. Mary Ann Savage and Mrs. Adelaide Savage. Occupying a special seat of honor on the platform was Mrs. Elizabeth Steel[e] Stapley, who has the distinction of being the first white child born in Utah (Aug 9, 1847)," the *Washington County News* reported.[79]

"At exactly 11 o'clock President Harding arrived amid cheering and handclapping from the crowd, which he smilingly acknowledged."[80] The twenty-four carloads of people in his party included Secret Service men, stenographers, correspondents, photographers, and representatives of Pathé News, Fox Film Company, International News Reel Company, Keystone View Company, and Pictorial News. Following them were representatives of the major newspapers, already beginning to be displaced by movies, films, and newsreels. Harding's official party was followed by forty cars of eager and curious Utahns. A St. Louis sunburn the president received three days earlier covered his fatigue and yellow pallor. "Senator Reed Smoot and Governor Mabey introduced him and Mrs. Harding to the pioneers and others seated on the platform, the president and his lady showing much interest in the medals worn by them and in Mrs. Stapley, the first white woman born in the state," the paper explained.[81]

A photographer took a picture of the platform guests including broad-lapped Elizabeth in her gingham dress and flowered hat seated next to Harding's wife, "Duchess," with the President to the left of Mrs. Harding. Harding's face looks pasty and embalmed—he was suffering from painful hemorrhoids—an impression reinforced by the photographic hand tinting and eerily intensified by the funeral bouquets of flowers almost obscuring him.[82] Elizabeth later proudly had large copies of this picture made for each of her children—all the people in the photo except herself and President and Mrs. Harding airbrushed out.

In his brief address Harding paid tribute to Elizabeth and the other pioneers, saying,

> It takes courage for men and women to leave peaceful homes and lead out into the wilderness to build up homes for themselves and those to follow them. It is a great pleasure to me to meet you people of the south, to see your great country and what you have done. It must be a great satisfaction to you pioneers to have made the wilderness blossom by your efforts, and this must be your reward. Surely God had a purpose when he prompted these pioneers, and I have a reverent regard for them. I consider pioneering the greatest thing in the world; it takes energy and courage and gives greater satisfaction than anything else. There is no place in America can offer a finer company of Americans than I see before me now. I am prouder than ever of being president of such a country as ours. I am told that this is the first time a president of this country has visited you; they will come oftener in the future. I am happy to have met you and wish you all every success.[83]

After a few congratulatory remarks from Mrs. Harding and more photographs, sixty girls representing the towns of Toquerville, Hurricane, and LaVerkin placed a basket of fruit and a bouquet of roses in each of the cars belonging to Harding's official party. Toquerville's little Norma Bringhurst—chosen by a drawing—gave the president "a big beautiful hand-woven Indian basket" of Dixie fruit with a "horseshoe of flowers" from the community.[84] Showing every evidence of pleasure and gratitude, the affable president and his party went up to Zion's Park, stopping on the way in Virgin, Rockville, and Springdale to admire banners, flags, and bunting displayed in their honor.

In Springdale old John Dennett and A. D. Gifford led the village pipe and drum corps in a lusty welcome, just as they had done for Brigham Young so many years before.[85] The Springdale band followed the president to the park, where he and the sixty-nine members of his official party, and a crowd of more than seven hundred spectators, were entertained in turn by the Springdale martial band, the St. George brass band, and the Dixie band. They played Henry Fillmore's "Men of Ohio" as a personal tribute to the Ohio-born president, followed by renditions of "America," "Build Thee More Stately Mansions," "O Ye Mountains High," "Utah We Love Thee," "Pilgrims' Chorus," and "The Star Spangled Banner."

"Boys, that's fine!" the enthusiastic president told the musicians. "I used to play in the band myself." When the Springdale martial band finished one lively tune he admitted, "I've never heard better drumming in my life!" This completely won over the band members and one of them—a Democrat—wrote, "What more could we ask?"[86]

Recently widowed Rone Spillsbury, who began every sentence with the phrase, "By the gods," felt like he had finally been introduced to those deities when Governor Mabey astride Rone's sorrel horse joined Harding, wearing a large blue bandana and sans coat and tie, to ride up the Zion Narrows with Herbert Hoover, Senator Smoot, and Anthony W. Ivins of the LDS Church First Presidency. Here they admired the scenery for two hours, and later Harding commented that "the greatest creations of the Almighty in the majestic natural wonders of Zion National park . . . inspired a deeper religious conviction" in him. Finally at 4 p.m. the president left the park, he and his wife stopping in Toquerville again to shake hands with every single member of a huge crowd. (The President was so impressed with Zion Park that when he got to Yellowstone he compared everything to what he'd seen in Utah.[87])

Southern Utahns were enthralled with the incompetent, adulterous, and very handsome president. "A magnificent specimen of physical manhood,"

Dixie historian and St. George band member Andrew Karl Larson wrote. "We was all just thrilled," remembered Ella Batty Reeves, who shook hands with him that day in Toquerville, "we thought that was something that would never happen again."[88]

"He looked just what he is, a typical American," gushed the *Washington County News* about Harding.

> The president no sooner spoke than the hearts of the people responded. He was one of them and they realized it immediately. He has been with us, he has seen our choice section of country, he has seen and spoken to our pioneers and early settlers and the sons and daughters of those pioneers and settlers, and now he carries away with him their sincere love and a great admiration for his strong, manly character; they are one with him in his high aims and purposes for the betterment of mankind, and are grateful for the honor of his visit.[89]

The *News* ignored dissidents. Walt Anderson, grandson of John Steele's friend Martin Slack (and himself a World War I hero who was gassed in the Meuse-Argonne Offensive), had been chosen as a Republican delegate to the state convention the previous July, but in August announced himself as a Democrat and candidate for county assessor on that ticket. When Anderson said of Harding, "Somebody ought to shoot the old son-of-a-bitch!" he was put in jail until the President left the county[90] but was still popular enough to be elected to the Toquerville town council that fall. Other complainers included a few Republicans who were unhappy the president wasn't partisan enough.[91]

Five weeks later, alerted by a new device called the radio—the one Brig Jarvis Jr. had been demonstrating across the county[92]—the *Washington County News* carried Warren Gamaliel Harding's obituary. He was eulogized in the Hurricane Ward as "inspired by God in the many things he did," remembered as a man who "advocated prayer," and—in a judgment not confirmed by most historians—spoken of as a man whose administration had many accomplishments.[93] The wisdom of the folk, summed up by Ella Batty Reeves, was more subtle and self-serving. "Thank the Lord he didn't die while he was in Toquer!" "Yep," agreed her husband Lynn, "that's what the people said all along the route. Thank the Lord he didn't die while he was along in Utah."[94]

But for the Stapleys and Roundys the honor paid Elizabeth by this president not only confirmed her status as a celebrity, it was confirmation of God's words to her in her father's deathbed blessing that "thou art a chosen vessel of the Lord" who was "called upon to do a great and mighty work in these last days."[95] The "mighty work" of Elizabeth's old age was to serve as a reminder of the pioneer past Harding had praised so vigorously. She very happily became a living decoration on floats in the Pioneer Day parades.

11

"Just Getting Nothing"

Victor L. Sylvester

Vic Sylvester didn't have to go as far as his successful Gregerson cousins—and more distant cousin George Decker, onetime president of the Branch Normal School in Cedar City—to know the benefits of education.[1] Despite his claim that college was "a paid vacation," he admired his older brother Frank who graduated from the University of Utah and became principal of a Wyoming high school before moving into mine promoting like their Uncle Andrew F. Gregerson.[2] Vic's sister Vinnie, or Dick, graduated from a nursing program while Art Gregerson's cousin-wife, Maud—another of Vic's sisters—attended the Branch Normal in Cedar and was elected a student body officer.[3]

Since Vic wasn't able or willing to make his mark through school he didn't have a bank of intellectual equity to draw on for his dreams. Acquiring capital was a tricky, treacherous business when one started with so little in life, though Sarah had a small piece of land and a granary (which she used as a house) that her father gave her when they married.

Vic mostly herded sheep. This was a big and profitable business for southern Utah sheep men as wool sold for thirty-six cents a pound in 1922. But a hundred thousand sheep were sheared every year at the Hurricane plants alone so there wasn't any unclaimed Utah range, and Vic had inherited neither herds nor grazing rights. With a monthly salary of forty-five dollars and apparently no special business savvy, the sheep business would mean life as a herder while the riches of the industry were extracted by owners. His only chance for financial independence was to take a risk. It appears that sheepherding was temporarily behind him in 1920 when, despite his hatred of farming, he was listed in the 1920 census and on the birth certificate of his daughter as a farmer.

"Dry farming" was touted and Iron county farmers vied with each other to see how much they could grow without irrigation.[4] Sarah's cousin Will Reeves told the newspaper in 1908 he could raise twenty bushels of Touse to the acre and twenty-five of Red Chaff, his claims putting Kanarra in the forefront of wheat farming without irrigation.[5]

In late 1915, "Professors [J. W.] Paxman and [J. David] Sharp gave a public lecture here on the subject of Dry Farming," wrote the Kanarra newspaper correspondent. "There was a fairly good turn out at the meeting. A number of questions were asked by the farmers present and answered to their entire satisfaction by Mr. Paxman. At the close of the meeting the speakers were tendered a vote of thanks and requested to come again, when an opportunity presented itself."[6] That summer dry land corn was reported to be successful. In fall 1916, Kanarra's LaMar Graff won a fifty dollar prize at the county fair for "the best acre of dry land corn."[7] Dry land wheat and rye were "a pretty fair crop" in 1918, but later Kanarra farmers said "the dry grain was almost a total failure, due to rabbits and drought."[8]

Mushroom towns like Nada, Heist, Latimer, Prout, and Sahara seemed to self-generate in Iron County's west desert,[9] the homesteaders convinced that dry farming was the future. Enthusiasm was so widespread that even an unmarried lady caught it: "Miss Celia Weiss of Beryl, Utah, was a visitor in Parowan on Wednesday. Miss Weiss is a homesteader near Beryl and expects to leave for Salt Lake in a few days, where she will make final proof on her land. Later she will pay a visit to her family at Los Angeles, Cal."[10]

Vic, a handsome man, six feet tall with blue eyes like his grandfather Ebenezer Hanks, put an advertisement in the *Iron County Record* than ran from March 19, 1920, through April 16, 1920, announcing that he had made Homestead Entry Number 014040 on March 12, 1915, giving the legal description of his irregularly shaped claim (NW ¼ SW ¼, Section 27; SE ¼, E ½ SW ¼, SE ¼, NW ¼, Section 28; Township 37 South, Range 12 West, Salt Lake Meridian). He explained he had "filed notice of intention to make five-year proof, to establish claim to the land above described, before the Clerk of the District Court, at Parowan, Utah, on the 24th of April, 1920." His witnesses were all Kanarra men—Jewett Wood, Arthur M. Willis, Albert Davis, and his cousin William A. Berry.[11]

Unfortunately, after the World War agriculture entered a recession if not depression. There were extended droughts in southern Utah and the west desert towns mostly dried up and scampered away like tumbleweeds; Vic's Iron County homestead vanished. By fall 1921, he made a failed effort to find work in Carbon County,[12] and in December of that year he was listed as owing Iron County $5.12 in personal property taxes[13] (he was never shown as a landowner).

In late 1920, "Mrs. Victor Sylvester and Brother Ren Roundy went to Hurricane to spend the holidays with their parents and rest of the family," the county newspaper reported.[14] Jesse, who had been working in the Castle Gate blacksmith shop in Carbon County, joined them in time for the New Year's celebration. But Sarah was back in Kanarra by early February, when the Kanarra correspondent informed readers that: "Two debates will be held Friday night. First 'Be it resolved that Women should be paid the same wages for the same work as Men are.' Mrs. Zina Pollock, Mrs. Sadie Williams and Mrs. Sarah Sylvester, Negative side, Rees James Williams, Willard Canfield and Noel Williams, the affirmative."[15]

Sarah had enough family in Kanarraville not to feel isolated. Her brother Ren lived there and their sisters and parents often visited. Alice Isom Gubler Stratton remembered when she was a young girl how she and her sister Edith caught a ride with "Brother [Joel] Roundy" and his son Karl for her first trip to Cedar "in their stripped down, top-less Model T." They heard about "deadman's hollow" on the "narrow, steep and rocky" dangerous Black Ridge and were entertained by Joel with the story of the "dream gold mine." Just as they got over the ridge top "the car coughed, sputtered, then died. It was out of gas."

"I've been praying for the past five miles that we could stop," Joel said. "The gas feed was stuck and I couldn't slow down." Alice added, "We were probably doing at least twenty miles an hour."

Karl hiked up to Ren's ranch house—"playhouse," Alice said they called it because it was so tiny—while it misted and rained and Joel Roundy told Indian stories. Karl came back with a quart bottle and poured it into the carburetor but it wouldn't work. "Brother Roundy sniffed at the empty bottle. 'Coal oil,' he said."

Karl hiked back to the ranch house and got a white horse to haul the car to Ren's. Despite the tiny house they found Ren's sisters Reva, Reba, and Annis, who fed them sourdough biscuits and fried mutton and put them up for the night—"long, cold and crowded," Alice remembered. Next morning "Brother Roundy's oldest daughter, Sarah Sylvester, fixed breakfast for us and combed Edith's and my long, tangled hair. She kept sending me to the ditch to dip the comb until she got us braided slick for the rest of our journey. The round trip to Cedar took us three days, mostly just chugging along."[16] No doubt the guests were a welcome respite from boredom.

When President Harding paid tribute to the pioneering spirit it was still alive, and not just in a minuscule shack at the south end of Kanarra. The eastern Nevada desert—Pahranagat Valley—seemed to some a logical place to settle. The *Salt Lake Mining Review* described it as a marshy, wet valley heavy with waterfowl: the name meant "your feet in the water" in Paiute.[17]

The *Review* didn't mention the rabidly unfriendly desert but Johnny Keller of Sharp, Nevada, found it when he headed for the valley only to have his horse give out and end up on foot, lost and without water. He presented quite a sight to Alamo's William Lamb Jr., when he wandered into Big Spring. Lamb "was very much startled by a man advancing toward him who was divested of all his clothing and presented the gruesome spectacle of being covered with blood and dirt from head to foot. The visitor wore a pair of boots, the upper portion of which had been cut off. Other than the boots, the fellow was stark naked." Lamb, "a man accustomed to the desert," realized dehydration was the reason for his unannounced guest's dementia and unadorned appearance. Keller was turned over to Charles Kelly, "where he was given food and water and in a few hours became rational," and while not well, recovered enough to participate in the Fourth of July celebration a few days later.[18]

The proposed Pahranagat settlement site was four thousand acres of good quality soil fifteen miles south of Alamo that, it was said, could be irrigated by completing an eight hundred foot tunnel to Pahranagat Lake. Boasting mild weather—little snow and few frosts—as well as good natural springs within seven miles, plenty of timber in the mountains, and a railroad in nearby Elgin, Pahranagat seemed promising.[19]

The Pahranagat promoters were very respectable and included "James Jepson of Hurricane and Ben C. Grainger of Alamo, Nev., [who] arrived here last Sunday night from Alamo," reported the *Washington County News*, September 8, 1921. "Mr. Jepson, who is one of the pioneers of the Hurricane canal, of which he was the first president, went to Alamo to look over an irrigation project in the Pahranaget valley, his advice in the matter being considered of great importance in view of his experience."

The venture won Jepson's endorsement; he pronounced it "a splendid opportunity for homesteaders as the water for the first 1000 acres will cost but $25 per acre." (But maybe Jepson was just restless and looking for new ventures because he lost three thousand dollars in fruit from a late spring frost at home.)[20]

Vic Sylvester signed up for a Pahranagat homestead, going out alone in late 1921 or early 1922. "He worked out there, and spent about half of two years out there," his brother-in-law, Andrew Olds, remembered. Olds said Vic "had one horse, when he went out there," but made a special trip to Pintura (formerly Bellevue) to see his father Joe, who sold him a colt from the family gray mare. "She wasn't a mare that everybody wanted," Andrew said with understatement. "One day she'd work like hell and the next day she wouldn't. But anyway he bred her and he got a big, nice fine colt out of her, a blue colt . . . And he give Joe a hell of a good price for it. Joe stuck him, as his dad." Vic soon found the blue colt almost worthless.[21]

While he was gone in late 1921, Sarah sold her Kanarra property and moved to Hurricane. "Wherever you move, I'm going to move Sarah with you," Reba quoted Vic as telling Joel, "because I know you'll take care of her." According to the same source Vic explained that "I know if I don't get anything for her to eat, you'll feed her."[22] Sarah did depend on her parents while Vic was gone. "Sarah's father was a helping them out," Olds asserted. "They used to keep them in milk you know, and anything they needed. I talked to the old boy [Joel] a number of times, and he didn't have too much to say about Vic, but you could tell he was a different man than Vic was. You know, religiously and every other kind of way. He went out and got in society and went along with it. And Vic just went out," Olds laughed heartily, and then concluded abruptly, "he went in the wrong society."[23]

But the move to Hurricane wasn't Vic's idea. Vic and Sarah's daughters JoAnn and Nell both remembered family fights because Vic was angry at Sarah for selling her Kanarra home and moving south without telling him. Sarah was pregnant while Vic was in Nevada and she already had her hands full with the girls when Reba got back from an appendix operation in April 1922. Dr. Macfarlane advised Reba, "Don't get out and move around and do a lot."[24]

"Well," Reba said, "Sarah came there and left JoAnn. And the little brat slipped out and left. And Grandma says, 'That kid's gone, you go get her.' Well, when she saw me, she run. And I knew I never could catch her if I didn't run, so I run. That's the reason I can remember it." And then, laughing, she said of the two-year-old, "fat little toad running around there like that, and she got mad at me 'cause I brought her back!"[25]

When the time drew near for Sarah to have her next baby, Vic headed to Hurricane in his wagon; when it broke down and one of the horses became lame he walked the last part of the journey. "But I got there in time!"[26] he recounted with satisfaction of Gwen's birth on October 18, 1922.

Nell remembered when the family joined Vic in Pahranagat. The Hurricane trucker, Andrew Wood, whose pretty and talented wife—Laura Parker Wood—was a cousin and close friend of Sarah's, took them. "It broke down in a wash down in Nevada some place," Nell remembered, and "some guy come along in another truck, and he stopped to help and get the truck going. He had a little boy, and we'd jump on puddles all the while they were fixing the truck." When they got to their destination they set up housekeeping in a tent.[27]

JoAnn recalled that

> one of the earliest remembrances I have that I've been thinking about lately is we were going on a wagon and I guess we were going to Pahranagat, and the wagon was stopped. And I remember being behind a bush playing in the red sand and I heard my mother call me. I didn't answer her and I guess I couldn't answer her, the only time I remember not answering my mother when she called. I looked up and I saw her face over this bush against the sky, and I thought how pretty her face was. That's all that I can remember about that. And I guess that I was about two.[28]

Nell described the homestead as

> way out in the flats with nothing but sagebrush and—just wild and woolly . . . [We] had nothing but canned milk because the cow was dry. And that was when JoAnn wanted some milk and Mom said, "Well, you can't have it straight," and she said "Well then I want it bended!" So she got it bended with a little water. And mother had dried some peaches. She had them in a sack and they came up missing. And when mother opened the dresser drawer, there were all the peaches. The packrats had just carried them from the sack into the drawer, and packed them in there.
>
> . . . We lived in a tent. And I think he made a little garden spot. I know when we went back from there, go somewhere, they sent me to find the cow just before daylight and I couldn't see any cow. I could see this coyote trotting along side of me, and it scared me. And I went back to the house and told them I couldn't find the cow. So somebody else found her.
>
> . . . They had a big pond or lake or something there and he turned the water on, down on to whatever land he was farming, and I know that once it came out all loaded with fish. And we picked up fish for a whole day and they salted them down in barrels of brine and cured them that way. And I remember once that Dad was told about this cow getting into the pond, and had a rope on her horns, and she charged him . . . The cows would try to get down to the water and there'd be so much mud between the bank and the water that they'd get stuck in it.[29]

They lived on the farm until "it come time to go to school [and] the state of Nevada moved us into town because I was school age, so we could go to school there." Nell enjoyed school in Alamo, but even with the children of the homesteaders added to the children of the townsfolk the school was so small that two rows served the third grade, two the fourth grade, two boys made up the fifth grade, and the rest of the class was the sixth grade. "And these two boys that were in the fifth grade sometimes didn't show up, so we had extra time," Nell said. "We did have a handicraft class. It was more than we'd had in Utah. I made a basket with a little bottom and a couple of salt and pepper shakers and painted it all up pretty. We thought they were real pretty."[30]

Reba said Sarah, who had once taught school in Alamo, complained that Pahranagat "was away from everywhere. Not too many people out there. She'd rather be where there was more people, but that's what he wanted to do, that's what she done with him." Maybe Sarah didn't mind the failure. "She said she was glad to come back with us," Reba remembered, and said Sarah criticized Vic because "he don't know anything about farming."

"He went out there herding sheep down through that part of the country and somebody just kidded him into going out there and get on his own and see what he could do with hisself," Reba explained disparagingly of Vic's Pahranagat adventure. "He said he couldn't stick to it. He didn't know anything about the stuff. And it wasn't raising sheep. And it wasn't this and that and he didn't know much about it, and so he just give it up. And all the jobs he had, they told him what to do. And out there he didn't have a boss to tell him what to do."[31]

Vic "never got a nickel out of his time," asserted his brother-in-law, Andy Olds.

> They were going to build a big reservoir . . . Well, they just naturally never had anything to work with, that was all, and no money to back them. And this old man [Jepson] figured that you could go out there and work with old teams. It took money to feed them and this, that, and the other. And the whole damn shebang flew up. Vic told me, he said one time, he said, "Hell," he says, "I was down there a couple of years. Just getting nothing." They worked and they worked, and you know, that's a pretty damn slow business in them days. I've stood on the off side and watched a lot of them damned projects. They just don't pan out.[32]

Olds was right: the failing wasn't a personal one of Vic Sylvester's. There were broader causes as Vic's cousin Arvil Hanks Davis explained. "They had a canal going down in there, but it wouldn't hold. They did a lot of work there, and spent a lot of time and a lot of money. If they could have got it where they wanted, down in the desert to that land, they'd a really had something." The problem was "they got the water coming through, but it wouldn't hold. It was porous. It'd had to be cemented in there: that would of took a lot of doing. But if they could have got the water through there, they would have really had something. It would have been a real farming place. The water wouldn't hold. And I think there are still signs of that canal up there."[33]

"It didn't pan out or something," Nell explained. "I don't know why we moved back in the middle of the winter, but we did." "I think it was right around February [1924] that we came back from there back here in a wagon."[34]

But Pahranagat was imprinted on the minds of some of his children. "Purgatory is between St. George and Hurricane," laughed Nell, describing one of Utah's most aptly named geographical oddities. "When we came back from Alamo, I think it was in February, I think it was in the year I was in the fourth grade, and we came over that in the dark. And one side of the wagon the wheel would go up over a rock, and then the other side would go up over a rock, and I thought that was well named. It sure felt like Purgatory going across in the dark!"[35]

"Oh," responded her younger sister Gwen, remembering Alamo was in Pahranagat Valley, "Now I know. That's where that saying came in our family 'living out to Pahranagut-dut-dut-dut.'"

Nell remembered that "I went to the first half of the fourth grade in Alamo, and then we moved back and lived in Bellevue [now Pintura] the rest of the year . . . We went to Bellevue, and we lived in the north half of Aunt Gladys [Sylvester Olds]'s house the rest of the school year. I went to school in Toquerville on the school bus the rest of that year."[36] Vic, embittered, drove the bus—which was really a wagon—and the salary he drew was the closest he ever got to profiting from education. More cynical than ever, Vic was even less willing to risk anything on hopes or acknowledge that he had dreams.

"What would you do if you had a million dollars?" someone asked him.

"Buy a damn good sheep dog!" was the cynical reply.[37]

Vic was soon at the herd.

After Nell finished up the 1923–24 school year in Toquerville, Sarah moved her family back to Hurricane and lived in a tent on Kate and Joel's lot where Reba found her niece JoAnn charming. "Everybody thought that JoAnn was about the best yet, and she was good looking and she was sociable, and she was a little bit fiery," Reba remembered.

> She was pliable and she knew lot of things and a lot of them went to her and asked them to help her do this and help her do that and she did it.
>
> Some people she liked and some people she didn't and she wasn't going to let them run over her, and Sarah said, "I don't believe in holding my kids back like some people do," so she let them go forward. And she said, "You have to stand up for your own rights." She said, "I'm teaching them that they got to stand up for their own rights. They can't depend on anybody else." And so they did, they stood up for their own rights.
>
> JoAnn, oh, she'd help this kid out and that kid. And feel sorry for them, and she'd say, "Grandma, I feel sorry for this kid, I feel sorry for that, what can I do to help them?'" And they would tell her, Grandma would tell her what to do to see if she could help them this way. And when it come time for Christmas, birthdays, or things like that, JoAnn always put something on a piece of paper, got a little piece of cloth and made something out of it and give it to Grandma Stapley and my mother. None of the rest of them had that ability . . . She'd always make this, even just take a little piece of paper and draw a little figure on it. Just sign on it "I love you," or something like that. Well, they just worshipped that.[38]

"Their home was just as much home to me as mine was," Nell explained of her Roundy grandparents.[39] The older couple was still living in the lean-to fashioned into a house. JoAnn's other earliest recollections include the Roundy house on a hill on the west side of Hurricane, but the Sylvester children's constant presence at the Roundys peeved some of their cousins. Reba remembered:

> They'd come to dad's to play . . . 'course they was to our place quite a lot. The other kids would come, they all play together, "Oh yes, you go up there and Grandma will give you what you want but they don't give us what we want." And I heard them say that one day and I said, "Did Grandma ever turn you down for anything you ever asked for?" "No." "Then what makes you say that then?" "Well, because they're here all the time and they get this and they get that." And I said, "If you didn't have a dad to help you out, what would you do?" "Guess we'd come to Grandma's too," they said. But the rest of the grandkids was always jealous because they always come to dad's. But we come to understand that they had to have them there because their mother had to go out to make a living and somebody had to take care of them.[40]

JoAnn described the lean-to house once it had been enclosed. "I remember when his house had two rooms," she explained. "There was a north room and a south room. The north room was the kitchen and the south room was the 'other room.' That's the way we had houses in those days. We had a kitchen and an 'other room.' And Grandpa's bed and Grandma's bed was in the other room. And at one time there was a bed in the kitchen."

Joel's house grew. "I'm going over to get my house today, and I don't want you kids in the way," he told JoAnn.

"What do you mean you're going to get a house? How you going to get a house? You going to bring a house over here?" JoAnn peppered back.

"Yes," he said, "I'm going over and getting that house and bringing it over here."

"Is it already built?"

"Yes."

"How can you move a house?"

"Well, you just stay behind the fence and watch me. You'll find out how I can move a house."

"I don't see how you can move a house."

"I can."

Then Joel left and, JoAnn remembered,

> He got a four horse team on it, and they rolled it on logs some way, and I stayed right there by the almond tree and the scratchy [her sister Gwen interjected: "Himalaya"] Himalaya bushes, and I just watched and watched, and after a while, here I could see it coming on up the road there, a block and a half away, and I just watched. Well I was just thrilled to death to see that house come!
>
> But he already had a foundation built. He had a cement foundation in the front of the house, and then he brought that up there, and however they did it, there was only about three or four guys and they moved that house right on the foundation and they fitted it right up against the house . . .
>
> And so that made a four room house. And they had two rooms on the north and two rooms on the south and this house had one door on the east and then he cut a door in to match the door that went into the kitchen and put together right there so that it had a door on the east that went right straight through to the kitchen and then it had a door in between the two rooms.[41]

At first they paid their neighbors, the Girnzy Strattons, for water and hauled it home. Reba explained why they got running water. "After a while, why, Grandma couldn't get out at night to the bathroom, so, we didn't have any water, we didn't have water for a long time. A little over a year we didn't have water. We carried our water up there to wash and to drink and everything else. But then we finally got tap water up there. We brought it from Mina Hinton's through this way"—and here she motioned diagonally—"through the block. We finally got the tap water up there." Joel dug a trench through Hintons' orchard and up the hill where the pipe was laid.[42]

That made it a lot easier for not just Elizabeth but the whole family. Still, Elizabeth wanted a lot of care and by the early twenties Reba did most of it.

> Mother went—I don't know whether she went to Relief Society or some entertainment downtown. It was on a Saturday. [Elizabeth said,] "You can't go. I got to have my bath." And I said, "I'll give her a bath." And she said, "No, you can't give me a bath." And I said, "I can give you a bath!" And Mother said, "Let her try it!" She hated to let us kids try things. "Let her try it," she said. "I'm sure she can make it." Well, I was twenty!
>
> And she said, "Well, I'm not going to have a bath! You're not going to bathe me!" And I says, "Grandma! All women are alike. You haven't got as much as I've got." "How do you mean that?" "I've got an appendicitis scar on my stomach and you don't have." "Well, that's right," she said. And I said, "That is right. Now I'm going to bathe you.
>
> So I got the water and I got it warm and I got the number three tub and set it down and put about a foot of water in the tub. So that's when I put her feet in the tub and I put the little stool in there for her to sit on and I said, "Now here's the wash rag, you wash the front of you and I'll wash the back." Well, that was fair enough, so she washed the front of her, washed her face, and so on, and I took the wash rag an washed her back. Then I said, "Now here's a chair you can lean up against while I wash the back of your legs." And she said "All right, all right." And so then we finally got her in and got her out and got her dressed and when she got dressed she said, "Well, I never was bathed like that before!" I said, "Well, there's always a different time for everything."
>
> [When Elizabeth was dressed,] I says, "Reva bring it in. Don't be taking it off somewhere's." And she says, "What are you going to do now?" And then I says, "Oh, we're going to doll you up and make you look good." So Reva come in and she had—face cream, we face creamed her

face, we face creamed her neck. And I says, "We got the lamp—we got the—ah—curling irons and we get them hot and we're going to curl your hair all over your head." That's the way everybody else did, was just curl it all over. And she said, "You're not going to do that," and I said, "Oh yes we are!" So we creamed her face and we curled her hair with the curling irons [which they had] on the chimney, down the chimney. We had it right down on the caldron and it got hot. And we curled her hair and we curled it all over, the top here, and curled her hair here and down.

[Reba described her grandmother's hair.] Oh, it was thick. She had thick hair, and she had a lot of it. She always combed it back this way with a bob in the back. Well, we put the bob in the back, but then we curled it before we got the bob . . . She had auburn hair. I says, "That's where the kids come with the red hair." Aunt May's kids nearly all had red hair. And I said, ah, she had auburn hair. She had it cut off and she wore a wig for a long time. It was way down to here [motioning down to her hips]. "That's the Irish in me!" [Elizabeth explained].

[When the girls were done Elizabeth said,] "Give me a looking glass!" and so we gave her a looking glass and let her see what she looked like, and she said, "Oh! It's been a long time since I curled my hair. I don't think I ever did," she says. So, she says, "You can curl my hair any time you want to," even in the weekdays she'd say, "Are you going to curl my hair?" We'd say, "Yes, if you want it curled we'll curl it."

We combed it, and we dolled her all up in a clean outfit and set her in a chair. We put lipstick on her, we put rouge on her, and we curled her hair up and we dressed her up and everything. "Now you just look nice; nobody knows you." [When Kate got home Reba told her,] "Make her believe you don't know her."

When Mother come she says, "Is that you?" and she says, "Yes, that's me." "Why," she said, "I've never seen your hair put like that before!" [Reba chuckled.] She says, "Well, I'm a young lady now!" So whenever Mother wanted to go anywhere's else she says, "If the twins will help me; if the twins will stay here with me together, you can go." So they said all right. So after that whenever the—they wanted to take her anywhere, "Will you stay with me?" "Yeah we'll stay with you." "Now curl my hair up!" [Reba chuckled again.] So we curled her hair up. And we made her look nice and she looked clean and she looked in her chair like—a young lady 'cause she had her hair all curled up. And she said, "I don't

> get my hair curled up, only when the twins bother me." So then, that's the way she—after that she was okay. She would let us go, because she knew we knew how to do things and she knew that we would do them to suit her. And, she was all right and she said, to my dad, "You want to take her off somewhere's? Go take her off," she says, "as long as you leave the twins with me." So we—that's the way we done her.[43]

JoAnn explained other improvements to the Roundy house. "I remember when grandma and grandpa put their ceiling in with factory. They finally got enough joists to go across the ceiling, close enough so they could put the factory on." Factory—unbleached low-grade muslin—was nailed to the walls and ceiling and

> then what you do after that is that you get some calcimine, which is a powdered paint. You mix it with water and then you take a brush or a broom or something like that and paint all this factory with it. Well, the thing that happens with it is, as this factory gets wet it kind of sags and then as it dries it shrinks because it's unshrunk. And so it gets really tight on the wall. And so you put paint on it, and there it is all covered with it, so you've got a nice little painted inside made out of cloth.[44]

The *Washington County News* reported in 1925, "Born, March 27, to Mr. and Mrs. Sylvester, a girl; all concerned getting along nicely."[45] "Ruth was born in the middle of the day & Gwen & I were at Grandma's—of course," JoAnn wrote many years later. "Reba, I think, was the one who told us the doctor had left us a red headed baby sister. I sure don't remember much about her as a little baby. It seems to me she was pretty & good natured." Ruth soon joined JoAnn as an object of Vic's ire. "I can remember that when Ruth was born, he didn't like her," JoAnn said,[46] and Reba said Vic argued, presumably jestingly, that "there's no redheaded kid in my family. She doesn't belong to me." But formidable Elizabeth Stapley, auburn before her hair turned white, countered that she had known Vic's grandmother Sarah Jane Casper Hanks Burnell (also partly Scots-Irish) very well, and Sarah Jane had red hair.[47] This quick rebuttal probably increased Vic's detestation of "Old Lady Stapley."

Ruth's memories of her father were even less flattering than JoAnn's. Asked what Vic was like, this normally vivacious woman said very softly that he had "a terrible temper," and asserted "I think he never grew up until after my mother died," explaining "Sometimes he would have tantrums and act childish.

Better not get in his way. He's knocked me down and kicked me in the ribs before."[48]

Vic's sister "Aunt Dick" Sylvester Leeds found Vic and Sarah's children adorable when she visited in the latter part of 1927. Writing to her husband George, she stated, "My brother Victor came from the mountains just as I was leaving Pintura for St. George so he went there with me—LaVell took us in the car and we had dinner with Maud and then came here as Victor had to go back to work in a few days." She added, "He had come down to see me hadn't seen me for twelve years—he & Sara have four of a kind, Nell—Joan[,] Gwen and Ruth."[49]

"Dick" recalled this trip in a letter to Vic's children on June 27, 1962: "When I visited Victor and Sara in the fall of '27—Ruth was the baby and a doll. Rex had notified his mother that he was on his way. Sara took me over to the [LaVerkin hot] springs and we had a good time. She told Victor, 'Dick got in that hot water and wallered like a hog.' I sure did and I would like to do it again."[50]

Sarah's first boy, Rex, was born after the school year ended, on June 3, 1928, while the family was living in the Porter house across from Ianthus Spendlove. JoAnn remembered that "Ruth pulled up Spendloves' flowers because West S[pendlove] pulled up ours. Also Ruth set fire to the house but she didn't really mean to," and the fire was soon under control.[51] Because Rex—a future Air Force Major—had a double crown Sarah argued prophetically that "he would travel all over the world and travel a lot." This prediction resulted in much guffawing from family and neighbors.[52]

The family "pecking order" is shown by the children's nicknames. Nell was still Vic's little "Tommy," and JoAnn was derisively called "Weeping Willow" and "Bawl Baby" because of her penchant for tears. Vic's favorite, Gwen, was known as "Itty Bit" or "Half Pint." Ruth was "Red," Vic's judgment on her temper and temperament. Rex wasn't nicknamed by the family, but at school they called him "Deacon" for his ancestor, Shadrach Roundy, who had held important Mormon Church offices.[53]

The family tensions were tough for JoAnn. She "had a nervous breakdown because of home conditions," asserted her school friend, Florence Beatty Leavitt,[54] while Reba said the condition developed after four-year-old JoAnn and her sister Gwen were buried under the collapsed walls of the Roundys' chicken coop. "Little Johaan [*sic*] Sylvester received a very badly broken and bruised leg Saturday when a wall which her grandfather was building fell on her and her baby sister. The baby escaped uninjured," reported the *Washington County News* in 1925.[55]

"They brought her up to Cedar where we were working," Reba explained. "She was wiggling all over the place."[56] JoAnn elaborated: "I was sick with nervous disorders, stomach upsets, I had St. Vitus dance, what you call chorea or something like that. Anyway, it was a nervous disorder." They futilely took her tonsils out to see if that would help; the chiropractor wasn't any help, either.[57]

Vic was rarely at home, and JoAnn told of the time she and Gwen were playing outside when a man came up with a suitcase in hand. "We were just—stood and gawked at him, because nobody ever came up that way with a suitcase clear out to the edge of town."

"Well, hello," he said.

"Hello," they replied.

"Is your daddy home?" he asked.

JoAnn replied, "No, my daddy's not home."

The stranger answered, "Well, I think he is." Then the girls knew he was not only strange, but crazy.

"Well, he is *not*!" they insisted.

"Oh, you go in and ask your mother if your daddy's not home," the man persisted.

"Oh don't be silly," JoAnn answered. "We know our daddy's not home!"

Of course, it was Vic.[58]

Both Vic and Sarah loved to sing, and there were pleasant evenings when Vic—slender and muscular, dressed in gabardine-type clothes with sporty russet-brown dress shoes and his small, tender feet askew—sat with Sarah—big-boned and square-jawed, wearing the dark blues or soft creams or grays that she favored, her long narrow feet up—while they sang in joyful harmony. "They sang one song that I cried every time that they sang it, called 'For Sale a Baby,' and I cried over that all the time," JoAnn remembered. "And they laughed and laughed because they thought that was so funny that I could cry about that song. It was a very, very sad song. And then they sang songs about somebody's goat that was a real funny song. And all those popular-type songs that were popular from that time, I guess from about 1900 on."[59]

Vic's repertoire included "Mother's Prayer at Twilight," "Bill Grogan's Goat," and "When Johnny Comes Marching Home." When Nell tape-recorded Vic singing many years later, she asked him to warble her favorite, "Mighty like a Rose," one of the racist songs popular among whites in the early twentieth century.[60]

"About the happiest time I ever saw in our house was when mom and dad were singing around the stove and it was about time for us to go to bed,"

JoAnn recalled wistfully, and then added sadly, "But that was a long, long, long time ago."[61]

There were other pleasures, especially going to Kanarra's famed Fourth and Twenty-Fourth of July dances. "[We'd] get there around noon, I think, then we'd watch the races, people and horse, especially horse," JoAnn wrote nostalgically.

> Everybody in Kanarra was a horse race fan and most had horses to race. I still love horse races. There was no age discrimination there it seemed to me. All the kids played with and took care of the little kids. We would visit with all (I mean ALL) our relatives. Dad's aunt Irona (aunt Ronie to us) Hanks Davis lived there and a lot of his cousins. Also mom's aunts and uncle and cousins too numerous to name (besides I've forgotten most of their names) lived there so it was really a family reunion.[62]

Reba added that "If they had a dance they danced all week. Then they went to New Harmony and danced all week and then they come back and danced again. So they had a lot of dances."[63]

JoAnn wrote that:

> After the fireworks, or during[,] as most of the kids let off firecrackers all day, the crowd would congregate at the outside wooden arena, the band would start up, and everybody (EVERYBODY WHO COULD STAND) would dance. The men in the orchestra took turns dancing, playing in the band, and slipping out for a drink. There was a lot of drinking going on among a certain group. The kids would dance with each other or with the grownups. As they became tired or sleepy, they would either go home if they lived in Kanarra and were old enough to stay alone, or they would just find a place in some wagon or on a quilt near the wagon, and go to sleep. Next thing they knew, the wagon was moving and, half asleep, they would murmur a word or two and go back to sleep until they got home. We didn't get home until first light of dawn since the dance usually lasted until two—four o'clock.[64]

(Afterward the rapscallion Kanarra boys would scavenge the dance site—the Coble Crest Pavilion was built for dancing in 1934—for discarded cigarette butts.)

"They were the old time dances," Reba remembered. "Quadrilles, hopscotch [Schottische], and the Highland fling, Virginia reels, there was another one—the two step—but I can't remember the other one. Now the two step was a hard dance . . . They had waltzes then too. They had trots, too, turkey trots."[65]

But even the dances could turn ugly. Florence Beatty Leavitt said that Vic would "get out on the dance floor, and he'd get one of the girls to dance with him and then he would just high step it and just slap his feet on the floor and just—just make a fool of himself! And it always embarrassed me for them."[66] JoAnn remembered a time she and Gwen went to the dance in Hurricane with their father and

> he kind of disappeared and we couldn't find him, and we didn't know what to do. We looked all over for him, and we couldn't find him, and the dance was almost out . . . And then as we went out the first door of the gymnasium into the hall, why he came up. And oh, he looked terrible! Oh, he was just all bloody and beat up, so we went home with him. He'd gone out and he'd seen these two guys or three guys picking on one guy—and it made him mad. Now he very seldom got into a fight—this is the only time I remember him getting into a fight with people, you know, anybody he knew. But he got mad and he started getting on this guy. They just really—there was three against two of them, and he and the other guy lost of course. But when he opened his eyes and came too, he came back in the dance to get us. Boy, mom was really upset to see him in that mess. He had a bloody face, his hair was all messed up—and I mean, I *never* saw my father's hair messed up. Ever. His hair just never did get messed up.[67]
>
> . . . We really got upset because then they'd go to dances with their friends and we couldn't go. [JoAnn remembered.] And that wasn't so bad but we always had to go tend somebody's kids so that the somebodies could go with them to the dance . . . So then we would go to somebody's house to tend their kids and then six other couples would come along and drop their kids off there for us to tend. So we'd end up with ten or twelve kids to tend all night long. And sometimes, I'll tell you, it was all night long. And then they'd give us ten cents, or maybe fifteen, for this whole night's work and then we were expected that if there was any dirty dishes or any housework around that looked like it needed doing we were to do it . . . It got to be such a racket . . . Babysitting was just really an exploitation in those days.[68]

She added a sentence clarifying that she and Gwen each tended children, but not both together.

As Vic's dreams repeatedly dissolved, the joys of song and dance dissipated and he became angrier. JoAnn described her father as

> very hot-headed, very opinionated . . . Generally when they were together, a lot of the times they were having fights about this, that, and the other, yelling at each other. Mom always had all these magazines . . . dad didn't like cluttering up the house, so every time he came around he started yelling at her for having all this junk—these magazines—that should be burned. That is what they fought about if they couldn't find anything else to fight about. Later, I got to thinking they really enjoyed those fights! But we didn't. Kids didn't.[69]

The fighting between Vic and Sarah wasn't physical. They would

> holler at each other. They didn't throw things at each other, and they didn't hit each other. I guess each one was afraid if they hit the other one they would kill them, so they didn't hit them. I don't know. They sure did a lot of fighting. Mom was mad at dad because he didn't decide to do what he said he would—investigate and join the [Mormon] church. Dad was mad at Mom because when he left to go someplace she sold her house in Kanarra and moved to Hurricane. And then she always wanted a house, and I think that was one bone of contention that they never did get settled between them. And another thing was, dad said to me once long after momma died, "Two things I can't stand. A dirty house and a nagging woman." And I guess that's about what he had. Mom didn't keep the house too clean all the time, because she really didn't have much to keep clean with, or much decent furniture to keep up. We tried, but it never did look very, really neat, you know.[70]

Underneath the conflict was religion: Sarah and Vic worshipped different gods. Vic was a rough, practical man who herded obedient sheep throughout the Nevada-Utah-Arizona range. When he saw the Mormons in church devoutly praying for rain, he scoffed that if they wanted rain, they should live where it rained. He could not take seriously a stratified heaven, gold plates, and temple ceremonies. Sarah, in contrast, was a devout and practicing Mormon who regarded his views as sacrilegious, his Bull Durham as disobedience, and his inactivity as spiritually perilous.

"The only time he didn't get along fine, I guess, was mostly around his family or when something made him angry," JoAnn added. "He was very, very furious when he was angry. He had a terrible temper. It flared like a flash and was just really violent while he was angry. So we just kind of learned to lie low when he was around, or tried to."[71]

He "would whale the daylights out of us," she laughed nervously. "You talk about child abuse! He didn't hit Momma, but he sure spat his kids a lot, or whip them, or whatever you want to call it. So, he became violent. It was all right with me if he didn't live around home too much. Anything that I ever did made him angry. There wasn't anything I ever did in my life that ever pleased him. I can say that."[72]

Vic was willing to physically attack his children, but not able to give them much affection. "I never saw my father rock a kid in my life," asserted JoAnn, disputing her older sister Nell's more favorable memories. "I saw Gwen on his lap and I saw Nell on his lap. But Nell came and climbed up on his lap and I looked at her like she was going to get hit, but she didn't. And Gwen would climb on his lap when he was in real good moods singing. But he'd sing first, see. Listen to him sing, you'd know he was in a good mood. So you could come a little bit closer." She asserted with a squeamish laugh that if she'd climbed on his lap, "I'd have gotten knocked across the room!"[73]

Sarah was extremely sociable; she "was always visiting people," JoAnn remembered. "She had all kinds of friends in town and she was always over to their place and they were over to our place."[74]

Sarah's children grew up as part of an elaborate kinship of uncles, aunts, grandparents, and cousins, who helped give them an identity and some confidence. A few were like Vic Sylvester—angry and repellent—but most were cheerful and unconditionally approving. Joel Roundy, their grandfather, was more of a father than Vic was. An important and welcome part of their lives was provided by three women, in descending order of significance: Sarah, Kate, and Elizabeth.

12

"Continue to Increase"

Elizabeth Steele Stapley

Thursday morning, March 25, 1926, forty-six-year-old solemn-faced, slender Arthur Clinton Sechrest sent his son, thirteen-year-old Arthur Clifton Sechrest to school as usual. Mrs. Sechrest was in Southern California at a daughter's wedding and the hired man, Osmon Patten Williams, was already working in the field. Sechrest warmed his feet in the oven of his newly built two-story frame house a mile and a half north of the nearest Kanarra home, put on his house slippers, then pattered to the bedroom door and drove a nail into the jam. He hung a rifle on the nail, stood between the rifle and the bed, pulled the trigger and sent a bullet through his brain.[1]

Later that day Osmon Williams found a chair in front of the open oven door in the kitchen where Sechrest had warmed his feet. When Williams went into the bedroom, he found Sechrest's body slumped by the door with a bullet hole in the forehead. He summoned morose Horace Roundy, onetime slide trombone player in the town orchestra and, most important for this occasion, constable.[2] Roundy in turn called the registrar of vital statistics, Will C. Reeves who signed all birth and death certificates.[3] Reeves's son Lynn was invited along because he had sometimes partied at the shy Mr. Sechrest's with Arthur Junior and was considered knowledgeable about the layout of the home.

That wasn't enough for Kanarra townsfolk and naturally they insisted justice of the peace, Jimmy Stapley, come along. Stapley didn't want to go. At sixty-one he was prematurely aged—bald, nearsighted, and feeble. He had been out with a horse and plow tilling the garden for the spring planting until his worried wife, Hattie—seeing his condition—insisted he rest. When Stapley's presence was demanded he went along with the crowd in Bishop Reese J. Williams's Model A Ford sedan (the bishop was invited because he had a car).

Kanarra's cautious but curious legal community found Sechrest in overalls and a checked shirt lying in a large, well-furnished bedroom. There wasn't a lot of blood and they gravely speculated "that maybe he was opposed to the [daughter's] marriage or something." Lynn Reeves added, "I don't know whether there was anything to that or not." The verdict, as recorded in the death certificate signed by both Will C. Reeves and Dr. J. W. Bergstrom: "Suicidal—gun shot wound in head." Jimmy Stapley began to look through the outbuildings. "As he come out to the pump house, for some reason he reeled and went down," Lynn remembered. Reeves explained that "we didn't have no idea how serious it was."[4]

"He'd had a stroke," recalled Jimmy's daughter, Lenna Stapley Williams. "They put him back in the car and took him home and he never did gain consciousness," dying of "apoplexy" on March 29th, his cousin Will Reeves signing another death certificate.[5] When Jimmy died, his mother Elizabeth, his sister Kate, and Kate's daughter Sarah went to Kanarra to help. His funeral drew friends from Iron and Washington counties including Dixie Stockgrowers' Bank cashier Kumen Williams, a Kanarra boy who made good in St. George; blue-eyed Joseph W. Prince, a onetime New Harmony boy married to a Kanarra girl named Isabelle Williams; and Dilworth Snow, a miller, singer, and son of Washington County's famed stake president, Edward H. Snow.[6] (Kumen was soon back for the burial of his mother, Martha Williams.)[7]

John Alma Stapley's daughter Leola Stapley Anderson pressed the folds in Uncle Jimmy's temple robe for his burial while Elizabeth grimly and censoriously supervised. "Grandma set there—boy, you pressed every one just right," Leola said, gritting her teeth with frustration even in recounting the story. Jimmy's widow, Hattie, came to Leola's defense, telling Elizabeth that Leola was "just right."[8]

Elizabeth was as angry at Jimmy as she was bereaved. "She said if he'd a been taken care of right, why he wouldn't have had the stroke," Reba asserted. "But he eat too much salt, and he had a stroke and he never came out of it." The fault was "his own. She says, 'he ate too much salt and he'd ought to a stopped it. Nobody to blame but hisself. He knew what he was doing.'"[9]

Joel spoke at his childhood friend and brother-in-law's funeral. Like others, he lauded "the usefulness and integrity of the deceased, and his abiding faith in the gospel." *The Iron County Record* meant to praise Jimmy Stapley as well, but the effort was unconvincing when an erroneous headline gave Stapley a new last name, proclaiming that "Services for James S. Davis" were held in Kanarra on March 31st.[10]

Elizabeth lost other family members in the 1920s, the biggest disaster when a large group of men entered Mine Number 2 at Castle Gate on the chilly morning of Saturday, March 8, 1924. Shortly after, three explosions blew up the mine and killed 172 people, including so many from Kanarra that Provo's *Daily Herald* headlined a story, "Funerals at Kanarra."[11] Among the dead were Elizabeth's impish grandson Leland Campbell Stapley, who inherited her red hair and her mother's maiden name; Vic Sylvester's cousin Andrew Berry; and two nephews and a grandnephew of Joel J. Roundy.[12]

In June 1923, M. M. Steele traveled south to Hurricane to speak at sacrament meeting and probably saw his sister Elizabeth for the last time. He moved to Salt Lake City to stay with his daughter Emily Steele Jensen and died there September 18, 1923, apparently of acute cardiac dilation. His hometown newspaper, Panguitch's *Garfield County News*, celebrated him as "one of the best and most respected citizens of this city" and "a prominent factor in the development and growth of Southern Utah."[13]

Elizabeth's sister Susie Bringhurst was a fixture in Toquerville as a midwife—she even delivered Victor Sylvester's sister Gladys.[14] On her fifty-sixth birthday the town gave her a surprise party. Her bishop-husband, William A. Bringhurst, owned the general store—which he rebuilt in 1908—was a leader in the Democratic Party, sat on the school board, and provided grumpy leadership to the town. He was one of the very few Utahns who got a Civil War pension, having served ninety days in a volunteer cavalry unit under Lot Smith offering protection from Indians.[15]

Susie was a church leader and she and Elizabeth kept in touch, the *Washington County News* reporting in May 1909 that "Mrs. Elizabeth Stapley of Kanarra is the guest of her sister, Mrs. S. A. Bringhurst."[16] Susie's husband was getting old and was struck with what was thought to be the "grippe" or flu, but turned out to be Bright's disease. He struggled on for several months and then his children were summoned. When he died on March 8, 1912, his funeral was a big event; he had been bishop over thirty-eight years and three current bishops—David Hirschi of Rockville, Samuel Isom of Hurricane, and Morris Wilson of La Verkin—as well as future bishop Walter Slack of Toquerville and Stake President Edward H. Snow were among those at his services. In the next stake conference, President Thomas P. Cottam, "referring to the death of the late Bp. Bringhurst of Toquerville said he believed Bp. Bringhurst had been a bishop longer than any other bishop in the Church." The obituary was honest enough to juxtapose two of Bringhurst's important life experiences with the government: "Bishop Bringhurst served a term in the state penitentiary for conscience sake and was a pensioner of the government for services rendered [in the Civil War]."[17]

"Mrs. Susann A. Bringhurst is intending to leave for Salt Lake City next Thursday to make her future home," reported the *Washington County News* soon after the bishop's death.

> The whole ward will participate in a farewell entertainment in her honor tonight given under the auspices of the Relief association of which she is one of the presidency. Mrs. Bringhurst is the widow of the late Bp. Wm. A. Bringhurst and has been an active member of our community and as such leaves with the best wishes of all for her success in her new field of action. Four of her children are residents of Salt Lake county.[18]

She rarely visited Toquerville after that but did give a recitation at the "Old Folks reunion" in September 1915.[19] She also returned in October 1921 to visit her daughter Ann Augusta Bringhurst Naegle, at which time her old friends were happy to see her: "The Relief Society entertained Mrs. Susan Bringhurst on the 3rd inst.," reported the *News.*[20] Certainly she would have visited her sister Elizabeth in Hurricane at this time and seen her niece Kate as well. However, in late May 1925, the newspaper reported that Mrs. Susan Bringhurst of Salt Lake had fallen and broken her hip. "It will be months before she can take a step, and it is believed by her physicians that she will never be able to walk again. Mrs. Bringhurst is seventy-four years old, and had been a citizen of this place [Toquerville] until about ten years ago. Much hope is held for her recovery."[21]

Susie's daughter Ann went to Salt Lake to take care of her. Ann was back in Toquerville soon but left again in October, the newspaper reporting she "left for Salt Lake on the 25th. On her return home she will bring her invalid mother, Mrs. Susanna Bringhurst, here to spend the winter." Staying in Toquerville wasn't permanent because Susie went back to Salt Lake County, dying August 18, 1927, in Taylorsville from a cerebral hemorrhage.[22]

Elizabeth's grandson Harold, son of her son John A., who had survived pneumonia in 1925, was thrown from a horse and killed in 1928. "Marks of the horse's feet in the vicinity where he was found by [his brother] Arvil indicated that the animal had bucked and pitched Harold from the saddle, his foot catching in the stirrup and preventing him from getting away from the horses feet," reported the *Iron County Record* on October 6. "It was evident, too, that he had been dragged a considerable distance, and that the horse had kicked him in the head, crushing the skull badly."[23]

Maybe these calamities made Elizabeth more anxious to be in her old Kanarra home for—after nearly ten years—she moved back to be with her brother Almy. Lenna Stapley Williams was a Kanarra teacher during the 1929–1930 school term, earning $800 a year. She found Elizabeth trying.

> She did stay at home for a little while when I was teaching school . . . I would get her breakfast and sometimes she would fiddle around and I couldn't get her to go home in time for me to get to school, you know. And that was upsetting to me. I'd have to send the kids with her, to get her home . . . I couldn't take school time to wait on Grandma. And that's what she couldn't stand, she wanted someone right there. And if she wanted something done she wanted it done right now. I couldn't do that . . . She didn't stay very long, though. She soon went [back] to Hurricane with Aunt Kate.[24]

Almy and Elizabeth were the only ones of their generation left; Almy now a public fixture in Kanarra standing behind his white picket fence chawing tobacco. When a stranger asked Dee Stapley for directions to Almy Steele's place he was told, "You go right on up this street and you see a man standing there chewing the pickets, why that's him."[25]

John Alma visited Elizabeth in Hurricane in July 1930[26] but caught bronchitis in February 1931 and became so sick he was taken to Cedar City. He "was stricken Saturday morning at 5:00 o'clock with cerebral hemorrhage, and five hours after the attack passed away" on February 21.[27] His nephew and namesake, John Alma Stapley, provided the information for the death certificate but seemed to be so unacquainted with his own grandmother that he reported—or the registrar, Alex H. Rollo, misreported—the deceased's mother was "Sarah Canbell" born in "England"; Almy was said to be a retired farmer.[28]

The obituary in the *Iron County Record* was more accurate, reporting "the deceased was born in Parowan, April 6, 1854, and was known to many people throughout the southern part of the State. He with his parents suffered all the hardships of the early settlement of this country. In his later years he lived in Kanarra, and was always highly respected, being a man of integrity, honest[y] and faithfulness," and that "the body was taken to Kanarra for internment, funeral services being held Sunday."[29] The family had a handsome if simple flat monument put over the grave.

Elizabeth, now the only one of her parents' children left, found her brittle bones were subject to more accidents. Reba remembered:

> Reva and I was taking care of her one day, and they was a little crack like that [in the floor], that the board had been broken. And we said, "Oh, come on, use your crutches! Don't be sliding that chair along there!" We got her to use her crutch, and she put her crutch in that hole [and fell] and broke her wrist, right here. And then while she went up North to stay with her kids one summer, why, she fell and broke this hip here, and another time she went up, she broke it right here. So she always pushed her chair in front of her, she never would use her crutches. Unless she was going out to a car, or something like that.[30]

Nevertheless, Catherine Campbell Steele's network of descendants burgeoned. All but two of Kate and Joel's children were married in the 1920s and did their part to contribute to the expanding family network. After his war service, Kate's Jesse Roundy joined his cousin Leland C. Stapley and townsman Jewett Wood in Castle Gate where he worked as an assistant in the blacksmith shops until Christmas, when he went to Hurricane to be with Joel and Kate for the holidays. Instead of going back to Carbon County, Jesse took up part of his father's Kanarra farm—he had met a pretty brown-haired young Hurricane girl and apparently didn't want to get so far away from home he couldn't court.

Nancy Lillian Eagar, a Hurricane eighth grade graduate went to Salt Lake City in June 1919 to care for her sister Jetta, who was receiving treatment at LDS Hospital. By 1920 she worked in Jim Judd's Hurricane drugstore for a dollar a day arranging shelves, decorating windows, and cleaning up.[31] Joel and Kate were anxious for her to meet Ren, who, as Lillian's sister Hazel Eagar Bringhurst remembered, "was getting kind of old!"[32]

The Stanworths and Roundys were "old time friends," and in 1920, just before the Hurricane Fair called Peach Days, Joel went over to see Lillian's mother, Nancy Alice Nutter Hinton Eagar Stanworth. Lillian remembered:

> We only had two rooms, and I went in the kitchen and he and I yelled back and forth . . . He was always a kidding me anyway, and he said, "Well I've got three boys that's coming down for Peach Day and you have your choice." He says, "I've got a missionary, a soldier-boy, and just

> a boy" [referring to Ren, Jesse, and Golden]. I said, "Well I'll take the soldier-boy." He says, "Oh, I wanted you to take the missionary," and I said, "No, the soldier-boy." Never thought any more about it.[33]

That night at the dance Lillian asked the ticket taker, "Where are the Roundy kids?" and was directed to them. Stella or Annis introduced Jesse. "I want you to meet Lillian, Jesse."

"Hello Lillian, how are you, can I have this dance?" was the bold reply.

> That was the beginning [Lillian laughed]. So then he introduced me to the other brothers and they each one asked for a dance. So we went on dancing, and there happened to be just four dances and there was only three of them so he asked me for the last dance and I said, "Yes, I'll dance with you." So I went on in with him to the last dance and while he was dancing he says, "Will you take me home?" and I said, "Yes, I'll take you home." He says, "You know where I live?" and I said, "Yes I know where you live, I'll take you home." So when the dance got out, why, we went out of the dance hall and the rest of them come with us and when we got out in the middle of the street he just whirled me around!
>
> I'm not going to let you take me home" [Jesse announced]. "I'm going to take you home."[34]

They loved to waltz and Lillian said of the two-step, "There's not a prettier dance anywhere and me and my husband we used to have more fun dancing when we was going together and after we was married. We used to just dance! And he was a janitor to the Kanarraville ward, for years, and he always managed the dances, and he could dance, boy, he knew how!"[35] Lillian's sister Hazel Eagar Bringhurst agreed that Jesse was "full of fun."[36]

The result was reported in the newspaper in 1921: "Mr. Jesse C. Roundy of Kanarra and Miss Nancy Lillian Eagar of Hurricane were married in the temple here [in St. George] Oct. 14."[37] "I married the wrong Roundy according to them," Lillian laughed, because they wanted her to marry Ren. "You're not marrying the one I want you to," Joel said, and she answered gaily, "I know I'm not, but I'm marrying the one I want." Reba remembered "everybody got married they chivareed." Lillian had a lot of friends and "they'd just make a big fuss and they'd get a bunch of cars and go around them and tag them all around and everything . . . honk the cars and yell and scream and sing. And I don't know, everything you could think of."[38]

Kate's daughter Stella was soon involved in a romance. Tight-lipped Ellis Russell was from Grafton, a town that the generally sympathetic Presbyterian missionary and Princeton graduate Claton Rice described as a "sleepy, off-the-road little Mormon village, [where] one found a lack of physical improvements and a lethargy which made St. George a flourishing metropolis by comparison. Dust and flies were ever present." There wasn't a future for the little village—it's long been a ghost town—and at the time of his courtship, Ellis was the mail carrier between Hurricane and Cane Beds. When I interviewed him he refused to characterize family members ("Listen, I'm not going to pass my opinion on anybody") but he did explain how he met Stella. "I was working for Albert Mathis over at Harmony."[39] Ellis's close-mouthed views reflected Albert Mathis's cogent advice: "In the course of human life five things observe with care, of whom you speak, to whom you speak, and how, and when and where."[40] (Sarah had worked for Mathis's wife years before; she didn't live by the same principles.)

Still, Ellis told me something: "I went over there [to Kanarra] to a dance one night. It was a last day of school program or something like that. I remember that, and it was over to Kanarra. That's when I met her. Oh, it was about, about 1917 or '18, right in there, I can't say for sure." Ellis had worked for Mathis "all summer, and never did go to see her, just met her to a dance one night, you know, when I was over there to a dance or two, and then after they moved down to Hurricane, why, we got better acquainted. You know how it goes from there."[41]

Ellis had a beautiful singing voice, but Reba laughed that he "just looked like any other guy. He was a little bit backward, and just a little bit different than we were." She thought "he didn't get out and do this and that. He was scared to make the effort. If he had a chance to put something there to make it bigger, and bring good money in, he wouldn't do it, because he was afraid he'd lose it."[42]

"Ellis Russell and Stella Roundy were married in the St. George temple Friday," reported the Hurricane correspondent to the *Washington County News* on October 5, 1922. "The groom is the son of Mr. and Mrs. Albert Russell and the bride is the daughter of Mr. and Mrs. Joel Roundy, both of this place, and are highly respected. We wish them a successful and happy life."[43] Ellis enjoyed the wedding ceremony but didn't appreciate the consequent chivaree. "He was hotheaded," Reba said. "You know how hotheaded he is, and the more he got hot, the hotter he spoke, why the more the people come out . . . He got mad at them, told them to get for home, and they just kept right on and she says, 'You might just as well be still. They'll go home quicker.' So he shut up."[44]

Kate's son Golden Roundy went on a mission in October 1921. He thought he was going to Oklahoma but ended up in Bluewater, New Mexico. "That was a little funny deal there," Reba remembered. Golden was supposed to also visit Colorado and he told the district mission president, "I haven't been up to Colorado for a long time, I ought to go up there."

"I think the church wants you right here," countered the president, adding, "The church wants you to marry that widow with two kids."

"This district president's told me to marry a woman out here," Golden wrote home to his parents.[45]

The woman was Clarinda Whetten Tietjen, born in Mexico and one of twenty-five children of a rancher, Mormon bishop, and polygamist named John Thomas Whetten, who played the fiddle while Clarinda accompanied him on the piano. They escaped Mexico with Pancho Villa on their trail and ended up in a lumber shed in El Paso before landing in a tarpaper house in Bluewater.[46]

Clarinda's first husband was Alma Tietjen.

> He courted me in a black top buggy pulled by a high spirited bay team. Alma was tall, light complected, a real good dancer, and a good mixer. I doubt if Alma ever saw a stranger. He rode lots of broncos and rode them well. His whole life was cattle and horses. We had lots of fun dating each other and attending the many parties and dances. We got along well and I accepted without hesitation, when he asked me to marry him. October 8th, 1912, we were married in the Salt Lake Temple.

An accident with a wagon on January 30, 1919, left Alma dead from a broken neck. His pretty bride found herself a widow with two fatherless children and a ranch to run.[47] She finally sold the land, bought a home in Bluewater for $800, and lived there five years.

> My whole life began to change one night when I attended a cottage meeting and met Elder Golden P. Roundy who was serving in the Western States Mission" [she recalled]. He made a great impression on me that night. He had such a great love for people and showed so much concern and compassion for those around him. We both knew it was love from the start but we held those feelings back and just enjoyed the group fellowshipping—and there was lots of that. The missionaries were very welcome in our home and I took great delight in baking goodies for

> them. Golden was District Leader at the time and his territory included part of Colorado and part of New Mexico, so he was kept busy and never let his personal feelings interfere with his call as a missionary. He loved the work and later became Branch President in Bluewater. President Knight later said that he felt inspired to send Elder Roundy to Bluewater. I am eternally thankful that he did.

Golden was released from his mission and back in Hurricane by Sunday, May 4, 1924, when he "bore a splendid testimony of the gospel" at church.[48] He spoke again on May 11 when "a special program was given in Sunday school in honor of the mothers. In the afternoon high tributes were paid the mothers by the following speakers, Golden Roundy, Jeremiah Johnson, and Bishop Naples of Vernal."

But he didn't hang around Hurricane, as Clarinda recalled. "After Golden was released, he returned home for nearly a month the longest month I could remember. Then he came back to Bluewater. We wasted no time in expressing our feelings for each other. Since I was sealed to Alma, we could not go to the temple so we chose to be married at Rehoboth Mission, near Gallup, New Mexico by President Noak, former mission President."

They were married on May 31, 1924, and when Clarinda met Joel and Kate she was taken with them.

> I loved Golden's parents at first sight. His father was a Patriarch and he was true to his calling. His mother was so sweet to me and I have throughout all my life cherished this relationship. They had a small plot of ground that they farmed and had fruit and nut trees and grapevines and we enjoyed bushels of sweet fruit, nuts and vegetables, always tied tight with a ribbon of love. Since Golden's and my birthdays were both in June, for years we could look forward to a lug of delicious Bing cherries in the mail—oozing and dripping with their goodness. It was a treat we all looked forward to and enjoyed.

After Jesse married and left Kanarra, Ren was lonely and asked his brother Karl to join him. "When he was home him and Ren was always close together," Reba remembered. "Ren had always took care of him when he was a kid. So he went down there, why Ren says 'Come on up and stay with me.' So Karl went up with them and they went over to New Harmony to the dances." Karl met New Harmony's Erma Condie. "She claimed she was the belle of the town up there, and she was the main one, and everybody liked her," Reba explained. "She's not bad looking . . . They went together back and forth and finally ended up getting married" on September 8, 1927, and unlike some family members, stayed in Hurricane.[49] "He was always the spoiled baby," his niece and Sarah's daughter Gwen said. Gwen's sister JoAnn agreed that Karl "always wanted everything his way," but confessed laughingly that she loved her grandfather Joel so much that she felt like Joel's children "should kind of bow down and crawl on their knees to him because to me he was just practically perfect, and Grandma too."[50]

Annis, the most like her sister Sarah with her seamstress skills, was working in Cedar City as a dressmaker in the mid-twenties and convinced Reba and Reva there was work in town so the twins moved up to join her.[51]

> Reva got a job down to the authorities [Reba remembered]. And I didn't have a job and so they [said] come up and help us with the dressmaking. So I went up and helped them for a month or two at the dressmaking and I worked then for the Corrys. But we just lived a block off from the main street and we had this big house and there was upstairs, there's a big main room an there's a loft back in the back and we slept in the back.
>
> . . . It had snowed, and they was snow all over the ground, and all at once there was a knock come on the door and here's some boys and girls that come up. "Come on. We want to get you to go for a sled ride." And we said we don't know who you are. "Well, then nothing like finding out," he said. "Come on. Get your coats on, let's go for a sleigh ride." So we said okay, so we put our coats on and went out and Darwin Condie was driving the team. And we rode around town quite a little bit, then we made a sharp turn and that flew the sled on its side. Then we was all freezing to death, so we come back up to our apartment. And the people downstairs, she was an English woman, and oh, that was terrible making all that noise and everything. And they said, "Well, when we get warm we'll leave." So they got warm. We had coal and stuff for the fire and so they left and she thought we was too noisy."[52]

"And that's where we first met. She [Reva] met [George] Burdett [Webster] and I met Yegg [Naze Edgar Bryant] and Annis just went along for the fun of it." "Yegg" was a jug-eared, long-faced truck driver. Burdett had grown up in Cedar doing any kind of work he could get: sheep shearing, hauling wood, laying track for the railroad, and even found time to spend a year at the Branch Normal School.

"Every time we had a snow storm, why, they'd come for us and—'Let's go for a sleigh ride,'" Reba remembered. "Sometimes they would see how fast they could take the turns and to see how many they could spill from the sleigh." The group also enjoyed picture shows every night.

After Golden got settled in New Mexico he wrote his sister Annis: "Why don't you come out and see me?" Reba explained that "Annis was a dressmaker and she'd earned some money, and Karl was working around here and there and, 'Why don't we go out and see him?' he says. And so they got Karl, and got a car and so they went out to see him and while they was out there, why she met this man, Golden's wife's brother-in-law"—Albert "Al" Valdemar Tietjen, whose brother Alma was Clarinda's first husband—a bronco busting one time Mormon missionary to Mexico who claimed to have had breakfast with Pancho Villa. Like his brother, Al was a big man, six foot four, and an athletic wrangler.[53] "She said she got word that that was supposed to be her husband," Reba said, "and he got word that was supposed to be his wife. So they went together and she come back home and then they got married [December 6, 1927], then she moved out there."[54]

Albert and Alma were sons of E. A. Tietjen, one of six famed Mormon Indian missionaries, the most well-known being Jacob Hamblin;[55] but also including Hamblin's brother Edwin Hamblin, Dan Jones, Thales Haskell and Ira Hatch. Alma's stepmother and one of E. A. Tietjen's wives was Amanda Hatch, daughter of Ira Hatch by his Navajo wife Sarah or Maraboots Dyson, sister of Peokon and daughter of Spaneshanks.[56]

This relationship to the Navajo people proved advantageous because Al and Annis became successful running Indian trading posts, at one time owning them at Smith's Lake, the Painted Desert, and Tohachi. A bust in the wool market nearly wiped them out, but they were able to hang on to Tohachi. In addition, Al became a bank director.

Annis and Golden were remembered by the new generation in Hurricane as exotics who sometimes came to visit from far away New Mexico, and Al and Annis always brought elegant gifts of Indian blankets and beautiful hammered silver jewelry.

"Then Annis got married and Reva and I lived there alone for a year, and then she got married" to Burdett Webster. The wedding drew only the announcement in the newspapers that they'd taken out a wedding license, the kidnapping of Juvenile Judge George A. Mitchell by a delinquent named Ernest Murie crowding out lesser news.[57]

"We didn't know until after Reva was married that they couldn't tell us apart," Reba explained. "We knew that we stayed in our room quite a little bit longer some nights than we did other nights, but after Reva got married, why Burdett told them we had to wait until we smiled, then they could tell us apart."

Reba's own courtship wasn't successful. Yegg was a younger maternal first cousin to their old Kanarra nemesis Rachel Griffin Roundy, and Joel believed Rachel inherited genetic defects through her mother's people, the Harrises, who were also Yegg's mother's family. "I hope you're not going to marry the guy that you're with," Joel cautioned her. "No way, no way will I marry him," she assured her father. She didn't love Yegg.

"Now you got your wife, but I didn't get the other one," Yegg complained to Burdett. When Burdett passed this on to Reba she said, "You just tell him to go find him another woman. I'm not going to marry him."[58] And eventually that's what he did.

Reba was her niece JoAnn's favorite. "She tells you what's what . . . But she tells you what you need to know. She helps you when you need it and she loves you. So Reba was one of these people I always felt I could depend on, even if she did tell me I was off in a dream world and I had to get practical and down to earth, learn how to live." Reva seemed more distant. "I never did know if she liked me or not," JoAnn explained. "That always makes a difference to me. So we didn't have the open communication that we had with Reba," and she remembered Reva's husband Burdett as "not very religious" but "a good, kind man."[59]

These marriages resulted in additional grandchildren for Kate and Joel, fulfilling God's promise to Elizabeth through her father's blessing that "thy posterity shall be exceeding numerous and continue to increase." "I was six or seven years old before I found out he wasn't everybody's grandpa," Gwen recalled. "He was just our Grandpa Roundy, but everybody in town called him Grandpa Roundy, the kids and the adults, and sometimes even in church they would say Grandpa Roundy."[60]

And many of those who called him Grandpa were not doing so as a courtesy, as JoAnn learned.

> I used to get kind of provoked when we'd go downtown and we'd start out with Grandpa and me or maybe Grandpa and Gwen and me and by the time we were halfway to town, there'd be ten other kids there

> and they'd all shove me right out and they'd all be right up against him. I figured I was a little bit special, because he was my Grandpa. Then a little later on, all these kids were calling him "Grandpa" and I'd say, "He's not your Grandpa."
>
> "Yes, he is my Grandpa."
>
> "No, he isn't."
>
> "Oh yes" [Joel interjected], "yes, I'm their Grandpa, too."
>
> "Where did those little snots come from?" [JoAnn thought to herself] They're not his. Then I found out, yes. But you see, Nell and I are his oldest grandkids. And then Gwen and after Gwen, a whole bunch of them. And so, about the time that Gwen was big enough to call him Grandpa, or a little bigger than that, there was LoRal [Russell] and Kay [Roundy] and all these other kids that he hadn't been their Grandpa until I was big enough and I really got kind of jealous, because I thought, "Where did all of these kids come from that say he's really their Grandpa and he's only my Grandpa and Nell's?"[61]

Joel's storytelling won him great applause from his children and grandchildren. He had been involved in drama in his younger days and was remembered in Kanarra as a great raconteur. He learned to memorize melodrama scripts, "And then when he was out herding sheep he learned to read the Bible and the Book of Mormon and study it. And when he come back, he set us kids in a corner and translated these Book of Mormon stories like the Bible stories so you could understand them," recalled Reba. "That's where we learned to tell these stories. I can remember more than once us kids getting in a corner while mother was getting supper or getting breakfast or getting ready for bed and us kids were in the way. He'd put us in a quilt down on the floor and all the neighbor's kids'd come in and he'd tell these stories. That's where he started." He also had piles of magazines, like the *Juvenile Instructor,* which could be a source of children's stories.

He acted his stories out with gestures, facial manipulation, and vocal intonation. "He certainly had a good relationship with an audience," remembered his granddaughter Gwen. "I've sat in those little groups myself when I was a kid and every kid was just right on edge . . . He could really tell the scary stories and that was what he loved telling the best." She explained, "He could tell coyote stories and cougar stories that would make the hair stand up on the back of your neck," and added, "and he'd talk like this," she whispered, "and he'd just get you so interested and go 'Ah!'" she shouted. "He'd scare you half to death or reach over and grab a kid by the hand quick. And every kid and everybody else loved to hear his stories." She explained that "he was such a story teller that that's what he'd do when he went home teaching. It'd take him a whole week to do his home teaching because he'd stop and tell stories to kids like an hour, an hour and a half, every place he went, so the kids would see him coming on the street or at church and they would say, 'When you coming home teaching? When you coming home teaching?'"

"He was everybody in the story and he was the narrator," JoAnn said. It was a common sight to see him in Hurricane, sitting on a clump of Bermuda grass on a red ditch bank, surrounded by a dozen silent and attentive children, two or three on his lap, some leaning over his shoulders, and all quietly spellbound while Joel's long thin hands gestured gracefully and his voice rose and fell, his neat white and blue striped overalls ("overhauls") breathed in and out with the modulations of his thin body, a pencil eraser peeking attentively out of his pencil pocket, the black leather thong to his turnip watch rolling in tune with his rhythmic cadences. He was once invited to tell stories on the radio in Cedar City but, without a visible audience he lost his magic touch and the attempt was a failure.[62]

"Grandpa was, I think, the world's most perfected tease," Gwen recalled.

> He could tease anybody and not make them mad and that's an art in itself and he used to say about the kids, they used to get so excited about seeing him, they'd come over close to him and he'd take a hold of their shoulder and say, "Turn around and let me kick ya," and every kid would turn around and let him kick them. He'd just stick his tongue out between his teeth and grunt, "Uh, uh," like he was really going to kick them hard and they'd just stand there . . . and he'd take hold of their shoulders and they'd turn around and let him kick them, he'd take the side of his foot and put it against their butt just barely tapping them.[63]

JoAnn's journal of May 20, 1979, added:

> Grandpa had some personal sayings such as "Ho, you don't love me." "Yes, I do" the child would answer. "How much, then?" "Oh, a whole bushel" or "A hundred haystacks full." He always taught us to measure love by hay loads—no wonder we still say "I love you tons." Hay was measured in bales, tons, and stacks. Or he'd say "You don't *whant* that." When I was in high school, he asked me to correct his English and if I

> heard him say anything incorrect (grammar wise) to tell him the correct way. He was in his late 70's or so but any time I corrected him, he would repeat it once or twice and very seldom did he use that error again.[64]

There were other joys associated with Grandpa Roundy. Gwen talked about Joel's granary, so weathered the wood was silvered. "Maybe that's why I love weathered wood now that I think about it," she said. "All of his books were in the granary and that's where I spent most of my time," JoAnn remembered.

> He had magazines from the 1880s on for the church magazines. He had *The Young Women's Exponent*,[65] which later became the—right now they call it the *New Era*. It was the mutual magazine and it was a little magazine, and they had *The Relief Society Magazine* and they had the *Juvenile*, which eventually became *the Juvenile Instructor*, which became *The Instructor*, and it was a Sunday School magazine. All the Sunday School lessons were in there plus a lot of very interesting things for kids, like word games and find the mistakes and how many things in this picture begin with an "M" or something, you know. So I had a lot of fun reading those.[66]

"The thing that was so neat to play in there," Gwen recalled, "is that you could lift up the lid to the grain bin and put your arms down in all that wheat and it would just slide over your arms as you lifted it up and then you'd bail down in again, and it was just really neat. We loved that."

"They grew their own wheat," Gwen explained, "then they'd take it to the mill and have it ground." Hurricane boasted the only flour mill in Washington County, established in 1915 by the canal company. On January 1, 1928, J. Wilson Imlay sold it to Joseph W. Webb, and Webb ran it for the next twenty years. The mill was modern, capable of holding up to eight thousand bushels of wheat and a thousand bushels of barley, and could grind four grades of cereal.

Gwen recalled:

> I can remember going up to that mill . . . That flour mill just seemed like the most fairyland kind of a place that I can ever remember because the ceilings just went on forever. You could look up there and see clear through up through the floor to the next story. And the ladder went up through the middle of it, and you could see up there two stories high—and the stories were high at that—and then these big old stones grinding

> and it was a terrible lot of noise when nothing else was mechanized. Cars were around by then, but we didn't have the motors all around our house like we do now.

The waterwheel was equally fascinating. "You could see it all happening! And it was marvelous! They had this water that would come through and turn the great big wheel and it was a marvelous place to go. This wheel would be like two times as tall as a kid, you know." But the ultimate fun was the floor, dusted with a thin sprinkling of flour. "You can't walk anywhere without making tracks in the white dust," Gwen said, speaking as if she were back in the old mill. "That was kind of fun, so we'd get down and make hand tracks, too!"[67]

This large multigenerational family had conflicts. JoAnn thought some of Joel's children took advantage of him. "They would come up and dump their kids on and they'd come without warning and eat. I guess they were supposed to but they didn't seem to ask first. That would have been okay, but Grandma being sick like that and they would ask to do things for them without pay or anything. And we all, all ate off them."[68]

If the uncles and aunts and cousins didn't give the new generation enough family, there were also great-aunts and great-uncles, like John A. Stapley, who JoAnn remembered as a cheerful tease, and great-great-aunts and great-great-uncles, like Almy Steele when he was still living on in Kanarra, a kindly old man. (Eventually JoAnn inherited his tiny New Testament, which wasn't worn out with study.) Likewise, for the Sylvesters there was an equal number of paternal kin.

Though family members died—sometimes tragically like Leland Stapley, and more often from causes associated with old age, as did Jimmy Stapley—the children being born to the new, fifth generation of Catherine's descendants guaranteed that this family would continue to multiply and spread across the Southwest—Utah, Arizona, and New Mexico. On November 16, 1890, John Steele had written to his Australian niece that the tiny adobe home in Toquerville wasn't large enough for Catherine's posterity;[69] by the 1920s the Toquerville Ward itself couldn't hold everyone descended from that frail yet powerful woman.

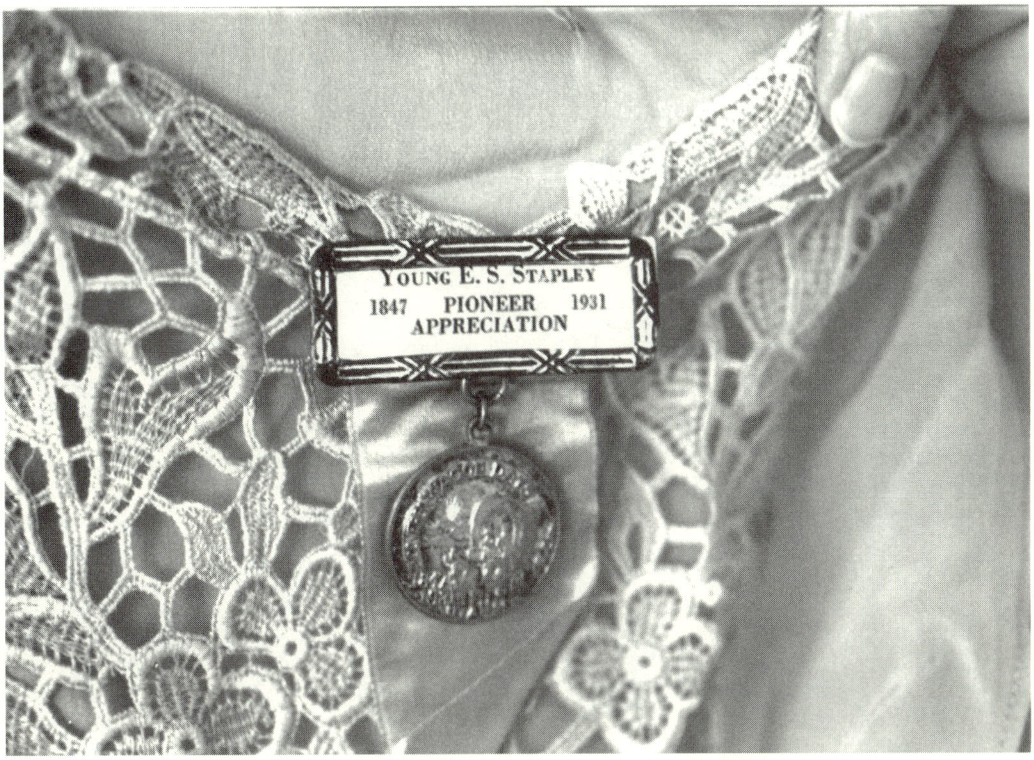

FIGURE 29. Close up of medallion on Elizabeth Stapley's dress. Courtesy of Josephine Kay Garfield.

FIGURE 30. Ordinary patchwork pieces by Young Elizabeth Steele Stapley. Courtesy of Josephine Kay Garfield.

FIGURE 31. Stapley Family reunion, Young Elizabeth Steele Stapley in center; Sarah Catherine "Kate" Roundy behind her to her right; probably Mary Kay left of Kate.

FIGURE 32. Sarah Catherine "Kate" Stapley (Roundy) and James Steele Stapley.

FIGURE 33. Mary “May” Elizabeth Stapley (Kay) and Sarah Catherine “Kate” Stapley Roundy.

FIGURE 34. Back, left to right: Joel Jesse Roundy, Sarah Elizabeth Roundy (Sylvester), James Lorenzo Roundy, Sarah Catherine “Kate” Roundy; front, left to right: Jesse Roundy, Rebecca Annis Roundy (Tietjen).

FIGURE 35 (opposite). Joel Jesse and Sarah Catherine Roundy homestead in Kanarraville. Illustration courtesy of Brad Lee Wolverton.

JOEL JESSE & SARAH CATHERINE ROUNDY HOMESTEAD, Kanarraville, Utah pre-1920s.

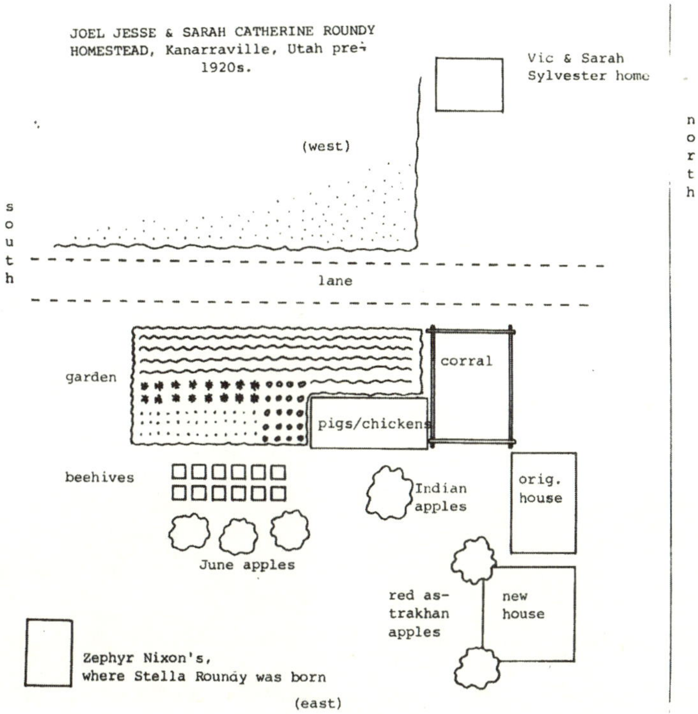

Joel Jesse & Sarah Catherine Roundy house in Kanarraville, pre-1920

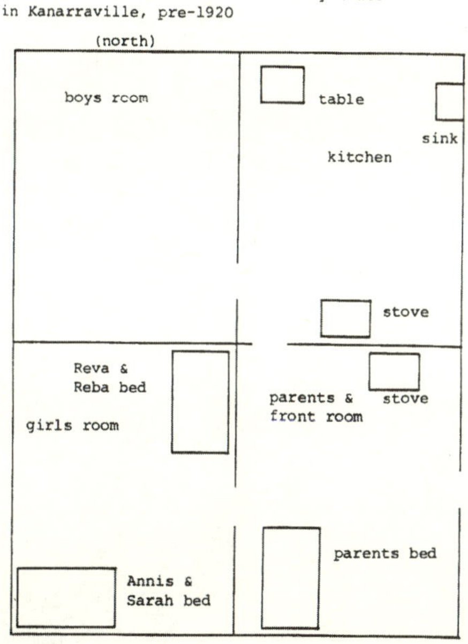

FIGURE 36. Estella "Stella" Roundy (Russell) and Annis Roundy (Tietjen).

FIGURE 37. Reva Roundy (Webster) and Reba Roundy (LeFevre).

FIGURE 38. Left to right: Golden Roundy, Estella Roundy, Annis Roundy, Joel Roundy, "Kate" Roundy, with the new car.

FIGURE 39. Joel Jesse Roundy and Sarah Catherine "Kate" Roundy, fiftieth wedding anniversary, 1937.

FIGURE 40. Sarah Catherine "Kate" Roundy, Joel Jesse Roundy, and JoAnn Sylvester Bate kissing her grandfather.

FIGURE 41 (opposite). Sarah Catherine "Kate" Roundy letter to Reba Roundy LeFevre.

Hurricane May 15 1949

Dear Reba & Karl

It seems a long time since I heard from you but I think it was just before you left to go to Old Mexico I thot I would wait untill you got back to answer but no doubt you have been back a long time before you get your release It wont be long now, which way will you come by Denver or by Goldens and Annise I know you will have to go to Salt Lake to Report and I guess it will be about as short one way as the other.

Gwen and Family were here for mother day went to St George Sunday morning and back home that nite she took Joann home with her. and I got a card from Max posted the 8 from Max on the 8 at from Oakland Calif so I guess she didnt stay long but I havent heard from any of them since.

FIGURE 42. Sarah Elizabeth Roundy (Sylvester).

FIGURE 43. Back, left to right: Jesse C Roundy, Sarah Elizabeth Roundy (Sylvester), James Lorenzo Roundy; front, left to right: Golden Roundy, Estella "Stella" Roundy (Russell), Rebecca Annis Roundy (Tietjen).

FIGURE 44. Sarah Elizabeth Roundy (Sylvester) and James Lorenzo Roundy while attending Murdock Academy, Beaver.

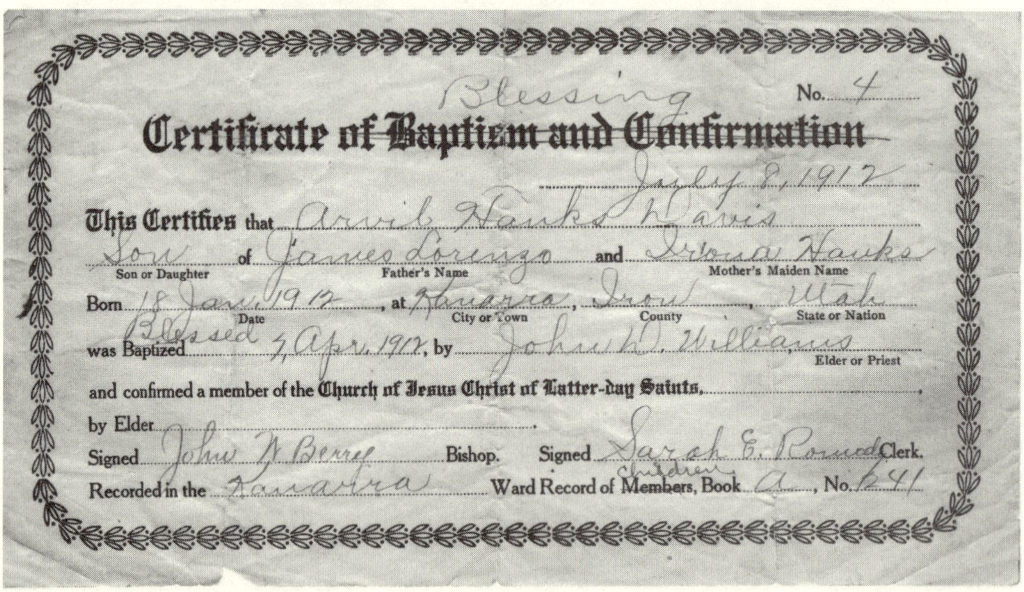

Blessing No. 4

Certificate of Baptism and Confirmation

July 8, 1912

This Certifies that Arvil Hanks Davis

Son of James Lorenzo and Irona Hanks

Son or Daughter | Father's Name | Mother's Maiden Name

Born 18 Jan. 1912, at Kanarra, Iron, Utah

Date | City or Town | County | State or Nation

was Baptized Blessed 4 Apr. 1912, by John W. Williams

Elder or Priest

and confirmed a member of the Church of Jesus Christ of Latter-day Saints,

by Elder

Signed John W. Berry Bishop. Signed Sarah E. Roundy Clerk.

Recorded in the Kanarra Ward Record of Members, children Book A, No. 641

FIGURE 45. The Murdock Academy Choir, 1910–11. The woman on the far right in front of the tree is Sarah E. Roundy (Sylvester).

FIGURE 46. Arvil Hanks Davis blessing certificate, signed by ward clerk Sarah E. Roundy.

FIGURE 47. Miners at Drum Mountain: back, left to right: Victor Sylvester, George Cropper, Reed Horton; front, left to right: Donald Hinckley, Peter Wilkins.

FIGURE 48. Kanarra Poultry Club, 1917: back, left to right: Sarah Davis, Eleanor Davis Pollock, Y. Elizabeth Stapley, Liza Wood, Sarah Sylvester (club president, holding hen), Kate Roundy, Lou Stapley; front, left to right: Rosella Pollock Christensen (holding son Maynard), Aaron Ingram, Naomi Wood Ingram (holding Eathel Ingram), Madge Stapley, Joseph Stapley, Nell Sylvester, Eve Nixon (holding magazine), Molly Williams.

FIGURE 49. Back, left to right: Ruth Sylvester (Pickering), Gwen Sylvester (Hunter); front, left to right: JoAnn Sylvester (Bate), Leon R Sylvester, Rex J Sylvester, Nell Sylvester (Stout) (Wilson).

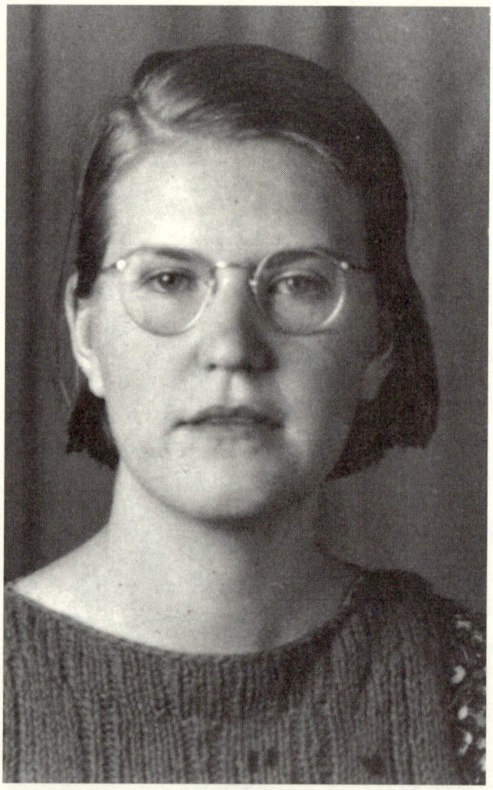

FIGURE 50. JoAnn Sylvester (Bate), 1938, the year her mother Sarah Elizabeth Roundy Sylvester died.

FIGURE 51. Maud Sylvester Gregerson with her brother Victor Leon Sylvester.

13

"She Only Had One Mother"

Sarah Catherine Stapley Roundy

"They are going about here in flying machines that in the future will soon take them to every distant part I suppose," Elizabeth's cousin Maryanne Campbell Wilson wrote M. M. Steele from Dublin on September 23, 1912. "Tho I will keep on the ground no matter what others do. I don't want to be a bird at all." And on April 8, 1919, Maryanne explained, "I am sorry not to be present [at M. M.'s anniversary party] but except I could charter an aeroplane I couldn't reach your feast in time. Bye and bye we shall be able to visit our friends in America when the aeroplane mode of traveling becomes general."[1] By then the *Iron County Record* published a prediction with the subheading: "The Aeroplane Bids Fair to Become Popular for Pleasure, Business and Commercial Uses."[2] Elizabeth shared Maryanne's fascination with flight.

On August 4, 1926, Mahonri's son Elton Stapley drove to Kanarra to take his grandmother Elizabeth to celebrate her upcoming birthday in Delta. Joel noticed that he "never could go fast enough to suit her"[3] and Elton had the same experience. She "liked to ride, and she'd go any time you said 'go!' as long as she felt at all well." Not only that, but "You couldn't drive fast enough in an automobile for to get her to say, 'Hey, you better slow down!' like my mother did. Mother used to watch the speedometer—'You're going too fast!' But not Grandma Stapley!" This trip Elton "got plenty of chances to see how fast she'd let you go" in his 1922 Model T Ford. "If you went forty miles an hour, why, you was going part of that distance up and down because the roads were just wagon tracks then, in those days."[4]

Back in Delta "they was a old barnstormer from World War I, with his plane there in Delta, was flying around giving people rides just about a quarter of a mile from our home," Elton remembered, "and one of my brothers [Evelyn, called "Ebb"] met us in the car while I was coming back, bringing her [Elizabeth] back from Kanarra taking her to Delta for a visit, and she was seventy-nine years old then, I believe, and it was when we got there, and my kid brother had been over on the ground where this fellow was, a bare forty acres where this fellow was landing with his plane and taking people for rides."[5]

Ebb "was just a kid in his teens and he was anxious to see. He was quite enthused." The plane "was one of these old bi-planes, two-wing things. World War I planes." Ebb told the pilot, Roy Carl Oelze,[6] that "Grandma was coming. And he says, 'Well, bring her over. I'll give her a ride.' I'll be darned."[7] According to the *Millard County Chronicle*, "The airplane ride was planned by Mr. [Mahonri] Stapley in honor of his mother's 79th birthday," and "A little coaxing was necessary to induce the aged lady to take her first flight, but when introduced to Pilot R. C. Oelze, she lost all fear."[8] Oelze, a handsome aviator dressed in jodhpurs, lineman boots, and wearing a goggled cap, was operator of the San Diego Aeronautical School and scouting out Delta for a possible airport. He even convinced two boys from South Delta, Freeman and Mack Sly, the youngest only sixteen, to take a six-week aviation course in San Diego.[9]

Elton continued: "He come over, he saw us pulling in to the lot, and he come running over and he says, 'Grandma, would you like to go for an airplane ride?' 'I sure would!' she says. So she went over and this old guy took her for a ride."[10] She was probably flying in Oelze's 1980 pound Curtiss J. N. "Jenny" biplane, in which he flew Salt Lakers a few weeks later.[11]

"One is in a veritable fairyland," wrote Ray Pinney in the *Salt Lake Telegram* of his own flight, "where telephone poles are toothpicks; small lakes, the aftermath of a shower; animals, insects. Farming acreage stands out individually in varying hues, dependent upon the recent crop sown, each small farm a block in itself. An automobile, with an extremely blatant motor, riding on a sea of down, without obstacles to impede progress or with which to collide, were it possible, would be mild compared with the comfort, smoothness and pleasure of an air trip."[12]

The ride lasted no more than fifty minutes and Oelze was careful to avoid doing any tricks or stunts; Elizabeth loved it. "Boy!" enthused Elton, "that was her conversation piece for quite a few years after that. She had an airplane ride."[13] Oelze was already planning an experiment of stopping his plane in midair to see if a fifty foot silk parachute could bring it in safely. A follow-up story about the success of that stunt brought a reminder to readers of the *Chronicle* that "Pilot Oelze will be remembered as the aviator who was in Delta a few weeks ago and took hundreds of our citizens on their first aerial trip, among them being Mrs. Young Elizabeth Stapley, who was the first white child born in the state of Utah."[14] (Oelze died within a year from natural causes and his handsome widow Laura, who took on the more romantic name of "Lorenza," is believed to be the first woman to manage an aviation field when she replaced her husband. Unfortunately, after the Great Depression hit she found herself unemployed at age thirty-four, living with her parents.[15])

Reba said Elizabeth promptly "wrote home and told Mother that she had gone up in this plane, and Mother said, 'Ah! I hope it don't send her crazy.' A man from Virgin [William Henry Spendlove] went up and he was out of his head and he didn't know what he was doing for quite a while after that. And she said, 'I hope nothing's wrong with her.'" But Spendlove, who sometimes lived in Kanarra, had other reasons to be addled, like Sheriff Charles Worthen pulling 250 gallons of wine out of his cellar during Prohibition.[16]

Reba felt sure her grandmother would be fine from the airplane ride and said, "'Now don't worry until she gets back, it may not even affect her. She wants to go fast, maybe that's just the thing she wants to do.' But Mother did worry, and then when it was all over with, why, she wrote back and said, oh, that was the time of her life!"[17]

Elizabeth never lost the thrill she got from this ride. "Oh, the happiest I was when I was up in the air!" she exulted. "I got to go as fast as I wanted to! Just right. That was just right." Reba said "she bragged about it,"[18] and it became a staple in her repertoire of anecdotes. A typical story in the *Deseret News* quoted her as saying, "I had my only airplane ride when I was 80 [actually almost seventy-nine] years old. I always told them they never could drive automobiles fast enough. But that ride was just right."[19]

Maybe the celebrity was as important as the ride, because Reba remembered that Elizabeth "always enjoyed the attention. Anybody that come in to talk to her and just kind of flabber a little bit over her, why, it put an inch of fat on her. She was just right up in the air, she couldn't get over it for two or three days."[20]

Elizabeth also loved music. Her mother, Catherine, knew many Celtic dances and Kate and Joel had a player piano. "Stella learned to play the piano, and Reva and I played the piano. We'd learn to get the double handed piece we played." They also had a record player that had to be pumped and took rolls.[21]

The 1920s brought one great change for music lovers. The first public radio broadcasting began in the autumn of 1920, and by the end of the decade broadcasting stations covered the land and one-third of Americans had a radio. "When radio first came out, a young lady was trilling up & down the scale in high soprano," wrote Velma Stapley Rymer. "My brother Ebb never liked such music so in haste he turned the radio off saying, 'Good H—do we have to listen to that?' at which Grandma remarked, 'Why Evelyn, you'll hurt the poor woman's feelings!'"[22]

She loved western music, and when Reba bought a radio from stingy Henry Scholzen with money she got from her post office job, they managed to pick up KNX from California. Elizabeth fell in love with KNX's western string band, the Arizona Wranglers, snuggling close to the big boxy radio cabinet to listen. The fiddle players were "Slicker" Laverne Costello, "Hungry" Joe Ivans, "Dynamite" Len Dassey, "Nubbins" J. E. Patterson, "Irontail" Charles Hunter, with "Sleepy"' Carl Short on the harmonica and "Sheriff" Loyal Underwood doing vocal. The Wranglers sang "cowboy songs, and they just really made it up!" enthused Reba. "We was glad we found something that would interest her. They'd come on once a week. 'Is it time for them Wranglers to come on?' 'No.' 'You let me know. Now don't you let them get by without me knowing,' she'd say. So we'd tell her when it was going to come, and get her up, right up by it, so she could hear it."[23]

Elizabeth "liked everything fast. And they'd get in there and sing," Reba explained.

> She couldn't hear very much. I think maybe if we'd took her to the doctor and had the wax took out of her ears, she would have been better, but she wouldn't go. And the Arizona Wranglers come out and she liked that, oh that was really great! So every time they come, we'd put her as close as you and I are together and turn the thing on full blast, and she could hear it and she'd clap her hands and she'd yell, "Come on! Come on! Let's have some more!" She just really had fun with it.[24]

The Wranglers played in Delta in 1934 on their way to Salt Lake,[25] and no doubt some of her children or grandchildren were able to give her firsthand accounts of the performance.

"We sent and got the picture" of the Wranglers "so she could see what they looked like," Reba explained. They were dressed elegantly in broad cowboy hats, beaded vests, colorful shirts, hand-tooled boots, gaudy ties, and lush neck scarfs with leather chaps. A printed inscription on the photograph reads, "Best Regards from The Arizona Wranglers and 'The Sheriff.'" That made this elderly fan even more enthused. "Now get them Wranglers out here so I can see them," she'd order, and Reba would put the picture in her hands. "Now which one's playing?"

"We don't know. Can't see them," Reba would remind her. Elizabeth's enthusiasm continued unabated.[26]

Kate was more low-key. JoAnn remembered her grandmother as someone who liked flowered dresses, made sure the rooms were painted in nice light colors, and scrubbed her linoleum floors so vigorously that she eventually wore the designs off them. Kate was always kind, but JoAnn remembered once

> I was at Grandma's house and she wasn't home and of course, it was terrible, because I looked around to see if there was something to eat and I don't know why I did, because usually, when I went into their house and they weren't home I'd just go right back out again. But anyway, there was some honey there and I fixed some bread and some honey then I spread the honey on the bread and then I ate it. And I felt guilty for weeks because I stole their bread and honey. The thing of it was, it was so dumb because if they'd been there, Grandma would've given me bread and honey anyway.[27]

Kate was generally even tempered, but Reba argued that "you can't tell me that a woman can take care of her mother for twenty years, or forty years, and not get het up over something." Asked if it was hard for Kate to have her mother in her home for so many years, Reba verified, "Sure it was hard. She didn't have any breather, she had to do what her mother said . . . But she couldn't take it out on her mother, might take it out on somebody else." "Taking it out" meant Kate said "what she thought and that was it. She never kept it up." Kate "was a quiet woman, and she didn't get excited too quick. But she did get excited once in a while." She wasn't "outspoken. You had to work her up to it. But if she thought that you needed to be corrected, why she'd tell you why and why you shouldn't do it. Then you was not supposed to do it no more. But, I don't ever remember her getting too angry."[28]

"Grandpa had one habit that drove Grandma absolutely crazy," JoAnn explained.

> While she was setting the food on the table, he'd go somewhere and then we'd have to wait ten or fifteen minutes for him to come back to get his meal. And that just drove her up the wall because she'd always wait until he was washing his hands before she put it on the table, so that by the time his hands were washed, part of it was on the table. And he'd say, "Well, just a minute dear, I've got to go down off to Strattons' for something," or "Well, just a minute, I've got to go out and see something about those figs out there"—whatever. Seems to me like almost every time we ate, that was his excuse.

Kate had long since resigned herself to this habit, for as JoAnn says, "She didn't nag him much for being late to meals all the time, because she'd kind of given up on that."[29]

"Grandma used to get a little bit upset sometimes—I don't really blame her," Sarah's daughter Ruth said of Kate. "But so many Sundays, when it was warm weather, there'd sometimes be up to thirty kids come up there and want him to tell stories in the Sunday afternoon."[30]

Reba pointed out that when Joel "got tired with the kids why he went off and left them for mother to take care of," but "she said 'No. They come to see you, they didn't come to see me, now you take care of them. If you want them to go home tell them to go home!' 'I can't do that,'" he responded. Her answer was terse and practical. "Well then, take it and shut up!"[31]

Joel was proud of his horse-trading ability, a claim that Kate scoffed at with good-natured but justified skepticism. "He'd tell a million stories of the horses he'd trade," his grandson Leon recalled, and Kate would "cuss him out for bragging."[32] (The word "cussing" was metaphorical; Kate's language was always dignified.) A letter Joel wrote to Kate when she was visiting her sister May in Mona just before Christmas 1925, alludes to this. "So you think I got bit when I traded Bolley of[f]. I got 2 cows but one of them was a calf the cow I got is gentle to and younger if you want her for old Kate I will git her back for one Jersey." Kate's response is not known, nor her attitude to his naming a cow "Old Kate."[33]

Gwen, Sarah's third child, asserted her Roundy grandparents "had a difference of opinion occasionally, but then they believed in talking about it. They'd talk to each other about their differences of opinion and tell each other their opinion and not just get mad and go sulk or anything like that, or blow up and say terrible things . . . Grandma was a little bit snippy but she didn't say ignorant things, just what she did say was sometimes harshly said."[34]

According to Reba, when Martha and Albert Fitzpatrick moved to town and Mrs. Fitzpatrick alienated neighbors and fellow church members with her bossiness, Kate "didn't argue very much with her. Dad didn't argue with her either. Well Dad said what he thought, and what he didn't think, he didn't think."[35]

However Kate gave her some plain advice: "If you want to be friendly with people, be friendly. If you don't want to be friendly, do what you're doing."[36]

Joel teased her through occasional irritations. "He'd come up and put his arm around her when she was busy, and she'd say, 'Can't you see I'm busy?' And he'd say, 'Oh yeah, I can see that'—give her a little pat," Gwen reported.[37]

"And then he teased her incessantly . . . They had these private little names that none of us heard them say," Gwen explained.[38] JoAnn's best friend Florence Beatty Leavitt told about one of them. Kate "was little, and her name was Catherine and he called her Kitty. She pretended she didn't like it, but it tickled her, I think. 'My Kitten, my Kitty,' he'd call her."[39] (In one letter he called her "Steena.")

Sometimes Kate was just plain overworked. "Oh, Ma, go in and sit down," Reba would say, but Kate would answer, "No, I'll just do this," and then she'd keep going.[40]

In January 1919, while most of Kanarra was stricken with the flu, and again in December 1928, Kate had "flu-pneumonia" that according to Stella "left her with a weak heart. She suffered with that the rest of her life." That tightened the bonds between Sarah and Kate because Sarah was concerned about her mother's health. Gwen argued that there "was a closer bond between Sarah and her mother than there was between her mother and the other kids."[41]

The closeness of the women brought its own strains. "There was conflict there," JoAnn said. "Considerable conflict. However I think that Momma [Sarah] had a real need to mother her mother."[42] Sometimes they grumped at each other but they didn't argue out loud, never shouted, and the differences were quickly forgotten because of the many things they had in common.

JoAnn gave an example of Kate complaining that Sarah was "the most headstrong, contrary child I ever met in my life!" because even as a child she complained about the clothes Kate made her and had to make them herself. "And she's just so headstrong and so contrary."[43]

"But then another conflict between them was Grandma didn't like the way Momma talked to her kids," JoAnn added.[44] Florence Beatty Leavitt remembered being in the house when Ruth upset Sarah and Sarah turned to her and snapped, "Ruth, you red-headed son-of-a-bitch! If you do that again I'll slit your throat from ear to ear!" Florence was so shocked and embarrassed that she never forgot it, and she remembered that Sarah "talked to JoAnn a lot the same way."[45]

"I always felt so bad, because your mother used such hard language to you," Kate told JoAnn.

"Hard language? What do you mean?"

"Oh, she was always saying those terrible things to you." JoAnn had heard the blood-curdling threats so much that they didn't mean anything.[46]

The differences were also in approach. "Mom thought you could do anything for yourself," JoAnn said. "Grandma thought you ought to wait for some people to do some things. Not everything." Kate had more patience. But Sarah never tried to boss Kate. "Well, I'd like to see her try it!" laughed JoAnn. "Grandma would not be bossed!"[47]

Grandma "was just a little spitfire," Gwen explained. "She tried to hold her temper, under certain circumstances, but she could let it go when the family was there. I don't think any of the townspeople ever heard her. But the family heard her. She wasn't jawing all the time. I think she thought Mom was jawing all the time."[48]

Another problem, Gwen said, was Vic. "Even though they learned to appreciate dad, and Grandma and Grandpa both said that he'd done more for them than most of their kids, and they learned to really love him—but they had to defend him: to everybody. And so I think that there's always that little nagging situation there that they had to defend him. To townsfolks and other members of the family."[49]

Vic "wasn't a churchy man," Gwen explained. "But he certainly had his principles and he taught kids strict honesty, things like that, responsibility, ingenuity, and all those hard-work kinds-of-things. But I thought that Grandma always kind of felt bad about that, that he didn't believe exactly like she did. She wasn't angry with him, I think she felt bad about it, and she felt bad for Momma, because she knew Momma wanted the temple and it wasn't happening."[50]

"And she felt kind of bad because Momma never had a home after they left Kanarra," JoAnn added, "and she knew Momma wanted a home."[51] Kate's headstrong daughter was counterbalanced by her even feistier mother, Elizabeth, who continued to demand a lot of attention, especially after she became crippled.

Elizabeth "shuffled when she walked," JoAnn said of her great-grandmother.

> She'd slide one foot and then she'd slide the other one up to it, and then she'd kind of slide the heel around and then the toe and then the heel to get a little ways; then she'd slide the other one up to it. And that was when she was, like, she came to the door and the chair was a little too far for her to reach, she'd do that 'til she could reach the chair. Then she'd take hold of the chair and slide it along with her and that's the way she'd walk. She was so afraid of falling again. And she had crutches that she used sometimes. But just to get around the house, lots of times she just used the chair and slid around the house.[52]

Every night for dinner Kate fixed Elizabeth tea, a ritual JoAnn observed closely.

> Grandma Roundy had several little tables around the house, and come evening or something, then Grandma Roundy would fix tea for Grandma Stapley and she would get a little table and set it by where Grandma Stapley was sitting and she'd put a little cloth on it, nice little table cloth on it, and then she would make a little tray with bread and butter or maybe a piece of cake if she had it, or something like that. It was usually bread and butter, and then she'd put a little bowl with some kind of jam or jelly in it, and then she'd put a little plate that had cheese or something like that on, if she had cheese at the time. And then she'd bring this in and put this little tray there with a napkin and then she would a—meanwhile she would make the tea. She would bring the water to a boil and the minute it boiled she'd jerk it off that stove and pour it in the teapot over the tea. And it'd sit about five minutes, between five and ten minutes and then she'd pour it out, in the cup for Grandma Stapley. Then Grandma Stapley would sit there and eat this tea, it'd be about, oh, six or seven, five or six, depending on the time of the year, in the evening.

The tea, which had to be so particularly done, was Elizabeth's supper.[53]

"Almost everybody, at one time or another, had a little friction with Grandma Stapley," JoAnn asserted. "But I don't think Grandpa Roundy ever did. Grandma Stapley was a very bossy-type person." According to JoAnn, one reason Joel got along so well with Elizabeth was that he tried to do what she wanted. "I think that bossy people, in a way, if they think you're not going to do it, they're more bossy. If they know you are going to do it, they'll ask you as many things, but the first time they'll ask you in a nicer way maybe."[54]

Reba disagreed with JoAnn about that. "When she come to live with us eighteen years, and she went and told my dad to go outside—'Now you get this done, you get that done.' 'I can't do it yet.' 'You do it right now.' He said, 'I can't do it yet.' 'You do it right now.' He said, 'I can't do it right now.' And it was so he couldn't do it, he didn't do it."[55]

Elizabeth would "get a little bit aggravated with her [Kate] and when they got off to theirselves why Grandma would just rave and carry on and Mother would just let her rave and carry on, never said anything," Reba remembered.

Sometimes Elizabeth had other complaints, including "whatever somebody done that she didn't like, why she'd talk about it . . . mostly her kids. She'd talk about, 'Well, if they'd a done this or done that, things would of been different.' And Mother says, 'It's all past. Let's forget it.' But she didn't get it off her mind." The result was she would "get it out, and when she got it out then they'd come back in where the people was and she was good natured."[56]

Kate didn't complain to her mother. "Sometimes you could see that she was put out [with Elizabeth]," JoAnn explained. "You could always tell how Grandma [Kate] felt by looking in her eyes. If she was sick you could tell. Her eyes showed it. It wasn't her face, it was her eyes. Her eyes would start snapping if she got a little bit upset, irritated or something."[57]

Kate "had to work all the time, continually, and that's about all she ever done, is continually," Reba said. Reacting to her mother caused worse problems. "If Mother would cross her path, why, Grandma would get angry, then she—I don't know how you'd call it. She'd tell her that was the wrong thing to do, and she shouldn't be doing this, and she shouldn't be doing that, and make you feel like a two-cent piece."

"I still think I'm right but she thinks I'm wrong, so let her think it," Kate told Reba. "As long as she don't see me do it, why then that's all right." Elizabeth demanded Kate "do the way she wanted her to do. She should run her household like she run hers. But Mother didn't do it." Still, Reba remembered that "Mother was very patient with her and said she only had one mother and she was going to take care of her."[58]

And there were advantages to having Elizabeth around. She was witty, had a fine sense of humor, and got things done. "I've saw Grandma do a lot of work," Reba recalled. "She done all kind of housework in there, she straightened up her bed and she straightened up her house around there with her crutch. And she always wiped the dishes. Mother washed the dishes; she always wiped them . . . She was always busy."[59]

Elizabeth sometimes looked at her great-granddaughter JoAnn with a jaundiced eye. "She's a little fat little girl," the older woman commented and Reba confirmed, "She was. She was heavy set when she was a little kid. But she was like her mother, she was a little bit spunky." Elizabeth said, "I asked her to get me a drink of water and she said 'No.' So, that was all there was to it. Nothing went any further than that. If she wanted to help me okay, if you don't, you don't."[60]

JoAnn had happy memories of Elizabeth, especially as her sewing teacher. Catherine had been a skilled tailor, Elizabeth was a proficient quilter, and Kate took an interest in sewing; but Sarah used her sewing machine to supplement her income. It was interesting that this talent was taught to JoAnn by Elizabeth and not by Sarah.

JoAnn learned to cord wool from her great-grandmother Elizabeth and enjoyed watching the older woman knit. "Grandma Stapley could knit like a house afire! She'd knit as fast as Momma." She added that

> I always got along with her fine. She never yelled and hollered at me, even when she kind of scolded me or told me I did something that wasn't right and I should not have done that. But she didn't yell at me, she just told me. And I understood that she was telling me . . . so that I would know better, rather than telling me so that if they didn't take a stick to me I could take a stick to myself.[61]

"She was just so sweet to me," JoAnn concluded. "But she never would let me comb her hair, because she said I pulled her hair. And then Gwen would climb on a chair, stand behind her, comb her hair, comb her hair, it was just soft, like, like white silk thread. But Gwen could comb her hair because Gwen didn't pull her hair."[62]

Another granddaughter remembered Elizabeth as demanding. "No speck of dirt ever escaped Grandma's eagle eye," wrote Velma Rymer. "One day as she sat on a high kitchen stool to help us do dishes, one particular cauliflower-shaped pitcher was most difficult to clean, but Grandma would not wipe it until we had scoured the difficult parts to gleaming white."[63]

"You didn't treat her like a little kid," Reba said of Elizabeth.

> She had a very good memory. She had a good memory right up to the day she died. She could tell you a lot of things, the dates and everything . . . in thirty-six we started genealogy, and we asked her what her father and mother's name was. She give us her father and mother's names, she give us the birthdates, she give the names of all of their children and all of the birthdates and who they all married. Every one of them was right. So she had a good mind. She just didn't have good health. After she fell down she didn't exercise, she didn't get up and do this, and I thought she done pretty well.[64]

Velma Rymer insisted that "It was always a festive occasion when Grandma arrived," but admitted Elizabeth was something of a perfectionist, explaining,

"Her nature, altho stern, was gentle."[65] Elizabeth's son John Alma tolerated her foibles. "Dad always just—whatever Grandma said, he'd make the best of it," his daughter Leola Stapley Anderson said.[66]

"He'd just say, 'Well, if Mother wants to do it that way, why, that's the way we'll do it.' He never would make no fuss about it." Leola added that the family "really enjoyed her. We always thought that was fun to have Grandma come. Course she didn't stay very long at our place. And then she'd come and stay 'til she wanted to go home and then they'd take her home . . . but she liked to come up and look the town [Kanarra] over and like that."[67]

It was usually Elizabeth's son Mahonri Stapley or his children who took her north in the early summer, and as Mahonri's daughter Lella explained, "There always had to be a woman along" so Lella "was usually available."[68] Elton, Mahonri's oldest son, acknowledged that sometimes Elizabeth could be difficult, but said, "I don't know if I ever heard my dad or mother ever said they wished the time would come when she would pick up and go. We've had her in our home several times for several days in a time. But I guess we've all got our characteristics and some of them are liked and some of them are disliked by our neighbors and associates. So, guess there's none of us that are perfect."[69]

Josephine Kay Garfield's memories of her grandmother's arrival in Mona are particularly vivid. "She'd bring her feather bed and seven pillows and all her own bedding and her own jam," laughed Josephine. "She was a fussy old gal, and all of her clothes had to be washed before ours were and starched and ironed and she was really very fussy. She knit her own socks, stockings, you know, wool stockings."[70] Josephine's sister Elsie explained the seven pillows: "There were five at her back, one under her leg, and one under her arm. And sometimes it'd take you quite a while to get those pillows stacked so that she was just right comfortable!"[71]

"And then she always had a glass of soda water by her bed," Elsie added.

> And it was quite—quite a challenge to get her put away for the night. She used to get some kind of funny ideas. For instance, she got the notion that she wanted bakery bread. And so there was a little store down the street and then beyond that was a service station, and the—the Wonder Bakery truck would come and deliver bread to the store and then it would go on down and deliver it to the service station because they had—just a few things, you know. And so we'd have to go to the store and get the bread for her. And then, if the store was out of bread you'd go on down to the other—to the service station, get her a loaf of bread

> there. But she got it into her head that the bread at the service station was, ah, baked better. I think she called it soaped.

"We all catered to her," remembered Josephine. "My younger sister, she could do no wrong. But the rest of us, we had to toe the mark and then my brother, he was the only boy, and she used to say, 'Now that's your only brother, now you be good to him! You let him do this and that!'"[72]

The northwest parlor room with its own little stove was reserved for Elizabeth's Mona visit. Josephine remembered "We had to make muffins every morning for her breakfast, 'specially for her." The older woman would ask her daughter May to read to her and while May enjoyed reading, she found this experience frustrating. "I don't know what good it does to read to her," May complained, "she's looking out the window saying, 'Well look at that, Mary, look whose going down the road!'"[73]

Elizabeth interfered so much in the family life that one year May had to send her back to Hurricane early because May's son was getting too hard to handle. However, May was so good-natured her husband Jack called her "Easy," though he detested her mother. "Aunt May's husband, she couldn't get along too much with him," Reba said. "She didn't like the way he done. He never associated with her too much,"[74] and Josephine explained why. "She tried to tell him what to do when she first came up here and he resented it very much . . . So they didn't have much to do with each other."[75]

Josephine's sister Elsie agreed. "Grandma was, it was her nature to want to be in control. And it was my father's nature to control his own family," she chuckled. "But he was nice to her, and, ah, she'd come and spend summers with her, but I don't think they ever talked anything, much." He wasn't a talkative man in any case. The Kays did have a player piano and Grandma Stapley "had a wonderful memory" and "She used to sing 'Come Come Ye Saints,'" laughed Elsie. "It sounded awfully off-key to me but she was an old woman and we all sing off-key when we get old!"[76]

And Grandma could be helpful, especially with her nursing skills. "Well," Elsie continued,

> Grandma was quite a character. But I admire her. She might not of been the easiest person to get along with but I think she was a good woman and I think she did a lot of good. And you know, when I graduated from high school, of course in the spring, and I was going go on to school in the fall. And, they talk about her being a nurse and taking care of sick

> and all that. She knew how to make poultices and all sorts of things. And anyway that summer, oh I guess it must of been about the latter part of August, a bunch of us kids had built a bonfire and had a marshmallow roast. And so we were all—squatted down, you know, roasting our marshmallows. And I was just off to the side of one of the girls. Her marshmallow caught on fire, and she went like that [motioning], and it hit me right there . . . And hot. And I thought, oh I was lucky it didn't get in my eye . . . And Grandma was with us then, and I thought, oh, I'm going to have a scar the rest of my life. And Grandma had me cake that—saturated with—I'm not sure if it was olive oil or castor oil and you know I had no scar at all, from that . . . She always knew how to doctor you, and I thought she was quite a person.[77]

But still, Josephine's conclusion was predictable. "It was just—well—it was like we were set free when she left!"[78] In March 1930 the Kays were "set free" when Elizabeth and her son John A. "arrived [in Kanarra] Saturday evening on the Pickwick [i.e., the equivalent of a bus] from Mona, Utah, where sister Stapley has spent the winter with her daughter Mrs. Mary Kaye," reported the *Iron County Record* on March 26, 1930.[79] Kate and Joel Roundy probably drove up from Hurricane to get her because a week later the newspaper reported that "Mr. and Mrs. J. J. Roundy from Hurricane spent Sunday in town visiting old friends."[80]

Elizabeth, sensing the resentment she sometimes created, was occasionally disgruntled and lonely, sad over her dependence on her children. Reba said that the older woman argued "a lot of times she didn't know why Grandpa didn't come and get her. He died eighteen years before she did. But she says, 'I don't know why he's sticking over there so much, why don't he come and get me?'"[81] But she was destined to outlast the 1920s and live well into the era of Franklin Delano Roosevelt.

Though there were disagreements and sometimes bitterness, these women had the ability to make social events out of mundane activities, allaying tensions, and reinforcing cooperative goodwill. "In our family, Grandma would put a quilt on, and everybody would come quilting, all of her kids that could, her kids-in-law and stuff like that," JoAnn explained.[82]

> Anybody would come around quilting. That was a social event. When they killed the pig or the beef, that was a social event, everybody would get together, and oh, all these people around. When they had [LDS]

> conference people would come from Toquerville and LaVerkin, which were all our relatives, and they'd come over to conference, in their wagons, later on in their cars. But they'd make the Sunday, you know, when they weren't in church, they'd come up to Grandma's and we'd have a big social thing then . . . And then people would come a visiting, some of Grandma's relatives, Grandpa's relatives would come. Their brothers or sisters or whatever, [would] come down for a visit, and they'd stay for two or three weeks. And so there was a lot of just plain socializing.[83]

The 1920s brought many changes in the lives of these women, including the loss of most of their social status. In Kanarra they held important community positions: Elizabeth was a respected midwife, Kate served some years as president of the Relief Society, and Sarah's sojourn as ward clerk broke new ground in the callings available to women. In Hurricane Elizabeth still received solace from her celebrity status. Besides looking after Elizabeth, Kate and Sarah were involved almost exclusively in demands on them to care for others. The new technology of the twenties put airplanes and radio within the reach of working people; the future held out the hope of much more. But the patterns of gradual prosperity during the twenties were to be reversed in the tribulations of the Depression. The thirties were a challenge to survive.

14

"That Was Money in Her Pocket"

Sarah E. Roundy Sylvester

For Joel and Kate Roundy the 1920s had been a slow crawl out of an economic morass as they regained some of the ground they lost when they were defrauded of their brick bungalow. They started over with a three-wall shack but by the end of the decade had finished and then doubled it into a comfortable house. They had also built a barn, root cellar, chicken coop, and had laid out a large garden. Joel, a horticulturist whose heroes included George Washington Carver and Luther Burbank and who was close friends with Hurricane orchardist Amos Workman, had an unusual variety of nuts and fruits that he grafted himself. His garden included berries, shrubs, pomegranates, and a leafy green vineyard. Still, there were no riches to be won through agriculture.[1]

While farmers were making little money, some speculators were getting rich, like those at the top of the mining business. On August 15, 1928, the *Salt Lake Mining Review* reported that Vic Sylvester's mining-promoter brother, Frank Sylvester, was vice-president of the newly incorporated Tintic Peerless Mines Company with a capitalization of $1.6 million. The president, Judge Wilson Isaac Snyder, had written a book about mining (Utah's Snyderville Basin was named for the Judge's uncle, Samuel Snyder).[2] The Judge's brother Horace Greeley Snyder was married to Ada Sylvester, Vic and Frank's cousin,[3] and things looked good. "Prospects for Washington County Never Brighter," boasted the *Washington County News* on May 23, 1929.[4]

But that was before Thursday, October 24, 1929, when the stock market began to crumble. Officers of J. P. Morgan and Company, Chase National Bank, Guaranty Trust Company, Bankers Trust, National City Bank, and First National Bank reacted to the downturn by setting up a stock-buying pool of $240 million. That stabilized the market for two days. Herbert Hoover, president for only eight months, assured the country that business "is on a sound and prosperous basis" and shortly the bankers discreetly tried to dispose of the stocks they'd publicly purchased. But by Monday, October 28, the market fell again, and the next day was memorable "Black Tuesday" when the market collapsed. Between September 3 and November 13, shares in the fifty leading stocks and the twenty-five leading industrials dropped by nearly half.[5] By 1931 Horace Greeley Snyder's house had been foreclosed on, Judge Snyder was dead, and Frank Sylvester was starting over.

Before the effects of the Crash could be fully felt, the Sylvester family burden was temporarily lessened when fifteen-year-old Nell announced she intended to marry twenty-two-year-old Edwin Stout. She couldn't have chosen a more qualified husband if her goal was to marry someone with impressive family roots in historic and southern Utah Mormonism: he was descended from the Stouts, Giffords, DeMilles, and Knights, all important players in Mormon history.

Reba said Sarah told Nell, "'You're too young to get married.' And Vic says, 'Well you can get married if you want to. Go get married.'"[6] When, years later, Maud had a granddaughter marry before some folks thought she was ready, Dick wrote that "Victor said, 'It's up to them—if they think they are old enough they probably are. They can go to school just the same after they are married if they have time, and do what else it takes.'"[7] Reba says Sarah countered Vic by telling Nell, "You're too young to get married. You'd better wait a year or two."[8]

Sarah was aghast, but she and Nell didn't communicate very well. "We didn't get close like some mothers and daughters and talk about anything and everything," Nell remembered. "She used to threaten me when I stayed out too late but I invariably come home after dark." Nell was more reticent than Reba in discussing Sarah's reaction. Asked what Sarah thought, Nell responded with another question: "What would any mom think?" and said Vic argued that "if you're bound and determined just as well write you out a declaration of independence and let you do it."[9]

"She decided if her dad said she could get married, she got married," Reba added. "Now, she says, she missed all the happiness of her life. She missed all the getting together with the girls and the boys and everything else. She just missed that. So, she says, 'I'm not going to tell my kids to get married.' I says, 'Of course you won't, 'cause they're all married.'" Reba didn't think Nell was ready for marriage. "She says she don't know anything. She wouldn't hardly wash dishes to home, let alone when she got married."

"Grandma! Don't you think that's too young?" Reba questioned Elizabeth, the aging family matriarch.

"I have nothing to say!" Elizabeth answered grimly.

"How come?"

"Cause I was married when I was sixteen."[10]

The wedding took place on January 30, 1930, in Parowan. Vern Jim, the first baby, didn't arrive until January 31, 1931. "I lived for the first three months in the south bedroom of Grandma Roundy's house," Nell recalled. "Put a cook stove in there and I moved there until it was time to open up the sawmill and then we moved to the sawmill and my husband worked for the sawmill."[11]

At first the Crash didn't seem to affect Sarah's life. Her daughters JoAnn and Gwen laughed that they were "already so poor anyway" that "at first we didn't even notice the Depression."[12] But the surest indicators of poverty are the delinquent tax records. Joel paid his 1928 taxes early, but he was late in paying the thirty dollars that the Washington County assessor demanded in 1931 and taxes for the remaining years of the decade were a struggle.[13] So many taxpayers were behind that the Washington County schools ran out of money and had to close in April; teachers were paid in "tax anticipation warrants" instead of cash, which were sold—usually at a discount—and could be redeemed for taxes.

In early 1930 Hurricane townsfolk followed Herbert Hoover's suggestion to boost the economy by public works, completing street grading and graveling and planning both a new sewer system and sidewalks. The Wadsworth Theatre attempted to spur the local economy by promising to show "The Jazz Singer." In August the Second Annual Dixie Fruit Festival was held in Hurricane and Joel's Jersey cow won a prize.[14] That hardly augured of bad times and hardship, but in December the Bank of St. George took out a full page advertisement to remind nervous depositors the bank was solvent.[15] At the end of 1931 the *Washington County News* published the longest delinquent tax list in its history—eight pages of delinquencies in a newspaper that was normally eight pages long.[16]

"We are passing thro one of the hardest times that have ever come to the U.S.," wrote Sarah's cousin Cassie Fullmer Roundy on July 20, 1931. "Drowth bank failures, financial depression and ruin and we wonder if Christs coming isnt at Our doors."[17]

Vic's uncle Reverend Ebenezer J. Hanks, who scandalized the family by becoming a Presbyterian minister, wrote his sister Nellie from Rigby, Idaho, on December 20, 1931, "When I think of the number of people who have nothing coming in this winter I feel as tho we have a whole lot to be thankful for. At least we do not have to fear being either cold or hungry."[18] Nellie wrote their Kanarra sister "Rony" Davis after Christmas that "I would have liked to have sent ever body in our family something but surcomsances wouldent allow me to this year if I am still living next year and better times which we all hope for I don't want to forget enny of them . . . I am going to send a Dolla[r] in this letter and you take it and buy a little present for you."[19]

The local church house in rural Mormondom had always served temporal as well as spiritual purposes, and sermons by the lay clergy were as likely to include admonitions "to advertise Zion National Park and use all influence possible to get the Arrowhead Trail to come direct south to Hurricane,"[20] as warnings about sin. The sermons Kate and Joel listened to updated church members on the smallpox epidemic, estimated the damage done to the fruit crop by a late frost, and addressed economics. Members were advised to be thrifty, help the poor with their fuel bills, and get out of debt. George I. Spendlove "remarked on the financial and general business depression, which is world-wide," noted a clerk who was thrifty with words. "Wheat selling in some places as low as 22 cents a bushel. Suggested a reciprocity scheme. There was an overproduction of wheat cotton and other farm goods in the world. Suggested that now is a good time to buy up provisions and store for a time of want which is inevitable."[21]

Spendlove's suggestions stirred another man to link these problems with the Mormon world view. "Elder Hall followed somewhat in the same line of thought and related scripture showing that the present condition is in fulfillment of prophecy."[22]

While it was comforting to find religious authority for the Depression, it was more practical to revert to a barter economy where tithing was again paid in kind and "all wishing to go to the Temple can pay for their ride in Produce, Dried fruits 7 and 8 cents [per pound,] molasses per gallon .50[,] chickens at market price."[23]

It was odd—certainly unfair—that something as remote as the New York Stock Market should have any effect on the lives of Elizabeth, Kate, and Sarah. For generations they had been trained in frugality and were better prepared than the financial elites for hard times. Catherine Campbell Steele spent much of her life boiling soap from scraps of grease, making and washing bedding and clothing, tending a garden, tailoring, and preserving fruits, vegetables, and meat. Elizabeth's life was passed in the same way and naturally she made sure that Kate had a practical knowledge of the "domestic arts." Sarah learned much from her mother and grandmothers and taught the same to her children. It was during the severity of the Depression that these generations of women cooperated ever more closely to feed and clothe their families.

Because the federal government and the business sector drastically cut spending, no one entity held enough economic power to stimulate the economy.

As the situation continued to contract the Depression worsened, destroying Herbert Hoover's presidency. On March 4, 1933, Franklin Delano Roosevelt was inaugurated and some were so enthusiastic that they compared his advent to the coming of Christ. Kate and her family were strong Republicans and more restrained, though Joel voted for Roosevelt with great reluctance, prompted by a dream he had that Roosevelt must be elected.[24] Vic's Aunt Nellie Hanks Goold wrote hopefully from Burley, Idaho, March 13, 1933, "I will be glad when sumer comes again and hard times is over it makes my heart ac[h]e to see poor people I hop[e] changing Presidence will help."[25]

"Women were not really that much in politics," JoAnn explained, and added her great-grandmother Stapley "had her own work to do and things she did . . . it didn't make that much difference to her." Elizabeth, like Joel a Republican, talked about "things that happened to her, her environment, where she was living now." She didn't talk politics. Kate "had political opinions but I don't think she expressed them very often because I think sometimes they were not the same as Grandpa's." Then JoAnn added thoughtfully, "I think she thought Grandpa talked maybe too much about politics." Sarah argued, "Your vote is personal. You can talk politics all the time about anything, you can argue on whatever side you want. When you go to the polls you vote whatever your conscience tells you. And it's nobody's business and you don't tell anybody about it." JoAnn didn't know how her mother felt about the changes in government brought about by the "New Deal."[26]

"Changing Presidence" led to the most dramatic restructuring the United States government had seen since the Civil War. On his first full day as president, Franklin Roosevelt issued a call for a special session of Congress and declared a bank holiday to stabilize financial institutions. Within a hundred days he had driven through a farm relief bill, established the Civilian Conservation Corps to create jobs for 250,000 young men, established the Tennessee Valley Authority to revitalize the economies of seven southern states through better harnessing of hydroelectric power, passed mortgage foreclosure legislation, abandoned the gold standard, and initiated major agriculture and banking reforms.[27]

But even with government moving like it had never moved before, those hundred days didn't save the Sylvesters from their worst Depression experience. For some reason, in May 1933 they switched places with Sarah's sister Stella Roundy Russell and her husband Ellis, the latter family moving to Hurricane and the former to the Roundy Camp Creek farm just south of Kanarra. Once again the extended family pooled resources.

Spring 1933 wasn't the best time to go to Iron County. Cedar City doctors James S. Prestwich and his brother-in-law Arnold L. Graff were in Denver being convicted of defrauding the federal government of 11,500 acres in Garfield County, Colorado.[28] Luckily Dr. Menzies Macfarlane and his partner J. W. Bergstrom, who had helped deliver Sarah's daughter JoAnn, filled in for the indicted doctors because Vic's Aunt Rony Davis, who was sick all spring with heart problems, spent three weeks recuperating in Cedar.[29]

JoAnn remembered it was hard enough without townsfolk being out of sorts.

> That was rough! because we went up there right when school was out . . . and it was summer in Hurricane in May, and when we got there [at Camp Creek] it was winter still. It's about 3,000 feet higher. It was icy cold and wintery and we didn't have the kind of clothes at all for that kind of weather . . . We didn't have any money and we didn't have any warm clothes, and we didn't have much food, so we were up there trying to live on mostly nothing.

Gwen said that "the cow was dry and it was too cold for a garden. We ran out of flour, we ran out of bottled fruit, and we thought we'd starve to death before that cow come in."[30]

JoAnn related:

> Mom would go out and "steal" grain from the cows. We had some grain for the cows and had to cut it in half because we didn't think we had enough to last them till the grass came up. But there was still sleety, snowy, and wet, and Gwen and I had to take the cows out all day long. Grandpa had, across the road, he had a bunch of land that didn't really have much on it except it just grew up in weeds and stuff that they pastured and there was a lot of scrub oak and stuff there. Gwen and I'd take the cows—now there was a bridge over kind of a wash and we'd take the cows down in the wash and take them under the bridge instead of taking them across the highway. And then we would herd them all day long. We'd take matches and a little piece of paper if we could find one and try to keep warm. We'd go in the scrub oak and scrape the snow and stuff off and scrape until we could find some kind of leaves and little pieces of wood and stuff that looked like they might be dry enough that we could possibly get them to burn, make us a fire and try

> to keep our fingers warm over it and watch those dumb cows trying to find something to eat in the snow.

"At Camp Creek we were all hungry," JoAnn explained, and Gwen echoed

those sentiments. "I mean hungry! And cold." The food they had preserved was all gone and poverty made family tensions unbearably high. "Dad was cross as a bear because he didn't have any money and the rain and sleet wouldn't stop so he could get the plowing done," JoAnn wrote. They were living in what JoAnn characterized as a "miserable hut," a twelve-by-sixteen-foot, one-room log building with two double beds bunk style, and a cot (this may have been Ren's "playhouse"). Furnishings were limited to a cook stove, dresser, cupboard, trunk, chairs, and a wash stand.

With nothing for the family to eat but cheese and boiled grain, Vic plowed and planted potatoes and a garden and used all his pioneer know-how, trapping white squirrels and gathering pine nuts while waiting for the crops to come in. Sarah continued to "steal" grain from the cow.

"Dad bought one bag of Bull Durham tobacco and tried to make it last all summer because it cost a whole nickel," JoAnn wrote in an unfinished 1978 draft of her memoirs.

> One package of tobacco paper came with the bag but extras cost a penny. He would ration it out to one cigarette a day after supper and would put about half as much tobacco as usual in it. When the paper ran out, he used any paper around the house. He felt that he couldn't spend money on non-food or on pleasure when we were in such dire straits. He never did smoke a lot, only about 2 to 4 cigarettes a day. I thought at the time he was ornery and angry because he had to cut down on his smoking.

One of those cold, hungry days Sarah had an announcement for Vic: she was pregnant. "They tried to figure out what on earth they were going to do," Gwen recalled. "And it got hotter, and hotter, and hotter. And this one night—and we lived in this one-room cabin up there. And we had a double bed built bunk-style with two-by-fours, and we were on the top bunk, us kids . . . [and] Rex was over on a cot on the other side of the bed." Vic and Sarah "were standing up and arguing, and it got to this push and shove, and a few other things." Ruth woke up to see her father and mother quarreling violently and

Vic "pushing her at the door and kind of punching at her. I mean, not hitting her hard, but—you know." Gwen reached out and pulled Vic's hair to make him stop. This abruptly ended the fight, but it was so traumatic no one ever forgot it.

Shortly after, Vic told Sarah that he wanted a divorce. Sarah is said to have responded, "Okay, you can have a divorce, but you're going to pay for the keep of the kids." Reba said that his sentiments were, "Well, if he had to do that, he wouldn't get a divorce." Sarah and Reba had a long talk later about Sarah's marriage, and Sarah confessed that "Dad didn't want her to marry him in the first place, but she said, 'I married him anyway.' And she said, 'And I told him [her dad] I'd never complain.' She never complained of a thing."[31]

They survived the summer and JoAnn noticed a special sparkle in her mother's eye when she went in to Kanarra. Here were all her lifelong friends and almost everybody was related. Aunt Hattie Stapley, Jimmy's widow, lived in town and besides John's children coming to visit, Aunt Hattie's did as well. Leland Stapley's two orphaned boys, Eugene and Lee, came down from Salt Lake to spend the summer with their grandma Aunt Hattie. Other visiting Stapley cousins included Alenna Stapley Williams, Madge Stapley, Leola Stapley Anderson, Parley Stapley, Dee and Hazel Stapley, Zina Pollock, William and Sophia Stapley, and even Aunt May Stapley Kay's daughter Kathryn—named for Catherine Campbell Steele, the matriarch of them all. There were even more cousins on the Roundy side.[32]

Great-grandma Elizabeth Stapley, who was in Mona visiting Aunt May Kay, got sick and so Uncle John Stapley brought her to town where she spent part of the summer. The Kanarra Relief Society held a birthday party in August for her at Uncle John's: "Mrs. Stapley was the first white child born in Utah. Dainty refreshments were served to 40 guests. A pleasant time was had by all present."[33] Vic's Aunt Rony Hanks Davis was soon back from Cedar City convalescing and her daughter Viola and granddaughter Lorna dropped in, the latter an imaginative girl who was a favorite and age-mate cousin of JoAnn's.

While they missed Hurricane—and weren't there when Uncle Jesse Roundy was a candidate for the city council on the Democratic ticket (he embraced the New Deal and co-ops with a lot more enthusiasm than his more conservative relatives[34]), they had more extended family in Kanarra than anywhere else.

In late 1933 Sarah moved the family into a light orange-colored brick granary in Hurricane. (This wasn't new: when she first got married she'd lived in Joel and Kate's granary.) "The granary had a cement porch that was smooth and it was about like a ten inch step or something like that," Sarah's daughter Gwen remembered. "We used to play jacks on them with matches and that and it was just perfect for kids to play on. And they had a cellar down underneath that didn't have a cement floor, but we slept down there anyway, 'cause the granary was one big room, the bedroom was one corner, the kitchen was one corner and so forth and there was an outside bathroom."[35]

It was a relief to get back to Hurricane and the embrace of Kate. These women worked together—cooking, canning, quilting, and "a lot of that," JoAnn remembered.[36] "And dried fruit together, and picked fruit, and gardened, and all that stuff. We shared gardens."[37] Sarah "always grew a large garden wherever we lived," JoAnn recalled and when she was able to rent a house with fruit trees and lots of land, "Momma grew a gorgeous, fantastic garden."[38]

Sarah's youngest daughter Ruth confirmed that. "One thing Momma used to always have was a real good garden . . . Rex and I used to have to go out and weed in the garden, irrigate stuff [when] we weren't very old." Gwen related, "We used to have to carry a square of sacking or something with us when you pulled the weeds [and] you had to throw them in this sack to feed the pigs." She added that besides giving the weeds to the pig, "I can remember having to eat the darn pigweeds. I hated that! Oh how I hated them; no matter how much vinegar you put on them or anything else, salt and pepper and vinegar, I still hated them, but if that's all you had to eat, you ate pigweeds. You had to save those out of the weeds that you weeded out of the garden."[39]

They preserved the food they grew. "Mom would go up and help her mother [Kate] bottle and can a lot of food," JoAnn remembered, and Elizabeth would help by performing chores like shelling peas. They canned pickles together (all kinds—bread and butter, dill, mustard, and sweet pickles), fruits and vegetables, and bottled enormous quantities of food—at one time more than twelve hundred quarts of tomatoes, and other vegetables and fruits by the hundreds. Sarah also preserved pork and beef and churned butter. Her children remember skipping across the hot corrugated tin roofs ("Cat on a hot tin roof, nothing!" said Gwen), laying out slices of apples, pears, peaches, and apricots to dry. In later years they thought a two-year food supply simple by comparison with Sarah's code, which code was probably reinforced after their Camp Creek miseries.[40]

What they didn't grow, they got by gift or barter. Once a year Vic, Sarah, and their children took a trek to Grandpa Joe Sylvester's house in Pintura (formerly Bellevue) where they picked black, red, and yellow currants.[41] In Hurricane, Sarah and her children picked Himalaya berries on shares using long stockings to protect their arms from thorns and straw hats to protect their faces from sunburn. The buckets of berries were made into jams or pies.

Sarah worked for Hurricane merchant E. J. Graff and others harvesting almonds, pecans, and black walnuts on shares. "She went down there and got—a—nuts out to the field," Reba remembered. "She'd get them and bring them and take them home and hull them. And she'd take her kids with her. And the boys would get up in the field and knock them—up in the trees and knock them down and the girls would pick them up and put them in a sack. And then she got somebody to haul them up to her . . . Now some people thought she was crazy for doing that but that was money in her pocket."[42] When they hulled the nuts, they saved the shells to burn in the winter to supplement the woodpile. "We spent all summer getting ready for winter," sighed JoAnn.[43]

Sarah also sold berries or almonds she got on shares, sending Gwen and JoAnn to deliver them. "Now be sure you get this much money out of it," she'd caution. Gwen, more assertive than JoAnn, wouldn't accept excuses. If the buyer put her off, she'd announce, "I guess we'll have to take these back because Momma told us we had to get the money." That usually was enough to coerce the customers into paying.[44]

They raised chickens, had a cow, and sometimes a young beef and a pig or two. Neighbors gave them scraps of meat that were considered undesirable—beef brains, tongue, and liver, or a pig's head for head cheese. "My mother knew all about nutrition," JoAnn remembered.

> And she knew that the best parts of the meat for nutrition were the liver and the heart and the tongue and the brain and those kinds of things. And so nobody else would eat them. Everybody in town, when they killed their animals, almost everybody in town, would run over some of these meats to Momma. And several people made head cheese out of their pigs' heads but not a lot, but several so that we didn't get all the head cheese in town.[45]

Quilting was even more communal than food storage and something that Elizabeth, the clan matriarch, took a special interest in. Her granddaughter Velma Stapley Rymer remembered that "Quilt making was Grandma's hobby, all made by hand & flawless" and she recalled, "On one visit to Mona, on which I accompanied her, we sewed together. It was then she taught me to use a thimble, saying I'd never be a good seamstress unless I used a thimble. She also taught me to whistle as we worked. My sister LaRu sewed for the public and gathered many beautiful pieces of silk material. Grandma sewed these into a crazy patch quilt, embroidering around each piece with silk floss, in many fancy designs."[46]

Reba confirmed that Elizabeth would "set and sew quilt blocks by the yard"[47] but it was multiple generations of women who turned the blocks into quilts. JoAnn remembered her mother Sarah, grandmother Kate, and great-grandmother Elizabeth, along with lots of other women, gathered around the large quilting frame.

> I'd be in the room or else I would hide under the quilt as the quilt was—when they started. Usually by the time the quilt was finished I'd have to get out of the way 'cause the knees would be there. Grandma Stapley helped quilt; and Grandma Roundy and Momma [Sarah] and usually somebody else would be there. Reba or Reva and Reba, or Aunt Stella sometimes came up and helped quilt . . . They'd put a quilt on the frames [and] the corners of the frames would be over the chairs, and then we would tie them together . . . They'd get around the quilt [usually in the north front room]. They'd lay the quilts out and put them up and—the lining, they'd tie. Now, we didn't tack them down. We had holes in our quilting frames, and we just took the carpet warp, kind of thread, and we just sewed them onto the frames, because of the holes in the middle you could run the needle through there. Sometimes a fancy quilt would be marked and sometimes you just decide which blocks to go around, to quilt around and then quilt it. And so if you have a fancy quilt you usually put a fancy—what they call quilting pattern, and make the fancy lines there between them. And then usually they'd start in the place that was sticking out the furthest into the floor.
>
> Boy they had fun quilting! Everybody liked to quilt and they talked! They talked about everybody they knew in Cedar City and everybody they knew in Kanarra, and all their relatives, and—the whole—that was where the newspapers were! Family newspapers! And it was always, who had a baby and who was getting married and how so-and-so was getting along and whether somebody was sick and whether somebody's kid wasn't doing so well, they'd go into that. Somebody's husband'd be doing something—sick or, ah—something, and all these things and all about the babies they had and how they had them and they'd go into all kinds of details that I wasn't supposed to hear but they forgot I was there! And when the, somebody—the other kids'd come in from

> outside, why, [whispering] "Sh! There's somebody coming in!" So the other kids didn't get to hear all these things that I got to hear! [JoAnn laughed.]
>
> And then after we quilted a while, why, somebody'd get up and go in the other room and check on the beans or whatever we were figuring they'd eat—like they'd bake beans—no, they wouldn't bake the beans usually, they'd have the beans on the stove, they'd be cooking a great big pot of beans and maybe a pot of potatoes—Grandma [Kate] always liked to have a pot of potatoes for everyone's meal. And then maybe in the oven there'd be rice pudding and somebody, periodically, would check that stuff, and anything else that needed to be done, somebody'd get up to do it and then they'd come back to quilt. They didn't really sit and quilt all the time. Each person would get up and then they'd come back.[48]

This was women's work but JoAnn remembered that

> about the time Grandpa came in to eat—because he'd be out working—and sometimes he'd come in and have something done in between. But he'd be like out watering or out weeding, or working, whatever he was doing. Or sometimes he'd be out to the orchard, out to the ranch—farm . . . he'd come in for dinner; we had dinner at noon, so everybody'd leave the quilting table and we'd go get the table all set and everybody would have this lovely meal. Call the kids in and this good meal and after the dishes were washed somebody might be going back to quilting.

JoAnn reported that family matriarch Elizabeth "was the only one that mostly sat there for a while until she got tired and then, ah—but she liked to quilt. I don't know how long she quilted at a time."[49]

Elizabeth taught Kate sewing and schooled many others as well. "Grandma Stapley taught me to sew," JoAnn remembered with enthusiasm, and scoffed at the stories of her great-grandmother's imperiousness.

> I always loved Grandma Stapley. I read about—what you say about Grandma Stapley and I think, boy! That's not the way she was to me! I was a little teeny kid, I guess I was about three when she taught me to sew by hand. I could hold the needle and make a stitch. That's all I already knew. And Grandma had a little chair. Grandma Roundy had

> two little chairs in her house. One was Grandma Roundy's little chair when she was little, and one of them, I think, belonged to one of her kids when they were little. And I would sit in this little teeny chair by this real short rocker that Grandma Stapley was in, 'cause Grandma Stapley was short, and she had a little rocking chair that had short legs. Not really short, but a lot shorter than normal. And she'd sit there and I'd come up and she'd want me to come sit by her so I'd sit by her and she'd hand me these things to sew together and so I'd sew and she'd keep saying, "Oh that's pretty good now! Just try and make the stitches just a little bit littler!" And so I'd make the stitches a little bit littler, and I kept practicing on it and I'd get those stitches so little I thought that you couldn't get them any littler, only had one thread in each stitch, sort of you know. "Now you have to back stitch them every few stitches, too, so they'll stay!" [These tiny pieces of cloth were salvaged]—Some of them were half-squares like they were an inch and a half long and three-quarters of an inch deep. And she had real little teeny squares and half-squares 'cause she could not bear to waste two threads in a cloth. Cloth to her was more precious than gold. So I learned how to conserve cloth from her.[50]

Elizabeth still owned her spinning wheel: cloth *was* gold to her because she'd picked, carded, and spun cotton to make fabrics, dug Oose to dye it, and designed and sewn the subsequent garments. JoAnn's blocks could be used in quilts and Elizabeth's were so prized that one with a Log Cabin design was featured in 1987, at the LDS Museum of Church History and Art [now called the Church History Museum] in a display titled, "Stitches in Time: Latter-day Saint Quilts of Family and Faith."[51]

Catherine Campbell Steele was not forgotten in their quilting bees because, as JoAnn remembered, Catherine's picture hung in Kate and Joel's house.

> I think it was in the south room, but then after they put the other rooms on I think that it was in the front south room, where Grandma Stapley's bedroom was. And—I'm not sure. It seems to me like it had an oval frame. And it had her picture in it . . .
>
> [Catherine] had a very intriguing expression on her face and a very interesting face, so I looked at it quite a bit . . . Whenever I think about anybody from Ireland I think that that must be what Grandma Steele looked like. She had that—kind of an Irish face, to me, and I think

> that, looking at her, that I would have figured she must have had a red-headed complexion.
>
> I asked who it was an they told me . . . what sticks in my mind is that I was told that she was a very regal woman and she always walked very straight-backed and—like a princess or a queen, and looking at her face I can imagine that she, if anybody insulted her or anything like that, that she would just keep her head up in the air and ignore it . . .
>
> [The women in the family] seemed to have great respect for her and think that she was a special person. I never heard anybody say anything that would make anything any different than what I thought. It seemed like they all seemed to think that she was just somebody special; after all, she was a descendant of kings, and she felt that way. And that's the way they—that's the way they talked about her . . . Like she was—you know, like she was—really lived up to her ancestry. Course since I know [now] what kings are like, pretty much, [Joann laughed] but they didn't seem to know what kings are like.[52]

If her great-grandmother Catherine was perceived as perhaps a little aloof, Sarah's great sociability set her apart. She counted most of the women in Hurricane as her friends, and she visited with them "about religion, she talked about people . . . She talked about the—working for this person and that person," Reba remembered,[53] and the slender diary of Sarah's newly married niece Audrey Gregerson Gubler tends to confirm it. August 1, 1932: "Had company. Aunt Sara[h]."[54] Sarah also "worked for a whole lot of people in Hurricane," Reba reported.[55]

Sarah's visits could have an economic purpose; she often sold magazines and sometimes books. "She had to get out and earn her own," Reba explained.[56] JoAnn's friend Florence Beatty Leavitt recalled that "Sarah was just absolutely frantic about money most of the time. And she did quite a lot of—a—she made clothes for people. Did quite a lot of sewing and seamstress work, and did anything she could, she worked anywhere she could to make what money she could."[57]

This was also Reba's perception. Sarah "had to support her own kids. She went out and worked ten hours a day, eight and ten hours a day for old clothes."[58] Sarah's friend, schoolteacher Mattie Ruesch, confirmed this in her autobiography many years later: "While living here [in Hurricane], I had some help from a Mrs. [Sarah Elizabeth Roundy] Sylvester who did some sewing for me because of my busy hours teaching; and she accepted in payment some hand-me-down clothes, probably given to me by my California sisters."[59]

In making her own way, Sarah found many creative and innovative solutions because, as JoAnn remembered, she was a woman who "thought you could do anything yourself."[60] She was an extremely competent seamstress, something she had learned not only at home but at Murdock Academy and in one of her correspondence courses. It was a valuable skill for which she had an interest and ability since childhood.[61]

Listening to a dialogue between Sarah's daughters years later reveals the enthusiasm generated by Sarah's tailoring skills:

> NELL: She used to let me pick out my dresses, how I wanted them made, by this pair of sleeves and that blouse and that skirt.
>
> RUTH: And she could make them!
>
> GWEN: Right! We all had the great, grand privilege—you could go through the new catalogues as soon as they came, and pick out all the parts we wanted. She'd put them all in one dress if they'd match.
>
> RUTH: It was amazing, the things she could do! She was really fabulous.
>
> GWEN: They were a lot of fun.
>
> NELL: She made me a dress out of white muslin with pockets big enough to hold my books. Oh, that was neat.
>
> RUTH: Gwen, do you remember those—was it yellow, and pink, or was it with lavender in the back of the ruffles?—one was mine, one was yours—they were so cute.
>
> GWEN: Mine was pink and yours was yellow.
>
> RUTH: Yah, and mine had lavender around the ruffle parts—
>
> GWEN:—and they had the reverse on the part of the ruffle edging. And they were organdy, and they were Fourth of July dresses.
>
> RUTH: Darling dresses!
>
> GWEN: Oh, they were—just made us feel queenly. We had matching slips and panties and everything.[62]

"She made this little green silk dress, and she made it exactly how I wanted it," JoAnn recalled of another garment. "And it was so beautiful I'll never forget how proud I was of that dress because I was the only kid my age, I think, that had a silk dress."[63]

"She would dye materials," JoAnn continued. "Anything that wasn't the right color she'd go buy dye and she'd dye it. She didn't buy natural dyes very much except for onions to make yellow and one or two like that. She got the dye you buy in the store, Putnam's Dye and some other brand. They were really cheap, they were about seven cents or something and you could dye quite a bit of stuff with it."[64]

> And she would make over clothes, and she would tear them all apart, take all the seams undone, wash them, dye them, cut them out like she was cutting out new cloth and make brand new clothes out of them, so you never could tell whether the dress she made had been made out of remodeled cloth or brand new cloth, and during the Depression she did an awful lot of sewing for people in town because during the twenties everybody was rich you know, after the war they had this great big boom and the prices were high and people were buying twenty, thirty dollar dresses all over the place and they had all these fancy clothes and then all at once they didn't have any money at all. [And so] she would take the clothes and make them over, and then she would be paid for it with old clothes. It sounds terrible till you consider that old clothes were just really expensive material that had hardly been used and then out of that she made clothes for us.[65]

JoAnn explained, "And so we always wore somebody else's hand-me-downs and they never looked like hand-me-downs. We never took a hand-me-down and wore it the way it was. That was just nothing my mother would allow us to do with a dress that somebody else had given us and just wear it, unless it fit perfectly, and really very few things ever did that." At the time of her marriage Sarah bought a secondhand vertical feed sewing machine, which, Nell said, was "way ahead of its time in design," and it was on this that much of her work was done.[66] Sarah's cousin Elsie Kay Smith remembered visiting "Aunt Kate" and Grandma Stapley. Grandma gave Elsie some dress materials of a soft, voile-like muted plaid with a darker blue and a lighter blue and a little bit of yellow.

> [Sarah] said she would make it. And so I went down to her house and took the material and she—the—laid it out. I can't even remember that she held a pattern to me or anything! It seemed to me all she did was take the scissors and cut it out! Oh, I was real worried! And then she got out her sewing machine and away she went. And in no time at all she made me one of the cutest dresses I ever had. It seemed to me she just looked at and cut it out. And it had puffed sleeves and then it had little ruffles over the shoulders, and I don't know if it was a gathered or a flared skirt. And then a little sash inserted and came around with

> a bow in the back. And it was—it was the cutest dress, oh, I just loved that! And I was so impressed to think that she could cut out a dress by looking at me, and making it that way . . . I thought Sarah was the most clever person, and my mother [Aunt May Stapley Kay] always said she was, too . . . Oh, I think she had a mind of her own. They always said she did. But she was a very smart woman. And very, very talented.[67]

Sarah's handicraft talents also included Battenberg, netting, and centerpieces.[68] "Often she would make what she called 'white work,'" JoAnn recalled.

> Almost all of the cutwork she made put white thread on white cloth because that was the way cutwork was supposed to be. But when she'd embroider things, like she'd embroider table clothes and things, I think she forced herself when she was doing pillow cases to do them alike but when she was doing table cloths or something like that she'd change the colors on one of the corners or all the corners or something cause she didn't like to see the same thing over that many times.[69]

JoAnn's friend Florence remembered that once when

> it was almost Christmas time, and she had taken a piece of cloth so big—two or three feet square, and it had delicate flowers on it and she had embroidered them until they just almost looked real. And she was fixing it up. I don't know if she was going to make a pillow or a little throw or little cover or something but oh, it was beautifully done! [Sarah was] a hardworking person. She was always busy just working every angle she could and on anything she could and she would go and work for people . . . She was a very, very industrious person.[70]

Sarah didn't just make clothing, either. Her cousin Elsie Kay Smith recalled Sarah making "a baby rack" for Aunt May, which was a long board on which she painted pictures, maybe of flowers, and designed it to hold baby things. May hung it behind the bedroom door.[71]

"She made fancy crepe paper flowers and she dipped them in warm Parowax so that they just looked more real than the plastic ones in the store now," JoAnn recalled.[72] Ruth said that Sarah "could look at a little picture, so small you could barely see it, of a pattern, crocheting, or fating or anything like that" and "she'd get her old magnifying glass out, and she'd look it over and the next thing you know she'd be making it."[73]

She took a piece of glass, about eight by ten inches, painted a scene in black with a seated fairy sporting two little antennae and butterfly wings, the centers colored a light pink, with that same pink hidden among a tree branch above and shrubbery below; it was backed with tinfoil and cardboard, giving it a curious luminescence, becoming a beautiful—if since cracked—heirloom for her granddaughter and namesake, Sara Jo Bate Merrill.

Sarah made a beautiful needlework centerpiece that so impressed Kate that she argued "put it in the fair." "No," Sarah responded diffidently. Kate entered it under Joel's name, and so Joel Roundy won a prize in the "Ladies' Department" at the Second Annual Dixie Fruit Festival for "his" centerpiece.[74]

Sarah took a millinery course and remodeled and made hats, straw hats, and bonnets. "I remember when we were really little she made straw hats for Gwen and me," JoAnn said. "She sent and got some braided straw and she made us little straw bonnets that were so darling that I'll never forget them. Anybody that wanted their hat remodeled, and could afford it, or a friend of my mother's, came to her and she remodeled their hat to suit them." Through another correspondence course she learned about cooking, "so she was a marvelous cook and she knew all about nutrition . . . all the vitamins they had discovered up till then, what they were in and everything, and what you should eat."[75]

Vic liked sliced onions in vinegar and Sarah especially favored tomatoes, onions, and parsnips. Ruth said "she liked hominy and she liked to make salt-rising bread every once in a while." Gwen remembered her mother making "the best homemade mayonnaise-salad dressing," and Nell said Sarah had a special recipe for cabbage. "She had cream and vinegar and I think an egg in it, but I can't get mine to taste the same way." Tomatoes with bread crumbs and yum-yum cake with walnuts were Sarah's other special delicacies.[76]

Frugality extended to every part of Sarah's life. "There were lots of times I went to school and the last thing you did before you go to school is to put a new cardboard sole inside your shoe because there wasn't any leather sole there," Gwen remembered.

> 'Cause you got two pairs of shoes a year, one the Fourth of July and one for Christmas. And you saved your Fourth of July ones for school—you'd go barefooted from the Fourth of July until school—you could wear them on the Fourth and the Twenty-Fourth and then you put them

> away and then you got them out for [fall] Peach Days and then you got them out for school. And you'd wear your old cast-offs which were mighty poor, and that's where we first learned about that half-soling business. My, it was wonderful![77]

Half-soling meant getting "a rubber sole, and they'd send you the glue along with it, just like a rubber cement only a little tougher and you could buy them in children's, men's, and women's sizes and they came in stapled to a cardboard and you could buy that and put on your shoes and then they'd last a little longer. And everybody had their shoes half-soled. Everybody." Gwen explained that "you put them on your shoe and if it stuck out on the side you just trimmed it around."[78]

Washing was a duty turned into an opportunity. "I was probably about seven or eight," Sarah's son Rex said, and "I remember it was my job to go out and gather limbs off the street to build a fire to heat the water to wash with . . . Build an outside fire with a tub on it."[79] At first Sarah washed on a scrub board that as Gwen pointed out would "wear your fingers out, wear the clothes out." Washing was an all day job, and after it was completed the suds were used to scrub the floor, mopped up, and then put on the rose bushes. Kate always claimed the reason she had beautiful roses was "I put the wash water on there, not the rinse water but the soapy water, and it washes all the aphids away and it leaves a little skin of soap on it and so they don't come back."[80]

Tired of the wash board, Sarah found an electric washing machine at E. J. Graff's store for thirty-five dollars. She bought it for five dollars down and five dollars a month. "When dad found out that she'd gone on tick and bought a washing machine, he just about split his gusset," JoAnn remembered. "Well, she was in debt for something, and that was worse than going to hell. It's really terrible that she would go in debt during the Depression." Vic argued "It wasn't necessary. You could wash without a washing machine!" But despite his protests Sarah stuck to her decision and paid for it by taking in washing at two cents a pound.[81]

JoAnn summed up. Sarah "had very capable hands. If she'd ever had any problems with her hands I don't know what she'd have done." She was an active woman. "She moved a lot. She wasn't a 'sit-around' lady. She was always running. Well, she was always going gadding. Going here, going there, going do this, going do that; she was gardening. She was always making things for the house like table cloths, pillow cases; she was crocheting or embroidering or she did macramé . . . she did pointed needlework . . . she did lots of cutwork . . . she made lots of fancy pillow cases."[82]

Elizabeth, Kate, and Sarah's talents complemented each other and they enjoyed visiting together. Asked "What do you think your mother and your grandmother and Sarah had in common?" Reba said, "Oh, what was going around town. Sarah got out and found out what was going around town and Grandma talked to the older people, see how their kids was, and how the babies was and all that stuff and mother was the Relief Society president [in Kanarra] so she had to know everything too, so they helped her find out what she had to do."

Elizabeth liked to sit

> in the front room where she could see everything. And when she went in the kitchen she wanted to sit by the table so she could see everything went on. Now mother washed the dishes and grandma wiped them, all of the work that was done she was right close by mother. Seems like mother was the only one in the whole family that ever could do anything to suit her. She always depended on mother to do this and mother to do that. I done the work outside, and mother and her done the work inside."[83]

And as these women cooperated, Catherine peered over them from her oval picture frame and watched them beat back the Great Depression and raise the next generation of children—passing on the skills and talents that had been given them.

15

"The Queen Bee"

Sarah E. Roundy Sylvester

Reba, never a friendly witness when it came to her brother-in-law Vic Sylvester, blamed him for Sarah's poverty. "He took off work. They didn't have any bread, they didn't have any potatoes or anything like that and my dad would go buy a sack of flour and give them. He raised potatoes up to the [Kanarra] ranch and he give them potatoes. Give them stuff off and on all the time. They'd a starved to death if my dad hadn't a fed them." And then, after a long and thoughtful pause, Reba said, "[Vic] didn't work like our folks did . . . He'd work if you'd give him a good job. If he liked it, he worked it. He was a real good worker if he liked the job. If he didn't like it, why he was always complaining that he'd quit."[1]

Reba's view was disputed by Gwen and JoAnn, who said Vic worked long and hard but sometimes jobs weren't available. Their perspective is supported by contemporary evidence; he took jobs that were tough and sometimes dangerous.

Even Vic's anger at Sarah buying a washing machine "on tic" showed he was invested in the family financial decisions, yet in hard times they each had to do what they could. One of the jobs Vic took was cleaning the Hurricane canal, a dangerous proposition because so much of that canal is on high precipices, but it didn't work out well for him as this *Washington County News* story shows:

> Hurricane Man Suffers Injury
> —Victor Sylvester, 39, of Hurricane, was severely injured there Friday afternoon when he was caught in a landslide while cleaning the Hurricane canal two miles east of the Warm Springs resort.
>
> Sylvester, with Otto Stanworth and Powell Lee, were working to loosen a slide that had partly reached the canal. Sylvester was 50 feet above the canal on the steep mountainside trying to loosen the top of the slide of rock and earth, when suddenly the ground above him gave

> way, carrying him down the mountain. Several large boulders passed over him.
>
> He was unconscious when picked up by his companions and rushed to Dr. E. C. McIntyre's office at Hurricane. The seriousness of his injuries is impossible to determine at this time.[2]

JoAnn remembered this incident. "He was on this rock and so he tried to balance himself and not roll over and let the rock roll over him but he went down quite a ways, then he got thrown off the rock, and another rock cut him right in the top of his forehead and into his hair." His injuries seemed so serious that at first "they thought he was dead."[3]

> [Sarah] was just shocked. She wasn't home when they brought him home. She was with the neighbors or something and she saw this car, came running home and saw him laying there flat looking like he was dead you know. Blood on him. She really was all shook up. I guess this is where we learned you handle the situation and then you have your hysterics after everything is well. She never had hysterics and went to pieces until everything was all handled. She never went to pieces. She handled it but you could see she just got white and she was all shook up. And it was scary.[4]

But even the temporary sympathy brought by the accident wasn't long lasting and the tensions were rarely unnoticed. Vic's niece Sylvia Batty Hunt said Sarah "seemed to be always mad, to me. Always angry at somebody. And so that's the impression I always have had of her, of being an angry person, so that she reminded me of—I shouldn't say!" She chuckled, but she did say anyway, "the wicked old witch, but anyway she was just a wonderful person and she was a good cook." Sylvia saw a cheerful side to Vic. "Oh, Uncle Vic was something else. He was funny. He was loveable, but you always knew he was ready to crack a joke or tell you a story, and everybody loved him. Everybody loved him, but he was never really close to anyone that I know of. I mean, really close. He kind of kept himself apart, but he still let you know that he cared about you."[5]

JoAnn never felt Vic cared about her and like Nell never had a comfortable relationship with her mother. Vic couldn't have cared for Sarah's anger and he didn't appreciate JoAnn's emotional personality; instead he was mostly absent and seemed always resentful. But he was also on the lookout for a way to support his family and with his brother Frank on the rebound a new opportunity arose.

Elizabeth's talented nephew, M. M. Steele Jr., was jokingly called "the Mayor of Sawtooth" and "Hon," as in "your Honor" a shortened version of Mahonri. He was mentioned in the *Millard County Chronicle* for the rumored success of his gold strikes in the Sawtooth mining district in the Delta country. It was said he was getting sixty dollars a pan but he worked so hard he lost forty pounds.[6]

That created a lot of interest by other mining promoters. On June 16, 1932, the *Millard County Chronicle* reported that:

> E. H. Snyder, J. C. Jensen, F. [Frank] J. Sylvester, R. J. Evans and H. G. Snyder all from Salt Lake registered at the Cooper Hotel [in Delta] last week and visited the Sawtooth mining district. We have not learned their decision.
>
> There are a number of rumors current about the strikes there some conflicting others good. Considerable money is being spent whether it develops a mining district or not time will tell.[7]

Frank staked 130 claims over 2,500 acres and patented 1,000 of those in the Drum Mountains in Juab and Millard counties. This area with Tintic quartzite formations overlying shale, limestone, and dolomite had been worked over in the late 1800s; but Frank was able to get the wealthy onetime ambassador John Hays Hammond's Engineers Exploration and Mining Company to make a preliminary investment of $20,000. By November 30, 1933, the *Chronicle* reported:

> The first shipment of ore from the mine at Drum [Mountain] left this week for the smelter. The ore runs about $20 a ton in gold as well as containing silver and copper so that when the mine is being operated to full capacity it should be paying well.
>
> About forty men from Delta and the surrounding towns are employed there at present and according to Mr. Sylvester there will be more added as soon as they have the material there to work with.[8]

Sarah moved the family back to Hurricane in late 1933, which is probably about the time that Vic went to work for Frank at Drum Mountain in the Sawtooth mining district.

The only picture extant of Vic between childhood and middle age is a photo of him at the mine with George Cropper, crew-cut Reed Horton, chunky but short "Shorty" McDonald, and long-legged Peter Williams.[9] Andy Olds described this adventure in his usual salty way as "a little mining work" created because Frank would "pick up a damned old hole up here in the northern part of the state somewhere and sell stock in it and he finally got stuck and lost all of his money and his wife's too. You can't make that stuff good somehow or other . . . But Vic was working for him quite a long while, but he was working for him on a salary basis."[10]

Vic told Frank to take his money and "invest it and make money for helping me," because he wanted to build a house. Andy gave the sequel. "Well, he never did get the house built and he never accumulated the money either. I figured he come home and went through the money, I imagine, but he never did have a house, until way later."[11] Vic's aspirations for a better life were permanently jilted.

Meanwhile, Sarah's pregnancy was advancing.

> "We went home at noon one day," Gwen said, and there was Grandma Roundy and she was dishing up soup into bowls on the table. She said, "Hurry up, eat your dinner!" We knew we had a whole hour for lunch, and we had just moved a block. We couldn't understand what the big hurry was. And Grandma said, "Sit down and eat this." "It's too hot, Grandma!" "Eat it!" It wasn't like her to hurry us along that much, but anyway, "Eat it, hurry!" Momma was laying on the bed in the corner, and that was unusual for us to see someone laying on the bed and to find Grandma there; we didn't know what that was about. "Eat it!" So she rushed us off.
>
> When we got home that night we found out we had a baby brother. He'd come about—was it one-thirty? One-thirty in the afternoon [on February 23, 1934], so Grandma was really in a hurry for us to get out of there . . . We thought he was so darling. . . . When he opened his eyes they were so dark blue, and they still are.

Leon "was really long, and skinny," Gwen said—"and wrinkled," chimed in Nell. "Dad said Leon was like a dried-up apple," laughed Ruth.[12] (He might have been wrinkled as a baby but grew up to be a handsome man: Vic's sister Maud, not given to gushiness, wrote of the adult Leon, "You have heard the expression as handsom[e] as a Greek God, well that is what he is."[13])

Late that summer JoAnn cut her hand peeling peaches and Sarah filled the cut with sugar, bandaged it up—a trick JoAnn used later on her own children—and assigned her to dry peaches; being hurt didn't mean not working. When the job was finished Sarah let JoAnn go to Kanarra to stay for a week with Vic's peppery aunt Irona "Rony" Wealthy Hanks Davis. She received her odd name because her father, Ebenezer Hanks (Vic's grandfather), thought he was going to get wealthy manufacturing iron and because his first wife's mother was named Wealthy. "Miss Lorna Bracken of Cedar is here visiting her grandmother Irona Davis. Miss Joan Sylvester of Hurricane is also a guest of Mrs. Davis," the *Iron County Record* reported on August 2, 1934.[14]

"Boy, was that ever a neat break," JoAnn wrote; she loved being with Lorna, Viola Davis's illegitimate daughter by Sarah's cousin William Basil "Dill" Williams. Lorna "was there part of the time I was there and we had lots of fun. She knew how to tap dance and taught me and she was always putting on musical shows and being all the characters, except for the ones she could get the rest of us to play."[15]

Sarah and Vic's son Leon had a nephew three years older than him because Nell and Ed Stout's son Vern was born in 1931 (after nineteen hours or more of his mother Nell pacing the floor). Vern's birth made Elizabeth a great-great-grandmother and there were now five living generations in the family: Vern, his mother Nell, Grandmother Sarah, great-grandmother Kate, and great-great-grandmother Elizabeth. That was so unusual at that time that it warranted a picture and story on the front page of the *Washington County News*:

> The Hurricane chapter of the Daughters of the Utah Pioneers held a meeting and social on Monday, December 10th, at the home of Artie Reeve. The meeting was opened by Sister Sarah Wilson, one of the old pioneers of Hurricane. There were present five generations of the Mrs. Y. E. Steele Stapley family. Mrs. Stapely [*sic*], who is reported to be the first white child born in Utah is 87 years old. The youngest present [not Vern] was only two months. The afternoon was spent in playing games, dancing, singing and a program. James Jepson, the oldest pioneer gave a reading. Refreshments of Pioneer molasses cake, barley coffee, and apples were served to fifty-five guests and members.[16]

The five generation picture shows Vern, a bald, bundled up baby with his mouth agape in the lap of Elizabeth, with white hair and glasses, a toothless closed-mouth smile, dressed in a heavy dark dress with what appears to be white lace around her neck, seated in a wooden chair. Kate is over her right shoulder, also with glasses, in a long, light-colored dress and light sweater; directly behind Elizabeth is Sarah in a print dress, her hair brushed to one side and her long nose making her face look almost gaunt. To the right is Nell, wearing a cap nearly covering her head, her "Flapper" hairdo combed straight and exiting the back, also in a print dress with a modern hemline ending at the knee. (Recent Church President Joseph F. Smith Sr. would have been appalled, for clear back in 1916 he objected that "many of the fashions worn today had their origin in the houses of infamy of Paris, London and other centers of so-called civilization."[17])

Vic and Sarah struggled on. President Roosevelt's jobs programs were helping some people by the mid-1930s but Vic's sister Gladys Sylvester Olds wrote in 1936 to sister "Dick" Leeds, "On Victors birthday I went over and had supper with him. He has managed to keep off relief and this winter when there is so much [New Deal] project work around they wont give him a days work. He is so anxous to go on a job. It sure gets him down."[18]

Despite poverty, Sarah's love of life led her to enjoy cultural experiences. She enjoyed drama, loved to give readings, and was pleased when she had some money and could take her children to the movies. JoAnn was interested in drama, too.

> When we were little, like five or six or along in there, prices weren't too bad, and so we were getting along, with not too much hassle then. And we had to be careful but Mom could squeeze out a couple of eggs or a nickel or a dime or something so whenever the traveling plays came through town—I guess they called them Chautauqua's or something like that in New York or back east—but we just called them the traveling plays. There was one group that came through almost every year, a family, and they'd put on plays every night for a week, and then not on Sunday, and then for another week, and they'd put on during that time three different plays or something like that. And we got to go see them whenever we could get the money, Mom'd let us go to the traveling plays and stuff like that.

One of the groups that came through regularly earlier in the century was the Walters Stock Company, who were quite good. They eventually degenerated into a group called Scott's Comedians. "Oh, we went once or twice," JoAnn said. "We'd sit on benches, I mean, not pews like in church. Benches." "Backless benches," chimed in Gwen. "Backless benches," agreed JoAnn. "They'd stick them up there all around and we'd sit and watch the plays. I thought they were real fun, but . . . they only lasted a few years that I remember, and then they quit coming."[19]

The "Comedians" were no loss: Hurricane teacher Andrew Karl Larson said "the leading young man was passable, while the leading lady—she was good looking enough—spoke as if she had a mouthful of hot potatoes." To entice the public to attend they offered prizes for lucky numbers and had a loud-mouthed barker who sold patent medicine "guaranteed to cure all ills in the category of chronic disease."[20]

"When the traveling photographers would come to town, why, she'd wish she had enough money to get our pictures taken," JoAnn recalled of Sarah. Once JoAnn and Gwen wanted their pictures taken, but only Gwen was bold enough to ask.

"We don't have any money," was the predictable reply.

"Well, isn't there some way we could do it without money?"

"I hadn't thought about that," Sarah said, and according to JoAnn "she went down and talked to the guy and he took a chicken. Mom killed and cleaned a chicken for him and gave him a chicken—or two—to get Gwen's photograph taken."[21]

Besides dancing, Sarah served the Hurricane North Ward as a Beehive teacher, again bringing many of her talents into play. These were the youngest girls in the Mormon Church's Mutual Improvement Association. "I felt so bad cause I wasn't old enough to be in that class and I used to go in there where she taught her lessons and take it all in because I really wanted to be part of that class because she was the best teacher," Ruth remembered.[22]

"She was good," agreed sister-classmate Gwen.[23]

On July 24th one year the town decided to celebrate Pioneer Day by sponsoring the best parade ever seen in the history of Dixie. Every group was asked to participate, including Sarah's Beehive girls. "Well, let's see," she said, as she began to think about some striking costumes that would really stand out. Soon she had an idea. Why not present the girls as little bees? "So she made these costumes out of crepe paper and she put little wings on them and made them all into bees," JoAnn explained."[24]

In order to insure that each costume was right she made them all herself. And of course, as the teacher, she was to lead this parade of bees so she used the brown and yellow crepe paper to fashion a costume for herself as the Queen Bee. It was a potent symbol in this family where Elizabeth's imperiousness had been compared to both a queen and a queen bee, and Catherine claimed to be descended from queens.

"We were all little bees," Gwen said of the procession. "Little honey bees for the beehive, and she . . . walked along with her thirteen little bees in the parade."[25]

"I was so embarrassed!" laughed JoAnn. "My mother out there in those long skinny tights and striped bee bottoms!"[26]

Sarah had more of a sense of humor than her daughters, not only when she went dancing or dressed up for the parade, but as JoAnn pointed out, "If she was getting mad you could almost always say something, and if she laughed she wouldn't be mad any more. And she was always getting a kick out of something, the inconsistencies of people. I guess that's where I really learned to notice what people said and what people do and . . . laugh about word things, and how opposite they are sometimes."[27]

Ironically, Sarah didn't participate very much in formal church services. "Women didn't have to go to church as much then as they do now," JoAnn said. "They had little kids around home, you know, lots of times one of them would be sick or something, or they'd stay home and fix a big dinner for the dad when they got home from church. And that was the approved way." She added that Sarah "sent all us kids to church on Sundays. Sometimes she went."[28]

Kate also stayed home more often than she went to church. "After she got pneumonia that first time [1919] she wasn't able to do very much . . . so instead of her being able to go to church on Sunday she stayed home all Sunday morning, stood on her feet all morning Sunday from five o'clock in the morning to get a great big fat dinner ready for everybody that come popping in at noon so they could get back to church at two. And then she spent the afternoon washing up the dishes." JoAnn concluded with intended irony, "She wasn't well enough to go to church!"[29]

Sarah and the Roundys had a special treat in 1936 when Joel's sister Sarah "Sadie" Roundy Berry and her husband Tom and son Herbert visited, which Sadie recorded in a brief diary. "We left at 10 o'clock arriving in Holbrook [Arizona] at 12 o'clock left there about three arrived in Hurricane, Utah about 10 o'clock that night found the folks in bed. They were all well." "The folks" were the Roundys. "The next day was Sunday we went to Sunday School went from there to Sarah Selvesters and ate dinner and visited the afternoon."[30]

"Monday we visited among the relatives, Tuesday was wash day and election day. We went with the folks while they voted. We called in to see Jesse [Roundy] and family. The folks were Ironing on Wendesday." (Joel had voted for Franklin Delano Roosevelt once: he had three other chances, beginning with this one in 1936 but he never took advantage of it again.)

"Thursday we went to the St George Temple went throu two sessions," Sadie Berry wrote. "Friday Joel and wife took us riding around to show us the town then went down to see the hot springs. It was quite a sight to see . . . Saturday we are still at Joels to day but Oh! how the wind is blowing today and it sure [is a] cold wind . . . Sunday . . . It is nice today Joel and Reba have gone to meeting . . . Tuesday . . . Went and saw Uncle Joels other twin girl Reva."[31]

Despite Sarah's emotional distance from her daughter JoAnn, she had a strong influence. JoAnn wanted to be a choreographer and she and her best friend, Florence Beatty Leavitt, wrote poetry, created dances, practiced dance steps, and went to all the 1930s musicals they could. JoAnn mentally designed the sets for the dances as well as the clothes.[32]

Asked if her mother helped with that she said, "I don't know how to answer that. My mother never helped me design clothes. I designed when I was—be in the movies. I don't think she even saw them, to think about it," she laughed.

> But actually, her influence is what made all of us in the family know we could design clothes because whenever the new magazines [and] new catalogues came out and it was time to get school clothes or anything, Momma always had us look through the catalogue and pick out the clothes we wanted . . . And so we just never dreamed that we couldn't design clothes because we always had clothes—books around with fashions in. She took all these magazines and they all had clothes in them. Well, the ones she took, almost every one of them had some kind of fashion in them. The *Lady's Home Journal* was all full of *Vogue* patterns and *Vogue* designs, and *The Delineator* had patterns in the new fashions in them, and the *McCall's* always had patterns in them, so we had all these patterns coming into the house all the time, so, we were just raised, you know like farm kids learn how to farm because they're raised on the farm. We learned how to design clothes because we were raised in a house where that was common. Momma was always sewing.[33]

"We both have lots of interests," JoAnn said.

> We're interested in all kinds of things. I remember, I guess Gwen and I would be about fourteen or sixteen years old, some where's along in there and some guy was giving an anatomy class in town, and Momma said she'd like to go to that anatomy class. And so, she thought she would take it. And I asked her if I could go with her, and so Gwen asked if she could go with her, and so we all three went to this anatomy, and you know, kids, fourteen and sixteen are not too happy to be seen with their parents . . . But anyway we wanted to go enough that we went with our

> mother and we went to this class, and we learned all the bones in the body and it was actually more bones than other anatomy, it was a class on the skeleton. And we learned a lot about it and we really enjoyed it, all of us.[34]

The whole family loved to read and at one time the library was in Jesse Roundy's shoe shop.[35] "It was fun to go to the library and it was also fun to go to Uncle Jesse's," JoAnn remembered with a satisfied smile.[36] And though the library had a door directly to the sidewalk, the Sylvester children also always stopped in the shoe shop to see their cheerful uncle. "They had quite a few books there," JoAnn continued, "and eventually they had so many books that there was no way they could keep them all in there."[37] The library was then moved to onetime teacher Chauncey Sandberg's furniture store where a larger room was available.[38] (The Hurricane Co-Op moved into the library's old quarters as Democrat Jesse Roundy was a firm believer in cooperative principles.)

In her junior year in high school, 1936–37, JoAnn got a job perfectly suitable for her interests, working as a library assistant for Anna J. Wood in the Sandberg store location. "I think I was on the NYC program, I don't know what they call it now, it was a youth program where you earn money to go to school with," she recalled. "And I was there from the time school let out until six o'clock three times a week."[39]

Sarah was as delighted with the library as JoAnn. "She thought that was a great idea, to have a library, and she took us to the library," JoAnn said. "She went to the library, and so did we, see what was there, and when there was books there why we read them, she read them. I mean, you know, all those magazines were not really enough to read"—and here she and Gwen broke into loud chuckles at the thought of Sarah's huge collection of magazines.[40]

Magazines, and particularly women's magazines, led reform movements and promoted progressive change from Sarah's childhood on and were the major means of communication in her lifetime, designed to be appealing to women but of interest to men.[41] Sarah read voraciously and kept the magazines to read again.

She also checked out three or four books a week, especially "love stories and romances, and she liked Zane Grey books. I don't know why she liked Zane Grey books but she did." Sarah also enjoyed "biographies, and she liked science books, but there weren't very many science books there, and she liked the regular classics" such as Robert Louis Stevenson, and Jean Stratton Porter's popular novels (*Freckles; Girl of the Limber Lost*).[42]

Vic read all the westerns, and instead of checking books out from the library read "everybody's books that were in the house. You know, this is a family of compulsive readers!" JoAnn laughed. "He was just like the rest of us, if he saw writing, he read it. It was a family trait."[43] (Vic's mother Jane had also been an avid reader.) Joel and Kate read but not with the single-minded intensity of the Sylvesters.

Kate made everyone feel welcome, reader or not. "I liked Sister Roundy," Florence Beatty Leavitt said of Kate, explaining that "I called them Grandpa and Grandma Roundy. They knew I didn't have any grandparents, and so they told me, they said, 'Okay, we'll adopt you; you're one of our grandkids,' so I called them Grandpa and Grandma Roundy all the time." Kate "was little. Not very tall. Not little, she was fairly husky for as tall as she was, a quiet little. She had gray hair when I knew her but she was a pretty woman, little woman. I guess the Stapleys were quite little people. And I sure liked her."[44]

Elizabeth was "quite outspoken, quite feisty," Florence recalled, and

> I was just a little bit afraid of her, because she said what she thought. I mean, she just came out plain with whatever she thought, and sometimes it kind of almost scared me. I was afraid she would get after me for something I had done. Well, one afternoon Grandpa and Grandma Roundy had gotten books with little strips of different kinds of suiting material and dress material and stuff, and I guess it wasn't any good and they had given it to JoAnn and so JoAnn gave me a lot of the pages out of it and we were going to make doll clothes or something out of it. I can't remember just what we were going to do, but she handed me these and I started to go out and Sister Stapley wouldn't let me leave. "Oh, you're not leaving with that!" she told me. And so I just stopped, and she called JoAnn in and she said, "Can you see what she's taking? She's taking some of your stuff!" And she said, "Well that's all right Grandma, I gave it to her," so she let me go.[45]

Florence said JoAnn "seemed to get along all right with her. She seemed to think a lot of her. I think she was used to her, and I wasn't."[46]

Sarah was a lot scarier to JoAnn than her great-grandmother Elizabeth.

> The nearest thing I ever came to getting in real Dutch when I was out with somebody, was something that was completely spontaneous. Gwen and I went to the picture show and it got out at eleven o'clock. And we met one of our acquaintances who lived up the road from us

> about—several blocks—and another kid. There were two kids there, I guess we knew both of them. And they were just acquaintances. We'd never thought about them seriously in any way and they started talking to us about the new bridge that was getting built. And we were all interested in this new bridge because it was so big and so high, and everybody tells me now it's just a little teeny thing and they're building a new big one now, but anyway, they said "Why don't we walk out and look at it?" And so, never having a thought in our head, and completely forgetting that we'd been to the picture show and it was eleven o'clock at night, we just started walking and talking, and then we walked out to the bridge. And we looked at it, in the moonlight, and looked all over at it and talked and then we came back. And we came in the house and we didn't realize how late it was, we knew it was late. After we got almost home we remembered, ah! We went to the show! It's later than we think. So we tiptoed in real quiet, and Mom said, "Is that you kids?" and we said, "Yes." "Do you know what time it is?" We said, "No." "It's three o'clock" or something like that. And we said, "Oh it couldn't be!" "Well, it is! Where have you been?" So we told her what happened, and she was real mad because we went out—because of this one guy that was with us, because I guess she thought he had—wasn't a nice kid or something, I don't know. And, she was saying something about him and I—we said, "We don't know what you're talking about. He was nice." We just—the four of us just walked and talked and went out and looked at the bridge and talked and talked and came back. We didn't stop and do anything. They didn't put their arms around us. They didn't even hold our hands. They didn't think about being romantic, and neither did we. "Well," she said, "I don't want you running around with him." I never did know why she didn't want us running around with him, really.[47]

On March 11, 1937, Kate and Joel celebrated their fiftieth anniversary and held a Golden Wedding reception in Hurricane's Relief Society Hall. A number of Kanarra residents attended, the *Iron County Record* for March 18 recording, "Mr. and Mrs. John Stapley and family, William C. Reeves, Mrs. Susie Berry, Mrs. Mollie Williams, Mrs. Francis Williams, John Platt, Mrs. Vilda Davis and Mr. and Mrs. Charles Parker, Jr., went to Hurricane last Thursday to attend the Golden Wedding reception of Mr. and Mrs. Joel J. Roundy. Mr. and Mrs. Roundy are former residents of Kanarra. They lived here from childhood until about 18 years ago when they moved to Hurricane."[48]

Reba said the Roundys "had a big party. And everybody there and all of dad's—I was going to say all of his family, his brothers and sisters was there, but they weren't. The two in Arizona started. One of them got there but the other [Aunt Fannie Roundy Willis] had a car wreck and she broke her hip, and they took her back to Arizona—Snowflake, Arizona, and she didn't get to his party."[49]

But "they had a program and everything, and they had their picture taken the next day, and everybody in the town was invited, and, why, you wouldn't a thought they'd never had a celebration before! Everybody was coming out! They fed them and everything, and they got along okay. Everybody was happy. But they got a lot of presents and they said, 'We didn't need the presents.' They didn't tell them not to bring presents." Included with the presents were a hand-tinted print and a figurine of "two girls clinging together."[50]

This was a great occasion for Elizabeth. "I think they took her down and she went in the church house, the Relief Society room, and everybody come to greet her and everything. Oh, that was real happiness for her. She liked people. She liked people to talk to, she liked people to notify [notice] her. And she was happy. She was kind of tired, but then she got over it," Reba remembered. "That was one of her joyous days! Out in the public. Everybody come and we had all of her folks and that there and she saw them all, and oh, that was great, she said."[51]

Maybe in earlier years Sarah could have been comforting with her brisk efficiency, love of laughter, and sometime optimism. But her grip on mortality began loosening after Leon was born, crumbling under the onslaught of stress, poverty, varicose veins, failing kidneys, and a weak heart.

She was so ill at the anniversary that she had to be carried in and sat grimly for the family photograph, looking so angry and haggard that her daughters never showed anyone the picture without apologizing first. Still, she "set there and talked to people. She couldn't get out and move around. She didn't do anything only just sit there. Her and Grandma sit together. I can't remember, I had to do other things, I can't remember what was going on!"[52]

Luckily, she was interested in medicine and self-doctoring saved money. "She'd learned from her mother and grandmother about healing herbs and things like that," JoAnn said. She used Brigham tea as a tonic, senna for the bowels, green tea for diarrhea, ginger tea and catnip to calm nerves, and a flaxseed poultice for minor infections. "Always had mustard plasters for colds," JoAnn added.[53] (John Steele prescribed all of these but ginger tea, though mostly for different ailments.)

Hydrotherapy seems to have been brought to Iron County by a popular twenty-five-year-old Battle Creek-trained nurse, Laura Gertrude Tobiason (she preferred Gertrude, perhaps to distinguish her from her mother), who spent the winter of 1911–12 in Cedar City working at various occupations, from teaching health classes, putting on a vaudeville play, to lecturing on "First Years of Girlhood."[54] Maybe Sarah attended Gertrude's hydrotherapy class for she "used a lot of cold water. If you had a sore throat or anything like that she always took a cloth, wet it in cold water and swung it in the air for a few minutes to let it get colder and then wrapped it around your neck and put a dry towel around it and left it on. Any place that was inflamed she put a cold pack on it. That's what they called it, a cold pack."[55]

An eerie, toothless old woman in Hurricane, Margaret Augusta Anderson, made her own salve. "Everybody thought she was a witch or something," JoAnn said.

> All the kids were scared to go around her house. Momma sent me over there one day for some salve and I was scared to go over there because everybody had told me how mean she was. Just really mean. She'd come and put curses on kids and all kinds of stuff, you know. Well, I went over there anyway. I had to! It was either go down and take a chance on her wrath or take a chance on my mother's, so I took a chance on hers.
>
> But I knocked on the door, and I knew she'd come and scream at me, and she come at the door and opened it, and I said that my mother sent me over to buy some salve, and she said, "Oh. Well, come in." And so I went in and sat down on the chair and waited. And she went in the other room and after a while she came out and handed me a jar or whatever, and I gave her the dollar Momma gave me to give her. And I left and I couldn't see anything wrong with her. She didn't sound very witchy to me![56]

Sarah worried about Kate's health as much as her children's. "Mom checked up on Grandma every day," JoAnn explained. "Especially after she had pneumonia and got that bad heart. Momma checked up on her every day. She didn't want her to get cold, she wanted to be sure that she didn't get pneumonia again," and the two women dosed each other with digitalis and swapped herbal remedies.[57] Dr. E. C. McIntire "told her to put Denver mud on her," Reba explained of Kate's second pneumonia bout. "Put a mustard plaster on her," and added, "They could make a jacket so that the sleeves didn't let any air through them, and the neck didn't let any air through it, and you put a jacket on them and then, all over here, everything was just tight. No air or anything else in it" and besides that she "fed her a beefsteak once a day for two weeks." That "cured" her pneumonia. This, Reba was certain, meant "pneumonia couldn't get over your heart it—your heart's in the way. It stops it . . . So every year for three years, I put mustard plasters on her and Denver mud." After Annis left, Sarah took care of Kate's thick and naturally curly hair. "They curled it quite a lot for her," Reba remembered.[58]

Sarah was well enough to go with Joel and Reba to the funeral of Joel's cousin Quimby Roundy, a onetime missionary, World War I soldier, sheep man, and bishop of Alton who died in Kanab on October 1, 1937, at age forty-nine. "I don't know whether he'd been out with the sheep or been out in the forest. I don't remember," Reba said. "But he come back and he died with tick fever"—that is, Rocky Mountain Spotted Fever.[59]

"It was my dad" who wanted to go to the funeral, Reba remembered, because he hadn't been able to keep in touch regularly with his favorite "Aunt Tild" (Malinda Parker Roundy), who was Quimby's mother and Joel's Kanarra cousin (Quimby's father was also Joel's cousin). "But he didn't want to go alone so he took Sarah and I with him. We went up Cedar Mountain and down a little ways and over into Kanab. 'Cause that was the quickest way. But everybody was glad to see my dad. They said they liked to see my dad."[60]

When they got in the chapel Sarah said, "Look at all the wheat around this house!" because wheat was used as a theme to represent Quimby's life and "it was all decorated with wheat. And everything they talked about was—him out in the forest, him out in the country, taking care of the wheat. Taking care of the forest."[61] (Quimby was so well-liked his World War I army friend Homer Englestead named one of his sons Quim.[62])

Sarah, six months younger than this cousin, had known him casually for many years and was impressed with the symbolism and the services. "She said that was a good program for him, he'd been out in the country all his life and—everywhere's else, and he was right with what he was with."[63] (The family went all out for his funeral, spending $188.20 just for the mortician.[64])

Sarah's health deteriorated rapidly after that trip and by the next spring (1938), she made what turned out to be her final effort to do something special for JoAnn. JoAnn explained:

> When I graduated from seminary most of the kids voted to have long dresses for seminary graduation. Most of us didn't own long dresses.

There may have been three kids that had dresses that year that they'd got for the Junior Prom that were long dresses. But most of us didn't even own a long dress. So Momma used to buy cloth in bundles and remnants, so many yards in each piece of cloth, got them for a good price and when we got there we saw what we had. Because you couldn't choose the cloth, because it was just pieces of, maybe cotton or linen or wool. And she found this remnant, and she thought maybe if she pieced it she might could get me a dress out of it.

Well, I didn't want an old pieced dress to wear to seminary. And I wasn't very nice—well, I tried to be as nice as I could, but I didn't really like this idea at all. And it was voile, cotton voile . . . Once in a while you see a piece of voile, but you hardly ever see a piece of cotton voile. But you can almost see through it. It's a little more sheer than regular cloth. It's almost transparent. But not quite as transparent as nylon curtains and stuff like that. And it had big lavender and blue and purple flowers on it, all over it. And I thought, oh, to graduate in something like that, I thought that what I really wanted would be something like a plain piece of cloth out of something that was a little full in the skirt and stuff, and long and gorgeous, and—something like out of Ginger Rogers and Fred Astaire musicals [she laughed], is what I thought dresses should be like!

And then to top it all off, here, we had a petticoat under it because you could see through it. Now we call them slips, but then we called them petticoats. In our days petticoats were not full, they were straight up and down almost, underslips. Now what they call those slips and petticoats are full. But we didn't have anything to make that out of so she hunted up four or five old flour sacks that hadn't been used and she soaked them and soaked them and washed them, scrubbed them and got every bit of the color out of them. They used to print the brand name and the name of the flour and everything was printed right on the sack . . . and the sacks were made out of muslin. And so she got them all washed up good and cleaned and no stains on them. And then she dyed this cloth bright orange. Bright orange. And then she made this slip out of it. And I thought I'd die when she told me that she'd made this slip to go with it and it was orange and I saw it on the clothesline and I thought the very best thing that could happen to me is if I would go jump off the bridge or if I could just crawl in a hole or die or something, or have a rattlesnake bite me or break a leg or anything to keep me from going to

> graduation. I just couldn't imagine an orange flour-sack petticoat under a see-through voile dress covered with blue, pink, and lavender flowers.
>
> However, when she *made* me put it on, and then I looked in the glass, I was just shocked! To death! I could not believe how that orange brought out all the colors in there and the pinks had a glow like the sun. The lavender looked pinkish, and the blue looked lavender-like, and it was just the most gorgeous thing I ever saw in my life. And I decided it was just too bad that I had to be so stupid that I had to be forced to see that after it was made, and that I didn't have sense enough beforehand to see what it was going to be like, or even to trust her judgment that she knew what was what.[65]

JoAnn's seminary graduation dress was a spectacular success, shoring up her sometimes deflated self-assurance.

Hurricane High School's forty-nine member graduating class of May 25, 1938, was the largest in the school's history and JoAnn was chosen to speak in defense of art. Her family was immensely proud of the honor granted to JoAnn to be one of the valedictorians and several relatives came to hear her speak, but her mother was too sick to be among them. Kate and Joel "thought that was great!" she remembered, noting that "they never told me so, they didn't want me to get a swelled head of course," but she knew it anyway.[66]

Otherwise her graduation was typical of thousands of others that June. They heard the adult speakers outline the perils of life, one person cautioning them that in the future there would be plenty of spilled milk; when that happened the best thing to do would be to pick up and move ahead. It was advice the whole family could cling to in the future.

Sarah's life during the thirties was tough, but as JoAnn explained, "She didn't sit around and moan and cry and weep and 'poor pitiful me' about it, and she didn't expect anybody to feel sorry for her for anything. She wouldn't take anybody's pity."[67] Instead she found a lot of joy in her extended family and her many friends.

16

"Stern Looking but Well-Polished"

Elizabeth Steele Stapley

"My dear daughter Young Elizabeth Steele Stapley," a dying John Steele pronounced on December 6, 1903.

> In the name of the Lord Jesus Christ and in the Authority of the Holy Priesthood that the Lord has been pleased to generously bestow upon me even that of a minister to go forth and bestow blessings upon his own children and to confirm the same unto thee . . . Thou art Called to do a great and a mighty work in these last days, and were called to come forth in a very prominent time of the building up of the church in this day. You shall Yet live Many Years upon the earth . . . And thy posterity shall be exceeding numerous and continue to increase, and no power contrary to that of the Almighty shall have power over them.[1]

Elizabeth lived those "Many Years" John promised her under unabashed "white supremacy," born in the heyday of slavery in what became a slave territory.[2] She was ten years old when Supreme Court Chief Justice Roger Taney issued the Dred Scott decision ruling that African Americans "had no rights which the white man was bound to respect."[3]

Nineteenth-century Mormons, like Irish, Italians, and Eastern Europeans, were derided as "not white." Historian W. Paul Reeve, whose book on this subject is subtitled, *The Mormon Struggle for Whiteness,* explained: "Being white equaled access to political, social, and economic power."[4] Denying "whiteness" to Mormons was to disempower.

In 1948, ten years after Elizabeth's death, the courts confirmed Native Americans' right to vote. Chinese Americans had been allowed citizenship in 1943, but Japanese and other Asian-born Americans would not be granted the privilege until 1952. The Voting Rights Act of 1965, which tried to make real the promise of the Fifteenth Amendment that citizens could not be denied the right to vote because of "race, color, or previous condition of servitude" is still being contested.[5]

Because of white racial privilege and a history of belonging to a culture whose "whiteness" was called into question, Elizabeth's claim to be the first white person born in Utah resonated and had a contemporary meaning that is now hard to appreciate and can seem vaguely embarrassing.

The first published reference I've discovered to the accident of her birth was on March 30, 1864, in her marriage announcement in the *Deseret News*. It was restated in a paragraph in Edward W. Tullidge's *The Women of Mormondom*:

> Here may be very properly mentioned the first daughter of "Deseret"; or, more strictly speaking, the first female child born in Utah. Mrs. James Stopley [*sic*], now a resident of Kanarrah, Kane county, Utah, and the mother of five fine children, is the daughter of John and Catherine Steele, who were in the famous Mormon battalion. Just after their discharge from the United States service they reached the site of Salt Lake City (then occupied by the pioneers), and on the 9th of August, 1847, their little daughter was born. This being a proper historical incident, inasmuch as she was the first white child born in the valley, it may be interesting to note that the event occurred on the east side of what is now known as Temple Block, at 4 o'clock A. M., of the day mentioned. In honor of President Brigham Young, she was named Young Elizabeth. Her father writes of her at that time as being "a stout, healthy child, and of a most amiable disposition."[6]

A letter from John Steele to Wilford Woodruff was polished up and published in the *Deseret News* on August 4, 1888, and included the following:

> As it is comforting to recount the reminiscences of the past, when they bring pleasing recollections of having done our duty, and as there must always be a first, I have the honor of being the father of the FIRST CHILD BORN IN THE VALLEY.
>
> It was named after President Young, Young Elizabeth Steele, born August 9th, 1847, at 3:40 a.m. I also made the first lasts and the first gaiter boots that were made in these valleys. I can now say with pleasure that that same baby girl, then born, is a handsome matron, having married one Mr. James Stapley, and now lives at Kanarrah, Iron County,

> Utah Territory. She is the mother of five sons and two daughters, and is now a grandmother [of Sarah Elizabeth Roundy, later Sylvester].[7]

When Orson Ferguson Whitney's *History of Utah* was published in sumptuous gold-leafed volumes in 1892, Elizabeth was not forgotten. "The first white child born in Utah opened its eyes to the light on Monday, August 9th, 1847—two weeks and two days after the arrival of the Pioneers. This infantile re-inforcement was a girl, the daughter of John and Catherine Campbell Steele." The account noted, "The father John Steele, was a mason,[8] and according to his account, [he] built nearly one-third of the 'Old Fort' with his own hands, using a trowel made by Burr Frost out of a saw-blade."[9] (We leave it to the reader to contemplate the sense of humor of the parents of Mr. Frost.) In 1897, the fiftieth anniversary of the Mormon arrival in Utah also generated publicity about Elizabeth's birth.[10]

By the mid-thirties Elizabeth had lived a long life, firmly ensconced in her role as a living artifact and periodically "discovered" by enthused young historians interested in her reminiscences of pioneer days. She found her increasing celebrity energizing. When she went to Delta in the summer of 1931, she earned two paragraphs in the *Millard County Chronicle* about her visit to the State House Museum in Fillmore, with the headline, "First White Child Born in Utah Visits Old Capitol Museum":

> Mrs. Elizabeth Steele Stapley is the first white child born in Utah. She was born August 9 1847 just five days after her parents arrived [in Salt Lake Valley].
>
> She visited the old State House Museum at Fillmore last week and viewed the pioneer relics with great enthusiasm. There are relics of her own family on exhibit there and a case devoted to [her father] John Steele who was very prominent in southern Utah from about 1853 on for many years.
>
> Mrs. Stapley lives now in Hurricane and is related to the Steele families in Delta.[11]

The museum has books and family papers of her father's and swords that had belonged to her brother Mahonri M., her father John Steele, and her grandfather John Steele Sr., the old Peninsular War soldier.

She went to Salt Lake City's pioneer parade, newly named "Covered Wagon Days" on July 24, 1931. Her picture was published on the front page of the *Salt*

Lake Telegram with the caption, "Mrs. Elizabeth Young Steel[e] Stapeley [*sic*] of Hurricane, who held a seat of honor as the first while child born in Utah. Her birthday was August 9, 1847." She appears broad hipped, white haired, with glasses and wearing a violet dress—which still survives—made by her seamstress granddaughter Annis,[12] beautiful lace around the neck and pinned to it a medallion with a rectangular label, "YOUNG E. S. STAPLEY | 1847 PIONEER 1938 | APPRECIATION."[13]

Elizabeth partly blocks a sign behind her that says, "[Y]oung Steel Stapley . . . Child Born In Utah [August] 9[,] 1847." The temperature was 103 degrees and thirty-four people were overcome by the heat and one died, but—safely ensconced between the Battery A 145th Field Artillery and a hodgepodge group representing Father Escalante, miners, and Indians—she had no reported problems.

Elizabeth joined seventeen other 1847 pioneers—the youngest a childish 84—for an informal dinner sponsored by the Daughters of the Utah Pioneers at Hotel Utah, the most elegant hostelry in the state. While the crowds outside were weltering, "Robert Sweeten, 91, of Garland, now sightless, but possessing a remarkable memory, recalled how he left Canada in 1847 and after several months' travel by team, arrived at Council Bluffs, Iowa, early in 1847 and then set out across the plains with still more than a thousand miles to go before reaching Great Salt Lake valley," reported the *Salt Lake Tribune*. "He said that after arriving here, food was often scarce and the people had to subsist on whatever they could find. He told how he had eaten boiled roots of wild thistles, the leaves of nettles and the bulbs of sego lilies during the early years of the settlements." The story concluded that "Mrs. Stapley has the distinction of being the first white child born in Salt Lake. Her parents came to Utah July 29, 1847, and she was born August 9 of that year."

Her favorite part, besides the personal attention, was probably the air show, which boasted five air reserve corps planes under the command of Lt. C. T. Talbot doing loops, rolls, and a mock dogfight.[14]

Despite being described as of Mona in these stories, Elizabeth's trips north to visit her children in the summer were short respites for Kate. "She never stayed," Reba explained. "So she went down to Delta . . . to Uncle Will's, and Uncle Will's wife [Emmeline] says [to Will], 'I took care of my mother, you take care of yours.' And what did he do? Brought her down to Mother!"[15]

"She just wanted them to be on the straight path, and sometimes they just wanted to go and have a little fun," Reba explained of Elizabeth's grandchildren. They were especially intimidated by the way she talked.

> You see, she was brought up where there was nothing. And these kids all come in where there was something going on at night. There was Mutual and some other things, school nights and things, and they would go to that. And she didn't like that. "They should be home. They should be doing this. They should be doing that." When she lived with us we couldn't sit around and hold our hands. "No. You have to get something to do." And that's what she'd say to them. "Now get this done! Get that done!" And they didn't like it.[16]

The most detailed and informative report about Elizabeth ran in the *Deseret News* on February 28, 1935, headlined, "Noted Woman Found Living at Hurricane." Picking up the theme that church historians LeRoi C. Snow—a long-faced man with a gentle smile, much resembling his father, former Church President Lorenzo Snow—and tall and thin Preston Nibley had "found" Elizabeth, the paper asserted, "So modest and so retiring is she that her whereabouts has been almost lost track of and a state has forgotten to give honor to her . . . She was 'discovered' there [Hurricane] last week end."

Snow wrote that "when we drove into Hurricane and enquired for Mrs. Stapley we were told that she was living with her daughter Mrs. Roundy and the little frame home on top of a hill about a mile away was pointed out to us. Only a lane led from the road up to the house. It was a bright, sunny day, just after noon. It was very windy and we had driven through a dust storm all the way from St. George."

"In answer to my knock the door was opened by a genial, white haired lady [Kate], who was 70 [69] years old the previous Wednesday [26 October]." Snow wrote that,

> Beyond her, in the room, I saw almost a heavenly picture, the dearest, sweetest old lady it seemed that I had ever seen—the object of our trip to Hurricane. I didn't have to ask if this was Mrs. Stapley, but immediately beckoned to Preston [Nibley] and his wife [Anna] to come . . . There she sat, just as lovely and happy as though she had carefully prepared and had been sitting there waiting for our arrival. Everything was in order and spotlessly clean. Mrs. Stapley was very happy to see us and gladly entered into conversation. Her eyesight is good. She doesn't use glasses.[17] Her mind is active . . .
>
> While I was taking the two pictures of this wonderful, old lady[,] Preston carried on the conversation. After we left the house Mrs. Nibley's

> first words were: "Why she is just like a little cameo, like a beautiful piece of Dresden China."[18]

The historians sent a *Deseret News* reporter to get more details of Elizabeth's story, and she spoke to him of hard work when she was a girl, life in a two-room cabin, and her career as a midwife. "I knew Brigham Young very well as I worked in the St. George temple with him and when he and his party made their pilgrimage south I helped take care of them," she explained. "I still have my spinning wheel with which I spun so much cotton warp from which my children's clothes were made. We made dyes for coloring our clothes from oose (the century plant). We also used it for softening the water when we washed. I served many years as a teacher or counselor in the Relief society."[19]

The Depression had one useful effect for Elizabeth: with prompting by Sheriff Will Brooks's wife Juanita and support by the relief administrator of Washington County, onetime Kanarra school teacher and now stake president William O. Bentley, federal funding was awarded for the unemployed to copy Utah diaries and autobiographies and to interview the elderly.[20] This resulted in several histories of Elizabeth. Isaac E. Diehl, former editor of the *Mammoth Record*, also interviewed her at Aunt May Stapley Kay's home in Mona. Unfortunately, the questions that Diehl was supposed to use to prompt him to create a narrative only generated short answers so his interview wasn't very revealing though she did tell him, "I have been a rambler on the hills and enjoyed the early days in spite of the privations." As an experienced newspaper editor he could have done better, but maybe his seventy-five years were against him.[21]

Someone wrote an account of her life in 1931 or 1932 and twenty-year-old Virginia M. Lee of the WPA's Historical Records Survey made a careful typescript. This account says "Grandma Sessions was the midwife who looked after mother and child," but Elizabeth was born before Patty Sessions (seen as miserly for letting her buried flour rot rather than selling it to starving 1847 Pioneers[22]) reached Salt Lake Valley. Still, there were valuable recollections of her childhood, the move from Parowan to Toquerville, as well as early life in Kanarra when "the people lived in a fort for protection from Indians." This history also reported that "she studied obstetrics from Doctor Christophersons," although I haven't been able to identify him.[23]

Elizabeth wasn't obsessed with pioneer history, and explained to the *Deseret News* with some glee other thrills in her life, including her airplane ride, that "was just right." The visit with President Harding was ritually acknowledged, but perhaps his standing as a president is shown by his being remaindered to one sentence in the very last paragraph of a lengthy story. The *News* published a five-generation photograph: Elizabeth in her rocker, and Kate, Sarah, Nell, and Nell's infant son Vern.[24]

Katharine Miles Larson wrote a story for the *Washington County News* celebrating Elizabeth's eighty-ninth birthday, plagiarizing the *Deseret News* but giving the additional information that "according to Mrs. Stapley she has picked, carded and spun cotton yarn, baked in a fire place and on camp fires, stripped cane and made molasses. Her first cook stove was bought with the money that she made from dried peaches after their trees had come into bearing."[25]

"On the occasion of her ninetieth birthday Utah's first white child, Mrs. Young Elizabeth Steele Stapley, kept her visitors in an uproar of laughter as she recited many witticisms about the changes that have taken place since she was born on a buffalo robe in a tent in Salt Lake City, on Aug. 9, 1847," noted the *Salt Lake Tribune* on August 10, 1937. "She observed the day with friends at the home of her youngest daughter, Mrs. Mary E. Kay, of Mona. Despite her years, Mrs. Stapley is still active and alert." The story was accompanied by one of the most pleasing of her photographs, showing a smiling, toothless old woman with wire-frame glasses, a dark blouse with the collar circled by fine lace, her 1897 pioneer medallion used as a neck clasp.[26]

Katharine Larson's story was published in conjunction with the announcement from the Hurricane North Ward Daughters of the Utah Pioneers "that a name had been selected for their camp. In honor to Mrs. Elizabeth Stapley, 90 year old resident of Hurricane and Utah's first white child, her name had been chosen to represent them."[27]

Larson acknowledged the women of early Mormonism and mentioned Elizabeth's mother Catherine:

> Rarely is consideration given or contemplation placed upon the sturdy women who accompanied their young Mormon Battalion husbands along the trail to Santa Fe. Such selfless women were the bulwark of western migration. Their acquaintance with stark necessity was a matter of choice, not a subject for acclaim. They accepted each day's adventure as one step nearer the haven they were marching toward. Utah's first white child, Young Elizabeth Steel[e] was born to Catherine Campbell Steel[e], one of those serene souls that had traveled from Council Bluff to Bent's Fort on the Arkansas River and on into the mountains between Las Vegas and Santa Fe where they were disbanded, carrying with her the child that was eventually to be born in Utah August 9, 1847."[28]

After rehearsing some of the events of her life, the story concluded that

> now the Hurricane north ward D.U.P.'s have christened their camp for the little old lady with porcelain skin who sits, dressed immaculately, by her window and marks time. She has seen the building of a state, the rise of a religious group, the departure of hard times and the golden wedding of a daughter and son-in-law Mr. and Mrs. Joel Roundy. As Mr. Roundy states it, "It isn't every bridegroom that can boast the presence of his mother-in-law at the fiftieth anniversary of his wedding.["] Although ninety winters have left their trace since Young Elizabeth was named, there is a glow of lasting loveliness in her countenance that speaks of courage and contentment in the toilsome years that have passed.[29]

Elizabeth loved the attention. "Did you see my piece in the paper the other day?" she would query chance guests. "What do you think about it?"[30] Sometimes she didn't have to ask. The first time the five generation picture was published in the newspaper, Elizabeth received a letter postmarked Laketown, Utah, from Mrs. Zettie N. Kearl, a woman so amiable her friend Alice Mallory recorded Kearl "stayed for supper oh my how I did enjoy her. Shes so good and jolley Such good company She['s] a dear . . . she was better than Medican[e]."[31]

She must have been equally uplifting to Elizabeth: "Dear friend you will be suprized to hear from me," Mrs. Kearl wrote, "but I just had to write to you after seeing your picture of five generations in the news. I remember you well dear when Mother and I were in dear old Toquerville. I am Zettie Nebeker youngest child of Mary & John Nebeker." Now the pleased mother of twelve devout believers in the Mormon faith, Zettie was spending her last years in northern Utah. "How proud you must be of your lovely family," she wrote. "I sure congratulate you dear heart and I pray that the fathers blessings will ever be with you."[32] Certainly Elizabeth's father's blessing was.

This fan letter must have been pleasing; Elizabeth preserved it. More often the rare letters she received were from family. Seymour Stapley wrote after a family reunion on a typewriter he had not quite mastered, "We arrived home in splendid shape we carried the same air back home in our tires that we left with we did not have one puncture on the whole trip."[33] Daughter May wrote from Mona to Elizabeth and Kate complaining gently that, "We don't get any letters from you," and reporting the death of "Aunt Eliza" on her eighty-fourth birthday.[34]

If Elizabeth wouldn't write, she was verbally communicative. "To me Grandma was a dear, she taught me to whistle & to use a thimble," wrote her granddaughter, Velma Stapley Rymer.[35] Reba explained that Elizabeth "liked jokes and she liked to laugh. She liked to talk and have a good time . . . She'd tell jokes. She'd tell you a lot of things been going on through the day." Kate, Reba said, "was a little bit calmer than that. She didn't have time for all that frivolly stuff. She was tired. But Grandma just liked to talk to people. She'd talk and laugh and everything else. People would come to see her you'd think she was a little kid playing around." She "just had a good time when somebody'd come to see her."[36]

Leola Stapley Anderson's husband, Arthur, went to northern Utah with his brothers-in-law Joseph and Arvil Stapley. Elizabeth was in Mona then so the three men stopped to visit her and found she had lost none of her acerbity. "Arvil took me in and introduced me to her," Arthur said. "My name is Arthur, everybody called me Art—but she always called me Arch. And she said, 'Who is that you've got with you?' and Arvil says, 'Well that's Joe, Grandma. Don't you know Joe?' She says, 'No indeed! I don't know Joe, but I know Joseph!'"

Arthur stopped and laughed at Elizabeth for objecting to a nickname for Joseph while always mangling his, and explained, "That was the kind of a person she was! What she said was the law!"[37] But Elizabeth had named Joseph after her own son that died in infancy, and perhaps mangling Arthur's name was unintentional—Elizabeth's granddaughter Leola Stapley was married to Arthur; her granddaughter Lella Stapley was married to a man named Archie.

Elizabeth's imperiousness was evident to the family. The older folks enjoyed being seated in their rockers but where "Grandma sit she saw the stove and you had to have a fire," Reba said.

> Ah, she had to have—see the fire burning before she was satisfied. If you had a fire and it wasn't so she could see the fire—"You open the door so I can see it," so she [Kate] had to open the door so she could see it because all the stoves she's ever had was so she could see the fire, and the draft and everything else, you could see the fire, but when we got an oil stove we shut the door. She couldn't see it; we didn't have no fire . . . We didn't have any fire, but she was a sweating and the sweat was just rolling off from her, she said, "There's no fire!"[38]

Elizabeth was invited to the annual Blackhawk encampment honoring the veterans of that early Utah Indian war (from which her husband and her brother Almy had each drawn a pension). A photograph of her on a float at a Mona Blackhawk parade shows her seated in a soft overstuffed chair with May standing nearby and other family members surrounding her (stylish and public-spirited Erma Keyte[39] shades Elizabeth with a dainty parasol), the Utah flag appearing as a backdrop. A big bouquet of flowers hosts a sign announcing her name, her claim ("First White Child Born in Utah"), and her August 9, 1847, birthdate.[40]

Elizabeth's fear of the dark didn't abate with age. "She'd never go to bed without the light burning all night," Reba explained. "When she come down to Hurricane they was a street light down there, as long as she could see that street light, she was okay. But just the minute she couldn't see that street light, why, she was right out of bed screaming, 'I got to have a light! Got to have a light!'" and didn't calm down until a light was turned on for her.[41] Reba said the older woman "had to have me help her dress, she had help to have a bath, comb her hair, and take care of her like a little kid. She needed a lot of help."[42]

But Elizabeth was lonely. "She'd been a widow eighteen years, and she wanted to go to her husband. She liked all that stuff," Reba said, referring to the celebrity, "but she didn't like it because people didn't come to our place to visit her. We lived outside of town, on the outside of town, and she didn't have enough company. She'd been used to being the main one in the town because she was the midwife and all the people come to see her and everything when she was to home and when she was to our place in Kanarra."[43] But now the Roundys—and Elizabeth—lived on the west outskirts of town. "When we come down there [to Hurricane] it was just too hard to get up there, they didn't come."

Elizabeth was not only lonely, she was vulnerable. In the spring of 1933 she was so sick that the *Iron County Record* reported "Mr. and Mrs. John A. Stapley left Saturday for Mona to be at the bedside of Mr. Stapley's mother, Mrs. Elizabeth Stapley, who is very ill,"[44] but later that summer the *Record* said "Mrs. Elizabeth Stapley is here visiting her son John and family." The paper went on to report, "The Relief Society officer[s] entertained at a birthday party Tue[s]day afternoon at the home of Mr. and Mrs. John Stapley in honor of Mrs. Elizabeth Stapley who is 86 years of age. Mrs. Stapley was the first white child born in Utah. Dainty refreshments were served to 40 guests. A pleasant time was had by all."[45] Among the guests was her grandson William B. Stapley and his family, down from Castle Dale in Carbon County.

On February 19, 1938, fifty-eight year old Lucretia "Lou" Higgins Stapley's appendix ruptured. The wife of Kate's brother John A. Stapley, Lou was rushed to the Iron County Hospital in Cedar City. Two days later she was operated on for appendicitis and general peritonitis by Dr. M. J. Macfarlane, then president of the State Medical Association, the day after his office had been burglarized.[46] Lou died on February 24 of a cerebral embolism, with contributing conditions including chronic endocarditis and chronic nephritis.[47]

The family gathered from as far away as Millard County and as close as New Harmony for the Kanarraville funeral. The *Millard County Chronicle* named the Delta contingent as "Mr. and Mrs. M. M. Stapley, Clayton Stapley, Mr. and Mrs. Will Stapley and Mardin [Marden] Stapley."[48] Services were held by Bishop William Graff with Joel Roundy giving the prayer and Elizabeth's son Mahonri Stapley dedicating the grave.[49]

Mahonri's back was crippled with rheumatism, or as Reba called it, "rheumatic fever." A few weeks after the funeral he went to Hurricane to visit his sister Kate and see if she could help. "He had—the left leg here he couldn't hardly walk on it. So we put him to bed," Reba remembered.[50]

Kate was at a bit of a loss: "I don't know what we can do unless we just burn it out." "Let's try it," Mahonri said. Reba took over the work of treating Mahonri with hot packs on his hip "morning and night, and while he was there them three weeks it went right down his leg and out his toe." Reba thought the remedy worked: "We ran it right out his foot. He says, 'You chased it right out my foot and I don't have it anymore,'"[51] and Reba asserted it never came back.[52]

The Hurricane home was always crowded with Kate and Joel's visiting children and grandchildren as well as assorted friends but when John A. and his family came down March 27, maybe for solace after his wife Lou's death, they weren't greeted by the usual warm and comforting Dixie weather. March was so stormy that flooding was endemic, several roads were cut off, two men drowned when the highway collapsed, the main water line into Hurricane washed out leaving townsfolk without culinary water for several days, and "the Kanab mail and tourists at Zion Park were morrooned [marooned]."[53]

It was cold, Reba explained. "And they leave the door open and they go in and out and in and out" and Elizabeth caught "bronchial—bronchitis in the throat, that's all she had . . . She said, 'Don't know why they had to leave that door open, it's just killing me.'"[54]

When she got sicker the family sent for Dr. E. Clark McIntire and "he come up and looked at her, 'She's all right,' he said. She's just a week sick. He says, 'She's all right.'" The family wasn't impressed with McIntire and when Elizabeth got worse Reba reported his response was "'Everybody has to die.' Never give her anything. Just said, 'When her fingernails go blue, then you can come and tell me, she's going.' And we said, 'We won't tell you when her fingernails go blue, 'cause she's a midwife, and she keeps her finger this way,'" Reba clenched her fingers into her palm, "so you can't see them . . . she put a clench on her hands."[55]

And after she heard McIntire tell them to watch her fingernails "she knew that we was watching to see if her fingernails was going blue" so she kept them clenched. "And you go like this," Reba said, prying her clenched fingers apart with her other hand, "and she'd yank them back like this," clenching again.[56] Reba's summation: "She's always been taking care of the sick and she knew what that meant and she wasn't going to give you the privilege of seeing it."[57] That didn't stop Reba from trying: "I'd go like that," Reba said, pulling her own fingers back with her unclenched hand, "and she'd put them back up again and she'd hold her arms down and put them this way so you couldn't see her fingernails."[58]

When Elizabeth's condition worsened, she demanded Kate "'Get all the kids here! Get all the kids here!' Uncle Will Stapley was slow. 'Is Will here yet?' she asked. 'No,' Kate said, 'Will's not here.' 'Well, he'd better be getting here.' And in a day or two Uncle Will came."[59]

On the morning April 1, 1938, five days after she contracted pneumonia complicated by the bronchitis, the family was gathered around talking. Kate said breakfast was ready, "Got it all cooked."[60] Aunt May Kay told Reba, "Now you stay right here, and if Grandma needs anything you give it to her or else you come and tell us."[61]

When Reba and Elizabeth were alone, the older woman ordered, "Go in the other room." Reba refused: "I'm not going in the other room."

"Go in the other room," Grandma persisted.

"You heard Aunt May tell me to stay right here. I got to stay here."

After the family all got seated, Elizabeth demanded again, "Well, go on in the other room."

"No," Reba said.

"I can't breathe. Go on in the other room."

"That's not going to help you breathe."

"Okay."

Elizabeth, in the north part of the room, turned to the right and said, "Will you? Will you take me?"[62]

"I couldn't see a soul up there," Reba remembered. "Whether she was talking to her mother or to her husband or who she was talking to I don't know."[63]

Reba ran into the other room and announced, "If you want to see Grandma before she dies you better get in there 'cause she just asked them to take her." The family rushed pell-mell into the bedroom, Uncle John was the last to arrive and "by the time he got that far she was gone. So I said, 'From now on, you can die anyway. I'm not going to be scared dying or being around people. I can go just like that—why, better for them.'"[64]

What happened after Elizabeth died was startling to Reba. "She always set up, oh, she had about six or eight pillows behind her. She always set up because, after she had lockjaw she couldn't breathe. She was afraid to lay down. She was afraid if she laid down on the bed she'd smother to death. So she set up and Uncle John—this is what got me—Uncle John peeled the quilts back off from her, grabbed all those pillows back from behind her,"[65] saying, "Get them pillows out from behind her! Get them pillows out from behind her!"[66] Reba pulled the pillows out. Then John "jumped up on the bed and he held her legs" and

> took her by the shoulders to push her out straight. They had a hard time doing it. She'd stayed that way so much she'd got kind of set. And I thought he was going to kill her! I thought that was the meanest thing I ever saw anybody do. But I said to them, "You didn't have to do that so quick," and Uncle Mahonri says, "Yes we did." And Uncle Will says, "We sure did. If we ever got her straightened out we had to do it right then while she was relaxed." And they worked with her until they got her down straight.[67]

Actually John couldn't get her quite straight but after considerable effort she was able to lie in a half-moon posture.[68]

Reba remembered preparing the body for burial. "They had a board there and they put a sheet over it, and then Jesse said, 'I'll cut her right here under the arm and draw the blood out'" because "it helps to preserve the body. That's what morticians do . . ." Jesse cut the vein under her right arm, drained her blood into a basin, and poured it down the sink. "He had seen quite a few other people done that, so he just done what he seen other people do," Reba explained. "I don't know what else he done. But he put her out on here and stretched her out and put a sheet over her.[69]

> And then the Relief Society people came and bathed her and combed her hair, just like you was going to dress somebody else [her hair thick and long even at ninety]. They dressed her, and when they got her

> dressed, why, they got the [temple] robe on the wrong side. After they'd got gone, why Aunt May and Mother went in to see what she looked like. She had buttons down the back of her dress and they didn't want her to have any buttons down the back of her dress but—Mother and Aunt May didn't because they said it would hurt her back. But anyhow that's what she wanted so they give it to her. And they said she's got her robe on wrong. The robe was supposed to be this way, and they had it this way. So they said, "Well, we can do that," so they took the robe off and put it on right. Somebody told the Relief Society president [Grace Jepson], and the next morning they come up real early, they come up to change that robe and Aunt May said, "We already did it." "You had no right doing it!" she said. "That was our job. Now you had no right doing it!"[70]

Sarah was one who often sat up with the dead[71] but the age-old ritual was honored in Elizabeth's case by Reba. "Well," she explained, "the dogs howled, and the cats howled." It was just like when Elizabeth's husband, James Stapley, died. Sitting with the dead was more a "courtesy to the body and respect for it and for everybody else" than a fear the body would be mutilated.[72]

Elizabeth's death was proclaimed in newspapers across the state. "Death Claims Utah's First White Child," headlined the *Salt Lake Tribune* the morning after Elizabeth died, announcing the funerals would be held Monday at 11 a.m. in Hurricane, and again at 2 p.m. in Kanarra, where she would be interred.[73] The *Washington County News*, attributing her death to bronchial pneumonia, rehearsed her life's story and noted that "Mrs. Stapley has been given much joy in the notoriety that the incident of her birth has accorded. She led the parade in Salt Lake City when the first Covered Wagon Days were celebrated [in 1931], she had named for her in 1937, the Hurricane North Ward D.U.P."[74]

The *Salt Lake Tribune* ran an editorial on April 4, 1938, praising Elizabeth as an "honored lady" who was "the first white child born within the borders of an alien territory which became the forty-fifth member of the sisterhood of states . . . Mrs. Stapley's infant eyes had seen the Mexican flag hauled down and the Stars and Stripes unfurled instead"—well, at least theoretically—and the newspaper outlined the many changes that had taken place in the United States since Elizabeth's birth.

The funeral, conducted by Bishop Frank Johnson in the Hurricane North Ward, was impressive, and with ninety-nine living descendants there was no lack of a crowd. The first speaker, Richard A. Benson of Parowan, related a story about the time Elizabeth's feisty father, John Steele, threatened to fistfight Indian Chief Walker. Wilford Leany paid tribute to Elizabeth's own qualities. Maggie Nielson, of the Young Elizabeth Steele Stapley Daughters of the Utah Pioneers Camp, gave a generous eulogium of Elizabeth and summarized: "It would take a poet to do justice to the first white baby born in a buffalo robe, in a tent, in the state of Utah. She was sweet, charming, serene and like the autumn leaves she had taken on her glory. She had mastered the art of growing old beautifully." James Jepson, who knew Elizabeth as a child in Toquerville, finished the praise by lauding Elizabeth's "long, useful and faithful life."[75]

Great-granddaughter Ruthell Roundy Bryant recalled, "I was about five or six, I remember having to go to the funeral, and I remember crying my bloody eyes out because I didn't want to go to the funeral and carry flowers, but they had, I think it was the great-grandchildren, take the flowers. I didn't want to do that."[76]

The body was then transported to Kanarra where Bishop William Graff conducted services a second time. Kanarra people recalled her midwife and nurse services, the *Iron County Record* reminding readers, "Mrs. Stapley's ability as a practical nurse made her many friends among the Indians and white people. Many times she was the only person able to administer to the sick in Kanarra."[77]

The Kanarra choir sang "The End of a Perfect Day" and old friends John Platt, Wells Williams, and Heber Benson praised her good qualities. Following the services, Joel dedicated the grave.[78]

There was no doubt about her sanctity. Bishop Johnson asserted without hesitation that "Mrs. Stapley will take her place in the celestial kingdom because of her truth and honesty."[79] Ironically, one of the Kanarra mourners, a sixty-nine-year-old retired farmer with a touch of the flu named James Wallace Williams died that night of a sudden heart attack. "He was to the funeral and I don't know whether he talked or not. But he went home. And he says, 'I don't feel too good.' He died that night," Reba explained. "Everybody thought that was so strange to think he'd die that night."[80]

The reddish stone with black speckles that marks Elizabeth's burial place is circled by a wrought-iron fence. The simple inscription reads:

James Stapley — Y. Elizabeth
Nov. 4, 1838 — Aug. 9, 1847
May 19, 1920 — Apr. 1, 1948
STAPLEY

Elizabeth's granddaughter Leola Stapley Anderson noted that a cement vault covers James and Elizabeth because "rodents and everything was bad down there so they would do things like that."[81] But also buried inside the fence were the remains of Almy Steele, and like most of the graves in the cemetery, his are unprotected by a concrete cover.

Kate was philosophical about her mother's death. "She felt like she'd lived long enough," Reba said. "Grandma always wanted to die. 'If I could just die and get out of here!' she says, 'Just die and get out of here!' So Mother thought, well, maybe that's what she should do."

Elizabeth's granddaughter Velma Stapley Rymer recalled that "Grandma passed away the first year of my marriage. While attending the funeral, I thot how like her, her casket was. Stern looking but well polished and endurable."[82]

17

"Poverty and Progeny"

The Women

Liberated by Elizabeth's death, Kate and Joel planned a summer trip to New Mexico to visit their children, Annis Roundy Tietjen and Golden Roundy. Reba remembered Sarah had

> been feeling pretty good for two or three weeks and she said, "Now, when you go I want to go with you." Dad said, "That's good." She was planning on this trip, and two days before we got ready to go she got sick and she said, "I guess I won't go with you." We called the doctor in and he said, "I can't do anything for her. She's too far gone." So, she said, "you go on with your trip," and then she says, "I'll see you when you get back."[1]

Reba went with Kate and Joel as they visited relatives but their most exciting experience was when a serviceman hitchhiker "flagged us down and wanted a ride." Kate was concerned: "What if he holds us up? What if he kills us?" but Joel said, "Reba's in the back seat. She's got a butcher knife. She can stop him!"

So Reba sat there with the knife, watching the soldier. "I held it," she said. "I just kept moving it around and doing this and that. He was going back east. Said he was on furlough and to save money he thought he'd just hitchhike to get back. But we got a kick out of him and we talked with him. I think we took him down to Flagstaff. He said, 'Well, I might have to go on the train and go back up. I never would get there and back here in time.'"

They visited Gallup, New Mexico, in the middle of the Navajo Indian reservation, as well as Flagstaff and the little Mormon towns of Snowflake and Showlow. They also saw Arizona's Painted Desert, where Kate loved the stratified and multicolored layers of Triassic Chinle siltstone, mudstone, shale, and petrified logs from a prehistoric coniferous forest.[2]

Eventually they returned to Hurricane where they faced Sarah's worsening health and a doctor they distrusted. Dr. McIntire's explanation of his lifelong refusal to mail bills to his patients was, "If the people want to pay me, they will." Some of those patients believed he took an equally cavalier attitude toward healing. When Sarah had once developed an ulcer on her leg, he couldn't offer her any remedy so she found a prescription for a varicose vein salve in an old "doctor book." McIntire said it couldn't hurt and wrote her a prescription, which the druggist filled. Sarah took an old gas tank and filled one side with hot water and one with cold, put the salve on her legs and tightly bandaged them, then rotated her legs from hot to cold. This cure seemed to work because her legs healed.[3]

Reba said, "Sarah sent her [urine] test up [to Dr. McIntire] with the kids and he just never done anything with them."[4] JoAnn confirmed that charge. "Gwen and I took the samples in and I caught him pouring them down the drain without even looking at them."[5]

There was one capable health care professional who took Sarah's illness seriously. "Mother has always taken care of the sick," Reba explained. "She's never been out of it. See, Grandma died in April, and that was just a continuation of what she'd been doing all her life." Sarah moved into the Roundy home and Kate and Reba provided most of her care. "Mother done it. Dad was up to the farm [in Kanarra], and I had to milk the cows, I had to herd the cows, 'cause we didn't have any feed. So I herded the cows. And Sarah sat down here and when she wanted to get up, I couldn't pull her up, so I'd go this way. And she said, 'I don't want you to do that anymore, it hurts me.'"[6]

When JoAnn graduated from high school in 1938 all thoughts of college and her future were submerged into caring for her mother.

> JoAnn could pull her up. And I says, "Now your mother wants to be pulled up." Well, we went out on the lawn to sleep and I said, "JoAnn, it's so quiet here you can't hear your mother." "Well, I think I can," she said. But we went out, and so when Sarah yelled for help, why, JoAnn hadn't gone to sleep. She got up twice and helped her, but the third time she wouldn't wake up. So I went in, and I said [to Sarah] "JoAnn—I can't wake her up, so you'll have to let me. I'll try to move you without it hurting you." But I couldn't do it.[7]

As Sarah got worse Reba and Joel bought a refrigerator so they could give her ice. This was a big hit with the youngest grandchildren. "Makes ice!"

joyously exclaimed Sarah's son Rex, "And all the grandkids around there would go up and eat them ice cubes. They were a big deal."[8]

Sarah, sleeping in the bed her grandmother had died in, was in bed so much that Reba said they "put a rubber tube out of a tire [under her]. We made it small, and we filled it full of air so she could sit on it, and we covered it over so she wouldn't get bed sores."[9] Her illness was diagnosed as Bright's disease, or nephritis, and with the edema she bloated like her dying great-aunt Mary Campbell Fish Steele, and Mary's dying aunt, Jane Steele McClelland.[10] "She was heavy with the water," Reba explained. "But if she'd got rid of the water, she'd of been skin and bones. Maybe weighed twenty pounds or fifty."[11] Vic's sister-in-law Lena Stevens Sylvester came to visit in the fall of 1938 and later sadly described her. "Sarah had this—what is it?—they bloat up. She swelled up with water in her until she looked like a bloated cow. That poor thing suffered something miserable! Oh!"[12]

"We put her to a window, we had an east window in the room she was in," Reba said. Remembering how the chiropractor, Dr. Eilersficken, had them put burdock leaves on Elizabeth's legs to draw out the water and the swelling, they adapted that in hopes of helping Sarah.

> We put her over to the east window every morning, and covered her with [catalpa] leaves as the sun came up, and we drawed that water out of her. [The doctor worried about her skin bursting.] He said, "This scar right here, now you watch it, and if that breaks, you come running, because if you don't she'll just be skin and bones." But it never did break. We wouldn't let it break . . . We put her under the east window, right here, and rolled her bed right up to there, and uncovered her and put the catalpa leaves on her and the water just run in little drips like this down and [out of her arms and legs and] we kept the water from getting so big.
>
> When she found out she wasn't going to live, why, she wanted to talk to the bishop, so Dad went and told him that she wanted to talk to him. But she said, "I want to talk to you alone," but he said, "I have to have my witnesses," so Dad went and got the two counselors and they went in and we don't know what she said. [The family believed she had confessed and asked forgiveness for sin.]
>
> She didn't want to die. I don't say she was afraid. She didn't want to die and leave her kids. Said that Vic had a hard time when his mother died and her kids was about the same age and she didn't want to die. Because, she said, what would become of her kids?[13]

Only days before her death, she asked Kate, Reba, and JoAnn to promise that after her death they would not have her posthumously sealed to Vic in the Mormon temple. JoAnn recalls the scene as beginning in incoherence: "Now I don't want you to do that."

"Do what?"

"Well, you just see you don't do it."

"What are you talking about?"

"Well, I don't want you getting your dad and me sealed in the temple," and then she complained lucidly about Vic's lack of religiosity, his quarreling, and his refusal to build her a house. She summed up: "See that you don't do that! Don't ever do that!"

"Well, I won't."

Sarah repeated it to her mother and to Reba. Reba remembered her as lucid and coherent: "Now you promise me you won't do it!" she demanded. Both Kate and Reba also agreed.[14]

Of course, the implications to the devout were not lost on Sarah. Her grandmother Priscilla Parrish Roundy had pointed out years before that Mormon women who die and are not sealed to a husband in the Mormon temple "would be servants hear after."[15] Sarah was risking being a celestial menial in the Mormon patriarchal heaven. Only the intensity of her conviction could have won assent from the three believers who agreed to honor this last request to directly challenge God's misogynist curse.

By September 1938 she was so sick that the only thing that brought her comfort was to move her, and that was painful. According to Nell, she and JoAnn alternated nights taking care of their mother, but neither JoAnn nor Reba mentioned Nell so it's likely to have been toward the end of her illness, when they were so tired they weren't remembering everything. JoAnn and Reba described taking turns getting up in the night, turning her, propping her up with pillows, and taking care of the bedpan.[16]

Florence Beatty Leavitt, who lived near, visited on September 19. "It was just late, late afternoon," Florence remembered.

> And she said to Sister Roundy, she says, "Oh Mother, Mother, I'm so hungry. Hurry Mother, get me something to eat!" She was just rolling her head back and forth on the pillow and she said, "Hurry! Hurry, I just can't wait! I can't wait! I'm just so hungry!" And she just kept this up constantly for about a half an hour, and she kept saying to her, "Well, I'm hurrying, I'm doing the best I can." And she said, "What do you want?"

> and she said she wanted some warm cereal. And so she fixed it for her and fixed it in a glass, and she wouldn't touch it.[17]

Later that evening Sarah's lungs filled with water. "She'd heard the death rattles so many times that she knew that nobody ever lived with them," Reba said. "'Cause I've heard her say, 'Yeah, I went and set up with this person, and that person, and when they got the death rattles, you know darn well they're going." When Sarah got the death rattles she said ominously, "Death rattles. You have to die whether you want to or not when you hear the death rattles, when you hear the death rattles."[18]

Kate told Reba to get Uarda Knight, the buxom, Berkeley-trained county nurse.[19] When Miss Knight showed up, "Sarah was ranting around and she said, 'I got to die! I got to die! I've got to die!'" She couldn't move her legs because they were so heavy with water but she gestured with her arms and argued with God that "I've got two younger kids," and said of four-year-old Leon, "I've got to raise him. I've got him. I've got to raise him." Kate assured her, "We'll take care of him, now just don't worry. We'll take care of him."[20]

Kate turned anxiously and whispered to Miss Knight. "You're not going to kill her, are you?"

"No, I'm just going to put her to sleep and let her sleep it off."

Knight "gave her the shot and she quieted down and never did rally after that. She just kind of slept it out."[21] JoAnn said, "When she died, and we were all there, we could see what happened to her face. She was just miserable and then she just went 'Ahhhh' and she never breathed in again. And in a few minutes her face relaxed and she just looked so peaceful and happy and she hadn't looked that way for a long time."[22] Her death certificate reported she was fifty years old and had suffered from myocarditis (inflammation of the myocardium) and edema (fluid trapped in the body) for two years and acute dilatation of her heart for six months.[23]

"I didn't realize she was ready to go when she did," Nell remembered. "I didn't—I had just got home about seven o'clock in the morning . . . she died that day, but I didn't realize she was that bad. But the doctor [nurse, actually] had given her a sedative and I guess it was morphine. She didn't wake up again, I guess." She added, "When I went home that morning—or when I went home after she died—the neighbor asked me how my mother was and I couldn't for the life of me say she'd died. I just couldn't say it. So I said, 'She's better.' They've held it against me I guess, but I just couldn't do it. They were in their yard and I was in my yard and I would have had to holler it and I just couldn't."[24]

Did Sarah come to terms with life and learn to live with sadness and disappointment? "She never came to terms with anything! She fought them all her life!" laughed JoAnn,

> [right] up until the last few months of her life. She was somewhat like Ruth. She never gave up. That's why I say she was so persistent. She never gave up. Up until her last illness she was always thinking that dad would eventually—and, oh, she wanted a home of her own, she never did get her—the home that she wanted. I remember the house that she wanted. She kept it for years in a scrapbook or book, and I remember a lot about it, but I don't remember the floor plan. I remember it was a house that came out in the *Ladies Home Journal*, and it was designed by Frank Lloyd Wright and it was a fireproof home. It was all made out of bricks and cement and concrete, and stuff like that. And she kept that for all this time, and she said that he promised her he'd build her a house, and he promised her he'd join the church. And she was still hoping against hope, clear up until she got her last sickness, that these things would happen, and when they'd get mad and get in a fight, these are the things they'd talk about. There was a lot of that, too. And, so I think that she never did admit that she wouldn't get what she wanted. But I think . . . that she did not make quite the effort to do it herself, and that's why she didn't get it. Because everything she decided to do herself, she ended up doing. But she was waiting for dad to do these two things. And he didn't do them. So she didn't get them. So I think it was more that she was hoping against hope that he would live up to her beliefs in him, so that she would—so that she would, you know, she wouldn't have to be disappointed in him.[25]

The mortuary couldn't prepare the body. "They didn't dare," Reba explained. "If they'd cut her skin, all that water would run out. But they said we couldn't keep her. We'd have to bury her the next day. And I said, 'You don't have to bury her the next day!' And they said, 'What are you going to do?' and I said, 'We'll pack her in ice.' They said, 'Oh, you can't do that.'" But Reba got a bucket "and we filled it as full as we could fill it of ice, and we went around to the neighbors and got them to fill it a little bit, and put that right here on her stomach, and some around her, and she kept good for two days." They dressed her in white and from the shoulders up she looked natural.

"We just didn't want to bury her that quick. And she was heavy. Someone said that was the heaviest casket they ever lifted because it was all water. She never ate. She never ate for four or five months. All she had was a little bit of—maybe a spoonful or two of water and a lettuce leaf."

"I decided it was time for me to get over being scared," Reba said, "so I went in and fingled her all over." Then Reba slept in the bed Sarah had died in. "It was cold," Reba remembered, "and Leon left Nell's and come over to our place before we were up and Mother told him to go in there and get in bed with me so he came in to get in bed with me, and he just got in and started to get warm, and he said, 'Get out of here, Reba! Get out of here, Aunt Reba!' I said, 'What's the trouble now?' And he said, 'My mother died in this bed. You better watch out, you'll die too.'"[26]

Kate wasn't as philosophical about Sarah's death as she had been about her own mother's. "I don't know whether you'd say it was her time or whether they was forced to her," Kate said, "because the doctor didn't do anything for her, she had to die."[27] "It was the doctor's carelessness."[28]

For the first time in his life, Vic faced full responsibility for his children. He handled the death without diplomacy. Florence Beatty Leavitt, who often stayed over because she was friends with JoAnn, asked, "How's your wife?"

"She died last night."[29]

That was how the younger children learned of their mother's death.

Aunt Dick recalled Nell's response years later: "When Sara died Nell wrote and said, 'Our mother is gone and all we can do is just be the people she wanted us to become.'" Dick added, "They are certainly doing that."[30]

"I just returned from Hurricane, Toquerville and LaVerkin where I have been for a few days," Vic's sister Maud wrote Dick:

> Sara Sylvester died on the 19th and . . . was buried on the 21rst [*sic*] of this month. The poor girl has had a long drawn out illness besides a bad heart she has had complication of kidneys and liver. She has been at her mothers in bed for the last five months. She left five children under the age of 18 the youngest 4 years and O how she wanted to live to care for them. She was so strong willed its hard to think of her dying unless she wanted to.[31]

The *Washington County News*, in a story probably written by Hurricane correspondent Milda Isom, described Sarah Roundy Sylvester as

> an excellent seamstress having made a sort of profession or trade of this work . . . She was also a good artist and especially loved to do fancy

> work. She has always been an active church member having worked in the M.I.A., the relief society and genealogical department. She was a good donator to worthy causes. Her personal characteristics were of a type that will live forever in the memory of her friends and all who knew her. Her personality could not help but be a magnetic one being filled with love, honesty, ambition, humor, dependability and always a willingness to cooperate.[32]

That is probably a fair summation. No biographical sketches were written—except this unusually perceptive obituary—leaving the family with a mixed legacy: pride in Sarah's talents and accomplishments, but eventually an unwillingness to accept her command not to be sealed to Vic. Her interment was equally subdued. Sarah was buried in the dry, gravelly Hurricane cemetery with a small piece of wood inscribed, "Sarah Elizabeth Roundy Sylvester" pounded into the ground above her.[33]

Like her recently deceased grandmother, Sarah was a powerful and courageous woman, her talents circumscribed by poverty and progeny. Family stories were written about Sarah's mother and her two grandmothers (all written by women), but her story was never celebrated by family historians. She had hopes, she had failures, she had fears, but in the end she had courage to face her eternity without the man with whom she had unhappily shared her earthly life.

When JoAnn married and moved to Idaho she thought often of her grandmother Kate. "We shared," JoAnn paused, and then added thoughtfully, "I don't know. We knew each other, that's all. We understood each other. I shared with her the beautiful things she kept to look at," mentioning a glass pitcher, a fancy sugar bowl, and handmade pillow cases. "I asked her why she didn't use them because they were so pretty and I thought she ought to get them out and use them and she said, no, she didn't want to do that, she just wanted to keep them to look at. And I could understand that."[34]

Kate and Joel's home became a refuge for Sarah's children and the elder couple's birthdays and anniversaries brought extended family celebrations.[35] They visited granddaughter Gwen in Fillmore, Stapley relatives in Delta, and family in Bluewater, New Mexico.

Grandchildren went off to war and then on LDS missions. There were births, marriages, and, sadly, deaths. Kate's son Jesse passed away from stomach cancer; grandson Collins Russell, a Navy man who survived World War II, died in a car accident at age nineteen;[36] and JoAnn's two oldest children burned to death in a house fire a few months after the war's end. As Kate approached her eighties, family members worried more and more about her weak heart and increasing fragility. But Kate had one more job to do.

"My mother said she wouldn't die unless I was married," Reba recalled. That hadn't been Reba's plan. "I was going to stay and take care of my father and mother." Reba told her mother, "I don't want to get married," and she told herself, "I wasn't ever going to get married," but Kate directed, "You pray about a man."[37]

"Do you think the Lord would answer my prayer?" Reba questioned.

Well, there was only one response to that kind of question of a devout Mormon. "Yes, I think he'll answer your prayer all right."

The answer wasn't coming any too quickly, and when Kate and Joel were called to do temple work in St. George, Reba was unmarried, working, and living at home. Her parents met Jane Artimesia Robinson LeFevre Davis at the temple; Jane was born in Paragonah but was a longtime resident of Panguitch, where Kate's Uncle Mahonri Steele built "the House of Nine Gables." Besides Reba's Steele cousins, Jane would know some of her Roundy kin because Joel's grandnephew was Panguitch war hero Uvon Roundy. (Rifleman Roundy was "authorized to wear the European theater ribbon with three battle stars, Good Conduct medal, American theater ribbon, combat Infantryman's badge and the Victory ribbon," reported the *Garfield County News*.)[38]

As Kate and Joel were nearing the end of their temple mission around spring 1944, Jane told Kate, "My son's in the service and he's down in Georgia. He's operated on and he has to be in the hospital a whole month and he wants some good girl to write to him. Do you know of any?"

The son was a onetime Civilian Conservation Corps enlistee, thirty-nine-year-old Corporal Carl LeFevre: five foot ten inches, 145 pounds, stationed at Robins Field in Warner Robins, Georgia. Reba was two years older, nine inches shorter, and thirty or forty pounds lighter.[39]

"Well, I've got a daughter over there but I don't know if she'll write to him or not," Kate answered. She asked Reba to write and Reba refused.

> I told her if he wants to write to me that's all right but I'm not going to write to him. So she went back and she told Sister Davis that I wouldn't write. And she wrote to her son and told him I was here if he'd write to me and he wouldn't write either. So it went on for two months and she said, "Will you see if you can't get your daughter to write to him?" She said, "Well I don't know if I can or not." And so one day she came and she said, "Well he's in the hospital, why don't you write to him?"

> and I said, "Well I'm just not in the habit of writing to people I don't know." "Well, he's a Mormon." I said, "That's all right. I've heard of other people, too, that's wrote to people in the service, and"—this is where he had it over on me. And she said, "Well, when I come back you have the letter wrote and sent." So it worried me for a long time, and I thought, what can I write, what can I say that would be interesting to him? So on the 24th [of July 1944] I sit down and wrote a letter and told what the program was and what we were doing here on the 24th, and before I thought it had a chance to get there I got an answer right back. So I wrote another letter and I said, "Well, you'd better not take it too serious; I'm not too good a person, I just about killed a man once" [referring to friend Yegg Bryant nearly hanging himself when she was with him and the difficulty she had saving him]. So I wrote him a letter what I had done. I said—mother come back and she said, "Did you write?" and I said, "Yeah, but I don't think I'll ever get another letter now," I said, "I think everything's settled." Next day I got a letter [she chuckled].[40]

"Well, there must be something wrong with him," Reba told herself. But they kept up the correspondence. When Carl got home on leave ("Carl LeFevre is spending a furlough at the home of his mother, Mrs. Jane L. Davis," reported the *Garfield County News* on September 14, 1944[41]) he looked up his murderous pen pal. "He come in September on a furlough and he come in to Hurricane and visited a day and then he went back."[42] Kate was very taken with Carl, a rich-voiced bachelor who, despite two years at the Branch Normal Academy in Cedar City, joined his brother Eldon to farm their father's acres to avoid foreclosure during the Depression.

"That's the man you're to marry, that's the answer to your prayer," Kate said after she met Carl.

"Are you sure it is?"

"Yes."

"I'm not sure."[43]

There were some bumps in this romance. When Carl visited on leave and fell asleep during a show Reba "started to get up and was going to leave him" but the "showman" said, "You're not going to leave him here!" Reba waited. When the show ended and Carl woke up she said, "Well, I was going to go leave you but they told me not to. I says, 'They wouldn't let me go.' 'Well I'm glad they didn't,' he says. 'But,' he says, 'I go to sleep every time we are in a show!' He says, 'We learned that in the service.'"[44]

When Reba was a younger woman and working in Cedar, she had poor enough health that she had Dr. Frank H. Petty Jr. pull her teeth. She went for a year as a "gummer" and then got ill-fitting false teeth: "The people down in Hurricane," she remembered, "said that it was worse than if I'd left them alone or even gone without false teeth." By the end of 1944 she felt the courtship was serious enough she had her father take her to Salt Lake City on the bus where she got new, prettier teeth from Standard Union. "I'll learn to have them on a year before he [Carl] gets here," she said. Despite that, she was undecided and so, as she told devout LDS interviewer Fielding H. Harris in 1968, "I seen in a—dream world," which Harris corrected to vision, a word she used thereafter to describe seeing faces of three potential suitors on the east wall of her bedroom—Carl's face on top.[45] Also visible was the message: "You're going to marry the one on the top." The other two were Hurricane widowers who, Reba was advised, were "not going to live too long."[46] The next time Carl visited, she agreed to an engagement. Reba, now working in the school lunch program, was asked by a lady she worked with, "Where's your ring?"

"We don't have to have a ring."

"Oh yes, you do!"

She wrote Carl about this conversation and he sent her a ring.[47] They were married on March 23, 1946. After Sarah died, Reba had gone to the temple in January 1939, because she had health problems and folklore said that would help her heal. Joel told her that since she'd "been through the temple I had to get married in the temple, so Carl said all right, he'd get married in the temple, so I got him in the temple. I didn't have to do like some of the other sisters, have to coax him in, but he went with me."[48] Her choice—or God's—of a partner turned out to be happily everything she could want even though they never had children (God promised those in the post-mortal existence, Reba said).

They moved to his Panguitch farm but left later for a Mormon mission in Hatch, New Mexico, where they received the only letter I've seen from Kate Roundy, with a note added by Joel (Reba thriftily used the envelope to work out some math):

> Hurricane May 15 1949
> Dear Reba & Karl
>
> It seems a long time since I heard from you but I think it was just before you left to go to Old Mexico I thot I would wait until you got back to answer but no doubt you have been back a long time before you get your release It wont be long now. whitch way will you come by Denver

or by Goldens and Annises I Know you will have to go to Salt Lake to Report and I Guess it will be about as short one way as the other.

Gwen [Sylvester] and Faimely were here for Mothers day went to St George Sunday morning and back home that nite she took Joann [Sylvester Bate] home with her. and I got a card from Max [Bate] posted the 8 . . . from Oakland Calif so I guess she didnt stay Long but I havent heard from any of them since.

When I gave Estella your Picture she said she didnt deserve it for she hadent even written you a word and she was ashamed but she had let one thing after another come along untill it never got done but She was going to try as there was a few days grace yet. but she was very proud of it but Karl [Roundy] came up and I gave his to him and he was very proud to think he had a Sister on a Mission with her Husband.

He might have gone on a mission if he hadent got in satch a hurry to get Married but I guess where he is as just about as hard and he seems to do his best. they cant all do the same thing so it is nice to try to do all things that you are ask to do by so doing we learn more and have more experience. I havent been to church today but am feeling better than I did this morning. Estella came up after meeting and Pa has just taken her home. Roola has been sick since Friday with Sore throat or symptoms of Poleo or something but is better today she thinks she will be able to go to School Monday there is Measels hooping cough they took one or more cases of Poleo to Salt Lake. I think they are better as we havent heard of them. We heard today that Emanuel Standsworth died in Cedar City this morning of heart trouble. Estella brot me a graduation card of the Hurricane High School of [~~1949~~] Dale Russell. 8 P.M.

Thursday. May. 19. 1949.

I think the seminary class will graduate to night school will be out next Friday.

George Willson spent a few hours with us this afternoon, he is working in Zion now, his faimily is at home.

I will close for now as this is all the news I know of George said you could come down some time if he could get you a chance Reba and Carl will be home soon love to all as ever.

Mother

The ~~Raspberries~~ Straw berries are Ripe and lots of them come and have some

Please excuse silly mistakes we we'll [*sic*] I guess I had better write a word or two I am glad you went to Old Mexico to see the country things are looking p[r]etty good now the nuts trees and comeing full it looks like we will have more nuts this year than—any othre year aur ather hen came of with 3 chickens and one of them is Dead aur Roses and doing good th[e]y bock like they will all grow Sane of them looks like they are goaeng to blossem.

We are goung to have same Apricots this year and Figs to but the cherres are not to thick we had the bulldozer dig up our currants and we have planted that to Tomatoes I am leeting the ather go dry to try and Kill the crowfoot out I sure hope it will do it for there is lots of it. George shamo Said he had Some Cabbage and Collie flowers so we'll try and Keep them for you I hope thank for the Pucture it sure looks good to me Karl Roundy is working on the Black[r]idge for $10.00 a day and sometimes more I hope you [illegible—perhaps "ejoye']

From Daddy with Love and lots of it[49]

Six weeks later "was Sunday," JoAnn remembered,

and down there you have to irrigate when you can irrigate so he was irrigating this Sunday [June 26, 1949]. It came on Sunday every so many weeks so everybody could have one Sunday they had to irrigate, instead of the same person having to irrigate every Sunday. And he'd been to Sunday School in the morning. I wasn't there, but this is the way they'd told me. He went to Sunday School in the morning and he came home. And while Grandma was getting dinner on the table, he went out and changed the water—put the dams in and moved it over to another section so he could leave it while he went to church in the afternoon. And he came back in and Grandma was in the living room and he washed his hands and walked over—now right by the door between the living room and the kitchen was where the refrigerator was, and he walked over there, wiping his hands. And he got just to the refrigerator and he said, "Oh, Dearie, I've got such a pain in my chest. I can't hardly stand it." And he . . . just passed right out. Grandma jumped up and ran over there to see what was the matter with him, because he never falls down or anything like that, so she didn't really know what to do and she went outside and yelled at the neighbors and they came over and called the

> doctor [E. Clark McIntire] and—I guess—I don't know. The way I got it from all the excitement and the way people were talking and stuff, Workmans—one of them called the doctor and one ran over. Grandma was there waiting, while the doctor came in and didn't know what to do with him or anything. The doctor came and he was dead.[50]

The death certificate said he died two hours after a coronary occlusion and a contributing factor was "old age."[51]

Nell, like her sister JoAnn, was stunned. "When they came and told me that Grandpa had died, I thought they had misunderstood and Grandma had died, because Grandma had heart trouble for years and years," Nell remembered. The funeral was held in the North Ward chapel Wednesday afternoon. It was well attended, the *Washington County News* reporting that "the house was crowded to capacity and there were many beautiful flowers."[52] "Everybody, I think, in four counties was there to his funeral," JoAnn recalled.[53]

Joel was lauded for being "active in the church organizations, being teacher of the Deacon's Quorum for 40 years, and he had a 100 per cent record for ward teaching for 60 years." Besides his extended family, the newspaper reported, "Most of the Kanarra people attended the service."[54] The Kanarra correspondent for the *Iron County Record* confirms that "Several people from here attended the funeral of Joel J. Roundy at Hurricane last week."[55]

Kate "was really shocked because she had always thought that she would die before Grandpa," JoAnn remembered.

> In her patriarchal blessing or something it said she would always have the priesthood in her home so she really was shocked and she couldn't believe it. And she didn't ever want to go stay with her kids. I think, partly, because her mother stayed with her so much. She didn't ever want to go live with her kids, yet she had this bad heart and they wouldn't let her live alone, so Reba came from Panguitch and stayed with her for a couple of weeks, then she went up to Reva's in Cedar City to stay. And she stayed there a little bit and then she got the flu and she wouldn't get well. The doctor kept taking—giving her stuff. And since she didn't want to get well and she kept saying, "Oh, Pa, why don't you come and get me? Pa, why don't you come and get me?" And, you know it was really sad, because here they were trying to make her want to live and everything and all at once, the doctor said one day, "She'd get better. She could be well if she wanted to." She seemed to be quite a bit better,

> but then Reva went in and she was laying there and she just looked up and she said, "Oh, Pa! You've come to get me," and she just smiled and died. So she died a few weeks after he did. She just didn't want to keep on living. She didn't want to live with her daughters or be a burden to anybody or be any kind of a problem to anybody and, of course, she'd never lived without him.[56]

Dr. Reed Farnsworth reported on the death certificate she died from myocardial insufficiency, from which she'd been suffering for five years.[57] Family attributed her passing to what is now called broken heart syndrome: she lost her will to live.

Kate died "just 23 days after her husband's death," the *Washington County News* reported.[58] "When but 15 years of age she became secretary of the Relief Society and later became president and was a teacher in the organization for many years," reported the *Iron County Record*.[59]

The family was summoned again and the *News* reported the pallbearers "were five grandsons and one great grandson, Kent and Joel Webster, Douglas Roundy, Vernon Al Tietjen, Dale Russell and Leon Sylvester."[60] The concourse of friends and relatives at the funeral seems to have been smaller than Joel's but maybe the newspaper just didn't take the time to identify many mourners.

The old patriarchs and matriarchs were gone but Vic Sylvester lived twenty-four years after Sarah and mellowed as he got older. His son Leon, who didn't remember his own mother, had affectionate memories of his father, especially the summers they spent herding sheep. "Oh, he was serious," Leon recalled of Vic. "He knew a lot about horses. Knew a lot about sheep. And he was a good worker." Leon learned a lot about sheep, camping, cooking, what ranges to attend to where and why, horse and sheep traits, and got along well with Vic. Vic had "had a long life and done a lot of different kinds of work. So he knew a lot of things."[61]

Vic tried to make amends to Ruth; she recalled that long after she was grown up and was working Victor would drop by to visit. "He said he'd finally figured out what our trouble was. He said we were too much alike. But he said the main trouble was that he thought you had to break a child's spirit, and mine couldn't be broken. He said that I was never in my life, ever going to let anyone get the best of me, when I was a kid; I guess I never did."[62] She found solace, but not forgiveness, in that thought.

When JoAnn's marriage fell apart, Vic gave her blunt but not unkind advice to get a divorce and he provided money for a lawyer; he also paid to get her ramshackle house reroofed. Yet my most entrenched memory of Vic and my mother, JoAnn, is her saying she hated him—I didn't know one was allowed to hate parents and I quite liked him—but, puzzling to me, when he died in my eleventh year she cried at his funeral.

"I got to like him better," she explained when I asked why, and she treasured him telling her, "I used to think you kids would never amount to anything; I was afraid you'd all turn out rotten. But now you're all grown up and you turned out pretty good after all, all of you."[63]

The second to the last time I visited Aunt Reba she had begun suffering from what we later learned was Alzheimer's and she couldn't remember my name. "I don't know who you are; I been in the hospital six days and I can't remember anything" (she didn't know how old she was either). When I said "I'm Kerry," she questioned, "Terry? Yes; Terry," and looked cheerful at solving that puzzle.

I visited a second time a few weeks later to celebrate her ninetieth birthday and found her chasing a black cat out of her house with a broom; I confirmed the time and place of her party. When I got to the stake center for the celebration my Aunt Ruth was there, sad about her diabetes and happy to share pictures of her newest grandchild but not interested in seeing mine. Uncle Rex's wife Dena was pretty, as always, pleasant, and quiet as she set up tables, rolled fresh white paper over the old Masonite tops and taped it down, then put balloons on the jugs of punch mix. Nell, dressed in blue, was dragging along her misanthropic husband George while she talked piously about spending the week in the temple, but George gave her away by admitting they only "been here since Wednesday"—three days. Gwen, being the fussy schoolteacher she was, managed to give her brother Rex an assignment—to set up a Roundy reunion—and then relaxed while Reba was thrust into an overstuffed chair on a blue wooden stand where she looked a little puzzled and regal, but in danger of falling off.

"They took my memory away in the hospital," she told her niece, Helen Roundy Cannon, whom she didn't remember.

"I'm Kerry," I told her and she answered, "I thought you were Kerry," and while I was standing there she turned to Rex to say, anxiously, "I was chasing this black cat out of my house, and this man come up and said, 'Is it for 3 o'clock?' and I said yes, and he said, 'Over at the stake center?' and I said 'Yes.' I knew who he was, but I couldn't remember his name."

"Oh, don't worry about it," Rex said.

She seemed so anxious because of me, this stranger/nonstranger, that I didn't go back; or maybe I used that as an excuse not to visit again.

Nearly sixty-two years after Sarah's death, on Saturday, January 6, 2001 (after a poor night's sleep), I got up at 3:15 a.m.—and with two of my children, snacks, three books, and a new camera—left Salt Lake City at four a.m. for St. George.

Salt Lake Valley's winter inversion was worse than usual, the fog and smog so thick it was hard to see where we were until we got to Santaquin in southern Utah County. Dawn was just breaking when we reached Beaver but the landscape didn't quicken my heart until we were just past Leeds and saw the beautiful patches of roadside purple Bentonite clay, the low red sandstone hills of Silver Reef, and the blue and white Pine Valley Mountains.

By 8:20 a.m. we arrived at St. George's Vernon Worthen Park where we rested, the smell of burning pine from local fireplaces perfuming the air, the grass frosted white, and the Red Hill north of town still a dark early morning russet.

Driving to the Metcalfe Mortuary across the street from the local homeless shelter we made our way to ninety-six-year-old Reba's coffin in the funeral home. Her chin was up in such a freakish manner that it drew comments. She was wearing a white blouse and her green temple apron was lying on her lap which, she had once explained to me, represented Eve's fig leaf skirt. Her face was fuller than I expected.

I leaned over to get a closer look and was hit with the stench of funeral flowers.

Uncle Rex, always smiling, was cheerful, bald, a little jowly, and pleased to see everyone. Aunt Gwen—always the prettiest of my mother JoAnn's sisters—was white haired and Uncle Leon was still as slender as his father Vic.

There were about sixty people at the service including representatives of the extended Roundy and LeFevre clans, for Reba mothered many of us. Her nephew Kent Webster—son of her twin Reva—was short and balding but couldn't speak of his deceased brother Dono because it was too stressful.

My aunt Ruth Pickering, her neck waddled, suffering from diabetes, looked gaunt as a rooster except her heavy legs, which were bandaged with rough ace bandages like she had elephantiasis. She was invariably kind to me. Her husband, Perry, was a little overgrown and wobbly; his big eyes always looked very sad.

Nell, Sarah's oldest daughter, nearing eighty-six—one of my mother's other handsome sisters—was crippled with curvature of the spine since having her back broken, but still bustled about energetically.

The Mortuary Chapel was clearly built for Mormons. The benches were stacked with Mormon hymnals, and the leaded glass window under the vaulted ceiling on the west wall boasted a Mormon beehive, sego lilies, and crickets. These symbols recalled the first winter the Mormons spent in Salt Lake Valley—that winter following Reba's grandmother Elizabeth's birth in summer 1847.

Bishop Merton Lovell, his thin hair carefully stretched in a vain effort to cover the bald spot on his head, wearing black splayed glasses, made some announcements.

Chubby-cheeked David LeFevre, a pale man with ears like antennas, wearing a handsome white carnation in his lapel pocket, gave the invocation. A Roundy niece whose name I missed made comments and read Reba's obituary while Aunt Ruth, seated in front of me, read along with the help of a magnifying glass.

A trio of handsome LeFevre kin—David, Kenneth, and Loretta—sang, and then Rex gave brief remarks contesting his cousin's suggestion that Reba was a poor driver just because she'd driven into a ditch. (My daughter Jennifer whispered to my daughter Marilee that riding with Reba "was one of the more frightening experiences" in her life.)

Ben Holyoak, a pink-faced man with receding hair flecked with gray, spoke as Reba had requested twelve years earlier. He was genial, a onetime salesman who recalled the time that one of Reba's nephews was busy drawing a picture of heaven. "We don't know what heaven looks like," Reba told him. "When I get through you'll know what it looks like!" the nephew responded.

The bishop offered some words to ponder when he mentioned the Alzheimer's of Reba's last years: "I think a lot of Reba's test was our test." As he talked about the importance of visiting her even though she didn't know who we were I remembered guiltily my two visits six years earlier. My Uncle Rex Sylvester's barbershop quartette sang "How Great Thou Art" and Reba's nephew Darrell Roundy gave a closing prayer, ending the services.

As I drove back to Salt Lake I felt gloomy—maybe guilty about those visits I stopped making—and, unaccountably, a phrase from the Wicked Witch of the West rang through my head: "Oh, what a world! What a world! What a world!" Once home I looked at a little black ball of wool that had belonged to Young Elizabeth Steele Stapley—a gift from Reba—and realized that all our conversations about "The Women" were finished.

NOTES

INTRODUCTION

1. JoAnn Sylvester Bate to Kerry William Bate, December 3, 1986, in author's possession.
2. Leopold von Ranke, *History of the Popes, Their Church and State*, trans. E. Fowler, rev. ed. (New York: Colonial Press, 1901,) 1:xviii–xix.
3. I thank Brigham Young University's L. Tom Perry Special Collections for allowing me to read the original letters against my transcripts and those of Iona Poling and for allowing their use in this book. Iona modernized the punctuation, spelling, and paragraphing in her 1960s transcripts, but reading the originals I find she achieved remarkable accuracy; I'm very indebted to her.
4. Thomas Babington Macaulay, "The Task of the Modern Historian," in *Little Masterpieces*, edited by Bliss Perry (New York: Doubleday, Page and Co., 1906), 11.

CHAPTER 1

1. Juanita Brooks, *On the Ragged Edge: The Life and Times of Dudley Leavitt* (Salt Lake City: Utah State Historical Society, 1973), 41.
2. For a memo of this conversation, see Reba Roundy LeFevre, interview by Kerry William Bate, January 25, 1985, 4 (hereafter all interviews are with Kerry William Bate unless otherwise identified; transcripts have been provided to the Utah State Historical Society).
3. "First White Child Born in Utah Is Active at 88," *Deseret News*, February 28, 1935, 13, 20.
4. "Kanarra," *Iron County Record*, July 13, 1906, 1.
5. Jesse Peyton Warner, interview, June 21, 1985, 6.
6. A carat symbol [^] is used to note interlinear additions in the original manuscript.
7. John Steele to Catherine Campbell Steele, May 26, 1878, box 1, fd. 12, MSS 528, John Steele Collection, 1847–1936, L. Tom Perry Special Collections, Harold B. Lee Library, Brigham Young University, Provo, Utah (hereafter LTPSC); John and "Mahona" Steele's mission calls are published in "General Conference at St. George—Second Day," *Deseret News*, April 11, 1877, 156; "Missionaries," *Salt Lake Telegram*, April 8, 1877, 2.
8. John Steele to Catherine Campbell Steele, April 25, 1878, October 13, 1877, October 30, 1877, box 1, fd. 12, MSS 528, LTPSC.
9. Ileen J. Johnson and Wanda S. Cox, *The Memoirs of Mahonri Moriancumer Steele Jr.* (mimeographed, 1963), 5.
10. John Steele to Catherine Campbell Steele, January 30, 1878, box 1, fd. 12, MSS 528, LTPSC.
11. [Anonymous], "History of the Stapley Family," copy in author's possession.
12. I toured the house July 23, 1987, and several times since; Mattie Giasson, "Historic House Is Living Slice of Old West," *Daily Spectrum*, January 29, 1988, 5; National Historic Register, http://pdfhost.focus.nps.gov/docs/NRHP/Text/88000401.pdf.
13. Hazel Eagar Bringhurst, interview, July 23, 1987, 2.
14. John Steele to Catherine Campbell Steele, November 25, 1877, July 30, 1877, August 20, 1877, box 1, fd. 12, MSS 528, LTPSC.
15. John Steele to Catherine Campbell Steele, April 25, 1878, September 27, 1877, August 20, 1877, box 1, fd. 12, MSS 528, LTPSC. Paul Dean Proctor and Morris A. Shirts, *Silver, Sinners and Saints: A History of Old Silver Reef, Utah* (n.p.: Paulmar, 1991), 75–77; "Mahonri Steele (Panguitch Pioneer)," anonymous history at Daughters of the Utah Pioneers Museum, Panguitch, UT.
16. "Southern Utah Notes," *Salt Lake Democrat*, August 3, 1885, 4. It went on to malignantly add, "lacking in intelligence, influence and address, and capable only to rehash third-rate tabernacle doxologies and vituperation against outsiders."
17. Tenth Census of the United States, 1880, *Toquerville, Kane, Utah*, roll 1336, page 428D, enumeration district 28, Family History film 1255336, (Ancestry.com); "Census Enumerators," *Deseret News Weekly*, May 19, 1880, 254–55 (his son M. M. was the Panguitch area enumerator).
18. John Steele to Catherine Campbell Steele, December 18, 1877, January 30, 1878, box 1, fd. 12, MSS 528, LTPSC.

19. John Steele to Catherine Campbell Steele, February 17, 1878, June 21, 1877, box 1, fd. 12, MSS 528, LTPSC; Mahonri Moriancumer Steele to Catherine Campbell Steele, November 20, 1877, February 20, 1878, box 1, fd. 17, MSS 528, LTPSC. Donald R. Lancaster, "Dixie Wine," (master's thesis, Brigham Young University, August 1972), 73.
20. John Steele to Catherine Campbell Steele, March 11, 1878, box 1, fd. 12, MSS 6161, LTPSC.
21. John Steele to Catherine Campbell Steele, May 1, 1878, box 1, fd. 12, MSS 528, LTPSC.
22. John Steele private note signed September 12, 1878: "One day after date I promise to pay the Trustee in Trust for the Church of Jesus Christ of Latter day Saints Fifteen pounds 18/2 sterling" but with the notation across it, "Cancelled by order of Pres John Taylor", "Salt Lake City April 25, 1879" signed by clerk A. A. Anderson, photocopy in possession of author.
23. John Steele to Catherine Campbell Steele, May 1, 1878, box 1, fd. 12, MSS 528, LTPSC.
24. Wanda Steele Cox, *Journals of John Steele and Mahonri Moriancumer Steele* (Cedar City, UT: self-published, 1967), 2:23 (page numbers start over so for the last half 2:23 means section two, page 23) (July 25, 1877); John Steele to Catherine Campbell Steele, October 30, 1877, box 1, fd. 12, MSS 528, LTPSC.
25. Agreement to dissolve the Ould-Steele marriage, box 1, fd. 13, MSS 528, LTPSC; Maybelle Harmon Anderson, *Appleton Milo Harmon Goes West* (Berkeley, CA: Gillick Press, 1946), 1, 44, 46, 180, 182, 186; "Mrs. Mary Jane Harmon," *San Bernardino County [CA] Sun*, December 11, 1910, 57.
26. John Steele to Catherine Campbell Steele, February 17, 1878, box 1, fd. 12, MSS 528, LTPSC.
27. John Steele to Catherine Campbell Steele, August 15, 1878, box 1, fd. 12, MSS 528, LTPSC.
28. John Steele to Catherine Campbell Steele, November 25, 1877, May 26, 1878, September 1, 1878, January 30, 1878, April 25, 1878, box 1, fd. 12, MSS 528, LTPSC.
29. John Steele to Catherine Campbell Steele, November 25, 1877, box 1, fd. 12, MSS 528, LTPSC.
30. John Steele to Catherine Campbell Steele, January 30, 1878, box 1, fd. 12, MSS 528, LTPSC.
31. F. R. and G. Kinder, *The New [1839] Directory of the City of Londonderry, and Coleraine, including Strabane with Lifford, Newtonlimavady, Fortstewart and Fortrush* (Derby: Standard Office, 1839), 82.
32. Lorana Fish Mineer to Kerry William Bate, August 16, 1987, original in author's possession; Kinder, *The New [1839] Directory of the City of Londonderry*, 82.
33. John Steele to Letisha Todd, November 16, 1890, in author's possession; patriarchal blessing no. 131, copy in author's possession; Cox, *Steele Journals*, 2:11; Lorana Fish Mineer to Kerry William Bate, August 16, 1987, in author's possession.
34. Katherine [Katharine] Larson, "Young Elizabeth Steel[e] Stapley, First White Child Born in Utah, Honored by D. U. P.," *Washington County (UT) News*, December 16, 1937, 1, A.
35. http://www.cotyroneireland.com/wills/josepharbuckle.html; *Post-Office Belfast Annual Directory for 1843–44* (Belfast: J. S. Wilson, 1843), 53: "Michael Campbell, tobacco spinner, 7 Hope's court"; *Henderson's Belfast Directory and Northern Repository for 1846–47* (Belfast: John Henderson, 1846), 225: "[Michael] Campbell, tobacco spinner, 26, Bank lane"; *Belfast Directory 1849*: "M. Campbell, 26 Bank lane, tobacco spinner"; *Henderson's Belfast directory and Northern Repository* (Belfast: J. Henderson, 1850), 71, 188: "26 Bank Lane M. Campbell, tobacco spinner." That Catherine's father is the Michael Campbell, tobacco spinner or tobacconist, is shown by the marriage record of her sister Margaret that identifies her father as a tobacconist. Belfast 1849 marriages 1:210, Ireland Civil Registration.
36. *Martin's Belfast Directory for 1840–41* (Belfast: M. Martin, 1840), 223: "John Steele, shoemaker, 18 King-street." Cox, *Steele Journals*, 2:4 shows Eliza Campbell's husband James Hamilton was a blacksmith. Strabane 1848 Marriages, 10:234, Ireland Civil Registration: "Margaret Campbell and James Johnston," describing the latter's occupation. Rebecca Campbell married James Boyd, who was described in his obituary as a whitesmith, accessed August 3, 2015, http://www.cotyroneireland.com/burial/StrabaneDeaths1850-69.html (this source does not identify which newspaper particular obituaries are drawn from). John Steele to Catherine Campbell Steele, prob. September 5, 1877, box 1, fd. 12, MSS 528, LTPSC; Vicary Gibbs and George Edward Cokayne, eds., *The Complete Peerage of England, Scotland, Ireland, Great Britain and the United Kingdom* (London: St. Catherine Press, 1910) 1:172. Annesley had 24,350 acres in County Down as well as other large holdings.
37. Anthony Richard Wagner, *English Genealogy* (Oxford: Clarendon Press, 1972), esp. chapter 4; also Wagner's *Pedigrees and Progress Essays in the Genealogical Interpretation of History* (London: Phillimore, 1975), esp. 92.

38. "Graduates of Columbia," *New York Times*, June 13, 1895, 3; *Columbian 1896* (n.p.), 59; Herman A. Knox, ed., *Who's Who in New York*, 7th ed. (New York: Who's Who Publications, 1917–18), 631. Arthur Knox was also in the *New York Times* as the attorney who took a deposition from former President Theodore Roosevelt in a lawsuit, see "Roosevelt Alters 'Fads' Testimony," *New York Times*, March 31, 1909, 4.
39. From the *New York Times*: "Knox-Bartley," November 12, 1897, 7; "Ascribes Success Partly to Chance," December 14, 1924, 5; "W. E. Knox, Head of Bowery Savings, Ends Life in Bank," February 5, 1927, 1, 6; "W. E. Knox Brooded over Minor Thefts," February 6, 1927, 22; "1,000 Gather at Bier of William E. Knox," February 2, 1927, 19. Knox, *Who's Who in New York*, 632.
40. Thomas Chapman, *Who Was Buried in James Madison's Grave? A Study in Contextual Analysis* (master's thesis, William and Mary College, 2005), The Montpelier Foundation, accessed January 11, 2014, https://www.montpelier.org/sites/default/files/Who%20Was%20Buried%20In%20James%20Madison's%20Grave.pdf, 18, 50, 153n9, 153–54; William Fletcher Boogher, *Gleanings of Virginia History* (Washington, D.C.: n.p., 1903), 252; Raleigh Travers Green, compiler and publisher, *Notes on Culpeper County, Virginia* (Culpeper, VA: 1900), 135–44, 153; "Dr. John Knox," *Richmond (VA) Dispatch*, August 24, 1889, 1; "Dr. John Knox," *The Daily (Richmond, VA) Times*, August 24, 1889, 4; "Virginia News," *Alexandria (VA) Gazette and Virginia Advertiser*, August 24, 1889, 2.
41. "Knox-Margaret," *New York Times*, April 6, 1934, 23; and "Accident is Fatal to Margaret Knox," April 7, 1934, 15.
42. *Matier's Belfast Directory 1835–1836*, (n.p.: 1836), 29: "Campbell, Mrs., dressmaker, 7, King-street."
43. Estella Roundy Russell, "Biography of Sarah Catherine Stapley [Roundy]," 1; Eighth Census of the United States, 1860, *Philadelphia Ward 3, Philadelphia, Pennsylvania*, roll M653_1153, page 386, image 392, Family History film 805153, (Ancestry.com); Tenth Census of the United States, 1880, *Chicago, Cook, Illinois*, roll 185, page 304A, image 0002, enumeration district 12, Family History film: 1254185 (Ancestry.com). When Catherine's sister Margaret married James Johnston in 1848 he was described as a widower but she was described, as was usual in those records, only as full age and a spinster. Strabane 1848 Marriages, 10:234, Ireland Civil Registration.
44. *Martin's Belfast Directory for 1840–41*, 223.
45. *Post-Office Belfast Annual Directory for 1843–44*, 53: "Michael Campbell, tobacco spinner, 7 Hope's court"; *Henderson's Belfast Directory and Northern Repository for 1846–47* (Belfast: John Henderson, 1846), 225: "[Michael] Campbell, tobacco spinner, 26, Bank lane"; *Belfast Directory 1849*: "M. Campbell, 26 Bank lane, tobacco spinner"; *Henderson's Belfast Directory and Northern Repository* (Belfast: J. Henderson, 1850), 71, 188.
46. William Campbell to M. M. Steele Sr., April 21, 1910; Maryanne Campbell Wilson to M. M. Steele Sr., April 8, 1919, September 23, 1912, copies of transcripts of these letters made by Iona J. Poling in author's possession.
47. Rachel Connelly to John Steele, June 4, 1888, box 1, fd. 27, MSS 528, LTPSC (mentioned in several other letters of Rachel as well); James Steele Stapley to John Steele, April 15, 1892, box 1, fd. 22, MSS 528, LTPSC; "Holywood, Ireland," Wikipedia, accessed July 24, 2015, *https://en.wikipedia.org/wiki/Holywood*: "Holywood is famous for its maypole at the crossroads in the centre of town. Its origin is uncertain, but according to local folklore it dates from 1700, when a Dutch ship is said to have run aground on the shore nearby, and the crew erected the broken mast to show their appreciation of the assistance offered to them by the townsfolk. The maypole is still used for dancing at the annual May Day fair."
48. Cox, *Steele Journals*, 1:52–53.
49. Pensioners' Affidavit, John Steele Sr., April 27, 1816, box 1, fd. 11, MSS 528, LTPSC.
50. Cox, *Steele Journals*, 2:1; [J. Cecil Alter], "Extracts from the Journal of John Steele," *Utah Historical Quarterly* 6, no. 1 (January 1933): 3; Pensioners' Affidavit, John Steele Sr., April 27, 1816. John Sr. was described then as being forty-two years old and a Chelsea Hospital pensioner.
51. For Beckwith, see David A. Hales, "The Renaissance Man of Delta: Frank Asahel Beckwith, *Millard County Chronicle* Publisher, Scientist, and Scholar, 1875–1951," *Utah Historical Quarterly* 81, no. 4 (Spring 2013): 86.
52. Frank Beckwith Sr., "Valuable Relics Found in Old Trunk," *Millard County Chronicle*, July 24, 1930, 1, 8; Frank Beckwith Sr., "From the Journal of Elder John Steele," *Millard County Chronicle*, September 1, 1932, 4; [Frank Beckwith Sr.], "Moki Bread Made of Mesquite 70 Years Old," *Millard County Chronicle*, August 18, 1932, 4.
53. Reba Roundy LeFevre, interview, May 23, 1987, 6.

54. John Steele to Catherine Campbell Steele, May 26, 1878, box 1, fd. 12, MSS 528, LTPSC.
55. Cox, *Steele Journals*, 1:1; Alter, "Journal Extracts," 3.
56. Rev. Thomas Morgan, ed., *Recollections of My Life and Times: An Autobiography by the Rev. James Morgan D. D., Late Minister of Fisherwick Place Church, Belfast, with Selections from His Journal* (Belfast: William Mullan, 1874); Thomas Hamilton, "Morgan, James, D. D.," in *The Dictionary of National Biography*, edited by Sir Leslie Stephen and Sir Sidney Lee (London: Oxford University Press, 1960) 13:918–19. Morgan performed the marriage of Catherine's brother Robert Campbell to Isabella Martin (1848 Marriages Belfast, 2:763, Ireland Civil Registration) and Steele noted in his diary Morgan's genealogical statistics.
57. Cox, *Steele Journals*, 1:1–2.
58. Reba Roundy LeFevre, interview, July 29, 1978, 31.
59. Robert Campbell to John Steele and Catherine Campbell Steele, November 3, 1890, box 2, fd. 27, MSS 528, LTPSC.
60. Cox, *Steele Journals*, 1:1–2.
61. Terryl L. Givens and Matthew J. Grow, *Parley P. Pratt: The Apostle Paul of Mormonism* (Oxford: Oxford University Press, 2011), 103–4 report this booklet "became the principal vehicle presenting Mormonism to the Latter-day Saint faithful and the general public alike, and it was elevated to near canonical status."
62. Alter, "Journal Extracts," 3; "England and Wales Census, 1851," Glasgow, St Enoch, roll *CSSCT1851_155*, page 7, line 4, enumeration district 7.
63. Cox, *Steele Journals*, 1:1–2.
64. Ibid.; Alter, "Journal Extracts," 3–6.
65. Russell, "Biography of Sarah Catherine Stapley [Roundy]," 1; Alter, "Journal Extracts," 4.
66. Cox, *Steele Journals*, 1:2.
67. Ibid.
68. Ibid.
69. Ibid., 1:3–4; Will Bagley, ed., *The Pioneer Camp of the Saints: The 1846 and 1847 Mormon Trail Journals of Thomas Bullock* (Spokane, WA: Arthur H. Clark, 1997), 25.
70. Reba Roundy LeFevre, interview, July 29, 1978, 28–29; July 23, 1987, 1–2; November 18, 1988, 4; October 6, 1989, 8–9; May 5, 1990, 4.
71. Norma Baldwin Ricketts, *The Mormon Battalion: U.S. Army of the West, 1846–1848* (Logan, UT: Utah State University Press, 1996); David L. Bigler and Will Bagley, eds., *Army of Israel: Mormon Battalion Narratives* (Logan: Utah State University Press, 2000), which includes a section excerpting John Steele's Mormon Battalion journal; Sherman L. Fleek, *History May Be Searched in Vain: A Military History of the Mormon Battalion* (Spokane, WA: Arthur H. Clark, 2006). Brigham Young himself had doubts about Battalion members: "I know the lowest scrapings of Hell were in that Bot. [Battalion], notwithstanding there was some good men among them," see John D. Lee, *A Mormon Chronicle: The Diaries of John D. Lee, 1848–1876*, edited by Robert Glass Cleland and Juanita Brooks (San Marino, CA: The Huntington Library, 1955), 1:6–7 (March 11, 1848). Unless otherwise noted the account of the Battalion relies on the Cox and the Alter publications of John's journals.
72. John Steele, "Toquerville June 15 1891," incomplete draft on the back of a form letter from *The Contributor* dated October 15, 1889, and addressed "To Our Agents", box 1, fd. 12, MSS 528, LTPSC. A completed typescript is in Cox, *Steele Journals*, 1:56.
73. Cox, *Steele Journals*, 1:3–4; Alter, "Journal Extracts," 17.
74. [J. Cecil Alter], "Extracts from the Journal of John Steele," *Utah Historical Quarterly* 6, no. 1 (January 1933): 10.
75. Hess's version is that approaching the authorities was his idea and he asked Steele to accompany him. John W. Hess, "John W. Hess, with the Mormon Battalion," *Utah Historical Quarterly* 4, no. 2 (April 1931): 50–51; Reba Roundy LeFevre, interview, July 29, 1978, 29.
76. Reba Roundy LeFevre, interview, July 29, 1978, 29; July 23, 1987, 2–3; October 6, 1989, 28–30; May 5, 1990, 4–6.
77. Alter, "Journal Extracts," 17.
78. The classic—and enormously readable—economic history of the Kingdom of God is Leonard Arrington, *Great Basin Kingdom: An Economic History of the Latter-day Saints, 1830–1900* (Lincoln, NE: University of Nebraska Press, 1968); also see Leonard J. Arrington, Feramorz Y. Fox, and Dean L. May, *Building the City of God* (Salt Lake City: Deseret Book, 1976).
79. Ronald O. Barney, *The Mormon Vanguard Brigade of 1847: Norton Jacob's Record* (Logan, UT: Utah State University Press, 2005), 226–30; Bagley, *The Pioneer Camp*, 243–44.
80. Barney, *Mormon Vanguard Brigade*, 228–30; David L. Bigler, *The Forgotten Kingdom: The Mormon Theocracy in the American West, 1847–1896* (Spokane, WA: Arthur H. Clark, 2005), 39.
81. "Town Talk," *Salt Lake Herald*, February 12, 1897, 8; Will Bagley, *The Pioneer Camp*, 253; Reba Roundy LeFevre, interview, July 29, 1978, 29–30.
82. Bagley, *The Pioneer Camp*, 253.

83. International Society Daughters of Utah Pioneers, *Pioneer Women of Faith and Fortitude* (Salt Lake City: Publishers Press, 1998), 2:1061–62.
84. Bagley, *The Pioneer Camp,* 182.
85. Cox, *Steele Journals,* 1:24; Alter, "Journal Extracts," 18; John Steele manuscript book of verse that former owner Gary Hall Callister labeled "Book #1"; John Steele to Wilford Woodruff, July 30, 1888, Wilford Woodruff Collection, Church History Library, The Church of Jesus Christ of Latter-day Saints, Salt Lake City, Utah, (hereafter CHL); Journal History of the LDS Church, August 9, 1847, CHL.
86. Cox, *Steele Journals,* 1:24; Alter, "Journal Extracts," 18; Joseph Fish, *The Pioneers of the Southwest and Rocky Mountain Regions,* edited by Seymour P. Fish (Salt Lake City: J. Fish Smith; and Provo: Seymour P. Fish, 1972) says she was originally named Young Elizabeth Deseret Steele (162), which despite Fish being her brother-in-law is incorrect; Biographical Sketches, CR 100 18 17:16:13 E. Stapley, CHL; Reba Roundy LeFevre, interview, May 5, 1990, 1–3; John Steele to Wilford Woodruff, July 30, 1888, Wilford Woodruff Collection, CHL; Journal History of the LDS Church, 9 August 1847, CHL; Beckwith Sr., "From the Journal of Elder John Steele," 4.
87. Alter, "Journal Extracts," 16–17.
88. J. Steele to W. Woodruff, July 30, 1888, Wilford Woodruff Collection, CHL; Journal of Carl A. Badger, September 9, 1905, to January 23, 1907 (see September 26, 1905), in Carlos Ashby Badger Papers, MSS 1298, LTPSC; Rodney J. Badger, *Liahona and Iron Rod* (Bountiful, UT: Family History Publishers, 1985), 275 (September 26, 1905).
89. "Journal of Sarah De Armon Pea Rich," 77 (actually, as pointed out by Guinevere Thomas Woolstenhulme, this is an autobiography), typescript, accessed March 11, 2011, http://www.boap.org/LDS/Early-Saints/SRich.html. Guinevere Thomas Woolstenhulme, "'I Have Seen Many Miracles,' Sarah De Armon Pea Rich," in *Women of Faith in the Latter Days, Volume One, 1775–1820,* edited by Richard E. Turley Jr., and Brittany A. Chapman, (Salt Lake City: Deseret Book, 2011), 271, also 281–82 for the Riches sharing with a Battalion family in need.
90. Alter, "Journal Extracts," 18–23; Cox, *Steele Journals,* 1:24–29.
91. Alter, "Journal Extracts," 23.
92. Andrew Jenson, "History of the Salt Lake City Tenth Ward," CR MH 9051, CHL; "Tenth Ward Historical Record of Members, Etc." LR series 11, reel 1, CHL.
93. Cox, *Steele Journals,* 1:28.

CHAPTER 2

1. [J. Cecil Alter], "Extracts from the Journal of John Steele," *Utah Historical Quarterly* 6, no. 1 (January 1933): 23–24; Wanda Steele Cox, *Journals of John Steele and Mahonri Moriancumer Steele* (Cedar City, UT: self-published, 1967), 1:29.
2. Leonard Arrington, *Great Basin Kingdom: An Economic History of the Latter-day Saints, 1830–1900* (Lincoln, NE: University of Nebraska Press, 1968), 122–29; Janet Burton Seegmiller, *A History of Iron County* (Salt Lake City: Utah State Historical Society and Iron County Commission, 1998), 41–56; Morris A. Shirts and Kathryn H. Shirts, *A Trial Furnace* (Provo: Brigham Young University, 2001); Luella Adams Dalton, *History of the Iron County Mission Parowan, Utah* (n.p., 1965); and for the prelude to settlement, see William B. Smart and Donna T. Smart, *Over the Rim: The Parley P. Pratt Exploring Expedition to Southern Utah, 1849–50* (Logan, UT: Utah State University Press, 1999).
3. Alter, "Journal Extracts," 23–24; Cox, *Steele Journals,* 1:29.
4. William R. Palmer, "Indian Names in Utah Geography," *Utah Historical Quarterly* 1, no. 1 (January 1928): 9–10.
5. Unless otherwise noted, life for the Steeles in Parowan up to Steele's Las Vegas mission is from Alter, "Journal Extracts," 23–28, and Cox, *Steele Journals,* 1:24–35.
6. Anonymous, "The Life of Henry Lunt Family Together with a Portion of his Diary," (BYU typescript), 156–57; also see 66 (November 13, 1853).
7. James H. Martineau to George A. Smith, May 30, 1855, MS 1322, George Albert Smith papers, Incoming Letters 1855, Church History Library, The Church of Jesus Christ of Latter-day Saints, Salt Lake City, Utah, (hereafter CHL).
8. John Steele to Catherine Campbell Steele, October 3, 1855, box 1, fd. 12, MSS 528, John Steele Collection, 1847–1936, L. Tom Perry Special Collections, Harold B. Lee Library, Brigham Young University, Provo, Utah (hereafter LTPSC). For a well-informed account of John Steele's Las Vegas mapmaking—complete with reproductions of several of his maps—see Richard Francaviglia, *Mapmakers of New Zion: A Cartographic History of Mormonism* (Salt Lake City: University of Utah Press, 2015), 104–9.
9. John Steele to George Albert Smith, October 1, 1855, MS 1322, George Albert Smith Papers, Incoming Letters, 1855, CHL.

10. Donald G. Godfrey and Rebecca S. Martineau-McCarty, eds., *An Uncommon Common Pioneer: The Journals of James Henry Martineau, 1828–1918* (Provo, UT: Religious Studies Center Brigham Young University, 2008), 45.
11. Gene A. Sessions, *Mormon Thunder: A Documentary History of Jedediah Morgan Grant* (Urbana: University of Illinois Press, 1982), 169–71.
12. Ronald O. Barney, *The Mormon Vanguard Brigade of 1847: Norton Jacob's Record* (Logan, UT: Utah State University Press, 2005), 228–30.
13. Ibid.; Robert Glass Cleland and Juanita Brooks, *A Mormon Chronicle: The Diaries of John D. Lee, 1848–1876* (San Marino, CA: Huntington Library, 1955), 1:6–7 (March 11, 1848), 1:69 (6 August 1848); Scott G. Kenney, *Wilford Woodruff's Journal: 1833–1898* (Midvale, UT: Signature Books, 1984), 5:276–78, 576 (May 23, 1861); John G. Turner, in his superb biography, *Brigham Young* (Cambridge, MA: Belknap Press, 2012) cites numerous examples of Young's violent language, 121–22, 153, 185–88, 211–12, 259–62, 284–86, and 349–50.
14. George A. Smith [by clerk Leo Hawkins] to John Calvin Lazelle Smith, December 26, 1853, MS 5164, James Henry Martineau Letters, 1855, CHL. Martineau, a fascinating figure, was closely associated with John Steele in Parowan. A useful autobiography of Martineau is published in Edward W. Tullidge, *Tullidge's Histories*, 2 (Salt Lake City: Juvenile Instructor, 1889): 68–79 (John Steele directing a standoff with Indians is related on page 71); "Autobiographies of James Henry Martineau and his Future Wife, Susan Ellen Johnson," typescript (Provo, UT: Brigham Young University, 1956); Godfrey and Martineau-McCarty, eds., *An Uncommon Pioneer: The Journals of James Henry Martineau, 1828–1918*, 45.
15. Jesse Nathaniel Smith to James Henry Martineau, January 2, 1856, fd. 1, MS 4786, James Henry Martineau Collection, CHL.
16. John H. Krenkel, ed., *The Life and Times of Joseph Fish, Mormon Pioneer* (Danville, IL: Interstate Printers and Publishers, 1970), 71–72.
17. Copy in possession of author; this poem is dated February 11, 1901, but is consistent with the early marriage of most of his daughters.
18. Krenkel, *Joseph Fish*, 77, 88. For a biographical account of Mary Campbell Steele Fish, see Silas L. Fish and Seymour P. Fish, "Mary Campbell Steele Fish" in *Family of Joseph Fish (1840–1926) Genealogical and Biographical Stories and Sketches*, edited by Seymour P. Fish and Vera P. Fish (Provo, UT: J. Grant Stevenson, 1970), 67–71 (the authors did not have access to Mary's letters in the John Steele collection, box 1, fd. 20, MSS 528, LTPSC).
19. Joseph Fish, "Joseph Fish 1840–1916," 39, MS 649, CHL.
20. Thomas LeFevre was one of the six deputies who arrested John D. Lee in Panguitch for his part in the Mountain Meadows Massacre according to Robert Kent Fielding, comp. and ed., *The* Tribune *Reports of The Trials of John D. Lee for the Massacre at Mountain Meadows* (Higganum, CT: Kent's Books, May 2006), 9; Ileen Johnson, *The Ancestry and Descendants of Mormon Pioneer William LeFevre of Utah* (n.p.: William LeFevre Family Organization, n.d.), 1–4. John Steele's papers include one with this notation: "Thom. Lefever, born Croland Linking-Shire, England, January 29, 1838 Ma[r]y C. Steele, born Belfast Co. of Antrim, Ireland 23 December 1840 Married by President G. A. Smith, Feb. 7, 1856, at Parowan at the house of John Steele, at 15 min. past 4 p.m. Witnesses: Richard Benson, William Lefevre, Sidney Burton, and John Steele," copy in possession of author.
21. "Journal of Rachel Andora Woolsey Lee, 1856–1860," (copied by Brigham Young University Library, 1970), 30 (February 15, 1857).
22. Cleland and Brooks, *Diaries of John D. Lee*, 2:89 (November 14, 1867).
23. Krenkel, *Joseph Fish*, 72.
24. John Steele to Catherine Campbell Steele, April 23, 1856, box 1, folder 12, MSS 528, LTPSC.
25. Reba Roundy LeFevre, interview, February 23, 1990, 6–7.
26. "Panguitch," *Deseret News*, July 4, 1891, 16–17.
27. Ardis E. Parshall, "'Pursue, Retake, and Punish': The 1857 Santa Clara Ambush," *Utah Historical Quarterly* 73, no. 1 (Winter 2005): 64–86, esp. 64–76; I thank Ardis E. Parshall for responding to questions. The attackers were apparently after Betts and Ambrose. Also see Elizabeth Oberdick Anderson, ed., *Cowboy Apostle: The Diaries of Anthony W. Ivins, 1875–1932* (Salt Lake City: Signature Books, 2013), 141–42; Ronald W. Walker, Richard E. Turley Jr., and Glen M. Leonard, *Massacre at Mountain Meadows* (Oxford University Press, 2008), 138–39; John Hyde Jr., *Mormonism: Its Leaders and Designs* (New York: W. P. Fetridge, 1857), 106–7, which Parshall points out has demonstrable errors; John Doyle Lee, *Mormonism Unveiled; Including the Life and Confessions of the Mormon Bishop, John D. Lee; (written by himself) and complete life of Brigham Young . . .* (St. Louis, Mo.: M. E. Mason, 1891), 273–74 (Parshall suggests this was added to Lee's account by his attorney and editor, William W. Bishop).

28. Sarah D. Rich to Catherine Campbell Steele, March 2, 1857, box 1, fd. 28, MSS 528, LTPSC.
29. John L. Smith to George A. Smith, November 2, 1857, MS 1322, George A. Smith papers, Family letters, CHL.
30. Utah Territorial Militia series 2210 reel 5, Utah State Archives documents 327 (August 8, 1853), 332 (August [10?], 1853), 333 (August 7, 1853), 355 (August 25, 1853), 357 (August 27, 1853); Evelyn K. Jones, *Henry Lunt: Biography and History of the Development of Southern Utah* (Provo, UT: BYU Family History Copy Center, 1996), 152–58. Those charged and convicted of mutiny were William Hunter, George Hunter, John Gregory, William Adshead and David Stoddard. Parowan Stake president John C. L. Smith "testified that he heard John Gregory tell Lt. Col. Jas. A. Little that he would talk when where, and as he pleased, and that he was ready to organize in a company to go to California." Richard Varley was acquitted. Brigham Young granted the others clemency, Daniel H. Wells in a letter to George A. Smith commenting "pursue this case no further in consideration of the [securing penitence] of the offenders and the strong interest felt by the people in their behalf . . ." (355). Jones quotes George K. Bowering's journal, October 8, 1853, "As several of the brethren are dissatisfied with things, and the Government of Affairs in the presiding offices being tyrannical in their rule, they are preparing to go to California . . . October 16: Some of our California brethren started out today" (158).
31. Besides John Steele's papers, I have relied on Walker, Turley, and Leonard, *Massacre at Mountain Meadows*; Will Bagley, *Blood of the Prophets: Brigham Young and the Massacre at Mountain Meadows* (Norman: University of Oklahoma Press, 2002); Juanita Brooks, *The Mountain Meadows Massacre* (Norman: University of Oklahoma Press, 1974); Will Bagley, *Innocent Blood: Essential Narratives of the Mountain Meadows Massacre* (Norman: Arthur H. Clark, 2008); Shannon A. Novak, *House of Mourning* (Salt Lake City: University of Utah Press, 2008); Lee, *Mormonism Unveiled.* Especially useful for John Steele's role in the council that allegedly tried to prevent the massacre, see Richard E. Turley Jr. and Ronald W. Walker, *Mountain Meadows Massacre: The Andrew Jenson and David H. Morris Collections* (Provo: Brigham Young University Press and Salt Lake City: University of Utah Press, 2009), 278, where a photograph of John Chatterley's holograph letter to Andrew Jenson is presented. John Steele's son-in-law wrote an account of the Massacre in Joseph Fish, "History of Enterprise," typescript (Salt Lake City: Family History Library, 1967), 10–12, 95.
32. Fielding, *The Tribune Reports*, 110; Krenkel, *Joseph Fish*, 69.
33. Journal of Carl A. Badger, September 9, 1905 to January 23, 1907, September 26, 1905, MSS 1298, Carlos Ashby Badger papers, LTPSC; Rodney J. Badger, *Liahona and Iron Rod* (Bountiful, UT: Family History Publishers, 1985), 275 (September 26, 1905). Dame was weak-willed, see Krenkel, *Joseph Fish*, 69; Fielding, *The Tribune Reports*, 21. James Henry Martineau acknowledged Dame's unpopularity when he wrote his wife November 9, 1858, from Santaquin, "Uncle Benjamin [Johnson] is no longer President here . . . The affair was like Br. Dame's, somewhat. Cause, dissatisfaction of the people . . ." See fd. 6, MS 4786, James Henry Martineau Collection, CHL.
34. William H. Dame Papers, James Henry Martineau's "Parowan Stake History Book," January 3, 1860, Utah State Historical Society, Salt Lake City, Utah (hereafter USHS).
35. Walker, Turley, and Leonard, *Massacre at Mountain Meadows*, 187–209; Bagley, *Blood of the Prophets*, 382–89; Bagley, *Innocent Blood*, 144–47.
36. Cox, *Steele Journals*, 1:35.
37. Maryanne Campbell Wilson to M. M. Steele Sr., September 23, 1912, transcript by Iona J. Poling in author's possession.
38. Susan E. Martineau to James Henry Martineau, May 30, 1858, fd. 5, MS 4786, James Henry Martineau Collection, CHL.
39. Photocopy in author's possession.
40. John Steele to Leticia Todd, February 2, 1893, transcript copy in author's possession.
41. Joseph Fish to Catherine Campbell Steele, December 9, 1874, box 1, fd. 20, MSS 528, LTPSC.
42. Fielding, *Tribune Reports of The Trials of John D. Lee*, 75.
43. Orvel Morgan Allen (1805–1893) of Toquerville was known as "O. M." See Allen's biography, accessed February 21, 2016, at http://www.themorrisclan.com/GENEALOGY/ALLEN%20Orval%20Morgan%20F120b.html.
44. John Steele to Catherine Campbell Steele, February 17, 1878, MSS 528, LTPSC.
45. Dr. S. Husted, to Hon. Mr. Black, December 1887, in the J. Steele pension file for Mormon Battalion service, Utah State Archives, Salt Lake City; *R. L. Polk Medical and Surgical Directory of the United States 1886* (n.p.: R. L. Polk, 1886), 899.
46. Journal of Levi Savage, March 23, 1877, typescript at Dixie University, John D. Lee Collection. The

transcriber of Savage's diaries did them in small sections, starting the pagination over each time; hence, it's easier to find a source by date than page number.

47. Badger Journal, September 26, 1905; Badger, *Liahona,* 275 (September 26, 1905).
48. John Steele to Catherine Steele, June 4, 1877, MSS 528, LTPSC.
49. Reba Roundy LeFevre, interview by Tonia Ann Bate, July 21, 1983, 29; "Young Elizabeth Steele Stapley," copied by Virginia M. Lee, 1.
50. "Young Elizabeth Steele Stapley," 1.
51. "Mrs. Young Elizabeth Stapley, First White Child Born in Utah, Dies at Hurricane," *Washington County News,* April 7, 1938, 1, 6.
52. Isaac E. Diehl, "Young Elizabeth Steele Stapley answers to Pioneer Personal History Questionnaire," B 289, box 10, 3, WPA Biographies, USHS; for her father's interactions with the Native Americans, see especially Frank Beckwith Sr., "Tovach and his Son," *Millard County Chronicle,* May 21, 1931, 4; "Moki-Chee-po-pope," *Millard County Chronicle,* December 31, 1932, 4. His Paiute Indian Dictionary, which Beckwith quotes from, is now in the John Steele Collection, box 1, fd. 3, MSS 528, LTPSC.
53. "Young Elizabeth Steele Stapley," 2.
54. Reba Roundy LeFevre, interview, January 24, 1987, 6; and July 29, 1978, 30.
55. Reba Roundy LeFevre, interview, May 9, 1985, 5–6.
56. Reba Roundy LeFevre, interview, July 23, 1987, 14.
57. John Steele to Catherine Campbell Steele, April 23, 1856, MSS 528, LTPSC.
58. "First White Child Born in Utah, to Observe Birthday," *Washington County News,* August 8, 1935, 1, 5; Helen Thurber Dalton, "History of John Calvin Lazelle Smith," 1975, 25–28, MS 5515 1, CHL; I have also benefitted from seeing a photograph of Smith in the William R. Palmer Collection, Southern Utah University (hereafter SUU); Krenkel, *Joseph Fish, Mormon Pioneer,* 18, 24, 42–43, 49; William R. Palmer, "John Calvin Lazelle Smith," No. 1-I-H/9-n/xviii f, 19–623, William R. Palmer Collection, SUU.
59. Washington Irving, "The Legend of Sleepy Hollow," 2, accessed February 17, 2016, http://www.eastoftheweb.com/short-stories/UBooks/LegSle.shtml.
60. John Calvin Lazelle Smith to E. W. Thompson, June 22, 1855, MS 1322, George Albert Smith papers, Incoming Letters, 1855, CHL.
61. Palmer, "John Calvin Lazell Smith"; Robert Proctor, *The History of Panguitch* (n.p.: n.p., 2014), 1–6.
62. "First White Child," *Washington County News,* August 8, 1935, 1, 5; she married Samuel Hamilton—"Aged Resident [Margaret Jane Meeks Hamilton] Passes Away," *Iron County Record,* March 17, 1932, 1.
63. Her obituary—as Susan West Smith—is posted on findagrave.com.
64. Isaiah Moses Coombs Journal, 169 (January 27, 1861); 115 (May 29, 1861); 137 (September 30, 1862); 138 (October 1, 1861); 150 (November 26, 1861); 153 (December 11, 1861), Isaiah Moses Coombs Collection, 1834–1886, MS 1198, reel 1, CHL.
65. Coombs Journal 118 (June 10, 1861, July 11, 1861); 124 (July 16, 1861); 133 (September 12, 1861), CHL.
66. Ibid.; Pratt M. Bethers, *A History of Schools in Iron County, 1851–1970* (privately published, 1972), 153–56 gives some of the early history of schools in Parowan but is weak on dates.
67. Isaiah Moses Coombs Journal, 169 (January 27, 1861); 138 (October 1, 1861), CHL; also see Sandra Dawn Brimhall, "Friends At All Times: The Correspondence of Isaiah Moses Coombs and Dryden Rogers," *Utah Historical Quarterly* 77, no. 2 (Spring 2003): 151–65.
68. Isaiah Moses Coombs Journal, 169 (January 27, 1861); 150 (November 26, 1861), CHL; Kenney, *Wilford Woodruff's Journal,* 5:576 (May 23, 1861); Krenkel, *Joseph Fish,* 143; "Persons Cut off the Church," Parowan Minute Book, March 18, 1874, CHL. "I presume that you have he[a]rd of [Bishop Warren's son] George warren and Frank [Fish] takeing one hundred and fifty head of stock that did not belong to them . . ."—Mary Campbell Steele Fish to John and Catherine Campbell Steele, February 7, 1874, MS 24404, John Steele Correspondence, CHL.
69. Kenney, *Wilford Woodruff's Journal,* 4:276–78 (May 19, 1854) and (May 21, 1854) where this day's entry's last lines are transcribed "I spent the night with T Bullock at Brother S[teels?]. 20 miles."
70. Nevada W. Driggs, "When Captain Fremont Slept in Grandma McGregor's Bed," *Utah Historical Quarterly* 41, no. 2 (Spring 1973): 178–81, esp. 180; Mary Lee Spence, "The Fremonts and Utah," *Utah Historical Quarterly* 44, no. 3 (Summer 1976): 286–302, esp. 299; Mary Spence, ed., *The Expeditions of John Charles Frémont: Travels from 1848 to 1854* (Urbana and Chicago: University of Illinois Press, 1984), 3:458–64, 475, 485–86; Helen Thurber Dalton, "History of John Calvin Lazelle Smith," 25–28, MS 5515 1, CHL; Solomon Nunes Carvalho, *Incidents of Travel and Adventure in the Far West,* edited by Bertram Wallace Korn (Philadelphia: Jewish Publication Society of America, 1954), 200–5, 276 mentions that John Steele was then mayor.
71. Isaiah Moses Coombs Journal, 161 (January 5, 1861); 163–65 (January 16, 1861); 133 (September 12, 1861),

CHL: "She then went on and railed out against polygamy and said I shouldn't have another daughter of hers and if I ever took another wife she would take Fanny away from me and bring the Devil into my family . . ."

72. Hyrum S. Coombs to Isaiah Moses Coombs, August 22, 1863, MS 1198, reel 4, Isaiah Moses Coombs Collection 1834–1886, CHL. Coombs remained friends with Steele, writing in his journal on Sunday, July 12, 1863, "Bro. Jno. Steele called on me this morning. He was one of the Mormon Battalion & is now on the way to the city to attend a festival of that honored body to be held on the 15th inst." (Coombs Journal, reel 1, 104).
73. "Young Elizabeth Steele Stapley," 2.
74. Cox, *Steele Journals,* 1:44.
75. David L. Bigler, *The Forgotten Kingdom: The Mormon Theocracy in the American West, 1847–1896* (Spokane, WA: Arthur H. Clark, 2005), 51.
76. Cleland and Brooks, *Diaries of John D. Lee,* 1:298.
77. Laney (also Leany) figures in a conjectural story that Mormons killed three members of John Wesley Powell's exploration expedition. See Dr. Wesley Pratt Larsen, "The 'Letter' Or Were the Powell Men Really Killed by Indians?" *Canyon Legacy,* no. 17 (Spring 1993): 12–19; Loren Webb, "SUU Professor Raises Questions about Deaths," *The Daily Spectrum,* October 22, 1993, B1. I disagree with Dr. Larsen's premise. Despite the issues raised in Laney's letter to Steele, the latter mourned Laney's death, wrote his obituary, and to console Steele his son M. M. wrote, "I am wonderfully well pleased that Elder Laney bore so good a character at his demise. He was one of the Lords Noblemen and I am confident there will be hardly a hairs weight ~~in the scale~~ against him when put into the scales as his surroundings will be taken into consideration. Peace to his ashes." Mahonri Moriancumer Steele to John Steele, January 10, 1892, photograph of letter in author's possession.
78. John Steele to Catherine Campbell Steele, July 30, 1877, MSS 528, LTPSC. John was referring to his onetime Parowan townsman James McGuffie, who in a recent interview in the *New York Herald* asserted, "John Steel, of Tokerville, who was ordered to assassinate poor Sherman, one of Fremont's men, in 1854, and whose body was left for wolves to eat, was called by Brigham at last spring's conference to go on a mission to Europe. He is an Irishman and may be round on the Green Isle, where his mother is, if she is not dead." "Brigham Young's Infamy," *New York Herald,* July 6, 1877, 2. But earlier McGuffie claimed that Sherman was taken away by Barney Carter, Job Hall, Charles Y. Webb, and "Old Man Gold" [Samuel Gould] and that "It was not long before old Gold began to boast that he had laid Sherman out with his pistol. Afterward he boasted many times to John Rogerson, who lives in Parowan, and Josiah Rogerson, telegraph operator at Beaver, that he shot Sherman when he was on horseback and left him at the mouth of a canyon for the wolves to eat." "Mormon Rascality!," *Salt Lake Tribune,* May 18, 1877, 3, reprinted from the *New York Herald,* May 12, 1877.
79. Utah Territorial Militia, series 2210, reel 5, Utah State Archives, documents 327 (August 8, 1853), 332 (August [10?], 1853), 333 (August 7, 1853), 355 (August 25, 1853), 357 (August 27, 1853).
80. Cleland and Brooks, *Diaries of John D. Lee,* 1:298. The fall in Parowan morale was reported in a letter from James Lewis to Apostle George Albert Smith, March 15, 1859: "The spirit that once reigned here has departed Stealing lying cheating &c drinking Whiskey seems the order of the day." MS 1322, Incoming Letters, J–L, 1859, George A. Smith papers 1834–1877, CHL.
81. Calvin C. Pendleton to William H. Dame, June 5, 1861, B-103, box 28, fd. 18, Juanita Brooks Collection, USHS.
82. Cox, *Steele Journals,* 1:44; [Frank Beckwith Sr.], "Valuable Relics Found in Old Trunk," *Millard County Chronicle,* July 24, 1930, 1, 8.
83. "The Family moved to Kanarra, where they lived only a short time then moved into Toquerville." [Anonymous], "Mahonri Steele (Panguitch Pioneer)," in Daughters of the Utah Pioneers Museum, Panguitch, UT. Note this would be the "first" Kanarraville, the town was relocated in 1866 by Bishop Lorenzo Wesley Roundy. Andrew Jenson, "Kanarra, Utah," CHL.
84. John Steele, 9–10, Utah Histories, Bancroft Library, University of California, Berkeley, History of Toquerville written by John Steele on June 26, 1880, microfilm copy, CHL.
85. Ibid.; "Notes and Incidents of an Excursion in Washington County," *Deseret News,* September 17, 1862, 91.
86. Seth Johnson to James Henry Martineau, December 19, 1876, MS 4786, fd. 10, James Henry Martineau Collection, CHL.
87. "Young Elizabeth Steele Stapley," 2; Cleland and Brooks, *Diaries of John D. Lee,* 2:7. For the flood's effect on the little town of Santa Clara, see Todd Compton, "The Big Washout: The 1862 Flood in Santa Clara," *Utah Historical Society Quarterly* 77, no. 2 (Spring 2009): 108–25.

88. "Young Elizabeth Steele Stapley," 2; Cleland and Brooks, *Diaries of John D. Lee,* 2:7.
89. George Armstrong Hicks, "A Life among the Poor of Utah," in *Playing with Shadows: Voices of Dissent in the Mormon West,* edited by Polly Aird, Jeff Nichols, and Will Bagley (Norman, OK: Arthur H. Clark, 2011), 171.
90. W. Paul Reeve, "'A Little Oasis in the Desert': Community Building in Hurricane, Utah, 1860–1920," *Utah Historical Quarterly* 62, no. 3 (Summer 1994): 223, quoting from Dean L. May, Lee L. Bean, and Mark H. Skolnick, "The Stability Ratio: An Index of Community Cohesiveness in Nineteenth-Century Mormon Towns," in *Generations and Change: Genealogical Perspectives in Social History*, edited by Robert M. Taylor Jr., and Ralph J. Crandall (Macon, GA: Mercer University Press, 1986), 155.
91. John Steele to Letisha Todd, February 2, 1893, photocopy in author's possession.
92. John Steele to Letisha Todd, March 21, 1891, transcript in author's possession.
93. John Steele to Letisha Todd, August 2, 1897, transcript in author's possession.
94. John Steele to Letisha Todd, September 16, 1899, transcript in author's possession.
95. John Steele filled out a biographical form for "The History of Utah, Historian Office, 60 E. South Temple St., Salt Lake City," and retained a copy, photocopy in author's possession. This is a thorough list of his extensive and impressive church and civic activities.
96. Reba Roundy LeFevre, interview, October 6, 1989, 10; and May 5, 1990, 12–13.
97. Cleland and Brooks, *Diaries of John D. Lee,* 2:20 (June 12, 1866).
98. Godfrey and Martineau-McCarty, *An Uncommon Pioneer,* 257 (May 2, 1881).
99. Ibid., 111 (April 1860).
100. Sarah D. Rich to Catherine Campbell Steele, March 2, 1857, box 1, fd. 28, MSS 528, LTPSC.
101. Isabella Wilkin to John and Catherine Campbell Steele, December 15, 1870, box 1, fd. 28, MSS 528, LTPSC.
102. Catherine's great-granddaughter, Josephine Kay Garfield, who then owned this clothing, allowed me to photograph and take measurements on January 25, 1989.
103. Photo provided by the late Josephine Kay Garfield.
104. Journal History of the Church of Jesus Christ of Latter-day Saints, 7 April 1877, 3, minutes of a conference held in St. George where Wilford Woodruff speaks. (Minutes kept by Samuel Bleak): "Apostle Geo. Q. Cannon read the following list of missionaries . . . To Europe: . . . John Steele, Toquerville; Mahonri M. Steele, Panguitch." CHL.
105. Cox, *Steele Journals,* 2:76.
106. Katherine [Katharine] Larson, "Young Elizabeth Steel[e] Stapley, First White Child Born in Utah, Honored by D. U. P.," *Washington County News,* December 16, 1937, 1, A.
107. Reba Roundy LeFevre, interview, May 23, 1987, 7; July 22, 1989, 23–24; and November 18, 1988, 1–3.
108. Ileen J. Johnson and Wanda S. Cox, *The Memoirs of Mahonri Moriancumer Steele Jr.* (mimeographed, 1963), 5–6.
109. James Steele Stapley to John Steele, September 10, 1891, box 1, fd. 22, MSS 528, LTPSC.
110. Cox, *Steele Journals,* 1:1.
111. Emily Steele Jensen's 1933 application for membership in the Daughters of the Utah Pioneers, accessed November 2, 2013, http://johnsonfamilyhistorystories.blogspot.com/.
112. John Steele to Catherine Campbell Steele, October 13, 1855, box 1, fd. 12, MSS 528, LTPSC.
113. John Steele to Catherine Campbell Steele, November 25, 1877, box 1, fd. 12, MSS 528, LTPSC.
114. Cleland and Brooks, *Diaries of John D. Lee,* 1:7 (March 11, 1848).
115. Dove Menkes, "A Young Man Goes West: The 1879 Letters of Leonard Herbert Swett," *Utah Historical Quarterly* 75, no. 3 (Summer 2007): 212.
116. David A. Dye, *Sacred Scribe: Entries from the Journals of Leonard John Nuttall* (Mona, UT: Hindsight Publishing, 2008), 119 (August 7, 1899).
117. Toquerville Relief Society Account Book, 1868–1903, 1 (June 11, 1868); Toquerville Relief Society Minute Book, 1870–1877 (March 4, 1869); Toquerville Relief Society Book, 1878–1882, 107 (January 1881); Toquerville Relief Society Minute Book, 1886–1889, 2–3 (January 1, 1886); and 6–7 (1887), LR 9225, series 14, CHL.
118. Toquerville Relief Society Minutes, 1886–1889, 88 (October 6, 1887); 66 (May 7, 1891); 78 (November 26, 1891); [undated], 142; 148 (1890), CHL; George Spilsbury, M[artin]. Slack, "Correspondence: Lies Refuted," *Deseret News,* June 6, 1877, 283.
119. Toquerville Relief Society Minutes, 1886–1889, 77 (December 1, 1887), CHL.
120. Toquerville Relief Society Minute Book, 1882–1884, 113 (September 3, 1885), CHL.
121. Toquerville Relief Society Account Book, 1868–1903, 1 (June 11, 1868); Relief Society Minute Book, 1882–1884, 10 (January 1882); and 11 (March 2, 1882); Toquerville Relief Society Book, 1878–1882, 119

(undated but 1882). For mention of the magnolia motif, see Toquerville Relief Society Book, 1870–1877, January 15, 1874 through May 10, 1874, CHL.

122. Toquerville Relief Society Account Book, 1868–1903, 1 (June 11, 1868); Relief Society Minute Book, 1882–1884, 13 (July 8, 1882), CHL.
123. Toquerville Relief Society Book, 1870–1877, April 6, 1870, CHL.
124. I have examined the rolls of all the relevant Toquerville Relief Society Books, which are remarkably complete.
125. Toquerville Relief Society Book, February 18, 1869; December 5, 1869; February 20, 1872; May 8, 1873; March 5, 1874, CHL.
126. Toquerville Relief Society Book, 1870–1877, September 30, 1877; and August 5, 1877, CHL.
127. Toquerville Relief Society Book, 1878–1882, 134 (February 16, 1882).
128. John Steele to Catherine Campbell Steele, May 26, 1878, MSS 528, LTPSC.

CHAPTER 3

1. John Steele to Letisha Todd, March 21, 1891, transcript in author's possession.
2. M. Slack to Hon. S. A. Thomas, October 16, 1869, 3179–80, no. 2130, TE-0 00.4, box 4, Utah State Archives.
3. Edwin Kenneth Slack, interview, October 16, 1987, 9 (all interviews are with Kerry William Bate unless otherwise designated).
4. John Steele's records as justice of the peace document the conflicts listed in this paragraph. See probate papers, box 2, fd. 13, MSS 528, John Steele Collection, 1847–1936; L. Tom Perry Special Collections, Harold B. Lee Library, Brigham Young University, Provo, Utah (hereafter LTPSC).
5. Toquerville General Minutes, 94 (March 20, 1898), Church History Library, Salt Lake City, Utah (hereafter CHL); Journal of Levi Savage, June 7, 1896, copy at Dixie University Special Collections, St. George, Utah (sometimes the typist of this journal misreads her first name as "Betty"); Toquerville Relief Society Account Book, 1868–1903, 104 and following, CHL.
6. Mahonri Moriancumer Steele to John and Catherine Campbell Steele, August 9, 1879, box 1, fd. 17, MSS 528, LTPSC.
7. John H. Krenkel, ed., *The Life and Times of Joseph Fish, Mormon Pioneer* (Danville, IL: Interstate Printers and Publishers, 1970), 240.
8. John Steele to Susan Steele Bringhurst, February 17, 1878, box 1, fd. 12, MSS 528, LTPSC.
9. Mahonri Moriancumer Steele to John and Catherine Campbell Steele, August 12, 1883, box 1, fd. 17, MSS 528, LTPSC.
10. Jane Catherine Steele Jensen to John Alma Steele, January 1, 1883, box 1, fd. 16, MSS 528, LTPSC.
11. Andrew Jenson, *Latter-day Saint Biographical Encyclopedia* (Salt Lake City: Western Epics, 1971, repr., Salt Lake City: Andrew Jenson Historical Company, 1901), 1:543, 821.
12. Reba Roundy LeFevre, interview, July 23, 1987, 8.
13. Robert Glass Cleland and Juanita Brooks, *A Mormon Chronicle: The Diaries of John D. Lee, 1848–1876* (San Marino, CA: Huntington Library, 1955), 2:109 (November 23, 1868).
14. Delphina "Della" Catherine Fish Smith, "Reminiscences and Diary," ca. 1928–1933, MS 5197, 20–21, CHL.
15. Gary Topping, ed., *Gila Monsters and Red-Eyed Rattlesnakes: Don Maguire's Arizona Trading Expeditions, 1876–1879* (Salt Lake City; University of Utah Press, 1997), 108–9, cited in Gary Topping, "Another Look at Silver Reef," *Utah Historical Quarterly* 79, no. 4 (Fall 2011): 306. What Della and Maguire described probably wasn't Dixie wine but "white-eye," made from the leftover wine pumice and peach and molasses refuse. "A Trip through Southern Utah," *The Weekly Kansas Chief* (Troy, KS), December 24, 1896, 2.
16. John Steele probate records, box 2, fd. 13, MSS 528, LTPSC.
17. John Steele to Catherine Campbell Steele, August 15, 1878, box 1, fd. 12, MSS 528, LTPSC.
18. Reba Roundy LeFevre, interview, July 23, 1987, 6–7.
19. John Steele to Catherine Campbell Steele, November 25, 1877, box 1, fd. 12, MSS 528, LTPSC.
20. Mahonri Moriancumer Steele to Catherine Campbell Steele, February 20, 1878, box 1, fd. 17, MSS 528, LTPSC.
21. Ibid.
22. Krenkel, *Joseph Fish*, 88, 138–39, 152, 155.
23. Reba Roundy LeFevre, interview, February 23, 1990, 6–7.
24. Krenkel, *Joseph Fish*, 120–21.
25. Ibid., 155–56; Smith, "Reminiscences," 15.
26. Smith, "Reminiscences," 12.
27. Mary Campbell Steele Fish to Jane Catherine Steele, [no month given] 13, 1874, box 1, fd. 17, MSS 528, LTPSC.
28. "Nathaniel Goodman," accessed July 15, 2015, https://familysearch.org/photos/stories/2327829.

29. "Sketch of John Peter Jensen, Read October 14, 1930, Directed by himself. Edited and corrected by Rex Jensen," accessed February 18, 2016, https://familysearch.org/photos/stories/21673768.
30. Smith, "Reminiscences," 20.
31. "Sketch of John Peter Jensen."
32. Raymond Mahonri Jensen, "Life of Raymond Mahonri Jensen," Utah State Historical Society, Salt Lake City, Utah (hereafter USHS).
33. Jane C. Jensen to C. Steele, May 2, [1883?], box 1, fd. 16, MSS 528, LTPSC.
34. Smith, "Reminiscences," 23–24.
35. Edwin Kenneth Slack, interview, November 17, 1988, 14.
36. "Toquerville Relief Society Account Book, 1868–1903," 7, 102 (February 5, 1894); 103 (July 6, 1893); 104 (22 January 1894); 110 (1895); 111 (1895); n.p. (1896 and also November 15, 1896–1898, 1901); "Toquerville Relief Society Minute Book, 1870–1877," August 9, 1877, unpaged accounts for Susan Bringhurst; "Toquerville Relief Society Book, 1878–1882," 33 (October 18, 1878); 79 (January 30, 1879); 107 (January 1881); 117 (October 6, 1881); 119 (January 9, 1882); 135 (February 24, 1882); 155 (February 10, 1882); "Relief Society Minutes, 1878–1879," 10 (January 8, 1882), CHL.
37. Edwin Kenneth Slack, interview, October 16, 1987, 12–13.
38. Toquerville Relief Society Minute Book, 1882–1884, 41–42 (July 5, 1883); Toquerville Ward Relief Society Minute Book, 1889–1890, 48 (August 7, 1890), CHL.
39. Susa B[ringhurst] to Mahonri Moriancumer Steele, on or after November 24, 1909, box 1, fd. 17, MSS 528, LTPSC.
40. Mary Campbell Steele Fish to Jane Catherine Steele Jensen, September 1, 1874, box 1, fd. 20, MSS 528, LTPSC.
41. Reba Roundy LeFevre, interview, July 23, 1987, 11.
42. Ibid.
43. Reba Roundy LeFevre, interview, January 24, 1987, 6; and July 23, 1987, 14.
44. "First White Child Born in Utah Is Active at 88," *Deseret News,* February 28, 1935, 13, 20.
45. "Young Elizabeth Steele Stapley," 1, copied on October 23, 1936, at Ogden, Utah, by Virginia M. Lee of the Historical Records Survey, WPA, USHS.
46. Katherine [Katharine] Larson, "Young Elizabeth Steel[e] Stapley, First White Child Born in Utah, Honored by D. U. P.," *Washington County News,* December 16, 1937, 1, A.
47. Now in author's possession.
48. Reba Roundy LeFevre, interview, July 29, 1978, 30.
49. Larson, "Young Elizabeth Steel[e] Stapley," 1, A.
50. John Burke and John Bernard Burke, *A Genealogical and Heraldic History of the Extinct and Dormant Baronetcies of England, Ireland, and Scotland* (London: John Russell Smith, 1844), 503–4 (page 503 is misnumbered 530); Stapley genealogical records in author's possession.
51. Information about the Stapleys in Australia, their participation with LDS missionaries and sailing to the United States can be found in William Layne Woolf, ed., *The Private Journal of William Hyde* (mimeographed, no date), 61–78; [Anonymous], "History of the Stapley family," revised manuscript, 1–2, copy in author's possession.
52. [Anonymous], "History of the Stapley family," 1–2.
53. Louise Slack, "Mary J. Bringhurst," (1935), 1, typescript dictated autobiography of Bringhurst, Washington County Library, St. George, Utah, M270-07 Bringhurst.
54. Cleland and Brooks, *Diaries of John D. Lee,* 2:109 (November 23, 1868).
55. Reba Roundy LeFevre, interview, May 1, 1986, 14–15; and July 29, 1978, 30.
56. Joseph H. Pollock, "How Navajo Lake Got Its Name," (July 1930), 2–4, copy in author's possession; Dr. William R. Palmer, *Forgotten Chapters of History: A Series of Talks Given over Radio Station KSUB Cedar City, Utah 1951,* no. 52, (Logan: Merrill Library and Learning Resources Program, October 1978), 1:1–3, (December 30, 1951).
57. James Stapley family Bible, "Family Record. Marriages," photocopy in author's possession; Larson, "Young Elizabeth Steel[e] Stapley," 1, A; Lella Stapley Maxfield, "History of James Stapley and His wife, Young Elizabeth Steele," 4, copy in author's possession.
58. George A. Hicks, "A Polygamous Bishop's Wicked Act," *The Salt Lake Tribune,* September 19, 1910, 3. Hicks claims that "Willes [Willis], in a short time afterwards, moved to Arizona, where he took to heavy drinking and later died of delirium tremens."
59. Larson, "Young Elizabeth Steel[e] Stapley," 1, A.
60. John Steele to George A. Smith, February 28, 1864, MS 1322, George A. Smith papers, 1834–1877, incoming correspondence 1864, CHL.
61. "Married," *Deseret News,* March 30, 1864, 209, 212.
62. Isabella Wilkin to John and Catherine Campbell Steele, March 27, 1868, box 1, fd. 28, LTPSC. Ostensibly Wilkin was also writing to John but the tenor of the letter suggests otherwise.
63. James Stapley family Bible, "Family Record. Births."
64. John V. Long, "Progress of President Young and Company," *Deseret News,* September 24, 1862, 104. For an interesting report on the challenges of the

geography of the Black Ridge, see Todd Compton, "Conquering the Black Ridge: The Communitarian Road in Pioneer Utah," *Utah Historical Quarterly* 82, no. 3 (Summer 2014): 222–33.

65. "Young Elizabeth Steele Stapley," 2.
66. Elizabeth Wood Kane, *Twelve Mormon Homes Visited in Succession on a Journey through Utah to Arizona*, edited by Everett L. Cooley (Salt Lake City: Tanner Trust, University of Utah Library, 1974), 114–15.
67. James Stapley family Bible, "Family Record. Births"; Estella Roundy Russell, "Biography of Sarah Catherine Stapley [Roundy]," 1.
68. "First White Child Born in Utah Is Active at 88," *Deseret News*, February 28, 1935, 13, 20.
69. John Steele kept numerous lists of alleged medical cures and the owner of his papers, Gary Hall Callister, allowed me to photocopy the list and take an inventory of Steele's books.
70. Reba Roundy LeFevre, interview, July 23, 1987, 13.
71. Gary Hall Callister allowed me to take photographs of this book.
72. Reba Roundy LeFevre gave Elizabeth's two medical books to my sister Tonia Ann Bate, who generously passed them on to me.
73. Frederick Hollick, *The Matron's Manual of Midwifery* (New York: American News Company, 1848), v–vii.
74. Rulon Berry Platt, interview, October 4, 1986, 8.
75. George W. Middleton, *Memoirs of a Pioneer Surgeon* (Salt Lake City: Publishers Press, 1976), 74–75. Elizabeth undoubtedly knew Middleton and her brother M. M. owned a copy of Middleton's (1911) *Embers, A Play in One Act* (in the Steele family trunk when I inventoried it).
76. Edwin Kenneth Slack, interview, November 17, 1988, 14.
77. Rulon Berry Platt, interview, October 4, 1986, 11.
78. Lynn Reeves and Ella Batty Reeves, interview, April 21, 1987, 12.
79. Sylva May Davies Williams, interview, July 24, 1987, 5.
80. Reba Roundy LeFevre, interview, January 24, 1987, 4–9, 21–22.
81. John had a booklet in his trunk called *Solar Biology*.
82. Horton Howard, *An Improved System of Botanic Medicine. Founded upon Correct Physiological Principles; Together with an Illustration of the New Theory of Medicine to which is Added, a Treatise on Female Complaints, Midwifery, and the Disease of Children in Three Volumes* (Columbus, Ohio: published by Horton J. Howard, 1836).
83. These books are in author's possession.
84. Laurel Thatcher Ulrich, *A Midwife's Tale: The Life of Martha Ballard, Based on Her Diary, 1785–1812* (New York: Alfred A. Knopf, 1990), 40.
85. Reba Roundy LeFevre, interview by Tonia Ann Bate, June 12, 1983, 1–2; LeFevre, interview by Tonia Ann Bate, August 4, 1985, 16–27; Rulon Berry Platt and Leila Platt Heap, interview, July 26, 1985, 52–58; JoAnn Sylvester Bate and Gwen Sylvester Bate, interview, June 26, 1985, 1–2; J. Cecil Alter, ed., "Journal of Priddy Meeks," *Utah Historical Quarterly* 10 (1942): 151.
86. Reba Roundy LeFevre, interview by Tonia Ann Bate, June 19, 1983, 6–7; LeFevre, interview by JoAnn Sylvester Bate, September 22, 1983, 3–4; Betina Lindsay, "Women as Healers in the Modern Church," in *Women and Authority Re-emerging Mormon Feminism*, edited by Maxine Hanks (Salt Lake City: Signature Books, 1990), 439–60; Linda King Newell, "A Gift Given: A Gift Taken," *Sunstone* 6, no. 4 (September–October 1981): 16–25; and D. Michael Quinn, "A Response," ibid., 26–27; Chris Rigby Arrington, "Pioneer Midwives," in *Mormon Sisters*, edited by Claudia L. Bushman (Salt Lake City: Olympus Publishing, 1976), 43–65.
87. Reba Roundy LeFevre, interview by Tonia Ann Bate, June 19, 1983, 6–7; LeFevre, interview by JoAnn Sylvester Bate, September 22, 1983, 3–4.
88. Rulon Berry Platt, interview, October 4, 1986, 14.
89. Claudia Beames, typist, "Historical Sketch of My Life, John Johnson Davies" (St. George: Works Progress Administration typescript, 1936), 27, 29, 39–40, 45, 62–63, 87, 115–16, 118–19; Ulrich, *A Midwife's Tale*, 40.
90. Reba Roundy LeFevre, interview, January 24, 1987, 8; and April 29, 1988, 13–14; LeFevre, interview by Tonia Ann Bate, July 21, 1983, 7; LeFevre, interview by JoAnn Sylvester Bate, September 22, 1983, 22–23; Jesse Lenard Warner, ed., "Samuel "H" Roundy History" (n.p.: 1933), 6–7, copy in author's possession; Kanarraville General Minutes, 1878–1905, 160 (January 1, 1899), CHL; Kanarraville Relief Society Minutes, 1895–1915, 23 (February 1899), CHL.
91. Reba Roundy LeFevre, interview by JoAnn Sylvester Bate, September 22, 1983, 23.
92. Voyle L. and Lillian S. Munson, *A Gift of Faith: Elias H. Blackburn* (Eureka, UT: Basin/Plateau Press, 1991).
93. Middleton, *Memoirs*, 74–75; William R. Palmer, "George Wood," dated "May 9/[19]43", Southern Utah University Special Collections, Cedar City, Utah; also in the saintly line of biography is June Wood Danvers and Esther Wood Hankins, "George Wood" (1987), USHS.

94. Middleton, *Memoirs*, 13; William Tarbet Stapley, "Autobiography," 11–12, copy in author's possession.
95. Leola Amelia Stapley Anderson, interview, November 21, 1987, 12.
96. Sophia Parker Stapley, *Together Again: An Autobiographical History* (Oakland, CA: Third Party Associates, 1976), 155.
97. Reba Roundy LeFevre, interview, January 24, 1987, 1–13, esp. 12.
98. Ibid., 4.
99. Leola Amelia Stapley Anderson, interview, November 21, 1987, 63.
100. Fredrick Wilford Balser, interview, May 28, 1988, 9.
101. J. Cecil Alter, "Addendas," *Utah Historical Quarterly* 10 (1942): 41–42.
102. "Kanarraville General Minutes, 1914–1922," 75–76 (19 December 1916), filed slightly out of order, CHL. Grant worked hard to improve his voice, see Bryant S. Hinckley, *Heber J. Grant: Highlights in the Life of a Great Leader* (Salt Lake City: Deseret Book, 1951) 45–50.
103. "Kanarraville Relief Society Minutes, 1895–1915," 123 (December 7, 1911) ("Lecture Harriett Balser Subject Why are Desease germs Important . . ."); 129 (November 1, 1912) (Ella Reeves lectured on "Diptheria" and "it was discussed by members of the class"); 130 (December 5, 1912); 134 (August 9, 1913), CHL.
104. "District Court Doings," *Parowan Times*, January 31, 1917, 1.
105. Rulon Berry Platt and Leila Platt Heaps, interview, July 26, 1985, 24–25; Reba Roundy LeFevre, interview, October 4, 1990, 1–4; Verna Platt Davis, interview, October 4, 1990, 1–7; Lyman de Platt, *The Platt Family History* (Highland, UT: Benjamin Platt & Mary Greaves Family Organization, 1979), and rev. ed. (St. George, UT: The Teguayo Press, 1998). Lyman de Platt was generous enough to send me an electronic copy of this book.
106. Rulon Berry Platt and Leila Platt Heaps, interview, July 26, 1985, 25.
107. Leonard Davis, interview, October 16, 1987, 7.
108. "Kanarraville," *Iron County Record*, February 9, 1917, 1.
109. De Platt, *The Platt Family History*.
110. Reba Roundy LeFevre, interview, January 4, 1990, 6.
111. Verna Platt Davis, interview, October 4, 1990, 1–7.
112. Ibid.
113. For this and what follows about Poincum and U-wink-ipe, see Stapley, *Together Again*, 83, 95; Larson, "Young Elizabeth Steel[e] Stapley," 1, A; "First White Child Born in Utah Is Active at 88," *Deseret News*, February 28, 1935, 13, 20; Reba Roundy LeFevre, interview, May 2, 1986, 16; LeFevre, interview by Tonia Ann Bate, July 28, 1985, 26–27 and February 1, 1988, 17–18; for photographs of U-wink-ipe ("Mary") and "Poinkum," see http://contentdm.li.suu.edu/cdm4/item_viewer.php?CISOROOT=/palmer&CISOPTR=557&CISOBOX=1&REC=1; Alva Matheson, *Cedar City Reflections*, 2nd ed. (Cedar City, UT: Southern Utah State College Press, 1974), 3; Ether Wood, "Biography," copy in author's possession; also http://brentprince.blogspot.com/2009/02/biography-of-ether-wood.html#!/2009/02/biography-of-ether-wood.html. An alternate version says Elizabeth made burial clothes out of "Aunt May's" graduation dress, see Leola Amelia Stapley Anderson, interview, November 21, 1987, 12. This Poincum may be the same Poincum who was husband of Eliza, who was briefly a Native American wife of Jacob Hamblin, see Todd Compton's outstanding biography, *A Frontier Life: Jacob Hamblin, Explorer and Indian Missionary* (Salt Lake City: University of Utah Press, 2013), 235.
114. Reba Roundy LeFevre, interview by Tonia Ann Bate, July 28, 1985, 26.
115. Sylva Davies Williams, interview, July 24, 1987, 5; Verna Platt Davis, interview, October 4, 1990, 1–5.
116. Leola Amelia Stapley Anderson, interview, November 21, 1987, 12–13; Reba Roundy LeFevre, interview, February 1, 1988, 18; LeFevre, interview, May 1, 1986, 30–31; "State's First White Baby Expires at 90," *Salt Lake Telegram*, April 2, 1938, 2. Reba Roundy LeFevre showed me the burial spot of the twins on April 30, 1986.
117. Reba Roundy LeFevre, interview, May 5, 1990, 10–11; JoAnn Sylvester Bate, interview, June 22, 1991, 1–2.
118. Reba Roundy LeFevre, interview, January 24, 1987, 17.

CHAPTER 4

1. The top story of the house has since been removed.
2. "Cobble Crest—a Hidden Treasure," Preservation Round Up Blog, accessed February 19, 2016, http://www.utahheritagefoundation.com/component/k2/item/523-cobble-crest-%E2%80%93-a-hidden-treasure#.VsdtU_IrKhc.
3. M. M. Steele to John Steele and Catherine Campbell Steele, August 12, 1883, box 1, fd. 17, MSS 528, John Steele Collection, 1847–1936, L. Tom Perry

Special Collections, Harold B. Lee Library, Brigham Young University, Provo, Utah (hereafter LTPSC).

4. "Land Entries," *Salt Lake Herald,* June 24, 1899, 3; *R. L. Polk and Company's Utah State Gazetteer 1903–04* (Salt Lake City: Tribune Job Printing, 1903), 515–18.
5. M. M. Steele to John Steele, June 17, 1888, copy in author's possession; "Richard Palmer Record Book, 1881–1882," 9–11, 15–16, 22, 40, 54, 154, 157, no. 1, box 2, fd. f3-b1, William R. Palmer Collection, Southern Utah University Special Collections, Cedar City, Utah (hereafter SUUSC).
6. Brent Pace Prince typed and generously posted the Kanarra and Harmony Stock Company Minute Book, 1874–1898, online and it shows that at the meeting adopting the bylaws, November 19, 1874, "On motion of L. M. Willis and Secnd by J Stapley, L. H. Redd was elected as 2nd Director." brentprince.blogspot.com/2008/10/harmony-kanarra-stock-raising-company.html.
7. William Tarbet Stapley, "Autobiography," (original untitled) typescript, edited by Kerry William Bate (Salt Lake City: 1987), 2.
8. From the *Iron County Record:* "Kanarra," July 24, 1903, 1; "Kanarra," August 14, 1903, 1; June 11, 1904, 1; "Stake Conference," July 09, 1904, 4; "Cedar City and Vicinity," September 7, 1906, 4; September 14, 1906, 2; "Local Items," June 18, 1909, 4, May 13, 1910, 4; "Kanarraville," July 19, 1912, 8. Amy L. Van Cott and Allen W. Leigh, *Generations of Websters* (Cedar City, UT: The Thomas Webster Family Organization, 1960), 66, 164; William R. Palmer to Dr. Herbert E. Gregory, June 9, 1942, no. 1, I-H/4-g/ii, fd. 16-b16, SUUSC; Charles Kelly, ed., *Journals of John D. Lee 1846–47 and 1859* (Salt Lake City: University of Utah Press, 1984), 205–6 (May 14, 1859).
9. Lynn and Ella Batty Reeves, interview, April 23, 1987, 7–8; all interviews are with Kerry William Bate unless otherwise indicated.
10. Elton Williams Stapley, interview, October 16, 1987, 1–2.
11. "Rennet is a complex of enzymes produced in stomachs of ruminant mammals which is used in the production of most cheeses," accessed January 27, 2015, https://en.wikipedia.org/wiki/Rennet.
12. Reba Roundy LeFevre, interview by Tonia Ann Bate, August 9, 1985, 5–7; W. E. Carroll, "Cheesemaking in the Home," *Iron County Record,* July 30, 1915, 1, 8; and "Make Your Own Cheese is Advice of Utah AC," November 14, 1919, 4.
13. Reba Roundy LeFevre, interview by Tonia Ann Bate, August 9, 1985, 5–7.
14. Rulon Berry Platt, interview, October 4, 1986, 22–23.
15. Leola Stapley Anderson, interview, November 21, 1987, 17–18.
16. "Notice to Water Users," *Iron County Record,* March 25, 1921, 5; and "Kanarraville," August 2, 1912, 8; "John Johnson Davies," 49, 51, Utah State Historical Society, Salt Lake City, Utah (hereafter USHS); Blair Maxfield, unrecorded interview by Kerry William Bate, April 5, 1990, 1.
17. Blair Maxfield, interview, April 5, 1990, 1.
18. James Stapley Family Bible, "Family Record. Marriages," photocopy in author's possession.
19. James Stapley to John Steele and Catherine Campbell Steele, October 2, 1886, MS 24404, John Steele Correspondence, Church History Library, The Church of Jesus Christ of Latter-day Saints, Salt Lake City, Utah (hereafter CHL).
20. Kanarraville Relief Society Minutes, 1889–1897, unpaginated, May 5, 1892, CHL.
21. Kanarraville Relief Society Minutes, 1889–1897, December 17, 1893, CHL.
22. Kanarraville Relief Society Minutes, 1889–1897, January [?], 1894; Kanarraville YMMIA Minutes, 1878–1890, 87 (February 13, 1886), CHL.
23. Reba Roundy LeFevre, interview, October 4, 1990, 7.
24. Stapley, "Autobiography," 5.
25. Joseph Fish said the deputies who helped the Deputy Marshall with Lee's arrest were "some of the noted thieves and whiskey bloats of the county and it became a common saying that if a prosecution was started against a cattle thief he would come out a Deputy Marshall." John H. Krenkel, ed., *The Life and Times of Joseph Fish, Mormon Pioneer* (Danville, IL: Interstate Printers and Publishers, 1970), 155. Among those "thieves and bloats" was Mary's first husband, Thomas LeFevre. See Robert Kent Fielding, comp. and ed., *The* Tribune *Reports of The Trials of John D. Lee for the Massacre at Mountain Meadows* (Higganum, CT: Kent's Books, 2006), 9.
26. Krenkel, *Joseph Fish,* 154–56; Joseph Fish to Catherine Campbell Steele, December 9, 1874, box 1, fd. 20, MSS 528, LTPSC.
27. John Steele to Catherine Campbell Steele, December 18, 1877, box 1, fd. 12, MSS 528, LTPSC.
28. Krenkel, *Joseph Fish,* 155.
29. John Steele to Catherine Campbell Steele, December 18, 1877, box 1, fd. 12, MSS 528, LTPSC.
30. Stapley, "Autobiography," 3, 7–8.
31. Estella Roundy Russell, "Biography of Sarah Catherine Stapley [Roundy]," 1–2, copy in author's possession.

32. Reba Roundy LeFevre, interviewed by Tonia Ann Bate, July 26, 1985, 14.
33. Delphina "Della" Catherine Fish Smith, "Reminiscences and Diary," ca. 1928–1933, MS 5197, 19–25, CHL.
34. Smith, "Reminiscences," 19–25; for a biographical sketch, see Joseph Fish Smith and Lillian F. Smith, "Della Fish and Joseph W. Fish Family" in *Family of Joseph Fish (1840–1926): Genealogical and Biographical Stories and Sketches,* edited by Seymour P. Fish and Vera P. Fish, (Provo, UT: J. Grant Stevenson, 1970), 127–34; for her living with her Steele grandparents, see Ibid., 377.
35. Smith, "Reminiscences," 23–25.
36. Fish and Fish, *Family of Joseph Fish*, 195–96.
37. Reba Roundy LeFevre, interview by Tonia Ann Bate, July 26, 1985, 14–15.
38. "First White Child Born In Utah Is Active at 88," *Deseret News,* February 28, 1935, 13, 20. Reba LeFevre tells a similar story with her grandfather James Stapley as the inventor of the boot straps, see Reba Roundy LeFevre, interview by Tonia Ann Bate, July 26, 1985, 16–17.
39. "You Run No Chances When You Buy a Range from Us," *Iron County Record,* January 31, 1913, 8. The Mrs. James Stapley referred to here may be Mrs. James Chattle Stapley.
40. Sylva May Davies Williams, interview, July 24, 1987, 4; and June 27, 1988, 3.
41. It was addressed to "Aunt Libbie." Elizabeth saved a similar Valentine's card from Sylva's sister Elva; copies in author's possession.
42. Rulon Berry Platt, interview, October 4, 1986, 22.
43. Reba Roundy LeFevre, interview, January 24, 1987, 24.
44. Reba Roundy LeFevre, interview by Tonia Ann Bate, June 12, 1983, 5–6.
45. Rulon Berry Platt, interview, July 28, 1987, 22.
46. Rulon Berry Platt, interview, July 12, 1987, 57.
47. Reba Roundy LeFevre, interview, May 2, 1986, 6.
48. Lynn and Ella Batty Reeves, interview, October 15, 1987, 37.
49. Sophia Parker Stapley, *Together Again: An Autobiographical History* (Oakland, CA: Third Party Associates, 1976), 85.
50. Young Elizabeth Stapley to C. Steele, [March, 1883], box 1, fd. 15, MSS 528, LTPSC. This letter says Sarah Stapley Reeves had a daughter born Monday. Reeves had two daughters born on a Monday: Phebe born September 29, 1879, and Amanda born March 19, 1883. From the context of the letter it is obvious it was written early in the year, so it is most likely March 1883.
51. Young Elizabeth Steele Stapley to John and Catherine Campbell Steele, May 8, 1888, MSS 528, LTPSC.
52. Copy in author's possession.
53. Ileen J. Johnson and Wanda S. Cox, *The Memoirs of Mahonri Moriancumer Steele Jr.* (mimeographed, 1963), 5–6.
54. Mary named her daughter Catherine Delphina but "Della" switched the order.
55. Josephine "Josie" Fish Barraclough to Catherine Campbell Steele, May 20, 1888, box 1, fd. 20, MSS 528, LTPSC.
56. Della Fish [Smith] to Catherine Campbell Steele, June 10, 1884, box 1, fd. 20, MSS 528, LTPSC.
57. Frances Fish Carson to Catherine Campbell Steele, April 29, 1882, box 1, fd. 20, MSS 528, LTPSC.
58. Frances Fish Carson to Catherine Campbell Steele, July 8, 1882, box 1, fd. 20, MSS 528, LTPSC.
59. Josephine "Josie" Fish Barraclough to John Steele and Catherine Campbell Steele, December 9, 1883, box 1, fd. 20, MSS 528, LTPSC.
60. Josephine "Josie" Fish Barraclough to Catherine Campbell Steele, April 18, 1884, box 1, fd. 20, MSS 528, LTPSC.
61. Emily Abbott Bunker to Catherine Campbell Steele, July 21, 1877, box 1, fd. 18, MSS 528, LTPSC.
62. Emily Steele to John and Catherine Campbell Steele, June 11, 1882, box 1, fd. 18, MSS 528, LTPSC.
63. Jane Catherine Steele Jensen to Catherine Campbell Steele, May 2, [1883?], box 1, fd. 16, MSS 528, LTPSC.
64. John Steele to Sarah Catherine Stapley and James Steele Stapley, February 28, 1878, copy in author's possession.
65. Reba Roundy LeFevre, interview, July 23, 1987, 4.
66. Rather, it was when I originally wrote this sentence; a house has since been built there.
67. John Steele to Letisha Todd, August 2, 1897, transcript in author's possession.
68. Reba Roundy LeFevre, interview, July 29, 1978, 31.
69. Ibid.
70. Reba Roundy LeFevre, interview, May 9, 1985, 7.
71. Reba Roundy LeFevre, interview, October 16, 1987, 1; and May 23, 1987, 7.
72. Josephine Kay Garfield, interview, May 26, 1988, 3.
73. Kanarraville Sunday School Minutes, 1882–1896, 42 (March 6, 1887); 73–74 (December 25, 1887); 103 (January 6, 1889); LR 4305, no. 3, 14–15, CHL; Kanarraville Relief Society Minutes, 1895–1915, 17 (January 6, 1898), CHL: "Bro. James Stapley . . . Said we should try to educate our children and improve our minds."
74. Reba Roundy LeFevre to Kerry William Bate, July 12, 1982, in author's possession.

75. Kanarra teachers and comments about them are in Stapley, "Autobiography," 4, 6–7.
76. "Kanarra Pioneer [Harriet Berry Stapley] Entertains Children with Stories of Life," *Iron County Record,* December 21, 1944, 7; Scott G. Kenney, *Wilford Woodruff's Journal: 1833–1898* (Midvale, UT: Signature Books, 1984), 7:563–65; George W. Middleton, *Memoirs of a Pioneer Surgeon* (Salt Lake City: Publishers Press, 1976), 27–30; John Henry Davies, *Among My Memories,* 8 (undated mimeographed typescript), copy at USHS; for additional information, see the following from the *Iron County Record:* "Quarantine Was Observed," January 26, 1906, 1; "City Council Proceedings," February 9, 1906, 8; "Political Nonsense," October 19, 1906, 2; "A Nice Piece of Work," December 10, 1909, 4; December 22, 1911, 8; "Things in General," December 29, 1911, 8; "Eugene Schoppmann," (obituary) April 26, 1912, 1. Schoppmann had been a surveyor, mapmaker, teacher, health officer, and chairman of the Iron County Democratic party.
77. Stapley, "Autobiography," 6–7.
78. Leon R Sylvester, SueZanna Wittwer Sylvester, Gwen Sylvester Hunter, Nell Sylvester Stout Wilson, Ruth Sylvester Pickering, interview, August 6, 1983, 33 (Ruth Sylvester Pickering speaking).
79. "Kanarra Pioneer [Harriet Berry Stapley] Entertains Children with Stories of Life," *Iron County Record,* December 21, 1944, 7. She errs in thinking Schoppman "drifted" out; he had a distinguished public career in Cedar City after his Kanarraville sojourn.
80. Kanarra YMMIA Minutes, 1878–1890, 81–82 (January 16, 1886); 82 (January 19, 1886); 92 (March 16, 1886); Kanarra YMMIA Minutes, 1890–1901, 56 (December 22, 1896); 89 (April 24, 1898); 92 (November 6, 1898); 100 (December 18, 1898), CHL.
81. Reba Roundy LeFevre, interview by Tonia Ann Bate, July 28, 1985, 41.
82. Ibid., 40.
83. Ibid., 40–41.
84. A scholarly but very readable and interesting study of evolving Mormon theology is Terryl L. Givens, *Wrestling the Angel: The Foundations of Mormon Thought; Cosmos, God, Humanity* (Oxford: Oxford University Press, 2015).
85. Toquerville Relief Society Book, 1886–1889, 61 (May 7, 1887), CHL.
86. Kerry William Bate and JoAnn Sylvester Bate, eds., *Ebenezer Joseph Hanks Manuscripts and Letters* (Salt Lake City: typescript, 1979), 191. Copy at CHL.
87. John M. Dunning, "Pioneer Day at Panguitch," *Deseret Weekly News,* August 11, 1886, 3.
88. M. M. Steele to John Steele and Catherine Campbell Steele, January 9, 1887, February 17, 1887, and August 4, 1887, box 1, fd. 17, MSS 528, LTPSC. The pressure put on polygamists is illustrated in part by the following newspaper sentence: "After fruitless searching on the morning of the 26th ult., of the residences of J. W. Crosby, Jr., M. M[.] Steele, Joseph C. Davis and James Harris, Sr., the officers put whole families under lock arrest, by simply telling them they had better not leave their premises or they would be arrested." "Deputies in the South," *Salt Lake Herald,* May 8, 1887, 8. For interesting studies of Mormon polygamy, see Richard S. Van Wagoner, *Mormon Polygamy: A History* (Salt Lake City: Signature Books, 1986) and B. Carmon Hardy, *Solemn Covenant: The Mormon Polygamous Passage* (Urbana and Chicago: University of Illinois Press, 1992). For Joseph Smith's polygamist relationships, see Todd Compton, *In Sacred Loneliness: The Plural Wives of Joseph Smith* (Salt Lake City: Signature Books, 1997).
89. "I some times get a letter from Mary Ellen, who is very much in love with her parents, & suppose she is to young to leave them." M. M. Steele to Catherine Campbell Steele, October 13, 1877, box 1, fd. 17, MSS 528, LTPSC.
90. Joseph Fish to John Steele, October 13, 1887, box 1, fd. 20, MSS 528, LTPSC.
91. "Panguitch," *Deseret News,* June 2, 1900, 7; Wanda S. Cox and Mrs. Doyle Steele, "Emily Bunker Steele," copy in author's possession.
92. Mahonri M. Steele to John Steele and Catherine Campbell Steele, September 4, 1887, box 1, fd. 17, MSS 528, LTPSC.
93. Stan Larson, *Prisoner for Polygamy: The Memoirs and Letters of Rudger Clawson at the Utah Territorial Penitentiary, 1884–87* (Urbana and Chicago: University of Illinois, 1993), 212; D[avid]. Spilsbury, "Letter from Toquerville," *Deseret Weekly News,* April 18, 1888, 217: "Our worthy Bishop, Wm. A. Bringhurst, was captured Feb. 14th and is now serving his time." Dr. Wesley P. Larsen, a Toquerville historian, after interviewing old-timers was quite certain that Richard T. Higbee turned Bringhurst in for the reward.
94. Joseph Fish to John Steele and Catherine Campbell Steele, December 31, 1886, box 1, fd. 20, MSS 528, LTPSC. The Toquerville ladies were also upset with Dalton's death, the minutes recording "Five of the Sister[s] Met at the appointed time Dec 16 our

Pres and councler E N Slack Encora Batty Mary F Lamb and E W Lamb But hearing of the Mu[r]der of Br Edward Dolton we felt as sad we adj[o]urned our meeting for 3 Weeks." Toquerville Ward Relief Society Minutes, 1886–1889, 34 (December 16, 1886), CHL.

95. Joseph Fish to John Steele, May 15, 1888, box 1, fd. 20, MSS 528, LTPSC.
96. Lella Stapley Maxfield, "History of James Stapley and his wife, Young Elizabeth Steele," 2, copy in author's possession.
97. Rulon Berry Platt, interview, May 19, 1982, 34.
98. Harriet Arvilla Ford Woodbury, interview, October 16, 1987, 11.
99. John Steele to Catherine Campbell Steele, December 18, 1877, box 1, fd. 12, MSS 528, LTPSC.
100. Ibid.
101. Reba Roundy LeFevre, interview, October 16, 1987, 8.
102. Reba Roundy LeFevre, interview, July 29, 1978, 7–8; LeFevre, interview by Tonia Ann Bate, June 19, 1983, 9. Kate was presented with a card on one side of which was a color picture of two pigeons and on the other a scientific-style report on these birds. Around the outside of the report is handwritten, "to S. C. Stapley by the Sup'ts Kanarra Sunday School," original in author's possession.
103. Reba Roundy LeFevre, interview, July 29, 1978, 7; Kanarra YMMIA Minutes, 1878–1890, 38 (1882), CHL.
104. William Charles Reeves, "History of Kanarra," (ca. 1940), 1, copy in author's possession.
105. Reba Roundy LeFevre, interview, July 29, 1978, 7 (Reba miscalls him "Wilfred" in this interview); LeFevre, interview by Tonia Ann Bate, June 19, 1983, 9; LeFevre, interview by Tonia Ann Bate July 21, 1983, 3 (calls him "Lewis"); LeFevre, interview by JoAnn Sylvester Bate September 22, 1983, 7 (calls him "R. C."); LeFevre, interview by Tonia Ann Bate July 26, 1985, 17; Church records confirm his name: Kanarra YMMIA Minutes, 1878–1890, 36 (February 4, 1882), CHL.
106. Reba Roundy LeFevre, interview, July 29, 1978, 9; LeFevre, interview by Tonia Ann Bate, June 19, 1983, 9.
107. Reba Roundy LeFevre, interview, July 29, 1978, 2. A good biographical account is in Everett Ellsworth Roundy, *The Roundy Family in America* (Dedham, MA: 1942), 300ff.
108. Maria Ward [pseudonym], *Female Life among the Mormons* (New York: Derby and Jackson, 1856), 9–11. Michael Homer and Massimo Introvigne speculated that Elizabeth Cornelia Woodcock Ferris, the wife of Benjamin G. Ferris (who was Utah Territorial Secretary between 1852–53), was the author of this book. But *History Detectives* (a PBS documentary television series), taking that assertion into account, tried and failed to solve the mystery of the authorship, see http://www.pbs.org/opb/historydetectives/blog/how-we-solved-it-stylometric-analysis/. We do know that the author was familiar with Spafford, New York, naming real people and events, though her book is mostly fictional. Spafford town historian and Roundy cousin George Knapp Collins accepts the historicity of "Ward's" book, undoubtedly because the Spafford portion, with which he was concerned, was basically correct. See George Knapp Collins, *Spafford, Onondaga County, New York* (Onondaga Historical Association, 1917), 47–51.
109. Elizabeth Wood Kane, *Twelve Mormon Homes: Visited in Succession on a Journey through Utah to Arizona* (Salt Lake City: Published by Tanner Trust Fund, University of Utah Library, 1974), 116.
110. Daniel Wells, Erastus Snow, and Brigham Young Jr. to Prest. B. Young, May 26, 1876, box 43, fd. 20, reel 56, Brigham Young Letters, CHL. The letter described Roundy's death; his body was never found.
111. Reba Roundy LeFevre, interview, July 29, 1978, 2.
112. Reba Roundy LeFevre, interview by Tonia Ann Bate, June 19, 1983, 8–9; and October 12, 1984, 8.
113. Kanarraville Sunday School Minutes, 1886–1892, 3 (March 28, 1886, April 4, 1886), CHL.
114. Ibid., 4 (April 4, 1886).
115. Ibid.
116. Ibid., 26 (October 3, 1886).
117. From what I've labeled "Notebook 1," JoAnn Sylvester Bate journal entry, Thursday, May 10, 1979, original in author's possession.
118. Reba Roundy LeFevre, interview, July 29, 1978, 7, 14, 26.
119. Kanarraville Sunday School Minutes, 1886–1892, 58 (1887), CHL.
120. Joseph Fish to John Steele and Catherine Campbell Steele, April 28, 1887, box 1, fd. 20, MSS 528, LTPSC.
121. Reba Roundy LeFevre, interview by Tonia Ann Bate, July 26, 1985, 17.
122. Orson Ferguson Whitney, *Popular History of Utah* (Salt Lake City: Deseret News Press, 1916), 369.
123. Reba Roundy LeFevre, interview, October 16, 1987, 14.
124. Reba Roundy LeFevre, interview by JoAnn Sylvester Bate, September 22, 1983, 5.

125. Kanarraville YMMIA Minutes, 1878–1890, 98 (January 25, 1890), CHL.
126. Reba Roundy LeFevre, interview by Tonia Ann Bate, June 19, 1983, 11.
127. "Kanarraville," *Iron County Record,* March 15, 1917, 4.
128. Reba Roundy LeFevre, interview by Tonia Ann Bate, July 21, 1983, 10–11.

    > Johnny was a bachelor who was always looking for that one rich widow, but never quite found her. He traveled practically all of his life and during his travels he found Kanarra and stayed with Bishop Berry. He became fond of him and his people, and when he died, he left his money in a will to the Kanarra people in the care of their Bishop. He wanted it used for the good of the poor people of the town. When Wells Williams was Bishop, his father died and he bought his father's farm for the church with the Coonsler [*sic*] money.

    Marilyn Lovell, *History of Kanarraville* (Kanarraville, UT: Kanarraville, Utah Beta Chi Chapter of Beta Sigma Phi, 1980), 20–21; David Spilsbury, "High Tribute Paid to Memory of Friend [John Kinsley/Kunzler]," *Washington County News,* February 9, 1922, 5; David Spilsbury, "Correction," March 2, 1922, 1.
129. Reba Roundy LeFevre, interview by Tonia Ann Bate, July 26, 1985, 40.

CHAPTER 5

1. http://www.findagrave.com/cgi-bin/fg.cgi?page=gr&GRid=22581216; also see [Untitled], *Iron County News,* January 31, 1891, 8, when Dr. Brown was considering relocating to Cedar City.
2. I visited the site on April 23, 1987; Joan Norman Williams, conversation with Kerry William Bate, July 24, 1987.
3. Lynn and Ella Batty Reeves, interview, April 23, 1987, 24 (all interviews are with Kerry William Bate unless otherwise indicated).
4. George W. Middleton, *Memoirs of a Pioneer Surgeon* (Salt Lake City: Publishers Press, 1976), 13.
5. William Tarbet Stapley, "Autobiography," (original untitled) typescript, edited by Kerry William Bate (Salt Lake City: 1987), 11–12, copy in author's possession. This is the source for the story of Sarah Elizabeth Roundy's birth.
6. Reba Roundy LeFevre, interview, July 29, 1978, 8.
7. Reba Roundy LeFevre, interview by Tonia Ann Bate, July 28, 1985, 37. As late as 1926, Dr. M. J. Macfarlane reported 44 percent of the children he examined in Iron County had enlarged thyroids. Robert Olesen, "Distribution of Endemic Goiter in the United States as Shown by Thyroid Surveys," *Public Health Reports,* 41 (November 26, 1926): 2702.
8. Photocopy of John Steele's medical prescriptions in author's possession.
9. Harriet Arvilla Ford Woodbury, interview, October 16, 1987, 31–32.
10. Rebecca Berry death certificate at http://www.archives.utah.gov/research/indexes/20842.htm.
11. Thelma Berry Lovell, interview, July 27, 1988, 10.
12. Rulon Berry Platt and Leila Platt Heap, interview, July 26, 1985 49–50; Reba Roundy LeFevre, interview by Tonia Ann Bate, July 28, 1985, 36–37; Voyle L. Munson and Lillian S. Munson, *A Gift of Faith: Elias H. Blackburn* (Eureka, UT: Basin/Plateau Press, 1991); "Close of a Brilliant Career. Patriarch Elias H. Blackburn Lays Down Life's Labors at 81," *Deseret News,* April 16, 1908, 5.
13. Kanarraville General Minutes, 1878–1905, 162 (November 5, 1899), Church History Library, The Church of Jesus Christ of Latter-day Saints, Salt Lake City, Utah (hereafter CHL); Munson and Munson, *A Gift of Faith,* 227, 230 mentions healing "Big Neck" or goiters; "Kanarra: Death of a Pioneer [Myron Shadrach Roundy]," *Deseret News,* February 13, 1902, 7.
14. Reba Roundy LeFevre, interview by Tonia Ann Bate, July 28, 1985, 36–37.
15. The patriarchal blessing was given October 18, 1900, in Loa, and included: "blest shall be your body & blest shall be your spirit & blest to continue your motherhood & blest that the present troubles of the body shall be overcome by faith & you shall live to continue your labors" (except the typist in all but the last use of the word 'blest' inadvertently typed "blrst"), photocopy of typescript in author's possession.
16. Rebecca Alenna Stapley Williams, interview, February 1, 1988, 4.
17. Josephine Kay Garfield, interview, May 26, 1988, 4.
18. Mahonri Moriancumer Steele to John Steele and Catherine Campbell Steele, June 17, 1888, copy in author's possession.
19. John Steele's brother-in-law, noticing his penchant for digressions tactfully wrote, "Of course when you write you can fill up a whole lot of papers with quotations from the scriptures Which makes your letters look very big and at the same time you seem to have forgotten that you have written the same

thing over and over again but a good tale is nothing the worse of being told over again I intend to send you a paper with this letter and hope you will write soon again and forgive me for writing so seldom." Robert Campbell to John Steele, March 1890, box 1, fd. 27, MSS 528, John Steele Collection, 1847–1936, L. Tom Perry Special Collections, Harold B. Lee Library, Brigham Young University, Provo, Utah (hereafter LTPSC).

20. John Steele to Letisha Todd, November 16, 1890, photocopy in author's possession.
21. "Meeting House Burned," *The [Provo, UT] Evening Dispatch*, February 11, 1891, 4.
22. Letisha Todd to John Steele, May 5, 1891, box 1, fd. 24, MSS 528, LTPSC.
23. John Steele to Letisha Todd, March 21, 1891, transcript in author's possession.
24. "Eliza Roxcy Snow," accessed August 7, 2015, https://en.wikipedia.org/wiki/Eliza_R._Snow.
25. Toquerville Relief Society Minutes, 1886–1889, (May 7, 1887); and 77 (post-December 5, 1887), CHL.
26. Toquerville Relief Society Minute Book, 1889–1890, 52 (October 2, 1890); and 58 (December 4, 1890), CHL.
27. Journal of Levi Savage, January 11, 1891, typescript at Dixie University, John D. Lee Collection (hereafter DU). The transcriber of Savage's diaries did them in small sections, starting the pagination over each time; hence, it's easier to find a source by date than page number.
28. Mahonri Moriancumer Steele to John and Catherine Campbell Steele, February 12, 1891, MS 24404, John Steele Correspondence CHL.
29. Toquerville Relief Society Minute Book, 1889–1890, 65 (April 1, 1891), CHL. This minute book, despite its title, includes the year 1891.
30. Savage Journal, June 16, 1891, DU.
31. Toquerville Relief Society Minute Book, 1889–1890, 99 (July 3, 1891), CHL.
32. Toquerville Relief Society Minute Book, 1889–1890, 148, CHL.
33. John Steele, June 15, 1891, partial draft, box 1, fd. 12, MSS 528, LTPSC; Wanda Steele Cox, *Journals of John Steele and Mahonri Moriancumer Steele* (Cedar City, UT: self-published, 1967), 1:55–57.
34. [Anonymous], "Short History of John Steele Jr. and Catherine Campbell Steele," 2. This is a useful history but the conclusion is conventional.
35. Reba Roundy LeFevre, interview, October 6, 1989, 10; and May 5, 1990, 12–13; Savage Journal, June 1891, DU.
36. Todd Compton, "Conquering the Black Ridge: The Communitarian Road in Pioneer Utah," *Utah Historical Quarterly* 82, no. 3 (Summer 2014): 222–33.
37. William C. McGregor, "Catharine Campbell Steele," *Deseret News*, June 22, 1891, 8; William C. McGregor, "The Late Sister Steele," *Deseret News*, June 25, 1891, 8; "Died," *Latter-day Saints Millennial Star* 53 (August 3, 1891): 496; "Died," *Latter-day Saints Millennial Star* 53 (August 17, 1891): 528.
38. Joseph Fish, *The Autobiography of Joseph Fish by Himself, with Notes by His Sons Silas and Jesse* (Lulu: 2009), 137.
39. http://www.findagrave.com/cgi-bin/fg.cgi?page=gr&GSln=STEELE&GSfn=catherine&GSbyrel=all&GSdyrel=all&GSst=47&GScnty=2784&GScntry=4&GSob=n&GRid=11697387&df=all&.
40. Savage Journal, June 21, 1891, DU.
41. Mahonri Moriancumer Steele to John Steele, July 13, 1891, MS 24404, John Steele Correspondence, CHL.
42. This was in turn given to Reba Roundy LeFevre, who gave it to the author.
43. James Steele Stapley to John Steele, July 29, 1891, box 1, fd. 22, MSS 528, LTPSC.
44. Ibid., September 10, 1891.
45. Reba Roundy LeFevre, interview, October 16, 1987, 23–24.
46. [Anonymous, but written by one of M. M. Stapley's daughters], "History of Mahonri Moriancumer Stapley," 1–2, copy in author's possession; Rebecca Almeda Williams Stapley, "A Short Sketch of the Life of Rebecca Williams Stapley," 1–3, copy in author's possession; "Delta Couple Invites Their Friends to Golden Wedding Celebration," undated, unidentified news clipping in author's possession.
47. Elton Williams Stapley, interview, October 16, 1987, 8; April 14, 1989, 17.
48. "Kanarra," *Iron County Record*, June 11, 1904, 8.
49. William Tarbet Stapley, "Autobiography," 21–22. From the *Iron County Record*: "Kanarra Kinks," January 9, 1903, 1; "Kanarra Kinks," January 23, 1903, 1; "Kanarraville," August 2, 1912, 8; "Kanarraville," May 31, 1912, 8.
50. Reba Roundy LeFevre, interview by Tonia Ann Bate, July 26, 1985, 11–12.
51. From the *Iron County Record*, "Kanarra Letter," September 15, 1911, 1; "Kanarra Letter," December 22, 1911, 5; "Kanarra Letter," March 15, 1912, 5; "Another Pioneer [Lucretia Groves] Laid Away," March 15, 1912, 5 (Joel Jesse Roundy spoke at Mrs. Groves's funeral); "City and Local Happenings," May 17, 1912, 5; "Kanarraville," May 17, 1912, 8; "City and Local Happenings," May 24, 1912, 5; "County Solons in Regular Session," September 7, 1917, 1; "Lost,"

October 12, 1917, 5; "Kanarraville," January 25, 1918, 5; "Kanarraville," June 7, 1918, 4; "Many Cases Heard in District Court," July 4, 1919, 1:

> An affidavit was filed charging that Veleris Groves, Holier Groves, Annie Groves and Lewis Groves, residents of Kanarra, were insane. A hearing was had in which Drs. Burton and Bergstrom were present and made such examination as is usual in such cases, and certified that the parties were insane and proper subjects for treatment in the State Mental Hospital, and the court remanded them to that institution, where they were immediately taken. Upon their arrival the doctor in charge of the hospital refused to receive them for reasons that he has not yet made known.

"Commissioners' Doings," *Parowan Times*, July 23, 1919, 4; and "District Court Report," June 25, 1919, 1, 8; from the *Iron County Record,* "Commissioners' Regular Meeting," December 19, 1919, 1; "[Iron County] Financial Statement," August 6, 1920, 5; "Special Road Committee," July 22, 1921, 1: "The clerk was instructed to write the governor of the condition of the Groves family at Kanarra and ask the state to take care of them as soon as possible"; "Monthly Meeting of Commissioners," November 25, 1921, 1. Eventually they were lodged in the State Mental Hospital. When the U.S. 1930 Federal census was taken, Heber A., Lewis M., and Wesley T. Groves were inmates. Reba Roundy LeFevre, interview by JoAnn Sylvester Bate, September 22, 1983, 40.

52. "Fusion Suggested," *Salt Lake Tribune,* September 2, 1908, 8. A "Fusion Ticket" of Socialists and Democrats were expected to run against the Republicans in Wayne County. James S. Stapley's surname is misspelled "Stopley."
53. "Kanarraville," *Iron County Record,* May 31, 1912, 8.
54. Kerry William Bate, "Diary of Mary Elizabeth (May) Stapley, a Schoolteacher in Virgin, Utah," *Utah Historical Quarterly* 60, no. 2 (Spring 1992): 158–67; "What is Going on in Utah," *Salt Lake Tribune,* December 16, 1903, 8. From the *Iron County Record*: "Among the School Children," February 27, 1904, 5; "Among the School Children," March 5, 1904, 4; "Kanarra," December 9, 1904, 3; "Kanarra," March 17, 1905, 5; "Kanarra," May 12, 1905, 5; "Kanarra," October 6, 1905, 5; "Local Happenings," July 13, 1906, 1; "Kanarra, Utah," September 28, 1906, 1; "Kanarra, Utah," December 28, 1906, 1; "Kanarra Letter," January 14, 1910, 1; *Iron County Record Supplement,* "Kanarra Letter," June 11, 1909, 1.
55. Findagrave.com for Thomas Hawker (1813–1905) and Charlotte Stapley Hawker (1823–1913), Pioneer Memorial Cemetery, San Bernardino, CA (though the account of Charlotte's alleged husbands is confusing); from the *San Bernardino County Sun*: "Pioneer [Thomas Hawker] Goes to Long Rest," April 28, 1905, 4; "Birthday Surprise for Great-Grandmother [Charlotte Stapley Hawker]," March 30, 1911, 6; "Mrs. Charlotte S. Hawker, Aged 91, Is Called to Final Rest," August 19, 1913, 2. No death certificate was issued for Thomas Hawker.
56. Kanarra Ward Record, 1905–1913, 48 (July 21, 1907): "The time was taken up by James Stapley who gave a brief account of his visit to California where he and his daughter Mary went to visit his two sisters and attended the National Education Association at Los Angeles," CHL.
57. "Certificates Are Granted by State School Board," *Salt Lake Tribune,* April 4, 27, 1909, 14; Kanarra Ward Record, 1905–1913, 48 (July 21, 1907), CHL.
58. Josephine Kay Garfield, interview, May 26, 1988, 9.
59. "Local and General News," *Washington County [Utah] News,* December 15, 1910, 4: "Mr. and Mrs. [James] Stapley and son and daughter, Will and Mary, of Kanarra, are city visitors . . . County Clerk Woodbury issued a marriage license this morning to John S. Kay of Mona, and Mary Stapley of Kanarra."
60. Reba Roundy LeFevre provided me a photocopy of William Tarbet Stapley's poem, in which he wrote "I'm 81"; William Tarbet Stapley, "Autobiography." [Untitled], *Iron County News,* January 17, 1891, 8; from the *Iron County Record,* "Local Items," November 21, 1903, 8; "Kanarra," byline March 3, 1904 (but misfiled electronically as page 11 under November 11, 1904); September 17, 1904, 8; "Home Missionary List," September 29, 1905, 5; "Home Missionary List," October 6, 1905, 8; "Parowan Letter," October 21, 1910, 1; "Jury List for 1911," January 6, 1911, 1; "Parowan News Items," August 11, 1911, 1; "Things in General," August 29, 1911, 4; "Where Does the Fault Lie?," October 20, 1911, 5; "Notice for Publication," 7; "The Missing Rib," March 1, 1912, 1; Mary C. Reeve, "A Tribute of William T. Stapley" ("on his 80th birthday" reads the second line), copy provided author by Reba Roundy LeFevre. "Delinquent Tax List," *Washington County News,* December 9, 1909, 2; "News of Our Neighbors," *Millard County Chronicle,* January 25, 1912, 1; Reba Roundy LeFevre, interview by JoAnn Sylvester Bate, September 22, 1983, 18–20.
61. "A Gala Day," *Iron County Record,* April 16, 1909, 1, lists the members of the Kanarra baseball team;

"Kanarraville," *Iron County Record,* March 17, 1916, 5, lists the members of Kanarra's east and west side teams; Reba Roundy LeFevre, interview by Fielding H. Harris, October 3, 1968, 12 of my transcript (Dixie University has since independently transcribed this interview); LeFevre, interview, July 29, 1978, 21–22; LeFevre, interview by JoAnn Sylvester Bate, September 22, 1983, 8.

62. Reba Roundy LeFevre, "Short Life History [of James Lorenzo Roundy]," 1, copy in author's possession.
63. Reba Roundy LeFevre, interview by Fielding H. Harris, October 3, 1968, 11.
64. Reba Roundy LeFevre, interview, July 29, 1978, 8–9.
65. Lynn and Ella Batty Reeves, interview, April 23, 1987, 33.
66. Reba Roundy LeFevre, interview by Tonia Ann Bate, July 21, 1983, 11.
67. Ibid., 9, 11.
68. Hazel Eagar Bringhurst, interview, July 23, 1987, 13.
69. Lynn and Ella Batty Reeves, interview, April 21, 1987, 15; Reba Roundy LeFevre, interview by Fielding H. Harris, October 3, 1968, 12.
70. Reba Roundy LeFevre, interview, July 23, 1987, 38–40; she was close enough to Nixon to refer to her as "Aunt Zeph," see Reba Roundy LeFevre, interview, January 28, 1989, 18.
71. "Cowardly Poisoning at New Harmony," *Iron County Record,* May 19, 1922, 8; "Kelsey Found Not Guilty by Murder Jury," *Salt Lake Telegram,* April 14, 1923, 2 (details of the story can be traced in this newspaper); Dr. Lloyd Wayland Macfarlane, *Dr. Mac The Man, His Land, and His People* (Cedar City, UT: Southern Utah State College Press, 1985), 275–79; Stephen L. Prince, *Gathering in Harmony* (Spokane, WA: Arthur H. Clark, 2004), 247–54.
72. Reba Roundy LeFevre, interview, January 24, 1987, 2–3.
73. William Tarbet Stapley, "Autobiography"; "Local Cullings," *Iron County News,* December 20, 1890, 8: "William Stapley of Kanarra, while out in the mountains hauling wood, fell from his load and rolling under the wagon the wheels passed over and broke one of his legs. The young man was contemplating entering the Academy here as a student after the holidays. We sincerely hope the accident may not be so bad as reported and that Will may still be able to carry out his educational project." "Intermountain Nuggets," *Salt Lake Tribune,* January 27, 1904, 3.
74. "Kanarra," *Iron County Record,* February 13, 1904, 5; also "Kanarra," apparently from a missing portion of March 5, 1904, issue but misfiled in the online version with November 21, 1903, 11 (the byline is dated March 3, 1904); William Tarbet Stapley, "Autobiography," 15.
75. "Kanarra," *Iron County Record,* February 13, 1904, 5; Reba Roundy LeFevre, interview, July 29, 1978, 21.
76. Reba Roundy LeFevre, interview, May 2, 1984, 14.
77. Reba Roundy LeFevre, interview, July 22, 1989, 12.
78. Karl G Roundy, interview, June 20, 1981, 10–11.
79. [Untitled], *Iron County Record,* October 24, 1903, 1; Fredrick Wilford Balser, interview, May 24, 1988, 1; and May 28, 1988, 1–2.
80. Reba Roundy LeFevre, interview, June 27, 1988, 23–24.
81. [Untitled], *Iron County Record,* October 24, 1903, 1; Fredrick Wilford Balser, interview, May 24, 1988, 1; and May 28, 1988, 1–2.
82. Reba Roundy LeFevre, interview by Tonia Ann Bate, July 28, 1985, 33–34.
83. Reba Roundy LeFevre, interview, November 7, 1981, 3–4; LeFevre, interview by Tonia Ann Bate, July 28, 1985, 31–33.
84. Reba Roundy LeFevre, interview by Tonia Ann Bate, July 26, 1985, 23; LeFevre, interview, July 29, 1978, 2.
85. Reba Roundy LeFevre, interview by Tonia Ann Bate, July 28, 1985, 3.
86. Reba Roundy LeFevre, interview by Fielding H. Harris, October 3, 1968, 10.
87. Julia Allyn, "Bee-Keeping for Women," *Ladies Home Journal,* 9 (April 1891): 4.
88. Reba Roundy LeFevre, interview by Tonia Ann Bate, June 12, 1983, 5–6.
89. "Bee Inspector on Rounds," *Parowan [UT] Times,* April 26, 1916, 1; from the *Iron County Record,* "To Bee-Keepers," September 8, 1916, 5; "Bee Keepers, Attention," March 5, 1915, 1; "Bee Keepers' Meeting," April 5, 1918, 8; "Doings of County Commissioners," July 5, 1918, 1; "Business of the Commissioners," October 31, 1919, 1; "Financial Statement," August 6, 1920, 5; Reba Roundy LeFevre, interview by Fielding H. Harris, October 3, 1968, 8; LeFevre, interview by Tonia Ann Bate, June 12, 1983, 5–6; LeFevre, interview by JoAnn Sylvester Bate, September 22, 1983, 1–2; Allyn, "Bee-Keeping for Women," 4.
90. Reba Roundy LeFevre, interview, May 9, 1985, 3.
91. Reba Roundy LeFevre, interview by Fielding H. Harris, October 3, 1968, 8–9; LeFevre, interview, July 29, 1978, 20; LeFevre, interview, May 2, 1984, 3–4; LeFevre, interview, April 5, 1990, 1–5; "Kanarra Notes," *Iron County Record,* April 4, 1924, 5.
92. Reba Roundy LeFevre, interview, July 29, 1978, 25.

93. Reba Roundy LeFevre, interview by JoAnn Sylvester Bate, September 22, 1983, 10–11.
94. JoAnn Sylvester Bate, interview, August 17, 1980, 8A–8B.
95. Reba Roundy LeFevre, interview by JoAnn Sylvester Bate, September 22, 1983, 14.

CHAPTER 6

1. John Steele to James Duffin, January 31, 1897, photocopy in author's possession.
2. John S. Haller Jr., *The People's Doctors: Samuel Thomson and the American Botanical Movement, 1790–1860* (Carbondale and Edwardsville, IL: Southern Illinois University Press, 2000), 287–88 for Thomsonian principles.
3. "Fatal Accident," *Deseret Weekly News,* November 23, 1894, 780.
4. John Steele to Frank J. Cannon, 1896, photocopy in author's possession.
5. John Steele to Letisha Todd, August 15, 1901, photocopy in author's possession.
6. "I am sorry to hear that my Aunt is confined to bed, & hope that under these trying circumstances she may have the best of all consolations which come from God, & I trust that your Rheumatism may shortly pass away." William Martin Campbell to John Steele, December 28, 1890, box 1, fd. 27, MSS 528, John Steele Collection, 1847–1936, L. Tom Perry Special Collections, Harold B. Lee Library, Brigham Young University, Provo, Utah (hereafter LTPSC).
7. Wanda Steele Cox, *Journals of John Steele and Mahonri Moriancumer Steele* (Cedar City, UT: self-published, 1967), 2:76–77.
8. Joseph L. Heywood to John Steele, December 10, 1891, photograph of letter in author's possession.
9. David Milne to John Steele, September 16, 1891, photograph of letter in author's possession.
10. Cox, *Steele Journals,* 2:62, 77; "Found His Wife Insane," *Salt Lake Tribune,* June 4, 1899, 5; Matilda Booth to J. Steele and "Lizzie," February 14 [1895?], box 1, fd. 14, MSS 528, LTPSC; marriage license, box 1, folder 14, MSS 528, LTPSC; Weber County Marriages Book, 2:472, entry no. 946; John Steele to Wilford Woodruff, July 15, 1896, Wilford Woodruff Collection, Church History Library, Church of Jesus Christ of Latter-day Saints, Salt Lake City, Utah (hereafter CHL).
11. "Toquerville to the Fore," *Deseret News,* April 18, 1893, 8.
12. Cox, *Steele Journals,* 2:77.
13. Oliver Ames Goold to John Steele, September 19, 1893, photocopy in author's possession.
14. Levi Savage, Journal, July 7, 1895, typescript, John D. Lee Collection, Dixie University, St. George, Utah. The transcriber of Savage's journals did them in small sections, starting the pagination over each time; hence, it's easier to find a source by date than page number.
15. John Steele to Wilford Woodruff, July 30, 1896, Wilford Woodruff Collection, CHL.
16. John Steele v. Tamar E. Steele (2nd D.C. Utah 1895), photocopy in author's possession.
17. This journal, mostly written in pencil, runs from July 14, 1897 through August 31, 1897 and is the source for the account of this visit unless otherwise noted; box 1, folder 10, MSS 528, LTPSC.
18. Reba remembered the younger Reese Williams as "Don't interfere with me. I get my feelings hurt too often." Reba Roundy LeFevre, interview by Tonia Ann Bate, July 21, 1983, 10–11.
19. John Steele to "Latita" Todd, August 2, 1897, transcript in author's possession.
20. Some sources about this wife and the difficulties of her sons can be found in the following *Salt Lake Tribune* articles: "Boys Happy in Jail," February 13, 1898, 8; "Given Another Chance," February 24, 1898, 8; "City and Neighborhoods," July 16, 1898, 8; "Found His Wife Insane," June 4, 1899, 5; "City and Neighborhood," July 19, 1898, 8; "Woman Said to Be Insane," October 19, 1899, 6; "City and Neighborhood," November 11, 1899, 8. "Says Three Boys Robbed the Store," *Salt Lake Telegram,* July 19, 1907, 3. The U.S. Federal censuses for 1900 and 1910 list Elizabeth Renick as an inmate at the Provo State Insane Asylum. Elizabeth Renick death certificate at http://www.archives.utah.gov/research/indexes/20842.htm. Besides John's diaries, the best sources for this marriage are the letters from "Lizzie" and her family in box 1, fd. 14, MSS 528, LTPSC.
21. "Parowan | Pioneer Celebrations," *Deseret News,* January 18, 1902, 7.
22. John Steele to Letisha Todd, August 15, 1901, photocopy in author's possession. A carat symbol [^] is used to note interlinear additions in the original manuscript.
23. Journal History of the Church of Jesus Christ of Latter-day Saints, 26 March 26, 1903, 6, quoting minutes of a meeting of the First Presidency held in the Salt Lake Temple that morning, CHL.
24. "Taylor," *Holbrook Argus [AZ],* March 28, 1903, 4.
25. "Shumway," *Holbrook Argus [AZ],* March 28, 1903, 4.

26. Joseph Fish to John Steele, April 27, 1903, box 1, fd. 20, MSS 528, LTPSC.
27. Josephine "Josie" Fish Barraclough to John Steele, July 8, 1903, box 1, fd. 20, MSS 528, LTPSC.
28. "Sketch of John Peter Jensen, Read October 14, 1930, Directed by himself. Edited and corrected by Rex Jensen," copy in author's possession, accessed February 18, 2016, https://familysearch.org/photos/stories/21673768.
29. "Kanarra," *Iron County Record*, August 14, 1903, 1; and "Kanarra," July 24, 1903, 1.
30. Reba Roundy LeFevre, interview, January 24, 1987, 21–22 (all interviews with Kerry William Bate unless otherwise identified).
31. John Steele's medical remedies, photocopy in author's possession.
32. Reba Roundy LeFevre, interview, April 29, 1988, 1; May 1, 1986, 6–7; January 24, 1987, 21–22; July 23, 1987, 1–21.
33. Elsie Kay Smith, interview, July 7, 1992, 13, 41.
34. Copy in author's possession.
35. Kanarraville Ward Record (Sacrament Meeting Minutes), 239 (January 19, 1902), CHL: "Bro John Steele of Toquerville was called to the stand and occupied the time upon general principles mostly." "Kanarra," *Iron County Record*, December 26, 1903, 5 (Kanarra byline December 16, 1903, and December 24, 1603 [*sic*, 1903]). The December 12, 1903, issue would have had the earlier article referred to in the December 16, 1903, byline, but that issue of this newspaper is missing. There are no preserved copies of the *Washington County News* for this time frame. "Parowan | Pioneer Celebrations," *Deseret News*, January 18, 1902, 7. His *Deseret News* obituary, almost certainly written by M. M. since it was bylined Panguitch, reports he moved to Kanarra in December, "Panguitch. Death of John Steel[e]," *Deseret News*, February 4, 1904, 14.
36. "Kanarra," *Iron County Record*, December 26, 1903, 5.
37. "Another Pioneer Gone," *Deseret Evening News*, January 5, 1904, 9.
38. "What Is Going on in Utah," *Salt Lake Tribune*, January 13, 1904, 3; "Snap Shots at Utah," *Salt Lake Telegram*, January 13, 1904, 6, reprinted from the missing January 9, 1904, *Iron County Record*; "Panguitch. Death of John Steel[e]," *Deseret News*, February 4, 1904, 14. The Logan paper reported "Father John Steele, who died at Kanarra last week, had the distinction of being one of the Mormon battalion, a pioneer into the Salt Lake valley, a pioneer into the Parowan valley, and the father of the first baby girl born in Salt Lake." "Utah State News," *Logan Republican*, January 23, 1904, 2.
39. Alice Louise Reynolds, "Woman's Intellectual Renaissance," *Young Woman's Journal* 10 (January 1899): 5.
40. Reba Roundy LeFevre, interview, May 1, 1986, 5–6.
41. Reba Roundy LeFevre, interview, January 24, 1987, 27.
42. Ibid.
43. Leonard Davis, interview, October 16, 1987, 2–3.
44. Leola Stapley Anderson, interview, November 21, 1987, 21.
45. Lella Stapley Maxfield, "History of James Stapley and His Wife, Young Elizabeth Steele," 2, copy in author's possession.
46. "Dr. E. Smith, Dentist," *Iron County Record*, January 9, 1903, 1; and [Untitled], May 7, 1909, 6; Noble Warrum, ed., *Utah since Statehood*, 4 vols. (Chicago and Salt Lake City: S. J. Clarke, 1919), 4:799–800.
47. Reba Roundy LeFevre, interview, October 16, 1987, 8–10.
48. Leola Stapley Anderson, interview, November 21, 1987, 17.
49. Reba Roundy LeFevre, interview, May 23, 1987, 27.
50. Ibid., 16.
51. Reba Roundy LeFevre, interview, May 9, 1985, 4.
52. Ibid., 5.
53. Reba Roundy LeFevre, interview, October 16, 1987, 5.
54. Leola Stapley Anderson, interview, November 21, 1987, 15.
55. Ibid., 16.
56. Elton Williams Stapley, interview, October 16, 1987, 5–6.
57. Leola Stapley Anderson, interview, November 21, 1987, 13.
58. Elton Williams Stapley, interview, October 16, 1987, 5.
59. Rebecca Alenna Stapley Williams, interview, February 1, 1988, 7.
60. Reba Roundy LeFevre, interview by Tonia Ann Bate, July 21, 1983, 29.
61. Elton Williams Stapley, interview, October 16, 1987, 6.
62. Reba Roundy LeFevre, interview, July 23, 1987, 28.
63. Gwen Sylvester Hunter, interview, June 25, 1981, 5.
64. Reba Roundy LeFevre, interview, January 24, 1987, 26.
65. Edwin Kenneth Slack, interview, November 17, 1988, 5.
66. "Court Proceedings," *The Union [St. George, Utah]*, May 7, 1896, 1; "Fifth District Court," *Salt Lake Tribune*, May 6, 1896, 5.

67. Diane Parkinson and John Parkinson, *James Parkinson of Ramsey: His Roots and His Branches England—Australia—America* (Austin, TX: Historical Publications, 1987), 106.
68. Edwin Kenneth Slack, interview, November 17, 1988, 6.
69. Toquerville Relief Society Account Book, 1868–1903, 102 (February 5, 1894); 103 (6 July 1893); 104 (January 22, April, December, 1893); 111 (1895); disbursements (April 30, November 15, 1897, 1898), CHL.
70. Toquerville General Minutes, 94 (March 20, 1898), CHL: "Several of the Brethren Spoke about Zettie Stapley keeping a disorderly house."
71. "Court Proceedings," *The Union [St. George, Utah]*, May 7, 1896, 1; "Fifth District Court," *Salt Lake Tribune*, May 6, 1896, 5.
72. "Court Proceedings," *The Union [St. George, Utah]*, September 12, 1896, 1; "Judge Higgins at St. George," *Salt Lake Tribune*, September 9, 1896, 5–6 (Zettie's husband is called "Joseph" on page 6).
73. "Sent to Asylum," *Salt Lake Herald*, September 8, 1899, 5. She is miscalled "Letta" Stapley in this report.
74. Parkinson and Parkinson, *James Parkinson*, 106.
75. The U.S. Federal census for 1900 in Toquerville, Washington County, UT, with Regula Naegle head of household.
76. Dr. Wesley Pratt Larsen, *A History of Toquerville* (n.p.: self-published, n.d.), 1:99–100.
77. Reba Roundy LeFevre, interview, June 27, 1988, 20–21.
78. Kerry William Bate, ed., "Diary of Mary Elizabeth (May) Stapley, a Schoolteacher in Virgin, Utah," *Utah Historical Quarterly* 60, no. 2 (Spring 1992): 164.
79. "Kanarra," *Iron County Record*, April 23, 1904, 5.
80. Ibid.; "Kanarra," *Iron County Record*, December 2, 1904, 2; and "Kanarra, Utah," September 28, 1906, 1; U.S. Federal 1910 census of Beaver, Beaver County, UT, with Elizabeth Limb head of household. From *The [Beaver County] Weekly Press:* [Crack-A-Jack Advertisement], March 27, 1914, 8; Ibid., April 3, 1914, 8; "Neighborhood Notes," October 29, 1915, 8; "East Ward Over Top," November 22, 1918, 5; "Wiliam Limb," January 3, 1919, 1; "Items of Interest," October 21, 1921, 6; [Untitled], November 11, 1921, 5; "Local and Personal Mention," November 25, 1921, 2; "Local and Personal Mention," April 7, 1922, 2; "Locals," February 16, 1923, 8; "Notice of Private Sale," March 23, 1923, 5; "Notice of Private Sale," April 6, 1923, 5. William Limb death certificate at http://www.archives.utah.gov/research/indexes/20842.htm.
81. Photocopy in author's possession.
82. Elton Williams Stapley, interview, October 16, 1987, 6.
83. Reba Roundy LeFevre, interview, April 23, 1987, 24–25.
84. Scott G. Kenney, *Wilford Woodruff's Journal, 1833–1898*, 9 vols. (Midvale, UT: Signature Books, 1984), 8:216, note on bottom of page.
85. "Kanarra Letter," *Iron County Record*, December 15, 1911, 1; and "Kanarra Letter," December 22, 1911, 5.
86. Reba Roundy LeFevre, interview, July 23, 1987, 24–26; LeFevre, interview by Tonia Ann Bate, July 28, 1985, 3–4; and January 24, 1987, 19–20.
87. Velma Stapley Rymer to Kerry William Bate, August 14, 1971, in author's possession.
88. Rebecca Alenna Stapley Williams, interview, February 1, 1988, 8–9.
89. Reba Roundy LeFevre, interview, January 24, 1987, 5, 19–20.
90. Ibid., 22–24.
91. From the *Iron County Record:* "Operations at Macfarlane Hospital," April 26, 1918, 5; "Kanarraville," May 3, 1918, 4; "Kanarraville," August 9, 1918, 4.
92. Dr. Lloyd Wayland Macfarlane, *Dr. Mac: The Man, His Land, and His People* (Cedar City, UT: Southern Utah State College Press, 1985), 89: "The 'delicate' or 'serious' operations performed under the less-than-ideal surgical conditions existing in Cedar City rarely went beyond appendectomies, hernia repairs, uterine suspensions, and hysterectomies."
93. "Kanarraville," *Iron County Record*, May 3, 1918, 4.
94. From the *Iron County Record:* "Sale Cheap," August 16, 1918, 4; "Sale Cheap," August 23, 1918, 4; "Sale Cheap," August 30, 1918, 5.
95. Reba Roundy LeFevre, interview, January 24, 1987, 4–5.
96. "Kanarra Letter," *Iron County Record*, December 10, 1909, 1; and "Kanarra Letter," December 24, 1909, 1; Edwin Kenneth Slack, interview, November 17, 1988, 12–13; "Toquerville," *Washington County News*, February 19, 1914, 5; Rhea Higbee Wakeling, "History of Rhea Higbee, Wife of Alva T. Wakeling," *Isaac Higbee and Sophia Somers Family Magazine* 3 (1958): 245F (also see 245D); he is listed as undertaker on George Casper Batty's (May 30, 1900–May 28, 1907) death certificate, http://www.archives.utah.gov/research/indexes/20842.htm.
97. "Kanarra Letter," *Iron County Record*, December 10, 1909, 1.
98. Edwin Kenneth Slack, interview, November 17, 1988, 12–13.

99. "Toquerville," *Washington County News,* February 19, 1914, 5.
100. Reba Roundy LeFevre, interview, January 24, 1987, 5.
101. Estella "Stella" Roundy Russell, interview by Gwen Sylvester Hunter, June 20, 1981, 2.
102. Harriet Arvilla Ford Woodbury, interview, October 16, 1987, 1–4, 6–8, 20.
103. Ibid.
104. Reba Roundy LeFevre, interview, January 24, 1987, 5; and April 24, 1987, 8.
105. From the *Iron County Record:* "Kanarra Letter," July 23, 1909, 1; "Kanarra Letter," March 4, 1910, 1; "Kanarra Letter," August 12, 1910, 1; "Kanarra Letter," August 19, 1910, 1; "Notice," August 26, 1910, 1; "Things in General," October 7, 1910, 6; "Kanarra Letter," November 25, 1910, 1; "Kanarraville," December 2, 1910, 1; "Kanarra Letter," January 20, 1911, 1; "Kanarra Letter," February 17, 1911, 4; "Kanarra Letter," March 31, 1911, 2; "Correspondent Feels Jolly," May 5, 1911, 1; "Kanarra to the Front," May 12, 1911, 1; "Kanarraville," May 10, 1912, 10; "Kanarra Letter," April 26, 1912, 1; "Seriously Injured in Rabbit Hunt," February 13, 1913, 5; "Retires from Plumbing Firm," April 4, 1913, 8; "Kanarraville," April 18, 1913, 8; "Another Serious Gun Accident," January 2, 1914, 1; "Kanarraville," January 26, 1917, 8.
106. Maxfield, "History of James Stapley," 1–2.
107. Reba Roundy LeFevre, interview, April 23, 1987, 8–9.
108. Ibid.; Reba Roundy LeFevre, interview, May 1, 1986, 1–3; October 6, 1989, 1–4; November 18, 1988, 34–35; November 19, 1988, 16–18; May 5, 1990, 7–10; LeFevre, interview by JoAnn Sylvester Bate, June 17, 1988, 5–6.
109. Reba Roundy LeFevre, January 24, 1987, 4–5.
110. Ibid., 5.
111. Rebecca Alenna Stapley Williams, interview, February 1, 1988, 7.
112. Reba Roundy LeFevre, interview, February 23, 1990, 7.
113. Reba Roundy LeFevre, interview, January 24, 1987, 5.
114. Reba Roundy LeFevre, interview, April 23, 1987, 9–13.
115. Reba Roundy LeFevre, interview, February 23, 1990, 13.
116. "Kanarra," *Iron County Record,* December 8, 1905, 1.
117. "Kanarraville," *Iron County Record,* February 20, 1914, 10.
118. Leola Stapley Anderson, interview, November 21, 1987, 18.
119. Rebecca Alenna Stapley Williams, interview, February 1, 1988, 6.
120. Leola Stapley Anderson, interview, November 21, 1987, 18.
121. Ibid., 61.
122. "Kanarraville," *Iron County Record,* May 1, 1914, 7.
123. "Our Homecoming," *Parowan Times,* October 27, 1915, 1.
124. Andrew Jenson, *Latter-day Saint Biographical Encyclopedia,* vol. 1 (Salt Lake City: Andrew Jenson, 1901, rprt. Salt Lake City: Western Epics, 1971), 543, 821.
125. When M. M. Steele, in his role as counselor in the stake presidency, gave a sermon at the Circleville LDS Church he was reported as saying, "I hope the people will vote the [Republican] ticket straight," which earned multiple indignant headlines in the *Salt Lake Tribune:* "Church Does Counsel Voters | Remarkable Attempt to Deliver Vote. | Priesthood Instructs Churchmen to Vote Republican Ticket. | Meeting Held in Meeting-House at Circleville That Attracts Much Attention," November 4, 1904, 2.
126. Robert Proctor, *The History of Panguitch* (privately printed, 2014), fourth page of the series of photographs on unnumbered pages following page 28; "Governor Spry Names Appointees," *Richfield Reaper,* March 17, 1911, 1. At a meeting in Panguitch, M. M. Steele Jr., introduced Governor Heber M. Wells and Hon. George Sutherland, senator and future U.S. Supreme Court Justice. See "Great at Panguitch," *Salt Lake Tribune,* October 15, 1900, 5. John F. Chidester—who drew up John's divorce papers—was a colleague and crony. See "Panguitch Republicans," *Salt Lake Tribune,* March 28, 1900, 3.
127. "Democratic Candidates," *Salt Lake Telegram,* September 27, 1902 (Catherine later married Job Riding and went by "Cathren"; "Rio Grande Pushing South," *Salt Lake Telegram,* December 21, 1903, 3.
128. "Our Homecoming," *Parowan Times,* October 27, 1915, 1.

CHAPTER 7

1. Rulon Berry Platt, interview, July 12, 1987, 52 (all interviews by Kerry William Bate unless otherwise indicated).
2. Reba Roundy LeFevre, interview, May 23, 1987, 26; Lynn and Ella Batty Reeves, interview, October 15, 1987, 45; for a thorough account of the story of the murder of William Shanks Berry and others, see Bruce Crow, *A Land of Strangers: Cane Creek*

Tennessee's Mormon Massacre and Its Tragic Effects on the People Who Lived There (Lewisburg, TN: AMH Press, 2013).

3. Rulon Berry Platt, interview, July 12, 1987, 44.
4. Reba Roundy LeFevre, interview, October 16, 1987, 18.
5. "Meeting House Burned," *The [Provo, UT] Evening Dispatch,* February 11, 1891, 4.
6. From the *Iron County Record:* "An Exciting Election," July 17, 1903, 1; "Kanarra Kinks," April 3, 1903, 1; "Leeds, Utah," July 31, 1903, 1; "Kanarra," December 26, 1903, 5; "Kanarra," March 26, 1904, 5; "Kanarra," June 25, 1904, 1; "Kanarra," December 2, 1904, 2.
7. Reba Roundy LeFevre, interview by JoAnn Sylvester Bate, September 22, 1983, 11; and July 29, 1978, 21.
8. "In Aug. 1971 Rosella Christensen . . . ," 1, paper in author's possession; William Charles Reeves, "History of Kanarra," (ca. 1940), 5, copy in author's possession.
9. *Southern Branch of the State Normal School of the University of Utah. Cedar City, Utah. 1905–1906* (1905), 4, 7–8, 10, 12, 17–19, 33–34, 36–39.
10. I thank Sheila Johnson of the Branch Normal School successor institution, Southern Utah University, for providing me Sarah's school transcript, September 2, 2014; for the Wesleyan University grade chart, see http://www.wesleyan.edu/registrar/general_information/grade_chart.html.
11. Kanarra Ward Record, 1905–1913, 13 (4 Mar 1906); 29 (11 Nov 1906); 54(November 10, 1907); 77 (8 November 1908), Church History Library, The Church of Jesus Christ of Latter-day Saints, Salt Lake City, Utah (hereafter CHL); from the *Iron County Record:* "Cedar City and Vicinity," June 22, 1906, 5; "Kanarra Letter," April 12, 1912, 4; "Kanarra Letter," April 19, 1912, 4; Kanarra YMMIA Minutes, 1901–1913, 115 (March 19, 1907); 26 (December 6, 1902); 33 (February 14, 1903); 87 (November 9, 1905); 95 (November 20, 1906); 96 (November 25, 1906); 115 (March 19, 1907), CHL. (The YLMIA Minutes are missing for this time period.)
12. Reba Roundy LeFevre, interview, May 1, 1986, 15; and May 9, 1985, 7–8. Reba also described the town Sarah taught in as Caliente (July 29, 1978, 21–22) and as Callio (interview with JoAnn Sylvester Bate, September 22, 1983, 11). Sarah Elizabeth Roundy Sylvester's obituary records "Callio," but a search doesn't reveal any Nevada town by that name, see "Services Held Wednesday for Sarah E. Sylvester in Hurricane," *Washington County News,* September 22, 1938, 1.
13. From the *Iron County Record:* "Kanarra Letter," December 10, 1909, 1; "Kanarra Letter," December 24, 1909, 1; "Kanarra Letter," January 14, 1910, 1; "Eighth Grade Graduation Exercises," June 10, 1910, 1. From the *Washington County News:* "Local and General News," March 12, 1908, 8; "Forestry Service Examination," April 30, 1908, 1; "Local and General News," October 22, 1908, 8; "Kanarra," October 29, 1908, 1; "Local and General News," August 12, 1909, 8; "Local and General News," October 14, 1909, 8; "Local and General News," May 12, 1910, 4; "Local and General News," June 16, 1910, 4.
14. Rulon Berry Platt, interview, May 19, 1982, 18–19.
15. Reba Roundy LeFevre, interview by JoAnn Sylvester Bate, September 22, 1983, 12–13.
16. "List of Graduates," *Iron County Record,* May 28, 1909, 1.
17. From the *Iron County Record:* "Kanarra Letter," January 21, 1910, 1; "Kanarraville," December 27, 1912, 8.
18. James Walter Goldthwait, *Diary of Western Trip 1902,* edited by Bob Oldham (Burnsville, NC: Ad Lib Press, 1982), 101. Goldthwait also wrote that "Prof. Hickman is a young man—grad of Ann Arbor." Goldthwait, himself a young man, used Toquerville as the base for his geology work in southwestern Utah and stayed at the "Stapley House"—the "hotel" run by James Stapley's brother Charles and his wife, Sarah Parkinson Stapley.
19. From the *Iron County Record:* "Kanarra Letter," August 19, 1910 1; "Winter Course in B. B. B. Y. U.," December 6, 1907, 1; "Murdock Academy," September 3, 1909, 1; Kanarra Ward Record (Sacrament Meeting Minutes), 1905–1913, 77 (November 8, 1908), CHL.
20. The following references are for the next several paragraphs about Murdock: Reba Roundy LeFevre, interview, July 29, 1978, 21–22; from *The [Beaver County, UT] Weekly Press*: "Keep the Good Work Going," January 14, 1910, 1; "New Building Week at the Murdock Academy," January 14, 1910, 1; "Briefs," January 21, 1910, 1; "Work on New School Building to Be Resumed," April 15, 1910, 1; "Murdock Sends Eight Men to Salt Lake Meet," May 13, 1910, 1; "Murdock Academy Graduates Hold Exercises at School Tuesday Evening," May 27, 1910 1; "Commencement Week," May 27, 1910, 1; "Murdock Academy Victorious," May 27, 1910, 1; "Girl's Opinion of Beautiful City," June 3, 1910, 1; "Briefs," August 26, 1910, 1; "Briefs," October 21, 1910, 1; "Briefs," October 28, 1910, 1; "M. A. Notes," January 5, 1911, 1; "Manual Training," February 3, 1911, 1; "Rev. Goshen to Lecture," March 17, 1911, 1; "Briefs," March 24, 1911,

1; "Briefs," April 7, 1911, 1; "Briefs," April 28, 1911, 1; "Schools Doing Fine Work," May 12, 1911 1; "Commencement Week at M. A.," May 19, 1911 1; "Certain Victory for Murdock," May 19, 1911, 1; "Murdock Wins State Track Meet," May 26, 1911, 1; "Briefs," May 26, 1911, 1; "Largest in Its History," June 2, 1911, 1; Murdock Academy student records, 1898–1922, LR 596 23, CHL.

21. Larry R. Gerlach, "Alma Richards's Olympic Leap of Faith Revisited," *Utah Historical Quarterly* 82, no. 2 (Spring 2014): 133–50. This is a thorough and interesting account of his Olympic career and reputation.
22. Reba Roundy LeFevre, "Things I Remember as a Child," (January 30, 1982), 1, original in author's possession.
23. Rulon Berry Platt, interview, May 28, 1982, 8.
24. "Artist Voices Objections to Sugarloaf Defacement," *Washington County News*, November 15, 1923, 1.
25. Leola Stapley Anderson, interview, November 21, 1987, 31, 51.
26. "New Harmony," *Washington County News*, August 31, 1911, 3.
27. Reba Roundy LeFevre, interview, January 24, 1987, 12; for Roma's birthdate, see Ancestry.com.
28. From the *Iron County Record*: "Kanarraville," April 11, 1913, 8; "Kanarraville," April 18, 1913, 8; "Kanarraville," June 20, 1913, 5.
29. Kanarra YMMIA Minutes, 1890–1901, 28–29 (February 13, 1894); 110 (February 26, 1899); 58–59 (17 January 1897); 63 (February 14, 1897); 68 (March 16, 1897); 92 (November 6, 1898), CHL; Sophia Parker Stapley, *Together Again: An Autobiographical History* (Oakland, CA: Third Party Associates, 1976), 84.
30. "'05 Halowe'en Song," Neils Albert Anderson Papers, Special Collections, Southern Utah University, Cedar City, Utah (hereafter SUUSC).
31. Rulon Berry Platt, interview, May 19, 1982, 16; Kanarra YMMIA Minutes, 1890–1901, 139 (March 4, 1900): "Instrumental music by David L. Davies and Henry Pollock. We were then favored with a song by Sarah Roundy and Hulda Pollock"; also Kanarra YMMIA Minutes, 1901–1913, 9–10 (February 5, 1902): "We were favored with a song by Rocina Williams Laura Parker and Sarah Roundy. After which the young men retired to their room," CHL. Reba Roundy LeFevre, interview by JoAnn Sylvester Bate, September 22, 1983, 30.
32. JoAnn Sylvester Bate, interview, August 17, 1980, 8A.
33. Kanarra Ward Record, 1905–1913, 5 (December 3, 1905); 55 (November 10, 1907; 113 (February 27, 1910); 135 (January 22, 1911), CHL.
34. Reba Roundy LeFevre, interview by Tonia Ann Bate, July 28, 1985, 1, 12; Marilyn Lovell, *History of Kanarra* (Kanarraville, UT: Kanarraville Utah Beta Chi Chapter of Beta Sigma Phi, June 1980), 22; Opal Pollock Williams, *Kanarra Is a Pretty Little Town* (privately printed, 1984), 8–9.
35. Kanarra Ward Record, 1878–1905, 264 (September 24, 1902), CHL.
36. "Regular Conference of Parowan Stake," *Iron County Record*, March 19, 1915, 1, 5.
37. Reba Roundy LeFevre, interview by Tonia Ann Bate, July 21, 1983, 2.
38. Bessie Davis and David Elmer Davis, interview, October 25, 1985, 1.
39. Reba Roundy LeFevre, interview by JoAnn Sylvester Bate, September 22, 1983, 28.
40. Leola Stapley Anderson, interview, November 21, 1987, 5.
41. Lynn Reeves and Ella Batty Reeves, interview, October 15, 1987, 21.
42. Harriet Arvilla Ford Woodbury, interview, October 16, 1987, 5.
43. "Frank [Anderson] and Lenard Slack, our hired man are in Kanarra to-night. They are attending the wedding dance given by Albert Davis and Hannah Reeves." Neils Albert Anderson to Amy Deslie Lowe [Anderson], December 11, 1908, Neils Anderson Papers, SUUSC.
44. Lynn and Ella Batty Reeves, interview, October 15, 1987, 27; "Why Do Cedar Dancers Prefer Parowan and Kanarra," *Iron County Record*, January 26, 1939, 4.
45. "Kanarra," *Iron County Record*, February 6, 1904, 5.
46. Reba Roundy LeFevre, interview by Tonia Ann Bate, June 19, 1983, 11–13.
47. Reba Roundy LeFevre, interview, July 29, 1978, 9–10; LeFevre, interview by JoAnn Sylvester Bate, September 22, 1983, 8–9.
48. Rulon Berry Platt, interview, August 2, 1985, 1, 4.
49. Lela Berry Pollock, interview, March 22, 1983, 12.
50. "The Missing Rib," *Iron County Record*, March 1, 1912, 1; "Marriage Licenses," *Salt Lake Tribune*, February 22, 1912, 7.
51. John S. McCormick and John R. Sillito, *A History of Utah Radicalism: Startling, Socialistic, and Decidedly Revolutionary* (Logan, UT: Utah State University, 2011) gives an overview of socialism in Utah. Donald Urie, socialist, was elected Cedar City mayor in fall 1911. Another socialist, Percy Wilkinson, also won as treasurer the same year, but was unable to hold office because he was not a qualified elector, see "Election Returns," *Iron County Record*,

November 10, 1911, 1; and "Things in General," November 17, 1911 8. Socialist Joseph T. Wilkinson won as mayor of the college student body in Cedar City, see "Wilkinson Wins," *Iron County Record*, July 14, 1911, 1. Evelyn K. Jones and York F. Jones, *Mayors of Cedar City* (Cedar City, UT: Cedar City Corporation, 1986), 159–68, 183–96; Thomas G. Alexander, "Political Patterns of Early Statehood," in *Utah's History*, edited by Richard D. Poll *et al.* (Provo: Brigham Young University Press, 1978), 418–21; from the *Iron County Record:* "Kanarra to the Front," May 12, 1911, 1; "Kanarra," June 25, 1904, 1; "Kanarra Installing Telephone System," April 18, 1913, 5.

52. "Serious Riot in Salt Lake," *Iron County Record*, August 15, 1913, 1.
53. "Portland Police to Arrest Women," *Iron County Record*, August 22, 1913, 1; "Dispute over American Flag is Cause of Downtown Riot; Four are Shot; I. W. W. is Held as Gunman," *Salt Lake Herald*, August 13, 1913, 1.
54. "Kanarra Letter," *Iron County Record*, August 12, 1910, 1. By August 24, 1912, nine households had gas lights including Joel Jesse Roundy, see the following from the *Iron County Record:* "Kanarra Letter," April 26, 1912, 1; "Local Patriotism and Civic Pride, 7; "Kanarra to the Front," May 12, 1911, 1; "Kanarra," June 25, 1904, 1; "Kanarra Installing Telephone System," April 18, 1913, 5; "Kanarra Letter," August 12, 1910, 1.
55. "Kanarra," *Iron County Record*, July 7, 1905, 6.
56. From the *Iron County Record*: "Local Items," July 3, 1903, 13; "Telephone is Here," August 14, 1903, 1; "Kanarra," February 13, 1904, 5; "Kanarra," June 25, 1904, 1; "Kanarraville," August 24, 1917, 4: "Reese Williams, John Stapley and Sam Pollock have taken over the Farm News Telephone system. The shareholders gave up their stock rather than help pay off a note owing by the company." "Kanarraville," *Iron County Record*, June 20, 1913, 5; Reba Roundy LeFevre, interview by Tonia Ann Bate, July 21, 1983, 13–14.
57. Neils Albert Anderson to Amy Deslie Lowe [Anderson], July 28, 1908, Niels Anderson Papers, SUUSC.
58. Reba Roundy LeFevre, interview, July 21, 1987, 13.
59. Kanarraville General Minutes, 1905–1913, especially see the minutes from 164–200 (April 14, 1912–December 9, 1913); Kanarraville General Minutes, 1914–1922, see minutes from beginning through January 18, 1914, CHL.
60. Thelma Berry Lovell, interview, June 27, 1988, 11.
61. Reba Roundy LeFevre, interview by JoAnn Sylvester Bate, September 22, 1983, 17–20.
62. Kanarra Ward Record, 1905–1913, 179 (Sacrament Meeting); 169 (June 9, 1912); 172 (July 7, 1912); 178 (Fast Day, September 1, 1912); 180–81 (October 1, 1912), CHL.
63. John Steele to Catherine Campbell Steele, May 27, 1877, box 1, fd. 12, MSS 528, John Steele Collection, 1847–1936, L. Tom Perry Special Collections, Harold B. Lee Library, Brigham Young University, Provo, Utah.
64. Kanarra General Minutes, 1905–1913, 166 (May 5, 1912); 182–83 (October 13, 1912); 170 (June 23, 1912); 196–97 (September 14, 1913); 199 (October 26, 1913); 198–99 (October 12, 1913); CHL; from the *Iron County Record*: [Untitled] April 22, 1910, 1; "Normal Notes," April 29, 1910, 1; "Normal Notes," May 6, 1910, 1; "Twelfth Annual Commencement," June 2, 1911, 1; [Untitled], August 23, 1912, 8; "Several Christmas Weddings Announced," December 27, 1912, 5; "Kanarraville," March 14, 1913, 8; "Kanarraville," April 4, 1913, 8; "Kanarraville," May 16, 1913, 5: "Band members will present Mr. Andrus with a $22 chair which is in honor of his labors in establishing a band here."; "Twenty-One Take Teachers Examination," August 8, 1913, 4; "Kanarraville," October 10, 1913, 5.
65. Kanarra General Minutes, 1905–1913, 186 (February 2, 1913); 169–70 (June 16, 1912); 172 (July 7, 1912), CHL.
66. Reba Roundy LeFevre, interview by JoAnn Sylvester Bate, September 22, 1983, 39.
67. Kanarra General Minutes, 1905–1913, 182–83 (October 13, 1912), CHL.
68. Ibid.
69. Kanarraville YWMIA Minutes, 1893–1900, 32 (January 28, 1896); Kanarra YMMIA Minutes, 1890–1901, 78 (January 29, 1898); 92 (November 6, 1898); 102 (January 8, 1898 [1899]); 133 (February 4, 1900), CHL.
70. Reba Roundy LeFevre, interview by Tonia Ann Bate, July 28, 1985, 31.
71. Ibid.
72. Ibid., 31–34; Plorn Jones Williams, interview, April 14, 1989, 14–16.
73. Rulon Berry Platt, interview, October 4, 1986, 16–19; Rulon Berry Platt and Leila Platt Heap, interview, July 26, 1985, 47–49.
74. Kanarra General Minutes, 1905–1913, 184 (December 29, 1912), CHL.
75. Rulon Berry Platt and Leila Platt Heap, interview, July 26, 1985, 59.

76. "New Harmony," *Iron County Record*, March 17, 1922 (supplement), 1; from the *Washington County News:* "New Harmony," September 25, 1913, 5; "New Harmony," March 30, 1916, 5; Reba Roundy LeFevre, interview by JoAnn Sylvester Bate, September 22, 1983, 14–15 identifies him as "George" Schmutz and also says a man named Hammond from New Harmony was interested in Sarah; Reba Roundy LeFevre, interview by JoAnn Sylvester Bate, September 22, 1983, 11, 20–21, 27–28.
77. Rulon Berry Platt, interview, October 4, 1986, 27.
78. Reba Roundy LeFevre, interview by JoAnn Sylvester Bate, September 22, 1983, 12–13.
79. Rulon Berry Platt, interview, May 19, 1982, 18.

CHAPTER 8

1. Joel H. Johnson to "Dear Children," April 25, 1869, in James Henry Martineau Collection, MS 4786, fd. 8, Church History Library, The Church of Jesus Christ of Latter-day Saints, Salt Lake City, Utah, (hereafter CHL). Johnson was then Bellevue postmaster. Geologist James Walter Goldthwait mentions Andrew F. Gregerson's "splendid orchard of apples, peaches, apricots etc." in Bellevue. See James Walter Goldthwait, *Diary of Western Trip 1902*, edited by Bob Oldham (Burnsville, NC: Ad Lib Press, 1982), 104 (July 31, 1902); and in a return visit, "At G[regerson]'s spread blankets out in shade of mulberry trees by stone wall & tried to take a nap, but hosts of flies prevented anything beyond a semi-conscious condition," 107 (August 1, 1902).
2. Victor's grandfather James Sylvester was a musician and poet who published a song, "I Am Going Away to Zion," on May 4, 1849, see John Freeman, "Collections of Songs," MS 1526, fd. 2, CHL; also see Maureen Smith Bryson and Kerry William Bate, *The Lives and Letters of the Sylvesters and Nicholsons* (Provo: Community Press, 1997), 57, 65. Victor's great-grandfather, William Nicholson, also wrote poetry (Ibid., 555); his great-uncle, Joseph Nicholson, was a musician (Ibid., 559); and Victor's grandfather's first cousin, Harry Nicholson, was an actor under the name "William Ashton" (Ibid., 563). Aping Tennyson refers to Herbert Nicholson's, "Alfred, Lord Tennyson 'In Memoriam,'" (Ibid., 593). Charles Sylvester's son John, also an engineer, was mentioned in British Prime Minister William Ewart Gladstone's earlier diaries, see M. R. D. Foot, ed., *The Gladstone Diaries, 1833–1839* (Oxford: Clarendon Press, 1968), 2:52 (August 2, 1833).
3. Ian Inkster and Maureen Smith Bryson, *Industrial Man: The Life and Works of Charles Sylvester* (Las Vegas: Jackpot Graphics, 1999).
4. Robert Glass Cleland and Juanita Brooks, *A Mormon Chronicle: The Diaries of John D. Lee, 1848–1876* (San Marino, CA: Huntington Library, 1955), 1:69 (August 6, 1848).
5. Scott G. Kenney, *Wilford Woodruff's Journal, 1833–1898*, vol. 5 (Signature Books: Midvale, UT, 1984), 276–78, 576 (May 23, 1861).
6. See "Beyond Science Fiction—NASA Tests Human-Robot Cooperation in Utah Desert," accessed July 11, 2015, http://www.nasa.gov/centers/ames/research/exploringtheuniverse/utah_robots.html; for a broader look at the NASA-Utah connection, see Thomas C. Chidsey Jr. and Rebecca M. E. Williams, "Why Are There Utah Names on Mars?," Utah Geological Survey, *Survey Notes* 47 (May 2015): 10–13.
7. "Local Items," *Iron County Record*, April 3, 1903, 1, and advertisement for "Lund Cedar and St. George Stage Co.," April 4, 1903, 4; David Spilsbury, letter to the editor, *Washington County News*, January 11, 1917, 8.
8. Bryson and Bate, *Lives and Letters*, 4.
9. "Mrs. [Jane Sylvester] Dies from Attack of Rheumatism," *Iron County Record*, July 23, 1904, 1 (page wrinkled at headline); reprinted from the *Dixie Advocate*, a newspaper that seems not to have survived.
10. Kerry William Bate and Maureen Smith Bryson, *The Joseph Sylvester Family Letters, 1882–1989* (Las Vegas: Maureen Smith Bryson, 1998), 424.
11. The marriage is reported in the online copy of the *Iron County Record*, "St. George and Locality," filed in the issue of December 5, 1903, 13, but because it reports the license was issued December 14 and the couple was married in 1904, not 1903, this page is probably part of the missing December 23, 1904, issue.
12. Bate and Bryson, *Joseph Sylvester Family Letters*, 489–92.
13. "Judge Chidester is Called to the Great Beyond," *Richfield Reaper*, July 7, 1917, 1; "Judge Chidester is Called Hence," *Iron County Record*, July 13, 1917, 1; Andrew Karl Larson to "Aunt Till," January 5, 1955, in Andrew Karl Larson Papers, MS B 144, box 2, fd. 5, Utah State Historical Society, Salt Lake City, Utah.
14. Kent Olds shared this observation with author on October 29, 1984.
15. Bate and Bryson, *Joseph Sylvester Family Letters*, 535.

16. Edwin Kenneth Slack, interview, October 16, 1987, 1–2 (all interviews are by Kerry William Bate unless otherwise indicated).
17. Arthur and Lottie Dodge Olds, interview, April 22, 1987, 1.
18. Ibid., 5.
19. Charles Andrew Olds, interview, October 11, 1984, 1; July 30, 1984, 9.
20. Edwin Kenneth Slack, interview, October 16, 1987, 2.
21. Rulon Berry Platt, interview, August 2, 1985, 24.
22. Edwin Kenneth Slack, interview, October 16, 1987, 2.
23. Charles Andrew Olds, interview, July 30, 1984, 1.
24. "A Trip through Southern Utah," *The Weekly Kansas Chief* (Troy, KS), December 24, 1896, 2.
25. Charles Andrew Olds, interview, July 30, 1984, 30.
26. Maud Sylvester Gregerson, undated manuscript page, copy in author's possession.
27. "Washington News," *Washington County News,* October 20, 1910, 3, and "Republican County Ticket and Platform," October 20, 1910, 1.
28. From the *Washington County News*: "Official Election Returns," November 12, 1908, 3; "Republican County Convention," September 22, 1910, 2; "Republican Convention," October 13, 1910, 1; "Republican County Ticket and Platform," 1; "Unofficial Election Returns," November 10, 1910, 1; "Official Vote in Washington County," November 17, 1910, 1.
29. Maud Sylvester Gregerson, undated, unnumbered manuscript page, copy in author's possession.
30. "Local and General News," *Washington County News,* April 2, 1908, 6.
31. Charles Andrew Olds, interview, July 30, 1984, 11.
32. Ibid., 4.
33. Bate and Bryson, *Joseph Sylvester Family Letters,* 243.
34. Maud Sylvester Gregerson, undated manuscript page, copy in author's possession.
35. Charles Andrew Olds, interview, July 30, 1984, 4.
36. Rulon Berry Platt, interview, May 19, 1982, 19.
37. Rulon Berry Platt, interview, May 28, 1982, 4.
38. Leon R Sylvester, SueZanna Wittwer Sylvester, Gwen Sylvester Hunter, Nell Sylvester Stout Wilson, and Ruth Sylvester Pickering, interview, August 6, 1983, 3.
39. Rulon Berry Platt, interview, May 28, 1982, 4.
40. From the *Iron County Record*: "Kanarraville," April 4, 1913, 8; "To Be Married," June 6, 1913, 1; "Parowan," June 6, 1913, 4; "Kanarraville," June 6, 1913, 4; [Untitled], July 11, 1913, 1; "Kanarraville," August 1, 1913, 4; "Kanarraville," August 8, 1913, 8; "Happily Married," August 15, 1913, 5; Reba Roundy LeFevre, interview, July 29, 1978, 22; LeFevre, interview by Tonia Ann Bate, July 21, 1983, 3; Lynn and Ella Batty Reeves, interview, January 16, 1988, 11.
41. "Kanarraville," *Iron County Record,* August 15, 1913, 8.
42. "Regular Conference of Parowan Stake," *Iron County Record,* March 19, 1915, 5.
43. Priscilla P. Roundy to Jane [Parrish Lindsay], January [1910], photocopy and transcript in author's possession.
44. Reba Roundy LeFevre, interview, October 16, 1987, 3.
45. Arthur and Lottie Dodge Olds, interview, April 22, 1987, 6–7, 11–12.
46. Rulon Berry Platt, interview July 12, 1987, 51–54.
47. Reba Roundy LeFevre, interview, January 25, 1985, 4.
48. "Toquerville," *Washington County News,* July 3, 1900, 1: "Toquerville, July 3rd. Victor Sylvester came to town the other day from the Danish ranch with a broken arm. Bro. Steel[e] set the broken limb." "Wanted to go to Toquer," Victor's daughter Gwen wrote in some cryptic notes when her father shared some of his early autobiography, "[His] Dad wouldn't let him so he went out in the meadow and tried to catch the horse. He had a good hold on the mane & the horse started spinning around—he went round & round then finally let go—He lit on the ditch bank & broke his arm—Then his Dad had to take him to Toquer anyway—Old man [John] Steele set his arm & put on splints," Bryson and Bate, *Lives and Letters,* 512–13.
49. Rulon Berry Platt and Leila Platt Heap, interview, July 26, 1985, 34.
50. Rulon Berry Platt interview, May 19, 1982, 18.
51. Rulon Berry Platt, interview, May 28, 1982, 5.
52. Charles Andrew Olds, interview, October 11, 1984, 11.
53. John Steele to Catherine Campbell Steele, May 1, 1878, box 1, fd. 12, MSS 528, John Steele Collection, 1847–1936, L. Tom Perry Special Collections, Harold B. Lee Library, Brigham Young University, Provo, Utah.
54. Wanda Steele Cox, *Journals of John Steele and Mahonri Moriancumer Steele* (Cedar City, UT: self-published, 1967), 2:6 (June 7, 1877).
55. Elton Williams Stapley, interview, April 14, 1989, 31; Sylvanus Stall, *What a Young Man Ought to Know* (Philadelphia: W. Briggs, 1897). Western novelist Frank Robertson had a similar experience with his

father when he was reading this book, see Frank C. Robertson, *A Ram in the Thicket* (Moscow, ID: University of Idaho Press, 1994), 258.

56. "National Educators Oppose Sex Hygiene," *Washington County News*, August 6, 1914, 1.
57. "Health Officer Coming," *Washington County News*, December 16, 1920, 1, and "Carrying the University of Utah to the People," December 23, 1920, 1.
58. Reba Roundy LeFevre, interview by Tonia Ann Bate, August 9, 1985, 8–9.
59. [Untitled], *Young Woman's Journal* 7, no. 9 (June 1896): 427; *Young Woman's Journal* 2, no. 2 (1890–1891): 56–62.
60. Reba Roundy LeFevre, interview by Tonia Ann Bate, August 9, 1985, 8–9.
61. "Kanarraville," *Iron County Record*, February 21, 1913, 8, and "Kanarraville," October 3, 1913, 5; William Berry Stapley, World War I draft registration card, available online at Ancestry.com; Bruce Crow, *A Land of Strangers: Cane Creek Tennessee's Mormon Massacre and Its Tragic Effects on the People Who Lived There* (Lewisburg, TN: AMH Press, 2013).
62. "Kanarraville," October 3, 1913, *Iron County Record*, 5.
63. Reba Roundy LeFevre, interview, January 25, 1985, 4; June 17, 1985, 1–11.
64. Reba Roundy LeFevre, interview, October 16, 1987, 22–23.
65. "Funeral Services for Stapely [*sic*] Infant," *Iron County Record*, June 11, 1920, 1; Richard Weldon Stapley death certificate (June 6, 1920) at http://www.archives.utah.gov/research/indexes/20842.htm. "District Court Cases Continued," *Iron County Record*, April 23, 1920, 1, and "Three Sentenced on Guilty Pleas," September 17, 1920, 1; Reba Roundy LeFevre, interview with JoAnn Sylvester Bate, September 22, 1983, 33–34.
66. Claton S. Rice, *Ambassador to the Saints* (Boston: Christopher Publishing, 1965), 88–90.
67. "Get Busy—or Lose," *Parowan Times*, May 3, 1916, 4.
68. "District Court Cases Continued," *Iron County Record*, April 23, 1920, 1; and "Three Sentenced on Guilty Pleas," September 17, 1920, 1.
69. JoAnn Sylvester Bate, interview, August 11, 1982, 36–37.
70. Reba Roundy LeFevre, interview by JoAnn Sylvester Bate, September 22, 1983, 16; Gwen Sylvester Hunter, interview, January 26, 1985, 1; "City and Local Happenings," *Iron County Record*, November 7, 1913, 4.
71. Marriage certificate for Victor Leon Sylvester and Sarah Elizabeth Roundy lists as witnesses Annis Roundy and Florence M. Joseph, copy in author's possession. From the *Iron County Record*: "Parowan," [supplement] October 15, 1909, 1; "Notice," December 3, 1909, 1; "Kanarra Letter," December 10, 1909, 1; "Parowan Letter," March 4, 1910, 1; "Kanarraville," July 19, 1912, 8; "Stake Conference Well Attended," September 27, 1912, 1 (picture of Marsden); [Untitled], June 6, 1913, 1; "Happily Married," August 15, 1913, 5; "Parowan Department," December 26, 1913, [online issue filed under December 19, 1913, as page 17]; "Prominent Man [L. N. Marsden] Died in Hospital Friday Morning," October 24, 1931, 1; "Large Crowd Pays Tribute to Marsden," October 28, 1931, 1, 4.
72. Charles Andrew Olds, interview, July 30, 1984, 13.
73. "Kanarraville," *Iron County Record*, November 14, 1913, 5.
74. From the *Washington County News*: "New Harmony," October 3, 1912, 3; "Local and General News," September 19, 1912, 8; "New Harmony," July 11, 1912, 2. For Barney's physical description—medium height, stout build, blue eyes, dark brown hair—see World War I draft registration card, available online at Ancestry.com; "Daniel Barney Obituary," [Idaho Falls] *Post-Register*, March 6, 1958, 15.
75. Kanarra YMMIA Minutes, 1901–1913, 167 (November 9, 1913), CHL.
76. Lynn Reeves and Ella Batty Reeves, interview, April 21, 1987, 3.
77. Reba Roundy LeFevre, interview by JoAnn Sylvester Bate, September 22, 1983, 16.
78. Ibid., 18.
79. The *Iron County Record* is missing between May and December 1914, but the weather is described by the New Harmony correspondent to the *Washington County News* in late June: "New Harmony," *Washington County News*, July 9, 1914, 5; Reba Roundy LeFevre, interview by JoAnn Sylvester Bate, September 22, 1983, 16; Leon R Sylvester, SueZanna Wittwer Sylvester, Gwen Sylvester Hunter, Nell Sylvester Stout Wilson, and Ruth Sylvester Pickering, interview, August 6, 1983, 16–17.
80. Bate and Bryson, *Joseph Sylvester Family Letters*, 40–41.
81. Ibid., 32.
82. Leola Stapley Anderson, interview, November 21, 1987, 15.
83. Ibid., 33.
84. Nell Sylvester Wilson, interview, June 22, 1984, 13–14.

85. From the *Iron County Record*: "Notice for Publication," March 19, 1920, 7; "Notice for Publication," March 26, 1920, 7; "Notice for Publication," April 2, 1920, 7; "Notice for Publication," April 9, 1920, 7; "Notice for Publication," April 16, 1920, 7.
86. Neils Albert Anderson to Amy Deslie Lowe [Anderson], December 3, 1908, Neils Albert Anderson Papers, Special Collections, Southern Utah University, Cedar City, Utah.
87. Rulon Berry Platt, interview, May 28, 1982, 2.
88. A picture of the women in the club was provided to me by Reba Roundy LeFevre, who also identified the club members. From the *Iron County Record*: "Kanarraville," April 7, 1916, 5; "Kanarraville," August 18, 1916, 1; "Kanarraville," October 20, 1916, 1; "Kanarraville," February 2, 1917, 5; "Kanarraville," February 9, 1917, 1; "Kanarraville," March 29, 1918, 4.
89. Lynn and Ella Batty Reeves, interview, January 16, 1988, 1–2.
90. Ibid., 8–9.
91. "Announcement," *Everybody's Poultry Magazine*, March 1917, 235.
92. "Kanarraville," *Iron County Record*, April 2, 1915, 1.
93. "Classified Advertisements," *Everybody's Poultry Magazine*, March 1917, 326–29; and Henry P. Schwab, "Everybody's Chats," March 1917, 350.
94. "Kanarraville," *Iron County Record*, February 2, 1917, 5, and "Kanarraville," February 9, 1917, 1.
95. Leola Stapley Anderson, interview, November 21, 1987, 27–29.
96. Reba Roundy LeFevre, interview, January 15, 1987, 34.
97. JoAnn Sylvester Bate, interview, August 17, 1980, 8A.
98. From the *Iron County Record:* "Kanarraville," April 7, 1916, 5; "Kanarraville," August 18, 1916, 1; "Kanarraville," October 20, 1916, 1; "Kanarraville," February 2, 1917, 5; "Kanarraville," February 9, 1917, 1.
99. Leola Stapley Anderson, interview, November 11, 1987, 28.
100. "Kanarraville," *Iron County Record*, March 29, 1918, 4.

CHAPTER 9

1. "Joseph T. Wilkinson Honored by Posterity," *Iron County Record*, March 30, 1917, 1; and "Active Useful Career is Ended," August 8, 1919, 1; Evelyn K. Jones and York F. Jones, *Mayors of Cedar City* (Cedar City, UT: Southern Utah State College, 1986), 107–14.
2. Estella "Stella" Roundy Russell, interview by Gwen Sylvester Hunter, June 20, 1981, 2–4.
3. "Hurricane," *Washington County News*, March 29, 1917, 5.
4. From the *Iron County Record:* "Local Items," March 26, 1909, 4; "Normal Notes," October 15, 1909, 1; "Things in General," April 7, 1911, 4; "Things in General," August 11, 1911, 4; [Untitled], September 15, 1911, 4; "Normal Notes," April 26, 1912, 4; "Athletic Team Goes to Win," May 24, 1912, 2; "City and Local Happenings," July 12, 1912, 5; [Untitled], August 23, 1912, 1; "City and Local Happenings," August 23, 1912, 5; "Several Christmas Weddings Announced," December 27, 1912, 5; [Untitled], April 11, 1913, 6; "Twenty-One Take Teachers' Examination," August 8, 1913, 4; "City and Local Happenings," August 29, 1913, 4; "B. A. C. vs. All-Stars," November 28, 1913, 1; "Modena," March 20, 1914, 4; S. R. Wilkinson, "What is Drudgery?" April 17, 1914, 6; "Cedar City Happenings," May 22, 1914, 10; S. R. Wilkinson, "Physical Education in the Public Schools," January 29, 1915, 5; "District School Meet at Murdock Academy," April 30, 1915, 1; "How Cedar City Will Celebrate," July 16, 1915, 1; [Untitled], August 20, 1915, 1; "Cedar City Happenings," December 17, 1915, 8; "Cedar City Happenings," June 15, 1917, 8; "Local Briefs," August 3, 1917, 8; [Untitled], July 5, 1918, 3; [Untitled], August 9, 1918, 3; "Local Briefs," September 13, 1918, 4; Reba Roundy LeFevre, interview, July 29, 1978, 22–23 (all interviews are with Kerry William Bate unless otherwise indicated).
5. Fredrick Wilford Balser, interview, May 28, 1988, 20. Sandra Dawn Brimhall and David A. Hales, "Frances R. Burke: Toquerville Presbyterian Missionary," *Utah Historical Quarterly* 72, no.2 (Spring 2004): 164–65 says a similar line was applied to John R. Wilkinson who married a Toquerville girl and refused to give a wedding dance until he was hoisted on a fence pole and forced to pay up. (Brimhall and Hales cite Mark Pendleton and Jacob Trapp, "Mission Bell Retired," an unpublished manuscript in their possession. I haven't been able to find such a John R. Wilkinson in preliminary research and wonder if he might actually be Stephen R., who married a Toquerville girl.)
6. "Cedar City News Letter," *Parowan Times*, November 15, 1916, 1.
7. "Co. Commissioners to Provide Poison," *Iron County Record*, January 12, 1917, 1. Neither Estella Roundy Russell nor Reba Roundy LeFevre named the trustee, but the school board member who lived in Kanarra was James W. Williams.

8. Estella "Stella" Roundy Russell, interview by Gwen Sylvester Hunter, June 20, 1981, 2–4.
9. Ibid.
10. Reba Roundy LeFevre, interview, January 24, 1987, 6.
11. Kanarraville Relief Society Minutes, 1895–1915, vol. 2, 23 (February 9, 1899), Church History Library, The Church of Jesus Christ of Latter-day Saints, Salt Lake City, Utah (hereafter CHL).
12. Sophia Parker Stapley, *Together Again: An Autobiographical History* (Oakland, CA: Third Party Associates, 1976), 99.
13. Reba Roundy LeFevre, interview by Tonia Ann Bate, July 26, 1985, 14–15.
14. Kanarraville Relief Society Minutes, 1895–1915, vol. 2, 33–34 (February 3, 1900), CHL.
15. Kanarraville Relief Society Minutes, 1889–1897, vol. 1, [unpaginated], February 6, 1890, February 20 [1890], and March 20, [1890]; Kanarraville Statistical Report, July 31, 1890, and April 3, 1890, CHL.
16. Kanarraville Relief Society Minutes, 1889–1897, vol. 1, [unpaginated], February 7, 1894; 1895–1915, vol. 2, 5 (October 30, 1895), CHL.
17. Kanarraville Relief Society Minutes, 1889–1897, vol. 1, [unpaginated], June 7, 1894, CHL.
18. Ibid., March 17, 1892, May 19, 1891, and November 19, 1892; 1895–1915, vol. 2, 12 (January 28, 1897), CHL.
19. Kanarraville Relief Society Minutes, 1895–1915, vol. 2, 12 (January 28, 1897), CHL.
20. Kanarraville Relief Society Minutes, 1889–1897, vol. 1, [unpaginated], January [?] 1894, CHL.
21. Kanarraville Relief Society Minutes, 1895–1915, vol. 2, 14 (March 4, 1897), CHL.
22. Ibid., 18 (January 19, 1898); 18 (February 4, 1898); 32, financial report ending December 31, 1899; 21 (June 5, 1899); 38 ("April" 1900), CHL.
23. Ibid., 82 (June 8, 1905), CHL.
24. Ibid., 91, CHL.
25. Ibid., 122 (November 3, 1911) reports the reorganization and the positions assigned to each new officer, CHL.
26. Thelma Berry Lovell, interview, June 27, 1988, 10; Kanarraville Relief Society Minutes, 1895–1915, vol. 2, 122 (November 3, 1911), CHL. Frances Williams's first name was usually spent Francis, whether that's correct I don't know.
27. Reba Roundy LeFevre, interview, January 15, 1988, 43–44; Marilyn Lovell, *History of Kanarraville* (Kanarraville, UT: Kanarraville Utah Beta Chi Chapter of Beta Sigma Phi, 1980), 20; Thelma Berry Lovell, interview, June 27, 1988, 2, 5–6.
28. Harriet Arvilla Ford Woodbury, interview, January 31, 1988, 8; Lynn and Ella Batty Reeves, interview, January 16, 1988, 13–14; Reba Roundy LeFevre, interview, January 15, 1988, 24.
29. Kanarraville Relief Society Minutes, 1895–1915, vol. 2, 124 (March 7, 1912), CHL.
30. Thelma Berry Lovell, interview, June 27, 1988, 2, 5. This was apparently when they got firewood for the meeting house. Albert Anderson wrote his fiancé from Anderson's Junction, "Yesterday they had a wood hauler's supper and dance." Neils Albert Anderson to Amy Deslie Lowe (Anderson), August 18, 1908, Neils Albert Anderson Papers, Special Collections, Southern Utah State University, Cedar City, Utah.
31. Kanarraville Relief Society Minutes, 1895–1915, vol. 2, undated financial statement following page 130 (December 7, 1913), CHL.
32. Reba Roundy LeFevre, interview, February 1, 1988, 27–31.
33. Fredrick Wilford Balser, interview, May 28, 1988, 11.
34. Reba Roundy LeFevre, interview by Tonia Ann Bate, July 28, 1985, 34; Estella Roundy Russell, "Biography of Sarah Catherine Stapley [Roundy]," 1, copy in author's possession.
35. Kerry William Bate, *The Ebenezer Hanks Story* (Provo: M.C. Printing, 1982), 209–10; "City and Local Happenings," *Iron County Record*, August 30, 1912, 5.
36. Byron David Stout, ed., *The Diaries of David Fisk Stout* (self-published, n.d.), esp. 393 for this time frame; "Rockville," *Washington County News*, September 19, 1912, 4; from the *Iron County Record*: "City and Local Happenings," September 6, 1912, 7; "Kanarraville," 10; "Kanarraville," October 4, 1912, 8; Kerry William Bate and Maureen Smith Bryson, *The Joseph Sylvester Family Letters, 1882–1989* (Las Vegas, NV: Maureen Bryson, 1998), 24.
37. "City and Local Happenings," *Iron County Record*, August 30, 1912, 5; and "Kanarraville," August 30, 1912, 8.
38. "Kanarraville," *Iron County Record*, September 6, 1912, 10.
39. [Untitled], *Washington County News*, May 26, 1910, 1: "Among thirty Relief Society nurses who were awarded diplomas last Thursday evening at Salt Lake City appears the names of two Washington county ladies, Phoebe Allen and Vinnie Sylvester." "Gives Diplomas to Nurses," *Salt Lake Herald*, May 21, 1910, 12; "Nurses of Relief Society Graduated," *Salt Lake Telegram*, May 20, 1910, 3 (Vinnie was one of the "independent" nurses, not a "Relief

Society" nurse); for a biographical sketch of Lovinia Sylvester Leeds, see Maureen Smith Bryson and Kerry William Bate, *The Lives and Letters of the Sylvesters and Nicholsons* (Provo: Community Press, 1997), 496–503.

40. "Kanarraville," *Iron County Record*, October 4, 1912, 8.
41. "Delinquent Tax List," *Iron County Record*, November 29, 1912, 3.
42. "Kanarraville," *Iron County Record*, October 4, 1912, 8.
43. Reba Roundy LeFevre, interview by Tonia Ann Bate, July 28, 1985, 34.
44. Ibid., 35.
45. Thelma Berry Lovell, interview, June 27, 1988, 2.
46. Reba Roundy LeFevre, interview by JoAnn Sylvester Bate, September 22, 1983, 36–37.
47. Kanarraville Relief Society Minutes, 1895–1915, vol. 2, 145 (February 4, 1915), CHL.
48. Maryanne Campbell Wilson to M. M. Steele, January 1, 1915 (misdated 1914), transcript by Iona J. Poling in author's possession.
49. Sylva May Davies Williams, interview, June 27, 1988, 5.
50. From the *Iron County Record*: "City and Local Happenings," July 26, 1912, 5; Kate Macfarlane, "Our Public Library," December 26, 1913, 22 (filed in the online version with the issue of December 19, 1913, includes a picture of Mrs. Watson); "Republican Ladies Page," November 3, 1916, 4.
51. From the *Iron County Record*: "Republican Ladies Page," November 3, 1916, 4; "Democratic Ladies Page," November 3, 1916, 5; "Sweeping Democratic Victory," November 10, 1916, 1.
52. "Sweeping Democratic Victory," *Iron County Record*, November 10, 1916, 1.
53. "Local and General News," *Washington County News*, October 1, 1914, 8.
54. "We Share This Opinion," *Iron County Record*, November 10, 1916, 1.
55. "War Clouds," *Iron County Record*, February 9, 1917, 4.
56. Sylva May Davies Williams, interview, June 27, 1988, 5.
57. "Kanarraville," *Iron County Record*, April 20, 1917, 7.
58. "Kanarra," *Iron County Record*, June 1, 1917, 5.
59. Leland Campbell Stapley, World War I draft registration card, available online at Ancestry.com.
60. "Kanarra," *Iron County Record*, June 8, 1917, 5.
61. "Liberty Loan Roll of Honor," *Iron County Record*, June 15, 1917, 1.
62. "Kanarra," *Iron County Record*, July 6, 1917, 5.
63. "Conscription List for Iron County," *Iron County Record*, July 27, 1917, 1; and "Draft Board Still Examining," August 17, 1917, 1.
64. "Men Who Will Fight our Battles," *Iron County Record*, August 24, 1917, 1.
65. Shirley Sylvester death certificate at http://www.archives.utah.gov/research/indexes/20842.htm; Reba Roundy LeFevre, interview, July 23, 1987, 30–33; and January 28, 1989, 19–21.
66. Reba Roundy LeFevre, interview, July 23, 1987, 30–33; and January 28, 1989, 19–21.
67. Ibid.
68. "2nd Contingent of Men Depart," *Iron County Record*, September 21, 1917, 1; and Thomas Lund, "From Lund to Camp Lewis," September 28, 1917, 1.
69. Leola Stapley Anderson, interview, November 21, 1987, 36.
70. "Kanarraville," *Iron County Record*, June 14, 1918, 4; Rebecca Alenna Stapley Williams, interview, February 1, 1988, 14.
71. Stapley, *Together Again*, 220.
72. Lorenzo Wendell Davis, World War I draft registration card, available online at Ancestry.com.
73. Wells Allison Williams, World War I draft registration card, available online at Ancestry.com.
74. "New Iron Co. Registrants," *Iron County Record*, September 20, 1918, 1.
75. "District Exemption Board Reports on Appeal Cases," *Iron County Record*, September 21, 1917, 1; ElRoy Smith Jones, *John Pidding Jones: His Ancestors and Descendants* (Salt Lake City: American Press, 1972), 232–40; "Memorial Services for our Gold Stars," *Iron County Record*, February 21, 1919, 1; "Gives Up Life," *Parowan Times*, August 28, 1918, 1.
76. John Wallace Stewart, World War I draft registration card, available online at Ancestry.com.
77. Moroni Kleinman, World War I draft registration card, available online at Ancestry.com.
78. Moroni Kleinman, "One of Our Marine Boys Writes to his Mother," *Washington County News*, December 27, 1917, 1.
79. Ibid.; "First Dixie Boy to Lose Life on Battlefield," July 25, 1918, Moroni Kleinman, Utah State Archives and Records Service, Salt Lake City, Utah; Moroni Kleinman, World War I draft registration card, available online at Ancestry.com.
80. From the *Washington County News*: "Registration List June 5, 1917," June 21, 1917, 1 (his full name was John Wallace Stewart); "Washington County's Registration," July 19, 1917, 5; "Toquerville," August 2, 1917, 5; "Toquerville," October 24, 1918, 5; "Marines

Had a Good Time on Christmas," February 20, 1919, 5; "Toquerville," February 27, 1919, 5; "Local and General News," February 27, 1919, 8; "Toquerville," September 4, 1919 (paper misdated on front page but hand corrected), 5; John Wallace Stewart, World War I draft registration card, available online at Ancestry.com.

81. From the *Iron County Record:* "Kanarraville," September 28, 1917, 4; "Kanarraville," July 5, 1918, 4; Leland C. Stapley, "Thru Fire of Hell without a Scratch," February 14, 1919, 1; "War Experiences from Iron County Soldier's Diary," April 18, 1919, 2.
82. "Second Liberty Loan Subscribers," *Iron County Record,* November 16, 1917, 4; and "Liberty Loan Roll of Honor," April 26, 1918, 8.
83. Rebecca Alenna Stapley Williams, interview, February 1, 1988, 14–15.
84. Kanarra General Minutes, 1914–1922, 90 (September 2, 1917), CHL.
85. Ibid., 112 (June 26, 1918 [1919]), CHL.
86. "Red Cross is in Financial Straits," *Iron County Record,* March 15, 1918, 1.
87. Reba Roundy LeFevre, interview, February 1, 1988, 24–26.
88. "Cedar Ladies Do Red Cross Work," *Iron County Record,* January 11, 1918, 1.
89. Reba Roundy LeFevre, interview by Tonia Ann Bate, July 28, 1985, 34; and May 23, 1987, 22.
90. Lynn and Ella Batty Reeves, interview, January 16, 1988, 21.
91. Rebecca Alenna Stapley Williams, interview, February 1, 1988, 15.
92. Reba Roundy LeFevre, interview, February 1, 1988, 30.
93. From the *Iron County Record*: "Red Cross Ladies Are Still Active," March 1, 1918, 1; "Red Cross Is in Financial Straits," March 15, 1918, 1; "Kanarraville," March 29, 1918, 4.
94. "Successful Red Cross Campaign," *Iron County Record,* June 22, 1917, 1 (note there are two page ones in this issue, I'm referring to the second page one in the online copy).
95. Ibid.; "Kanarraville," *Iron County Record,* June 7, 1918, 4. For a useful account of Utah women during World War I, see Miriam B. Murphy, "'If Only I Shall Have the Right Stuff': Utah Women in World War I," *Utah Historical Quarterly* 58, no. 4 (Fall 1990): 334–50.
96. Reba Roundy LeFevre, interview by Tonia Ann Bate, July 28, 1985, 34.
97. Kanarra General Minutes, 1914–1922, 100 (March 17, 1918), CHL.
98. Belle Case La Follette and Fola La Follette, *Robert M. La Follette: June 14, 1855–June 18, 1925* (New York: MacMillan, 1953), 1:626–44; "Satan Abdicates in Favor of Kaiser," *Iron County Record,* November 30, 1917, 2.
99. From the *Iron County Record*: "Local Defense Committees," November 30, 1917, 2; [Untitled], January 4, 1918, 2; "Apparently No Cause for Suspicion as Spy," April 5, 1918, 4; Emily Crane Watson, "Library Notes," April 12, 1918, 8; Reba Roundy LeFevre interview, by Tonia Ann Bate, July 21, 1983, 1. U.S. Federal census 1900 for San Francisco, California with Eilersficken as head of household; "Hypnotism," *San Francisco Call,* November 21, 1902, [want ads], 12. Apparently he had a wife previous to May Stout for "Mrs. Eilersficken, formerly Miss Mott, clairvoyant medium; readings daily, 25c, 50c" offered her services from the same 34 and Sixth Street address (Ibid). May Stout had previously been married to a man surnamed Cabbage, accessed August 26, 2015, https://familysearch.org/ark:/61903/1:1:XL4R-6X9. "Your Rheumatism," *Los Angeles Herald,* July 26, 1908, pt. 4:4; and [Untitled], August 9, 1908, 4:3. Samuel T. Black, *San Diego County, California: A Record of Settlement, Organization, Progress and Achievement* (Chicago: S. J. Clark Publishing, 1913), 2:326 gives a very useful biography of Eilersficken. The *Report of the Attorney General of California* shows case number 409: "F. B. C. Eilersficken—San Diego. Illegal Practice, Medicine, April 23, 1915" (70), with the case pending appeal on December 31, 1915; [Untitled], *Parowan Times,* December 19, 1917, 8, and business advertisement on same page; "$25 Reward," *Parowan Times,* April 24, 1918, 8. May Stout Eilersficken—apparently not related to the well-known Utah Stout family—qualified for the DAR by her descent from Ensign James Morgan of Middlesex County, NJ (National Society, Daughters of the American Revolution. *Daughters of the American Revolution Lineage Books* (152 Vols.), database online at Ancestry.com. Eilersficken's World War I draft registration card was dated October 7, 1918, and gives his permanent address as 1504 Monroe Avenue, San Diego, CA, but explains he was then living in Beaver, Utah. World War I draft registration card, available online at Ancestry .com; "Mystery Revealed," *Beaver County Weekly Press,* March 7, 1919, 8.
100. Reba Roundy LeFevre, interview by JoAnn Sylvester Bate, September 22, 1983, 23–26 (inadvertently there is no page 25 in this transcript).

101. From the *Iron County Record*: "The Lid is Off—The Ban is Lifted," February 7, 1919, 1; "Kanarra," February 14, 1919, 5; "Memorial Services for our Gold Stars," February 21, 1919, 1; "Kanarra," March 7, 1919, 3; [Untitled], May 9, 1919, 2, [Untitled], May 9, 1919, 4; "Soldier's Day Big Success," May 23, 1919, 1, 4.
102. Kanarra General Minutes, 1914–1922, 112 (June 26, 1918 [1919]), CHL.
103. Reba Roundy LeFevre, interview, October 12, 1984, 14.
104. Kanarra General Minutes, 1914–1922, 112 (June 26, 1918 [1919]), CHL.
105. Reba Roundy LeFevre, interview, January 15, 1988, 32; LeFevre, interview by Tonia Ann Bate, June 19, 1983, 10–11.
106. Kanarra General Minutes, 1914–1922, 117–18 (May 18, 1919), CHL.
107. Leola Stapley Anderson, interview, November 21, 1987, 22.
108. "Kanarra," *Iron County Record*, February 7, 1919, 8.
109. "Local Items," *Iron County Record*, April 4, 1919, 8; Reba Roundy LeFevre, interview, July 29, 1978, 31–32.
110. Reba Roundy LeFevre, interview by Tonia Ann Bate, August 4, 1985, 36; From the *Iron County Record*: [Untitled], June 28, 1918, 6; "For Sale-Miscellaneous Wanted," April 18, 1919, 5; [Untitled], June 28, 1918, 6; [Untitled want ads], April 18, 1919, 5; "For Sale-Miscellaneous," May 30, 1919, 8: "FOR SALE.—New No. 10 Royal Typewriter—$50.00—F. Eilersficken, Kanarraville. Adv. 1w." This is the only time we find his name associated with Kanarra. He was in Beaver before he went to Parowan and moved back to Beaver by November 1918 ([want ad], *Beaver County Weekly Press*, November 22, 1918, 8) and left Beaver May 1, 1919 ("Chiropractor Leaves," *Beaver County Weekly Press*, May 2, 1919, 1). He must have stayed at least a few weeks in Kanarra in May 1919, when he was trying to sell his typewriter. It was likely then he examined Young Elizabeth Steele Stapley. Reba Roundy LeFevre, interview by JoAnn Sylvester Bate, September 22, 1983, 25–26.
111. "Kanarra," *Iron County Record*, May 2, 1919, 2.
112. Reba Roundy LeFevre, interview by Tonia Ann Bate, July 28, 1985, 2.
113. "Toquerville," *Washington County News*, September 4, 1919 (front page of newspaper is misdated August 28, 1919), 5.
114. Leola Stapley Anderson, interview, November 21, 1987, 13–14.
115. From the *Iron County Record:* "Kanarra," August 1, 1919, 8; "Kanarraville," October 3, 1919, 8; "Kanarra," February 7, 1919, 8; "Kanarra," March 7, 1919, 3; "Kanarraville," December 5, 1919, 5; "Kanarra," February 7, 1919, 8; "Kanarra," February 14, 1919, 5; "Locals," June 20, 1919, 3.
116. From the *Iron County Record*: "Kanarra," June 13, 1919, 3; "Kanarra," August 1, 1919, 8; "Kanarra," January 23, 1920, 5; "Kanarra," February 27, 1920, 3.
117. From the *Iron County Record*: "Kanarra," August 1, 1919, 8; "Kanarra," January 23, 1920, 5; "Kanarra," February 27, 1920, 3; "Local Column Overflow," *Washington County News*, June 10, 1920, 4.
118. Reba Roundy LeFevre, interview by Tonia Ann Bate, June 12, 1983, 7.
119. "Kanarra," *Iron County Record*, January 23, 1920, 5.
120. Ibid.
121. Ibid.
122. Rulon Berry Platt, interview, May 19, 1982, 35.
123. From the *Iron County Record*: "Kanarraville," November 28, 1919, 4; "Kanarraville," December 5, 1919, 5; "Kanarraville," December 19, 1919, 8; Joseph W. Summerhays, et al., *Jubilee History of Latter-day Saints Sunday Schools, 1849–1899* (Salt Lake City: Deseret Sunday School Union, 1900), 259 shows Joel J. Roundy became Kanarra Sunday School Superintendent, November 19, 1899. Reba Roundy LeFevre, interview by Tonia Ann Bate, July 21, 1983, 21–25.
124. William Grant Platt, "Kanarraville," *Iron County Record*, January 2, 1920, 8.
125. "Castlegate Disaster is far Reaching," *Washington County News*, March 13, 1924, 1.
126. Reba Roundy LeFevre, interview, May 2, 1984, 1–2.
127. Reba Roundy LeFevre, interview, January 24, 1987, 28; and May 23, 1987, 25.
128. From the *Iron County Record*: "Kanarraville," January 16, 1920, 8; "Kanarra," October 29, 1920, 5; "Kanarra," December 31, 1920, 7; "Kanarra," February 4, 1921, 8; "Twenty-Nine Get B. A. C. Diplomas," May 27, 1921, 1.

CHAPTER 10

1. James Jepson Jr., "Memories and Experiences of James Jepson, Jr.," 25–26, B-103, box 16, fd. 1, typescript, Juanita Brooks Collection, Utah State Historical Society, Salt Lake City, Utah (hereafter USHS); John Steele to James Jepson, Jwnly [July] 1, 1893, transcript by Iona J. Poling in author's possession; James Jepson to James G. Bleak, June 17, 1900, MS B 144, box 9, fd. 29, Andrew Karl Larson Papers, USHS; "Second District Court," *Salt Lake*

Tribune, September 22, 1883, 4; [J. Cecil Alter], "Extracts from the Journal of John Steele," *Utah Historical Quarterly* 6, no. 1 (January 1933): 25. For the founding of Hurricane, see Andrew Karl Larson, *I Was Called to Dixie* (Salt Lake City: Deseret News Press, 1961), 382–402; Douglas D. Alder and Karl F. Brooks, *A History of Washington County from Isolation to Destination* (Salt Lake City: Utah State Historical Society and Washington County Commission, 1996), 193–97; William R. Palmer, "The Hurricane Canal," No. 1, I-H/q-a/xiii f8-b22, William R. Palmer Collection, Southern Utah University; Alice Gubler Stratton, *The Story of the Hurricane Canal* (Hurricane, UT: Hurricane Valley Pioneer Heritage Park Foundation, 1992); Leila Larson, "The Origin and Growth of Hurricane," Washington County Library, St. George, Utah. Lucy J. Isom, *History of James Jepson, Sr. and his wife, Eleanor Nightingale* (privately published, ca. 1962). Jepson was brother-in-law to John Steele's son Mahonri Moriancumer Steele, and John joined others in petitioning to get Jepson released from prison for an accidental murder (John's June 10, 1884, letter to Governor Arthur L. Thomas, accompanied by the petition, is in the Utah State Archives, no. 2130, TE-0 00.4, box 13; for the murder, see "The Homicide," *Salt Lake Herald*, January 6, 1883, 8).

2. Estella Roundy Russell, interview by Gwen Sylvester Hunter, June 20, 1981, 1.
3. Reba Roundy LeFevre, interview by Tonia Ann Bate, July 28, 1985, 46–47.
4. "Kanarraville," *Iron County Record*, June 7, 1918, 4; and "Kanarraville," June 28, 1918, 4; Reba Roundy LeFevre, interview by Tonia Ann Bate, June 19, 1983, 1–2.
5. Reba Roundy LeFevre, interview by Tonia Ann Bate, July 28, 1985, 47.
6. Ibid.
7. "Twenty-Nine Get B. A. C. Diplomas," *Iron County Record*, May 27, 1921, 1; "LaVerkin," *Washington County News*, January 15, 1920, 4.
8. From the *Washington County News*: "LaVerkin," January 15, 1920, 4; "LaVerkin," January 8, 1920, 5; "LaVerkin," January 29, 1920, 1; "Toquerville," January 29, 1920, 4; "Hurricane," January 29, 1920, 5; "Toquerville," February 19, 1920, 5; "Many Homes Invaded by Influenza Scourge," February 12, 1920, 1.
9. "Pres. E. S. Romney Called," February 13, 1920, *Washington County News*, 1; and "Erastus Snow Romney Passes Useful Life," February 19, 1920, 1. From the *Iron County Record*: "Bulletin Report on Health Conditions," February 6, 1920, 1; "Influenza Claims Its First Victim," February 6, 1920, 1; "Wife and Mother Called by Death," February 6, 1920, 1; "Local Happenings," February 13, 1920, 8; "Kanarraville," February 20, 1920, 5; "Kanarra," February 27, 1920, 3; "Kanarra," March 12, 1920, 3; Reba Roundy LeFevre, interview by Tonia Ann Bate, June 19, 1983, 2.
10. "Kanarraville," *Iron County Record*, February 20, 1920, 5; and "Kanarra," February 27, 1920, 3. "Utah Pioneer of 1847 is Dead at Kanarra," *Deseret News*, February, 27, 1920; Leonard J. Arrington, "The Influenza Epidemic of 1918–19 in Utah," *Utah Historical Quarterly* 58, no. 2 (Spring 1990): 165–82.
11. From the *Washington County News*: "Fruit Trees in Blossom," February 26, 1920, 1; "Beneficial Rains," February 26, 1920, 1; "Unusual Weather," April 22, 1920, 1; "LaVerkin," March 18, 1920, 5; "Hurricane," April 1, 1920, 5; "Hurricane," April 8, 1920, 1.
12. "Kanarra," *Iron County Record*, February 27, 1920, 3; Reba Roundy LeFevre, interview, July 29, 1978, 31 (all interviews are with Kerry William Bate unless otherwise indicated); LeFevre, interview by Tonia Ann Bate, July 21, 1983, 31–32.
13. "LaVerkin," *Washington County News*, April 15, 1920, 5; Hurricane Ward Records, Sacrament Meeting Minutes, CR 3983 11, no. 2, 11 (April 11, 1920), Church History Library, Church of Jesus Christ of Latter-day Saints, Salt Lake City, Utah (hereafter CHL); Hurricane Relief Society History and Minutes, 1920 rolls and June 1, 1920, Minutes, CHL.
14. From the *Washington County News*: "Hurricane," August 14, 1919, 1; "District Court," August 21, 1919, 1; "Hurricane," October 9, 1919, 5. As late as 1924, when Elmer Bradshaw wanted to put up a pool hall, he built it in Virgin. "Hurricane," *Washington County News*, July 17, 1924, 5.
15. "Hurricane," *Washington County News*, October 23, 1919, 5.
16. Virgil D. White, *Index to Indian Wars Pension Files, 1892–1926* (Waynesboro, TN: National Historical Publishing, 1987), 2:1468. His pension was granted October 11, 1917. "Veterans of Indian War Allowed Pensions," *Ogden Standard Examiner*, April 5, 1918, 8. James Stapley made a 160-acre land entry in 1899, section 18, township 28 south, range 12 west, see "Land Entries," *Salt Lake Herald*, June 24, 1899, 3.
17. Reba Roundy LeFevre, interview by Tonia Ann Bate, August 4, 1985, 37.
18. "Kanarra," *Iron County Record*, February 27, 1920, 3.
19. Reba Roundy LeFevre, interview, May 23, 1987, 7–8.
20. Reba Roundy LeFevre, interview, July 29, 1978, 12–23.

21. James Stapley death certificate at http://axaem.archives.utah.gov/cgi-bin/indexesresults.cgi?RUNWHAT=IDXFILES&KEYPATH=IDX208420076027.
22. "Hurricane for Roads and Reclamation," *Washington County News*, May 27, 1920, 1.
23. Leola Stapley Anderson, interview by James Clive Davis, November 24, 1979, 62 (I've transcribed this and included it with the interview I did with Mrs. Anderson on November 21, 1987). Kanarraville General Minutes, Book D, 1914–1922 (January 4, 1914, to March 19, 1922), 131–32 (May 21, 1920), CHL.
24. Rebecca Alenna Stapley Williams, interview, February 1, 1988, 5, 12.
25. Reba Roundy LeFevre, interview by Tonia Ann Bate, August 4, 1985, 37.
26. "District Court Proceedings," *Iron County Record*, September 30, 1921, 1; and "Probate and Guardianship Notice," November 4, 1921, 4. For an advertisement for Shay & Lunt, see Ibid.
27. Reba Roundy LeFevre, interview by Tonia Ann Bate, August 4, 1985, 12.
28. Reba Roundy LeFevre, interview, January 15, 1988, 15–16; "Hurricane," *Washington County News*, November 18, 1920, 5.
29. White, *Index to Indian Wars Pension Files*, 2:1471. His pension was granted June 18, 1917. "Veterans of Indian War Allowed Pensions," *Ogden Standard Examiner*, April 5, 1918, 8.
30. Reba Roundy LeFevre, interview by Tonia Ann Bate, August 4, 1985, 37.
31. Harriet Arvilla Ford Woodbury, interview, October 16, 1987, 8.
32. Leola Stapley Anderson, interview, November 21, 1987, 31.
33. Elsie Kay Smith, interview, July 7, 1992, 29–30.
34. Ibid., 30.
35. "Kanarra," *Iron County Record*, October 29, 1920, 5 (Kanarra byline October 26, 1920). Joan Sylvester birth certificate in author's possession, signed by registrar W. C. Reeves; "Bergstrom-Pond Nuptials," *Iron County Record*, October 8, 1920, 1.
36. Reba Roundy LeFevre, interview by Tonia Ann Bate, August 4, 1985, 34.
37. "Hurricane," *Washington County News*, November 18, 1920, 5.
38. Reba Roundy LeFevre, interview, January 24, 1987, 25–26; LeFevre, interview by Tonia Ann Bate, July 21, 1983, 32–33.
39. "List of Junior High School Graduates," *Washington County News*, May 5, 1921, 1.
40. "Hot Weather," *Washington County News*, July 1, 1926, 5; and "Veyo," July 1, 1926, 5.
41. Reba Roundy LeFevre, interview, May 1, 1986, 1–4
42. Reba Roundy LeFevre, interview, May 9, 1985, 4.
43. "Hurricane," *Washington County News*, April 28, 1921, 5.
44. Reba Roundy LeFevre, interview, November 19, 1988, 12.
45. "Melbourne DeMill" [obituary], *Salt Lake Tribune*, April 22, 1950, 18; "Melbourne DeMill" [obituary], *Salt Lake Telegram*, April 22, 1950, 14; "South Ward Sustains New Bishopric," *Richfield Reaper*, May 21, 1931, 1; from the *Washington County News*: "Rockville," January 21, 1909, 4; "Springdale Doings," March 17, 1910, 4; "Hurricane," May 8, 1913, 4; "Liberty Loans Oversubscribed in Utah," November 1, 1917, 5; "Hurricane Prospering, Many New Buildings," August 23, 1917, 1; Reba Roundy LeFevre, interview by Tonia Ann Bate, June 19, 1983, 5–6; and May 2, 1984, 1, 6.
46. "Local Happenings," *Iron County Record*, January 30, 1920, 8.
47. "Hurricane," *Washington County News*, April 26, 1923, 5.
48. Reba Roundy LeFevre, interview by Tonia Ann Bate, June 19, 1983, 5–6; and May 2, 1984, 1, 6.
49. "Local Happenings," *Iron County Record*, January 30, 1920, 8; "Hurricane," *Washington County News*, April 26, 1923, 5; from the *Washington County News*: "Grafton," January 15, 1920, 5; "LaVerkin," November 24, 1921, 5; "Rockville," November 24, 1921, 5; "Hurricane," November 24, 1921, 6; "Short Creek," February 23, 1922, 5. "Final Rites Held for Victim of Truck Accident [Joseph Haslam]," *Iron County Record*, December 19, 1935, 5; Joseph Ezekiel Haslam death certificate at http://www.archives.utah.gov/research/indexes/20842.htm. Reba Roundy LeFevre, interview by Tonia Ann Bate, June 19, 1983, 5–6; and May 2, 1984, 1, 6.
50. Reba Roundy LeFevre, interview, May 1, 1986, 45–46.
51. "Hurricane Making Substantial Growth," *Washington County News*, September 25, 1924, 1.
52. Reba Roundy LeFevre, interview, May 1, 1986, 46.
53. "Hurricane," *Washington County News*, January 3, 1924, 5; Reba Roundy LeFevre, interview, May 9, 1985, 43.
54. Reba Roundy LeFevre, interview, May 1, 1986, 48.
55. "Kanarra Notes," *Iron County Record*, February 4, 1924, 2; Reba Roundy LeFevre, interview, April 5, 1990, 1–5; and May 2, 1984, 3–4.
56. For Reba's own appendicitis, see "Hurricane," *Washington County News*, April 13, 1922, 5; Reba

Roundy LeFevre, interview by Fielding H. Harris, October 3, 1968, 9.

57. Ibid.
58. Ibid.; Reba Roundy LeFevre, interview, May 5, 1990, 19; LeFevre, interview, October 12, 1984, 10; LeFevre, interview, April 5, 1990, 1–4; Dr. George Russell Aiken, interview, April 7, 1990, 9–10; George Russell Aiken, *The Doc Aiken Story: Memoirs of a Country Doctor* (n.p., 1989), 77; Reba Roundy LeFevre, interview, May 2, 1984, 3–4.
59. Dr. George Russell Aiken, interview, April 7, 1990, 9–10.
60. Reba Roundy LeFevre, interview, May 2, 1984, 1–2.
61. Ibid.
62. Ibid., 5.
63. For Harding's fatal western trip, see Robert K. Murray, *The Harding Era: Warren G. Harding and His Administration* (Minneapolis: University of Minnesota Press, 1969), 438–51; and Francis Russell, *The Shadow of Blooming Grove: Warren G. Harding in His Times* (New York: McGraw-Hill, 1968), 576–92, esp. 577–78. For a gossipy account of Harding's wife, see Carl Sferrazza Anthony, *Florence Harding: The First Lady, the Jazz Age, and the Death of America's Most Scandalous President* (New York: William Morrow, 1998).
64. Senator Reed Smoot's important role in Harding's Utah trip is outlined in Smoot's diary, Book 33: 43 (April 11, 1923); 46 (April 18, 1923); 46 (April 2, 1923); 48 (April 26, 1923); 49 (Apr 30, 1923); 50 (May 2, 1923); 51–52 (May 7, 1923); 61 (June 5, 1923); 62–63 (June 8, 1923); 64 (June 11, 1923); 66 (June 15, 1923); 67 (June 17, 1923); 70 (June 21, 1923); 71 (June 23, 1923); 71–72 (June 25–26, 1923); 73 (June 27, 1923), MSS 1187, box 4B, Reed Smoot Papers, L. Tom Perry Special Collections, Harold B. Lee Library, Brigham Young University, Provo. Utah.
65. Reba Roundy LeFevre, interview, October 12, 1984, 21; and January 15, 1988, 32–33; LeFevre, interview by Tonia Ann Bate, August 4, 1985, 32–33.
66. "Republicans Meet," *Iron County Record,* September 14, 1906, 1.
67. The following are useful sources for President Harding's Zion's Park visit: "A Great Day for Utah's Dixie," *Washington County News,* June 28, 1923, 1; "Southern Utah Gives Glad Welcome to Nation's Chief Executive," *Iron County Record,* June 29, 1923, 1; from the *Washington County News*: "Zion's Park Included in Harding's Itiner'y," May 31, 1923, 1; "President Harding Coming to Zion Park," June 14, 1923, 1; "Pres. Harding Sure to Visit Zion Park," June 21, 1923, 1; "The President in Zion National Park," (reprinted from the *Salt Lake Tribune*) July 5, 1923, 4; "Springdale," July 5, 1923, 5; "Mrs. Harding Game, but She Balks at Riding Zion Horse," *Ogden Standard Examiner,* June 28, 1923, 1–2; "President and Mrs. Harding Pay Visit to Our State," *Richfield Reaper*, 1, 4, 11; from the *Salt Lake Telegram:* "Pres. Harding Impressed by Park Scenery," June 28, 1923, 1; E. J. David, "Harding Sees Scenic Masterpieces," June 28, 1923, 2; "Wonderland of Utah Viewed by Nation's Chief," *Salt Lake Tribune,* June 28, 1923, 1, 3; Andrew Karl Larson, *The Education of a Second Generation Swede* (Salt Lake City: Deseret Press, 1979), 321–24; Eldon Larson to Karl and Katharine Larson, October 7, 1969, MS B144, box 2, fd. 5, Andrew Karl Larson Papers, USHS; Andrew Karl Larson, "Zion National Park with Some Reminiscences Fifty Years After," 16–19, Ibid., box 9, fd. 27 (I have used the most marked-up draft). The final version was published, A. Karl Larson, "Zion National Park with Some Reminiscences Fifty Years Later," *Utah Historical Quarterly* 37, no. 4 (Fall 1969): 409–25.
68. "A Great Day for Utah's Dixie," *Washington County News,* June 28, 1923, 1.
69. Ibid.; Larson, *Education of a Second Generation Swede,* 321–24; Eldon Larson to Karl and Katharine Larson, October 7, 1969, MS B144, box 2, fd. 5, USHS; Andrew Karl Larson, "Zion National Park with Some Reminiscences Fifty Years after," 16–19, Ibid., box 9, fd. 27; A. Karl Larson, "Zion National Park with Some Reminiscences Fifty Years Later," *Utah Historical Quarterly* 37, no. 4 (Fall 1969): 409–25.
70. Edwin Kenneth Slack, interview, April 29, 1988, 10–11; "A Great Day for Utah's Dixie," *Washington County News,* June 28, 1923, 1.
71. "A Great Day for Utah's Dixie," *Washington County News,* June 28, 1923, 1: "American Legion boys in uniform, most of them with medals, one of whom, a young man named Peterson, was conspicuous because of the number of medals and two crosses" (Peterson was Naegle's birth surname).
72. "Toquerville," *Washington County News,* January 11, 1923, 5.
73. "District Court," *Washington County News,* April 21, 1921, 1; "Toquerville," November 1, 1923, 4.
74. Edwin Kenneth Slack, interview, April 29, 1988, 10.
75. "Governor's Chauffeur Is Reported Lost," *Salt Lake Telegram,* June 28, 1923, 2; "Two Policemen Left Behind by President," June 28, 1923, 11.
76. "The President in Zion National Park," *Washington County News,* July 5, 1923, 3, quoting the *Salt Lake*

Tribune; E. J. David, "Harding Sees Scenic Masterpieces," *Salt Lake Telegram*, June 28, 1923, 2: "There was not a little regret expressed as the auto caravan passed a deserted winery. There were some in the party who were moved to refer to Omar Khayyam's epic concerning the jug of wine."

77. "Lawbreakers Pay Penalty," *Washington County News*, January 3, 1924, 1.
78. Nell Murbarger, *Sovereigns of the Sage* (Palm Desert, CA: Desert Magazine Press, 1958), 190. Murbarger's story is based on her interview with Toquerville resident Lorine Lamb Higbee.
79. "A Great Day for Utah's Dixie," *Washington County News*, June 28, 1923, 1.
80. Ibid.
81. Ibid.; "Southern Utah Gives Glad Welcome to Nation's Chief Executive," *Iron County Record*, June 29, 1923, 1.
82. Mike R. Winder and Ronald L. Fox, *When the White House Comes to Zion* (American Fork, UT: Covenant Communications, 2011), 57 shows a hand-tinted picture of President Harding with, among others, Young Elizabeth Steele Stapley.
83. "A Great Day for Utah's Dixie," *Washington County News*, June 28, 1923, 1.
84. Norma Bringhurst Empey, interview by Fielding H. Harris, June 30, 1969, 31 (transcript at Special Collections, Dixie University, St. George, Utah).
85. "Springdale," *Washington County News*, July 5, 1923, 5; "Wonderland of Utah Viewed by Nation's Chief," *Salt Lake Tribune*, June 28, 1923, 3.
86. Larson, *Education of a Second Generation Swede*, 321–24; A. Karl Larson, "Zion National Park with Some Reminiscences Fifty Years Later," *Utah Historical Quarterly* 37, no. 4 (Fall 1969): 409–25.
87. "Zion Park Praises Echo from Presidential Party While in Yellowstone," *Washington County News* (reprinted from the *Deseret News*) July 12, 1923, 1.
88. Lynn and Ella Batty Reeves, interview, October 15, 1987, 75–77.
89. "A Great Day for Utah's Dixie," *Washington County News*, June 28, 1923, 1.
90. Edwin Kenneth Slack, interview, April 29, 1988, 11.
91. "Republican Co. Convention," *Washington County News*, July 6, 1922, 1; and "Announcement," August 10, 1922, 1; Peg Mcentee, "WWI Soldier's [Walter Anderson] Purple Heart Awarded to His Grandson," *Salt Lake Tribune*, July 27, 2013, A1–A4; Whitney Evans, "Family Accepts Purple Heart Almost 100 Years after Service," *Deseret News*, July 27, 2013, B1–B6; *Congressional Record—Senate*, July 23, 2013, S5834 https://www.congress.gov /congressional-record/2013/7/23/senate-section /article/s5834-2?q=%7B%22search%22%3A%5B %22walter+anderson%22%5D%7D&resultIndex=3. Anderson had a distinguished career in Salt Lake, becoming a Democratic county commissioner.
92. From the *Washington County News*: April 12, 1923, 8; July 26, 1923, 1; "Enterprise Carnival was Big Success," August 2, 1923, 1; "Nation Mourns Death of Beloved Leader," August 9, 1923, 1. By the next year Jarvis had turned radio salesman.
93. From the *Washington County News:* "Local and General News," August 2, 1923, 1; "Nation Mourns Death of Beloved Leader," August 9, 1923, 1; "Memorial Service for Pres. Harding," August 16, 1923, 1.
94. Lynn and Ella Batty Reeves, interview, October 15, 1987, 77.
95. Copy in author's possession.

CHAPTER 11

1. Hans Gregerson, "Andrew Ferdinand Gregerson," 13–14 (May 19, 1975), Edna Gregerson Collection, Dixie University Library, St. George, Utah; Maureen Smith Bryson and Kerry William Bate, *The Lives and Letters of the Sylvesters and Nicholsons* (Provo: Community Press, 1997), 374–438; Althea Gregerson Hafen, *The Life of Andrew Ferdinand Gregerson* (self-published, n.d.), 2, 4, 8. Neils Albert Anderson to Amy Deslie Lowe, December 11, 1908:

    > While getting some rocks out of the road, who should I see but Arthur Greagerson. He was sober this morning. We talked for a while. He wanted to know what I "had done with that Lowe girl." Now, why should he connect our names in any way? Poor Arthur! He seems to be going down the hill without putting on the brake . . . 8:30 P.M. Now I will try to finish this letter to-night. I see I was telling you about Arthur. This is the first I have seen him for three years. He looks somewhat the worse for his having followed the life of a minor. Mineing isn't a good occupation for some young men. I feel sorry for Arthur. He was exceptionally bright.

    Neils Anderson Papers, Special Collections, Southern Utah University (hereafter SUUSC).
2. For Victor's siblings, see Bryson and Bate, *The Lives and Letters of the Sylvesters and Nicholsons*, 472–551.
3. "Normal Notes," *Iron County Record*, February 26, 1909, 2; and "Normal Notes," March 30, 1909, 1.

4. J. W. Paxman, "The Great Southern Utah Dry-Farm District: Kanarra, Cedar and Parowan Valleys, Iron County," *Parowan Times*, March 7, 1917, 5; J. W. Paxman, "Dry Farming in Utah Valley," *Iron County Record*, May 22, 1914, 1; Neils Albert Anderson to Amy Deslie Lowe, June 28, 1908: "We shall cut grain this coming week. It is all dry land grain but it has done much better than any we have ever irrigated," Neils Anderson Papers, SUUSC.
5. "Dry Farming. Kanarra to the Front," *Deseret Farmer*, August 15, 1908, 4.
6. "Kanarraville," *Iron County Record*, January 1, 1915, 1.
7. "Crowds See County Fair," *Iron County Record*, September 15, 1916, 1.
8. "Kanarraville," *Iron County Record*, August 30, 1918, 4.
9. Janet Burton Seegmiller, *A History of Iron County Community above Self* (Salt Lake City: Utah State Historical Society, Iron County Commission, 1998), 101, 173, 175, 179, 182–83; also see Carlton Culmsee's aptly named article, "Flimflam Frontier: Submarginal Land Development in Utah," *Utah Historical Quarterly* 32, no. 2 (Spring 1964): 91–98, which discusses Nada in Iron County.
10. "Parowan," *Iron County Record*, September 15, 1916, 5.
11. From the *Iron County Record*: "Notice for Publication," March 19, 1920, 7; "Notice for Publication," March 26, 1920, 7; "Notice for Publication," April 2, 1920, 7; "Notice for Publication," April 9, 1920, 7; "Notice for Publication," April 16, 1920, 7.
12. "Kanarra," *Iron County Record*, September 23, 1921, 5.
13. "Delinquent Tax List," *Iron County Record*, December 9, 1921, 9.
14. "Kanarra," *Iron County Record*, December 31, 1920, 7.
15. "Kanarra," *Iron County Record*, February 11, 1921, 8.
16. Alice Isom Gubler Stratton, *Look to the Stars*, 37–38, accessed August 5, 2013, http://www.aarongifford.com/alice/looktothestars/chapter07.html. Stratton dates this 1919, but Joel Roundy still lived in Kanarra then.
17. William R. Palmer, "Indian Names in Utah Geography," *Utah Historical Quarterly* 1, vol. 1 (January 1928): 11; "History of Hiko and Pahranagat Valley," *Salt Lake Mining Review*, December 30, 1920, 26.
18. "Keller's Sad Plight; Lost on Desert," *Washington County News*, July 15, 1915, 1.
19. "Bidding for Homeseekers," *Washington County News*, September 8, 1921, supplement, 1.
20. Ibid.; from the *Washington County News*: [Untitled], September 15, 1921, 1; "Local and General News," October 6, 1921, 8; "Hurricane," August 3, 1922, 7; "Hurricane," June 14, 1923, 5 [7 online copy]; "Hurricane," June 28, 1923, 7; "Local and General News," November 29, 1923, 10.
21. Charles Andrew Olds, interview, July 30, 1984, 24 (all interviews by Kerry William Bate unless otherwise indicated).
22. Reba Roundy LeFevre, interview, July 30, 1984, 2.
23. Charles Andrew Olds, interview, July 30, 1984, 25.
24. Reba Roundy LeFevre, interview by Tonia Ann Bate, August 4, 1985, 42–43; LeFevre, interview by Tonia Ann Bate, July 28, 1985, 44; LeFevre, interview, April 23, 1987, 13; "Hurricane," *Washington County News*, April 13, 1922, 5.
25. Reba Roundy LeFevre, interview, January 15, 1988, 11; LeFevre, interview by Tonia Ann Bate, August 4, 1985, 43.
26. JoAnn Sylvester Bate and Gwen Sylvester Hunter, interview, June 26, 1985, 16.
27. Nell Sylvester Wilson, interview, June 22, 1984, 5.
28. JoAnn Sylvester Bate, interview, August 17, 1980, 1.
29. Nell Sylvester Wilson, interview, June 22, 1984, 3–5. For purposes of clarity I have rearranged the sentences in the first paragraph.
30. Ibid., 4.
31. Reba Roundy LeFevre, interview, July 30, 1984, 1–2.
32. Charles Andrew Olds, interview, July 30, 1984, 24.
33. Arvil Hanks Davis, interview, August 8, 1982, 9; and January 24, 1985, 1.
34. Leon R and SueZanna Sylvester, Gwen Sylvester Hunter, Nell Sylvester Stout Wilson and Ruth Sylvester Pickering, interview, August 6, 1983, 1.
35. Ibid.
36. Ibid.
37. Leonard Davis, interview, October 16, 1987, 1.
38. Reba Roundy LeFevre, interview, May 2, 1984, 6–8.
39. Nell Sylvester Wilson, interview, June 22, 1984, 6.
40. Reba Roundy LeFevre, interview, May 2, 1984, 12–13.
41. JoAnn Sylvester Bate and Gwen Sylvester Hunter, interview, June 26, 1985, 12.
42. Reba Roundy LeFevre, interview by Tonia Ann Bate, August 4, 1985, 31; and May 5, 1990, 6–7.
43. Reba Roundy LeFevre, interview, May 1, 1986, 6–7.
44. JoAnn Sylvester Bate, interview, August 17, 1980, 16.
45. "Hurricane," *Washington County News*, April 9, 1925, 5 (this issue is missing from the Utah digital newspaper collection but is in the microfilmed collection at the Utah State Historical Society, Salt Lake City, Utah).

46. JoAnn Sylvester Bate, "If I Had It to Do Over Again: The Story of My Life, Book 1," unpaginated in a yellow Mead spiral notebook in author's possession.
47. Reba Roundy LeFevre, interview, May 2, 1984, 8; LeFevre, interview by Tonia Ann Bate, July 21, 1983, 29; and July 23, 1987, 36; and February 1, 1988, 5.
48. Ruth Sylvester Pickering, interview, May 4, 1984, 7.
49. Kerry William Bate and Maureen Smith Bryson, *The Joseph Sylvester Family Letters, 1882–1989* (Las Vegas, NV: Maureen Bryson, 1998), 54.
50. Ibid., 337.
51. Bate, "If I Had It to Do Over Again."
52. Ibid.
53. Leon R and SueZanna Sylvester, Gwen Sylvester Hunter, Nell Sylvester Stout Wilson and Ruth Sylvester Pickering, interview, August 6, 1983, 17; JoAnn Sylvester Bate, first interview, September 14, 1983, 8–9.
54. Florence Beatty Leavitt, interview, April 27, 1988, 22–23.
55. "Hurricane," *Washington County News*, March 5, 1925, 5.
56. Reba Roundy LeFevre, interview, May 2, 1984, 13.
57. JoAnn Sylvester Bate, interview, August 17, 1980, 4–5.
58. JoAnn Sylvester Bate, interview, August 24, 1980, 1.
59. JoAnn Sylvester Bate, first interview, September 14, 1983, 7; and August 24, 1980, 2.
60. Recording provided by Nell Sylvester Stout Wilson to author June 20, 1981.
61. JoAnn Sylvester Bate, interview, August 24, 1980, 2.
62. JoAnn Sylvester Bate, "Once Is Enough My Life," Typescript (1978), 1, copy in author's possession.
63. Reba Roundy LeFevre, interview, July 21, 1983, 2.
64. Bate, "Once Is Enough My Life," 1–2.
65. Reba Roundy LeFevre, interview, July 21, 1983, 2; "Why Do Cedar Dancers Prefer Parowan and Kanarra," *Iron County Record*, January 26, 1939, 4.
66. Florence Beatty Leavitt, interview, April 27, 1988, 16.
67. JoAnn Sylvester Bate, interview, August 24, 1980, 11–12.
68. Ibid., 12.
69. Ibid., 3.
70. Ibid.
71. Ibid., 7.
72. Ibid.
73. JoAnn Sylvester Bate, first interview, September 14, 1983, 6–7.
74. JoAnn Sylvester Bate, interview, August 17, 1980, 8A.

CHAPTER 12

1. "Suicide Near Kanarra," *Iron County Record*, March 26, 1926, 1; Lynn Reeves, interview, June 27, 1988, 1–9 (all interviews are by Kerry William Bate unless otherwise indicated).
2. "Kanarra," *Iron County Record*, September 20, 1918, 4.
3. Arthur Clifton (Clinton) Sechrest, death certificate at http://www.archives.utah.gov/research/indexes/20842.htm. Jimmy's daughter Alenna said her father was called out to Sechrest's because he was a notary public (Rebecca Alenna Stapley Williams, interview, February 1, 1988, 18–19) but the newspaper shows Jimmy had been appointed justice of the peace in 1922, see [Untitled], *Iron County Record*, November 10, 1922, 1. If Stapley served a four-year term he would still have been justice of the peace in March 1926.
4. Lynn Reeves, interview, June 27, 1988, 6.
5. James Steele Stapley death certificate at http://www.archives.utah.gov/research/indexes/20842.htm. "Services for James S. Davis [Stapley]," *Iron County Record*, April 9, 1926, 1; and "A Correction [of the Davis/Stapley name]," April 16, 1926, 1; Rebecca Alenna Stapley Williams, interview, February 1, 1988, 18–19.
6. Thomas G. Alexander, *Edward Hunter Snow: Pioneer—Educator—Statesman* (Norman, OK: Arthur H. Clark, 2012) is a useful biography of Snow, a pivotal figure in southwestern Utah in his day.
7. From the *Washington County News*: [Untitled], April 1, 1926, 1 [note: this issue is not digitized but can be consulted on microfilm at the Utah State Historical Society, Salt Lake City, Utah]; "Local and General News," April 1, 1926, 8; "Dixie Pioneer Passes to Heavenly Rest," April 8, 1926, 1; "Mother of Kumen D. Williams Passes Away at Kanarra," April 22, 1926, 1.
8. Leola Stapley Anderson, interview, November 21, 1987, 37–38.
9. Reba Roundy LeFevre, interview, January 15, 1988, 43–44.
10. "Services for James S. Davis [Stapley]," *Iron County Record*, April 9, 1926, 1; and "A Correction," April 16, 1926, 1.
11. "Funerals at Kanarra," *[Provo] Daily Herald*, March 13, 1924, 2; E. J. David, "Survey at Castle Gate Fails to Disclose Financial Distress among Victims' Dependents," *Salt Lake Telegram*, March 13, 1924, 1.

12. "Kanarra," *Iron County Record,* April 4, 1921, 8; Sophia Parker Stapley, *Together Again: An Autobiographical History* (Oakland, CA: Third Party Associates, 1976), 221; Ronald G. Watt, *A History of Carbon County* (Salt Lake City: Utah State Historical Society, Carbon County Commission, 1997), 149–53; "Fate of Host of Utah Miners Is Yet Undisclosed," *Helena Independent,* March 10, 1924, 1–2; Saline Hardee Fraser, "One Long Day That Went On Forever," compiled by Marianne Fraser, *Utah Historical Quarterly* 48, no. 4 (Fall 1980): 379–89. From the *Salt Lake Telegram* on March 11, 1924: Harvey Hancock, "Hope Wrecked, Loving Hearts Wait for Dead," 1; "Rescue Crews Find Battered Forms of Dead," 1, 7; E. J. David, "Castle Gate Victims Die Instantaneously from Terrible Blast," 1, 7; "List of Dead," 1; "Iron County Towns Mourn Miner Dead," 7; "Mine Passage Described as Great Canyon," 7; "Coal on Walls Coked by Heat," 7 (note: page 7 is page 13 on the digital file). Especially useful is W. DeVere Pollock's "The Castle Gate #2 Coal Mine Explosion," December 25, 1991, written in the form of a letter, he describes what William B. Stapley was doing that day, copy in author's possession.
13. "Hurricane," *Washington County News,* June 14, 1923, 5 (because this newspaper has a supplement the electronic copy of the page is 7); Mahonri M. Steele death certificate at http://www.archives.utah.gov/research/indexes/20842.htm; "M. M. Steele, Sr., Passes Away at Salt Lake," *Garfield County News,* September 21, 1923, 1; and [Untitled], September 28, 1923, 5.
14. Maud Sylvester Gregerson, undated, untitled manuscript, copy in author's possession; "Toquerville," *Washington County News,* May 7, 1908, 1.
15. Kenneth L. Alford, ed., *Civil War Saints* (Provo, UT: Religious Studies Center, BYU, 2012), 435–36.
16. "Toquerville," *Washington County News,* May 13, 1909, 2; and "Toquerville Loses Charming Young Lady," September 16, 1909, 5.
17. From the *Washington County News*: "Toquerville," February 1, 1912, 3; "Toquerville," February 15, 1912, 1; "Toquerville," February 22, 1912, 1; "Toquerville," February 29, 1912, 3; "Branch Normal Notes," March 7, 1912, 1; "Toquerville," March 14, 1912, 4; "Local and General News," March 14, 1912, 8; "Saints in Conference," March 21, 1912, 1; "Eventful Life Closed," March 21, 1912, 1; "Toquerville," March 21, 1912, 3. William A. Bringhurst death certificate at http://www.archives.utah.gov/research/indexes/20842.htm. Josiah Granville Leach, *History of the Bringhurst Family with Notes on the Clarks, De Peyster and Boude Families* (Philadelphia: J.P. Lippincott, 1901), 86 and picture facing same. For Bringhurst saving a half-buried, three-year-old Piute toddler, see "Piute Barbarity," *Harrisburg [PA] Telegraph,* August 6, 1879, 3.
18. "Toquerville," *Washington County News,* August 8, 1912, 2; and "Toquerville," August 15, 1912, 5.
19. "Toquerville," *Washington County News,* September 23, 1915, 5; and "Toquerville," September 30, 1915, 3.
20. "Toquerville," *Washington County News,* October 6, 1921, 5 (her Christian name is given as "Sussane").
21. "Toquerville," *Washington County News,* May 28, 1925, 5.
22. "Toquerville," *Washington County News,* October 29, 1925, 5; Susan Bringhurst death certificate at http://www.archives.utah.gov/research/indexes/20842.htm.; "Susan Bringhurst," *Salt Lake Telegram,* August 19, 1927, 21. Her name has been given as Susann, Susanna, and Susan. It is Susan in her death notice. She appears to have been named for Susan Smith Adams (wife of Orson Bennet Adams). Adams, like Catherine Campbell Steele, was a laundress in the Mormon Battalion and she and her husband were also early Parowan settlers. See Mary E. Adams, "A Short Sketch of the Life of Orson B. and Susan Adams Smith," accessed August 10, 2015, http://www.cedarcity.org/DocumentCenter/View/7591.
23. "Kanarra," *Iron County Record,* February 13, 1925, 5; and "Kanarra Boy Killed by Horse," October 26, 1928, 1; "Young Horseman Gravely Injured," *Ogden Standard Examiner,* October 4, 1928, 2; "Kanarra Man Injured When Thrown from Horse," *Salt Lake Telegram,* October 25, 1928, 7; "Rider Falls, Foot Catches," *Salt Lake Tribune,* October 24, 1928, 15.
24. "Teachers for Next Year Approved by the Board," *Parowan Times,* May 1, 1929, 1; Rebecca Alenna Stapley Williams, interview, February 1, 1988, 11.
25. Leola Stapley Anderson, interview, November 21, 1987, 19–20, 60.
26. "Kanarra News," *Iron County Record,* July 16, 1930, 5.
27. "John A. Steele Suddenly Stricken," *Iron County Record,* February 25, 1931, 1.
28. John Alma Steele death certificate at http://www.archives.utah.gov/research/indexes/20842.htm.
29. "John A. Steele Suddenly Stricken," *Iron County Record,* February 25, 1931, 1.
30. Reba Roundy LeFevre, interview by Tonia Ann Bate, August 4, 1985, 35.
31. Nancy Lillian Eagar Roundy, interview by Fielding H. Harris, October 16, 1969, 3–6, original at

Special Collections, Southern Utah University, Cedar City, Utah (pagination is based on my transcript, not the transcript at Dixie University); from the *Washington County News*: "Co. 8th Gde. Graduates," April 30, 1914, 1; "Hurricane," March 16, 1916, 5; "Hurricane," June 15, 1916, 5; "Hurricane," June 12, 1919, 6; Hazel Eagar Bringhurst, interview, July 23, 1987, 7–9.

32. Hazel Eagar Bringhurst, interview, July 23, 1987, 8.
33. Nancy Lillian Eagar Roundy, interview by Fielding H. Harris, October 6, 1969, 16.
34. Ibid.
35. Ibid., 15.
36. Ibid.
37. Nancy Lillian Eagar Roundy, interview by Fielding H. Harris, October 6, 1969, 17; "Local Column Overflow," *Washington County News,* October 20, 1921, 4; Reba Roundy LeFevre, interview by Tonia Ann Bate, August 4, 1985, 1.
38. Reba Roundy LeFevre, interview, February 1, 1988, 2; LeFevre, interview by Tonia Ann Bate, August 4, 1985, 1.
39. Ellis Russell and Zona Russell Jensen, interview, January 22, 1985, 1–2; Claton S. Rice, *Ambassador to the Saints,* (Boston: Christopher Publishing House, 1965), 79; from the *Washington County News*: "Virgin," March 2, 1916, 5; "Grafton," January 1, 1920, 5; "Grafton," May 11, 1922, 5; "Hurricane," June 8, 1922, 5; "Local and General News," October 5, 1922, 12; "Hurricane," October 5, 1922, 9; "Cane Beds," May 3, 1923, 1; Reba Roundy LeFevre, interview by Tonia Ann Bate, July 28, 1985, 47–48.
40. "New Harmony," *Washington County News,* November 26, 1925, 5.
41. Ellis Russell and Zona Russell Jensen, interview, January 22, 1985, 1–2.
42. Reba Roundy LeFevre, interview by Tonia Ann Bate, July 28, 1985, 48.
43. "Hurricane," *Washington County News,* October 15, 1922, 8.
44. Reba Roundy LeFevre, interview, February 1, 1988, 3–4.
45. Reba Roundy LeFevre, interview by Tonia Ann Bate, July 28, 1985, 48–49; "Kanarra," *Iron County Record,* October 14, 1921, 4.
46. "Clarinda Whetten Tietjen Roundy, 18 June 1891–19 April 1980," history recorded by Rinda Roundy Bell and posted online at John Amasa Whetten Family Histories, accessed May 25, 2012, http://sites.google.com/site/whettenhistory/john-thomas-whetten/clarinda-whetten (quotes that follow from her are from this source).
47. Ibid.; Gary Tietjen, *Ernst Albert Tietjen: Missionary and Colonizer* (Bountiful, UT: Family History Publications, 1992), 376–93.
48. "Hurricane," *Washington County News,* May 15, 1924, 4 (this issue is not on the Utah digital newspaper website but is on microfilm at the Utah State Historical Society).
49. Reba Roundy LeFevre, interview, January 15, 1988, 6.
50. JoAnn Sylvester Bate, interview, August 11, 1982, 24.
51. Reba Roundy LeFevre, interview by Tonia Ann Bate, August 4, 1985, 3–4.
52. Ibid., 5–6, 9.
53. Tietjen, *Ernst Albert Tietjen,* 406–13.
54. Reba Roundy LeFevre, interview by Tonia Ann Bate, August 4, 1985, 3.
55. The definitive study of Hamblin is Todd Compton, *A Frontier Life: Jacob Hamblin, Explorer and Indian Missionary* (Salt Lake City: University of Utah Press, 2013).
56. "Tribute to Edwin Hamblin," *Washington County News,* February 5, 1925, 1; Tietjen, *Ernst Albert Tietjen,* 43.
57. Reba Roundy LeFevre, interview by Tonia Ann Bate, August 4, 1985, 5–8; and July 29, 1978, 25–28. Amy L. Van Cott and Allen W. Leigh, *Generations of Websters,* (Cedar City, UT: Thomas Webster Family Organization, 1960), 237–39; "Marriage License Issued," *Parowan Times,* September 12, 1928, 1; and "Judge Driven Four Hours at Gun Point," September 12, 1928, 1. "Marriage License Issued," *Iron County Record,* September 14, 1928, 2; and "Youthful Gunman," September 14, 1928, 1.
58. Reba Roundy LeFevre, interview by Tonia Ann Bate, August 4, 1985, 4–9; and July 29, 1978, 25–28.
59. JoAnn Sylvester Bate, interview, August 11, 1982, 24.
60. Gwen Sylvester Hunter, interview, June 25, 1981, 7–8.
61. JoAnn Sylvester Bate, interview, August 27, 1980, 11–12.
62. The following are sources for the description of Joel Jesse Roundy and his storytelling: Reba Roundy LeFevre, interview, July 29, 1978, 9–10; and April 29, 1988, 12, 16; and October 4, 1990, 7; Gwen Sylvester Hunter, interview, June 25, 1981, 7; Verna Platt Davis, interview, October 4, 1990, 8; Harriet Arvilla Ford Woodbury, interview, October 16, 1987, 6–7; Lynn Reeves and Ella Batty Reeves, interview, April 21, 1987, 14; Rulon Berry Platt, interview, July 12, 1987, 43; Leonard Davis, interview, October 16, 1987, 1–2; Sylva May Davies Williams, interview, July 24, 1987, 9–10; Varsel Clair

Roundy, interview, January 28, 1989, 6–8; Ferl Leola Davis Zohner, interview, July 22, 1989, 7–8; Ellis Alonzo Russell and Zona Russell Jensen, interview, January 22, 1985, 3, 5–6, 9; Ruthell Roundy Bryant, interview, February 5, 1985, 1; Jesse Kay Roundy, interview, February 11, 1985, 1; Rulon Berry Platt and Leila Platt Heap, interview, July 26, 1985, 46 (Leila Platt Heap speaking); Rex J Sylvester, interviewed by Tonia Ann Bate, April 3, 1984, 7–8; Ruth Sylvester Pickering, interview, May 4, 1984, 2.

63. Gwen Sylvester Hunter, interview, June 25, 1981, 5.
64. JoAnn Sylvester Bate Journal, 20 of my transcript (May 20, 1979), copy in author's possession.
65. This conflates two magazines; the *Young Woman's Journal*, which was the YMMIA magazine, and the *Women's Exponent.*
66. JoAnn Sylvester Bate, interview, August 27, 1980, 4.
67. Gwen Sylvester Hunter, interview, June 25, 1981, 20–21; from the *Washington County News*: "Hurricane Locals," January 5, 1928, 4; "First Class Product Turned out by the Hurricane Mill," February 16, 1928, 4; "Hurricane Flour Mill," June 27, 1929, 2; Ralph L. Webb, "Hurricane Flour Mill," in *Hurricane Hintons and Spendloves from England to the Rocky Mountain Zion*, edited by Cherrie Gubler Naegle (Toquerville, UT: 2007), 324–25, also see picture on page 236.
68. JoAnn Sylvester Bate, interview, August 11, 1982, 25.
69. John Steele to Letisha Todd, November 16, 1890, transcript in author's possession.

CHAPTER 13

1. Maryann Campbell Wilson to Mahonri M. Steele, September 23, 1912, and April 8, 1919, transcripts by Iona J. Poling in author's possession; for M. M. and Emily Bunker Steele's fiftieth wedding celebration, see "Golden Wedding Anniversary," *Millard County Chronicle,* April 24, 1919, 1, which includes a picture of each.
2. "New Age of Travel Seen Just Ahead," *Iron County Record,* February 21, 1919, 3.
3. Reba Roundy LeFevre, interview by JoAnn Sylvester Bate, September 22, 1983, 3.
4. Elton Williams Stapley, interview, April 14, 1989, 7–8, 24 (all interviews are with Kerry William Bate unless otherwise indicated).
5. Ibid.
6. [Untitled], *Our Navy,* November 1917, 29: "The following have recently been advanced to chief petty officers with acting appointments."
7. Elton Williams Stapley, interview, April 14, 1989, 7–8, 24; William Tarbet Stapley, "Autobiography" (original untitled), edited by Kerry William Bate, typescript (Salt Lake City: 1987), 23.
8. "Utah's First White Child Takes Airplane Ride at 79," *Millard County Chronicle*, August 5, 1926, 1; "First Woman Born in State Rides in Air Plane," *Salt Lake Tribune,* August 8, 1926, 1; "Plane Ride Gift to Utah Pioneer," *Ogden Standard Examiner,* August 8, 1926, 7.
9. From the *Millard County Chronicle*: "Parachute Experiment Successful," August 26, 1926, 1; "Famous Flyers Visit Delta," September 23, 1926, 1 (picture of R. Carl Oelze in his flying uniform); "'Wings' Flyer Plans U.S. Tour," October 28, 1926, 1; "Freeman and Mack Sly Take to the Air," November 4, 1926, 8.
10. Elton Williams Stapley, interview, April 14, 1989, 7–8, 24.
11. [Untitled], *Salt Lake Telegram*, August 25, 1926, 1; and "Two Lads Take First Flight, Twenty Others Get Thrill," August 23, 1926, 13.
12. "Two Lads Take First Flight, Twenty Others Get Thrill," *Salt Lake Telegram*, August 23, 1926, 13.
13. Elton Williams Stapley, interview, April 14, 1989, 7–8, 24.
14. "Parachute Experiment Successful," *Millard County Chronicle,* August 26, 1926, 1; from the *Salt Lake Telegram*: "Huge Parachute Plane Safeguard," August 21, 1926, 1; "Plane is Landed from Midair," August 24, 1926, 1; "Complete Safety of Airplane Travel Is Assured by Parachute Landing," August 25, 1926, 1; "Aeronautics: Plane Parachute," *Time,* September 6, 1926 (accessed online February 18, 2011); "Plane Is Safely Landed by Giant Parachute," *Popular Mechanics,* November 1926, 705–7.
15. In the 1930 U.S. Federal Census for Los Angeles, CA, Oscar W. Lovan is listed as head of household with Lorenza Oelze, "stepdaughter" age 34 in the household; but in the 1900 census for East Castle Rock, CA, she is listed as born May 1895 and his daughter.
16. Reba Roundy LeFevre, interview with Tonia Ann Bate, August 9, 1985, 10; and April 23, 1987, 19; from the *Washington County News*: "Virgin," February 1, 1912, 3; "Local and General News," 4; "LaVerkin," February 8, 1912, 1; "District Court," June 6, 1912, 1; "LaVerkin," June 13, 1912, 3. There was a contemporary and apparently less imbibing William Spendlove in Hurricane.
17. Reba Roundy LeFevre, interview with Tonia Ann Bate, August 9, 1985, 10; and April 23, 1987, 19.

18. Ibid.
19. "First White Child Born in Utah Is Active at 88," *Deseret News,* February 28, 1935, 13, 20.
20. Reba Roundy LeFevre, interview, April 23, 1987, 18–19.
21. Reba Roundy LeFevre, interview by Tonia Ann Bate, August 9, 1985, 25.
22. Velma Stapley Rymer to Kerry William Bate, August 14, 1971, in author's possession.
23. Reba Roundy LeFevre, interview, May 2, 1986, 9–13; LeFevre, interview by Tonia Ann Bate, June 19, 1983, 3–4.
24. Ibid. Reba gave me the photo of the Wranglers that had belonged to her grandmother.
25. "Arizona Wranglers Visit Delta," *Millard County Chronicle,* September 27, 1934, 1; "Another Stage Show Coming to Orpheum," *Salt Lake Tribune,* September 30, 1934, D-9.
26. Ibid.; Reba Roundy LeFevre, interview, May 2, 1986, 9–13; LeFevre, interview by Tonia Ann Bate, June 19, 1983, 3–4.
27. JoAnn Sylvester Bate, interview, August 27, 1980, 17.
28. Reba Roundy LeFevre, interview with Tonia Ann Bate, August 9, 1985, 25.
29. JoAnn Sylvester Bate, interview, August 27, 1980, 9.
30. Ruth Sylvester Pickering, interview, May 4, 1984, 2.
31. Reba Roundy LeFevre, interview, April 29, 1988, 11–12.
32. Leon R Sylvester, interview, June 26, 1984, 17–18.
33. Joel Jesse Roundy to Sarah Catherine Roundy, December 15, 1925, original in author's possession, transcript in Reba Roundy LeFevre, interview, July 22, 1989, 35.
34. Gwen Sylvester Hunter, interview, June 25, 1981, 4.
35. Reba Roundy LeFevre, interview, October 6, 1989, 35–38; and June 27, 1988, 7–9; JoAnn Sylvester Bate and Gwen Sylvester Hunter, interview, June 26, 1988; and August 27, 1988, 32–33. Albert Emil Fitzpatrick, interview by Fielding H. Harris, April 16, 1968; Martha Roselia Landon Fitzpatrick, interview by Fielding H. Harris, April 14, 1968 mentions Joel Jesse Roundy as a patriarch and Mrs. Fitzpatrick says after consultation with Roundy ("the patriarch") they sold their place in Hurricane and moved to St. George "and we've thoroughly enjoyed it" (I have not transcribed these interviews located at Southern Utah University Special Collections, Cedar City, Utah).
36. Reba Roundy LeFevre, interview, October 6, 1989, 35–38; and June 27, 1988, 7–9.
37. Gwen Sylvester Hunter, interview, June 25, 1981, 5.
38. Ibid., 4–5.
39. Florence Beatty Leavitt, interview, April 27, 1988, 14.
40. Gwen Sylvester Hunter, interview, June 25, 1981, 5.
41. Estella Roundy Russell, "Biography of Sarah Catherine Stapley [Roundy]," 3, copy in author's possession; "Kanarra," *Iron County Record,* February 7, 1919, 8; [Untitled], *Washington County News,* January 3, 1929, 5; JoAnn Sylvester Bate and Gwen Sylvester Hunter, interview, June 26, 1985, 29.
42. JoAnn Sylvester Bate and Gwen Sylvester Hunter, interview, June 26, 1985, 29.
43. Ibid., 30.
44. Ibid., 31.
45. Florence Beatty Leavitt, interview, April 27, 1988, 10–11.
46. JoAnn Sylvester Bate, interview, August 11, 1982, 26.
47. JoAnn Sylvester Bate and Gwen Sylvester Hunter, interview, June 26, 1985, 29–31.
48. Ibid., 31.
49. Ibid., 31–32.
50. Ibid., 32.
51. Ibid.
52. JoAnn Sylvester Bate, interview, June 17, 1988, 5.
53. Ibid.
54. JoAnn Sylvester Bate, interview, August 11, 1982, 28.
55. Reba Roundy LeFevre, interview, May 9, 1985, 3.
56. Ibid.
57. JoAnn Sylvester Bate, interview, August 11, 1982, 29.
58. Reba Roundy LeFevre, interview, May 9, 1985, 5.
59. Reba Roundy LeFevre, interview, April 29, 1988, 16–18; and April 12, 1989, 5–6.
60. Reba Roundy LeFevre, interview, October 16, 1987, 12.
61. JoAnn Sylvester Bate, interview, June 17, 1988, 4–11.
62. Ibid., 5.
63. Velma Stapley Rymer to Kerry William Bate, August 14, 1971, copy in author's possession.
64. Reba Roundy LeFevre, interview, May 9, 1985, 5–6.
65. Velma Stapley Rymer to Kerry William Bate, August 14, 1971, copy in author's possession.
66. Leola Stapley Anderson, interview, November 21, 1987, 14, 20–21.
67. Ibid.
68. Lella Stapley Maxfield, "History of James Stapley and his wife, Young Elizabeth Steele," 5, copy in author's possession.
69. Elton Williams Stapley, interview, October 16, 1987, 9.
70. Josephine Kay Garfield, interview, May 26, 1988, 2–6, 13.
71. Elsie Kay Smith, interview, July 7, 1992, 6, 9–11, 14–15.
72. Josephine Kay Garfield, interview, May 26, 1988, 2.

73. Ibid., 5–6.
74. Reba Roundy LeFevre, interview, April 23, 1987, 5.
75. Josephine Kay Garfield, interview, May 26, 1988, 11.
76. Elsie Kay Smith, interview, July 7, 1992, 14–15.
77. Ibid., 6, 9–11, 14–15.
78. Josephine Kay Garfield, interview, May 26, 1988, 5.
79. "Kanarra News," *Iron County Record*, March 26, 1930, 8.
80. "Kanarra News," *Iron County Record*, April 5, 1930, 4.
81. Reba Roundy LeFevre, interview, July 23, 1987, 26.
82. JoAnn Sylvester Bate, interview, August 24, 1980, 13.
83. Ibid.

CHAPTER 14

1. JoAnn Sylvester Bate, interview, August 11, 1982, 14; August 17, 1980, 13 (all interviews are with Kerry William Bate unless otherwise indicated). Thelma C. Anderson, *Workman Family History* (Salt Lake City: Publishers Press, 1962), 137, 145–48; from the *Iron County Record*: "Roll of Honor," October 4, 1912, 1; "City and Local Happenings," 5; [Untitled], May 16, 1913, 1; from the *Washington County News*: "Fire at Hurricane," March 16, 1922, 1; "Hurricane," March 23, 1922, 5; "Hurricane," March 15, 1923, 5.
2. From the *Salt Lake Mining Review*: "Dips, Spurs and Angles," April 30, 1919, 39; "Around the State," June 15, 1919, 43; "Mining Talent Plans Development in New Section of Tintic," January 30, 1928, 7; "Here and There around the State," February 15, 1928, 17. "Delinquent Notice. Notice Lily Mining Company," *Godwin's Weekly*, March 24, 1918, 14.
3. Maureen Smith Bryson and Kerry William Bate, *The Lives and Letters of the Sylvesters and Nicholsons* (Provo, UT: Community Press, 1997), 159–69.
4. "Prospects for Washington County Never Brighter," *Washington County News*, May 23, 1929, 1.
5. Arthur M. Schlesinger Jr., *The Crisis of the Old Order, 1919–1933* (Boston: Houghton Mifflin, 1957), 158.
6. Reba Roundy LeFevre, interview, May 9, 1985, 12–13; and July 23, 1987, 12–13.
7. Kerry William Bate and Maureen Smith Bryson, *The Joseph Sylvester Family Letters, 1882–1989* (Las Vegas, NV: Maureen Bryson, 1998), 255.
8. Reba Roundy LeFevre, interview, May 9, 1985, 12–13; and July 23, 1987, 12–13.
9. Nell Sylvester Wilson, interview, June 22, 1984, 4–5.
10. Reba Roundy LeFevre, interview, May 9, 1985, 12–13. Reba reported her grandmother said, "fifteen and a half," but she was sixteen so I've corrected the quote.
11. Nell Sylvester Wilson, interview, June 22, 1984, 7.
12. JoAnn Sylvester Bate and Gwen Sylvester Hunter, interview, June 26, 1985, 20.
13. "Delinquent Tax List," *Washington County News*, December 12, 1929, 5; and "Delinquent Tax List," December 10, 1931, 11.
14. From the *Washington County News*: "Hurricane Plans Improvements," January 23, 1930, 1; "'The Jazz Singer' Coming to Wadsworth Theater," January 23, 1930, 1; "Hurricane Celebration Well Attended," August 28, 1930, 4.
15. "Condensed Report of the Condition of the Bank of St. George," *Washington County News*, December 11, 1931, 4; Thomas G. Alexander, *Edward Hunter Snow: Pioneer—Educator—Statesman* (Norman, OK: Arthur H. Clark, 2012), 221–24.
16. "Delinquent Tax List," *Washington County News*, December 10, 1931, 11.
17. Cassie Fullmer Roundy to "Dear children grand children and great grand children," July 28, 1931, copy in author's possession.
18. Bate and Bryson, *Joseph Sylvester Family Letters*, 61.
19. Ibid.
20. Hurricane Ward Records, 2 (January 4, 1924); 123 (January 1, 1926); 134 (March 29, 1926), LR 3983 11 14, no. 3, Church History Library, Church of Jesus Christ of Latter-day Saints, Salt Lake City, Utah (hereafter CHL); Hurricane North Ward, vol. 5, 1928–1933, 122–23 (December 25, 1932); 130 (April 1931), CR 3891 11 no. 2, CHL.
21. Hurricane North Ward, vol. 5, 1928–1933, 144 (August 23, 1931), CHL.
22. Ibid.
23. Ibid., 188 (December 18, 1932), CHL.
24. JoAnn Sylvester Bate, interview, June 17, 1988, 8–9, 21–22.
25. Bate and Bryson, *Sylvester Family Letters*, 63.
26. JoAnn Sylvester Bate, interview, June 17, 1988, 17–18.
27. For more about Roosevelt's "hundred days" see Jonathan Alter, *The Defining Moment: FDR's Hundred Days and the Triumph of Hope* (New York: Simon & Schuster, 2006).
28. "Four Accused of Land Fraud," *Washington County News*, January 19, 1933, 4; from the *Iron County Record*: "Local Physicians Facing Land Fraud Charges in Denver," June 1, 1933, 1; "Dismissal of Case Denied," June 8, 1933, 5; "Will Be Resentenced on September 11th," June 22, 1933, 5; "Receive Stiff Fines for Land Fraud," September 14, 1933, 1; "Utah Doctor is Sentenced," *Ogden Standard Examiner*,

June 10, 1933, 1; "Four Accused of Land Fraud," *Salt Lake Tribune*, January 14, 1933, 3; "Appeals Case to the Supreme Court of the United States," *Iron County Record*, June 15, 1933, 4. Graff was originally sentenced to eighteen months at Leavenworth but resentenced to a $1,800 fine.

29. "Kanarra News," *Iron County Record*, May 11, 1933, 4; and "Kanarra News," June 8, 1933, 7.
30. The following is the source for the next several paragraphs about Camp Creek unless otherwise noted: JoAnn Sylvester Bate and Gwen Sylvester Hunter, interview, June 26, 1985, 36, 44–47; Gwen Sylvester Hunter, interview, June 25, 1981, 18.
31. Reba Roundy LeFevre, interview, July 30, 1984, 6; LeFevre, interview by JoAnn Sylvester Bate, September 22, 1983, 15.
32. Citation for this and the following paragraph: from the *Iron County Record*: "Kanarra News," April 27, 1933, 7; "Kanarra News," May 18, 1933, 4; "Kanarra News," June 1, 1933, 1; "Kanarra News," June 8, 1933, 7; "Kanarra News," June 22, 1933, 8; "Kanarra News," June 29, 1933, 4; "Kanarra News," July 20, 1933, 5; "Kanarra News," August 3, 1933, 3; "Kanarra News," August 10, 1933, 5; "Kanarra News," August 17, 1933, 5; "News from Kanarra," August 24, 1933, 5; "Kanarra News," September 21, 1933, 4; "Kanarra News," October 5, 1933, 5; "Kanarra News," October 12, 1933, 5; "Kanarra News," October 19, 1933, 5; "Both Parties Nominate Tickets at Hurricane," October 26, 1933, 1; "News From Kanarra," November 2, 1933, 5; "Kanarra News," December 14, 1933, 4.
33. "Kanarra News," *Iron County News*, August 17, 1933, 5.
34. "Both Parties Nominate Tickets at Hurricane," *Iron County Record*, October 26, 1933, 1.
35. Leon R Sylvester, SueZanna Wittwer Sylvester, Gwen Sylvester Hunter, Nell Sylvester Stout Wilson and Ruth Sylvester Pickering, interview, August 6, 1983, 15.
36. JoAnn Sylvester Bate and Gwen Sylvester Hunter, interview, June 26, 1985, 29.
37. Ibid.; Nell Sylvester Wilson, Gwen Sylvester Hunter and JoAnn Sylvester Bate, interview, June 6, 1988, appendix A, 14.
38. JoAnn Sylvester Bate and Gwen Sylvester Hunter, interview, June 26, 1985, 27.
39. Leon R Sylvester, SueZanna Wittwer Sylvester, Gwen Sylvester Hunter, Nell Sylvester Wilson, and Ruth Sylvester Pickering, interview, August 6, 1983, 20.
40. JoAnn Sylvester Bate, interview, August 17, 1980, 14; Leon R Sylvester, SueZanna Wittwer Sylvester, Gwen Sylvester Hunter, Nell Sylvester Wilson, and Ruth Sylvester Pickering, interview, August 6, 1983, 21.
41. JoAnn Sylvester Bate, interview, August 17, 1980, 12; Leon R Sylvester, SueZanna Wittwer Sylvester, Gwen Sylvester Hunter, Nell Sylvester Stout Wilson and Ruth Sylvester Pickering, interview, August 6, 1983, 21.
42. Reba Roundy LeFevre, interview, July 22, 1989, 9–10.
43. JoAnn Sylvester Bate, interview, August 17, 1980, 14.
44. JoAnn Sylvester Bate, first interview, September 14, 1983, 5; June 1, 1986, 10–11.
45. JoAnn Sylvester Bate, interview, August 17, 1980, 14–15.
46. Velma Stapley Rymer to Kerry William Bate, August 14, 1971, copy in author's possession.
47. Reba Roundy LeFevre, interview, April 29, 1988, 18.
48. JoAnn Sylvester Bate, interview by Tonia Ann Bate, October 31, 1989, 14–16.
49. Ibid., 16.
50. JoAnn Sylvester Bate, interview, June 17, 1988, 4–5.
51. "Stitches in Time Exhibit," *Quilter's Newsletter Magazine*, February 1988, 10.
52. JoAnn Sylvester Bate, interview, June 22, 1991, 1–2.
53. Reba Roundy LeFevre, interview by JoAnn Sylvester Bate, September 22, 1983, 33.
54. Brian Gubler, ed., *Audrey Gregerson Gubler Personal Diary, 1 Jan 1922 thru 24 Jun 1942* (n.p.: 1989), 11–12 (August 1, 1932, also see September 2, 1932).
55. Reba Roundy LeFevre, interview by JoAnn Sylvester Bate, September 22, 1983, 33. Notice also JoAnn's comments about her mother.
56. Reba Roundy LeFevre, interview, July 30, 1984, 3.
57. Florence Beatty Leavitt, interview, April 27, 1988, 9.
58. Reba Roundy LeFevre, interview, July 30, 1984, 3; and October 6, 1989, 38–39.
59. Matilda Woodbury Ruesch, *Hi-Lites and Lo-Lites: Autobiography of (Mattie Ruesch) Matilda Woodbury Ruesch*, (St George, UT: n.p., 1966), 44, 46; Reba Roundy LeFevre, interview by JoAnn Sylvester Bate, September 22, 1983, 30–31.
60. JoAnn Sylvester Bate and Gwen Sylvester Hunter, interview, June 26, 1985, 30.
61. Ruth Sylvester Pickering, interview, May 4, 1984, 8–10; Gwen Sylvester Hunter, interview, June 25, 1981, 9; Reba Roundy LeFevre, interview by JoAnn Sylvester Bate, September 22, 1983, 10–11, 21.
62. Leon R Sylvester, SueZanna Wittwer Sylvester, Gwen Sylvester Hunter, Nell Sylvester Stout Wilson and Ruth Sylvester Pickering, interview, August 6, 1983, 7.

63. JoAnn Sylvester Bate, interview, June 1, 1986, 3.
64. JoAnn Sylvester Bate, "Good Things I Remember about Mama," Appendix A in Nell Sylvester Wilson, Gwen Sylvester Hunter, and JoAnn Sylvester Bate, self-interview, June 6, 1988, 13–14; and August 17, 1980, 8B; Reba Roundy LeFevre, interview, May 1, 1986, 41; Leon R Sylvester, SueZanna Wittwer Sylvester, Gwen Sylvester Hunter, Nell Sylvester Stout Wilson and Ruth Sylvester Pickering, interview, August 6, 1983, 38.
65. JoAnn Sylvester Bate, interview, August 17, 1980, 8B.
66. Nell Sylvester Wilson, June 22, 1984, 2.
67. Elsie Kay Smith, interview, July 7, 1992, 28–29.
68. "Prize Winners at County Fair," *Iron County Record,* September 21, 1917, 1; "Exhibits at Fair Excellent," *Parowan Times,* September 19, 1917, 1 (both newspaper stories identify her only as "Mrs. Sylvester"); JoAnn Sylvester Bate, first interview, September 14, 1983, 10–11.
69. JoAnn Sylvester Bate, first interview, September 14, 1983, 10; JoAnn Sylvester Bate, "Good Things I Remember about Mama," Appendix A in Nell Sylvester Wilson, Gwen Sylvester Hunter and JoAnn Sylvester Bate, interview, June 6, 1988, 13–14.
70. Florence Beatty Leavitt, interview, April 27, 1988, 11–12.
71. Elsie Kay Smith, interview, July 7, 1992, 27–28.
72. JoAnn Sylvester Bate, interview, August 17, 1980, 8B.
73. Leon R Sylvester, SueZanna Wittwer Sylvester, Gwen Sylvester Hunter, Nell Sylvester Stout Wilson and Ruth Sylvester Pickering, interview, August 6, 1983, 7.
74. "Hurricane Celebration Well Attended," *Washington County News,* August 28, 1930, 4: "Ladies Department—center piece—first J. J. Roundy"; Reba Roundy LeFevre, interview, January 16, 1988, 10–11.
75. JoAnn Sylvester Bate, interview, August 17, 1980, 8B.
76. Leon R Sylvester, SueZanna Wittwer Sylvester, Gwen Sylvester Hunter, Nell Sylvester Wilson, and Ruth Sylvester Pickering, interview, August 6, 1983, 14–15.
77. Ibid., 10.
78. Ibid., 9–10.
79. Rex J Sylvester, interview by Tonia Ann Bate, May 3, 1984, 1.
80. Nell Sylvester Wilson, Gwen Sylvester Hunter, and JoAnn Sylvester Bate, interview, June 6, 1988, 6.
81. JoAnn Sylvester Bate, interview, August 17, 1980, 8B–9.
82. JoAnn Sylvester Bate, first interview, September 14, 1983, 10–11; Reba Roundy LeFevre, interview by JoAnn Sylvester Bate, September 22, 1983, 30–33.
83. Reba Roundy LeFevre, interview, April 12, 1989, 5–6.

CHAPTER 15

1. Reba Roundy LeFevre, interview, July 30, 1984, 15 (all interviews are by Kerry William Bate unless otherwise indicated).
2. "Washington County Man Suffers Injury," *Washington County News,* March 3, 1932, 6; "Hurricane Man Suffers Injury in Earth Slide," *Salt Lake Tribune,* February 29, 1932, 7; Kerry William Bate and Maureen Smith Bryson, *The Joseph Sylvester Family Letters, 1882–1989* (Las Vegas, NV: Maureen Bryson, 1998), 61–62n28.
3. JoAnn Sylvester Bate, first interview, September 14, 1983, 1–2.
4. Ibid.
5. Sylvia Batty Hunt, interview, July 10, 1992, 19.
6. "Mayor [M. M. Steele] of Sawtooth Visits Poverty Flat," *Millard County Chronicle,* January 14, 1932, 8 (where "Hon" is described as "Urbane handsome affable"); and "Delta," June 3, 1932, 1.
7. "Six Mining Men Visit Sawtooth Field," *Millard County Chronicle,* June 16, 1932, 1.
8. From the *Millard County Chronicle*: "Mining Ground in Western Juab Will Be Developed Immediately," October 19, 1933, 1; "First Shipment of Ore Sent from Drum," November 30, 1933, 1; also see "Mine At Drum Well Underway," December 14, 1933, 1; "Gathering Mineral Specimens at Drum," May 17, 1934, 1; "Output Increased at Utah Central," *Salt Lake Telegram,* April 2, 1936, 16; "Output Increased at Utah Central," *Salt Lake Tribune,* April 3, 1936, 24; and "Business Briefs," April 24, 1936, 21.
9. Photo of Drum Mountain mining crew in author's possession.
10. Charles Andrew Olds, interview, July 30, 1984, 12.
11. Ibid.
12. Leon R Sylvester, SueZanna Wittwer Sylvester, Gwen Sylvester Hunter, Nell Sylvester Wilson, and Ruth Sylvester Pickering, interview, August 6, 1983, 10, 15–16.
13. Bate and Bryson, *Joseph Sylvester Family Letters,* 304.
14. "Kanarra News," *Iron County Record,* August 2, 1934, 6 (the story is in the margin of the newspaper

and JoAnn's last name is almost impossible to read); JoAnn Sylvester Bate, "Once is Enough," 2–3, original in author's possession.

15. Bate, "Once is Enough," 2–3.
16. "Hurricane Daughters of Utah Pioneers Hold Meeting," *Washington County News*, December 20, 1934, 2.
17. "[torn] Turning Backward," *Iron County Record*, April 14, 1916, 4.
18. Bate and Bryson, *Joseph Sylvester Family Letters*, 69.
19. JoAnn Sylvester Bate and Gwen Sylvester Hunter, interview, June 26, 1988, 59.
20. Andrew Karl Larson, *The Education of a Second Generation Swede* (Salt Lake City: Deseret Press, 1979), 441–42.
21. JoAnn Sylvester Bate, interview, June 1, 1986, 13.
22. Leon R Sylvester, SueZanna Wittwer Sylvester, Gwen Sylvester Hunter, Nell Sylvester Wilson, and Ruth Sylvester Pickering, interview, August 6, 1983, 6.
23. Ibid.
24. JoAnn Sylvester Bate, first interview, September 14, 1983, 1–2.
25. Leon R Sylvester, SueZanna Wittwer Sylvester, Gwen Sylvester Hunter, Nell Sylvester Wilson, and Ruth Sylvester Pickering, interview, August 6, 1983, 3, 6–7.
26. JoAnn Sylvester Bate, first interview, September 14, 1983, 1–2.
27. JoAnn Sylvester Bate, interview, June 1, 1986, 8.
28. JoAnn Sylvester Bate, first interview, September 14, 1983, 6.
29. Ibid.
30. Transcript of diary in author's possession.
31. Ibid.
32. JoAnn Sylvester Bate, manuscript in author's possession; JoAnn Sylvester Bate, interview, June 1, 1986, 7; June 17, 1988, 3; August 3, 1988, 1; Florence Beatty Leavitt, interview, April 27, 1988, 1, 3–4; Bate and Bryson, *Joseph Sylvester Family Letters*, 74–77 (includes a photo of the letter).
33. JoAnn Sylvester Bate, interview, June 17, 1988, 4. Also see Florence Beatty Leavitt, interview, April 27, 1988, 2.
34. JoAnn Sylvester Bate, interview, June 1, 1986, 12.
35. JoAnn Sylvester Bate and Gwen Sylvester Hunter, interview, June 26, 1988, 13. An excellent history of the library is Audrey Ballard, "History and Development of Hurricane Library since Inauguration in 1934 Related," *Washington County News*, February 29, 1940, 1, 8; also from the *Washington County News*: "Pickett Contributes to Hurricane Library," February 2, 1939, 1, 6; Katharine Larson, "Hurricane," October 27, 1938, 5: "J. M. Hinton, Victor King and Jesse Roundy left Tuesday evening for Cedar Mountains where they will cut logs for lumber to be used in the construction of the new library and city hall soon to be built in Hurricane."
36. JoAnn Sylvester Bate and Gwen Sylvester Hunter, interview, June 26, 1988, 13.
37. Florence Beatty Leavitt, interview, April 27, 1988, 2; JoAnn Sylvester Bate, interview, June 17, 1988, 13.
38. "County Teachers," *Washington County News*, August 31, 1916, 1; and "Hurricane," November 16, 1922, 5; JoAnn Sylvester Bate and Gwen Sylvester Hunter, interview, June 26, 1988, 13–14.
39. JoAnn Sylvester Bate and Gwen Sylvester Hunter, interview, June 26, 1988, 3.
40. Ibid., 10.
41. Edward Bok, *The Americanization of Edward Bok*, edited by W. David Lewis (Chicago: R. R. Donnelley and Sons, 2000), xvii–xviii, xxvii–lii.
42. JoAnn Sylvester Bate and Gwen Sylvester Hunter, interview, June 26, 1988, 11.
43. Ibid., 11–12.
44. Florence Beatty Leavitt, interview, April 27, 1988, 14.
45. Ibid.
46. Ibid., 15–16.
47. JoAnn Sylvester Bate interview, June 1, 1986, 14.
48. "Kanarra News," *Iron County Record*, March 18, 1937, 4; Reba Roundy LeFevre, interview by JoAnn Sylvester Bate, September 22, 1983, 12.
49. Reba Roundy LeFevre, interview, January 15, 1988, 3–5.
50. Ibid., 3.
51. Ibid., 4.
52. Ibid.
53. JoAnn Sylvester Bate and Gwen Sylvester Hunter, interview, June 26, 1985, 2.
54. From the *Iron County Record*: "Hydrotherapy," November 10, 1911, 4; [Untitled], January 26, 1912, 1; "Things in General," February 2, 1912, 8; "Normal Notes," February 16, 1912, 8; "Normal Notes," February 23, 1912, 1; "City and Local Happenings," May 31, 1912, 5; "Gertrude Tobiason Dies of Neuralgia," *Salt Lake Tribune*, April 28, 1916, 12.
55. JoAnn Sylvester Bate and Gwen Sylvester Hunter, interview, June 26, 1985, 2.
56. Ibid., 2–3.
57. Ibid., 4, 32–33.
58. Reba Roundy LeFevre, interview by Tonia Ann Bate, June 12, 1983, 7–8.
59. "Alton," *Kane County Standard*, October 1, 1937, 8; and "Final Rites for Bishop Roundy," October 8,

1937, 1; Quimby Roundy death certificate signed by Dr. George R. Aiken with the decedent's first name as "Quinby" at http://www.archives.utah.gov/research/indexes/20842.htm; Everett Ellsworth Roundy, *The Roundy Family in America* (1942; repr., n.p.: Shadrach Roundy Family Organization, 2000), 244, 434, 484; Reba Roundy LeFevre, interview, February 23, 1990, 1–4.

60. Reba Roundy LeFevre, interview, February 23, 1990, 1–4.
61. Ibid.
62. Homer Young Englestead, interview by Fielding H. Harris, October 13, 1969 (I have only partially transcribed this interview, hence no page number), original at Southern Utah University Special Collections, Cedar City, Utah. In listing his children Englestead said, "After Maggie was Quim, I called him Homer Quim, Q-u-i-m. I named him Quim after a buddy of mine in the service [World War I], Quimby Roundy . . . we were so close in the service . . ."
63. Reba Roundy LeFevre, interview, February 23, 1990, 1–4.
64. *1936–41 Pickett Mortuary Funeral Record*, original at the Family History Library in St. George, Utah, entries chronologically arranged.
65. JoAnn Sylvester Bate, interview, June 1, 1986, 4–5.
66. "Student Body Officers Meet at Hurricane," *Washington County News*, May 19, 1938, 1, 3; JoAnn Sylvester Bate, interview, August 3, 1988, 2. For more on JoAnn's high school graduation, see JoAnn Sylvester Bate and Gwen Sylvester Hunter, interview, June 26, 1988, 38–39; JoAnn Sylvester Bate, interview, May 15, 1984, 2; Florence Beatty Leavitt, interview, April 27, 1988, 18–19.
67. JoAnn Sylvester Bate, interview by Tonia Ann Bate, June 1, 1986, 16.

CHAPTER 16

1. Copy in author's possession.
2. W. Paul Reeve, *Religion of a Different Color: Race and the Mormon Struggle for Whiteness* (New York: Oxford University Press, 2015), 142–43: "The US Congress created Utah as a territory in 1850, as part of a broader compromise that year that admitted California into the Union as a free state and allowed popular sovereignty to determine the issue of slavery in New Mexico and Utah territories. Legislators in both Utah and New Mexico opted for systems of unfree labor." Utah never adopted Southern slave codes.
3. Dred Scott v. Sandford, 60 U.S. 393 (1857), accessed August 12, 2015, https://en.wikisource.org/wiki/Dred_Scott_v._Sandford.
4. Reeve, *Religion of a Different Color*, 3. Culture, ethnicity and religion were considered race defining in the nineteenth century. Reeve sums up: "Mormon [perceived] behavior—fanaticism, adherence to theocratic rule, ignorance, sexual promiscuity, plural marriage, fawning subservience, and violence—produced race" (262).
5. Denise Oliver Velez, "Fighting Back against the SCOTUS Voting Rights Decision," *DailyKos*, Sunday, August 4, 2013, http://www.dailykos.com/story/2013/8/4/1228116/-Fighting-back-against-the-SCOTUS-voting-rights-decision.
6. Edward W. Tullidge, *The Women of Mormondom* (1877; repr., Salt Lake City: n.p., 1975), 443.
7. John Steele, "Pioneer Reminiscences," *Deseret Evening News*, August 8, 1888, 480. I have also benefited from reading the original letter in the Wilford Woodruff Collection at the Church History Library, Salt Lake City, Utah.
8. John Steele's actual trade was shoemaker.
9. Orson Ferguson Whitney, *History of Utah* (Salt Lake City: George Q. Cannon and Sons, 1892), 1:351–52. Also, in 1892 the *Salt Lake Herald* ran a story and mentioned the birth: "The little one was named Young Elizabeth Steele—Young for President [Brigham] Young, and Elizabeth for Queen Elizabeth of England. She is now the wife of James Stapley of Kanarra, Iron county." "The Story of the Pioneers," *Salt Lake Herald*, December 24, 1892, 2; LeRoi C. Snow, "Pioneer Celebration," *Improvement Era*, 25 (1922): 1023.
10. "A Young Pioneer," *Deseret News*, February 11, 1897, 5; "Town Talk," *Salt Lake Herald*, February 12, 1897, 8; and later, "Daughters Draw List of Fifty-One Living Pioneers," *Salt Lake Tribune*, July 25, 1929, 10; and "Tablet to Pioneers Will be Unveiled at Capitol," March 2, 1933, 16.
11. "First White Child Born in Utah Visits Old Capital Museum," *Millard County Chronicle*, July 16, 1931, 1.
12. In 1988 this dress was owned by Josephine Kay Garfield who reported that "Aunt Kate" said Annis must have been ill when she made it but neither of us found any flaw in it. Josephine had another dress belonging to "Grandma Stapley" that was a dark suit with a fish scale pattern. From the nap of the neck to the waist it was sixteen and a half inches and had solid stays. It measured fifty-eight inches from the nap to the hem, with sleeves twenty-three inches at the top. The skirt was forty-one and a half

inches from top to hem, with a waist of thirty-one inches. Josephine Kay Garfield allowed me to photograph it January 25, 1989.

13. "Huge Throngs See Greatest Spectacle in Utah History," *Salt Lake Telegram*, July 24, 1931, 1 (also see stories on page 8); "Thin Ranks of Pioneers Enjoy Banquet," *Salt Lake Tribune*, July 25, 1931, 1, 6, 8.
14. "Thin Ranks of Pioneers Enjoy Banquet," *Salt Lake Tribune*, July 25, 1931, 8.
15. Reba Roundy LeFevre, interview by Tonia Ann Bate, July 28, 1985, 46; and October 6, 1989, 5.
16. Reba Roundy LeFevre, interview, April 23, 1987, 5–6 (all interviews are by Kerry William Bate unless otherwise indicated).
17. Reba explained that Elizabeth's eyesight was good "til she got old, up to about ninety—up to about eighty-five. She would read but she held it quite close to her eyes." Reba Roundy LeFevre, interview, April 12, 1989, 5.
18. "First White Child Born in Utah Is Active at 88," *Deseret News*, February 28, 1935, 13, 20. For critical comments on LeRoi Snow as a historian, see Dennis B. Horne, *Latter Leaves in the Life of Lorenzo Snow* (Springville, UT: Cedar Fort, 2012), 15–16.
19. Ibid.
20. Juanita Brooks, "Jest a Copin'—Word F'r Word," *Utah Historical Quarterly* 37, no. 4 (Fall 1969): 375–95, esp. 381.
21. Isaac E. Diehl, Young Elizabeth Steele Stapley, B 289, box 10, WPA Biographies, Utah State Historical Society, Salt Lake City, Utah (hereafter USHS); "Utah's Oldest Printer [Isaac E. "Ikie" Diehl] Dies in Provo Age 79," *Ogden Standard Examiner*, July 16, 1940, 4.
22. Priddy Meeks relates the story of the buried flour; he thought Patty's actions may have been influenced by her husband. See J. Cecil Alter, ed., "Journal of Priddy Meeks," *Utah Historical Quarterly* 10 (1942): 165–66. John Steele had tremendous resentment against Sessions and some other well-off pioneers. On January 1, 1848, Patty Sessions recorded in her journal: "Mr Sessions myself and a number of others spent new years at Br Millers Br Jackman was there he said it was the best meeting he ever had it was the best new years I ever spent we feasted then blesed and was blessed." Donna Toland Smart, ed., *Mormon Midwife: The 1846–1888 Diaries of Patty Bartlett Sessions* (Logan, UT: Utah State University Press, 1997), 105. On the same day Steele complained bitterly in his journal, "From Christmas unto the present, and before it, there has been party after party, one spree after another and dancing, all those that had aplenty were invited to come and share their plenty, but none of those that were considered destitute were invited to partake of their plenty, when they well knew that there were many of their brethren the soldiers, who were literally starving." Ileen J. Johnson and Wanda S. Cox, *The Memoirs of Mahonri Moriancumer Steele Jr.* (mimeographed, 1963), 25–27. Smart, the editor of Sessions's diaries, confirmed that Sessions often seemed "just plain miserly" but disagreed with the charge. Smart, *Mormon Midwife*, 26.
23. "Young Elizabeth Steele Stapley," copied by Virginia M. Lee, 3, original at USHS.
24. "First White Child Born in Utah Is Active at 88," *Deseret News*, February 28, 1935, 13, 20.
25. Katherine [Katharine] Larson, "Young Elizabeth Steel[e] Stapley, First White Child Born in Utah, Honored by D. U. P.," *Washington County News*, December 16, 1937, 1, A.
26. "Birthday Saddened by News of Death," *Salt Lake Tribune*, August 10, 1937, 9.
27. Larson, "Young Elizabeth Steel[e] Stapley," 1, A.
28. Ibid.
29. Ibid.
30. Reba Roundy LeFevre, interview, January 16, 1988, 8.
31. Alice Emma Quibell Dean Mallory, "Five Year Diary," November 25, 1946, in author's possession.
32. Zettie N. Kearl to Elizabeth S. Stapley, April 30, 1931, copy in author's possession.
33. Seymour Stapley to Joel Jesse Roundy, October 27, 1930, addressed to "Dear Brother and Kin" but listed on the bottom of the page are all recipients: Y. E. Stapley, J. J. Roundy, Jessie [Jesse] C. and Reba Roundy, Serah [Sarah] Sylvester and Nell Stout, copy in author's possession.
34. May Stapley Kay to Elizabeth Stapley, December 3, 1930, copy in author's possession. I have not been able to identify "Aunt Eliza."
35. Velma Stapley Rymer to Kerry William Bate, August 14, 1971, original in author's possession.
36. Reba Roundy LeFevre, interview, May 1, 1986, 57.
37. Leola Amelia Stapley Anderson, interview, November 21, 1987, 14.
38. Reba Roundy LeFevre, interview, November 19, 1988, 5.
39. "Erma Crawforth," *The [Nephi, UT] Times-News*, undated but after April 26, 2004, accessed July 31, 2015, http://www.nephitimesnews.com/0404/042804/obits.htm.
40. Copy of picture provided me by Velma Stapley Rymer. Josephine Kay Garfield identified Erma Keyte.

41. Reba Roundy LeFevre, interview by Tonia Ann Bate, July 28, 1985, 3–4.
42. Reba Roundy LeFevre, interview, May 9, 1985, 4.
43. Reba Roundy LeFevre, interview, January 15, 1988, 6.
44. "Kanarra News," *Iron County Record,* April 27, 1933, 7.
45. "Kanarra News," *Iron County Record,* August 17, 1933, 5.
46. "State Centralization of Hospital Being Attempted," *Iron County Record,* March 3, 1938, 1; and "Macfarlane-Bergstrom Offices Burglarized," March 3, 1938, 4.
47. Lucretia Higgins Stapley death certificate at http://www.archives.utah.gov/research/indexes/20842.htm.
48. "Kanarra News," *Iron County Record,* March 3, 1938, 10; "New Harmony," *Washington County News,* March 10, 1938, 6; "Attend Funeral," *Millard Country Chronicle,* March 3, 1938, 1.
49. "Kanarra News," *Iron County Record,* March 3, 1938, 10.
50. Reba Roundy LeFevre, interview, May 1, 1986, 8.
51. Ibid.; Reba Roundy LeFevre, interview, October 6, 1989, 19.
52. Reba Roundy LeFevre, interview, October 6, 1989, 19.
53. "Recent Storms Highly Valuable to Farms and Ranges," *Iron County Record,* March 10, 1938, 1; "East End of County Suffers Heavy Loss from Storms," *Washington County News,* March 10, 1938, 1, 3.
54. Reba Roundy LeFevre, interview, May 1, 1986, 7–11.
55. Ibid., 7.
56. Ibid., 8.
57. Ibid., 9.
58. Ibid., 7.
59. Ibid., 8.
60. Ibid.; also October 6, 1989, 19.
61. Reba Roundy LeFevre, interview, May 1, 1986, 8.
62. Ibid.; October 6, 1989, 19.
63. Reba Roundy LeFevre, interview, July 29, 1978, 14.
64. Reba Roundy LeFevre, interview, May 1, 1986, 8.
65. Ibid., 9.
66. Reba Roundy LeFevre, interview, October 6, 1989, 19.
67. Reba Roundy LeFevre, interview, January 15, 1988, 5–6; also see October 6, 1989, 20.
68. Reba Roundy LeFevre, interview, May 1, 1986, 9.
69. Ibid., 10.
70. Ibid.
71. Reba Roundy LeFevre, interview, July 29, 1978, 13.
72. Reba Roundy LeFevre, interview, May 1, 1986, 12.
73. "Death Claims Utah's First White Child," *Salt Lake Tribune,* April 2, 1938, 1–2.
74. "Mrs. Young Elizabeth Stapley, First White Child Born in Utah, Dies At Hurricane," *Washington County News,* April 7, 1938, 1, 6.
75. Ibid.
76. Ruthell Roundy Bryant, interview, February 5, 1985, 2.
77. "First White Child Born in Utah Dies at Hurricane," *Iron County Record,* April 7, 1938, 5.
78. Ibid.
79. "Mrs. Young Elizabeth Stapley, First White Child Born in Utah, Dies At Hurricane," *Washington County News,* April 7, 1938, 1, 6.
80. Reba Roundy LeFevre, interview, July 29, 1978, 14–15; LeFevre, interview by JoAnn Sylvester Bate, September 22, 1983, 27.
81. Leola Stapley Anderson, interview, November 21, 1987, 4.
82. Velma Stapley Rymer to Kerry William Bate, August 14, 1971.

CHAPTER 17

1. Reba Roundy LeFevre, interview, May 1, 1986, 36 (all interviews are by Kerry William Bate unless otherwise indicated).
2. "Painted Desert (Arizona)," *Wikipedia,* accessed August 12, 2015, https://en.wikipedia.org/wiki/Painted_Desert_(Arizona); Reba Roundy LeFevre, interview by Tonia Ann Bate, July 26, 1985, 8–10; and May 1, 1986, 36–40.
3. Reba Roundy LeFevre, interview, May 1, 1986, 36.
4. Reba Roundy LeFevre, interview, January 15, 1988, 3.
5. JoAnn Sylvester Bate and Gwen Sylvester Hunter, interview, June 26, 1988, 53.
6. Reba Roundy LeFevre, interview, May 1, 1986, 40–41.
7. Ibid.
8. Rex J Sylvester, interview by Tonia Ann Bate, May 3, 1984, 5.
9. Reba Roundy LeFevre, interview, May 1, 1986, 40–41.
10. John Steele to Catherine Campbell Steele, December 18, 1877, box 1, fd. 12, John Steele Collection, 1847–1936, L. Tom Perry Special Collections, Harold B. Lee Library, Brigham Young University, Provo, Utah.
11. Reba Roundy LeFevre, interview, May 1, 1986, 40–41.
12. Lena Stevens Sylvester, interview, July 26, 1984, 8.

13. Reba Roundy LeFevre, interview, May 1, 1986, 34–41.
14. Reba Roundy LeFevre, interview, July 30, 1984, 11; JoAnn Sylvester Bate, interview, August 11, 1982, 31–32; and Bate, first interview, September 14, 1983, 14–15.
15. Priscilla Parrish Roundy, Venice, [Utah], January [1910] to Jane Parrish Lindsay, copy of typescript in author's possession.
16. Nell Sylvester Wilson, interview, June 22, 1984, 8–9; Reba Roundy LeFevre, interview, May 1, 1986, 40–41.
17. Florence Beatty Leavitt, interview, April 27, 1988, 13–14.
18. Reba Roundy LeFevre, interview, July 29, 1978, 13–14, 16.
19. "Miss Uarda Knight, Public Health Nurse to Retire," *Washington County News,* November 12, 1964, 1.
20. Reba Roundy LeFevre, interview, July 29, 1978, 13–14, 16; LeFevre, interview by JoAnn Sylvester Bate, September 22, 1983, 36–37; April 5, 1990, 25–26; May 1, 1986, 33–34; JoAnn Sylvester Bate, interview, August 11, 1982, 14, 33.
21. Reba Roundy LeFevre, interview, November 18, 1988, 7.
22. JoAnn Sylvester Bate, interview, August 11, 1982, 33.
23. Sarah Sylvester death certificate at http://www.archives.utah.gov/research/indexes/20842.htm.
24. Nell Sylvester Wilson, interview, June 22, 1984, 8–9.
25. JoAnn Sylvester Bate, interview, June 1, 1986, 16.
26. Reba Roundy LeFevre, interview, July 29, 1978, 14–15; LeFevre, interview by JoAnn Sylvester Bate, September 22, 1983, 37–38.
27. Reba Roundy LeFevre, interview, January 15, 1886, 6.
28. Reba Roundy LeFevre, interview, February 1, 1988, 7.
29. Rex J Sylvester, interview by Tonia Ann Bate, May 3, 1984, 5. Florence Leavitt could not recall this event and Rex was uncertain about her name, but given the circumstances it fits.
30. Kerry William Bate and Maureen Smith Bryson, *The Joseph Sylvester Family Letters, 1882–1989* (Las Vegas, NV: Maureen Bryson, 1998), 299.
31. Ibid., 73.
32. "Services Held Wednesday for Sarah E. Sylvester in Hurricane," *Washington County News,* September 22, 1938, 1, 5; Kerry William Bate, "Promise to Grandma," *Dialogue: A Journal of Mormon Thought* 19, no. 4 (Winter 1986): 123–36.
33. Rex J Sylvester replaced this with a conventional tombstone.
34. JoAnn Sylvester Bate and Gwen Sylvester Hunter, interview, June 26, 1988, 66–67.
35. From the *Washington County News*: "Young Elizabeth Steel[e] D. U. P. Camp Holds Reorganization Meeting," November 2, 1944, 1; Audrey Ballard, "Hurricane," June 20, 1940, 4; Julia Whitney, "Hurricane," October 31, 1940, 4A; Mrs. Thomas Hinton, "Hurricane," November 30, 1944, 4; Wilhelmina Hinton, "Hurricane," March 14, 1946, supplement; Wilhelmina Hinton, "Hurricane," April 18, 1946, 6; Wilhelmina Hinton, "Hurricane," May, 23, 1946, 12; Wilhelmina Hinton, "Hurricane," June 13, 1946, 8; Wilhelmina Hinton, "Hurricane," June 20, 1946, 6; Wilhelmina Hinton, "Hurricane," August 1, 1946, 12; "Mr. and Mrs. Joel J. Roundy Enjoy Family Dinner-Birthday Party on Nov. 29," December 5, 1946, 6; Wilhelmina Hinton, "Hurricane," December 5, 1946, 14; "Mr. and Mrs. J. Roundy Celebrate 60th Wedding Fete on March 11," March 20, 1947, 1; Wilhelmina Hinton, "Hurricane," August 14, 1946, 6; "Elizabeth Steele DUP Meeting," November 27, 1947, 11; Wilhelmina Hinton, "Hurricane," December 4, 1947, 3, 11; Wilhelmina Hinton, "Hurricane," December 11, 1947, 10; Wilhelmina Hinton, "Hurricane," March 18, 1948, 4.
36. "Funeral Services Held for Collins Russell in Hurricane Tuesday," *Washington County News,* August 22, 1946, 1.
37. Reba Roundy LeFevre, interview by Fielding H. Harris, October 3, 1968, 13 of my transcript; LeFevre, interview by Tonia Ann Bate August 4, 1985, 8–10; LeFevre, interview, July 22, 1989, 4–5, 27.
38. "Our Men and Women under the Colors," *Garfield County News,* April 25, 1946, 1.
39. Carl and Reba LeFevre, interview by Jarald Keith LeFevre, December 28, 1971, untranscribed tape in author's possession; Carl's military service is outlined in the *Garfield County News*: "Seven from County Leave for Service with Armed Forces," January 7, 1943, 1; "Our Men and Women under the Colors," September 23, 1943, 5; "Our Men and Women under the Colors," March 30, 1944, 1; "Our Men and Women under the Colors," September 14, 1944, 1; "Our Men and Women under the Colors," March 15, 1945, 1; "Our Men and Women under the Colors," March 22, 1945, 1; "Our Men and Women under the Colors," September 27, 1945, 1.
40. Reba Roundy LeFevre, interview by Fielding H. Harris, October 3, 1968, 14.
41. "Our Men and Women under the Colors," *Garfield County News,* September 14, 1944, 1.
42. Reba Roundy LeFevre, interview, October 3, 1968, 15.

43. Ibid.
44. Reba Roundy LeFevre, interview, October 6, 1989, 47.
45. Reba Roundy LeFevre, interview, October 3, 1968, 15.
46. Reba Roundy LeFevre, interview, April 29, 1988, 6.
47. Reba Roundy LeFevre, interview by Fielding H. Harris, October 3, 1968, 15.
48. Ibid.
49. Original letter in author's possession.
50. JoAnn Sylvester Bate, interview, August 27, 1980, 15; "Joel J. Roundy Dies in Hurricane," *Washington County News,* June 30, 1949, 6; and "Joel J. Roundy Service is held in North Ward," July 7, 1949, 6; Nell Sylvester Wilson, interview, June 22, 1984, 8.
51. Joel J. Roundy death certificate at http://www.archives.utah.gov/research/indexes/20842.htm.
52. "Joel J. Roundy Dies in Hurricane," *Washington County News,* June 30, 1949, 6; and "Joel J. Roundy Service is held in North Ward," July 7, 1949, 6.
53. JoAnn Sylvester Bate, interview, August 27, 1980, 15.
54. "Joel J. Roundy Dies in Hurricane," *Washington County News,* June 30, 1949, 6; and "Joel J. Roundy Service is held in North Ward," July 7, 1949, 6; untitled transcript of Joel Jesse Roundy funeral services in author's possession reports that author, professor, and historian Ivan J. Barrett, then Hurricane seminary principal, praised Roundy as "considerate of others, he was gentle, he lightened the burden of others, he was humble minded, he was courageous, a sweet temper. It takes a person with a sweet temper when he is tired to forget the fatigue and play and talk with the little kids. It surely does! His entire life was for others—in the service of others," 6.
55. "Funeral Services Held for Zion Park Stake Patriarch," *Iron County Record,* June 30, 1949, 4.
56. JoAnn Sylvester Bate, interview, August 27, 1980, 16; "Sarah C. Stapley Roundy Dies in Cedar City; Services in Hurricane," *Washington County News,* July 28, 1949, 6.
57. Sarah Catherine Roundy death certificate at http://www.archives.utah.gov/research/indexes/20842.htm.
58. "Sarah C. Stapley Roundy Dies in Cedar City; Services in Hurricane," *Washington County News,* July 28, 1949, 6.
59. "Funeral Rites Held for Catherine Roundy," *Iron County Record,* August 4, 1949, 3.
60. "Sarah C. Stapley Roundy Dies in Cedar City; Services in Hurricane," *Washington County News,* July 28, 1949, 6.
61. Leon R Sylvester, interview, June 26, 1984, 12–13.
62. Ruth Sylvester Pickering, interview, May 4, 1984, 11.
63. JoAnn Sylvester Bate, interview, August 11, 1982, 31.

BIBLIOGRAPHY

LIST OF ABBREVIATIONS

CHL	Church History Library, Church of Jesus Christ of Latter-day Saints, Salt Lake City, Utah
LTPSC	L. Tom Perry Special Collections, Harold B. Lee Library, Brigham Young University, Provo, Utah
SUUSC	Southern Utah University Special Collections, Cedar City, Utah
USHS	Utah State Historical Society, Salt Lake City, Utah

MANUSCRIPT COLLECTIONS

Anderson, Neils Albert. Papers. SUUSC.
Badger, Carl A. Journal, 1905–1907. LTPSC.
Biographical Sketches. CHL.
Brooks, Juanita. Collection. USHS.
Coombs, Isaiah Moses. Collection, 1834–1886. CHL.
Freeman, John. Collections of Songs. CHL.
Hurricane Relief Society, History and Minutes. CHL.
Hurricane Ward Records, Sacrament Meeting Minutes. CHL.
Hurricane North Ward. 1928–1933. CHL.
Journal History of the Church of Jesus Christ of Latter-day Saints. CHL.
Kanarraville General Minutes, 1878–1905. CHL.
Kanarraville General Minutes, 1905–1913. CHL.
Kanarraville General Minutes, 1914–1922. CHL.
Kanarraville Relief Society Minutes, 1889–1897. CHL.
Kanarraville Relief Society minutes, 1895–1915. CHL.
Kanarraville Sunday School Minutes, 1882–1886. CHL.
Kanarraville Sunday School Minutes, 1886–1892. CHL.
Kanarraville YMMIA Minutes, 1878–1890. CHL.
Kanarraville YMMIA Minutes, 1890–1901. CHL.
Kanarraville YMMIA Minutes, 1901–1913. CHL.
Kanarraville YWMIA Minutes, 1893–1900. CHL.
Larson, Andrew Karl. Papers. USHS.
Martineau, James Henry. Collection. CHL.
Mormon Battalion Service Files. Utah State Archives, Salt Lake City, Utah.
Murdock Academy Student Records, 1898–1922. CHL.
Palmer, William R. Collection. SUUSC.
Parowan Minute Book, CHL.
Savage, Levi. Journal. John D. Lee Collection. Dixie University.
Smith, Delphina "Della" Catherine Fish. "Reminiscences and Diary." Ca. 1928–1933. CHL.
Smith, George Albert. Papers. CHL.
Smoot, Reed. Papers. LTPSC.
Steele, John. Correspondence. CHL.
Steele, John. Papers. LTPSC.
"Tenth Ward [Salt Lake City] Historical Record of Members, Etc." CHL.
Toquerville General Minutes, CHL.
Toquerville Relief Society Account Book, 1868–1903. CHL.
Toquerville Relief Society Minutes, 1870–1877. CHL.
Toquerville Relief Society Minutes, 1878–1882. CHL.
Toquerville Relief Society Minutes, 1882–1884. CHL.
Toquerville Relief Society Minutes, 1886–1889. CHL.
Toquerville Relief Society Minutes, 1889–1890. CHL.
Utah Territorial Militia. Series 2210, Reel 5. Utah State Archives.
Woodruff, Wilford. Collection. CHL.
Young, Brigham. Letters. CHL.

NEWSPAPERS AND WEBSITES

Adams, Mary E. "A Short Sketch of the Life of Orson B. and Susan Adams Smith." http://www.cedarcity.org/DocumentCenter/View/7591.
Alexandria [VA] Gazette and Virginia Advertiser. 1887–1910. http://chroniclingamerica.loc.gov/lccn/sn85025007/.
Beaver County Weekly Press. 1881–1929. http://digitalnewspapers.org/newspaper/?paper=Southern+Utonian+and+Beaver+City+Press.
"Beyond Science Fiction—NASA Tests Human-Robot Cooperation in Utah Desert." http://www.nasa.gov/centers/ames/research/exploringtheuniverse/utah_robots.html.
"Clarinda Whetten Tietjen Roundy, 18 June 1891–19 April 1980." Recorded by Rinda Roundy Bell. http://sites.google.com/site/whettenhistory/john-thomas-whetten/clarinda-whetten.

"Cobble Crest—A Hidden Treasure." Preservation Round Up Blog. http://www.utahheritagefoundation.com/component/k2/item/523-cobble-crest-%E2%80%93-a-hidden-treasure#.VsdtU_IrKhc.

Daily Herald [Provo, UT]. 1935–1977. http://www.newspapers.com/browse/#244|h3ueIEHxE.

Daily [Richmond, VA] Times. 1886–1889 http://chroniclingamerica.loc.gov/lccn/sn86071854/.

Daughters of the American Revolution Lineage Books. 152 vols. [database online] Provo, UT: The Generations Network, 2000.

Deseret Farmer [Provo, UT]. 1908–1909. http://digitalnewspapers.org/newspaper/?paper=Deseret+Farmer.Online.

Deseret News. 1850–1910. http://digitalnewspapers.org/newspaper/?paper=Deseret+News.

Evening Dispatch [Provo, UT]. 1891–1895. http://digitalnewspapers.org/newspaper/?paper=Evening+Dispatch.

Everybody's Poultry Magazine. https://archive.org/details/usda-everybodyspoultrymagazine.

Garfield County [Panguitch, UT] News. 1923–2005. http://digitalnewspapers.org/newspaper/?paper=Garfield+County+News.

Goodwin's [Salt Lake City, UT] Weekly. 1902–1919. http://digitalnewspapers.org/newspaper/?paper=Goodwins+Weekly.

"Goodman, Nathaniel." https://familysearch.org/photos/stories/2327829.

Harrisburg [PA] Telegraph. 1914–1919. http://chroniclingamerica.loc.gov/lccn/sn85038411/1919-12-31/ed-1/seq-1/. 1866–1948. http://www.newspapers.com/browse/#607|hJQqL9Igb.

Helena [MT] Independent. 1889–1894. http://chroniclingamerica.loc.gov/lccn/sn83025308/.

[Helena] *Independent Record*. 1874–1999. http://www.newspapers.com/browse/#128|hOH4nmurj.

Holbrook Argus [AZ]. 1900–1913. http://chroniclingamerica.loc.gov/lccn/sn94051342/.

Iron County [Cedar City, UT] Record. 1890–1979. http://digitalnewspapers.org/newspaper/?paper=Iron+County+Record.

Irving, Washington. "The Legend of Sleepy Hollow." http://www.eastoftheweb.com/short-stories/UBooks/LegSle.shtml.

Kane County [Kanab, UT] Standard. 1912–1950. http://digitalnewspapers.org/newspaper/?paper=Kane+County+Standard.

Logan [UT] Republican. 1902–1921. http://digitalnewspapers.org/newspaper/?paper=Logan+Republican.

Los Angeles [CA] Herald. http://chroniclingamerica.loc.gov/newspapers/?state=California&ethnicity=&language=. 1873–1910. http://www.newspapers.com/browse/#627|hw5zL4tL1.

Martin's Belfast Directory for 1841–2. Belfast: Matthew Martin, 1841. http://streetdirectories.proni.gov.uk/media/3WLWxMNE-xIbq1NBCRQvdQ..a?ts=HpXQdHMACCHq8zO1D5omvy7ptGu76G6-rdhoQ7gryjE.a.

Millard County [Delta, UT] Chronicle. 1910–1947. http://digitalnewspapers.org/newspaper/?paper=Millard+County+Chronicle.

New York Times. 1851–1922. http://www.newspapers.com/browse/#138|hC8P-Uzi2.

Ogden [UT] Standard Examiner. 1879–1927. http://digitalnewspapers.org/newspaper/?paper=Ogden+Standard.

Parowan [UT] Times. 1915–1945. http://digitalnewspapers.org/newspaper/?paper=Parowan+Times.

Prince, Brent Pace. Kanarra and Harmony Stock Company Minute Book, 1874–1898. brentprince.blogspot.com/2008/10/harmony-kanarra-stock-raising-company.html.

Richfield (UT) Reaper. 1906–1940. http://digitalnewspapers.org/newspaper/?paper=Richfield+Reaper.

Richmond (VA) Dispatch. 1884–1903. http://chroniclingamerica.loc.gov/lccn/sn85038614/. 1852–1953. http://www.newspapers.com/browse/#891|h2eM8toXb.

Salt Lake [City, UT] Democrat. 1885–1887. http://digitalnewspapers.org/newspaper/?paper=Salt+Lake+Democrat.

Salt Lake [City, UT] Herald. 1870–1920. http://digitalnewspapers.org/newspaper/?paper=Salt+Lake+Herald.

Salt Lake Mining Review. 1889–1929. http://digitalnewspapers.org/newspaper/?paper=Salt+Lake+Mining+Review.

Salt Lake [City, UT] Telegram. 1902–1905. http://digitalnewspapers.org/newspaper/?paper=Salt+Lake+Telegram.

Salt Lake [City, UT] Tribune. 1871–1919. http://digitalnewspapers.org/newspaper/?paper=Salt+Lake+Tribune. 1890–1977. http://www.newspapers.com/browse/#267|hC5Nar_YU.

San Bernardino County [CA] Sun. 1894–1988. http://www.newspapers.com/browse/#864|hzDjqKkoh.

San Francisco Call. 1895–1913. http://chroniclingamerica.loc.gov/lccn/sn85066387/. 1890–1913. http://www.newspapers.com/browse/#465|hHPgOGo6l.

Stratton, Alice Isom Gubler. *Look to the Stars*. http://www.aarongifford.com/alice/looktothestars/chapter07.html.

Thomas, Hayward. *Reminiscences and Journal*. https://history.lds.org/overlandtravels

/sources/12845048123732110642/thomas-hayward -reminiscences-and-journal-14-16.

Union [St. George, Utah]. 1878–1898. http://digitalnewspapers.org/newspaper/?paper=The+Union

Utah State Archives. Death Certificates, 1905–1964. http://www.archives.utah.gov/research/indexes/20842.htm.

Washington County [St. George, UT] News. 1898–1945. http://digitalnewspapers.org/newspaper/?paper=Washington+County+News.

Weekly Kansas Chief (Troy, KS). 1872–1883. http://chroniclingamerica.loc.gov/lccn/sn82015484/. 1872–1899. http://www.newspapers.com/browse/#805|hxILHZSuo.

Wesleyan University Grade Chart http://www.wesleyan.edu/registrar/general_information/grade_chart.html.

World War I Draft Registration Cards, 1917-1918. Database online at Ancestry.com.

PERIODICALS

Allyn, Julia. "Bee-Keeping for Women." *Ladies Home Journal* 9 (April 1891): 4.

Alter, J. Cecil. "Addendas." *Utah Historical Quarterly* 10 (1942): 41–42.

———. "Extracts from the Journal of John Steele." *Utah Historical Quarterly* 6, no. 1 (January 1933): 3–28.

———. "Journal of Priddy Meeks." *Utah Historical Quarterly* 10 (1942): 143–223.

Arrington, Leonard J. "The Influenza Epidemic of 1918–19 in Utah." *Utah Historical Quarterly* 58, no. 2 (Spring 1990): 165–82.

Bate, Kerry William. "Diary of Mary Elizabeth (May) Stapley, a Schoolteacher in Virgin, Utah." *Utah Historical Quarterly* 60, no. 2 (Spring 1992): 158–167.

———. "Promise to Grandma." *Dialogue: A Journal of Mormon Thought* 19, no. 4 (Winter 1986): 123–36.

Brimhall, Sandra Dawn. "Friends at All Times: The Correspondence of Isaiah Moses Coombs and Dryden Rogers." *Utah Historical Quarterly* 77, no. 2 (Spring 2009): 151–65.

Brimhall, Sandra Dawn, and David A. Hales. "Frances R. Burke: Toquerville Presbyterian Missionary." *Utah Historical Quarterly* 72, no. 2 (Spring 2004): 156–66.

Chidsey, Thomas C., Jr., and Rebecca M. E. Williams. "Why Are There Utah Names on Mars?" Utah Geological Survey, *Survey Notes* 47 (May 2015): 10–13.

Compton, Todd. "The Big Washout: The 1862 Flood in Santa Clara." *Utah Historical Quarterly* 77, no. 2 (Spring 2009): 108–25.

———. "Conquering the Black Ridge: The Communitarian Road in Pioneer Utah." *Utah Historical Quarterly* 82, no. 3 (Summer 2014): 222–33.

Culmsee, Carlton. "Flimflam Frontier: Submarginal Land Development in Utah." *Utah Historical Quarterly* 32, no. 2 (Spring 1964): 91–98.

Driggs, Nevada W. "When Captain Fremont Slept in Grandma McGregor's Bed." *Utah Historical Quarterly* 41, no. 2 (Spring 1973): 178–81.

Fraser, Saline Hardee. "One Long Day That Went on Forever." Compiled by Marianne Fraser. *Utah Historical Quarterly* 48, no. 4 (Fall 1980): 379–89.

Gerlach, Larry R. "Alma Richards's Olympic Leap of Faith Revisited." *Utah Historical Quarterly* 82, no. 2 (Spring 2014): 133–50.

Hess, John W. "John W. Hess, with the Mormon Battalion." *Utah Historical Quarterly* 4, no. 2 (April 1931): 47–55.

Larsen, Wesley Pratt. "The 'Letter' or Were the Powell Men Really Killed by Indians?" *Canyon Legacy* 17 (Spring 1993): 12–19.

Larson, A[ndrew] Karl. "Zion National Park with Some Reminiscences Fifty Years Later." *Utah Historical Quarterly* 37, no. 4 (Fall 1969): 409–25.

Menkes, Dove. "A Young Man Goes West: The 1879 Letters of Leonard Herbert Swett." *Utah Historical Quarterly* 75, no. 3 (Summer 2007): 204–19.

Murphy, Miriam B. "'If Only I Shall Have the Right Stuff': Utah Women in World War I." *Utah Historical Quarterly* 58, no. 4 (Fall 1990): 334–50.

Newell, Linda King. "A Gift Given: A Gift Taken." *Sunstone* 6 (September–October 1981): 16–25.

Olesen, Robert. "Distribution of Endemic Goiter in the United States as Shown by Thyroid Surveys." *Public Health Reports*, 41 (November 26, 1926): 2702.

Palmer, William R. "Indian Names in Utah Geography." *Utah Historical Quarterly* 1, no. 1 (January 1928): 5–26.

Parshall, Ardis E. "'Pursue, Retake, and Punish': The 1857 Santa Clara Ambush." *Utah Historical Quarterly* 73, no. 1 (Winter 2005): 64–86.

Quinn, D. Michael. "A Response." *Sunstone* 6 (September–October 1981): 26–27.

Reeve, W. Paul. "'A Little Oasis in the Desert': Community Building in Hurricane, Utah, 1860–1920." *Utah Historical Quarterly* 62, no. 3 (Summer 1994): 222–45.

Reynolds, Alice Louise. "Woman's Intellectual Renaissance." *Young Woman's Journal*, 10 (January 1899): 5.

Spence, Mary Lee. "The Fremonts and Utah." *Utah Historical Quarterly* 44, no. 3 (Summer 1976): 286–302.

Topping, Gary. "Another Look at Silver Reef." *Utah Historical Quarterly* 79, no. 4 (Fall 2011): 300–16.

Wakeling, Rhea Higbee. "History of Rhea Higbee, Wife of Alva T. Wakeling." *Isaac Higbee and Sophia Somers Family Magazine* 3 (1958): 245A–245J.

BOOKS

Aiken, Russell. M.D. *The Doc Aiken Story Memoirs of a Country Doctor.* Self-published, 1989.

Alder, Douglas D., and Karl F. Brooks. *A History of Washington County from Isolation to Destination.* Salt Lake City: Utah State Historical Society and Washington County Commission, 1996.

Alexander, Thomas G. *Edward Hunter Snow: Pioneer—Educator—Statesman.* Norman, OK: Arthur H. Clark, 2012.

———. "Political Patterns of Early Statehood." In *Utah's History,* edited by Richard D. Poll, Thomas G. Alexander, Eugene E. Campbell, and David E. Miller, 409–28. Provo: Brigham Young University Press, 1978.

Alford, Kenneth L., ed. *Civil War Saints.* Provo, UT: Religious Studies Center, Brigham Young University, 2012.

Alter, Jonathan. *The Defining Moment: FDR's Hundred Days and the Triumph of Hope.* New York: Simon and Schuster, 2006.

Anderson, Elizabeth Oberdick, ed. *Cowboy Apostle: The Diaries of Anthony W. Ivins, 1875–1932.* Salt Lake City: Signature Books, 2013.

Anderson, Maybelle Harmon. *Appleton Milo Harmon Goes West.* Berkeley, CA: Gillick Press, 1946.

Anderson, Thelma C. *Workman Family History.* Salt Lake City: Publishers Press, 1962.

Anonymous. "History of Mahonri Moriancumer Stapley." Copy in author's possession.

———. "History of the Stapley Family." Copy in author's possession.

———. "Mahonri Steele (Panguitch Pioneer)." Daughters of the Utah Pioneers Museum, Panguitch, UT.

———. "Short History of John Steele Jr. and Catherine Campbell Steele." Copy in author's possession.

Anthony, Carl Sferrazza. *Florence Harding: The First Lady, the Jazz Age, and the Death of America's Most Scandalous President.* New York: William Morrow, 1998.

Arrington, Chris Rigby. "Pioneer Midwives." In *Mormon Sisters,* edited by Claudia L. Bushman, 43–65. Salt Lake City: Olympus Publishing, 1976.

Arrington, Leonard J. *Great Basin Kingdom: An Economic History of the Latter-day Saints, 1830–1900.* Lincoln, NE: University of Nebraska Press, 1968.

Badger, Rodney J. *Liahona and Iron Rod.* Bountiful, UT: Family History Publishers, 1985.

Bagley, Will. *Blood of the Prophets: Brigham Young and the Massacre at Mountain Meadows.* Norman: University of Oklahoma Press, 2002.

———. *Innocent Blood: Essential Narratives of the Mountain Meadows Massacre.* Norman: Arthur H. Clark, 2008.

———. *The Pioneer Camp of the Saints: the 1846 and 1847 Mormon Trail Journals of Thomas Bullock.* Spokane, WA: Arthur H. Clark, 1997.

Barney, Ronald O. *The Mormon Vanguard Brigade of 1847: Norton Jacob's Record.* Logan: Utah State University Press, 2005.

Bate, JoAnn Sylvester. "Good Things I Remember About Mama." Appendix A, in Oral History Reminiscing: Nell Sylvester Wilson, Gwen Sylvester Hunter and JoAnn Sylvester Bate, June 6, 1988. Copy in author's possession.

———. "If I Had it to Do Over Again: The Story of My Life, Book 1. Copy in author's possession.

———. Journal. "Notebook 1." Copy in author's possession.

———. "Once Is Enough My Life." Typescript. 1978. Copy in author's possession.

Bate, Kerry William. *The Ebenezer Hanks Story.* Provo: M.C. Printing, 1982.

Bate, Kerry William, and JoAnn Sylvester Bate, eds. *Ebenezer Joseph Hanks Manuscripts and Letters.* Salt Lake City: typescript, 1979. CHL.

Bate, Kerry William, and Maureen Smith Bryson. *The Joseph Sylvester Family Letters, 1882–1989.* Las Vegas, NV: Maureen Bryson, 1998.

Bethers, Pratt M. *A History of Schools in Iron County, 1851–1970.* Privately published, 1972.

Bigler, David L. *The Forgotten Kingdom: The Mormon Theocracy in the American West, 1847–1896.* Spokane, WA: Arthur H. Clark, 2005.

Bigler, David L., and Will Bagley, eds. *Army of Israel: Mormon Battalion Narratives.* Logan: Utah State University Press, 2000.

Black, Samuel T. *San Diego County California: A Record of Settlement, Organization, Progress and Achievement.* Chicago: S. J. Clark, 1913.

Bok, Edward. *The Americanization of Edward Bok,* edited by W. David Lewis. Chicago: R. R. Donnelley and Sons, 2000.

Boogher, William Fletcher. *Gleanings of Virginia History.* Washington, D.C., 1903.

Brooks, Juanita. *The Mountain Meadows Massacre.* Norman, OK: University of Oklahoma Press, 1974.

———. *On the Ragged Edge: The Life and Times of Dudley Leavitt.* Salt Lake City: Utah State Historical Society, 1973.

Bryson, Maureen Smith, and Kerry William Bate. *The Lives and Letters of the Sylvesters and Nicholsons.* Provo: Community Press, 1997.

Burke, John, and John Bernard Burke. *A Genealogical and Heraldic History of the Extinct and Dormant Baronetcies of England, Ireland, and Scotland.* London: John Russell Smith, 1844.

Carvalho, Solomon Nunes. *Incidents of Travel and Adventure in the Far West.* Edited by Bertram Wallace Korn. Philadelphia: Jewish Publication Society of America, 1954.

Chapman, Thomas. *Who Was Buried in James Madison's Grave? A Study in Contextual Analysis.* Master's thesis, William and Mary College, 2005.

Cleland, Robert Glass, and Juanita Brooks. *A Mormon Chronicle: The Diaries of John D. Lee, 1848–1876.* San Marino, CA: Huntington Library, 1955.

Collins, George Knapp. *Spafford Onondaga County, New York.* Onondaga Historical Association, 1917.

Compton, Todd. *A Frontier Life: Jacob Hamblin, Explorer and Indian Missionary.* Salt Lake City: University of Utah Press, 2013.

———. *In Sacred Loneliness" The Plural Wives of Joseph Smith.* Salt Lake City: Signature Books, 1997.

Cox, Wanda Steele. *Journals of John Steele and Mahonri Moriancumer Steele.* Cedar City, UT: self-published, 1967.

Cox, Wanda S., and Mrs. Doyle Steele. "Emily Bunker Steele." Copy in author's possession.

Crow, Bruce. *A Land of Strangers: Cane Creek Tennessee's Mormon Massacre and Its Tragic Effects on the People Who Lived There.* Lewisburg, TN: AMS Press, 2013.

Dalton, Helen Thurber. "History of John Calvin Lazelle Smith." 1975. CHL.

Dalton, Luella Adams. *History of the Iron County Mission Parowan, Utah.* N.p.: n.p., 1965.

Danvers, June Wood, and Esther Wood Hankins. "George Wood." 1987. USHS.

Davies, John Henry. *Among My Memories.* Self-published, 1937.

Davies, John Johnson. "Historical Sketch of My Life, John Johnson Davies." Typescript. St. George: Works Progress Administration, 1936.

Diehl, Isaac E. Young Elizabeth Steele Stapley answers to "Pioneer Personal History Questionnaire." Salt Lake City: Works Progress Administration Biographies, 1936. USHS.

Dye, David A. *Sacred Scribe: Entries from the Journals of Leonard John Nuttall.* Mona, UT: Hindsight Publishing, 2008.

Fielding, Robert Kent, comp. and ed. *The Tribune Reports of The Trials of John D. Lee for the Massacre at Mountain Meadows.* Higganum, CT: Kent's Books, 2006.

Fish, Joseph. *The Autobiography of Joseph Fish by Himself with Notes by His Sons Silas and Jesse.* N.P., Lulu: 2009

———. "History of Enterprise." Typescript. 1967. Family History Library, Salt Lake City, Utah.

———. "Joseph Fish 1840–1916." Typescript. CHL.

Fish, Seymour P., ed. *The Pioneers of the Southwest and Rocky Mountain Regions.* Vol. 1. Published by J. Fish Smith, Salt Lake City and Seymour P. Fish, Provo: 1972.

Fish, Seymour P., and Vera P. Fish. *Family of Joseph Fish (1840–1926) Genealogical and Biographical Stories and Sketches.* Provo, UT: J. Grant Stevenson, 1970.

Fleek, Sherman L. *History May Be Searched in Vain: A Military History of the Mormon Battalion.* Spokane, WA: Arthur H. Clark, 2006.

Foot, M. R. D., ed. *The Gladstone Diaries, 1833–1839.* Oxford: Clarendon Press, 1968.

Francaviglia, Richard. *Mapmakers of New Zion: A Cartographic History of Mormonism.* Salt Lake City: University of Utah Press, 2015.

Givens, Terryl L. *Wrestling the Angel: The Foundations of Mormon Thought: Cosmos, God, Humanity.* Oxford: Oxford University Press, 2015.

Godfrey, Donald G., and Rebecca S. Martineau-McCarty, eds. *An Uncommon Pioneer: The Journals of James Henry Martineau, 1828–1918.* Provo, UT: Religious Studies Center, Brigham Young University, 2008.

Goldthwait, James Walter. *Diary of Western Trip 1902.* Edited by Bob Oldham. Burnsville, NC: Ad Lib Press, 1982.

Green, Raleigh Travers. *Notes on Culpeper County, Virginia.* Culpeper, VA: self-published, 1900.

Gregerson, Hans. "Andrew Ferdinand Gregerson" (May 19, 1975). Edna Gregerson Collection, Dixie University Library, St. George, Utah.

Gubler, Brian, ed. *Audrey Gregerson Gubler: Personal Diary, 1 Jan 1922 thru 24 Jun 1942.* 1989. Copy in author's possession.

Hafen, Althea Gregerson. *The Life of Andrew Ferdinand Gregerson.* Self-published, undated.

Haller, John S., Jr. *The People's Doctors: Samuel Thomson and the American Botanical Movement, 1790–1860.* Carbondale and Edwardsville, IL: Southern Illinois University Press, 2000.

Hamilton, Thomas. "Morgan, James, D. D." In *The Dictionary of National Biography,* edited by Sir Leslie Stephen and Sir Sidney Lee, 13:918–19. London: Oxford University Press, 1960.

Hardy, B. Carmon. *Solemn Covenant: The Mormon Polygamous Passage.* Urbana and Chicago: University of Illinois Press, 1992.

Henderson's Belfast Directory and Northern Repository for 1846–47. Belfast: John Henderson, 1846.

Henderson's Belfast Directory and Northern Repository. Belfast: J. Henderson, 1850.

Hicks, George Armstrong. "A Life among the Poor of Utah." In *Playing with Shadows: Voices of Dissent in the Mormon West,* edited by Polly Aird, Jeff Nichols, Will Bagley, 61–209. Norman, OK: Arthur H. Clark, 2011.

Hinckley, Bryant S. *Heber J. Grant: Highlights in the Life of a Great Leader.* Salt Lake City: Deseret Book, 1951.

Horne, Dennis B. *Latter Leaves in the Life of Lorenzo Snow.* Springville, UT: Cedar Fort, 2012.

Hyde, John, Jr. *Mormonism: Its Leaders and Designs.* New York: W. P. Fetridge, 1857.

Inkster, Ian, and Maureen Smith Bryson. *Industrial Man: The Life and Works of Charles Sylvester.* Las Vegas: Jackpot Graphics, 1999.

International Society Daughters of Utah Pioneers. *Pioneer Women of Faith and Fortitude.* Salt Lake City: Publishers Press, 1998.

Jensen, Raymond Mahonri. "Life of Raymond Mahonri Jensen." Copy in author's possession.

Jenson, Andrew. "History of the Salt Lake City Tenth Ward." CHL.

———. *Latter-day Saint Biographical Encyclopedia.* Salt Lake City: Andrew Jenson Historical Company, 1901. Reprint, Salt Lake City: Western Epics, 1971.

Jepson, James, Jr. "Memories and Experiences of James Jepson, Jr." Typescript. Juanita Brooks Collection. USHS.

Johnson, Ileen. *The Ancestry and Descendants of Mormon Pioneer William LeFevre of Utah.* N.p.: William LeFevre Family Organization, n.d.

Johnson, Ileen J., and Wanda S. Cox. *The Memoirs of Mahonri Moriancumer Steele Jr.* Mimeographed, 1963.

Jones, ElRoy Smith. *John Pidding Jones: His Ancestors and Descendants.* Salt Lake City: American Press, 1972.

Jones, Evelyn K. *Henry Lunt Biography and History of the Development of Southern Utah.* Provo, UT: BYU Family History Copy Center, 1996.

Jones, Evelyn K., and York F. Jones. *Mayors of Cedar City.* Cedar City: Cedar City Corporation, 1986.

Journal of Discourses. 26 vols. Liverpool: F. D. Richards, 1854-1886.

Kane, Elizabeth Wood. *Twelve Mormon Homes Visited in Succession on a Journey through Utah to Arizona.* Edited by Everett L. Cooley. Salt Lake City: Tanner Trust, University of Utah Library, 1974.

Kelly, Charles, ed. *Journals of John D. Lee, 1846–47 and 1859.* Salt Lake City: University of Utah Press, 1984.

Kenney, Scott G. *Wilford Woodruff's Journal, 1833–1898.* Midvale, UT: Signature Books, 1984.

Knox, Herman A., ed. *Who's Who in New York.* New York: Who's Who Publications, 1917–18.

Krenkel, John H., ed. *The Life and Times of Joseph Fish, Mormon Pioneer.* Danville, IL: Interstate Printers and Publishers, 1970.

La Follette, Belle Case, and Fola La Follette. *Robert M. La Follette, June 14, 1855–June 18, 1925.* New York: MacMillan, 1953.

Lancaster, Donald R. "Dixie Wine." Master's thesis, Brigham Young University, 1972.

Larsen, Wesley Pratt. *A History of Toquerville.* Vol. 1. Self-published.

Larson, Andrew Karl. *The Education of a Second Generation Swede.* Salt Lake City: Deseret Press, 1979.

———. *I Was Called to Dixie.* Salt Lake City: Deseret News Press, 1961.

———. "Zion National Park with Some Reminiscences Fifty Years After." Andrew Karl Larson Papers, USHS.

Larson, Leila. "The Origin and Growth of Hurricane." Copy at the Washington County Library, St. George, Utah.

Larson, Stan. *Prisoner for Polygamy: The Memoirs and Letters of Rudger Clawson at the Utah Territorial Penitentiary, 1884–87.* Urbana and Chicago: University of Illinois, 1993.

Leach, Josiah Granville. *History of the Bringhurst Family with Notes on the Clarks, De Peyster and Boude Families.* Philadelphia: J.P. Lippincott, 1901.

Lee, John Doyle. *Mormonism Unveiled; Including the Life and Confessions of the Mormon Bishop, John D. Lee; (written by himself.) and complete life of Brigham Young . . .* St. Louis, Mo.: M. E. Mason, Pub., 1891.

Lee, Rachel Andora Woolsey. Journal, 1856–1860. Copied by Brigham Young University Library, 1970.

LeFevre, Reba Roundy. "Short Life History [of James Lorenzo Roundy]." Copy in author's possession.

———. "Things I Remember as a Child." 1982. Copy in author's possession.

Lindsey, Betina. "Women as Healers in the Modern Church." In *Women and Authority: Re-emerging Mormon Feminism*, edited by Maxine Hanks, 439–60. Salt Lake City: Signature Books, 1990.

Lovell, Marilyn. *History of Kanarraville.* Kanarraville, UT: Kanarraville Utah Beta Chi Chapter of Beta Sigma Phi, 1980.

Macaulay, Thomas Babington. "The Task of the Modern Historian." In *Little Masterpieces*, edited by Bliss Perry. New York: Doubleday, Page and Co., 1906.

Macfarlane, Lloyd Wayland. *Dr. Mac: The Man, His Land, and His People.* Cedar City, UT: Southern Utah State College Press, 1985.

Martin's Belfast Directory for 1839. Belfast: M. Martin, 1839.

Martin's Belfast Directory for 1840–41. Belfast: M. Martin, 1840.

Martineau, James Henry, and Susan Ellen Johnson Martineau. "Autobiographies of James Henry Martineau and his Future Wife, Susan Ellen Johnson." Typescript. Provo, UT: Brigham Young University, 1956.

Martineau, James Henry. "Parowan Stake History Book." William H. Dame Papers, USHS.

Matheson, Alva. *Cedar City Reflections.* Cedar City, UT: Southern Utah State College Press, 1974.

Maxfield, Lella Stapley. "History of James Stapley and His Wife, Young Elizabeth Steele." Copy in author's possession.

May, Dean L., Lee L. Bean, and Mark H. Skolnick. "The Stability Ratio: An Index of Community Cohesiveness in Nineteenth-Century Mormon Towns." In *Generations and Change: Genealogical Perspectives in Social History*, edited by Robert M. Taylor Jr. and Ralph J. Crandall, 141–58. Macon, GA: Mercer University Press, 1986.

McCormick, John S., and John R. Sillito. *A History of Utah Radicalism: Startling, Socialistic, and Decidedly Revolutionary.* Logan, UT: Utah State University, 2011.

Middleton, George W. *Memoirs of a Pioneer Surgeon.* Salt Lake City: Publishers Press, 1976.

Morgan, Thomas, ed. *Recollections of My Life and Times: An Autobiography by the Rev. James Morgan D. D. Late Minister of Fisherwick Place Church Belfast with Selections from His Journal.* Belfast: William Mullan, 1874.

Munson, Voyle L., and Lillian S. Munson. *A Gift of Faith: Elias H. Blackburn.* Eureka, UT: Basin/Plateau Press, 1991.

Murbarger, Nell. *Sovereigns of the Sage.* Palm Desert, CA: Desert Magazine Press, 1958.

Murray, Robert K. *The Harding Era: Warren G. Harding and His Administration.* Minneapolis, MN: University of Minnesota Press, 1969.

Novak, Shannon A. *House of Mourning.* Salt Lake City: University of Utah Press, 2008.

Palmer, William R. *Forgotten Chapters of History: A series of Talks Given over Radio Station KSUB, Cedar City, Utah, 1951.* 1: no. 52, December 30, 1951. Logan: Merrill Library and Learning Resources Program, October 1978.

———. "George Wood." 1943. William R. Palmer Collection. SUUSC.

———. "John Calvin Lazelle Smith." William R. Palmer Collection. SUUSC.

———. "The Hurricane Canal." William R. Palmer collection. SUUSC.

Parkinson, Diane, and John Parkinson. *James Parkinson of Ramsey: His Roots and His Branches, England—Australia—America.* Austin, TX: Historical Publications, 1987.

Pickett Mortuary Funeral Record. Family History Library, St. George, Utah.

Platt, Lyman D. *The Platt Family History. Highland, Utah: The Benjamin Platt & Mary Greaves Family Organization.* 1979. Revised, St. George, UT: Teguayo Press, 1998.

Pollock, Joseph H. "How Navajo Lake Got Its Name." July 1930, William R. Palmer Collection. SUUSC.

Pollock, W. DeVere. "The Castle Gate No. 2 Coal Mine Explosion." December 25, 1991. Copy in author's possession.

Post-Office, Belfast Annual Directory for 1843–44. Belfast: J. S. Wilson, 1843.

Prince, Stephen L. *Gathering in Harmony.* Spokane, WA: Arthur H. Clark, 2004.

Proctor, Paul Dean, and Morris A. Shirts. *Silver, Sinners, and Saints: A History of Old Silver Reef, Utah.* N.p.: Paulmar, 1991.

Proctor, Robert. *The History of Panguitch.* N.p.: n.p., 2014.

Reeves, William Charles. "History of Kanarra." Ca. 1940. Copy in author's possession.

Rice, Claton S. *Ambassador to the Saints.* Boston: Christopher Publishing, 1965.

"Richard Palmer Record Book 1881–1882." William R. Palmer Collection. SUUSC.

Ricketts, Norma Baldwin. *The Mormon Battalion: U.S. Army of the West, 1846–1848.* Logan: Utah State University Press, 1996.

R. L. Polk and Company's Utah State Gazetteer, 1903–04. Salt Lake City: Tribune Job Printing, 1903.

R. L. Polk Medical and Surgical Directory of the United States 1886. N.p.: R. L. Polk & Co., 1886.

Robertson, Frank C. *A Ram in the Thicket.* Moscow, ID: University of Idaho Press, 1994.

Roundy, Everett Ellsworth. *The Roundy Family in America.* Dedham, MA: n.p., 1942.

Russell, Estella Roundy. "Biography of Sarah Catherine Stapley [Roundy]." Copy in author's possession.

Ruesch, Matilda "Mattie" Woodbury. *Hi-Lites and Lo-Lites: Autobiography of Matilda Woodbury Ruesch.* St. George, UT: n.p., 1966.

.Schlesinger, Arthur M., Jr. *The Age of Roosevelt: The Crisis of the Old Order, 1919–1933.* Boston: Houghton Mifflin, 1957.

Seegmiller, Janet Burton. *A History of Iron County: Community Above Self.* Salt Lake City: Utah State Historical Society, Iron County Commission, 1998.

Sessions, Gene A. *Mormon Thunder: A Documentary History of Jedediah Morgan Grant.* Urbana: University of Illinois Press, 1982.

Shirts, Morris A., and Kathryn H. Shirts, *A Trial Furnace.* Provo: Brigham Young University, 2001.

"Sketch of John Peter Jensen." Copy in author's possession.

Slack, Louise. "Mary J. Bringhurst." Typescript. 1935. Washington County Library, St. George, Utah.

Smart, Donna Toland, ed. *Mormon Midwife: The 1846–1888 Diaries of Patty Bartlett Sessions.* Logan, UT: Utah State University Press, 1997.

Smart, William B., and Donna T. Smart. *Over the Rim: the Parley P. Pratt Exploring Expedition to Southern Utah, 1849–50.* Logan, UT: Utah State University Press, 1999.

Spence, Mary, ed. *The Expeditions of John Charles Frémont: Travels from 1848 to 1854.* Urbana and Chicago: University of Illinois Press, 1984.

Stall, Sylvanus. *What a Young Man Ought to Know.* Philadelphia: W. Briggs, 1897.

Stapley, James. Family Bible. "Family Record. Marriages." Photocopy in author's possession.

Stapley, Rebecca Almeda Williams. "A Short Sketch of the Life of Rebecca Williams Stapley." Copy in author's possession.

Stapley, Sophia Parker. *Together Again: An Autobiographical History.* Oakland, CA: Third Party Associates, 1976.

Stapley, William Tarbet. "Autobiography." Transcribed and edited by Kerry William Bate. Salt Lake City: 1987. Copy in author's possession.

Steele, John. Utah Histories. Bancroft Library, University of California, Berkeley.

Stout, Byron David, ed. *The Diaries of David Fisk Stout.* Self-published, n.d.

Stratton, Alice [Isom] Gubler. *The Story of the Hurricane Canal.* Hurricane, UT: Hurricane Valley Pioneer Heritage Park Foundation, 1992.

Summerhays, Joseph W., et al. *Jubilee History of Latter-day Saints Sunday Schools, 1849–1899.* Salt Lake City: Deseret Sunday School Union, 1900.

Tietjen, Gary. *Ernst Albert Tietjen: Missionary and Colonizer.* Bountiful, UT: Family History Publications, 1992.

Topping, Gary, ed. *Gila Monsters and Red-Eyed Rattlesnakes: Don Maguire's Arizona Trading Expeditions, 1876–1879.* Salt Lake City: University of Utah Press, 1997.

Tullidge, Edward W. *Tullidge's Histories.* Salt Lake City: Juvenile Instructor, 1889.

Turley, Richard E., Jr., and Ronald W. Walker. *Mountain Meadows Massacre: The Andrew Jenson and David H. Morris Collections.* Provo: Brigham Young University Press, 2009.

Turner, John G. *Brigham Young.* Cambridge, MA: Belknap Press, 2012.

Ulrich, Laurel Thatcher. *A Midwife's Tale: The Life of Martha Ballard, Based on Her Diary, 1785–1812.* New York: Alfred A. Knopf, 1990.

Van Cott, Amy L., and Allen W. Leigh. *Generations of Websters.* Cedar City, UT: Thomas Webster Family Organization, 1960.

Van Wagoner, Richard S. *Mormon Polygamy: A History.* Salt Lake City: Signature Books, 1986.

Wagner, Anthony Richard. *English Genealogy.* Oxford: Clarendon Press, 1972.

———. *Pedigrees and Progress: Essays in the Genealogical Interpretation of History.* London: Phillimore, 1975.

Walker, Ronald W., Richard E. Turley Jr., and Glen M. Leonard. *Massacre at Mountain Meadows.* New York: Oxford University Press, 2008.

Ward, Maria [pseudonym]. *Female Life among the Mormons.* New York: Derby and Jackson, 1856.

Warner, Jesse Lenard, ed. "Samuel H Roundy History." 1933. Copy in author's possession.

Warrum, Noble, ed. *Utah since Statehood.* 4 vols. Chicago and Salt Lake City: S. J. Clarke Publishing, 1919.

Watson, Caddie Slack. *Slack Family History.* Provo, UT: J. Grant Stevenson, [1965?].

Watt, Ronald G. *A History of Carbon County.* Salt Lake City: Utah State Historical Society, Carbon County Commission, 1997.

Webb, Ralph L. "Hurricane Flour Mill." In *Hurricane Hintons and Spendloves from England to the Rocky Mountain Zion,* edited by Cherrie Gubler Naegle. Toquerville, UT: 2007.

White, Virgil D. *Index to Indian Wars Pension Files, 1892–1926.* Waynesboro, TN: National Historical Publishing Company, 1987.

Whitney, Orson Ferguson. *History of Utah.* 4 volumes. Salt Lake City: George Q. Cannon and Sons, Publishers, 1892–1904.

Williams, Opal Pollock. *Kanarra Is a Pretty Little Town.* Privately printed, 1984.

Winder, Mike R., and Ronald L. Fox. *When the White House Comes to Zion.* American Fork, UT: Covenant Communications, 2011.

Woolf, William Layne, ed. *The Private Journal of William Hyde.* Mimeographed. N.p.: n.p., n.d.

Woolstenhulme, Guinevere Thomas. "'I Have Seen Many Miracles,' Sarah De Armon Pea Rich." In *Women of Faith in the Latter Days,* edited by Richard E. Turley, Jr., and Brittany A. Chapman, 1:271–85. Salt Lake City: Deseret Book, 2011.

INDEX

Index